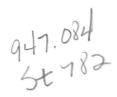

ANNALS OF COMMUNISM

Each volume in the series Annals of Communism will publish selected and previously inaccessible documents from former Soviet state and party archives in a narrative that develops a particular topic in the history of Soviet and international communism. Separate English and Russian editions will be prepared. Russian and American scholars work together to prepare the documents for each volume. Documents are chosen not for their support of any single interpretation but for their particular historical importance or their general value in deepening understanding and facilitating discussion. The volumes are designed to be useful to students, scholars, and interested general readers.

# Stalinism as a Way of Life

## A Narrative in Documents

### Lewis Siegelbaum and Andrei Sokolov

*Documents Compiled by Ludmila Kosheleva, Larisa Rogovaia, Lewis Siegelbaum, Andrei Sokolov, Vladimir Telpukhovsky, and Sergei Zhuravlev*

*Text Preparation and Commentary by Lewis Siegelbaum, Andrei Sokolov, and Sergei Zhuravlev*

*Translated from the Russian by Thomas Hoisington and Steven Shabad*

Yale University Press

New Haven and London

This volume has been prepared with the cooperation of the Russian State Archive of Social and Political History (RGASPI) of the State Archival Service of Russia in the framework of an agreement concluded between RGASPI and Yale University Press.

Designed by James J. Johnson and set in Sabon and Melior types by The Composing Room of Michigan, Inc., Grand Rapids, Michigan.
Printed in the United States of America by Vail-Ballou Press, Binghamton, New York.

*Library of Congress Cataloging-in-Publication Data*

Stalinism as a way of life : a narrative in documents / Lewis Siegelbaum and Andrei Sokolov ; documents compiled by Ludmila Kosheleva . . . [et al.] ; text preparation and commentary by Lewis Siegelbaum, Andrei Sokolov, and Sergei Zhuravlev ; translated from the Russian by Thomas Hoisington and Steven Shabad.
    p.   cm.
Includes bibliographical references and index.
ISBN 0-300-08480-3 (cloth : alk.paper)
    1. Soviet Union—History—1925–1953—Sources.   I. Siegelbaum, Lewis H.   II. Sokolov, A. K.   III. Kosheleva, L.   IV. Zhuravlev, Sergei.

DK267 .S69386   2000
947.084—dc21                                                                              00-032074

A catalogue record for this book is available from the British Library.

Yale University Press gratefully acknowledges the financial support given for this publication by the Lynde and Harry Bradley Foundation, Inc., Joseph W. Donner, Austin H. Furse III, the David Woods Kemper Memorial Foundation, Jeremiah Milbank, Roger Milliken, the National Endowment for the Humanities, the John M. Olin Foundation, Inc., the Open Society Fund (New York), Karen Pritzker, Robert Pritzker, Lloyd H. Smith, and Keith Young.

# Contents

# Acknowledgments

In working on this project, my greatest debt of gratitude is, of course, to Andrei Sokolov. His perspicacity, scholarly rigor, hospitality, and sense of humor
triumphed over the extremely difficult circumstances in which he, like other
Russian scholars, is compelled to work and live. I also would like to express
my thanks to Sergei Zhuravlev for his outstanding contributions to this volume and to the directors and staffs of the Russian State Archive of Social and
Political History, the State Archive of the Russian Federation, the Russian
State Archive of the Economy, and the other archives cited in this volume.

At Yale University Press, Jonathan Brent obtained the necessary funding and
provided vital encouragement for the project. I greatly appreciate his support,
as well as that of his project assistants, Timothy Sergay and Vadim Staklo, and
other members of his staff. Dan Heaton performed the task of editing the manuscript with both professional vigor and humor. I also wish to thank the
anonymous readers of the first version of the manuscript for refusing to toler-
ate its weaknesses.

This project was blessed with the services of two outstanding translators,
Thomas Hoisington and Steven Shabad. Their rendering into English of
Sokolov's prose and the documents—many of which were written in substan-
dard Russian—showed the greatest sensitivity and imagination. Their profes-
sionalism was infectious, and their tracking down of the most obscure geographical and lexicographical references went far beyond the call of duty.

Sheila Fitzpatrick and Ronald G. Suny read the typescript of the Russian version in its entirety, and the latter also read and provided needed advice on my introduction; Jeffrey Burds and William Chase shared with me their approaches to scholarly collaboration; Larry Holmes, David Prestel, and Elvira Wilbur answered a few historical, linguistic, and geographical queries.

All deserve my thanks, as do Leslie Page Moch and Daniel Orlovsky for their much needed emotional support and equanimity during periods of personal crisis. I also am grateful to the International Research and Exchanges Board (IREX), the National Endowment for the Humanities (NEH), the Center for the Study of Russia and the Soviet Union, and Michigan State University's College of Arts and Letters for making possible my research in Moscow and Andrei Sokolov's trip to East Lansing.

Except where specified otherwise, all illustrations are used with permission of Center for Contemporary History, Institute of Russian History, Russian Academy of Sciences.

With the exception of Andrei Sokolov, none of the organizations or people mentioned here is responsible for the views expressed in this book.

*Lewis Siegelbaum*

# Notes on Transliteration and Terminology

In transliterating from Russian to English we have used a modified version of the standard Library of Congress system in the text and documents. Hard signs have been omitted, and the following changes have been imposed for proper names.

In the final position:
    ii in the LOC system becomes y (Trotsky, not Trotskii)
    iia = ia (Izvestia, not Izvestiia)
In the initial position:
    E = Ye (Yezhov, not Ezhov)
    Ia = Ya (Yaroslavsky, not Iaroslavsky)
    Iu = Yu (Yudin, not Iudin)

On first usage, the names of institutions are given in the original Russian (in italics) followed by the English translation in parenthesis. In the case of initials and acronyms, the full Russian title is given in parentheses followed in brackets by the English translation. These terms may be found in the Glossary and Abbreviations. Strict Library of Congress transliteration is used in source notes and for words or phrases that are translated in the text.

# A Note on the Documents

The overwhelming majority of documents used or cited here are from Russian archives listed below. Russian archival documents are cited and numbered by collection (*fond* or f.), inventory (*opis'* or op.), file (*delo* or d.), and page (*list* or l., or in plural, ll.): thus, for example, RGASPI, f. 17, op. 114, d. 608, ll. 140–141.

Some of the documents were too long to be reproduced in full in this volume. Our editorial excisions are given by standard ellipsis dots: . . . Where substantial sections have been omitted, a brief description of the excised portion is given in brackets [ ]. All information in brackets is provided by the authors or, where indicated, by the translators.

All documents cited here exist in the archives either as original typescripts or manuscripts, or, in the case of many of the letters and summary reports, as typed copies. The status of each document is indicated immediately following the archival citation. Unless otherwise noted, we have tried to render in translation the original punctuation, syntax, and deviations from standard spellings. In cases where Russian and English words are similar, misspellings in the Russian are rendered similarly in English. When the word *criminal* is rendered as *crimanil,* for example, it reflects a similar transposition of the *a* and the *i* in the original. In other cases, we have supplied a plausible misspelling of a word whose Russian equivalent was misspelled in a way not easily reflected in the English. Thus *padarok* (incorrect spelling of *podarok*) is rendered as *presints* instead of *presents, chiasto* (incorrect spelling of *chasto*) is given as *oftin* rather than *often,* and so on.

In this volume documents from the following archives are used:

GARF — *Gosudarstvennyi Arkhiv Rossiiskoi Federatsii* [State Archive of the Russian Federation]

RGAE — *Rossiisky Gosudarstvennyi Arkhiv Ekonomiki* [Russian State Archive of the Economy]

RGASPI — *Rossiisky Gosudarstvennyi Arkhiv Sotsial'noi i Politicheskoi Istorii* [Russian State Archive of Social and Political History]

TsGAODM — *Tsentral'nyi Gosudarstvennyi Arkhiv Obshchestvennykh Dvizhenii g. Moskvy* [Central State Archive of Social Movements in the City of Moscow]

TsKhDMO — *Tsentr Khranenia Dokumentov Molodezhnykh Organizatsii* [Center for the Preservation of Documents from Youth Organizations]

TsMAM — *Tsentral'nyi Munitsipal'nyi Arkhiv g. Moskvy* [Central Municipal Archive of the City of Moscow]

# Glossary and Abbreviations

| | |
|---|---|
| arshin | Russian unit of length equal to two feet, four inches |
| ASSR | *Avtonomnaia Sovetskaia Sotsialisticheskaia Respublika* [Autonomous Soviet Socialist Republic], an administrative unit within a Union republic and corresponding to the territory indigenous to an ethnic group after which it was named |
| Cheka | All-Russian Extraordinary Commission for Combating Counterrevolution and Sabotage (1918–22), succeeded by GPU |
| desiatina | Russian measure of area, equal to 2.7 acres |
| edinolichniki | independent farmers remaining outside collective farms |
| FZMK | *Fabrichno-zavodskoi mestnoi komitet,* local factory and shop committee of a trade union |
| Glavlit | *Glavnoe upravlenie literatury* [Chief Directorate of Literature], organ of literary censorship |
| Glavpolitprosvet | *Glavnoe upravlenie politicheskogo prosveshchenia* [Chief Directorate of Political Education] |
| gorkom | *gorodskoi komitet,* city committee of Communist Party |
| GPU | *Gosudarstvennoe politicheskoe upravlenie* [State Political Administration] (1922–32) |
| GULAG | *Gosudarstvennoe upravlenie lagerei* [State Administration of Labor Camps], the labor camp system |

| | |
|---|---|
| IKP | *Institut krasnykh professorov* [Institute of Red Professors] |
| ispolkom | *ispolnitel'nyi komitet,* executive committee (of soviet) |
| ITK | *Ispravitel'naia trudovaia kolonia* [Corrective Labor Colony] |
| kolkhoz | collective farm |
| Kolkhoztsentr | Kolkhoz Center, the coordinating agency for national collectivization |
| Komsomol | All-Union Leninist Youth Organization |
| krai | administrative territory roughly equivalent to oblast' |
| kraikom | *krainoi komitet* [krai committee of Communist Party] |
| Kul'tprop | Committee for Culture and Propaganda |
| lishentsy | people who were disenfranchised on the basis of their class origins or functions within the tsarist regime |
| MGK | *Moskovsky gorodskoi komitet* [Moscow City Committee of Communist Party] |
| MOPR | *Mezhdunarodnaia organizatsia pomoshchi bortsam revoliutsii* [International Organization for Assistance to Revolutionary Fighters], founded in 1922 by the Comintern to provide material and moral support to victims of "White terror" and their families |
| MTS | *Mashino-traktornaia stantsia* [machine-tractor station] |
| Narkompros | *Narodnyi komissariat prosveshchenia* [People's Commissariat of Education] |
| Narkomput' | *Narodnyi komissariat putei soobshenii* [People's Commissariat of Ways and Communications] |
| Narkomtiazhprom | *Narodnyi komissariat tiazheloi prolmyshlennosti* [People's Commissariat of Heavy Industry] |
| Narkomzdrav | *Narodnyi komissariat zdravlenia* [People's Commissariat of Health] |
| Narkomzem | *Narodnyi komissariat zemledelia* [People's Commissariat of Agriculture] |
| NKID | *Narodnyi komissariat inostrannykh del* [People's Commissariat of Foreign Affairs] |
| NKPros | *See* Narkompros |
| NKRKI | *Narodnyi komissariat raboche-krest'ianskoi inspektsii* [People's Commissariat of Workers' and Peasants' Inspection] |
| NKVD | *Narodnyi komissariat vnutrennykh del* [People's Commissariat of Internal Affairs], from 1934 the successor to the OGPU |

NKYu            *Narodnyi komissariat yustitsii* [People's Commissariat of Justice]
NKZ             *See* Narkomzem
nomenklatura    people chosen by Party apparatus to serve in various responsible positions
obkom           *oblastnoi komitet* [oblast' committee of the Communist Party]
oblast'         administrative unit, province
OGIZ            *Obedinennoe gosudarstvennoe izdatel'stvo* [Association of State Publishing Houses]
OGPU            *Obedinennoe gosudarstvennoe politicheskoe upravlenie* [Unified State Political Administration], the political police (1932–34), successor to the GPU
okrug           an administrative unit between the raion and the oblast'. By 1930 the USSR was divided into 246 such units. Most were dissolved in the 1930s.
ONO             *Otdel narodnogo obrazovania* [Board of Public Education]
Orgburo         *Organizatsionnoe biuro* [Organization Bureau of TsK VKP(b)]
orgnabor        organized recruitment (of laborers)
otkhodniki      migrant laborers
Politburo       *Politicheskoe biuro* [Political Bureau of TsK VKP(b)]
politotdel      *politicheskii otdel* [Political Department], attached to MTS and sovkhozes during 1933–34
pood            Russian unit of weight equal to thirty-six pounds
raiispolkom     *See* RIK
raion           administrative district subordinate to oblast' or krai
RIK             *raionnyi ispolnitel'nyi komitet* [district executive committee]
RKKA            *Raboche-Krest'ianskaia Krasnaia Armia* [Workers' and Peasants' Red Army]
sazhen'         Russian unit of length equal to seven feet
sel'kor         unpaid, voluntary newspaper correspondent in the village
SNK SSSR        *Sovet Narodnykh Komissarov SSSR* [Council of Peoples' Commissars of the USSR]
sovkhoz         state farm, employing wage labor
Sovnarkom       *See* SNK SSSR
STO             *Sovet Truda i Oborony* [Council of Labor and Defense]

| | |
|---|---|
| TsChO | *Tsentral'no-Chernozemnaia Oblast'* [Central Black Earth Oblast'] |
| TsIK | *See* VTsIK |
| TsKK | *Tsentral'naia Kontrol'naia Komissia* [Central Control Commission of VKP(b)] |
| TsK VKP(b) | *Tsentral'nyi komitet Vsesoiuznoi Kommunisticheskoi Partii (bol'shevikov)* [Central Committee of the All-Union Communist Party (Bolsheviks)] |
| VKP(b) | *Vsesoiuznaia Kommunisticheskaia Partia (bol'shevikov)* [All-Union Communist Party (Bolsheviks)] |
| VLKSM | *See* Komsomol |
| VSNKh | *Vsesoiuznyi sovet narodnogo khoziaistva* [All-Union Council of the National Economy] |
| VTsIK | *Vsesoiuznyi tsentral'nyi ispolnitel'nyi komitet* [All-Union Central Executive Committee (of Soviets)] |
| vydvizhenets | promotee of working-class or peasant background |

# Introduction

## Lewis Siegelbaum

SEVERAL YEARS AGO, the Russian Museum in St. Petersburg assembled an exhibition on the art of the Stalin era. Taking up three floors of the museum, the exhibition, "Agitation for Happiness," comprised gigantic canvases in oils bearing such titles as *S. M. Kirov Takes the Parade of Physical Culturists* (A. N. Samokhvalov, 1935), and *Glory to the Great Stalin* (Yu. P. Kulach et al., 1950); smaller paintings of industrial and agricultural life teeming with purposeful activity; sculptures cast in bronze of muscle-bound workers, Red Army sentries, and proud, determined schoolchildren; and the stuff of everyday life: medals and postage stamps, tea sets and chess sets, inkwells and ceramic figurines. So much exhortation, so many figures striding confidently into the radiant future, so much health, well-being, and happiness! It was enough to make one nostalgic for those times.

The compilers of the exhibition's catalog anticipated just such a reaction. They pointed out that this art had contributed to the strengthening of a "regime of terror, the victims of which consisted of many millions of innocent people." "It would be cynical," they wrote, "to underestimate by nostalgic or fashionable postmodern interpretations the seriousness of guilt of this destructive art that befogged consciousness, or to evaluate it from a safe historical distance in terms of taste." We must, they insisted, "look behind the facade of its staging and understand by whom and in relation to whom this manipulation of emotions was realized."[1]

These are strong words that bear tribute to the power of art—even (or especially?) "totalitarian art"—to move or sway. Stalin's rule was not only a "regime of terror" but, so the compilers imply, of seduction. Even while it destroyed, it also created via its "agitation for happiness" a make-believe world, one in which millions believed themselves to be happy. In this Land of Oz, consciousness was "befogged," making it impossible to look behind the facade. Only now, with our critical (if not "safe historical") distance, can/must we investigate who did what to whom.

Although Stalin died nearly fifty years ago, his is an unquiet ghost. The system and empire over which he presided for a quarter-century lie in ruins, and the methods he employed have by now been universally condemned. Yet the exhibitors of art that glorified him will not permit us simply to view it; they instruct us in how to understand it, unintentionally echoing the Leninist formula of *kto-kogo* (who-whom) in the process. Perhaps it is unfair to chide them for their didacticism. The weight of the Stalinist past lay heavily upon the (now ex-) Soviet people for so long that the anxiety associated with displaying its art is understandable.

The documents contained in this volume are also artifacts of the Stalin era. They span the 1930s, the period of Soviet history from Stalin's "Great Turn" toward full-scale collectivization and industrialization to the Nazi invasion of the Soviet Union in June 1941. This was a period of massive social transformations. It also was when the political system—variously termed totalitarian, Stalinist, state socialist, or just Soviet—assumed a form that was to persist until the late 1980s. The magnitude of the changes and the dynamism of the state that engineered them inevitably shaped the lives of all those who lived through this decade—and many who failed to do so. But shaped how? Were all Soviet citizens terrorized and/or seduced? What other effects did the state have on citizens' thinking and behavior, and vice versa? How useful is it to counterpose the state to society—"them" versus "us," as it were—when virtually all able-bodied urban adults were employed by the state, and the urban-based intelligentsia rarely rubbed shoulders with collective farmers?

For several decades following the Second World War, American and more generally Western Sovietology viewed the Stalin era through the prism of totalitarianism.[2] Under Stalin, it was argued, the Soviet Union became a full-blown totalitarian society in which formal legality was a mere smokescreen for the dictatorship of the Communist Party and the caprice of its general secretary. Purging, the execution or consignment to labor camps of invented enemies, and the forcible resettlement of ethnic minorities to Central Asia were but the most obvious forms of totalitarian repression. Collective farms, officially hailed as an advancement over small-scale private agriculture, represented yet another form of incarceration, a "second serfdom" for the peasantry. More generally, the totalitarian regime exercised its rule through social "atomization" and massive and unrelenting "indoctrination."

Within this conceptual framework there was room for subtle analysis of the inner workings of the Soviet state and the mainsprings of both "terror and progress."[3] Yet ultimately the totalitarian school offered a mirror image of official Soviet representations and was no less absolutistic in its rendering of Soviet reality. Neither employed Stalinism as an analytical category, as both tended to regard the Soviet Union's evolution as the fulfillment of its Leninist potential. Throughout this foundational period of Soviet studies in the West, only a few works departed from this Sovietological consensus.[4]

It was not until the late 1970s that the state-centeredness of this approach began to yield to social historical investigation and the previously heretical notion of social support for the regime. This support was located in distinct social groups, particularly within a generational cohort to whom the prodigious expansion of state power under Stalin appealed. Whether inspired by the lofty aim of marching in step with progress or the more selfish motive of rising rapidly up the social scale, young, mostly semieducated workers provided the shock troops "from below" for collectivization, industrialization, and cultural revolution. The turn toward social conservatism, evident from the mid-1930s onward, could thus be explained in terms of the consolidation of power by these *vyd-*

*vizhentsy* ("promotees"). It was they who would emerge in the post-Stalin era as Milovan Djilas's "New Class," or as what Sheila Fitzpatrick called the "Brezhnev generation."[5]

If social historians complicated the story told by a previous generation of Sovietologists, other scholars more directly challenged the usefulness of the totalitarian conceptualization. Relying heavily on the Soviet press and the Smolensk Party Archive, which had been captured by the Germans in 1941 and subsequently by the Americans, these "revisionists" rejected the self-advertised image of the Stalinist state as monolithic and all-powerful. It was, in their view, riddled with internal tensions and contradictions. It was, indeed, a weak state, whose leaders thrashed about to discover the reasons for its ineptitude and found them among almost innumerable "enemies of the people."[6] This was a version of Stalinism and the Great Purges so closely identified with it in which Stalin played a much reduced if not exactly passive role.

Neither upward mobility nor a weak state figured in the work of Moshe Lewin, whose thrust is perhaps best characterized as a variant on modernization theory. Stalinism, for Lewin, represented an extreme, indeed pathological, form of etatism, of the party's self-appointed "task of wrenching rural Russia out of the shell into which it had hid from the ravages of earlier calamities and of pushing it up into the twentieth century." Stalin's agenda for the "telescoping of stages," relentlessly pursued via a bacchanalia of experimentation, campaigns, and "jolts and tilts," ironically accentuated the backwardness he sought to overcome: in the course of the First Five-Year Plan (1928–32), the cities were "ruralized"; the party was transformed into a predominantly administrative and managerial organ ("economized"); and the entire socioeconomic system was "archaicized." Not until this "quicksand society" had had a chance to solidify—that is, not before the 1950s—could one discern the rudiments of a civil society.[7]

The scholarship discussed thus far was produced without the benefit of access to Soviet archives. This became possible only toward the end of the 1980s. The ability to sift through files in both party and state archives—to examine the Stalin era at close range, as it were—has had a profound effect on Western historiography, an effect that is likely to continue for some time to come.[8] Before considering current understandings of the Stalin era that come out of this research and indicating how this book relates to them, I must explain the origins and nature of the present volume.

Nearly ten years ago, Professor Andrei Sokolov of the Institute of History of the (then) Soviet Academy of Sciences assembled a team of researchers and archivists in Moscow to select documents from recently declassified archives pursuant of two projects. One involved compiling letters in the form of a documentary narrative covering the first decade or so of Soviet power. This project resulted in the publication of *Golos naroda: Pis'ma i otkliki riadovykh sovetskikh grazhdan o sobytiiakh 1918–1932 gg.* (Voice of the people: Letters and commentary of ordinary Soviet citizens about events in the years 1918–1932).[9] The second essentially took up where the first left off. My own involvement in the latter project began in the summer of 1993, when I traveled to Moscow to meet with Professor Sokolov, Sergei Zhuravlev, and several of the archivists to discuss the methodology of selecting documents and the themes and chapters of the volume, and to examine documents they already had selected. On this and subsequent visits, I also worked in the archives, selecting additional documents for consideration. Professor Sokolov spent November 1996 in East Lansing, during which time I read the entire manuscript that he and Zhuravlev had prepared. Professor Sokolov in turn read a draft of my introduction for the English-language edition.

It was agreed from the outset that while Sokolov had full responsibility for the Russian edition, I would have free rein in revising the text for the English-language edition. Before submitting the manuscript to the translator, I eliminated some of the documents and edited the commentary. Then, working from the translations, I made further cuts, added some passages of my own, and inserted explanatory and bibliographic notes where necessary. The Russian version was published in 1998.[10]

The documents selected for this volume were those which we thought best illustrated the kinds of written communication among Soviet citizens, between them and party and state officials and institutions, and among officials themselves during the 1930s. Unlike others published in the Annals of Communism series, these documents are purposefully eclectic. They represent several genres of writing (letters, summary reports, minutes of meetings, memoranda) by individuals with varying degrees of literacy from nearly all walks of Soviet life. All appear in English translation for the first time.

This, then, is a volume of social history that allows peasants and workers, intellectuals and the uneducated, adults and children, women and men, Russians and those of other national groups, the downtrodden and the elite to tell their own stories in their own words. They "speak Bolshevik" (some better than others), as well as other languages.[11] They complain and beseech, and are both elliptical and shockingly blunt. They proclaim their unswerving dedication to building socialism and their horror at some of the things that are done in its name. Taken together, they reveal, unwittingly for the most part, the social values, codes of conduct, stereotypes, pathologies, and, yes, hopes and fears that produced and were produced by this most traumatic decade in Soviet history.

Making sense of this polyphony of voices is a challenge. To facilitate this most important of tasks, we assembled the documents in the form of a thematically structured narrative. The themes were suggested by the goals that the state placed on the agenda for Soviet society. These are highlighted by the titles we have given to the chapters, which are taken from contemporary expressions, stock propaganda phrases, and clichés, each bearing sizable semantic weight. Although we employ them ironically, we are far from oblivious to the role they played as distinctive social and political indicators, or to the often painful and cruel realities that lay behind them. Why these goals were put on the agenda, how they were formulated, and what strategies were adopted for their achievement are subjects addressed in numerous political histories of the period. They receive relatively little attention from us. Rather, the emphasis is on the "processing" of these goals—that is, how their pursuit, born of impatience and unrealizable expectations, interacted with existing customs, beliefs, relationships, and practices to further complicate already harried lives.

Our narrative begins with the "socialist offensive" of the late 1920s and early 1930s. This refers to the launching of various "fronts"—industrialization, collectivization, "tractorization," mech-

anization of the Donbass, cotton planting, godlessness, proletarianization of literature and the cinema, and so forth—in full accordance with all the rules of military operations. We then turn to
cadres, who, as Stalin's famous slogan had it, were to "decide
everything." Documents in this chapter relate to the multitudinous
and often mutually contradictory tasks assigned to party and state
functionaries, and why they invariably were performed so badly.
The draft of the Stalin Constitution of 1936, the subject of the third
chapter, occasioned something akin to a national referendum on
the Stalinist version of socialism. Seizing the opportunity presented
by the constitution's incorporation of a language of rights, letter
writers and participants in formal discussions projected their own
ideas, hopes, and resentments onto the document. Their comments
and suggestions thus provide an unusual, though not entirely
transparent, glimpse into popular mentalities.

A society of abundance—of "love and plenty"—or at least one
in which the basic needs of its members are met, was what socialism historically vouchsafed. The documents in the fourth chapter
reveal not only the yawning gap between the assertion of socialism's achievement and quotidian experiences but the extent to
which that gap engendered much bewilderment, denunciation, and
repression. In the fifth chapter we return to the countryside to examine what "Bolshevik order" meant to the majority of Soviet citizens, the collectivized peasants and those on state farms. Although
not all the voices in this section are complaining, the picture portrayed of rural life is far from edifying. Our account ends with the
younger generation, those born after the 1917 Revolution, whose
childhoods were "happy" by decree. What living in the "land of
socialism" meant to them, how they responded to the world their
elders prepared for them to inherit, and how unpredictable their
fates could be makes for fascinating but also heartrending reading.

The nature and provenance of our sources deserve special attention. One of the chief revelations to come from the opening of Soviet archives is the sheer volume of letters received by newspapers,
as well as party and state leaders and institutions. We now know
that in the not atypical month of July 1935, *Krest'ianskaia Gazeta*
(The peasants' newspaper) received approximately 26,000 letters.
Mikhail Kalinin, who as president of the Central Executive Com-

mittee of the Soviets was one of the most frequent recipients of letters, received an average of 77,000 a year between 1923 and 1935. Throughout 1936 Andrei Zhdanov, Leningrad party secretary, received 130 letters a day. The regional party secretary in Dnepropetrovsk, Mikhail Khataevich, reported, perhaps with some exaggeration, that he received 250 letters every day.[12] Letters also poured in to other newspapers, municipal soviets, procurators' offices, the People's Commissariat of Internal Affairs (NKVD), party and state control commissions, and the offices of Politburo members and government leaders, including Stalin.

These letters contained complaints, petitions, denunciations, confessions, and advice. We have included examples of all these types of letters. The majority were sent by individuals who signed their names, for anonymous and collectively signed letters were frowned upon by authorities. Regardless of their motivations for sending letters, authors expected a response, and the archives indicate that some kind of response usually was forthcoming. Newspapers published only a tiny fraction of letters. More often, staffers forwarded them to appropriate agencies or wrote replies themselves. Individual leaders who received letters responded directly to some and forwarded others with comments and queries. The correspondence between Kalinin and Nadezhda Krupskaia reproduced in Chapter 6 (doc. 150) exemplifies the latter treatment.

Aside from individual letters, we also used summary reports (svodki) prepared by special information departments of the party, the Secret-Political Departments of the secret police, and newspapers. These were produced for "top secret" distribution to selected individuals in higher organs. They include information culled by the vast network of informants from conversations overheard, rumors, and other evidence of popular moods, as well as from letters sent to respective institutions. As other scholars have noted, the svodki produced by the secret police tended to emphasize the negative—that is, to unmask anti-Soviet or hostile thinking. This was less true of party and newspaper summaries.[13] Finally, we include reports produced by middle-ranking functionaries in the party and state based on their investigations of how certain campaigns such as collectivization were proceeding, and what conditions were like on collective farms, in prisons, schools, and institutions of higher learning. As with other documents, we are at least as concerned with the mentalities of those who wrote such reports as with the phenomena they describe.

Of course, there are limitations and caveats associated with the use of such material. First, the relation between what is described or alleged and what may actually have happened is complicated. The stories told in letters are just that: reconstructions that narrate a necessarily selective series of events, framed in a fashion that makes a point. This limitation, though, is also a potential advantage. Like the sixteenth-century letters of remission discovered by Natalie Zemon Davis in French archives, these documents are "fictions" created by their authors to tell what they "thought a good story was, how they accounted for motive, and how through narrative they made sense of the unexpected and built coherence into immediate experience."[14] Read as stories, they provide evidence of both the range of discursive strategies employed by their authors and the not inconsiderable influence of certain "master narratives," of which the author may not have been aware, on the (re)presentation of self. Moreover, because the documents were frequently acted upon, they "created" reality as well. This had real consequences not only for the author but also for the addressee and anyone implicated in the original communication.

A second limitation has to do with representativeness or typicality. In the strictest sense, each "case" presented in the documents is unique and none should be interpreted as representative of a universal condition. Nevertheless, patterns do emerge in the nature of complaints, accusations, and situations described. The commentary is designed to highlight those patterns, provide historical contextualization, and indicate our own interpretations of the documents. Where appropriate the full numbered documents are supplemented by quotations from other documents and references to still others.

Yet another dimension of representativeness is the happenstance of preservation. We cannot know what proportion of the letters sent to Moscow found their way into the archives. In the case of *Krest'ianskaia Gazeta,* letters survive from the years 1924–28 and again for 1938 but not in between. As for those incorporated into summaries, we obviously were dependent on the judgments of compilers and at least to some extent the categories under which they grouped letters. We discovered a marked preponderance of letters from the central Russian region, with roughly a third coming from Moscow oblast alone. Very few from outlying areas of the Russian republic, the republics south of the Caucasus, or Central Asia made their way into the summaries. It also should be noted that the quantity of summaries shrank from one year to the next, perhaps indicating greater reliance on other mechanisms for checking up on popular moods as the decade progressed. Then again, there was a definite animation in surveys of popular opinion whenever a major campaign was launched, as in the cases of the constitutional project in 1936 and the introduction of new party rules in 1939. Finally, in one instance we know that a folder of summaries from 1932 was designated for destruction in 1936 yet survived; nevertheless, we cannot know how many other files were indeed destroyed.[15]

Our own decision about which documents to include was often based on what we "thought a good story was." Here, though, the main criterion was not persuasiveness but rather the extent to which the story illuminated its author's subjectivity. We also preferred documents that referred to events/encounters allegedly experienced or witnessed by authors, though some containing more generalized observations are included as well. We chose illustrations that related to specific documents or events discussed in them.

We have tried to interfere as little as possible with the actual content of the sources. Thus, for the most part, errors of grammar and spelling in the documents have been maintained in the Russian edition and rendered as faithfully as possible in their English equivalents for this edition. The only exceptions are in cases where comprehension would otherwise have been inordinately impeded. This approach allows for maximum exposure to the variety and timbre of the voices directed at public institutions and emanating from within them in the 1930s. It limits our own voices to commentary that leads thematically from one document to the next. In this lies the difference of our book from a more familiar model of historical narration.

The documents tell us a great deal about Soviet society in the

1930s—perhaps above all that it did not come close to measuring up to the standards or goals set by its vanguardist tutors and that their efforts to shape or whip into shape maddeningly recalcitrant "elements" and forces intensified the gap. Much of the recalcitrance and disorderliness has come to be seen by historians of the period as evidence of resistance. Resistance, of course, is a big category with a substantial epistemological pedigree. It ranges from overt and often violent confrontation with authorities to more passive and hidden forms, famously characterized by James Scott as "arts."[16] Labor historians have long analyzed intentional slow-downs, "soldiering," and the like as endemic to a transnational working-class culture of resistance to speed-ups, de-skilling, and infringements on autonomy. Studies of slave, colonial, and peasant societies have highlighted dissimulation, jokes, the use of the language of authorities against them, and other "weapons of the weak" short of open defiance.[17] Even the sudden outbreak of violent rebellion has been shown to have had its origins and long-lasting effects in popular folklore, religion, and memory.[18]

Before the opening of the archives, documenting resistance of any kind in the Stalin era was not easy. Historians perforce were limited to reading between the lines of official pronouncements about kulak terrorists, wrecking, and sabotage; unverifiable reports that appeared in émigré publications; and some memoir literature. Mapping the social, temporal, and geographical landscapes of resistance and making judgments about its intensity and frequency were at best risky, and few ventured to do so.

On the basis of recent archival research, it has become clear that practically every major state initiative of the 1930s was accompanied by some form of popular resistance. In the case of full-scale collectivization, which commenced in late 1929, resistance was massive. It ran the gamut from insurgencies and other acts of violence, to murders of collectivizers and their local collaborators, to vociferous protests by women (the so-called *bab'i bunty*), frequently in connection with *raion* soviet decisions to close churches and/or confiscate church property, to the *razbazarivanie* ("squandering") of livestock and other property through slaughter and sale, the destruction of collective farm buildings, the liberation of arrested kulaks, the reacquisition of confiscated property, and the disbandment of collective farms.[19] In the longer term, more passive and furtive forms of resistance—Luddism, evasion, theft, ridicule, rumor, and so on—predominated.[20]

Even though the mapping of peasant resistance to collectivization remains incomplete, several questions can be asked about how to understand the phenomenon. Was this a case of the defense of tradition versus a particularly brutal form of enforced modernization? If so, to what extent did peasants invoke positive images from the prerevolutionary past—"Cossack freedom," for example—as opposed to what they defined as Soviet order and justice? With respect to the epidemic of disturbances in March 1930, what role did peasants' perceptions of the state's weakness or vulnerability play? If, as one scholar has argued, "peasant culture lived in peasant resistance," did peasants who collaborated with collectivizers or staffed the collective farms thereby put themselves beyond peasant culture?[21] Finally, what or against whom did peasants think they were resisting? Was it primarily individual authorities, their abuses of power, the entire project of collectivization, the Soviet government, or the apocalyptic Antichrist?[22]

Some of the same issues crop up in connection with working-class resistance. From one particularly well-studied case, a strike of textile workers in the Ivanovo Industrial Region in 1932, it is clear that the language of workers' rights in a socialist state was involved, as well as the legacy of prerevolutionary protests.[23] What is less clear is whether the strike represented a breakdown of tacit rules of social behavior occasioned by the failure of the state to conform to its self-assumed paternalistic responsibilities, or a "working up" of frustrations produced by the state's assumption of those responsibilities in the first place.[24] Here also, the issue of how to define resistance is important. Do we accept the regime's definition according to which violations of labor discipline were punished (sometimes) as anti-Soviet behavior, or do the motivations of the offender constitute the crucial criterion? Should refusals to conform to officially sanctioned behavior or to execute directives be included, or would this be trivializing the very concept of resistance?

The documents in this book can help to define the conceptual parameters of popular resistance. The "class enemy," a mainstay of

Bolshevik rhetoric, was ever present during the First Five-Year Plan. But, as revealed in the testimony presented by a worker to the First Congress of Shock Workers, the "enemy who is dressed in the same overalls as us" was harder to identify and combat (doc. 2). In all likelihood, this shock worker would have considered the letter sent anonymously from the Red Putilovets factory in Leningrad to the Central Executive Committee as written by the same "enemy." For despite their membership in the party, the authors denounce "the terrors and persecution of the peasants" and make common cause not only with the persecuted peasants but also with comrades Trotsky and Bukharin (doc. 9).

Class clearly was not at issue in the case of the youthful pranksters who defaced portraits of Stalin, declared that they wanted to be White Guards, scrawled swastikas on school property, and otherwise shocked their elders (see Chapter 6). This might be construed as resistance, and certainly was considered blasphemously anti-Soviet. But even if the signifiers were political, in all likelihood the targets were not. Many of the documents in the chapter on "Happy Childhoods" suggest the need to incorporate intergenerational relations in considering the nature of resistance.

As for peasants, the weapons of silence and laughter, effective in normal times, proved of limited use in a world turned upside down, where, as a letter to *Pravda* put it, "white is transposed into black, and black into white" (doc. 13). Rumors—that peasants who traveled to Moscow to plead their cause saw former landlords "sit[ting] in our central offices," that collective farmers were to be sent into industry and that foreigners would take their place—perhaps were more effective in confounding authorities (docs. 13, 19). Coming across the latter rumor makes it all the more poignant to read in a letter from a collective farmer of the Northern Caucasus (one of the areas most severely affected by famine) that "he who bolted in time for work in industry did well for himself" (doc. 24).

Bolting in the form of "self-dekulakization" was widely practiced during collectivization. In its aftermath, millions of peasants, predominantly young males, voted against collectivized agriculture with their feet. Out-migration thus occupied a major role in the repertoire of peasant responses, one that would have tremendous consequences for both Soviet agriculture and urban life.[25]

Whether it should be considered a form of "resistance," though, is more doubtful.

For peasants who remained in the countryside, resistance did become part of a way of life, something with which local and, more indirectly, higher authorities had to contend. It is indeed the chief reason why so many historians consider collectivization to have been a Pyrrhic victory for the state, and it would remain endemic to the "Bolshevik order on the kolkhoz" not only for the remainder of the 1930s but for decades thereafter. But resistance was only one dimension of Stalinism as a way of life in the countryside. Between the extremes of resistance on the one hand and full or abject compliance on the other lay the broad, gray area of adaptation and accommodation.[26]

From the documents it is possible to identify at least four strategies that fall within this area: lodging complaints about and otherwise denouncing abusive officials; suggesting revisions to Soviet laws; joining the white-collar or skilled blue-collar work force within the kolkhoz; and engaging in labor activism. If the first two strategies exemplify ways that peasants adapted to the collective farm system by trying to make the system adapt to them, the latter two suggest a greater degree of accommodation, though not necessarily the internalization of the regime's values. These strategies were not mutually exclusive, except that peasants appointed to the kolkhoz administration were not apt to denounce themselves as abusive.

In writing letters of denunciation and complaint, peasants ran the risk of persecution (especially if their communications were intercepted at the local level), but they also could instigate outside intervention leading to the prosecution or removal of offending officials. The complaint lodged by thirty-six independent farmers from the Mordovian Autonomous Oblast led to an investigation that resulted in sanctions against several raion officials (doc. 100). The woman who contracted gonorrhea after having been raped by the kolkhoz chairman provided a deposition that ultimately led to a five-year sentence against him (doc. 117). Letters denouncing abusers of power often referred to them as "kulaks," "scoundrels," and "swine." They also included references to class backgrounds, as in "son of a former elder who always tormented poor peasants," and they otherwise exhibited the importance of memory in kolkhoz politics. Terms derived from more recent or contemporary political discourse, such as "wrecker," "enemy of the people," "Polish spy," "fascist," and "Trotskyist," also cropped up in peasants' letters (and, especially during the Great Purge, in testimony before local courts), but these were more apt to be employed by local party members and administrative personnel than by rank-and-file collective farmers.[27]

The discussions occasioned by the draft of a new Soviet Constitution provided an opportunity for Soviet citizens to express their views on a broad range of issues. The published record of these discussions, replete with statistics on the number of meetings, speakers and proposals, and accounts of labor enthusiasm, not surprisingly presented a picture of overwhelming support for the principles embodied in the constitution. As with other public events, the demonstration of acclaim was an essential ingredient of "Soviet democracy," reinforcing the notion that the party was guiding the masses along the path toward the bright future.[28] But if the party leadership was not also genuinely curious about the public's response, it would be hard to explain why the NKVD and regional party organizations went to the trouble of transcribing and collating the discussions in fortnightly summaries to members of the Politburo and the Central Executive Committee's Presidium.[29] Whatever the case, and despite the limitations of selectivity and the categories under which comments were grouped, we must be grateful for these compilations. Likened by one historian to the *cahiers de doléances* of the French Revolution, the tens of thousands of comments on the constitution and suggestions for its revision are a rich source of information about popular attitudes.[30]

Even a cursory glance at the letters and statements reveals the sheer variety of interpretations and suggestions concerning individual articles. This was particularly the case among peasants. Although provisions relating to household and collective property (docs. 6–10) held great importance for *kolkhozniki*, questions of civic equality and economic justice occurred with remarkable frequency. Surely those who expressed the belief that the constitution meant a return of private property, reinstated full rights to dekulakized peasants and the clergy, abolished compulsory deliveries of foodstuffs, and guaranteed a multiparty system could not have been so deluded (docs. 62, 64, 65). Were they simply naive, misunderstanding the contents of the constitution and the intent of its authors?

In trying to answer this question, it may be worth recalling an earlier momentous act of the state, in this case, the tsarist state. The Emancipation Decree, which abolished serfdom in February 1861, was an extremely lengthy document, full of "legalisms, obscurities, and seeming contradictions." It occasioned all manner of interpretations among the affected peasantry after it was read out in the villages. From the standpoint of the authorities, those that construed the decree as granting *volia* (the peasants' long-cherished ideal of unrestricted freedom) were the most pernicious. Where the peasants persisted in their views, the regime did not refrain from unleashing massive force to disabuse or repress them. The same question might be asked of these peasants: did they really believe that the tsar, their "Little Father" *(batiushka),* wished them to be completely free but that landlords, officials, and priests were conspiring to hide the truth from them? Or was their insistence that emancipation meant true freedom a matter of the "peasants' substitute for politics, a pretext, which they otherwise lacked, to probe the intentions and determination of the regime"? If the peasants' "naive monarchism" was not simply a function of their ignorance, then we must entertain the notion that their misunderstanding was willful.[31]

Seen in this light, the promulgation of the constitution, not unlike that of the emancipation of the serfs seventy-five years earlier, created one of those rare moments when the role of the state in people's lives, if not their role in the life of the state, was open for reconsideration and could be queried. It was an opportunity to lodge a grievance, denounce a malefactor, spin out a pet theory, pour out one's soul. It may have been, as Professor Sokolov contends, "only an illusion of democracy," but lacking the real thing, participants in this conversation were determined to make their thoughts known.

Many peasant responses seem little removed from prerevolutionary times. A widow's contention that land—presumably the household garden plots to which kolkhozniki were entitled—

should be divided not according to the number of (male) workers but rather *na edoka* (by the number of consumers) repeats a demand that many in similar family circumstances made in connection with the emancipation settlement, even if in this instance the authority of Lenin is invoked (doc. 61). The ritualistic praise of Stalin that prefaced many of the responses echoes the naive monarchism of an earlier time, while the form in which at least one peasant letter writer expressed his suggestions is reminiscent of tsarist-era petitions (doc. 66).

This is not to say that nearly two decades of Soviet power left no trace. Complaints about their second-class status in the "socialist country of workers and peasants" and suggestions that the constitution permit peasants to be represented by trade unions and a party of their own, that it be accompanied by a general amnesty, that the death penalty be abolished, that all citizens enjoy the right to travel abroad for work and study, and that the entire "popular mass [be] lifted up and merge into one, as in physics" attest to a characteristically modern sensibility in which the rights of person figured prominently (docs. 66–68). By the same token, and only because of such a sensibility, was it possible to conceive of and call for depriving others (the "new Soviet bourgeoisie," "loafer-parasites") of such rights (doc. 69).

Thus far, I have referred to peasants monolithically. While this makes sense in terms of the solidarity that peasants often exhibited in the face of outsiders, that solidarity had its limits. Many of the sources of divisiveness within the village stemmed from collectivization. As indicated in the documents, these included divisions between kolkhozniki and independent farmers; between peasants who had joined kolkhozes during the first wave of collectivization and those who entered later; between indigenous residents and re-settled dekulakized families or, later still, deported nationalities; and between the families of peasant-migrants and those who stuck it out on the kolkhoz (docs. 15–16, 91, 122, 129). In time, tensions between these groups diminished, but other sources of tension persisted. Inter- and intrafamily feuds, one of the banes of village life, took on a new dimension as sides traded mutual accusations of "kulak" pasts or "anti-Soviet" behavior. In addition to such horizontal cleavages, the hierarchical structure of collectivized agriculture militated against solidarity. For while the legal category of kolkhoznik distinguished members of collective farms from other Soviet citizens, it obscured occupational and gender-based differences within the kolkhoz.

The white-collar elite, which included kolkhoz chairmen, accountants, business managers, brigade leaders, and the heads of various offices and departments, constituted a minimum of 5 percent of the kolkhoz population. Men made up the overwhelming majority of this group—approximately 75 percent by 1937. Men also predominated among the skilled blue-collar work force that included tractor drivers, combine operators, and blacksmiths. Like white-collar personnel, they (and in some cases, their families) were exempted from fieldwork, and, uniquely among kolkhozniki, they received a guaranteed income from the state. Still, for many blue-collar workers, a mechanical skill represented a one-way ticket out of the kolkhoz into labor-starved industry.[32]

Teachers and agronomists were also salaried, but as state employees typically did not belong to the kolkhoz. Whereas agronomy was another predominantly male profession, nearly half of rural teachers were women. Most women, however, were employed in fieldwork, livestock tending, cooking, and child care, jobs that tended to be at the bottom of the pay scale. Moreover, family responsibilities, which included the lion's share of work on the household plot, further limited women's income derived from the kolkhoz.

Conflicts within the kolkhoz village stemming from this gendered division of labor are illustrated in the documents from the Migulin Raion of the Azov–Black Sea Krai (docs. 117–18). This district—and indeed the entire Don region—presented particular challenges to Soviet authorities owing to the concentration of Cossacks, who were notoriously "counterrevolutionary."[33] The abuses of office perpetrated by various kolkhoz officials in the mid-1930s, however, were by no means unique to this area. Their misappropriation of kolkhoz funds, extortion rackets, and sexually predatory behavior toward kolkhoz women were depressingly common, as other documents make clear (docs. 119–21).[34]

Finally, labor activism, encouraged and rewarded by the party, the Komsomol, and, in the case of sovkhoz workers, their respective trade unions, was an adaptive strategy that also could disrupt village solidarities. As in industry, where the shock work and Stakhanovite movements originated, so in agriculture the overful-fillment of quotas by model workers represented a threat to infor-mally negotiated levels of effort and output. Consequently, those who achieved the status of shock workers, or after 1935 Stak-hanovites, ran the risk of ostracism or worse by fellow villagers. Bi-ographical information on activists and the criteria and procedures for "cultivating" them awaits further research, but it appears that at least initially many had served in the Red Army, had worked in industry, or otherwise had nonagricultural experience that de-tached them from the village. Such types were well represented among the delegates to the two Congresses of Outstanding Kolkhoz Workers in January 1933 and February 1935.

Also present at these congresses, though, were substantial num-bers of young women. Among them were Pasha Angelina, who had organized the first women's tractor brigade in the USSR, and Maria Demchenko, a combine operator who pledged to harvest five hundred centners per hectare (nearly four times the average yield) of sugar beets, and succeeded in doing so shortly after the second congress. For their prowess in these male-dominated me-chanical occupations, Angelina and Demchenko were lavished with material rewards and official adulation, becoming the most celebrated Stakhanovites in agriculture. In these respects they sym-bolized the new Soviet woman who owed her emancipation from the patriarchal family to collectivization and the wise leadership of Comrade Stalin.[35] This link between rural women—particularly young, unmarried women—and the regime was not entirely fic-tional. For among the less celebrated rural Stakhanovites and local "notables" (znatnye liudi) was a preponderance of women whose achievements as milkmaids, calf tenders, and fieldworkers put them in contact with outside authorities and earned them modest material rewards if not the respect of their fellow villagers.[36] Such was the case with Klavdia Maksimovskaia, a Northern krai milk-maid who wrote her "autobiography" in response to a request from her trade union's instructor to describe her material condi-tions and her needs (doc. 127).

The willingness of such rural notables as Maksimovskaia and

Ivan Sychov to play by the regime's rules suggests a considerable blurring of the boundaries between "us" and "them." But does this mean that these individuals not only had learned what they were expected to say and do but also had internalized the regime's values? Was there something else going on here besides the pursuit of a strategy? Perhaps we need to approach Stalinism as a way of life in terms of not only games and strategies but the formation of a Stalinist subjectivity.

This is the thrust of a second line of recent scholarly inquiry. "When it comes to Stalinism," writes Stephen Kotkin in his account of the steel city of Magnitogorsk, "what needs to be explained and subjected to detailed scrutiny are the mechanisms by which the dreams of ordinary people and those of the individuals directing the state found common ground in [the] Soviet version of the welfare state."[37] Kotkin characterizes this common ground, located at the intersection of the "grand strategies of the state" and the "little tactics of the habitat," as a distinctly "socialist civilization."

Kotkin's shift of the historical optic away from "what the party and its programs prevented [toward] what they made possible, intentionally and unintentionally," is enormously suggestive.[38] His focus on Stalinism's productive modalities of power (instead of its repressive and otherwise disabling dimensions) contains the potential for transcending the binary oppositions of who-whom, state and society, support and resistance, and orthodoxy and heresy that have been so deeply embedded in Sovietology. Yet as his critics have pointed out, he tends to treat individual subjects as already fully formed *before* they encounter the Bolsheviks' intentions, programs, and policies. They are capable of participating in, circumventing, or resisting the ideologically inspired grand strategies of the state, but they do not internalize them. This "assume[s] a high degree of detachment between the *subject* and its public performance, and the possibility of the pursuit of a personal agenda outside the Bolshevik system of meaning."[39] In other words, the "little tactics of the habitat," if not the "dreams of ordinary people," are rooted in an uncomplicated self-interest, whereas it is precisely the self that has to be examined.

Pursuing the worldview of the Stalinist subject requires a reconceptualization of subjectivity that is independent of its Western liberal moorings.[40] It means taking seriously the importance that individuals attached to "working on" themselves so as to embody the Soviet program of modernization and bring their heterodoxical thoughts into line with what they were expected—no less by themselves than by others—to believe. In this sense, the illiberal Stalinist self was just as much a site or "carrier" of Stalinism as were formal political institutions and rituals. Diaries offer rich possibilities for illuminating this site, and in the case of Stepan Podlubnyi, we see how one individual resorted to his diary as a "laboratory of his Soviet self."[41] But other kinds of materials have been used for a similar purpose. In the hands of one literary historian, for example, the notebooks, manuscripts, and other papers of a Stalin Prize-winning novelist, Vasily Azhaev, reveal the process by which "reforging is made possible; that is, by which coercion becomes desire."[42]

Our documents, less private than these sources, were written to be read and acted upon by someone else. Nevertheless, many illustrate the extraordinary degree to which Stalinist political culture could be personalized, and vice versa—that is, how the personal became Stalinized. Whether it was I. K. Karniush, the semiliterate peasant who rendered the history of the tsars and the revolution/civil war in the manner of a folktale before inserting his kolkhoz and himself into the narrative; or the aged P. P. Zagumennov, who after attending a study session devoted to the *Kratkii kurs istorii VKP(b)* [Short course in the history of the VKP(b)], ascribed to the book near miracle-working powers; or, again, Maksimovskaia, whose story of orphanhood, adoption by the state farm, near suicide, and rescue bore little if any relation to what she had been asked to write about, there is much evidence of a blending of the popular and the official, the familiar and the strange, the old and the new (docs. 73, 75, 127).

The familiar, even intimate tone of many of the letters also suggests the link between the personal and the political. This link often was forged through use of kinship and familial metaphors. One notes, for example, that letters sent to Mikhail Kalinin, president of the Executive Committee of the Soviets, addressed him as "all-Union elder" *(starosta)*—a term combining Soviet and village communal lexicons—and, more frequently, as "dear uncle" and "grandfather" (docs. 130, 132, 137–138, 148). Nadezhda Krupskaia, Lenin's widow and an important official in the RSFSR's Commissariat of Education, becomes "dear N.K.," whose "maternal/parental assistance" is craved (doc. 152). At a time when the status of real Soviet families was in flux and representations of the Soviet Union as a "great family" and Stalin as a great father were becoming more prevalent, these familial images assumed more than rhetorical importance.[43] Not only because dekulakization and terror dispersed families and produced so many orphans, but also because in Stalinist discourse the small nuclear family was encompassed by the big (all-Union) one, the distinction between metaphorical and blood relatives became blurred.

The organic conception of the state as well as the government's strongly pronatalist policy enabled one letter writer from Leningrad to concoct a vast scheme based on the principle that illness violated "the requirements of health discipline." The scheme included the establishment of a Commissariat of Work Capacity and Longevity that would head up campaigns to eliminate ignorance about health and unhealthy behavior. But that was not all. In the interests of producing the most healthy "civic progeny," women of childbearing age were to be categorized according to their health, with the highest category being that of Stakhanovite of childbearing production. Men would be registered by a childbirth bureau according to "the quality and fullness of their fertilizing agent." This bizarre eugenic project was proposed as an amendment to the constitution that would ensure "our homeland's might in every field that requires a capacity for work and longevity from citizens" (doc. 72).

This brings us both logically and chronologically to the "great terror," that paroxysm of state-organized/disorganizing butchery that no history of Stalinism can fail to address. Reviewing recent accounts of the terror can make one nostalgic for the simplicity and clarity of the classical interpretation of a paranoid ruler who ruthlessly exterminated former colleagues and millions of others in his unquenchable thirst for personal power.[44] The avalanche of new source materials and a more sophisticated understanding of the mechanisms of power have generated a plethora of new interpretations. Yet their sheer number and the fact that they all depart to a greater or lesser extent from the all-embracing sweep of the totalitarian model has meant that none has been able to replicate the earlier version in monopolizing the scholarly community's attention to the subject, much less in capturing the popular imagination.

Thus why "it" happened can be explained by power struggles between the Kremlin center and power holders on the periphery; by the embitterment of bureaucratic relations within the party-state machine occasioned by the ability of cadres to deflect disciplinary initiatives onto scapegoats; by the survival of large numbers of previously repressed individuals and those expelled from or reprimanded by the party, leading to the "logic" of the top leadership's desire to eliminate a potential "fifth column" in a time of increasing international tensions; by the party's "inquisitorial mind-set" that grew out of its theocratic responsibilities and the empowerment of the secret police with virtually unlimited power to hunt down and round up enemies; by a more generalized belief in the existence of spies, wreckers, and other "enemies of the people," whose elimination by the NKVD would truly make life better; by the nomenklatura elite's "corporate anxiety" feeding Stalin's suspicion of "enemies with party cards," which led to a replacement of "normal politics" by a "paranoiac war of all against all;" or by a combination of any or all of these explanations.[45] Yet another potentially valuable approach—aimed less at why the terror was initiated than at why so many people actively participated in it— emphasizes the discursive significance of "purification" and "degeneration" and the desire of Stalinist subjects to be among the pure.[46] The parabola of terror in particular regions, professions, and sectors of the economy is the subject of yet another whole literature, as is the more lugubrious question of the number of the terror's victims.[47] And we are just beginning to become aware of the extent of "mass operations" against recidivist criminals, former kulaks, religious sectarians, and members of diaspora nationalities.[48]

The documents in our volume speak to the popular dimensions of the terror: how it entered into the Stalinist way of life—and death—in the late 1930s. Several of the documents are in the form of denunciations, popular initiatives that were by no means peculiar to this period but took on an often lethal dynamic once the hunt for enemies became a national pastime. Whether inspired by a(n alleged) miscarriage of justice, professional jealousy, or instances of administrative high-handedness and incompetence, all employ the overheated language of wrecking, political banditry, "Trotskyist-Bukharinist scum and other vermin," and so forth that had become standard tropes of Stalinist political discourse (docs. 76–77, 109–10, 113). Other letters attack NKVD officers for perpetuating "horrors" or for having "completely let themselves go," but also, in one instance, written in the wake of N. Yezhov's removal as people's commissar, for having "overlooked real spies and saboteurs" (docs. 81, 83–85). Letters from relatives of arrestees are also represented. While some contest the accusations and sentences, others betray a willingness to sacrifice a spouse or a parent ("My father is guilty of something." "Am I supposed to drop dead just because I have a child from somebody who was sentenced to five years under Article 58?" "I don't know what my father was guilty of. . . . I only know that my mama is not guilty of anything.") in the interests of saving themselves or the other parent (docs. 82, 153–54).

Finally, there are documents relating to interethnic relations. This is a subject with little scholarly pedigree but one that has been developing rapidly since the breakup of the Soviet Union.[49] As many scholars have noted, nationality policy was a construction project (or "work in progress") throughout the prewar period, if not beyond. Nomenclature changed frequently, as did ethno-territorial boundaries and locations of particular nationalities on the continuum that stretched from the primitive (*plemena* [tribes]) to the modern (*natsii* [nations]). Correspondingly, "bourgeois nationalism" and "great-power chauvinism," epithets that crop up in our documents, changed meaning. If earlier in the decade intellectuals who were insufficiently enthusiastic about the proletarianization of their fellow nationals were accused of yearning for the pre-Soviet past (that is, were *bourgeois* nationalists), then by the late 1930s, bourgeois *nationalism* had come to mean insufficient enthusiasm for Russians as big(ger) brothers.[50] More generally, constructions of nationality had huge implications not only for the ethnographers, statisticians, and party and state officials who studied, counted, and ruled over the hodgepodge of peoples within (and sometimes spilling over) Soviet borders, but for the peoples themselves.

The documents mainly concern the situation on the ground, as it were. This ground had become extremely unstable in the late 1930s, owing to the worsening economic situation in the country, the wave of forced resettlements following Soviet annexations of new territory in the west, and the doubtful loyalties of those who were allowed to remain behind. National antagonisms flared up where new settlers (both voluntary and forced) pressed upon the already scarce resources, or where the refusal of a job could be interpreted as national discrimination. Yet we also find instances of hospitality toward the forcibly resettled and even more friendly relations. It would be interesting in this connection to know which was worst from the standpoint of those to whom the reports included here were sent: evidence of interethnic hostility, collusion among members of the same nationality in crimes (including draft evasion), or friendship between tainted exiles from "the former Poland" and collective farmers in Kazakhstan (docs. 92–94).

The picture we present of how Soviet citizens tried to navigate the "massive social transformations" of the 1930s is not a particularly happy one. Although it contains some streaks of light, the dominant tone is dark with a good deal of gray. It might be thought that our selection of documents and commentary linking them are tendentious, designed to cast aspersions on the moral character or level of civilization of "*Homo Sovieticus.*"[51] In other words, we run the risk of being accused of blaming the "many millions of innocent people" who were victims of a "regime of terror."

To such a charge, we would plead not guilty. Our plea would not be on the grounds that the documents speak for themselves and that we acted as mere ciphers for their transmission into print. Rather, we wish to emphasize several things. First, the institutional and cultural terrain through which people navigated was itself harsh and full of dangers. To some extent, this was historically conditioned. Even before the onset of the Socialist Offensive, there were plenty of reasons for resentment and apprehension stemming from the experiences of tsarist oppression, the civil war, the failure of the New Economic Policy (NEP) to vindicate sacrifices, and the way these experiences had been processed. If we did not know this already, the frequent references in the letters to incidents from the past and the terminology employed in describing them tell us so.[52] The offensive, though, intensified these feelings partly through the harshening of official policies and rhetoric, and partly through the harshening of daily life.

Secondly, at least some cadres who were schooled to oppose any "liberalizing" tendencies and observe stern vigilance either could not bring themselves to carry out policies which they knew to be inhumane or sought on their own initiative to ameliorate the effects of such policies. The rural soviet chairman who felt that he was "on the edge of a straight razor" because his refusal to collect additional taxes had earned him a reprimand from the party; the NKVD bureau chief who used his report of an attempted suicide to inform higher authorities of the dire food situation on the fourteen kolkhozes in his raion; and several whistleblowers seeking to halt abuses are examples of such officials (docs. 27, 31–33, 45, 118). Evidently, the situation was more complex than the epithets of a police state or "regime of terror" would suggest.

The Stalinist state surely used and abused its citizenry. But as our documents show, the reverse was also the case. Officials appropriated funds at their disposal for their own use and otherwise fed at the state's trough; aggrieved and ambitious citizens sent letters denouncing their tormentors (who may have been merely carrying out state policies), or offering their services so that they too could garner a meager share of the state's resources; youngsters sought intervention or at least guidance to see them through difficulties that the state itself had created, while their elders sought absolution and the remission of their fates. All to a degree acted as the offspring of a paternalistic state that regarded some as more deserving than others but claimed, in any case, to know what was in their best interests.

This is not to reject but rather to complicate the hoary distinction between the "state" and "society." The very title of our book is meant to suggest that what normally is thought of as political—a system or ideology—was something more, a lived reality or way of life. The way Soviet citizens lived, the variety of relationships they entered into and how they fashioned themselves in so doing, both shaped and were shaped by what Stalinism was. From the distance of sixty years and in the aftermath of the collapse of the system constructed in the 1930s it is easy to stand back and declare that Stalinism's ideological mainsprings, the promise of socialism, was a chimera that "befogged" consciousness. But whether those whose voices we have assembled believed in that promise or only pretended to do so, they had to work with what was given, namely the mad rush to build socialism. Thus, in addition to art that trumpeted the glories of Stalinism, we would point to another kind of art—that of surviving the stampede—and mourn those who got in the way.

# CHAPTER ONE

# The Socialist Offensive

THE YEAR 1929 marked the beginning of the full-scale collectivization of agriculture, the key element of what was, in the terminology of official propaganda, a "full-scale socialist offensive on all fronts."[1] The slogan, with its connotations of attack and advance, was absolutely typical of Communist rhetoric at this time. It eclipsed more gradualist and organic metaphors, such as growing into *(vrastanie)* socialism, which N. I. Bukharin and others had employed during the heyday of the New Economic Policy (NEP). Impatience with compromises, fear that the country was growing into capitalism rather than out of it, and disgruntlement among rank-and-file workers who bore the brunt of rationalization, economization, and other efficiency drives were only part of what constituted the crisis of NEP. Politically, the crisis followed upon Stalin's consolidation of power as general secretary and his faction's successive victories over the Left and Joint Oppositions within the party. Toward the end of 1927 the Stalinist "center" lurched leftward: it appropriated the recently silenced opposition's agenda for rapid industrialization based on massive investments in heavy industry, promoted campaigns for self-criticism and against bureaucratism within party and state organs, and otherwise intensified class-war rhetoric. Efforts by Bukharin, A. I. Rykov, and M. P.

Tomsky to tone down this rhetoric and minimize the danger of a "capitalist offensive" earned them the opprobrium of the Stalinists and the sobriquet of right opportunists.

The new policy was doomed to constant failures for which excuses had to be sought, for which the desired had to pass for the real. Trotsky called this "the policy of half-shut eyes," one that involved the application of the term *socialist* to everything that occurred inside the Soviet Union. But it is doubtful that anyone, including Trotsky, knew just what that new order should be, and what might result from naked ideas thrown onto the soil of a society bearing the burden of many years' trials and suffering from many evils and vices.

The Socialist Offensive began in accordance with all the rules of military operations. Battlefronts were declared: the Industrialization Front, Collectivization Front, Tractor Front, Ideological Front, Cultural Front, Antireligious Front, Literary Front, and so forth. Each front had its "armies," "bases," heroes, and "saboteurs." Every ton of coal or iron produced, every village collectivized, every individual converted to godlessness, every "bourgeois" writer exposed was a victory for socialism. Thus could a young worker in the Moscow subway construction project write verses with the refrain: "As we fought then, in 1918, not sparing our young years / So we must fight now for each meter built."[2]

For storming the fortresses that the Bolsheviks could not fail to take, they needed mass support. At the beginning of 1929 a campaign was launched to develop nationwide mass socialist competitions in factories and plants, and among transport and construction workers. Socialist competition was declared to be one of the main battlefronts in the class struggle and a prerequisite for fulfilling the goals of the First Five-Year Plan. The competition's main form was the shock worker and shock brigade movement. As V. V. Kuibyshev, chairman of VSNKh (*Vyshii Sovet Narodnogo Khoziaistva* [supreme council of the national economy]) and one of Stalin's close comrades in arms, said at the first All-Union Congress of Shock Brigades in December 1929, the chief task of shock brigades was to create a new type of worker. Correspondingly, newspaper articles propagandizing the shock worker movement appeared with such titles as "A New Man Is Being

Born" and "A New Society Is Being Forged." According to Kuibyshev,

> Socialist competition and shock brigades constitute the most effective attack on the petty bourgeois psychology still strong in certain strata of the working class. They mark the end to the old rule of "Every man for himself and God for everyone." They deal a crushing blow to old work traditions, old habits, the old psychology cultivated for decades under capitalism. Precisely this makes socialist competition and shock brigades a unique front in the class struggle. . . . The lack of uniformity in the working class, naturally, adds extreme urgency to the task of the shock brigades, gives it a special importance because we must reeducate by means of the finest examples possible those strata of workers now pouring into the factories who are removing themselves from agriculture.

Kuibyshev also pointed out that socialist competition and shock brigades were meeting opposition from bureaucratic staff in the form of quiet sabotage and scornful attitudes.[3]

There can be no doubt that a substantial part of the working class was imbued with the competitive spirit, especially, as statistical information about shock workers testifies, young people and Komsomol members. At the First Congress of Shock Brigades more than 30 percent of the participants were people under age twenty-two, while those over forty made up only 15 percent.[4]

The sizable scope of the movement was achieved through clever use of exaggerated claims, healthy rivalry, the eagerness of the young to take part in anything new, and their desire to stand out, to appear in displays, on the pages of newspapers, at rallies, meetings, and assemblies. Hence the notion of competition as holiday and parade was constantly fanned by the press. Hence rush work, the race for figures, mass calls for and mobilization of shock workers. Shock brigades were formed to eliminate hitches in production. At many plants "antireligious shock brigades," Komsomol "light cavalry" detachments, and the like were active. In the Subway Project the women's "reformatory" shock brigade became famous for "reforming" men who were drunkards, absentee workers, and loafers. To fall behind women in work was something even the most inveterate rowdies could not suffer. The form of this work—collective shock work—was also characteristic of the spirit of the time, as it was of the working traditions of the Russian peasant commune *(obshchina)* and the artel: all together, all at once, all in one stroke, "One, two—heave! Once more—heave!"

Soviet historians created a large corpus of literature on the topic of socialist competition and published a great number of documents about work achievements, heroism, and worker self-sacrifice for maximal output during the first Five-Year Plans. Quite a few of the published documents clearly smack of journalistic cant, contain political twaddle, and repeat hackneyed expressions. In as much as they have already been published, there is no sense in citing them again. But we would like to pay heed nonetheless to several that convey the "aroma" of the epoch.

Here, for example, is an excerpt from the address of worker A. N. Voronin, speaking in the language of a "metalworker" to the First Congress of Shock Brigades:

---

## Document 1

Speech by A. N. Voronin to First Congress of Shock Brigades, December 1929. *Pervyi Vsesoiuznyi s"ezd udarnykh brigad (k tridts. s"ezda)* [first all-Union congress of shock brigades (for its thirtieth anniversary)], Moscow, 1959, pp. 127–128.

---

The worker-peasant government has decided to build on the remote steppes of Kazakhstan a railroad in order to connect Turkestan and Siberia. For this the government has allocated approximately two hundred million rubles and has given us the task of trying our best to build a railroad in five years, which will be called the Turkestan-Siberian Line.

We, the workers and the engineering and technical staff, taking into account the warlike and urgent need for this line, have decided that we will build it not in five years but 3.5. Accordingly we will shorten construction by eighteen months. We have said that we will build it at little cost, and build it well and solidly. Some hysterical persons have told you that we will not be able to build it quickly and solidly.

I will give you an example, Comrades. The example is a very important one. In the eighth construction section, at one time the fifth construction section, at the Alma-Ata station is Poganka Brook. Here was built a reinforced concrete bridge. Now when they finished constructing it and got it completely ready, a locomotive was brought up and stood six hours on this bridge, and in the final analysis it turned out that the bridge settled one thousandth of a meter. So the words of the hysterical ones were not justified.

It's all very well that the Turk-Sib builders succeeded in building the railroad fast, at little cost, and solidly, in spite of the doubts of the "hysterical ones." Often, though, accelerated production speeds were attained to the detriment of the quality of work completed. Frequent stoppages, production breakdowns, and difficulties putting newly completed projects into service are proof of this. As a matter of fact, the shock workers themselves inspired an ambiguous attitude on the part of other workers. This is the subject of an excerpt from G. B. Gelman's address to the First Congress of Shock Brigades on behalf of workers of the Proletariat's Victory *(Pobeda proletariata)* textile factory in the city of Yegorevsk. Criticizing management for not devoting enough attention to the problems of competition, he said, among other things:

## Document 2

Speech by G. B. Gelman to First Congress of Shock Brigades, December 1929. *Pervyi Vsesoiuznyi s"ezd udarnykh brigad (k tridts. s"ezda)*, Moscow, 1959, p. 100.

. . . It's necessary that those agreements we put together be comprehensible to the workers so that each worker who signs an agreement will know that in doing so he takes upon himself such and such obligations. We have achieved at our factory some two hundred cases of reduced production costs, in some departments workers voluntarily increased their productivity per shift, etc. Thanks to this, we carried out our tasks and even more. If the delegates here say that they intend to fulfill the Five-Year Plan in four years, then our workers have adopted that rate of speed needed to fulfill their Five-Year Plan in three years, for we have already cut costs by 21 percent and reduced the number of rejects.

Working in the foremost lines of the economic battlefront, one must not forget that we find ourselves amid the fiercest class struggle. I wish to present as an example the following facts: the workers of the dyeing division changed from one type of jigger to another, raising labor productivity by more than 100 percent. On the night shift a shock worker fell into the machine, and when he was being beaten by this jigger, when his legs were being broken, when he was being boiled in the hot dye, a worker standing nearby did not stop the machine. When the matter was investigated, it turned out that [the latter] was a well-to-do kulak.

Another instance. When the boiler room firemen were to start increased work shifts, they nearly tossed our initiator into the furnace.

We're not afraid of battling with the enemy we see, but the enemy who works along side us at a machine, the enemy who is dressed in the same overalls as us, this enemy we're afraid of. We can't for a minute forget that the class enemy is mighty powerful, and we will be victorious only by the fiercest struggle with him.

Significantly, all remarks against competition, regardless of the motives for making them, were subject to ruthless class-related judgment and considered intrigues of secret enemies of the Soviet government. Just who were these "enemies," "hysterical persons," "bearers of the petty bourgeois mentality," "backward workers," "bureaucrats," and so forth? Why were they against competition, and why was it necessary to fight them in the fiercest manner? Gelman's speech makes it quite clear why workers spoke out against competition: the unavoidable reduction in labor costs, tightening of the work schedule, increase in the physical intensity of work. But not only this. Storming and campaigning ran counter to the requirements of modern industrial production, with its steady pace, monotony, and precision. No wonder that competition produced its best results in situations where only wheelbarrows and spades were required, where everything depended on applying physical effort. Thus, whether competition and opposition to it should be treated solely in the sense of a struggle between the new and the old is open to doubt. Gelman points to one of the "enemies" of competition as a "former kulak" who had managed to find work in a factory. It is not hard to understand why the "former kulak" dipped an industrial front-runner in hot dye, but it is highly unlikely that all the stokers at the Proletariat's Victory factory were "former kulaks."

Soviet publications did not include documents that set forth the arguments of those objecting to shock work, nor of people who doubted the benefit of the movement. Mention is made, of course, of the existence of "whiners and those of little faith," of bureaucratism and overrigid organization of the movement that damaged "the Great Cause." There is really no mention at all of the degeneration of socialist competition when there were observed—against a background of impressive growth in the number of shock workers, shock brigades, factory shock departments and sections, and even of entire shock plants—production stoppages, standstills, falls in productivity, and so forth, and a resultant slowing down of the indicators of growth in the economy.

Let us look at a letter by a young Leningrad worker who, responding to a Komsomol appeal, went off to work at one of the shock construction sites of the First Five-Year Plan, Magnitka.[5] The letter was written in June 1931 and, after being subjected to a thorough examination, became an object of great attention on the part of political organs, never reaching the addressee:

## Document 3

Personal letter by a young Leningrad worker from Magnitogorsk, June 1931. GARF, f. 7952, op. 5, d. 172, ll. 59–60. Typed copy.

Hello, Uncle Fedia. Greetings from Magnitogorsk. Uncle Fedia, we arrived at the place here safe and sound. They did a poor job of meeting us at Magnitogorsk. We sat and waited a very long time for the bus to take us to the place we were going. Toward evening the bus came for us. Brought us to open country and left us. They showed us a tent in which there was nothing except the tent itself. The first night we slept on the bare ground, for the second they made sawhorses and paneling for us. We slept on the bare boards. The third day they sort of knocked together a floor in the tent for us out of boards. They handed us blankets and empty mattress cases, gave us straw, and we stuffed the mattresses. So began our camp life.

Uncle Fedia, here dinners in the cafeteria are eighty kopecks and a ruble ten kopecks and they're no good at all, so we have to go hungry, and there's nowhere else to get food. Uncle Fedia, they don't give us work by specialty since nobody knows when the machine installation will begin. Four days we did nothing, or sat in tents, or walked around looking for the bosses. Finally, they gave us something to do: building temporary housing. We raised a fuss and handed to the employment office a request to have our agreement annulled, but they came back to us with time conditions: if by 10 June they didn't give us work by trade and did not lodge us in temporary housing and did not distribute overalls to us, then on the eleventh the agreement would be voided. We're waiting until 15 June, and no matter what I'm coming back to Leningrad. So we've fallen into a trap. No matter how hard you try, you can't find a way out. Right now we're building temporary housing. But you can understand yourself what sort of carpenters we are. But otherwise there's no work. A large number of workers leave to go back to where they came from

## Document 3 *continued*

every day, but it's very hard to get out of here. They won't let you out for any-thing, but no matter what I'm coming back since life here is impossible: first of all, there's no work by trade, they don't give you overalls, the chow is aw-ful, we're living in tents, and the weather is cold and rainy all the time. The tents always leak and after a rain everything is soggy. Strong cold winds come down from the mountains so it's very cold to live in the tents, we're freezing, and the bosses don't give a damn. Now when we were being sent off, we heard pretty, sweet words. You're going, they said, to a shock construction project. They're waiting for you. The project (installation of machinery) can't proceed without you, they said. But in fact this is what is actually the case: we are not needed at all since there are many workers here and we're putting up tempo-rary housing.

Uncle Fedia, there is such a mess here that you wouldn't be able to make head or tail of it. Our big shots here are nothing but bureaucrats, there's com-plete confusion, you can't find anything anywhere.

Uncle Fedia, I'm going to stop writing for now. I'll write more later.

---

There can be no doubt that the letter is accurate. Indeed, the problems mentioned not only were not concealed but rather were featured in romanticized accounts of the First Five-Year Plan and "the heroic working life of our pathfinders." The creation of this myth is probably more the product of later years and the numerous books, movies, and memoirs that tell us about "roaring industrial-ization": plants springing up in empty places erected by the shock work of Soviet workers and engineers. But many sources depict a life quite unromantic. In the document cited above one finds noth-ing heroic—just muddle and disorder, and that at a construction site considered a model for the entire country, a distinctive symbol of the First Five-Year Plan. In the push to expand construction in the country, sanitary and epidemiological conditions took a sharp turn for the worse. In a memorandum to party bodies sent at the end of 1931, the People's Commissariat of Health *(Narkomzdrav),* citing very incomplete data, noted that morbidity in 1931 had in-creased from the previous year, typhoid fever had risen by 64 per-cent, typhus had doubled, and smallpox had tripled. Doctors at-tributed these catastrophic indicators to the mass concentration of people at new construction sites and to the unsanitary conditions and absence of elementary hygienic practices. In workers' tempo-rary housing each person was allotted less than one square meter of living space. Special inspections of the construction sites at Kuznetsk, Magnitogorsk, and Bobriki showed that instances of mass epidemics were concealed by site directors. In infirmaries at temporary living quarters that were inspected in winter, terrible cold prevailed, 5–6° C., along with filth, bedbugs, and lice. Because of interruptions in the water supply, sick people did not wash for days. At the Bobriki site it was revealed that for forty-seven sick people there were only eight spoons. The corpses of those who died were left in the infirmaries for up to four days, and when they were finally dispatched to the morgue, they were put on carts along with dishes, utensils, and food products. Mass outbreaks of venereal disease were recorded. At the Kuznetsk site alone it was revealed that there were twelve hundred patients with venereal disease. Tuberculosis was widespread.[6]

No wonder that the confrontation with reality caused the initial enthusiasm of the builders of the new society to dry up and be replaced by a profound disillusionment. What is more, in the sources one can trace the transition of such emergency situations into permanent features in the daily life of people at Soviet construction sites. But what in actual fact did "construction site" mean? It meant brick, cement, glass, machinery, and equipment that existed on paper but not at the site. Economically unfounded decisions resulted in plans coming apart at the seams. Soaring tasks, including among other things the approval of counterplans—a form of socialist competition in which workers proposed to outdo management's planned targets—that had no material underpinning, aggravated the confusion still more and had destructive consequences for the entire economy.

The general worsening of the economic situation in the country was accompanied by increased shortages, by much broader use of rationing (introduced at the end of the 1920s), by the closing of many private stores, large and small, and by a resultant flourishing of speculation on the black market. Life became increasingly burdened with diurnal concerns, deprivations, and difficulties, and this determined peoples' habitual behavior despite all the talk about high matters and sacrifices in the name of socialism.

The summary compiled from letters to *Pravda* for September 1930 included the report of a "promotee" *(vydvizhenets)* named

Tarasov about the supply situation in Moscow (which, incidentally, was better than in the country as a whole):

---

# Document 4

Letter to *Pravda* included in summary report "The Sukharevites Are in Charge," September 1930. RGAE, f. 7486s, op. 1, d. 102, ll. 242–243. Typed copy.

---

. . . The denizens of Sukharevka, of the Central, Smolensk, and other markets are experiencing spring, are they not? The secondhand dealers have truly bred like hell, haven't they? Occupying themselves now with the very lively resale business are seasonal workers and dairy sales women and invalids and some of the non-class-conscious workers with their wives and those sent to work at various construction projects. They employ a huge number of work methods. So here the cooperative's records have been cleaned up, here also entirely fake records, here two or more of these registers under one and the same name, here a false due date for your pregnant wife and here travel document abuse and unscrupulous use of someone else's ration books. It's got to the point that even a backward worker nearly five times in the course of a week or two stands [in line] for women's hose and, beating his breast, as a worker demands "Get it for me now. You are giving things to the profiteers. May you croak, give to me too." A whole mass of deathly ill invalids of one sort or another and people who have been patients at Kanatchikov's Summerhouse [the popular name for a psychiatric clinic in Moscow] have appeared and with extraordinary arrogance abuse their position: "Give to us or don't expect us to account for our actions."

What is more, in this "activity" there is a clearly marked tendency to remove from the Soviet state market any sort of goods by any means—and fast. Toss men's winter shoes on the market and let people buy as many as they want. Women will buy many pair each, in a few hours it will look like a fire has cleaned the shelves no matter how full they were.

"Someone" came up with the notion that you should take what's here today and take it no matter what the cost because on the morrow there won't be anything and who knows when it will appear again because, as they say, now it's all industrialization. In some cases it's even happened that store windows get broken, metal barriers are knocked down and there's a wild, inhuman crush. In the Central Department Store (in the retail part of Mostorg [Moscow trading firm] that's on the Petrovka) because of such uncontrolled force from this type of customer the fourth floor is in danger of collapse. The public is very definitely becoming more and more insolent with every day, and the ones who resell secondhand store goods are the first to unleash antagonism.

On 23 July in Mostorg's Store no. 5 that's at the Smolensk Market customers beat one woman clerk unmercifully. Another clerk was beaten so badly by customers that she had to be doused with water.

On 21 July in that store work went on thanks only to the presence of an entire detail of police. You work under siege and the thought of a very probable rout of the store doesn't leave the staff even for a minute. It's clear that this business is guided by those from Sukharevka who give their catchwords to the crowd. The huge Moscow group of activists should mobilize and crush these "Sukharevites."

Complaints about standards established for supplying workers, about huge lines in stores, about salesclerks hiding goods so that they can sell them on the side—such is the standard fare of these documents. Workers inveighed against increased prices for food and other essential items in 1931 and a subsequent increase in prices at worker cafeterias. The summary compiled apropos of this protest provides evidence of such discussions at the Moscow Electro-Plant *(Elektrozavod):* "Cafeteria no. 4. 'Those bastards jumped dinner prices up from thirty-seven to fifty-five kopecks. You really get fleeced for every meal. . . . ' Cafeteria no. 2. ' . . . OK, great, so this is how we'll build socialism sooner.'"[7]

An analysis of reports from various localities shows that nowhere in the country was the situation any better. Here, for example, is the report of a certain Buslaev from Mordovia, included in the same *Pravda* summary under the rubric of "How Profiteering Starts":

# Document 5

Letter to *Pravda* on supply situation in Mordovia, September 1930. RGAE, f. 7486s, op. 1, d. 102, l. 239. Typed copy.

The worker settlement of Vindrei in the Zubovo-Poliansk Raion of Mordovia Oblast was forgotten by the trade department and the consumer cooperative, and the Vindrei Sawmill in particular was forgotten.

The workers for their part made every effort to fulfill the industrial and financial plan and fulfilled it by more than 100 percent, but how are they supplied? The ration is received only by the worker, except for rye flour, his wife

## Document 5 *continued*

and small children receive nothing. Workers and their families wear worn-out clothes, the kids are in rags, their naked bellies are sticking out. You need to buy something badly, and where are you going to buy it? In the worker's co-op! A big waste of time. Nothing but empty shelves and bottles of perfume. At the market? The profiteers skin workers alive. A meter of calico costs thirty-five kopecks. The exact same calico now from a profiteer at the market costs a ruble thirty-five kopecks a meter. The workers are outraged that the profiteer has calico and other items, and in the worker's co-op there is nothing. I think it's clear what atmosphere may emerge at the plant, but surely there are ways to prevent it. All you have to do is have the right person put pressure in the right place.

---

This very demand that "the right person put pressure in the right place" is typical of the mentality of the time, reflecting the conviction that all problems can be solved by means of administrative and punitive measures. Archival sources from this period testify to growing social resentment. It is expressed in thousands of appeals to the authorities regarding the ever-increasing difficulties of buying food, the disgusting meals served in workers' cafeterias, and scandalous behavior occurring in lines. Ration portions established for various categories of the population were not met. For "trade" in coupons there simply wasn't enough food. Because of this, abuses and corruption by those in charge were frequent. Reports were received about people destroying stores and cooperative shops, about "women's riots."

A letter from worker B. N. Kniazev from Tula describes increased dissatisfaction and grumbling among workers and compares the working class to a horse that has been driven too hard:

## Document 6

Letter of complaint to *Pravda* from B. N. Kniazev, Tula, September 1930. RGAE, f. 7486s, op. 1, d. 102, l. 241. Typed copy.

---

The building of socialism is not done by Bolsheviks alone. It should not be forgotten that many millions of workers are participating in the building of socialism. A horse with its own strength can drag seventy-five poods, but its owner has loaded it with a hundred poods, and in addition he's fed it poorly.

## Document 6 *continued*

No matter how much he uses the whip, it still won't be able to move the cart.

This is also true for the working class. They've loaded it with socialist competition, shock work, overfulfilling the industrial and financial plan, and so forth. A worker toils seven hours, not ever leaving his post, and this is not all he does. Afterward he sits in meetings or else attends classes for an hour and a half or two in order to increase his skill level, and if he doesn't do these things, then he's doing things at home. And what does he live on? One hundred fifty grams of salted mutton, he will make soup without any of the usual additives, neither carrots, beets, flour, nor salt pork. What kind of soup do you get from this? Mere "dishwater."

Worker P. Skatov from Moscow wrote *Pravda* in the summer of 1930: "When they tell you that today there's a lecture at the shop on religion or some such thing, in response you sigh and spit because you don't want to listen to these highfalutin words. We've learned to speak a hundred times better than to do our work." An anonymous letter writer from the Donbass declared: "The press trumpets 'Give us coal, steel, iron, and so forth and so on. Shame on those who fail to fulfill the industrial and financial plan.' I say the following: dear newspaper trumpeters, 'Come and visit us in the Donbass. We'll treat you to a bottle of hot water (instead of tea), a hunk not of bread but something incomprehensible, boiled water without sugar, and then, dear friend, kindly go and mine the coal quota.'"[8] The difficulties were intensified by the offensive against the private sector involving as it did the elimination of several traditional forms of existence characteristic of the way of life of industrial and office workers in the provinces. This is the subject of an anonymous letter to *Pravda* from the city of Aktyubinsk in Kazakhstan:

## Document 7

Anonymous letter of complaint to *Pravda* from Aktyubinsk, Kazakhstan, 1932. RGAE, f. 7486s, op. 1, d. 236, ll. 11–12. Typed copy.

Comrade Editor, Please give me an answer. Do the local authorities have the right to forcibly take away the only cow of industrial and office workers?

## Document 7 *continued*

What is more, they demand a receipt showing that the cow was handed over voluntarily and they threaten you by saying if you don't do this, they will put you in prison for failure to fulfill the meat procurement. How can you live when the cooperative distributes only black bread, and at the market goods have the prices of 1919 and 1920? Lice have eaten us to death, and soap is given only to railroad workers. From hunger and filth we have a massive outbreak of spotted fever.

Having liquidated private tradesmen, the government suddenly discovered that basic things that were impossible to do without had begun to vanish. Unable to meet their burden, the restaurants, cafes, and snack bars, the barbers and hairdressers, the tailors and repair shops that had provided the everyday bases of existence closed shop. The influx of huge numbers of rural dwellers into the cities aggravated the shortages. It turned out that retail trade, eating establishments, and consumer services were indispensable. Like it or not, the question of organizing state-run institutions of trade, eating services, and everyday needs had to be addressed. At first, it seemed that here too the problems could be solved at a stroke by creating giant enterprises. In 1931 construction began for the Moscow meat processing and packing factory (subsequently the Mikoyan Plant), old candy and cookie factories were reconstructed, and a network of state stores, service shops, and workers' cafeterias was created. Attention focused initially on large industrial centers. But all these measures proved to be insufficient. The unwieldy state trading, public catering, and other state-run services and activities coped poorly. The disdainful attitude toward small things against the background of great political questions was telling. The term "for mass consumption" *(shirpotreb)* cropped up in the 1930s for merchandise produced to meet everyone's daily needs. It acquired a certain pejorative connotation and became a blanket term for inferior quality, which, along with poor services, crudity, and boorishness, found expression in lines such as "gobble up what you are served" and "there are lots of you, and I am but one woman here."

The documents make clear a gradual intensification of social conflict. Socialist competition sowed discord among workers, discord that was officially viewed as opposition to the new movement by backward strata in the working class. Workers' hostility intensified toward people from rural areas onto whom the leadership tried to shift blame for ever-increasing difficulties. Peasants escaping in great numbers to industrial work sites because of the mass collectivization effort and the dispossession of kulaks in the countryside were often regarded as parasites, human riffraff unfit for building socialism. Worker Cherkasov, for example, wrote about how "the old foxes run away from collectivization. In Moscow there's a great influx of peasants who don't want to be on collective farms. They are drunkards, crooks, and thieves. There are hundreds and thousands of them. They'll be a hindrance to us as we build socialism." Another report asserts that the Moscow horse park's workforce consists mostly of country people who "make their way via vodka and debauchery and influence [other] workers to do the same." The troubles at Magnitogorsk were explained by the fact that "kulaks have wormed their way in."[9]

How this attitude was perceived by young people coming to work in industry is described in a letter written in 1930 by I. P. Koniukhov from the village of Dubrovka in the Duminichi Raion, Sukhinichi Okrug of the Western Oblast:

---

# Document 8

Letter to *Pravda* from I. P. Koniukhov, Western Oblast, 1930. RGAE, f. 7486, op. 1, d. 100, l. 21. Typed copy.

---

Worker and peasant youth have taken this path with ardor to master it, to get to know one another on this path, to unite, so that by its end there is no division into workers and peasants, but one whole with proletarian consciousness and feeling. Starting down this path we see proof (we won't speak of what is put down on paper) of a new variety of anti-Semitism: persecution of the muzhik [a derogatory term for peasant]. They try to belittle peasants working at the plant by calling them "Hairy Muzhik." Nicknames like this say "How backward the countryside is."

---

The old workers, moreover, were hostile not only toward those with rural backgrounds but also toward those who, responding to mass appeals, had come from far away to work in industry. One of the documents tells how miners jeered Komsomol members mobilized for work in the mines of the Donbass, doing everything they could to drive them out. In mine no. 1 in Shcheglovka, Komsomol members "met with hostility. At first the miners cursed them, then they began to act openly against them. The cutting instructor deliberately sent them to work in a shaft tunnel not shored up. A collapse resulted. One [Komsomol member] was smothered, another suffered a broken leg, a third escaped with bruises. When they were going down the shaft to a tunnel at that same place, a machine operator started his cutter and a huge chunk of coal . . . knocked out the rib of one Komsomol member." Evidence of anti-Semitism is also reported. In mine no. 29 in Makeyevka "they terrorize Jews at every turn, threatening to kill them if they don't leave." Among mine workers, conversations of this type also took place: "Jewboys came to us from Berdichev. D'ya think they're really gonna work? They go into the mines wearing their coats, just like they're at a health resort. . . . Four hundred and fifty Komsomol members, all kikes, are coming to us in Budyonnovka. We'll see how well they're gonna work."[10]

Meanwhile, the Socialist Offensive picked up speed in rural areas, especially after the November 1929 party plenum. The leadership envisaged the wide-ranging effort to organize collective farms as a mighty avalanche that would sweep away kulak opposition, obliterating them as a group and paving the way to build socialism in the countryside. The kulaks, said Stalin, had to be hit so hard that they would not be able to stand on their own feet again. "This is what we Bolsheviks call a true offensive."[11]

Special collectivization staffs were formed at all levels. They included practically every available "proletarian activist." Their chief assignment: increase the number of collective farms being created. The initial idea was essentially to complete collectivization during the First Five-Year Plan. At the local level, however, campaigns that had set out to increase the pace of collectivization caught on, making for a race that often shortened projected collectivization schedules by a half or two-thirds.

Worker Zakharin from Leningrad sent Stalin a letter in which he reported that in his administrative zeal "the secretary of the Raion

Committee [raikom] in Gorodok [Vitebsk Okrug of the Belorussian Soviet Socialist Republic] worked himself into such a frenzy that, afraid of being behind others and driven by the wish 'to catch up and overtake,' in a special express [telegram] to the Okrug administration blurted out that his collectivization had been carried out a whole one hundred and six-tenths, written as '100.6%.' Try to catch up to him."[12]

Besides the problem of peasants being forcibly driven onto kolkhozes, everywhere there were "excesses." At a conference in the office of S. I. Syrtsov, Sergo Ordzhonikidze reported an incident in Ukraine: "The muzhiks were terribly upset when they heard that it looked as though there was a plan to collectivize hens. In one village the muzhiks, finding out about this, slaughtered 125 hens, bought plenty of vodka, and drank while eating the hens: 'Let's gorge ourselves with chicken while we still can.'"[13]

Opposition of the peasantry to collectivization in some places took the form of mass actions, rumors of which reached the city. Of course, not all workers were biased against the peasants, nor were all disdainful and contemptuous of those who had come from the countryside. Many of them still possessed abandoned farms and had relatives, friends, and acquaintances living there. The following letter, sent from Leningrad in March of 1930, bears witness to this.

---

## Document 9

Letter to Stalin and Kalinin (ostensibly) from workers at Red Putilovets factory, Leningrad, March 1930. GARF, f. 1235, op. 4, d. 47, ll. 164–165. Typed copy.

---

[*Translator's note:* Much of the spelling, punctuation, capitalization, usage, and syntax in this letter is that of a person with little education. To convey the meaning of the text fully, these characteristics are reflected only minimally here.]

To the Secretary and to the Head of the VTsIK (*Vsesoiuznyi Tsentral'nyi Ispolnitel'nyi Komitet* [All-Union central executive committee]) Stalin and Kalinin.

We, the workers of the Red Putilovets Plant, fifty in number, have discussed and have decided that we once and for all protest against the terors and persecutions of the peasants and the one who you deprive of the vote and consider them kulaks. We all as one, members of the VKPb [*Vsesoiuznaia Kommunisticheskaia Partiia (bol'shevikov),* All-Union Communist Party of the Soviet Union] have a tie with the countryside, to us write our fathers and brothers how they're deprived of the vote and are not asked if they are agreed to be on the kolkhoz or not, but right off the bat their property is taken away by the careerists, and they're driven into prisons the shame of Soviet power, as capitalists do not do as you do in a free country, you throw into prison those who worked from morning till late night, the toilers who've put their whole life into their home and into their farm. You've called them kulaks only because they slept on their fist [the literal meaning of *kulak*] not having a pillow to themselves in their home, You regard those as kulaks who made their farm prosper and gave income to the state. You drove them into cellars and want them to rot alive, these fathers and brothers of ours, and posted their grandson with a rifle to guard them like wild animals. We're indignant against this, for what have we fought, for what have we shed blood when we did not expect this, that our worker-peasant reign would torment our fathers and brothers so. Why then do we need the VKP since it makes life impossible for all of us?

They kill, throw people into prison, and take all that we have gained with hands hardened by toil. We demand an order be given immediately to the local organizations and stop the teror in our free country, pay attention what they're saying, all the Leningrad workers they're leaving the party only because nowadays everyone's being persecuted. No one has a liking for Soviet authority, but consider you torturers of the Russian people. Why do we have to do the five-year plan so thoroughly when we've become poor after such wealth as we have in Russia even if you take only sugar that they used to feed the pigs with, and now you can't buy it even if you have the money, and also our children are starving and we have absolutely nothing to feed them with. We want Comrade Trotsky to be right and Comrade Bukharin and other comrades, but you squeeze everyone tighter and tighter, you want to complete the five-year plan in four years. You like it that the Komsomol members shout, but they are really dumbbells and sheep who don't understand anything, and you must pay attention to all of the proletariat and peasantry now this is why they send you a thousand curses and consider you violators and not rulers of the Russian people. You've robbed all the capitalists and you have your hands on small-time property owners and on the peasants. You're sending millions of toilers before their time to the next world at the same time you are writing that we are a nation of free laborers. We didn't know that poor peasants will be shown so much respect. It seems like it would be better if everyone was a poor peasant and beggars. You can't get nothing from a poor peasant, a poor peasant is a loafer and that's just why he's poor he is used to getting everything from others for nothing. You are now collecting scrap metal and rags. Doesn't that mean that you're begging alms from workers? But what you

## Document 9 *continued*

ought to do is give to him. Where is the wealth that we inherited from the capitalists? Even the poor peasants, they are gasping, specially in the country they don't look a lump of sugar in the eye, why the hell a five-year plan when they don't let you live here and now, who have we built the damn five-year plan for. You are destroying millions of people. It's become ridiculous you forced registering of old men workers for the Party, and who doesn't join up you threaten to fire. . . .

One day I was talking with an elderly worker he openly declared how we now have a time of persecution of everybody they don't let you live out your days peacefully. There's a fact no one can deny. . . .

A stream of profanities and threats follows. The letter is actually one of many anonymous maledictions addressed to those in power found among archival documents. The language and style of the letter clearly indicate the milieu from which it came. Doubtless it is not a joint letter from workers at "Red Putilovets" but rather the opinions of one worker, obviously a member of that middle-aged generation whose fathers and brothers too still lived in the countryside. To the author of the letter young people, Komsomol members, are "dumbbells, sheep" who understand nothing about what's going on.

A report in the summaries of letters to *Pravda* entitled "Why Are You Silent About Your Crimes?" treats the same subject:

## Document 10

Letter to *Pravda* included in summary report "Why Are You Silent About Your Crimes?" 1930. RAE, f. 7436s, op. 1, d. 102, l. 228. Typed copy.

. . . When you begin reading newspapers, in particular *Pravda,* you automatically get upset that such a revolting and outrageous lie has been written, and who exactly is this lie written for? It's for us, the Russian workers. Did Lenin, or Marx, ever teach the party to lie so outrageously, so shamelessly, without blushing? You commit acts of violence against workers and peasants. You scribblers, you've enslaved us worse than the tsar and you write impudently, you lie that you are for us workers. It's time to drive you out, you vile creatures, so you won't enslave the peasants in Lenin's name.

You invented something called a kolkhoz that no one needs (even Stalin) [an allusion to Stalin's article "Dizzy from Success" (see below)]. You robbed people. People get rid of their livestock, and then you go and write in *Pravda* that they went [to the kolkhoz] voluntarily. In 1918 and 1919 they trusted you, you had the slogan: "factories and plants to the workers, all the land without payment to those who reap," but is that what has happened? . . .

---

Peasant opposition to collectivization forced the leadership to make several amendments to the way this policy was being pursued. In the article "Dizzy from Success," published at the beginning of March 1930, Stalin, condemning "excesses" in the kolkhoz movement, lumped blame for them on local officials. Contrary to the assertions of Soviet historiography, the documents indicate that the ebb of peasants from kolkhozes in the wake of the article failed to produce substantive change in kolkhoz-building methods. The "excesses" continued as before. Along with direct coercion, a method of economic compulsion termed "extra-hard assignments" was now applied. These put extremely heavy burdens on private peasant farms and were designed to force independent peasants *(edinolichniki)* into collective farms. As a peasant from the village of Dabuzha in Kaluga Okrug wrote to *Pravda:*

> They strip the grain from everyone without exception, they do not take into consideration whether the peasant has a surplus or not, and they've taken away two poods per month, including all that's needed for the household. . . . Life for the peasant, you can say, is bad to the last degree. They'll take everything from the peasant without exception, both grain and potatoes. And it's rumored that they'll also be taking meat and butter and eggs and ham. Wouldn't it be interesting to know where all this goes? Under these circumstances you mourn the former life when the markets all flourished and you could get everything you desired. Now everything has died off, though you write that in the factories and plants they manufacture more than they used to, but for some reason we have nothing: no cereals, no fish, no flour, no butter, nothing to wish for, in a word, there's nothing, no tea, no sugar; they've driven the price of shares [in village consumer societies] up to twenty-five rubles, and all the same there's nothing.[14]

In a letter written in 1932, M. Ye. Bocharnikova, a peasant woman from the village of Tiurino in the Troitsky Raion of the Central Black Earth Oblast *(TsChO, Tsentral'no-Chernozemnaia*

*Oblast')*, tells how "extra-hard assignments" often were set and carried out:

---

## Document 11

Letter on "extra-hard assignments" for independent farmers from M. Ye. Bocharnikova, Central Black Earth Oblast, 1932. RGAE, f. 7486s, op. 1, d. 236, l. 40. Typed copy.

---

The rural commission gave us the extra-hard assignment of [delivering] 150 poods of grain: a hundred poods of winter wheat and fifty poods of spring-sown wheat. I wasn't able to fulfill such an assignment in view of the fact that there are three in my family and we have three plots of land . . . in all fifteen sazhens. I delivered fifteen poods of grain, and that's the most I can do. . . . My husband is an old man of sixty-eight, unfit for work, and my boy is twelve, and I'm forty-seven. The commission didn't take our circumstances into consideration. They took our horse with its harness, the new harness we purchased and the young horse, our seven sheep, twenty-five poods of flour, two fur coats, two homespun coats, twelve arshins of ordinary cloth for leg wraps, one pair of felt leg wrappings, one curried hide, two pair of warm women's boots, one pair of leather men's boots, nine pieces of sun-bleached linen, four warm shawls, two sarafans, two mugs, four knives, two ropes, and so forth. When they came to take all these things, my husband wasn't home. I didn't want to let them take them. They hit me and tied me up, lay me face down and abused me. . . . They left me with nothing to my soul and they also took the seven solid boards that we had ready for our coffins, and one saddle and thirteen hens. I petition . . . to restore my house to me, that is, my hut, and return the property of mine indicated above.

---

Finding it impossible to run their farms, more and more independent peasants abandoned life in the countryside and went to work in industry. They were included in the category of "those who dekulakized themselves," added to the count of liquidated "kulaks" driven to the north in strings of carts and special railroad trains, a phenomenon that occasioned much weeping, moaning, and loss of life.

Governmental bodies were inundated with letters protesting against forced exile, attributing it to the tyranny of local authorities, the wicked tongues of neighbors, and so on. There were descriptions of the unbearable conditions under which exiles lived and references to the high mortality rate caused by disease and malnutrition, especially among children. Letters came from the Urals, from Eastern Siberia, and the Northern Krai. "Our husbands are separated from us," a group of women wrote to President Kalinin, on behalf of fifty thousand exiles.

> They are off lumbering somewhere, and we women, old people, and small children have been left behind to languish in churches. As many as two thousand of us have been packed into each church where plank beds have been put up three stories high so that there's always a steamy mist in the air. We have all become sick from this air and the drafts, and children under fourteen have dropped like flies, and there's been no medical assistance for all these sick persons. In the course of a month and a half as many as three thousand children have been buried in the Vologda cemetery, but now they've moved us from Vologda to crude makeshift dwellings at Kharov Station and at the 573 kilometer post on the Northern Railroad. Mikhail Ivanovich, if you could see how we live in these dwellings, you'd be horrified. If we had to spend a couple of years in these dwellings, not one of us would remain among the living. The dwellings were built in a wet place in the forest. They have water up to a quarter meter high in them. The dwellings were built out of crude boards and are thatch-roofed, so that the wind whistles all around. In each of them 150 of us have been packed. As for provisions, there's three-quarters of a pound of bread and no cooked food whatsoever. We brought a supply of food with us, but when they moved us, the local officials in Vologda took it away, and this is not including the pork fat [and] white flour we gave away. Now they give us nothing except hot water.[15]

Besides such protests, what was happening at times also elicited normal human sympathy and pity. The appearance of exiles in a number of northern cities could not help but be noticed by local residents. An especially large number of letters was received from Vologda, through which passed one of the main routes used to transport exiles. A group of the city's factory and office workers wrote Kalinin that exiles "were sent further on in terribly cold weather. Babes in arms and pregnant women rode in cattle cars pressed up against one another, and women gave birth to children on the spot (is this not cruel?); then they were thrown out of the cars like dogs and after that put up in churches and in dirty, cold barns where there is no place to move about. They are kept half starved, in filth and lice. . . . No wonder that every day as many as fifty die."[16] Other eyewitnesses, more often than not using assumed names, reported the same.

> The citizens of the city of Vologda request that you make certain that those exiled from various provinces are treated humanely. They are living in horrible, nightmarish conditions, worse than cattle. All the city's churches have been taken over . . . and peopled with those who have been exiled, and in them there is cold and hunger. The churches are not heated at all, plank beds are made of wet crude boards, and there are *children* in these conditions. The plank beds are built in three tiers, in the Prilutsk Monastery in six tiers. People fall off of them, they are buried like cattle—without coffins. The outhouses are small and people defecate out in the open. The threat of a typhus epidemic is inevitable. Protect Vologdites as well as exiles from pestilence.

In an anonymous letter to *Pravda* sent from Arkhangel'sk, it was pointed out that "it is one thing that we destroy the kulak in an economic sense; to then destroy their children in a physical sense is nothing short of barbaric. Here in the north children of those exiled are beginning to die by the dozens, the public is grumbling, . . . those exiled live in the most horrible conditions imaginable, a separate hut has been set up for sick children, they kicked the school out of its premises, eating places for those exiled have been closed, and the members of the cooperative are forbidden to help them; children's corpses are taken to the cemetery by threes and fours and even without coffins, just in boxes." Another letter with an illegible signature from the North Dvinsk Okrug of the Northern Krai contained the following plea: "Those who have been exiled need to be taken care of, they are on the brink of death; 'bigtime' criminals have it better than they, and these people have been exiled for sobriety, calloused work; exiled are poor, ordinary people who are being punished even though they are completely innocent."[17]

Even OGPU agencies directly responsible for dispossessing kulaks reported the abnormality of the situation and told of mass escapes. They placed the entire blame on management units that were using exiles as a labor force. In May 1931 the OGPU transferred administration of the special resettlement project entirely to a special GULAG administration. A series of centralization efforts were made to bring order to the resettlement process, but the situation showed little improvement.

Meanwhile, the exodus from rural areas became more and more widespread, furnishing construction projects of the First Five-Year Plan with cheap, in some instances virtually free, labor. What was it that forced people to flee collective farms, that "bulwark of socialism in the countryside"? The documents tell us how the kolkhoz system actually formed and why people did everything they could to escape a kolkhoz fate. To be sure, there were successfully organized kolkhozes. The press emphasized these examples of positive kolkhoz building, propagandizing them in every way possible. Close analysis of letters received from many collectives, however, shows that the beginning of almost every farm system was accompanied by a drop in production, muddles, organizational confusion, and fairly acute social conflicts. One of the letter writers alluded to above—from the village of Dabuzha in Kaluga Okrug—sent the following communication to *Pravda:*

---

## Document 12

Letter to *Pravda* on collectivization in Kaluga Okrug, 1930. RGAE, f. 7486, op. 1, d. 100, l. 55. Typed copy.

---

We used to only hear about them [collective farms], but now we know them all too well. We've now had a good look at how they operate. One collective is in our village, another is in the next village of Borankov. It's a commune, well, and what's going on there really makes you want to laugh and cry at the same time. They operate by arguing and cursing that often lead to fights. And why? Simply because some of them want to labor, to work, and others say straight out, "it's completely worthless," and that's the truth. I know that you'll say that it's the kulaks there who are spoiling the whole business. No, it's lazy people who don't want to work who spoil things. At the present we don't know what other collectives, or communes, are like. But our commune is no good at all. So it's obvious that there can be no improvement of life. And don't even bother to think about the possibility of increasing the harvest, to increase the harvest this way is out of the question. It's really obvious to everyone that I've been ruined today, and tomorrow the same thing will happen to my neighbor, and then who's going to improve the farming? It's crystal clear, no one. A state grain procurer came to us, and he began to force grain out of

## Document 12 *continued*

us. We told him then and there, "Listen, my dear man, you can take from us today, but tomorrow there'll be nothing to winnow because we won't want to get it ready."

The letter speaks directly to the absence of material incentives in kolkhoz work and to the disastrous consequences of forced liquidation of independent peasant farms. Meanwhile, newspapers continually reported how in this locality or that the peasants themselves passed resolutions about forming new kolkhozes, and how much more successfully they worked in comparison to independent peasant landholders. Use of the "success story" mechanism looms large in one of the letters sent to *Pravda* from the Lower Volga Krai. Objecting to the assertion that "all wishes for transfers to kolkhozes in the form of resolutions sent to the press were dispatched by collective farm members themselves," the author, "to counterbalance this, as proof of how such resolutions were drawn up," paints the following picture:

## Document 13

Letter to *Pravda* on collectivization in Lower Volga Krai, 1930. RGAE, f. 7486, op. 1, d. 100, l. 60. Typed copy.

In one village I went to an exhibition. Before looking at the exhibits we had to go to a big meeting. Speeches are given: a spokesman for the RIK [*Raionnyi Ispolnitel'nyi Komitet,* district executive committee], the agronomist, the supervisor of the reading room [*izbach*], the chairman of the rural soviet [*sel'sovet*] and its secretary. The RIK spokesman and the agronomist talk about successes of the state together with lavish praise of collective kolkhoz cultivation of the land and its advantages over private cultivation and so on. The members of the rural soviet speak about the achievements of that village. After finishing his speech while others were speaking, the RIK spokesman started composing a resolution about the desirability of organizing a land society. Having finished composing, he reads that the land society is going to promote the idea of contributing to a loan for industrialization in each peasant household; during the current year he wants to organize two large-scale collectives, etc. He finishes reading. Then he asks the peasants to speak from the floor, those in favor and those against. Everyone remains silent, no one says a word. The supervisor of the reading room gets up, repeats the question, again there is silence. The RIK spokesman says, "So, everyone's agreed?" Laughter in the crowd. Here you have an irrefutable picture of the self-inspired kolkhoz movement. Precisely this type of information is given to the press about the kolkhoz movement and the party acts upon it, a great amount of it is fake documentation invented and composed by those party members who pursue the personal goal of advancing themselves, and the peasant's silence results from unwillingness and fears of being accused of espionage, of exile, of being put in prison, fines, having to suffer confiscation, and having to pay various burdensome taxes.

Then a look at the exhibits. An example of the judging process: representing horticulture are apple trees two or three years old, some belonging to a private peasant and others from a kolkhoz. The chairman, an agronomist, having looked over the kolkhoz apple trees along with the judging committee, goes up to the peasant and says, "Although these apple trees both in the roots and in the crown are better than the kolkhoz ones, we should give precedence to the kolkhoz because of our class distinctions." Laughter again in the crowd. As a result the first prize goes to the kolkhoz, and the peasant gets a certificate of merit. So, because of our class distinctions white is transposed into black, and black into white, and you can see here how the judging is straight falsification. Peasant experts understood this fake judging and how the local authorities, using agronomists, aim to show agricultural achievement in their village and to show that such achievements supposedly occur not because of peasant experts but because of the activities of the local authorities. In point of fact no one made even the slightest effort to look into any aspect of the middle-sized peasant farm economy, nor was anyone willing to do more than compile official charts, and therefore exhibitions scheduled in many villages did not take place. The sentence dished out by the agronomist judging the apple trees is nothing more than subtle mockery of the party's class line. So this is what all educated people working in the Soviet Union survive on, and their slogan, like that of the peasants, is to own something. On account of this peasants say that former landowners sit in our central offices and hold power, taking vengeance on us for land and estates taken from them. Bearing this out are stories widespread among the peasantry like the following: from some village a lot of grain is demanded. Peasant advocates [*khodoki*] go to Moscow and ask that a lesser amount of grain be required of the village. When the person you need to ask about this is pointed out, they recognize him as their [former] landowner. When the advocates explain the reason they've come and the amount of the grain tax, the landowner says: "That's still too little. Everything should be taken from you and we'll take it because you took our land and estates from us. . . ."

It's hard to say whether the peasant advocates who asked that a "lesser amount" be requisitioned actually recognized their land-owner in the responsible official, but there are quite a few examples of how the kolkhoz reminded the peasants not only of landowners but serfdom as well.

Very often intrigue by "kulaks and other class-alien elements" was given as the reason why things were not going well on collective farms. This, incidentally, was the favorite plot in Soviet literature devoted to the kolkhoz movement in the early thirties. There were also murders of kolkhoz activists and beatings and sabotage of kolkhoz work. This is often communicated in confidential reports. M. P. Kichigin, a member of the *Krest'ianskaia Gazeta* (The peasants' newspaper) worker brigade and an associate member of TsK VKP(b), wrote the following:

## Document 14

Report of M. P. Kichigin on collective farm chairman in Central Black Earth Oblast [n.d.]. RGAE, f. 7486s, op. 1, d. 102, l. 296. Typed copy.

In 1928 a kolkhoz was organized in the village of Dubinka in the Lavrov Rural Soviet of the Shilovo Raion of Yelets Okrug of TsChO. Forty-two households joined it, but among them happened to be kulaks, such as G. A. Gubanov, former owner of a flour mill; P. P. Shein, former army officer; P. G. Shein, who before the revolution possessed land; and a series of others who joined the kolkhoz to avoid paying big taxes and being dispossessed, as should have been the case. The chief saboteur of "Victory" Kolkhoz is the chairman of this kolkhoz, Nikifor Arsentievich Mitrofanov, former army officer, a second lieutenant who from 1924 to 1927 had a retail grocery business and now, instead of doing decent work, does nothing but drink a lot and corrupt the other members of the kolkhoz.

His drunken escapades amount to outright hooliganism. For example, in 1929 during haymaking, drunk, with a group of kolkhoz members he trampled one woman, knocked on V. R. Sheinaia's and A. V. Sheinaia's doors and, when they wouldn't open their doors, ordered that the windows be broken, saying "She's getting this on account of me."

On St. George's Day [23 April] he rode a stud horse to death. Appeals have been repeatedly submitted to RIK, but all in vain since there's apparently a "solicitous hand" supporting him, and he, taking advantage of this, drinks hard every day, plays cards, keeping as much as nine hundred rubles of state funds on himself.

## Document 14 *continued*

When they asked him why he carries so much money with him, he answered: "The independent peasants want to put me through a Bartholomew's Night, therefore I'm always prepared to clear out of here with money."

At the kolkhoz there is a work brigade leader named Barsky who works as a accountant. He did a good job of putting in order the kolkhoz's accounts, which had been totally neglected since last year. Comrade Barsky made statements more than once to RIK about Mitrofanov without any results.

But there were, however, results.

They want to expel Barsky from the kolkhoz, and they'll achieve this goal of theirs unless their drunken "orgy" is stopped in time.

One more instance still of Mitrofanov's meanness. In the spring he bought a bull for breeding at the kolkhoz in the village of Torniasov and signed a bill to its owner for one hundred rubles more than he should have. It was made known to RIK, but with the same result.

---

Here is an interesting document that re-creates the panorama of kolkhoz construction in Belorussia:

---

## Document 15

Report to Kolkhoz Center on collectivization in Belorussia, 26 September 1930. RGAE, f. 7486s, op. 1, d. 102, ll. 226–225 ob. Typed original.

---

To Comrades [N. I.] Yezhov [at that time a deputy member of the Narkomzem of the USSR] and [T. A. ] Yurkin [president of the Kolkhoz Center *(Kolkhoztsentr)*]:

On the instructions of Comrade [G. F.] Grinko [at that time a deputy member of the Narkomzem of the USSR] I send you extracts from confidential reports of recent date concerning shortcomings in the kolkhoz movement in the BSSR so that instructors (Communists) sent to provincial raions of the BSSR will be acquainted with them and so that appropriate measures are taken to correct the shortcomings described by the facts cited below:

Signed: Shakhov

26 September 1930

Received by the Kolkhoz Center 27 September 1930.

In Starobinsk Raion of Bobruysk Okrug the chairman of "Colossus" Kolkhoz, G. Gerasimov, was a gangster in 1921 and dealt in contraband 1923–24. In Lepel' Raion the post of chairman of "Overcome" Kolkhoz is occupied by the former gangster and horse thief Vashchenko. In Kopyl' Raion of Minsk Okrug the chairman of "Communard" Kolkhoz, Vikenty Zenko, in the past was a Red Army deserter and for contraband activity served eight months in prison. In Vitebsk Raion of the same okrug the chairman of the Kolkhoz Named for the Red Army, Yermolaev, is the son of an Old Believer priest. In Mezhinsk Raion the chairman of the kolkhoz is a prominent kulak who before the revolution owned sixty-five *desiatina* of land.

In the "Spark of Socialism" and "Freedom" Kolkhozes in Rogachev Raion of Bobruysk Okrug, farming machinery is completely mismanaged.

In Zhitkovichi Raion of Mozyrsk Okrug the chairman of Detovsk Kolkhoz, Trantsevsky, sold off the kolkhoz's rye.

In Goretsk Raion of Orsha Okrug the secretary of "Fighter" Kolkhoz, Goshman, is selling off kulaks' belongings transferred to the kolkhoz and has transferred two hogs and twelve piglets to acquaintances as their personal property. He himself makes illegal spirits from kulak grain transferred to the kolkhoz.

In Krichev Raion of Mogilev Okrug, on account of the management's lack of administrative abilities, five hundred poods of grain taken from kulaks and transferred to the kolkhoz have perished.

In the Kolkhoz Named for Stalin in Sosnian Raion of Vitebsk Okrug the administration distributed manufactured cloth it had received among the prosperous peasants and the poor peasants got nothing. The chairman of the kolkhoz, Vasilievsky, took the best piece for himself.

In Tolochin Raion of Orsha Okrug the chairman of "Yasnaia Poliana" Kolkhoz, Pleskin, supplied his own relatives—peasants of average means—first with manufactured goods. As a result many poor peasants left the kolkhoz, but those of average means remaining on the kolkhoz announced: "You can all leave. We'll treat you to more vodka if you'll just leave."

The chairman of the Kolkhoz Named for the Twelfth Party Congress in Tolochin Raion of Orsha Okrug, Pekarsky, a worker from Minsk and a VKP(b) member, drinks heavily all the time and passes his time in drunken quarrels with members of the kolkhoz. In Kopyl' Raion, the chairman of the horticulture and vegetable farm artel, Sankovich, worker and VKP(b) member, treats the members of the artel crudely and manages the artel by issuing orders and decrees. His authority is not respected.

Members of the "Dawn" Agricultural Commune, celebrating a religious holiday at a cemetery, were to a man drunk. During the drinking bout the kolkhoz's threshing floor burned and many pieces of agricultural equipment were lost. At the Kolkhoz Named for Stalin in Surazh Raion, vodka is traded; the collective farm members often get outrageously drunk and commit violent acts.

At "Red Ray" Kolkhoz in Kliuchev Raion of Bobruysk Okrug, kolkhoz member Sadovsky, with the knowledge of the kolkhoz chairman, sold 150 poods of potatoes belonging to the kolkhoz. In connection with this the kolkhoz members say: "We don't have a collective farm but a place to be robbed, everyone takes what he can. Our leader knows about it and does nothing whatsoever."

In several raions when meadows were set aside for kolkhoz farmers, independent peasants declared a boycott of kolkhoz members. Peasant carpenters are refusing to work on kolkhoz building projects. During a fire at one of the kolkhozes (Krasno-Sloboda Raion of Bobruysk Okrug) the peasants said: "Why go there. If one or two kolkhozes burn, to hell with them, as long as people haven't been burned up."

In the village of Chizhevichi in Starobinsk Raion of Bobruysk Okrug relations between independent peasants and collective farmers have become very strained. Cattle of "Freedom" Kolkhoz have to stay in their sheds because independent peasants prevent them from being let out to pasture.

In the village of Rostkovo in Liadnensk Raion of Orsha Okrug, independent peasants proceeded to systematically mow meadows belonging to the "Red Day" Kolkhoz.

---

The picture that emerges is complex, contradictory, and unattractive. Not one to be explained by the intrigues of "class enemies" alone, it is rather the typical behavior of both the "most active members of the kolkhoz" and the "vanguard" of the working class (those twenty-five thousand sent out to the countryside to organize kolkhozes), "thievery of public property," and mass drunkenness, and clashes between collective farm members and those not on collective farms.[18] A report that collective farms were becoming a "bogeyman" for independent peasants comes from Velikiye Luki Okrug in Leningrad Oblast and from the Kolkhoz Named for the OGPU in the Tutayev Raion of Ivanovo Oblast.[19]

The "extra-hard assignment" was a Sword of Damocles hanging over not only each independent peasant but also each collective farm member who dreamed of preserving the vestiges of economic independence. In the village of Tryokhonetievo, Novosilsk Raion, the staff of the rural soviet led by deputy chairman Davydov forced bribes and drink from collective farm members, threatening those who refused with an extra-hard assignment and inflicting such on some collective farm members, taking their cows from them immediately as well. In their complaint about excesses, a group of collective farm workers wrote: "We have no choice but to request protection from the local authorities.... Our village consists of forty-eight households, all of them part of the collective farm. This year fifteen farms have been forced for made-up reasons to perform an extra-hard assignment. Absolutely everything was taken from these farms—sheep, hens, iron pots and pans, sackcloth, even chocks." In this instance the perpetrators were made to answer for these excesses.[20]

As we see, abuses in kolkhoz construction continued even after Stalin's article was published. Independent peasant P. N. Samsonov from the village of Lyubovka in Bondarsk Raion wrote that by June 1931 the kolkhoz consisted of sixty farms. Only fifteen farms were independent of the kolkhoz. According to Samsonov's report, the chairman of the rural soviet and the board of the kolkhoz, in an effort to attract the remaining farms to the kolkhoz, began going from house to house, demanding that the kolkhoz be joined. The independent peasants refused. Then the kolkhoz chairman, Petrov, and the schoolteacher, both drunk, appeared at Samsonov's door, arrested him, and locked him up in his own grain storage barn. They released him only after his thirteen-year-old son declared that the farm would join the kolkhoz. The other independent peasants were also arrested and kept under arrest for two days, released only after they applied to join the kolkhoz.[21]

K. V. Galkin from Chernushkin Raion of Ural Oblast reported that because of disorders on the "Thirteen Years of October" Kolkhoz, out of the 107 households that belonged to the kolkhoz, 24 households of poor peasants and families of Red Army soldiers had left. The disorders were "hard drinking bouts by all the board members. Forty of the one hundred horses were lost in the course of the winter, part of them perishing because they had been fed straw roofs, their normal feed having been plowed into a field in the fall. Out of one hundred sows and fifty young pigs, thirty-two remained. The rest had perished or had been slaughtered and eaten by board members and their relatives. The board members had butchered cows and horses for meat, giving none of it to the members of the kolkhoz." Complaints to the Raion Union of Kolkhozes *(Raikolkhsoiuz)* and even an article in the raion newspaper failed to bring any decisive action, and the board continued "to administrate," dividing the foodstuffs among their nearest and dearest. Fifteen desiatinas of land remained unsown.

Permission by the Raion Union of Kolkhozes to give kolkhoz land to independent peasants for cultivation had no effect. The kolkhoz did not permit anyone to work on this land and it remained idle.[22]

The flow of complaints grew: about state grain procurement excesses resulting in depleted seed grain and minimal food stocks on the kolkhozes; about the overdue return of cows taken in connection with obligatory meat deliveries; about the retention of personal property that had been confiscated for fines imposed for failure to fulfill erroneously prescribed extra-hard assignments relating to state procurements. A significant number of appeals concerned the compulsory collectivization of kolkhoz members' cows. Applications to leave kolkhozes continued to come in.

Departure from the kolkhoz, however, had become a big problem. In order to leave it for work in industry one had to have written permission from the kolkhoz or rural soviet administration. No wonder that in 1932 the flow of fugitives from the countryside declined sharply. A frequent recourse of kolkhoz authorities under these conditions was expulsion from the kolkhoz, which put a person in the complicated, practically hopeless situation of being a social outcast. Here, for example, is a typical report of such an expulsion:

---

## Document 16

Report on expulsion from a collective farm in Middle Volga Krai, 1932. RGAE, f. 7486s, op. 1, d. 236, l. 74. Typed copy.

---

N. D. Andrianov from the village of Boiarkino ("Laborer" Kolkhoz) in the Middle Volga Krai joined the kolkhoz in 1931; in April 1932 he went to Moscow and began work on the construction of the "Ball Bearing" [Sharikopodshipnik] plant as an unskilled laborer at a salary of seventy rubles. At the beginning of June he received notification that he and his wife had been expelled from the kolkhoz for departing without permission to find work. To his request for an official decision to be issued, he received the verbal response: "Since you didn't ask for our permission when you were leaving, don't ask us for it now." Meanwhile the requester's family remained on the kolkhoz and had to manage somehow to live.

---

Reports on this subject abound. Collective farm member M. P. Nesterov from the village of Norinskaia in Diatlov Rural Soviet of Niandoma Raion complained that he had been expelled from the kolkhoz because there had been a disruption in the state lumber procurement where he had been sent by the kolkhoz as a work brigade leader. Nesterov explained that, because of illness, he was unable to carry out his obligation connected with the state lumber procurement and had left for Moscow to earn a living, going to work for the MOGES (*Moskovskaia oblastnaia gidroelektrostantsiia* [Moscow Oblast hydroelectric power station]) project. The Raion Union of Kolkhozes, to which Nesterov's complaint was sent, simply remitted the decision of the kolkhoz board: "To leave Nesterov's wife Maria on the kolkhoz and [to compel her] to break ties with her husband, Nesterov." Collective farm member M. Ye. Suslin from the village of Almasovo in the Voznesensk Raion of Nizhni Novgorod Krai wrote that he had been expelled from the kolkhoz because of "row-upkicking," which manifested itself in his criticism at meetings of collective farm members with the kolkhoz board: the kolkhoz's stores of seed and other items were being expended, for example, and kolkhoz membership had been given to a kulak, the father-in-law of the kolkhoz chairman, who was exiled later on.[23]

Evidence of mismanagement, disgraceful goings on, and abuses of power is also given in the report about organizing work on collective farms compiled by *Krest'ianskaia Gazeta* in September 1930. In all fairness, it should be noted that the report contains information about six well-functioning collective farms that regularly fulfilled their planned state grain procurement and whose accounting books were in order. But a torrent of negative facts inundates the laconic, dry descriptions of these kolkhozes. Subjects discussed are the deleterious effect of wage leveling on pay for work and the poor way in which the kolkhoz's domestic animals and property were kept: "horses are skinny and dirty," "carts and sledges are in disrepair," "harnesses lie about without being looked after." A letter writer named Cherpukov from the village of Durnovka in Solntsev Raion of Kursk Okrug declares that "'Red Armor' Kolkhoz at the village of Pokrovka should be entered on the shirkers' list. The kolkhoz is parasitical. There's absolutely no accounting for work done, and everyone fills his own pocket." No work was going on, it is observed, because there was no discipline; the work brigade leader, instead of directing collective farm members to do work, went fishing. "The collective farm members drink heavily and curse, using foul language in the presence of women. The Komsomol cell delegated four Komsomol members to help the kolkhoz, but no one even noticed."[24]

Someone named Chvyryov described a general meeting at Streletsko-Pushkarsky Kolkhoz in Riazan Okrug. Items on the agenda included preparation for haying and approval of the minutes from a board meeting. In response to a request of the assembly, the matter of measuring work time was considered. As it turned out, the established method of counting was outrageous. Some people worked more and received less than others. Collective farm members were constantly cheated. Two carpenters on the kolkhoz each received forty rubles. One of them, Bokaryov, spent most of the workday strolling about the marketplace or sitting and smoking in the kolkhoz's business office. When collective farm members criticized members of the board, the board members immediately proposed that they try being board members themselves. The collective farm members were given reprimands without any reason.[25]

It was also hard for collective farm members in a material sense because they had been deprived of traditional sources of peasant wherewithal, and to them just as to city dwellers a system of rationing now applied, rationing, moreover, of an obviously "mongrel" variety.[26] As one letter observed:

---

## Document 17

Letter on rationing on collective farms, 1930. RGAE, f. 7486s, op. 1, d. 100, l. 120. Typed copy.

---

The peasant who has become a member of a kolkhoz, and with no ties besides to any other work, in his cooperative member booklet has the letter "V." The peasant who is a kolkhoz member and works in some establishment has the letter "B" in his cooperative member booklet. The letter "B" receives five meters of cloth per dependent, ten meters for himself as head of the household, 1,500 grams of sugar for each dependent. The letter "V" receives no cloth, and if he receives as much as five meters in the course of three months it has nothing to do with the size of his family, and two hundred grams of sugar a month for each dependent. Even the members of the VKP(b) themselves laugh at such an abnormality . . . and as a result what happens is that everyone tries to abandon the kolkhoz work of cultivating land and to secure his well-being somewhere at an industry.

Perhaps some party officials did actually laugh at the abnormality of such a policy. The document provides evidence of inequality among collective farm members who, not unlike independent peasants earlier, felt downtrodden. At issue was a phenomenon that became one of the most persistent in collective farm policy, one that was to have far-reaching consequences.

At the same time, in addition to required deliveries of agricultural products, numerous other requirements also applied to kolkhozes. Collective farm members complained that directive after directive came down from the authorities soliciting contributions to the share fund, making deductions for the special indivisible kolkhoz fund, demanding compulsory deposits in savings banks, recruiting tractor work brigades for machine-tractor stations (MTSes), and so forth.[27]

The situation on state enterprises in rural areas, state farms, government farms, and MTSes (of which there were still very few) was in no way better. One of the advantages of the New Countryside, according to the propaganda, was wide-scale use of mechanized labor. Equipment was scarce, however, and that available was of low quality. Maintenance personnel were virtually nonexistent, and nowhere were there enough spare parts. The leadership attempted to solve these objective problems by employing administrative and punitive measures. Source materials report that mechanics were tried for the shortage of spare parts, that "the best workers, up to their ears in soot, are deserting the tractor front," that personnel in repair shops changed daily. What is more, payment for work done by MTSes was onerous for collective farms. Collective farm workers feared that "the government will take the entire harvest for the work done by tractors."[28]

Once implemented, collectivization had a catastrophic effect on agricultural production. Animal husbandry suffered more than anything else because of the mass slaughter of cattle when peasants joined collective farms. The situation in grain production looked somewhat different. According to official data, in 1930 (a year of extraordinarily favorable weather conditions) eighty-four million tons of grain were harvested; seventy million tons were harvested in 1931, sixty-seven million in 1932, and sixty-eight million in 1933. Figures of this sort indeed seem considerable.[29] Their attainment, however, was against the background of a disintegrating independent peasant sector and of much organizational confusion in the building of kolkhozes. State grain procurement nonetheless grew steadily, thanks to intensified strong-arm pressure on the rural areas. This meant that less and less grain was left for village peasants' domestic use. Grain crops often passed by kolkhoz grain barns, going directly to state grain procurement points. The results were increasingly clear signs of pauperization and impoverishment in the rural areas—and the approach of famine.

A report from Krasnoiar Raion in Middle Volga Krai is typical: "The people of Tarasov village are starving; they are swelling up from starvation, and the other day one man died from hunger. Several have gone to the city of Kozlov in search of a living and to buy bread and at home, as during wartime, remain only women, children, and old men. Everyone is cursing Soviet power and going off to work in industry. We don't know how things will be with the third Bolshevik spring because not only will there be no seed, but there will not even be people and animal power."[30]

Reports about famine were received from Kazakhstan, from Leningrad Oblast, from the land of the Kalmyks. According to "illiteracy liquidator" V. I. Gaidamaka,

Nineteen thirty-one became a development year for our kolkhoz. In that year we brought in a harvest of about five hundred tons of grain, we sowed 625 hectares of winter wheat, and we improved our animal husbandry. We fulfilled the state grain procurement plan of 3,250 centners by 100 percent, but many collective farm members were left hungry all of 1932 because the five tons of grain put aside not only failed to provide food for three hundred collective farm dependents, but in addition the spring sowing area (890 hectares) remains unplanted. . . . The collective farm workers are leaving in groups to search for a living with the intention of later bringing their families to live with them. They leave at night so that the board members of the kolkhoz won't stop them and make them fulfill the many kolkhoz tasks that have not been completed. Also leaving are Komsomol members and candidate party members. During the last ten days about thirty men have left the kolkhoz. . . . The spring plan is threatened with failure.[31]

The same kind of letters came from North Caucasus Krai, in particular from the "Giant" State Farm on the Sal'sk steppe, the success of which had been widely propagandized in the press. From Chamlyk *stanitsa* (Cossack village), former Red Army soldier V. M. Kovalchuk, reported:

---

## Document 18

Letter from V. M. Kovalchuk on flight from collective farms in North Caucasus Krai, 1932. RGAE, f. 7486s, op. 1, d. 236, l. 8. Typed copy.

---

I write not as one who gives in to difficulties, not as an enemy of Soviet power, but as a man who fought for it.

In Chamlyk Raion there is one kolkhoz, second in size in the krai, that fulfills a three hundred thousand–pood state grain procurement, but the trouble is this socialist farm is melting like the spring snow, people are fleeing the kolkhoz for who knows where. At the kolkhoz they took all the grain away and left a little field corn for the people to live on. All this is the result of the kolkhoz's unavoidable disintegration, and what a disgrace that is!

The kolkhoz plants wheat and lives on corn. Everyone's mood is almost anti-Soviet. Dear comrades, now you go and take any one of us, set in front of us only field corn without any grease, dress us in rags, shoes without soles, and force us out to work on the steppe when the temperature is twenty-five degrees below zero; wouldn't any of you become a deviant and curse all and everything?

Here is one example. At the stanitsa we have some thirteen thousand hectares of land; before the revolution there were twelve thousand people, and now there are eight thousand. There has been a decrease in people, the rest don't have the strength to do the harvesting; as a result thousands of hectares of various crops are rotting on the steppe, overgrown with weeds.

The people have become pretty malicious, they look disapprovingly at the Communists, the Communist cell has lost its authority. Members of the party also. Now we have to meet contract requirements for delivery of hens, this also intensifies anger among the peasants. Out of people fighting for Soviet

## Document 18 *continued*

power they are now making people who are against Soviet power because every last kernel of grain has been taken from them and they have nothing to chew on. Every night seven to ten households abandon the stanitsa. This on account of the good life. I've permitted myself to express my opinion as one comrade to another, to the masses I speak differently, the way Soviet authority talks.

---

Here is an anonymous letter from Novocherkassk stanitsa:

---

## Document 19

Anonymous letter to *Izvestia* on rumors in North Caucasus Krai, 1932. RGAE, f. 7486s, op. 1, d. 236, ll. 4–5. Typed copy.

Dear *Izvestia* Newspaper, Tell me if it's true that there's a directive that all the collective farm workers be sent into industry and foreigners brought in to take their place. So allegedly the authorities take all the grain away and do not leave any for us to eat or plant, so that the collective farm members themselves have abandoned the kolkhozes and gone to work in industry. Further, they deprive all able-bodied workers of their rations so that they will croak faster and not impede the building of socialism. To the children of collective farm workers barley bread is given that is half bran, one hundred grams per child and nothing more because it's impossible to build socialism out of Russians so that only the strong remain and the weak croak.

That all collective farm workers went to work in industry is a correct policy, but regarding the weak it is not correct. Because the weakest of all are newborn children whose mother is starving and cannot give them the breast. This means [that only] children more than two years old survive, and there won't be any young.

We collective farm workers do not believe that the higher authorities want to take all our grain away, even the seed grain, we petitioned RIK, they send us to Novocherkassk Raion, there they don't even want to listen to us. It's already the beginning of March and our kolkhoz doesn't know if it's going to get grain for sowing or not. There's a real kolkhoz for you—without grain, without sowing! Dear *Izvestia* Newspaper, Don't you take away our faith that kolkhozes will lead us not to ruin but to a better life, and that if we starve, guilty are not the higher authorities but the local ringleaders. Dear *Izvestia* Newspaper, Let there be at least some good white bread for babes in arms, let there be some seed for sowing, otherwise things will get even worse.

Analogous letters came from Western Siberia, where in 1931, despite a poor harvest, the planned state grain procurement was fulfilled strictly. One letter writer urged newspapers not to anger the population by writing about starvation in India. In his opinion, the good life in the USSR could be found only in Moscow and Leningrad, whereas misery reigned everywhere else.[32]

Collective farm member A. P. Kokurin wrote from Mordovia:

---

## Document 20

Letter of complaint to *Izvestia* from A. P. Kokurin, Mordovia, 1932. RGAE, f. 7486s, op. 1, d. 236, l. 6. Typed copy.

---

I have a family of nine, and what did I have before the kolkhoz? I had all the produce I needed to feed my family, and fuel, and I clothed and shod them. Had a horse and three head of sheep. Delivered to the government twenty poods of rye, forty poods of millet, oats, potatoes, and hemp. I have worked on the kolkhoz, I have honestly earned 355 labordays, but I no longer eat bread but chaff and taters, we don't have enough to resole our shoes. My children have turned black from malnutrition. Respected editors, is there no way to leave the kolkhoz rather than perish there?

---

Worker A. P. Nikishin in his letter to VTsIK thus describes the condition of a specially subsidized kolkhoz in the Privolzhsky Raion of Middle Volga Krai, where:

---

## Document 21

Letter to VTsIK from A. P. Nikishin on starvation in Middle Volga Krai, 1932. RGAE, v. 7486s, op. 1, d. 236, l. 33. Typed copy.

---

. . . In the fall of 1930 the land was all plowed and the following spring sown, and the harvest OK, a good one. The time came to gather the grain, the collective farm workers reaped the harvest without any hitches, . . . but it came time to deliver to the state and all the grain was taken away. Even leaving a big percent of the grain wouldn't be enough to sow our land. Collective farm workers began to come to the board for their share. They were refused, there was no grain. . . . And at the end they stopped giving out shares to almost all of the collective farm workers. And at the present time collective farm workers with small children are perishing from hunger. They don't eat sometimes for a week and don't see a piece of bread for several days. People have begun to swell up because of hunger. Collective farm workers with great effort manage to get hold of some money, abandon their families and small children, and themselves go into hiding. And all the males have departed, despite the fact that in the near future the spring planting is coming. Horse power has almost all died, for 360 householders eighty horses were left, and those any day now are as good as dead. And collective farm workers, each expects to die any day now from hunger, and it's even worse for the poor independent peasants. The crops were taken away and everybody can barely move on their legs. . . . The same story in several kolkhozes of the raion, and this situation threatens to devastate the spring sowing campaign.

The directives for such policy came, naturally, from above, and the local leaders made every effort to carry them out. A citizen named M. Prokunin wrote:

## Document 22

Letter from M. Prokunin on starvation in Middle Volga Krai, 1932. RGAE, f. 7486s, op. 1, d. 236, l. 32. Typed copy.

On a casual trip through K[inel']-Cherkassy Raion of Middle Volga Krai, I drop in to the office of Comrade Kozurov, the chairman of the raion executive committee. In front of him stands at attention the chairman of a rural soviet [one of the Twenty-Five Thousand workers sent to the provinces] and reports: "In my rural soviet [of Kromov] the following situation has arisen: the collective farm workers have no bread, hungry stablemen are not feeding the cattle, they say 'I'm hungry and I'd rather sit at home on the roof of the stove.' The cattle are dying from malnutrition, the collective farm workers snatch parts of the carcasses and eat them." Chairman of the Raion Executive Committee Kozurov, [instead of] sharing his opinion, giving advice to the chairman, shouted: "Don't come to me any more with small matters like these. Have you lost your mind? You all got six poods and ate it all up, and village leaders are panicking, [and] you've come with this small matter. Today I will raise [the matter] of you at the meeting of the Raion Committee Bureau. We will reach practical conclusions on how you've handled the matter. Can you believe what he's complaining about? He has no bread on his kolkhoz, they eat carrion, I as RIK chairman receive seventeen kilograms of flour. I make do with

## Document 22 *continued*

it. And his rural soviet got six poods for the year and it's already gone. Don't come to me any more with small matters like this, or I'll have you tried." The poor chairman of the rural soviet left the office and began to cry, "How can I go back to my rural soviet? I don't dare show my face there." As bad luck would have it, the seasonal laborers returned from logging work in the Ul'ianovsk Raion; there, too, no bread had been given out.

For the local leader the critical situation on the kolkhoz probably was tiny compared to some of his tasks, tasks unknown to the chairman of the rural soviet. In 1932 the situation became even more complex. Ivan Litvinov from Novooskol'sk Raion of the Central Black Earth Oblast wrote to *Izvestia:*

## Document 23

Letter to *Izvestia* from I. Litvinov on refugees from Ukraine in Central Black Earth Oblast, 1932. RGAE, f. 7486s, op. 1, d. 236, l. 13. Typed copy.

Day after day all over our raion move starving Ukrainian peasants, collective farm members and independent peasants alike, in strings of carts. For any crust of bread whatsoever they part with all their belongings, footwear, clothing, or anything else they have. When you question them, they reply: "We had a good harvest, but Soviet authorities 'procured' our grain, put into effect their plans and tasks for us to the point that we were left without a pound of bread." When you ask them, "Who is to blame?" They answer "Soviet power, which has taken our grain away from us down to the last kernel, dooming us to hunger and poverty. It's worse than it was under serfdom."

I myself am a worker, a Komsomol member since 1928, and I wonder how the Ukraine can be hungry after a good harvest. We also have collective farms, and there's enough bread, but why is there such a situation of all places in the Central Black Earth Oblast? I direct the attention of *Izvestia* to this phenomenon because wherever "hungry carts" arrive they create a panic and provoke hostile speeches against Soviet power.

The same thing occurred in the Northern Caucasus. Ivan Gusev from the Budënny Kolkhoz in the Ol'khov Rural Soviet of Novocherkassk Raion wrote:

# Document 24

Letter from I. Gusev on food shortages in North Caucasus Krai, 1932. RGAE, f. 7486s, op. 1, d. 236., l. 12. Typed copy.

The members of the Kolkhoz Named for Budënny find themselves without grain, the grain we had was taken away by the former Shakhtin Raion, and Novocherkassk Raion says: "You gave it to us yourselves, hand over your documents. For food, they say, you'll get no grain, but we'll give you grain for planting." But whatever shall we do without bread, what will we have to eat until the next harvest?

He who bolted in time for work in industry did well for himself, he can live and has bread to eat, and the others made a dash for it, but late, written permissions are not being given now by the rural soviet, which says: "If you all leave, there will be no one to do the work." Now we are left naked, barefoot, two hundred grams of barley bread a day and we eat cabbage without butter. It's terrible to see a big strong man cry, and he cries because they deceived him with the kolkhoz, because he's left without a farm, without bread, without clothes, and he's lost his freedom.

We don't want anything, we'll give up our huts and home country, if they'd only give us permission to leave so we could go to industry. What's the point of us kicking the bucket in the kolkhoz from not eating?

---

Accounts submitted in the summer of 1932 report hot and dry weather. In a number of places crops perished, and in others low harvests resulted. There were reports that results were inflated, sown areas concealed, yields underestimated, that equipment frequently broke down, agricultural work was of low quality, kolkhoz fields were overgrown with weeds, harvesting was late, and, as a consequence, that losses in various places amounted to anywhere from 25 to 50 percent of the harvest. In Ukraine, it was reported, losses were aggravated by combine operators' low level of competence. Because of the dry weather fires were occurring on a mass scale. They were often attributed to arson. From everywhere at once came reports about the appearance of "barbers," collective farm workers who, in order to subsist, were "dragging sheaves off the kolkhoz fields."[33]

The leadership regarded these occurrences as acts of destruction and sabotage. In August 1932 a law was passed to protect socialist property. It prescribed draconian punishments for theft of and damage to state holdings: up to ten years' imprisonment, even the firing squad. Lists of "shirkers" designating kolkhozes, state farms, and raion organizations foiling projected plans found wide use. Extraordinary commissions were formed that took everything "down to the last straw" from kolkhoz grain barns, including seed depositories, in such grain-rich regions as Ukraine, North Caucasus, and the Volga region. There were wide-scale repressions against both peasants who did not fulfill planned grain deliveries and leaders unable to guarantee grain delivery procurements.

As a result, real famine broke out, taking millions of lives. The circumstances surrounding it are fully elucidated in fiction and in published source material. Described there are the various forms the "famine-scourge" of the winter and spring of 1932–33 acquired. All over the country hundreds of thousands of starving and impoverished peasants straggled, packing railroad stations and wandering about like phantoms in search of sustenance and alms. According to data found in the archives by N. A. Ivnitsky, toward the beginning of March 1933 OGPU agencies arrested 219,460 persons, for the most part peasants who had set out in search of a living. Of this number, 186,588 were sent back to where they had come from; the rest were brought to trial.[34]

Thanks in part to Mikhail Sholokhov's letters reporting the arbitrary exercise of power on the Don, the harassment of collective farm members, instances of torture, beatings, "swollen" and dying people, people "devouring not only fresh carrion but also destroying glanderous horses, and dogs and cats, even carrion that had been cooked down in tallow-producing shops which had no nutritional value," the Politburo passed a resolution in July 1933 acknowledging excesses in state grain procurement in the Veshin Raion.[35] Nonetheless, and despite Soviet scholars' silence on the subject, the famine long remained a source of popular bitterness, and among some Ukrainians was interpreted as the result of the regime's genocidal intent.

For peasants fleeing the hungry villages, Moscow and Leningrad were the most attractive destinations. Not surprisingly, these were the first cities to introduce limitations on the influx of new residents, or residential registration (propiska), and in December 1932 an internal passport system was introduced with the intent of impeding mobility. In spite of this, people found ways of "settling in" and anchoring themselves in these cities. These included acquiring counterfeit passports, stealing ration coupons or purchasing them on the black market, entering into fictive marriages, and other techniques known to illegal immigrants the world over.

The adaptation process was not easy for the new workers. Instances of drunkenness, idling, damage to machine tools and equipment, and industrial injuries became more frequent as new personnel arrived. These transgressions were usually explained as kulak intrigues, as conscious efforts to hinder the building of socialism. A summary entitled "The Class Enemy in Industry," compiled for the central and local press by the Department of Press and Information of SNK SSSR (*Sovet Narodnykh Komissarov SSSR* [council of People's commissars of the USSR]) and STO (*Sovet Truda i Oborony* [labor and defense council]) in 1930 includes such facts of "sabotage" as shoddy production, wedges and tacks shoved into machinery, machinery with sand and glass shards in it, and damage to gears. "At the Makeyevka Pipe Factory during a period of severe cold, idlers and malingerers poured water on the rails so that the car and crane wheels spun and they could rest. No one did anything to oppose this."[36]

Old conflicts traditional to relationships in factories also revived. The following is an anonymous report about a conversation supposedly overheard in passing at the "Female Worker" *(Rabotnitsa)* Factory in Leningrad:

---

## Document 25

Anonymous report of conversation at "Female Worker" factory, Leningrad, 1930. RGAE, f. 7486s, op. 1, d. 102, l. 212. Typed copy.

---

A couple of women workers talk to one another.

"Those damn bastards, they won't give you time off," says a weaver to her work pal.

"But where we are ain't so bad," says a young weaver wearing a red kerchief. "Not a single Komsomol member in our section, and when one shows up, we immediately make it hot for her." And, looking around nervously, she burst out into a shrill laugh.

## Document 25 *continued*

"Parasites like you oughta be driven out of the factory," declares a male voice addressing the women workers.

"Don't even bother to talk to him," says an elderly weaver, turning to a coworker. "He must be one of those promotees: has a pencil sticking out of his pocket."

"Can't you tell he's a Jew?" declares a third woman laconically after taking a good look at the facial features of the stranger. "Everyone knows who the Jews stand up for."

Whom the Jews stood up for remained unclear, but it is clear that in the factory anti-Semitic sentiments were rife. The promotees, we see, found themselves in the difficult position of being the principal bearers of Socialist Offensive ideas. As such they all too often found themselves the object of specialist-hating sentiments. The chaos and disorganization caused by experiments that they conducted could not help but provoke resistance, though passive, from the old specialists. At the same time, workers' hostility intensified toward an administration with representatives of the old cast still in its ranks, as a letter by someone named Bochkaryov from the raion center of Little Serdoba (Middle Volga Krai) demonstrates.

## Document 26

Letter from Bochkaryov, Middle Volga Krai, on specialists, 1930. RGAE, f. 7486s, op. 1, d. 100, l. 21. Typed copy.

We poor peasants haven't retreated from our post but have fought to the last drop. We finally took power into our own hands, as expected of us we switched to normal work, but then, however, the tsarist hangers-on saw at once what the deal was. They saw that our government paid for our toil as much as was needed to make a living. Then they began to enter our ranks to help us as specialists, and then snuck into our party as well. Now this is really the way all the tsarist hangers-on infiltrated the Soviet Union. The last year I was in the service, I keep a strict eye on this. They were infiltrating our lives by joining some of our trade unions, for example, our communication services union. In this union there was some specialist-bureaucrat who works in this business, at first as a specialist, and then he sneaks his way into the party, and then he's in charge of us. He immediately sees those who stand on the side of soviet power and immediately has those dismissed from the union. This is the way all specialists of this sort work their way into our party. Now I've been in classes six months in courses and for sure I can do any job he can [literally: "In any work I can outdrink him," meaning that the more vodka one can drink, the more respect one deserves]. When we went to repair the lines, I saw these types of specialists when we began to screw the hooks into the telephone poles, and what happens? I screw in three hooks, and he screws in one. I hold two poles, and he one, and all his work is that way, but just the same they've made him into my boss because he's the old specialist. Finally he dismissed all of us poor peasants from the union and put in his own types, those he wanted. Here's an example for you of how they climbed into our party. Now our party has begun to worry about purging its ranks. If you're going to purge the way you purged earlier, then you won't purge them. I'll tell you straight out why—and here's the reason: for each party member you need to do the purge in the place where he was born and where he grew up or where everyone knows him: who he is, if he's a landowner, a police chief, a priest's son, a police officer. They will know about all this in his native village. Now it's the right kind of purge when we purge the whole pack, then we will make socialism in our republic and be able to fulfill the Five-Year Plan. What's needed is to have our people, the poor peasants, everywhere. Then we will be able to keep our power in our own hands even if we know there are gangs around.

In essence, the letter describes the emergence of the "purge from below," one of the war cries during the first years of the Socialist Offensive. The main thrust was at Soviet institutions where "worker purge brigades" were active. Frequently a purge would turn into open persecution of people for social and political reasons. Conducting purges were young working-class people supposedly not burdened by the weight of the cursed prerevolutionary past. Clarifying one's class background and other credentials became part and parcel of every event of any significance in a person's life, be it admission to the party, admission to the Komsomol, or promotion to a leadership position. In 1933 public renunciations of fathers and mothers of alien social origin were organized at many Moscow plants.

Living space in cities being at a premium, the authorities sought to "cleanse" them of whole categories of people deemed socially alien or deviant. A major housecleaning in Leningrad of members of the former nobility who were not gainfully employed was one example. Campaigns were launched against homeless children, beggars, prostitutes, alcoholics, and hooligans. Cleaning up the behavior of all urban residents—part of the Stalinist civilizing mission—involved campaigns against such bad habits as smoking, hard drinking, cursing, and chewing edible seeds and spitting out the hulls.

The battle against use of profane and obscene language was widespread at new construction projects where there was a large group of strong-willed Komsomol members. At the best known Komsomol construction site of the 1930s, the Moscow Subway Building Project, the problem of profanity became especially acute after female Komsomol members were mobilized to work there. At first, transgressors were subjected to a ten-kopeck fine for each curse word or expression. But it quickly became clear that a whole army of inspectors had to be released from basic work duties just to collect fines. What is more, for the many who used bad language routinely the fine total began to exceed monthly pay. Realizing that "a Red Army attack" here would achieve nothing, activists decided to switch to a long-term moral siege using "lists of shirkers" and in-house newspapers.[37]

Utilization of female labor for heavy work originated during this time of industrialization. The top leadership of the party and Komsomol higher-ups knew how to take advantage of women's striving for emancipation, for equality with men. This was especially pronounced in the construction of the Moscow subway. The first women reported for work there in the summer of 1933, the result of the Second Komsomol Mobilization for the Construction Industry. Most upset by this were tunnel diggers, who claimed that a woman in the tunnel would bring misfortune. In the Subway Building Project in one tunnel alone some six hundred young women worked, among them shaft sinkers, concrete workers, and electrical workers. According to eyewitnesses, they worked passionately. One young woman challenged an old male worker to compete with her, and he couldn't keep up with her pace. But then neither could she: she strained herself and got sick.[38]

Supposedly at the initiative of the masses, a "Godless Five-Year Plan" was proclaimed. Closing of churches became widespread, priests were arrested and exiled. By the mid-1930s the number of Orthodox sanctuaries was reduced to one-quarter of that of pre-revolutionary times. Quite often at church closings there were fights between Komsomol members and believers, and cemeteries and grave markers were destroyed. Churches were converted into storehouses and clubs. In one a shooting gallery was opened, the icons serving as targets. A defining moment of the fight against religion was the blowing up of the Church of Christ the Savior in Moscow in December 1931.[39] It was one way of liquidating symbols of the "hated old times" and starting the "socialist reconstruction of the capital." Monasteries were closed, their elaborate compounds reverting to prisons, reformatories for minors, and exclusive Soviet institutions.

The press actively battled against such "obsolete" Christian precepts as obedience, virtue, humility, serenity, and meekness, ridiculing them unmercifully. Self-discipline, valor, courage, persistence, self-sacrifice, confidence in the morrow, loyalty to the party, hating enemies of socialism and the working class—these were the virtues posited instead. In a psychological sense, "socialist tenaciousness" became pivotal, and with it a large measure of fanatical conviction and devotion, all designed to replace the old religious sentiments. It seemed that no sphere of social life, not even the most intimate, was unaffected by the Socialist Offensive.

Popular were slogans calling for a critical recasting of the old bourgeois cultural heritage and creation of a new socialist culture. More often than not, however, this meant inculcation of crude cultural clichés and stereotypes designed to make the ideology of the Socialist Offensive comprehensible to the "wide masses of working people." Slogans proclaimed an all-out attack against hostile ideologies, tendencies, patterns of behavior, and traditions. Little by little anti-intellectualism—distrust of "the rotten intelligentsia" and "rotten liberalism"—took hold.

To help these ideas gain acceptance, campaigns were launched at the beginning of the 1930s by Stalin himself that criticized and reinterpreted accepted norms in philosophy, political economy, and history. The result was censure of "Rubinism" and "Deborinism" (supposedly dangerous tendencies in economics and philosophy, named for the leading scholars), as well as the Pokrovsky

school of history. Impetus was given to the "tireless work of eradicating inimical views and theories" and to affirming Comrade
Stalin as the sole source of authority in all realms. Literature, art,
and film during the Socialist Offensive underwent a process of organizational and ideological unification. The only correct and permissible directions, it was declared, were those that blended with
the new ideology and concepts of building socialism.

Not only were various schools and directions wiped out in scholarship and science, religious life, literature, and art, but the most
zealous adherents of the Socialist Offensive, those who tirelessly
struggled with actual deficiencies, were also persecuted. One of the
first sacrificed was none other than that "castigator of vices"
Demian Bedny ("Demian the Poor," pseudonym of peasant writer
Yefim Alekseevich Pridorov). At Stalin's prompting the Secretariat
of TsK VKP(b) in 1930 characterized his feuilletons as "slander of
socialism and the Russian working class." It was an object lesson
to other "slanderers of the USSR, of its past and of its present," as
Stalin wrote to Bedny on 12 December 1930. Sensing the direction
of the wind, poor Demian quickly dashed off a versified feuilleton
critical of himself: "Get going, Shoulder! Swing, Arm! If only a
single bright line! I turn to the left, I turn to the right. That's really
not good. Everywhere black lines: Vices! Vices! Vices!"[40]

In April 1932 TsK VKP(b) passed a resolution restructuring organizations of writers and artists. The setup of the existing professional associations, it observed, created "the dangerous potential
of transforming these organizations from a vehicle that would
maximally mobilize Soviet writers and artists for the tasks of building socialism into one that cultivated isolationism, of tearing writers and artists away from the political tasks of our times."[41] The
resolution created unions of writers, artists, composers, and archi-
tects, giving institutional organization to those working in the creative fields. Each union was a bureaucracy strictly controlled by
party organs, each directed by a secretariat made up of specially selected people loyal to the authorities and enjoying privileged status. Persons active in the arts who did not join or were expelled
from the unions were treated as social outcasts.

Another way of strengthening the principles of the new ideology
and culture was to toughen the organs of censorship. The main

purpose of Glavlit (*Glavnoe upravlenie literatury* [chief directorate of literature]), Glaviskusstvo (*Glavnoe upravlenie iskusstva* [chief directorate of art]), and Glavrepertkom (*Glavnyi repertuarnyi komitet* [chief theater repertory committee]) was to exercise ideological control over the activity of book publishers, editorial boards of newspapers and journals, and creative organizations; over exhibits being mounted, contests conducted, and films released; over the repertories of theaters, and so forth. During this period a tremendous number of scholarly studies and artistic and journalistic works that did not fit the new system of values lay on the shelves of special repositories.

As was the case on all Socialist Offensive fronts, notorious "excesses" were unavoidable. A. G. Rudnev, the director of the Central Library Named for Lenin in the Western Oblast (in the city of Smolensk), who for twelve years had painstakingly built the library's collection, complained to N. K. Krupskaia, deputy commissar of education for the RSFSR, that a purge committee had ordered him fired and put on trial for his lack of class-conscious vigilance, specifically, for the presence of forbidden literature in the library's holdings and of class-alien elements (twenty noblemen) on its staff.[42]

N. Maltsev, member of TsKK (*Tsentral'naia Kontrol'naia Komissia* [central control commission]) VKP(b), described how libraries were purged of books in a confidential memorandum:

## Document 27

Memorandum of N. Malstev to Ya. Rudzutak and Ye. Yaroslavsky on purge of libraries, 16 October 1932. RGASPI, f. 17, op. 114, d. 371, ll. 116–118 (verso). Typed original.

Libraries have been purged of pernicious and outdated literature by NKPros [*Narodnyi Komissariat Prosveshcheniia*, People's Commissariat of Education] without adequate instructions and control. The only instructions from *Glavpol[it]prosvet* [*Glavnoe upravlenie politicheskogo prosveshcheniia*, chief directorate of political education], dated 29 March 1930, present no defined order for book inspection and removal and are filled with ambiguities and obviously incorrect and harmful directives that could not serve as a practical guide for conducting a purge. Therefore in some oblasts (Moscow and

Leningrad) instructions solely for those oblasts appeared; more often than not, in view of the difficulty of this undertaking and the risks involved, the matter was allowed to take its own course, whatever happened would happen, and responsibility could be placed on those who actually carried out the work.

And what happened was very bad. At a meeting of those who conducted the purges, it came to light that more than 60 percent of all book holdings have been withdrawn. There are libraries in which the portion of books withdrawn reached 80 or 90 percent. Correspondence from very different corners of the USSR indicates that the classics of philosophy, science, belles-lettres, and even revolutionary Marxism have been removed: Marx, Engels, Lenin, Stalin, Tolstoy, Turgenev, Goncharov, Dickens, Hugo, resolutions of party congresses, reports of congresses of soviets, Sechenov, Timiriazev, Khvolson, Ivan Pavlov. The names of these "withdrawn" authors alone indicate criminal activity in the way the purge was conducted.

It is difficult to explain all this by lack of sophistication and stupidity in those carrying out the purge. It is one thing that in certain instances Lenin's books were withdrawn, for instance, because they were listed under the last name Il'in, or Marx's "Communist Manifesto" with Riazanov's foreword, but in many other instances this explanation breaks down.

Lists of works recommended for removal produced by purging committees in Moscow and Leningrad drawn up by "authoritative" and "educated" people give directions that in the provinces could lead to nothing else. Under "Philosophy" the Leningrad instructions propose that "idealistic philosophy should be removed entirely from circulation" (leaving only Kant's and Hegel's works). The works of bourgeois sociologists Spencer, Tarde, M. Kovalevsky, and Simmel are being withdrawn, as are Bukharin's *Istmat* [*Istoricheskii materializm,* historical materialism], Deborin, Kornilov, from the section of antireligious literature Kautsky's *Foundations of Christianity* and the titles of ninety books that I personally am unacquainted with but which include many surnames of Communists. From the "Social and Political" section Kautsky's *The Economic Doctrines of Karl Marx,* Luxemburg's *Accumulation of Capital,* Rosenberg's *Commentaries on Das Kapital,* Sabsovich, Borian's *State Control in the Soviet Union and in Western Europe,* Yaroslavsky, volumes 2 and 4, Nevsky, Kerzhentsev, Bogdanov's *Lessons in Political Economy,* Hilferding, Tugan-Baranovsky.

Under science, Bekhterev, Sechenov, Pavlov, many books about physics, chemistry, geology, and particularly biology.

The Moscow instructions differ little from the Leningrad ones. On seventy lists of books subject to removal to a special repository of the oblast library which were distributed throughout the Soviet Union without the knowledge of NKPros figure many books of great value. Listed here is all antireligious literature that unmasks religion by scientific fact alone, all trade union literature from the time before the trade unions were reorganized. Listed here are both Guesde and Jaurès, Vandervelde's *Condition of the Working Class in Belgium*, the Webbs, a whole series of books by Lozovsky, Tomsky, *Theses for the Fourteenth Congress* approved by the PB [Politburo], Friche's *History of the Labor Movement in the West*, Sechenov, Freud, Ditzen, Kollontai's *The New Morality and the Working Class*. The list for belles-lettres was drawn up in a completely arbitrary way. Why withdraw Hamsun, Dickens, Hauptmann, Zlatovratsky, Potapenko, Rostand, Oscar Wilde, Fet, Hugo, Sudermann, even Lunacharsky, Balmont, A. K. Tolstoy, and many, many others who by the humblest and most general assessment are on a higher level and less pernicious than the hundreds of junky kinds of belles-lettres that Gosizdat [*Gosudarstvennoe izdatel'stvo,* state publishing firm] puts out even now?

A kind of sadistic guardianship of the reader results from all this. The main instructions of Glavpolitprosvet are more restrained and balanced. But even according to them, "all prerevolutionary literature" concerned with upbringing and education, all prerevolutionary mathematics textbooks, all anthologies of Russian literature, collections of pieces for recitation, oral public reading and narration "should be removed from local public libraries and transferred to central and pedagogical libraries." In the category of belles-lettres removal of all books by Averchenko, Krestovsky, and Nemirovich-Danchenko is recommended, although works deemed "least unacceptable" can be kept, including Benoit's *Atlantis,* the famous Tarzan, and others.

There is a really terrible peril to all this because of the quite unacceptable and unregulated way in which the books were removed. What is the "central" library that is supposed to make the final decision about the fate of a book withdrawn, whether to throw it out or sell it? Is this a raion library, an oblast one? This decision has been left to the discretion of the local authorities. The Moscow Oblast Library created such centers in twenty-three spots. Glavpolitprosvet instructions propose that "all books deemed properly withdrawn—once two copies have been deposited in the archives and a selection made of those having potential value for research and specialized libraries—are to be sold unbound to factories for recycling into paper." No wonder that, following this, for example, in Morshansk they destroyed all philosophical literature taken from local libraries? There can be no doubt that such instances abound.

But this is not all.

According to the Glavpolitprosvet instructions, two copies of a huge number of books of great value are supposed to kept in the "archives" of a library. According to the instructions of Mosoblpolitprosvet [*Moskovskoe oblastnoe upravlenie politicheskogo prosveshcheniia,* Moscow Oblast directorate of political education] and MOSPS [*Moskovskii Sovet Professional'nykh Soiuzov,* Moscow council of trade unions] a "special repository" *(spetsfond)* was set up. In Leningrad a "closed repository." Except for books "worthy of being actively promoted to the reading masses," all other books not subject to the purge and removal process are to be put into these repositories. These books should be "kept separate from the main core [of books] in a special room or on separate shelves or in separate cabinets. Free access to them should not occur, catalogue cards for them are to be removed from the general catalog and maintained separately for reference purposes." The only possible meaning is that, after the official purge, readers can only use permitted books made available to them by a librarian at the latter's discretion, for there is no way for them even to know what else the library has (the catalog cards having been withdrawn).

All the instructions put great emphasis on the urgency of this work and the need to speed it up. Books were hauled to the Moscow Oblast Library by the truckload during the night; any organized receiving of them was out of the question. To tell what is what in such a mass of books is utterly impossible. An easy solution was sought and found: sell the books. The Oblast Library got itself a pretty good source of income out of the purge. The result? Secondhand book dealers all had books with uncanceled library identification stamps. This bacchanalia of stupidity was followed by a bacchanalia of stealing, for you couldn't have created a more irresponsible atmosphere for the bad element among library workers than by letting books with library identification stamps appear on the secondhand book market legally.

Characteristic in this business is not so much the Olympian composure and apathy of NKPros as the silence of the trade union community. During the time of the purge, from January 1930 on, "Red Librarian" [Krasnyi Bibliotekar'], VTsSPS's [*Vsesoiuznyi Tsentral'nyi Sovet Professional'nykh Soiuzov*, All-Union central council of trade unions] and NKP's [NKPros] special organ, besides publishing the above-mentioned instructions from Glavpolitprosvet, made note of the purge with only a single article, whose author, Timofeev, in June 1931 could still observe that even with the removal of 60 percent of book holdings there was still much pernicious and outdated literature in libraries and demanded that the purge be more intensive and broader and that the procedure for pulping books be simplified. No need for any approvals or carting books off. Just compile two copies of a simple list, a form for which he proposes on the spot, and the books can be pulped.

It's no wonder that the purge took place under pressure, ignoring completely the opinion of librarians. Noted were isolated instances of OGPU interference (in Tyumen and Kasimov) in the purge of book stacks. In Kasimov a OGPU agent took Bukharin's book *Istmat* from a student at an educational prep center for workers, and the librarian who produced the book for him was summoned to the OGPU and given a scolding.

VTsSPS in a resolution of its own published in the 4 September issue of the newspaper *Trud* [Labor] correctly noted the "quite obvious political harm" resulting from purge excesses. But the resolution is inadequate. First of all,

## Document 27 *continued*

though in its first paragraph VTsSPS categorically forbids trade union bodies from conducting a book purge, in the next it not only proposes that a "purge procedure" be developed but also institutes a procedure for continuing the purge: "Removal of books must be carried out by an authoritative commission headed by a member of the Presidium of FZMK [*Fabrichno-Zavodskoi Mestnyi Komitet*, (Local factory and shop committee]" and "the lists of books withdrawn should be approved by FZMK or by the boards of the Union," i.e., in actual fact VTsSPS made matters even more confusing and made removal of books following the purge procedure more irresponsible, for one should not trust any FZMK to make a decision about the fate of a book. One should also not deem adequate VTsSPS choices for a special commission to unmask those guilty of improperly removing books. The commission is supposed to include four library workers: one from VTsSPS, one from MOSPS, one from NKPros, and one from among the workers of the given library, some of whom could have been direct culprits in this whole business and not in a position to unmask persons who are genuinely guilty in a political sense of causing extraordinary political and material harm to the building of socialism and soviet power by their criminal purging activity. The activity of a commission such as this should not and cannot be limited to the libraries of unions alone.

Therefore I propose:

1. To put forward a proposal to TsK VKP(b) to stop immediately the purging, transportation, and reselling of books from all libraries.
2. To create as a body of TsKK's Presidium a commission to unmask the real culprits of criminal purging activity and to develop measures to liquidate the harmful consequences of this activity.

---

This document gives us a good sense of the direction taken by the ideological purge, of how, as a result, not only prerevolutionary Russian literature but also some of the greatest works of world literature were removed as reading options for the general public. What is more, Marxist works, which might be expected to have engendered some degree of understanding of what was going on, fared no better. To attribute all this entirely to stupidity and overcautiousness on the part of those who implemented the purge would hardly be meaningful, for the "bacchanalia" was initiated by high officials. No one ever questioned publicly the need for such a purge. But where does one draw the line between what should be allowed and what not, what could be read and what was not good for the building of socialism? Worse still, sometimes utterly incompetent people and organizations were enlisted to conduct the campaign. How other than by hypocrisy can one explain the protests against "excesses" by those leaders who were privy to the purge? The amusing side of the situation is that they would suddenly include themselves on the list of banned authors. And it makes their indignation with the "lazy and careless attitude" particularly understandable, as in the case of Yaroslavsky, "chief antireligious expert in the land of the Soviets" and author of works on the history of Bolshevism, who in a confidential letter to the Politburo reported:

# Document 28

Ye. Yaroslavsky to Politburo on library purge, 15 September 1932. RGASPI, f. 17, op. 114, d. 371, ll. 109–110. Attested copy, typed.

I have learned that during the past two years the book collections of almost all libraries have been virtually annihilated. This annihilation has been carried out under the banner of "purging" the collections of every kind of ideologically uncontrolled and pernicious literature based on general instructions published in 1930 by NKPros. The instructions were "made concrete" by certain ONO [*Otdel Narodnogo Obrazovaniia*, board of public education] lists and have produced the following results.

Removed was all antireligious literature unmasking religion on the basis of scientific data (in spite of Lenin's directions to use such literature widely), all trade union literature published before the Fifth Plenum of VTsSPS's Eighth Convocation [December 1928], literature about unemployment and round-the-clock shift work and about the transition to the seven-hour workday, almost all popular literature regarding cooperatives, regarding social insurance, labor protection, and the building of kolkhozes and state farms published before 1930–31, all idealistic philosophers—except for Kant and Hegel—and the works of Spencer, Simmel, Bukharin, and others on historical materialism and sociology.

Furthermore, "closed stacks" have been created, where books can be used only by party activists and students in higher educational institutions for party workers *(komvuzy)*. To these closed stacks have been transferred such books as Rosa Luxemburg's *Accumulation of Capital*, Hilferding's *Finance Capital*, books dealing with the history of the party by Nevsky, Kerzhentsev, and Yaroslavsky, on economic policy by Sarabianov, Kritsman, Tel', Tsiperovich, on physics by Timiriazev, Ioffe, on the study of reflexes by Bekhterev, Sechenov, Pavlov (member of the Academy of Sciences).

In Moscow Oblast alone 350,000 books were removed from trade union libraries in the city of Moscow during 1930–32. Stored in a warehouse on the Arbat in Moscow were 209,000 books taken out of raion libraries. All over Moscow and Moscow Oblast a special brigade consisting of Comrades Modestov, Etingof, Lebedinskaia, and Buzinier removed books: from the MONO [*Moskovskii Otdel Narodnogo Obrazovaniia*, Moscow board of public education] Library, [Sidney and Beatrice] Webb's *History of Trade Unionism* (Let me remind you that while living in exile, Lenin was translating the Webbs), Lozovsky's *Issues in the World Trade Union Movement* and also four other titles by the latter, Friche's *History of the Labor Movement in the West,* and others.

Several local boards of education, the Gudauta one, for example, went so far as to issue instructions to remove books such as Bebel's, Lassalle's, Plekhanov's *Our Differences,* the works of Marx and Engels, V. Il'ich's [Lenin's] *The Development of Capitalism in Russia,* and Stalin's *Articles on the National Question.*

In some libraries, in Leningrad in particular, works of Marx and Engels edited by Riazanov are being withdrawn and, because in many libraries there are no other editions of Marx, this means that they are withdrawing almost all works by Marx and Engels.

Here is more factual evidence to show the extent of the purging zeal. Removed from the library at Siniavinsk Peatbogs in Leningrad Oblast were Tolstoy, Turgenev, Goncharov, Korolenko, Bezymensky, Podiachikh, M. I. Kalinin, the "Communist Manifesto," Chernyshevsky, books by Lenin, and so forth. From the Central Library of the Communications Union in Leningrad books by Romain Rolland were removed, and this at a time when we are publishing Romain Rolland's letters and his appeal "War on War." Removed from the library of the Glass Plant Named for October 25th in the Western Oblast were books by Marx and Engels, Lenin, Stalin, Krupskaia, Yaroslavsky, Kerzhentsev, Krylenko, Bubnov, Demian Bedny, Bezymensky, Turgenev, Korolenko, Zhukovsky, and others.

All of us in the past became engrossed in our youth with books like Giovagnoli's *Spartacus*. In 1932 the Institute of Literary Criticism and Bibliography faulted this book and, understandably, it is now being removed by librarians who follow our reviews and bibliographical information, afraid to let books remain in libraries that this reviewer or that, sometimes an illiterate one, has condemned in the press.

As a consequence of all these books being removed and the utterly wild, scandalous "purge" of libraries, the staff of VTsSPS published in the 4 September 1932 issue, no. 206, of the newspaper *Trud* a resolution suspending this kind of "purge" and instructing VTsSPS's Public Culture Department to appoint a special commission to disclose those who were responsible for erroneously removing books from trade union libraries and for transferring books from trade union book holdings to local boards of public education and selling them.

## Document 28 *continued*

It seems to me that this resolution is wholly inadequate, and I propose:

That a commission of TsK and TsKK be appointed that will give more serious attention to this matter, taking an interest not only in trade union books but in the entire library network as well. NKPros here has committed, in my opinion, a serious error.

More detailed materials on this issue can be found in the Culture Department of VTsSPS.

---

Krupskaia also complained about excesses in the purge of libraries. In a letter to P. P. Postyshev she wrote: "Recently they established a *'N.D.M.'* collection, *"Ne Davat' Massam'* [don't give to the general public], where they dispatch 'suspicious publications' (including those of Hegel, Marx and Engels, Lenin). . . . The working and kolkhoz masses are treated like little children to whom one should give only topical propaganda leaflets and translated novels."[43]

There can be no question that as a result of measures taken the process of purging libraries was made somewhat more orderly, but the tight ideological control of publishing as well as of books acquired by public libraries and those being retailed remained unchanged. Special significance was attached to printed materials that people encountered on a daily basis. In this category were desk and wall calendars, which were designed to implant a definite perception of the world in a population as yet without much education. Calendars for factory and kolkhoz workers were published in mass editions. Special calendars were issued for party members, for shock workers, for Red Army soldiers, and so forth. The significance attached to this material and the extent to which ideological control was exercised over it are reflected in a memorandum to the Politburo dated 28 December 1932:

---

## Document 29

A. Stetsky to Politburo on tear-off calendars, 28 December 1932. RGASPI, f. 17, op. 114, d. 333, ll. 56–57. Typed original.

---

To: Comrade Stalin, Comrade Kaganovich, and Comrade Postyshev
Tear-off calendars for collective farm members and for the shock worker for

1933 have come out in "Sotsekgiz" [*Sotsial'no-ekonomicheskoe gosudarst-vennoe izdatel'stvo,* state social and economic publishing firm] editions. In four calendars that Kul'tprop MK [department of culture and propaganda of the Moscow Party Committee] looked through, three for kolkhoz members and one for workers, a series of faulty, confused formulations and the grossest political and technical errors were discovered. For example, in one of the calendars for kolkhoz members we find:

16 October, the slogan "The Collective Farm Should Be Highly Productive and at the Same Time Require of Its Members the Least Expenditure of Physical Labor . . . " [instead of "Highly Productive Labor"].

1 November, in a note, progressive piecework [payment for work on a graduated scale above the norm, which ran counter to the way work was then organized] is recommended as the best form of piecework.

21 September, a slogan printed "Improve Supplies to the Toilers—Don't Forget Undernourished Livestock."[44]

21 December, the biography of Comrade Stalin is given. In the text nothing is said about Comrade Stalin's role in the party and in the Proletarian Revolution.

In a calendar for collective farm workers who are learning to read:

18 January, it is recommended that seed stock be readied no later than 15 February instead of 15 January.

30 January, the slogan "Agricultural Pests Are Eating Up More of the Harvest Than Working People" [objectionable because it might cause people to think about how badly organized extermination of pests was or how poorly collective farm members were fed].

15 July, a note, "Fatten Up Livestock for Slaughter," opens with the words "Don't sell undernourished livestock to the government or kill it to feed collective farm workers."

In the calendar for shock workers:

6 January, a despicable citation taken from a pronouncement of enemies: "See, even among Bolsheviks there are people who reject the Stalinists' dizzying fantasies."

27 January, "In their degree of literacy . . . the Bashkir, Chuvash, Komi, Karelia, and other such republics have already outstripped those capitalistic countries most advanced in education (Germany, NAUS [North American United States], and others)" [objectionable perhaps because of references to the United States and Germany as countries foremost in terms of education, or perhaps because of the boldness of a lie too obvious to be credited].

9 February, in the word Stalinabad the "b" was left out [with the result that it could be read as "Stalin's Hell (Stalina ad)"].

9 March and 20 September, the left wing is identified with counterrevolutionary Trotskyism.

We have listed only part of the more glaring political blunders.

## Document 29 *continued*

In accordance with instructions from Kul'tprop, in all stocks of kolkhoz calendars the sheets with the grossest political mistakes will be removed and replaced with other sheets (one side of these will be filled by the date, the second side, where the text was, will be left blank).

In calendars already distributed in part, pages to be removed will be torn out and not replaced.

The shock worker calendar is still in production, and Kul'tprop has proposed appropriate textual corrections.

With the aim of improving publication of tear-off calendars for 1934, Kul'tprop takes it upon itself to:

1. Strengthen the editorial staff of tear-off calendars by appointing competent party workers (Comrade Kurskaia has been sent, negotiations are under way with a number of other workers);
2. Attract qualified editors from among party members and author-compilers to work on these calendars;
3. Propose that compilation of tear-off calendars for 1934 start early in 1933.

Director of the Department of Culture and Propaganda of Leninism, TsK VKP(b) A. Stetsky

At a special session of the Orgburo (*Organizatsionnoe biuro,* organization bureau) of TsK VKP(b) on 17 January 1933, a number of measures were outlined to correct the conditions under which tear-off calendars were published. Among them: identify and punish as quickly as possible those guilty of permitting mistakes, strengthen party control, and use the calendar's content to popularize achievements of the Five-Year Plan in both city and country.[45]

How one ought to cast light on these achievements and how much the idea of speed in the Socialist Offensive had encroached on censors' consciousness is illustrated by the following episode, one of many like it. A sentence from a novel about kolkhoz life by the Belorussian writer Lyn'kov, *Bredet Sivka medlenno* (Sivka trudges slowly), met with objections from the censor: "Why slowly, why not speedily, why isn't the poor horse happy along with the collective farm workers?" Moreover, an aura of secrecy surrounded everything, especially anything related to defense. Writer Shapovalov complained that Glavlit was deleting from literary works such "banned" words as *tank, unit (zveno), airplane,* and *frontier.*[46]

What forms various types of ideological control might take in the press and what consequences awaited those who conveyed information not in line with the official version are well illustrated, for example, by a memorandum of 28 May 1933:

## Document 30

A. Stetsky on lack of vigilance among TASS workers, 28 May 1933. RGASPI, f. 17, op. 114, d. 608, ll. 140–141. Typed original.

To the Secretaries of TsK VKP(b)
To the Politburo of TsK KP(b)
CC: Comrades Doletsky, Bukharin, and the Director of RATAU [*Russkoe Agenstvo Telegrafnykh Agenstv Ukrainy,* Russian language agency of the telegraph agencies of Ukraine], Comrade Lakizo.
On May 21st in *Izvestia* appeared the following item:
"INTERNATIONAL CONGRESS OF TEACHERS
Kiev, 20 May (TASS)—An international congress of teachers attended by more than three hundred delegates took place in the Education Workers Club.
To loud cheers Comrades Stalin, Molotov, Kaganovich, Kossior, Postyshev, Zatonsky, Thälmann, Dimitrov, and Stasova were elected to the honorary presidium of the congress.
Talks were given at the congress by representatives of revolutionary teachers in Germany, France, England, Poland, and Japan."
This news item was placed in *Ekonomicheskaia Zhizn'* [Economic life], *Komsomol'skaia Pravda* [Komsomol Pravda], *"Za kommunisticheskoe prosveshchenie"* (For a Communist education), *Tsentral'naia nemetskaia gazeta* (Central German gazette), *Lesnaia Promyshlennost'* (Lumber industry).
In actual fact no international congress of teachers took place. It turned out that local organizations in Kiev, in tune with their usual way of bungling mass work condemned by TsK VKP(b), made an evening devoted to the status of teachers in capitalist countries out to be a "congress" at which individual lecturers spoke for each country, an honorary "congress" presidium was chosen, and so forth.
This small occurrence calls for special attention because it reveals a lack of fundamental vigilance among TASS workers and newspaper editors.
Under work circumstances such as these there is the danger that staff of our news agencies and newspaper editors, including even the editorial staff of an official state organ, might permit even provocative items planted by our enemies to be published.
TASS received the wire cited above from the Ukrainian News Agency (RATAU). RATAU had received the wire from Kiev from Rabinovich (not a

party member), secretary of RATAU's bureau in Kiev. Comrade Leshevov (not a party member), a RATAU editor, and Comrade Kryzhanovsky (not a party member), who approved the dispatch without verifying the report, sent it on to TASS. At TASS the wire was edited by Comrade Gol'der (not a party member), and Comrade Sushchenko (a party member) approved its dispatch to newspapers also without verifying the facts of the report. In addition, this report was OK'd by NKID's [*Narodnyi Komissariat Inostrannykh Del,* People's Commissariat of Foreign Affairs] publication office, whose employee Comrade Yaroshevsky (a party member) also did not verify the credibility of the information. Penalties for RATAU's mistake were imposed on Comrade Deshevov (fired) and Comrade Kryzhanovsky (reprimanded).

I consider the measures taken to be insufficient.

I request that the question of TASS's inside information and its ties with the news agencies of the Union's republics be raised by Orgburo.

I request that the Politburo TsK KP(b) of Ukraine investigate RATAU's scandalous actions.

I propose that Comrade Doletsky remove Comrade Gol'der from work at TASS and issue a severe reprimand to Comrade Sushchenko

Director of the Department of Culture and Propaganda of Leninism, TsK VKP(b) A. Stetsky

---

The Socialist Offensive, especially in its initial phase, was characterized by a ruthless toughening of punitive policy on the part of the Soviet state. The number of those arrested by various state organs rose almost sevenfold between 1927 and 1933, from 76,983 to 505,256. The greatest growth occurred during 1930 and 1931, when people were arrested for political reasons, including "counterrevolutionary activities" and "anti-Soviet agitation." In 1932 and 1933, on the other hand, there was incredible growth in the number of those detained for violating other statutes, in connection first and foremost with the passage of the Law on Protection of Socialist Property of 7 August 1932 and with the fight against profiteering, embezzlement, and other such crimes.[47] Running parallel on a widening scale was "kulak exile." Joining the families of exiled "kulaks" were "those with origins in socially alien classes," ex-landowners, gentry, priests, and other "exes" revealed in the course of the Great Purges.

The network of camps, penal colonies, and special settlements *(spetsposeleniia)* began to enmesh the country. With the enlistment of forced labor, many of the problems of industrialization could be solved. Prisoners built canals, railroads, and industrial establishments. Many extracted gold and other precious metals. Labor in special settlements organized as collective and state farms was used to clear and then plow new lands. Many worked also in the coal and forest industries. The state proclaimed a policy of "reformation through forced labor." Those who actively showed their worth in "the building of socialism" had a good chance of being pardoned, rewarded, even allowed to continue their careers. In the 1930s the highly popular film *Zakliuchennye* (Prisoners) depicted the rapid reeducation at the Baltic–White Sea Canal Construction Camp of both criminals and political prisoners, transformed into active participants in building socialism. The actual picture was far less rosy.

Ingrained in the penitentiary system were those same practices that characterized everyday life in Soviet society: competitions, record-breaking efforts, maximal standards of output. The police also overfulfilled norms, as it were, arresting several times the number of people who actually received sentences. Thus in 1932 there were 410,433 arrests but only 141,916 convictions.[48] Among the remainder, many languished in prisons for months or even years awaiting the outcome of judicial deliberations.

A good idea of what was happening in those years can be gained from materials related to the August 1932 investigation of a penal labor colony in the city of Nizhni Novgorod—that is, of one of the many standard ITKs (*Ispravitel'no-Trudovye Kolonii*, penal labor colonies) inherited from the old NEP-era penal world.

---

## Document 31

Report on penal labor colony in Nizhni Novgorod, 10 August 1932. GARF, f. 1235, op. 141, d. 1369, ll. 84–81. Corrected original, typed.

---

To the Presidium of VTsIK, Comrades Kiselyov and N. Novikov,
To the Procurator of the RSFSR, Comrade Vyshinsky,
A Report On Conditions at the Penal Labor Colony in the City of Nizhni Novgorod
The Nizhni Novgorod labor colony, built to accommodate eight hundred

## Document 31 *continued*

persons, had 3,461 persons incarcerated in it on 1 August 1932. The overload is explained, first, by the fact that a lot of people are held for a long time under investigation and, second, by the fact that the people's judges hearing cases apply the full force of the law (for example, for embezzling one hundred rubles or for swindling someone out of six rubles and so many kopecks or the like they give one to two years of strict solitary confinement) and, thirdly, by the fact that Moscow sends so many (there are instances of children being sent). The living accommodations look like the proverbial herring barrel packed with people. Iron bedsteads are ____ in number.[49] Plank beds are furnished to ____ people, and the rest sleep on the bare floor. There are mattresses for only ____ persons in all, and no blankets or pillows. People sleep literally on bare plank beds. It's dirty and stuffy in the places of confinement.

The practice of confining prisoners by category is not always precisely observed. A worker, peasant, kolkhoz member brought for the first time to the House of Correction *(Ispravdom)* not infrequently finds himself among inveterate recidivists, prostitutes, and ruffians. For example, from rounds in the women's ward in one cell questioning revealed that here were repeat offenders and prostitutes with up to seven convictions, and here also were female factory workers and collective farmers with first convictions for stealing a goat or embezzling a hundred rubles, those still being investigated, and those simply taken into custody. During the inspection of the second ward, it became apparent that in cell no. 1 among working people deprived of their freedom were four repeat offenders. All newcomers to cell no. 1 are subjected to a thorough search and under the threat of a knife have everything of any value whatsoever taken from them, not even mentioning the pieces of dried bread they bring with them, which as a rule are plucked by robbers immediately after they arrive. The administration views this outrageous situation with great indifference, and for this reason prevailing opinion among the prisoners is that it's useless to complain. The head convict in the first ward, Razin, is a recid [recidivist thief], in the second ward, Lapshin, a recid, in the third, fourth, and fifth men convicted under paragraphs 162 and 193 of the Criminal Code [article 162 concerned theft; article 193, the last one in the 1926 Criminal Code, incorporated the 1924 Regulations on Crimes by Military Personnel], in the sixth Rachkov, a recid convicted six times over, etc.

Prisoners communicate freely between cells; here too the possibility of theft is not absent.

At the House of Correction five oversight committees [comprising representatives of various bodies and social organizations who looked after the condition of prisoners' space] have been formed, their work goes on without proper leadership, committees' sessions are very rarely attended by representatives of the Worker and Peasant Inspectorate, of Soviet social organizations, of the Gorsovet [*Gorodskoi sovet,* city council], Komsomol, and the Zhenotdel [*Zhenskii otdel,* the party's women's section]. At sessions up to eighty items are put up for consideration at one time. Oversight committee no. 3 may serve as an example. At the session of 1 July of this year, eighty-three items were considered; the session of 29 June considered eighty-six items. Using this approach, the work of an oversight committee becomes little more than pro forma, never going to the heart of matters.

The House of Correction has three hundred staff; thirty-three of them are members or associate members of VKP(b), four Komsomol members. Of all the Communists, only one deals directly with prisoners and that in his capacity as secretary of the VKP(b) cell.

The political and educational work, the very core of the House of Corrections' existence, is carried out very poorly. This work is killed by prison work activities and by inaction on the part of the administration. For 3,461 persons there are 760 newspaper subscriptions, 110 journal subscriptions. The club was designed for four hundred; 350 semiliterate persons are being taught. Vocational education was given to 263 persons in the first half of the year. The cultural service is wholly inadequate; it does not draw on the institutional and scientific strengths of Nizhni Novgorod. In their free time prisoners are pretty much left to their own devices. Observed were instances of card playing and telling of far-fetched stories hostile to the Soviet authorities.

In quantitative terms the House of Correction keeps growing, numbering now 3,461 persons, of which 1,750 are serving terms; 362 are prisoners in transit, and there are 1,467 persons under investigation, or 46.6 percent of the total [actually 42.3 percent; several other percentages in the document are incorrect. See below for a still lower figure for persons under investigation]. Among those under investigation are found many individuals who have been in prison four months or more without being indicted. After interrogations, a large number (up to sixty) of them . . . were sent on to the procurator. [A list follows of eleven individuals under investigation by OGPU who had been in prison for two to eleven months without their cases having been initiated.]

Who are the term prisoners? Workers: 293. Hired hands: 85. Poor peasants: 184. Peasants of average means: 273. Collective farmers: 131. Kulaks: 395. Idlers. 91. Office workers: 105. Of the numbers cited, those especially for workers, collective farmers, poor and middling peasant stick out the most. Why has this happened? Conversations with the prisoners and checks done on sentences show that the People's Courts were particularly generous in awarding prison terms for relatively small crimes. For example, for stealing a rooster an old woman of sixty-five was given three years' exile in remote provinces of the USSR, for stealing a goat, two years' incarceration. For stealing boots a sixteen-year-old lad was sentenced to two years in prison, for forging a check for six rubles a year and a half sentence, for a 400-ruble shortage in accounting for an advance, two years, for a hundred-ruble shortage, one year. For selling a half-liter of water as vodka the sentence was two years, etc.

The distribution of crimes committed by the prisoners is: counterrevolutionary crimes 83, gangsterism 17, hooliganism 232, bribery 43, job-related crimes 339, murder and bodily injury 184, robbery and grand larceny 212, cattle theft 45, arson and property damage posing a threat to public safety 57, illegal production and sale of alcoholic beverages 11, malevolent price increases 63, and failure to fulfill required extra-hard work assignments 111.

The age distribution of those arrested is: under eighteen, 83; age fifty to sixty, 119; over sixty, 82. The rest are between ages eighteen and fifty.

There are 1,407 persons being detained pending investigation, 243 by the People's Court [Narsud], 173 by the interrogating unit, 119 by the procurator, 723 by GPU bodies, 149 by other bodies.

In the case of GPU, the figure is now significantly reduced.

The stays of those being investigated in the House of Correction are: up to two months, 857; from two to three months, 229; and longer than three months, 321 persons.

As a result of my visits, prisoners and persons being interrogated submitted 780 appeals. All of these appeals have now been sorted by prisoner file and scrutinized by members of the krai court and the procurator. On their own authority they have already released several people from the House of Correction. After being considered, all appeals remaining without satisfactory resolution will go to the KraiKK-RKI [*Krai Kontrol'nyi Komitet-Raboche-Krest'ianskii Inspektorat,* krai control commission and workers' and peasants' inspectorate], where they will be reviewed anew; there's an agreement for this. All those petitions that pertain to VTsIK and the procurator of the republic will be sent there after an on-site investigation here has been completed.

Thirty-five appeals were received concerning the special prison block. In view of the fact that they all will be resolved locally, they were transferred to the OGPU krai chief.

From conversation with prisoners it turned out that many of them had filed requests to go home and help with the harvest. Of all those who so petitioned the observation committee released only fourteen for work in the fields.

The House of Correction's Industries

At the House of Correction the following enterprises function: a cabinet-making factory, a metalworking shop, shoe manufacturing and tailoring shops, a brick plant, cartage, a construction repair shop, and a crew that performs off-site work.

All together 1,827 persons are occupied with production work, 334 persons do maintenance, and there are 82 guards and firemen. Involved with one type of work or another are 64.8 percent, not working are 35.2 percent.

The production plan for 1932 was expressed as the sum of sales prices, 3,203,249 rubles. For the first six months the target was 1,529,788 rubles; realized in the first six months was 852,123 rubles, or 56.38 [actually 55.70] percent.

Labor output in man-days: according to plan 110,855 for the first six months; 79,741 days were actually put in, constituting 71.9 percent. Wages to be paid out (according to plan): 107,063 rubles; paid out (actual) were 76,742 rubles, or 71.67 percent.

In terms of labor productivity, seven rubles, sixty-one kopecks for one day's labor (according to plan), the actual was the sum six rubles forty-nine kopecks, or 85.87 [actually 82.28] percent. Average wage (according to plan), ninety-seven kopecks per day, actually paid out was 96 kopecks, or 99.7 percent.

Wages are paid properly in the form of credit slips for merchandise in prison stores, because 25 percent is retained for disbursement at time of discharge.

Total income for the first quarter of 1932 amounts to 93,860 rubles.

I am leaving out other areas of prison life from the present report in view of the fact that I was not able to familiarize myself adequately with them. I will say a few words about food. Prisoners who do not work receive 450 grams of bread, those that do eight hundred grams. Dinner is prepared in two cauldrons for those working and those not. Much unpeeled potato finds its way into the soup, delivery of food to the prisoner involves many stages. What finds its way to the prisoner is different from what was in the pot. That little fat that finds its way into the serving containers is all but lost in the process of pouring and ladling.

Medical care. For the whole colony four physicians are available; every day one physician is on duty at the outpatient receiving room. There are visits from 120 to 150 or more persons. Patients are received during a six-hour period. Clearly with a situation such as this one cannot say that the medical service is at a satisfactorily high level.

From all that is described the conclusion is obvious. With regard to the penal colony organizational measures must be undertaken, the number of service personnel must be increased. Decisive measures to speed up the interrogation process must be taken by the Office of the Procurator. All cases of persons under investigation must be audited. The verdicts and files of those convicted must be audited. Political and educational work must be raised to an appropriate level, and so forth. . . .

VTsIK Presidium Instructor Novikov

In addition, Novikov submitted to the OGPU a list of petitions that, in his opinion, involved matters pertaining directly to the authority of this body. The list gives one a notion of how arrests for "political reasons" occurred.

# Document 32

Report accompanying prisoner appeals, 10 August 1932. GARF, f. 1235, op. 141, d. 1369, ll. 91–90 (verso). Corrected original, typed.

Strictly Confidential
To the Chief of the Nizhni Novgorod Krai OGPU
Comrade Reshetov
CC: Krai-Procurator Comrade Ovoshchnikov
As a result of conversations with and a review of appeals received from prisoners in the special block, I make the following observations:

1. Some individuals have been under investigation for a very long time.
2. According to the prisoner appeals few airings are granted.
3. During visits to prisoners' cells newspapers, journals, and books were not visible.
4. Those arrested request that they be furnished salt, tobacco, and paper.
5. Several are worried about harvesting their grain.
6. One of the prisoners began a hunger strike 7 August; he demands that he be sent to a concentration camp.

The thirty-five appeals turned in are transferred to your office for a proper review because all the requests set forth in the appeals relate directly to your office.
—VTsIK Presidium Instructor Novikov

In the same folder, there is a document dated 14 July 1932 detailing an utterly outrageous episode that illustrates how the battle against homeless children and crime was conducted in Moscow during those years:

# Document 33

Memorandum to Vyshinsky on incarceration of minors, 14 July 1932. GARF, f. 1235, op. 141, d. 1369, ll. 89–89 (verso). Corrected original, typed.

To the Procurator of the Republic, Comrade Vyshinsky
In addition to our correspondence no. 7k5/365 of 28 May and no. 7k2/517 of 23 June regarding the question of minors, fifty-six in number, sent out of Moscow under guard, I write once again with the object of directing your attention to the abomination that has been committed against these children.
Briefly about the course of events: the Moscow joint committee that classi-

fies underage lawbreakers, having considered the question of dispatching this group of children, according to its own resolution of 20 April decided to dispatch them all to GUITU [*Glavnoe Upravlenie Ispravitel'no-Trudovykh Uchrezhdenii*, chief directorate of penal labor institutions] of NKYu [*Narodnyi Komissariat Yustitsii*, People's Commissariat of Justice]. In the month of April, GUITU sent all fifty-six under guard to Arzamas. Arzamas was not given advance notice of the dispatch of this party. At the Arzamas ITD [*Ispravitel'no-Trudovoi Dom*, reformatory] at this moment repairs were being done, and for this reason the children could not be domiciled and had to be sent on to the Nizhni Novgorod FZTK [*Fabrichno-Zavodskaia Trudovaia Koloniia*, factory and workshop labor colony], which was already filled beyond capacity.

But the situation was made considerably more complicated by the fact that, except for the 20 April resolution, no documents and decisions had been sent saying why the minors had been taken into custody and how long their term was.

The KUITU [*Kraevoe Upravlenie Ispravitel'no-Trudovykh Uchrezhdenii*, krai directorate of correctional institutions] head and the krai procurator's office during the first half of May wrote and sent telegrams to NKYu asking that the documents for the children in custody be sent. In their telegrams they threatened to release all the children if the documents were not sent. From the Office of the Procurator of the Republic they received the answer that they should refrain from releasing the children and send them on instead in compliance with the resolution, but in the resolution, I repeat once again, it was specified, "Send them to GUITU NKYu." Once again they received notification that the matter would be cleared up quickly.

The minors meanwhile began to starve and knife one another, bored with being in FZTK, [and] not waiting for the "quick" decision in the matter we, in spite of the Office of the Procurator of the Republic's prohibition, on our own began distributing the children, to the FZU [*Fabrichno-Zavodskoe Uchilishche*, factory workshop school], the Trudkommuna [*Trudovaia kommuna*, work commune], some we returned to their parents as having been illegally held, a few we released.

And, finally, in the first days of July we received from the Office of the Procurator of the Republic the 19 June resolution of the Standing Committee [*Dezhurnaia Komissia*] regarding the minors. According to this resolution, twenty-four of the fifty-six by committee decision were to be sent to work assigned by the Labor Board [*Otdel Truda*].

Comrade Vyshinsky, in our memorandum of 28 May we asked that suitable measures be taken against persons guilty of procrastination, but this matter has turned out to be considerably worse. . . .

Who thought it necessary to bring in twenty-four persons, fifteen- and sixteen-year-old children, send them under guard to Arzamas, then under guard

## Document 33 *continued*

to Nizhni Novgorod, keep them as prisoners for several months, and all this so that they could be sent to work assigned by the Labor Board?

Since when in the USSR has there been a procedure established for sending minors off to work in this way?

I request that this matter be investigated and a report drawn up of measures taken.

—Deputy Krai Procurator Ovoshchnikov

[On the document is a handwritten postscript:]

To the deputy secretary of VTsIK, Comrade N. Novikov

I am forwarding a copy of the krai procurator's memorandum. I ask that you take appropriate measures quickly. I report that as of [date undecipherable] the young children still had not been taken from the reformatory and have contact with adult criminal types. During visits with prisoners, I had occasion to see these children. They do not know why they in particular were sent, for there were many others. Report the results.

2 August 1932

VTsIK Instructor Novikov

---

Facts like these were not at all isolated. At first everything seemed simple: on 10 March 1931 it was decided to completely liquidate homeless children from Moscow's streets. Over a ten-day period all homeless children were to be rounded up and transferred to children's homes, work communes, and other institutions. It was calculated that there were 1,200 homeless children in Moscow, and project estimates were drawn up for distributing clothing, food, and other necessities. And that was to be the end of the matter.[50] But it turned out to be much more complex than that.

The process of giving some order to the activities of correctional and judicial bodies began in 1933. The number of mass "sweeps" declined; arrests were made to comply with legal practices. Space was freed up at places of imprisonment by releasing persons who had wound up there by chance. At the same time, tougher and tougher punishments were imposed. The number of guilty verdicts issued by courts jumped sharply: from 141,256 to 239,664. The population of the GULAG increased in 1933 by 176,000, in 1934 by 455,000, and in 1935 by another 330,000.[51] Thereafter, the campaign started to lose momentum, but this was only a prelude to the unleashing of mass operations in 1937.

The forced labor sector constantly grew. It acquired an organizational legitimacy of its own and became an important factor in the development of the economy. A substantial part of this sector was made up of "special resettled persons" *(spetspereselentsy)*, or, from 1934 on, "labor deportees" *(trudposelentsy)*, inhabitants of the special labor settlements that sprang up all over the country and became a means of forcibly colonizing the country's more remote territories. In 1933 nearly four hundred thousand "kulaks" and their families came to these settlements, double the previous year's arrivals. The total number of special resettled persons in the country declined by seventy thousand, the consequence of high mortality and mass flight. In the same year, for example, 152,000 settlers died and 246,000 fled.[52]

As comprehensive collectivization became more of a reality, "kulak exile" gradually shrank in scale. Between 1934 and 1937, the number of persons who came to the labor settlements declined annually, from 255,000 to 246,000 to 165,000 to 128,000. And by the end of 1937 the total population of the settlements was only 878,000, almost 450,000 less than at the end of 1931, when the number of special resettled persons reached its maximum.[53]

By the middle of the 1930s these settlers had to a degree "struck roots" in their new places. General education schools, vocational training schools, and technical secondary schools appeared in the labor settlements. And the original settlers' ranks were beginning to be diluted, the consequence of increases in the number of persons not on the books of the NKVD. (Supervision, economic arrangements, and other administrative questions in the labor settlements were carried out by NKVD command offices, and in the USSR as a whole by the GULAG Department of Labor Settlements.) In May 1934 civil rights were restored to labor deportees, and from January 1935 the right to vote. At the same time, from 1934 labor deportees were obliged to pay taxes and to pay off loans they had been given for the initial expenses of settling. However, the restoration of rights to labor deportees was far from complete. They did not have internal passports, they could not be drafted into the Red Army, and they did not have the right to return to the places where they used to live. Nonetheless, the number of people deserting the labor settlements on their own constantly increased.

The gradual move of people to more and more remote, severe, and thinly populated regions meant that areas like the arid steppes and the Arctic zones would have to be mastered, and this magnified the role of forced labor from penal-labor (ITL) camps, infamous for their brutal working and living regimens. In 1936 these camps contained, according to NKVD data, 821,000 prisoners. They became the principal means of developing new, hard-to-reach parts of the country and of utilizing cheap manpower in extreme conditions. Almost every camp had its own capital (chief camp) and suburbs (camp stations, camp centers [*lagpunkty*]). Remote Kolyma and its capital Magadan, which could be reached only by sea and then only during a certain period of the year, became the symbol of the GULAG. Supplementing the camps was a system of smaller and more numerous penal labor colonies (ITK) stretched across the entire country. According to NKVD data, in 1936 they held 375,000 prisoners.[54]

The Second Five-Year Plan was marked by a slowdown in the tempo of the Socialist Offensive, this against a background of incessant propaganda about the "outstanding achievements of the USSR on the battlefront of building socialism." The catastrophic consequences of the first years of Socialist Offensive, the chaos and disorder in the country, forced the Stalinist leadership to take decisive steps. The first symptoms of a change in policy can be traced to Stalin's speech to the country's economic leaders on 23 June 1931. Apparent was the influence of the most pragmatically oriented part of the party's economic nomenklatura. First-line production managers in particular strove to reduce the tensions that had developed during the previous period.

Stalin now spoke about the need for organized recruitment of labor on collective farms, eliminating wage leveling and labor fluidity, improving living conditions, placing cadres properly, and inculcating the idea of self-supporting enterprises. While calling for the creation of a new working-class intelligentsia, Stalin condemned persecution of specialists of the old school. At first specialists were returned to their former places under the supervision of OGPU bodies, then a "pardon" was declared for a number of individuals previously labeled "saboteurs" in view of their readiness to work for the good of socialism. Differential rates of pay were introduced, and salaries were made dependent on seniority. The practice of promotion by class of origin and political values *(vydvizhenstvo)* was made more difficult, for many promotees (specialists by practice alone) were simply inadequate to their tasks, and their actions served only to diminish the authority of the leadership. Steps were taken to strengthen discipline at work. In September 1932 individual work records were introduced in which all work transfers were noted; they were studied closely by personnel departments. By the Law of 15 November 1932 failure to appear for work became grounds for firing at a factory or plant, for taking away ration books, and for eviction from allotted living space. At the same time the government was forced to acquiesce to those few remaining vestiges of a free-market economy, such as the "kolkhoz market" and commercial trade.

The new Five-Year Plan coincided with the time when most of the projects planned earlier were supposed to be finished and beginning operations. Starting up newly completed plants immediately exposed a fundamental problem: the need to master modern equipment. In 1934 approximately a third of the equipment installed was idle because of organizational confusion and a lack of training, and of the remainder, only 40 percent was activated at full capacity. Even official Soviet sources testify to the enormous difficulties that arose in setting new plants into motion. A large role in overcoming them was played by the creation before the end of the First Five-Year Plan of the NII *(Nauchno-Issledovatel'skii Institut,* scientific research institute) system and of educational institutions linked closely to industry: plant technical colleges *(vtuzy),* technical secondary schools, technical and polytechnic institutes. The number of graduates of degree-holding specialists from institutions of higher education and technical secondary schools increased at the same time that the entire system of mass general and professional and technical education was being rebuilt. Based on primary education, made obligatory by the state, a wide network of FZO *(Fabrichno-Zavodskoe Obuchenie,* factory and plant training) schools and vocational and trade schools was created with programs of study ranging from half a year to two years. These schools trained workers for standard occupations, marking the beginning of the Soviet system of trades and technical education. Simultaneously, the network of schools providing the first years of secondary education (NSSh [*Nepolnaia Sredniaia Shkola,* seven-year schools]) and general secondary education (SSh [*Sredniaia Shkola,* ten-year schools]) was expanded considerably.

A contradictory phenomenon of this period was the Stakhanovite movement, which can be regarded as a kind of new wave of the assault mentality. In August 1935 miner Aleksei Stakhanov dug 102 tons of coal, exceeding the daily norm many times. Following Stakhanov's example, "heroes of the labor front" set records in other industries as well and were well rewarded for their achievements. In contrast to shock work's emphasis on strength-related and exhaustive forms of competition, the Stakhanovite movement was touted as a movement of industrial innovators who were achieving success thanks to improved organization of work and a thorough grasp of techniques. At the same time, higher authorities used the movement to maintain pressure on engineers, technicians, and managers of enterprises. As it happened, from the very beginning the movement conflicted with the developmental logic of the planned distribution system then entering a state of hypertrophy. Record mania led to the violation of the normal production process, to the overexpenditure of raw materials and supplies, to wear and tear of equipment. Quality of production suffered greatly. Resolutions demanding that records be set meant increased intensity of work, lowering wage rates, and increased output norms for other workers, which made Stakhanovites none too popular.[55]

Meanwhile, daily life in the Soviet Union did get a little easier. This was most noticeable in the capital. On 15 May 1935 the first line of the Moscow metro went into service. It was hailed as an example of socialism's achievements. Indeed, hadn't the entire country built the metro? Now the entire country celebrated its opening, and admired its efficiency and beauty. In 1934, in connection with the decision to abolish rationing on 1 January 1935, Moscow was witness to an unprecedented spectacle: along the streets passed "sausage parades" in the course of which various types of "Mikoyan sausage" were carried, along with red banners as a symbol of socialist prosperity. This was precisely when sausage became the criterion of material well-being for the Soviet family. A wide assortment of sausages in Moscow really did appear in the mid 1930s in connection with MIKOMS's production success.

These and other developments suggested that the extraordinary overexertions and enforced abstinence of the first Five-Year Plans need not continue forever. New forms of trade and consumer services that were introduced in 1934–36 were remote from the usual notions about the needs of the collective-oriented person, about disregarding delicacies and comfort. A series of decrees brought expanded networks of hotels, cafes, and restaurants, of barbers and hair dressers, and especially of shops for tailoring clothes and making footwear. Candy and cookie factories not only substantially increased their volume of production but also opened a group of speciality stores in the capital. The triumphal march of "Soviet champagne," relatively inexpensive and widely available, commenced. The struggle to cultivate consumerism at times assumed unusual forms. Thus on 11 June 1934, Mossovet (*Moskovskii sovet*, Moscow city council) passed a special resolution prohibiting the sale in stores of wine by the glass.[56] In the same year construction began outside of Moscow of a phonograph record plant. Even bakery shops developed new forms of service, introducing tasting displays of new products and home delivery of bread purchases. But especially vital changes for the better occurred in housing policy. Not long before, the communal apartment *(kommunalka),* in which there was no place for bourgeois individualism, was declared the ideal socialist form of habitation. But according to the new plan to reconstruct Moscow, approved in 1934, every family would live in a separate apartment with all the conveniences. Moreover, every member of the family was supposed to have his or her own room.[57] The new guidelines seemed positively fantastic, which is exactly what they were.

To be sure, some signs of political liberalization did appear in the mid-1930s. Highly indicative in this regard was a speech by L. Mekhlis, editor in chief of *Pravda*, a man well informed and near the top of the party hierarchy, to a conference of newspaper people on 13 August 1935. "We have encountered two instances of amnesty. This is very significant. If you're not afraid of big words, then you could speak of Soviet liberalism."[58] Knowing how cautious Mekhlis was, there can be little doubt that he was voicing the opinion of the leadership. And although the term "Soviet liberalism" didn't stick, little islands of liberalism, or, more exactly, liberal illusions, really did exist, and not only in the political sphere but in the economic and cultural ones as well. Significantly, the Seventeenth Congress of the VKP(b) was perceived by some delegates as an indicator of democratization. Thus a member of the Aktyubinsk obkom of the Komsomol named Nazarov, returning from the congress to his native city, took a certain liberty: during a celebration in the municipal garden Nazarov met acquaintances who asked him where he had been. He answered, "In Moscow." What had he done there? Nazarov astounded his listeners by answering, "I opened the Seventeenth Congress." How is that? There was no place to retreat so the Komsomol leader replied confidentially, "Here's how. I went to the congress, I see Stalin stumbling onto the podium blind drunk. I took him by the scruff of the neck, chucked him out, and opened the conference myself." The joke met with laughter, and inspired by its success, Nazarov repeated it to the next group of listeners. As a result, soon the whole town "knew the truth" about the opening of the Seventeenth Party Congress, but dispatched to Moscow on 1 November 1934 was a memorandum about this outstanding event addressed to A. S. Bubnov, the RSFSR commissar of education, and A. V. Kosarev, the secretary of the Komsomol.[59]

CHAPTER TWO

# "Cadres Decide Everything!"

THE COUNTRY'S LEADERS, also under the spell of the Socialist Offensive, were sometimes forced to work until they were on the verge of an emotional breakdown. The mighty task—to rouse the masses and lead them into battle—took its toll. In a letter to his wife written in May 1929, G. M. Krzhizhanovsky, chairman of Gosplan, described one of his speeches as follows: "What great times we are living through. . . . The great might of those at the bottom has been roused! A decisive historic force has emerged! The excitement and joy that come over me when I see this is beyond all description. I then wax poetic, and my audience felt this." His speech about the Five-Year Plan had ended with thunderous applause and the singing of the "Internationale." "There were even instances of hysterics," Krzhizhanovsky continued, noting that after he had given this type of speech, it took him a long time to return to normal. "I'm now weak and exhausted, but . . . I feel good. I've done what I should, made my tiny contribution to the great effort. Now let whatever is going to happen happen!" The forced wait in the trenches of NEP is over, he intimated; the party has roused everyone anew to the long-awaited battle, to the offensive against the enemy.[1] But far from all cadres in the land of the Soviets were equal to this "historic task."

103

At the beginning of the Socialist Offensive the composition of high-level cadres was still fairly diverse. Members of the Bolshevik elite of the older generation occupied the more important party and state administrative posts and headed the various public organizations. They knew how to fight for a cause, and without question this affected the way in which they carried out their duties. Because many of them were not on Stalin's side during the time of intraparty struggles in the 1920s, however, Stalin did not consider them reliable exponents of his General Line. Here and there high-level posts were occupied by "old" or "bourgeois specialists" whose political past was far from uniform. Some of them were completely apolitical; others had come from a wide spectrum of political parties, ranging from the Mensheviks to the Kadets (Constitutional-Democrats). Their views on what was happening in the USSR also differed. A substantial number of them sympathized with the party's "right wing," whose leaders Bukharin, Rykov, and Tomsky called for moderation and caution in transforming society.

But the largest group among the leaders, especially in the provinces, consisted of the new generation of Communists, those who had joined the party during the years of the revolution and civil war and had become part of the party's special ruling elite, the nomenklatura: people chosen by the party apparatus to serve in various responsible posts. In the course of the first postrevolutionary decade, they developed into a significant social stratum, flesh of the flesh of the society that begat them. This special elite constantly added new cadres, called at the time *vydvizhentsy*. At the beginning of the Socialist Offensive these were the ones on whom the party relied.

The promotees climbed up the rungs of power and command quickly and in great numbers. During the First Five-Year Plan the number of party members, the basic pool from which cadres were drawn, doubled, reaching 3.7 million in 1932. The promotees often lacked practical experience in directing work and handling crises; instead, they substituted administrative enthusiasm and bustle. In the interest of advancing their careers, promotees were quick to expose errors, real or imagined, by their superiors.

Basic qualifications for promotion were party membership,

"proletarian" origins, firm-handed implementation of the General Line, and faith in the course declared by Stalin. New cadres had to profess, if only in words, unshakable faith in the bright future consistent with the revolution's precepts and be prepared for the sake of this to make any sacrifice and subscribe to the belief that "there are no fortresses the Bolsheviks cannot take." Ascent up the career ladder depended on this. At the same time, the aspirations of this new cohort to seats of power and command inevitably led to conflicts with those who had succeeded earlier in occupying responsible posts. The general purge became one way of replacing cadres.

The decision to conduct a purge of the party and the state apparatus "under the control of the toiling masses" was reached at the VKP(b)'s Sixteenth Congress in May 1929. Couched in terms of combating bureaucratism and distortions of the party line, and of developing means of criticism and self-criticism, the purge was so widespread that it affected all Soviet institutions. An active part was played by worker purge brigades sent by factories and plants. At this stage, the purge was animated by the initial mood of the Socialist Offensive. Not infrequently it turned into public abuse of people for social and political reasons.

The first wave of the purge struck at various "deviators from the General Line," especially "right-wingers" whose views were in greatest conflict with the spirit of the time. A broad campaign was waged against them by the press, and they were "exposed" and condemned at assemblies and meetings everywhere. The November 1929 plenum of the TsK judged being part of the rightist deviation as incompatible with party membership. Over a short period 149,000 persons (11 percent of all party members) were expelled from the party, most accused of belonging to the rightist deviation. As a rule, this meant removal of those not liked by the new promotees. Most were forced to acknowledge their errors and omissions publicly. Refusal to do this would have meant an end to their careers. But this was not all. Sundry facts from a person's biography were subject to extensive investigation and could lead to most unpleasant consequences.

Here, for example, is an appeal to the Presidium of TsKK VKP(b) from a prominent executive, F. G. Kolgushkin, requesting reinstatement in the party.

# Document 34

Petition from F. G. Kolgushkin for reinstatement in party, 4 October 1930. RGAE, f. 8043, op. 11, d. 11, ll. 13–14. Typed copy.

Respected Comrades:

In March 1928 by decision of the TsKK's Presidium I was expelled from the ranks of the VKP(b) because I had concealed from the party, specifically when I was chosen at the Fifteenth Congress of VKP(b) to be an associate member of the TsK VKP(b), the fact that in 1911 after being convicted by the St. Petersburg Law Court under Article 102 for belonging to the RSDRP(b) [*Rossiiskaia Sotsialisticheskaia Demokraticheskaia Rabochaia Partiia (bolshevikov)*, Russian Social Democratic Workers Party (Bolshevik)], I had submitted an appeal addressed to the tsar and been pardoned.

As was the case in my previous appeals (of 1928 and 1929), I continue to consider this act of mine to be a most serious crime against the party, a base act, verily that of a renegade. I also consider that the punishment meted out to me in 1928 was correct and deserved. I swear to you that during the two and a half years I have borne this punishment, burdensome and horrible for a Bolshevik, I have not ceased to be a Bolshevik in all of my actions nor will I cease to be one, because I am a Bolshevik and because I must atone for my guilt in the eyes of the party.

I simply cannot remain longer in this position; it will be unbearable for me. How can I remain outside the party when a concentrated, all-out effort is required for the great feat of building socialism as it keeps developing?

I beg the Presidium of TsKK VKP(b) to return me to the ranks of the VKP(b). This will enable me to participate with even greater strength in the building of socialism, in the party's struggle to surmount problems, and to atone for my guilt. Until May 1929 I worked in Novosibirsk as deputy chairman of Sibkraisovnarkhoz [*Sibirskii kraevoi sovet narodnogo khoziaistva*, Siberian Krai economic council]. On 15 May 1929 the TsKK, in accordance with a request by the Siberian Regional Party Committee, passed a resolution entertaining the possibility of my returning to the party but asking the worker cell for comments. Following this, in May 1929, I was appointed chief of Kuznetskstroi [Kuznetsk construction project]. Organizing construction at a new location absorbed all my time. I had to move from Novosibirsk and was, successively, at the construction site in Tomsk and in Moscow. I was subsequently sent on an official trip to America to negotiate a contract with an engineering firm for building the Kuznetsk plant and to place orders for equipment. I spent eight months altogether in America and Germany. All this prevented me from formally rejoining the party in accordance with the TsKK's resolution of 15 May 1929. Now that I have returned from abroad I am scheduled to go to the Urals, to Uralmet [*Ural'skaia metallurgiia*, Ural metal production project]. It is clear that my work there will from the very begin-

## Document 34 *continued*

ning entail prolonged and frequent trips to plants where I will be asked to report on the functioning and organization of American plants. This will again encumber and drag out my rejoining the party and will also prevent me from working as effectively as I could as a party member.

I am unable to live and work merely as a specialist and once again ask TsKK to return me to the party. I spring from landless peasants and since childhood I have worked as a hired person, starting out as a shepherd.

---

So the petitioner feels that he cannot remain a mere "specialist," understanding perfectly well that this would mean an end to his service career. In this instance there was a positive outcome in deference to the post that Kolgushkin occupied, though the "shameful black mark" remained forever in his personal record. It was far less common, however, for appeals of this kind to have favorable outcomes in the wake of a party evaluation of past transgressions. No wonder the "personality explication" methods used by bureaucratic staff—collecting various statements, questionnaires, autobiographies, factual verifications, and so on— acquired ever greater significance. In the same file with Kolgushkin's petition, for example, is an appeal from Narkomtorg *(Narodnyi komissariat torgovli,* People's Commissariat of Trade) workers A. Amosov and P. Karavaev objecting to the restoration of party membership to their former colleague A. E. Gar:

---

## Document 35

Letter from Narkomtorg workers opposing colleague's reinstatement in party, 1930. RGAE, f. 0643, op. 11, d. 11, ll. 11–12. Typed copy.

---

In essence, we insist that the matter be reviewed for the following reasons: Citizen Gar declared to MKK [*Moskovskii kontrol'nyi komitet,* Moscow control committee] that he was a left-wing SR [Socialist Revolutionary] while in VIKZHEL' [*Vsesoiuznyi Ispolnitel'nyi Komitet Zheleznodorozhnikov,* All-Union executive committee of railroad workers] when he was chairing the strike committee of the railroad workers (September 1917). In fact, Gar was an inveterate right-wing SR, treating Bolsheviks and the proletarian revolution with fury and spite. As chair of the strike committee he kept calling off strikes to please [SR leader] Chernov and Kerensky. Therefore his declaration actually conceals and blurs his true counterrevolutionary role. In the October Days of 1917 in Moscow he worked at the Kadet headquarters of Colonel Riabtsev, whom he undoubtedly was actively helping. As a result of Gar's activities and those of the counterrevolutionary wing of the Moscow VIKZHEL' Bureau, a group of White Guards from Briansk Station broke through the rear line of our Red Army supporters during the October Days and on account of this treachery we lost many Bolshevik–Red Army men. After the October Days, had Gar fallen into Bolshevik hands he would have got it good, but he managed to sneak away in time. Many were ready to shoot him.

According to his petition, he actively helped the Bolsheviks in Khar'kov. To back this up, he gives as a reference a member of the underground revolutionary committee, Comrade Saveliev. Comrade Saveliev has written the following in response to a note from Amosov: "In my opinion Gar is not a counterrevolutionary but someone who looks after his own interests." Now this is actually what he is currently doing, as has been corroborated by the Narkomtorg Purge Commission. His departure for Khar'kov after the October Revolution is suspicious. He "slipped away" for sure from the Bolsheviks and only after Denikin made it hot for the Mensheviks and SRs did he carry out a couple of insignificant acts against Denikin, and now makes these acts out to be very revolutionary and unabashedly Bolshevik in nature.

He makes himself out to be a fully qualified engineer. He was elected to VIKZHEL' when he was a stationmaster on the Kazan line. At any rate, it turned out that he is not a fully qualified engineer.

The fact that he is now the chief mechanic at the Ridder zinc industrial complex in Kazakhstan apparently played a prominent role in TsKK's decision to rehabilitate him. However, he got there thanks to the patronage of Ridder's chief engineer, Comrade Stamo, an ex-left-wing SR, now a Communist working with the railroads, also a member of VIKZHEL', very confused about his left-wing SR days and in general a gullible person. Before this Gar was a Narkomtorg bureaucrat. Apparently he understands very little about what goes on at Ridder since this line of work is not something he has ever done before; his basic profession is that of a railroad worker and even here he is not fully qualified as an engineer. Again his characteristic sleight of hand is evident.

I have conversed more than once about Gar with my comrades in the Revolutionary Five who were in charge of seizing control of the railroads in the Moscow Division in October 1917 (Piatnitsky, Zimin, and others). All of them, along with the 1917 Bolsheviks of this region, become extremely indignant when they recall Gar and consider it erroneous and utterly wrong for the party to accept such a "Bolshevik" in its ranks, if you can call him that.

Therefore, we request that the party board [*partkollegiia*] review this matter anew, summoning all interested parties, for example, Comrade Karavaev from TsKK, Piatnitsky, Zimin, ex-left-wing SR Konstantin Lapsher, now a

## Document 35 *continued*

Bolshevik, and other persons. If the party board decides not to review this matter, I ask that it be submitted to the TsKK's Presidium.

As is evident, the petitioners gave more emphasis to Gar's political biography than to his professional qualifications. The fate of work at the Ridder ore deposits most likely did not concern them; they simply envied a more successful colleague. In those years more often than not people occupied various nomenklatura positions that had nothing to do with their field of specialization. It was characteristic of the general purge that a motley crew of new party members striving to make careers for themselves rushed to replace those "cleaned out." It is also apparent that special significance was attached to such petitions as this. The past acquired an ominous cast, and God forbid if it was tainted by non-Bolshevik attitudes and opinions. This would prompt waves of denunciations, slander based on rumor, and conversations which had to be cleared up and checked out. Under these circumstances a competitor could be smeared or otherwise pushed aside, optimizing one's own chances for advancement. Here, for example, is a typical denunciation, unedited, from the beginning of the purge, July 1929.

## Document 36

Letter to NK RKI denouncing Narkomfin employees, July 1929. GARF, f. A-406, op. 25, d. 128, ll. 108–109. Typed copy.

Strictly Confidential
To the People's Commissar of the Workers' and Peasants' Inspectorate
It is utterly incomprehensible why that element so alien and harmful to Soviet authority cannot be purged. Why, I answer, it's because responsible workers themselves cover up this ulcer and by the same token secretly sabotage our Soviet Union and assist the enemy.
Let's take an example: Narkomfin [*Narodnyi komissariat finansov*, People's Commissariat of Finance]—a known White Guard woman works there, the wife of ex–Staff Captain Svidersky, Aleksandra Prokofievna Sviderskaia—she's now calling herself by her maiden name again, Goncharova—works quietly in a Narkomfin branch office on Nastasinsky Lane. A certain Korolyov got her this job. He works in Narkomfin and occupies a prominent position

# Document 36 *continued*

there and lives with her and got her salary increased for this, claiming she was his wife. This White Guard woman's husband, ex–Staff Captain Citizen Svidersky, Vladimir Yurievich, with the help of MUUR [*Moskovskoe Upravlenie Ugolovnogo Rozyska,* Moscow criminal investigation administration] agent Nikolai Andralov, got to be director of a Mossel'prom [*Moskovskoe upravlenie sel'skoi promyslovoi kooperatsii,* Moscow rural cooperative administration] beer joint. In just a short period of time under that Denikinite director of Mossel'prom there were losses, and for that Narsud [*Narodnyi sud,* People's Court] of Khamovniki Raion sentenced him to two years in prison and disenfranchised him. And then, to save her own skin, his wife Aleksandra Prokofievna Sviderskaia quickly got some sort of divorce and took back her maiden name Goncharova and continues to work in Narkomfin and saboteurize Soviet authority. These two White Guardists, husband and wife, named Svidersky, helped Denikin, then fled to Bulgaria and returned to the RSFSR in 1924, and thanks to MUUR agent Citizen Nikolai Andralov received asylum and a safe refuge. This same Nikolai Andralov is a known bribe taker and shady character, poses as a representative of the OGPU, and engages in suspicious business. Citizen Goncharova-Sviderskaia, Aleksandra Prokofievna, Narkomfin employee, says that the time will soon come when we hang all the Communists and my husband will be a commander once again.

We know that they will purge many proletarians, and the wreckers themselves will stay because they know how to find a loophole, and in this way saboteurize and organize secret agitation against Sov-authority.

Andralov, Nikolai, the MUUR agent, has shady people coming to his apartment and settles their affairs. Korolyov, in Narkomfin, without squeamishness lives with the staff captain's wife and hides her. Well, no one can do anything. It's time to get busy and expose the ulcer, to purge from the Soviet system all the rot and body buyers, saboteurs and bribe takers; NK RKI [*Narodnyi Komissariat Raboche-Krest'ianskoi Inspektsii,* People's Commissariat of Workers' and Peasants' Inspection] should work secretly on this and expose the hiding place.

We request that Narkomfin purge all this scum and MUUR throw out bribe takers and tramps.

Ponamareva

A check of Narkomfin employees revealed no woman with the name Ponamareva. The letter nonetheless was forwarded to the commission formed to purge this institution.

Here is another document that resulted in a purge of staff at the VTsIK and Narkomzem of the RSFSR, a letter addressed to Stalin about S. N. Izvekov, a promotee of peasant origin, purportedly written by a group of his fellow villagers.

---

## Document 37

Letter to Stalin denouncing peasant promotee, 4 January 1930. GARF, f. A-406, op. 25, d. 131, ll. b/n-199. Typed copy.

---

Dear Comrade Stalin,

All the newspapers of our [Soviet] Union are filled to overflowing with articles about the fight against kulaks and kulak henchmen. We in the provinces fight using the slogan you unfurled and we fight not because we are afraid but because we are conscientious. Permit us to ask you and put before you our proletarian question. Are you fighting against kulaks and their henchmen in the center itself, in the very apparatus of Soviet power? You have no small number of them there. Take, for example, the Presidium of VTsIK, where there's not just a kulak but an arch-kulak. This is Stepan Nikolaevich Izvekov from Orel, known all over Orel District [uezd] as Styopa Izvekov. How he got there and how he made his way into VTsIK is very mysterious and strange. Isn't it miraculous? Has Grishka Rasputin been raised from the dead, he who in tsarist times made his way up to the tsar and ruled Mother Russia? Who exactly is this Styopka? A prosperous arch-kulak from Orel Province [guberniia] and District, Pokrov Volost, Ovsiannikov Village, who in the old tsarist times served in the army and after coming back from there served as a gendarme under Captain of the Provincial Investigation Department Schulz, infamous throughout the Orel area for reprisals against workers and peasants, especially during the memorable days of 1905. No better either was Styopka Izvekov, his coworker, who accurately fulfilled the orders of tsarist magnates by snuffing out workers and peasants. Many to this day still recall Styopka's reprisals, and who doesn't know about his mean tricks, and what things hasn't he dealt with; to count them all would be hard. And suddenly Styopka got himself into a position of Power, entered the circle of our proletarian leaders, the circle of the Rulers of the USSR, and became Stepan Nikolaevich, "Comrade Izvekov."

Comrade Stalin, there's no place for him there. Where there's a place for him is Solovki [the Solovetsky Islands, located in the White Sea at the entrance to Onega Bay, the site of the Northern Special-Purpose Forced Labor Camps (SLON), founded in 1922] or with his forefathers, given his old dirty tricks and the position he used to hold. Otherwise, many of the peasants among us who are still ignorant may come to the conclusion that all our proletarian Authorities are people like Styopka, that it's people like him who sit at the Center, and they'll sure be speaking the truth.

## Document 37 *continued*

Comrade Stalin, we peasants from the villages of Mostki, Lezhenki, Ovsiannikov, Fedorovka, Big and Little Kulikovka, Upper and Lower Shchekotikhin demand that you purge alien elements from our proletarian Government and not create the impression that it's kulak Styopka and people like him who sit on the VTsIK. We peasants demand that you not merely return him to the countryside but send him for his old mean tricks to Solovki and then even further.

Comrade Stalin, we peasants count on your firmness, count on the fact that you won't betray us and leave us alone, because in the provinces he and his henchmen have already planted informers. We are afraid that they are going to burn us out or might even kill us, for they are capable of doing this sort of thing.

Peasants Yefim Kotov, Yegor Novikov, Nikolai Nekrasov, Semyon Shchekotikhin, Andrei Ovsiannikov, Aleksei Shirobokov, Vasily Domov.

Comrade Stalin, we request that you respond to our request through the rural soviet or *Orel Pravda* and inform us how the purge of VTsIK staff is proceeding.

An investigation failed to confirm the facts reported in this letter. Indeed, it is patently obvious that the letter is a fabrication, of interest only because of the "incriminating material" amassed and the type of argument used to discredit someone.

An anonymous letter to M. I. Kalinin received in September 1931 discussed the purge in Abkhazia:

## Document 38

Anonymous letter to Kalinin on purge in Abkhazia, September 1931. RGASPI, f. 78, op. 1, d. 416, l. 1. Typed copy.

Soviet power [*sovvlast'*] is lacking in Abkhazia. Information sent to the press by worker-correspondents has been suppressed, the TsIK leadership has taken all responsibility away from the GPU and RKI.

A purge of the staff is now under way, but just what sort of purge is it that leaves saboteurs unscathed, gets rid of cleaning ladies and typists, and keeps trying to smoke out daughters of priests and tsarist bureaucrats? What good does this do? We in the purge brigade see how information exposing big fish is being swept under the carpet while small fish are caught, discredited, and their dirty linen washed in public. Is this really the way it's supposed to be?

## Document 38 *continued*

Our construction projects are going to pot, those at Tkvarcheli and Bzyb', but the leaders remained untouched, TsIK stands up for them. Defeatist landlords, former princes are esteemed—you're not allowed to offend them. Why, there are princes in the party; the workers and the poor peasants are surprised by this fact. That's the way it is here. TsK instructors Kozlov and Tseitlin came out here and made a lot of promises. What have these comrades done? You ask them, Mikhail Ivanovich. Make them account for themselves. Rumor has it that some people write to Moscow from here so we too decided to write— maybe somebody will investigate and find the root of the evil. We have to set this matter straight.

Among Abkhazians who know about this matter are TsIK member Comrade Agrba, State Prosecutor Comrade Kabakhia, and the chairman of the SPS [*Sovet Profsoiuzov,* council of trade unions] Comrade Abzianidze. Many Abkhazians have fled to Tiflis and other places because they were silenced.

We can't sign this, or life would be impossible for us, they would eat us up. We ask that serious attention be given to the matter. Crush the bootlicking and unscrupulous factions. In addition, disgraceful things are going on in the raions. Kulaks sit on RIKs [*Raionnye Ispolnitel'nye Komitety,* district executive committees], there are gangs, top-skimming, and bootlicking. Where are the construction and production rates, where is self-criticism, where is the Five-Year Plan? There are none of these. It wouldn't be a bad idea if you showed your fist more. There is no determination and discipline here.

---

A member of the purge work brigade doubtless wrote the letter. Many things described obviously existed: bootlicking, favoritism, private deals, "top-skimming"—that is, obtaining goods by bypassing the official distribution system, using one's position to advantage. The number of artful careerists in both party and state institutions was not small. Probably the best evidence of the relation between cadres genuinely devoted to their tasks who unquestioningly fulfilled party directives and persons joining the party for other reasons is provided by a concrete, real-life situation like the one produced by the decision at the beginning of the 1930s to eliminate the okrug as an administrative division.

At the end of the 1920s the territorial administration of the USSR was reorganized. Krais or oblasts, okrugs, and raions took the place of provinces, districts, and subdistricts *(gubernii, uezdy, volosti)*. Krais and oblasts were vast administrative units, and at this level managerial cadres belonged to the loftiest group of the party nomenklatura, entry into which was no small matter. Okrugs were somewhat like the former provinces. Many provincial centers became okrug seats, and work in the okrug system was considered prestigious, not far removed from the country's highest authorities. Raions were lesser administrative units, the seats of which were, as a rule, small provincial towns and villages that might not even appear on a map.

Very quickly it became clear that this system was extraordinarily cumbersome and unmanageable. In accordance with a resolution of the Sixteenth Party Congress and a TsK decree of 15 July 1930, okrugs were to be eliminated to achieve the goal of "maximal proximity of the party, soviet, cooperative, administrative, and supply apparatus to raion and village." An informational account of the control commissions' work in the okrugs compiled from reports of TsKK instructors sent to provincial areas paints the following picture:

---

## Document 39

Informational report on response to elimination of okrugs, 1930. RGAE, f. 8043, op. 11, ll. 22–23. Typed copy.

---

At the moment that the okrugs were eliminated, officials in a number of organizations experienced feelings of panic and a reluctance to go to the raions. KK Commissioner Il'ichev (in the Urals) stubbornly resisted going to a distant raion because "the wife won't go," "there're a lot of sick people there, she says." Korbotin (Tataria) considered his being dispatched to a raion as chairman of the raion control commission [PredRKK] to be "a most cruel and undeserved punishment."

In the Lower Volga Krai there were several instances of officials not wanting to go to a raion because "I found a better apartment in Saratov," "there're no shoes there," etc. These comrades were sent to a board of inquiry, and after "a lot of persuading" the board would succeed in getting them to agree to depart for the raions.

In Vladivostok out of 249 assigned to be transferred only 169 were given moving vouchers; the others showered the okrug [party] committee with petitions with all sorts of certificates attached about ailments, etc., doing everything possible to avoid going to a raion. Thirteen were sent to Beloiarsk Raion (in the Urals), but only two actually arrived.

In Leningrad Oblast out of 126 persons earmarked to leave for a raion, only twenty-nine went. The officials with most seniority absolutely refused to go to a raion; for example, the director of the organizational department [zavorgot] of the Lodeinoe Pole Trade Union Council, Smirnov, did not want to go to a raion.

A State Bank instructor (in Borisoglebsk) named Lifonovsky "went on leave" secretly, and his family even refused to divulge his address, claiming they didn't know it.

A Popov (Bezhetsk Okrug) fled from a raion, giving as the reason: "My wife doesn't like it here."

Moving raion staff to the village level also met with opposition from some party members. For example, in Shakhun Raion (Nizhni Novgorod) labor inspector Lakeev refused to become chairman of a vast rural soviet, claiming: "I am a raion worker, I will not walk ten versts on foot. There is no cooperative store in the rural soviet, you could die of starvation. People will laugh at me. I'm not the son of a priest, I can find work without a party card." And in the same place Belaev, the chair of the MK [*Mestnyi Komitet,* local committee], a high school graduate, was appointed RIK planner and refused: "My ideal is to become better qualified. They've worn me out with social service work. I don't want an official post the way the others do. If it turns out I lose my party card, well, I'm still no worse than other Communists."

---

Naturally, cadres like these were purged. But the old specialists were persecuted more than anyone else. The many production breaks and gaps were blamed on them. During 1930 and the beginning of 1931 trials were organized (for Gosplan and VSNKh staff, for members of the Toiling Peasants Party, for members of the Menshevik Union Bureau, and others). The majority of them took place behind closed doors. There were also "open" trials, however, fabricated jointly by the OGPU and judicial bodies. At the trial of the PromParty (*Promyshlennaia Partiia,* Industrial Party) the accused "confessed" that they had created an extensive underground organization of two thousand specialists with the alleged aim of initiating activities under the direction of infiltrators from abroad in order to disrupt the USSR's economy. At many enterprises specialists were fired and arrested. The Donbass mines, for example, lost more than half of their engineering-technical personnel at this time.[2]

Gradually, standard bureaucratic purge procedures for verifying petitions, letters, denunciations, questionnaires, and so forth emerged.

The writer Andrei Platonov makes note of this change at the beginning of the 1930s, describing the fate of a member from the nomenklatura of the 1920s who "served a long time in distant oblasts in various posts of the Union of Soviets and the Union of Consumer Associations and then returned to the country's center. However, they had managed to forget his status and credentials." It was as if he had become "obscure, indistinct, personally alien, and even somewhat dangerous. On his return he found an unfamiliar world of sections, secretariats, clusters of prominent executives, one-man management, and piecework. When he'd departed, it was a world of departments, subdepartments, broad collegiality, a world of meetings and planning for unknown times thirty years into the future. . . . Now that was a time from the past forgotten forever, a time in which opportunism had a chance to mature." So the responsible staff member was added to the list of "people without clearance." Two or three times a month the "uncleared" ones would come to an institution, receive their salary, and ask: "Well, how am I doing? Have I been cleared yet?" "'No,' was the answer they got, coming from persons who had been cleared already. 'So far we haven't received enough information about you to give you any kind of designation. We'll keep trying to clear your status up!'"

Platonov notes that new cadres were needed, "endowed with inherent talent and technical education," capable of "mercilessly expounding the reality" of class identification in order to transform the "grand design of the party into a maximalized mass man leading all those of his class forward—the same design that Lenin himself possessed before October of 1917"—to make the "new technical Bolshevism" a reality.[3] To grow cadres of this sort was no small task.

The introduction of centralized planning based on directives required the restructuring of the entire economic administrative system. At first characteristics clearly inherited from war communism were evident. Conglomerates, closely resembling the central administrative boards or chief directorates *(glavki)* from the years immediately following the revolution and betokening a bureaucratized economy, were created for state syndicates, which virtually monopolized supply and sales. All aspects of production were regulated from above—even down to such matters as standard worker pay scales. Enterprises were supposed to receive—in effect, free of charge—the appropriate stocks of raw materials and everything else according to a system of ration cards and orders. One-man management was introduced in factories, and managers of industrial enterprises were made directly responsible for fulfilling the state industrial and financial plan. The directors of the biggest construction projects and industries were now appointed from a special nomenklatura list. Thousands of suppliers went to all parts of the country, extracting resources, fighting for larger supplies, and looking longingly at the shipments going elsewhere. Cadres able to obtain all that was needed were highly valued. They knew how to demand, like Stalin himself.

The reaction of the nation's economic managers to these measures is contained in a report on the attitudes of delegates to the February 1931 Industrial Conference of VSNKh, a meeting attended by a great number of industrial officials. The report was compiled by an OGPU agent and sent to party organizations—a standard method of exercising control over cadres. The following are excerpts from the report:

## Document 40

OGPU report on attitudes of economic managers, 1931. RGASPI, f. 85, op. 1s, d. 143, ll. 1–2. Typed copy.

Debate occasioned by Comrade Ordzhonikidze's speech is now in its fourth day. The speech was pivotal to the work of the conference. Wearied by the debate, conference members are filling the House of Unions snack bar and corridors. They make it a point to go into the hall for the speech by Comrade [I. P.] Pavlunovsky [deputy chairman of VSNKh, responsible for defense industries], and when they hear applause, assuming that Politburo and government members Comrades Stalin and Molotov are speaking.

There's no consensus among conference members, the reason for this being their heterogeneous makeup. Group allegiance depends on where the member works and the type of work he does.

A number of people said the following: the reform of industrial management that created conglomerates was designed to bring administrators closer to actual production. However, because of the push to industrialize and shortages of materials, which pointed up the need for greater distribution planning, and also because credit reforms were misunderstood, the reform actually resulted in increased bureaucracy and a dilution of responsibility.

Now Comrade Ordzhonikidze makes the role of directors of enterprises and chiefs of construction crucial, giving them the right to conclude agreements and relieving them of the responsibility of overseeing supply departments.

The group that includes the nonparty delegation from Transcaucasia (Chichinadze, Ter-Asvatsaturov, and Melik Pashaev), along with Shablievsky, the recently appointed chair of the North Caucasian Krai Economic Council, says that a real boss has come onto the scene, changing everything and saying what everyone wanted to hear. Now everything hinges on accountability, one-man management, and supply. The laissez-faire attitude has come to an end: firm directives from the presidium [of VSNKh] have taken over.

In the lobbies no one talked about politics as such.

Genak (from VSNKh) finds that the talk at the congress consists mainly of platitudes. Directors don't shout "give us one-man management," but, silent and apprehensive, listen as "adopt one-man management" is shouted at them. . . .

Metigovsky, the director of the Saratov Raion power plant, is glad that I. N. Smirnov [expelled from the party in 1927 for his ties to Trotsky, reinstated in 1930 and employed in the VSNKh bureaucracy] with his proposal that supply be organized according to the model of Chusosnabarm [defense council plenipotentiary for army supplies in charge of the entire system of special, supradepartmental bodies (ChUSO), which supplied the Red Army during the civil war and period of war communism] has been criticized.

---

So the directors didn't shout "give us one-man management" but listened to others who shouted at them, "adopt one-man management." And yet one-man management, which made the director solely responsible for everything that happened at an enterprise, had its advantages, especially when the rhetoric of the Socialist Offensive conflicted with business interests. Some directors were courageous enough to act pragmatically. A good example can be found in the memoirs of Pyotr Fyodorovich Stepanov, former director of the Hammer and Sickle plant in Moscow. In connection with its reconstruction, the plant was required to take on the production of fine steel wire. Stepanov sent out scouts who found in an out-of-the-way place a small workshop run by a family named Zaitsev that did this sort of thing. Even though he knew that the workshop would be confiscated and the Zaitsevs labeled kulaks and resettled in the far north, the director took the risk of inviting them to the plant. "I gave them three hundred rubles and said that if they got things going, I'd give them a thousand rubles," recalled Stepanov. "These people went on to become the founders of the process for making fine wire. . . . The Zaitsev brothers not only got us started producing fine steel wire but they continued to come up with new inventions. They are craftsmen and the children of craftsmen, and their inventive skills began to develop in childhood." By taking the Zaitsevs into Hammer and Sickle, Stepanov saved them from deportation, something that caused many at the plant to scowl and also something that under the former management "triangle" (of director, secretary of the party organization, and chairman of the trade union committee) probably couldn't have happened. In this instance the director compelled the plant's party committee to accommodate him. And this set a precedent. Later on, when Hammer and Sickle set about producing new items, higher quality hardened steel was needed. Because the technology for this had yet to be mastered at the plant, Stepanov invited an officially licensed craftsman named Kran (an ethnic German), paid him, and Kran then set up the necessary production process at the plant.[4] How many leaders would have dared to be as resourceful and entrepreneurial as this to advance their business? Many worried about other problems, and let minor details of everyday life and corruption bog them down.

The practical realities facing managerial cadres in the provinces are described in their letters and petitions sent to TsKK-RKI. In June 1932 the senior investigator of the Odessa Oblast procurator's office, a man named Yegorov, reported:

---

## Document 41

"On violations of revolutionary legality in Odessa Oblast," June 1932. RGASPI, f. 613, op. 3, d. 135, ll. 1–7. Typed original.

---

Until April 1932 I worked in Khar'kov investigating the most important cases handled by the Procurator's Office of the Republic. When oblasts were being organized in Ukraine, I was transferred as senior investigator to the

## Document 41 *continued*

Office of the Odessa Oblast Procurator. During my brief sojourn in Odessa I encountered a number of very crude violations of revolutionary legality by those heading organizations in Odessa and by those running the Odessa Oblast Procurator's Office. Due to special circumstances, which I can explain separately if needed, I decided to appeal directly to TsKK VKP(b), bypassing Ukrainian organizations.

This past spring among work assigned to Senior Investigator Yestraikh of the Odessa Oblast Procurator's Office was a case involving major abuses of power in the "Moscow Tailoring and Knitted Goods" Artel: theft of merchandise, bribe taking, and other such crimes. Among those who should have been called in as defendants in connection with this case was a man named Todosiuk who had been found guilty of a number of crimes and was one of the leaders of the criminal band in question. However, Deputy Oblast Procurator Khimich, without any legal basis whatsoever, ordered Yestraikh not only not to include Todosiuk as a suspect but not even to question him. In accordance with Khimich's order, material about Todosiuk was singled out and set aside, and as a result the other defendants were sentenced to long periods of imprisonment, while Todosiuk continues to go scot-free. [Omitted is a section describing other unsuccessful attempts to make Todosiuk accountable.]

Meanwhile, after the "Moscow Tailoring and Knitted Goods" Artel [was shut down], Todosiuk landed himself a cushy job as director of a store closed to the public that serves the city council's staff exclusively, where he committed a number of new abuses of office. . . . But Todosiuk's crimes do not end here. Todosiuk is involved in yet another case dating from the time he served as director of a fur goods plant. [The illegal receipt of a tank of sulphuric acid is described next.] *One can only conclude that this failure to prosecute Todosiuk for repeated criminal activity is the result of his direct tie to a number of prominent staff members in the Odessa procurator's office and on the Odessa Control Commission who participated in the case and who are themselves customers of the city council's closed distribution store of which Todosiuk is the boss* [The special emphasis is Yegorov's, and was noted by TsKK.] This closed store is the best in the city in terms of quantity and choice of goods, and the scandalous things going on there have caused resentment among the workers for a long time. The same closed store, though labeled as being solely for the city council, in fact supplies various prominent Odessa party officials, and no one knows who authorized this. By the way, in Odessa in general I believe the directives for closed stores are stretched a great deal. Workers are undersupplied so that certain categories of prominent officials can have far more than is normal. The best closed stores, such as those for the city council, prerevolutionary political prisoners, and prerevolutionary political émigrés, supply the prominent officials of Odessa. In the store for prerevolutionary political prisoners the last thing you will find is prerevolutionary political prisoners, and in the store for political émigrés they are in fact the smallest group. Most of the customers work for the Odessa Trade Department and other institutions. The same is true with the city council store. Even the closed store for foreigners, for consuls, etc., "Insnab" [*Inostrannoe snabzhenie,* foreigners' supply], is supplying local council and party officials. [A discussion follows of unsuccessful attempts to investigate abuses in the closed store of the city council and also of judicial and investigative bodies concealing data about corruption and other abuses of office.]

One of the crudest violations of revolutionary legality has to do with the housing policies of the Odessa City Council. In February 1932, when oblasts were organized in Ukraine, Odessa became an oblast center, and space was needed to accommodate newly created oblast organizations and incoming staff. In dealing with this matter, local organizations blatantly ignored existing housing legislation, basing their actions on the applicability—condemned by Lenin—of a separate, "Kaluga" law because of alleged unusual local circumstances. The established order of evicting and resettling workers by legal procedure (with the exception of those instances strictly defined by law) was countermanded by Odessa's leaders. Instead, evictions and resettlement by administrative fiat were instituted. Class distinctions were totally disregarded; workers, specialists, scholars, and other toilers subject to eviction were treated arbitrarily and crudely in spite of privileges guaranteed them under the law. Evictions took place immediately after sought-out "objectives," i.e., rooms or apartments, had been found, and often people were resettled in housing that was clearly unsuitable. . . .

An example demonstrating how the Odessa officials cast aside all restraint is their system of "bonus awards" for finding an "objective" leading to eviction, the "award" being some of the rooms from which others had been evicted. [An example of eviction paid for with a bribe is cited.] To sum up, the bacchanalia of administrative evictions continued for several months in Odessa. Thousands of working people were resettled. The procurator's office, RKI, and city council received a mass of complaints about illegal resettlements and corrupt practices. However, the local [party] organizations failed to respond to these in any way. Only after *Pravda* published TsK VKP(b)'s resolution of 14 April containing details about how the Rostov City Council had tampered with housing policy did the "zeal" of the Odessa administrators abate somewhat. [Discussions follow about how this campaign was never condemned, about an attempt to save face by blaming "switchmen," and about how the campaign in fact continued but failed to achieve its object of accommodating incoming staff members. Many of the latter continued to live in hotels, the local nomenklatura cleverly using the campaign to their own advantage.]

Besides verifying statements and petitions and keeping an eye on high-level administrators, another purge method employed was wide-scale verification of party members. Such verification was conducted in the railroad industry in 1932. During the First Five-Year Plan, the railroads were strained to the limit. Chaotic, disorganized railroad traffic aggravated problems at both construction sites and industrial enterprises. This transport crisis was alleged to result from the intrigues of "wreckers" and "saboteurs," among them "former" or "bourgeois" specialists, and led to the "exposure" of 4,500 "saboteurs" in the first half of 1931. Promotees from the ranks of railroad workers got their positions. The following excerpts indicate what party verification materials demonstrated:

---

# Document 42

Party verification of railroad employees, 1932. RGASPI, f. 117, op. 114, d. 346, ll. 143–144. Typed original.

---

Renewed Activity by the Class Enemy and the Fight Against It

We possess a substantial number of facts pointing to renewed activity by class-alien, counterrevolutionary, kulak, SR, and Trotskyist factions that is manifested in deteriorating work discipline, declining work quality, and various incidents of sabotage and wholesale theft (on the Moscow-Kazan RR, SR factions in Ruzaevka, Alatyr', Penza, and Yudin; on the Moscow-Kursk RR, in Plekhanovo and Tula SR and Trotskyist terrorist groups with two "Communist" collaborators; on the North Caucasus RR, at Krasnodar Station a counterrevolutionary organization of men from former "haves": a priest, a tsarist military officer, a kulak, and a military bureaucrat, and others; on the Western RR, at Maloiaroslavets a counterrevolutionary bandit organization headed by bureaucrats from tsarist times with connections abroad, and a "shock worker" and his band of twenty-five).

Proof of sabotage: at the Maloiaroslavets repair shops repeated arson in the cabs of competing locomotives. In the October RR's Moscow shops competing engineers have been systematically harassed, sand poured into the axle boxes of their locomotives, and tools looted. Timetables on the Yekaterinsk RR were designed to sabotage, and the Siberian, Far East, and other lines have sabotage organizations.

In December on the Moscow-Kazan RR communication lines were damaged fourteen times, rendering the lines useless for a total of more than ten hours.

Recently, party organizers and cell members have significantly intensified their fight against the class enemy. For example, class enemies holding party cards have been exposed and expelled: six "Communists" from the cell at the Golutvino Shops of the Moscow-Kazan RR, a secret tie between the secretary of the party collective at Kurgan Station and kulaks. In Zlatoust the secretary of the Komsomol cell and the head of the technical propaganda office were exposed as kulak agents. The secretary of the party cell of workers also had a secret tie [with class enemies]. Secret enemies were exposed who had shielded themselves with party membership along the North Caucasian and Trans-Caucasian RRs, at the Krasnodar, Novocherkassk, Tikhoretsk, Baku, Nantlug, Akstafa, and other stations.

Recently, on many railroads (Perm, Moscow-Kazan, Omsk, Tomsk, Northern Moscow Belt Line) bands of thieves have been exposed by GPU and party organizations. More than 50 percent of these thieves are themselves railroad workers. In some instances bands are run by Communists (for example, one Petrov who worked for three years as cell secretary of the Moscow freight station on the October RR turned out to be the leader of a band of thieves).

However, to put it bluntly, the fight against the class enemy is still far from being sufficiently intense in day-to-day work. The vast majority of Communists are not exercising party vigilance at the high level needed, and in some instances in cells as well as among party organizers class vigilance and party alertness have obviously been blunted (in the party organizations of the Golutvino shops, the stations at Krasnodar, Moscow, and Penza, the Nizhni Novgorod and Moscow freight stations, Penza Station, the Maloiaroslavets Shops, and at other places).

In view of the facts cited here, we think the purge of the party on the railroads should have the highest priority, that new, broad, and thorough verifications should be carried out in conjunction with the GPU, and that class-alien and kulak elements should be chased out of the transportation industry.

What was happening in the country was sometimes given a different evaluation. Some of the party's economic nomenklatura began to call for more measured and cautious policies; others, reacting to mounting difficulties, became despondent and pessimistic. M. Matiukhin, director of the energy bureau of the Transmashtekh (*Transportnoe Mashino-Tekhnicheskoe*, transport machine technology) Conglomerate, reported the following to his friend and onetime colleague M. I. Kalinin:

# Document 43

Letter from M. Matiukhin to Kalinin on disarray in energy sector, 16 December 1932. RGASPI, f. 78, op. 1, d. 430, ll. 45–47. Original document.

The Early Hours of 16 December 1932

Dear Mikhail Ivanovich,

I'm of course very sorry that I haven't once written you but I've been busy building "the good life." In the summer, after a trip to the countryside, I kept intending to describe to you in a letter what I'd seen, but then decided not to, for my description one way or another would have had a different slant. Now, in a dark mood due to my son's sickness and having to keep watch at his bedside, I take up my pen to while away the time. I hope my writing will accomplish something. [Matiukhin's letter consists of two parts. The first includes his impressions from being in the countryside, to which we shall return later. Following is part two.]

I've always emphasized in my letters that the trouble with Soviet power is the fact that it gives rise to the vilest type of official—an official that carefully understands and carries out the general designs of the supreme authority, one that always heaps blame on the sinister machinations of the devil. This official never tells the truth because he doesn't want to distress the leadership. He gloats about famine and pestilence in the district or ward controlled by his rival. He won't lift a finger to try to help his neighbor. And so now I serve at the Transmashtekh Conglomerate. There are at present six plants in this conglomerate. I direct the energy bureau. I know well the two plants I've visited. Haven't had time to visit the others yet. I think that even you see now the impassable bog Soviet industry is mired in and the catastrophic disarray of the nation's energy sector. This is of very, very great concern to me because it's my work. People always talk about what ails them. Mikhail Ivanovich, no matter how disastrous the situation, nonetheless it can be alleviated here and there. You know (though it's kept secret from the likes of us, it's an open secret), that many of our plants that use energy from raion generating stations to operate have fairly powerful reserve stations. These reserve stations are kept idle in case of enemy attack. But the enemy has already attacked. That's obvious. No blockade could pose a greater threat than the energy disarray we see at present. [Here the energy shortages at the Kovrov and Kaluga plants are discussed in detail.]

And so, Mikhail Ivanovich, in 1933 the Kovrov and Kaluga plants will be in a state of paralysis. It's just bound to happen. I know where there are idle diesel engines. I'll take it upon myself to prove that they could and should be removed from where they are, and I want you to help me do this. I want to work toward overcoming the state of paralysis that's imminent as well as the one that already exists. Meanwhile all I see around me is loathsome politicizing, dirty tricks being played, and people being trapped for slips of the tongue. There's no end to the denunciations. You literally can't spit anywhere without hitting some revolting denouncer or liar in the puss. What have we come to? It's impossible to breathe. The less gifted a bastard, the meaner his slander. Of course, the purge of your party is none of my business, but I think that as a result of it the more decent elements still remaining in your party will be cleaned out. My observations relate to both party and nonparty milieus. Vile hypocrisy weighs one down like a horrible nightmare.

I'll close. Life has become very hard. My child is sick. Another is expected in one and a half to two months. The second time I married was inopportune. It's heartrending to look at a child who won't eat enough, while you're starving yourself for his sake. What lies ahead? If only the work were gratifying. But all you really do is write, write, write and give reports. And you have given the best years of your life to Work and the Revolution, yet you expect every day that this or that bastard is going to profit at your expense and rise in the ranks. A proletarian in the proletarian state is suspect, and any hypocritical bastard turned into a proletarian by the will of the Revolution can drown you in a teaspoon of water at any given moment. These are the times we live in. Things used to be worse, but they weren't so vile. So I ask you to see me officially for five or ten minutes for personal reasons as well as for the sake of the cause I serve. I want to prove to you with the full force of my will how good results can be achieved, if only to a small degree in a small area.

Yours, M. Matiukhin

Here we see an old specialist cadre who has become tired of the problems, sickness, unhealed wounds of the civil war, and the operations of the powers that be. From the letter it is evident that departmental self-interest has resulted from subdividing industry into branches and that the branch industries are competing with one another and struggling to influence the development of the centrally planned distribution system. To this old specialist the typical bureaucratic methods and modes of this struggle with their underlying political motives are revolting. As a result special nomenklatura clans formed around corporate interests, re-creating the military-mobilization economic model of Soviet power's early years. Adherence to this or that set of ideological postulates became the norm—and also a means of self-fulfillment.

These documents suggest that the situation was ripe for a new party purge, and this is precisely what was announced in January 1933. Member categories subject to expulsion were specified:

class-alien elements and enemies, "two-faced ones"—that is, those who say they are for but are actually against the basic party line— those who openly and covertly violate strict party discipline, those who jabber about the lack of realism in prescribed party plans, careerists, self-seekers, morally depraved members, and politically ignorant members unfamiliar with party rules, regulations, and programs. In the course of the purge, 18 percent of the party's members were expelled, and a further 15 percent left the party out of fear.

During the purge, documents were collected and carefully verified by appropriate organs. When discrepancies were noted or something seemed unclear, an explanation was demanded of the person undergoing verification or inquiries were dispatched to various institutions. Verification results, including the verified person's own written explanation and other clarifying information, were duly included in the personal file of the person being verified. The number of documents required for each personal file constantly grew until it included an assessment of qualifications for a given type of work, references, evaluation of previous work performed, documentation of Marxist education, personal attributes, and, finally, party references. In the file were also put denunciation letters, cadre verification results, and so forth.

During purge committee sessions questions were raised about participation in the revolutionary movement, party membership, and knowledge of Marxist-Leninist theory. In the personal file of SNK member B. I. Freiman, for example, there is an excerpt from the minutes of the 11 October 1933 session of a committee purging the party cell in the People's Commissariat of Communications of the USSR. The questions come from the committee and the answers from Freiman.

---

# Document 44

Excerpt from minutes of party purge committee within Narkomput', 11 October 1933. RGASPI, f. 17, op. 100, d. 64890, ll. 8–8 (verso). Typed original.

---

Question: Where exactly did you go through the Bolshevik hardening process?

## Document 44 *continued*

Answer: I was hardened as a Bolshevik while working in America, for I had close ties with the newspaper New World. Comrade Bukharin came to America and also worked for this newspaper.

Q: How did you master the theoretical principles of Bolshevism, by reading Lenin?

A: I've read Lenin, but not everything he wrote of course.

Q: What is the main tenet of Leninism?

A: Leninism is the extension of Marxism in the era of the dictatorship of the proletariat. [When the question "What is the main tenet of Leninism?" was repeated, Freiman said he didn't understand.]

Q: What is the dictatorship of the proletariat?

A: It is the revolutionary dictatorship of the proletariat and the poorest peasants.

Q: What is the difference between the dictatorship of the proletariat and the revolutionary-democratic dictatorship of the proletariat and peasantry?

A: It is power held jointly and equally by the proletariat and the peasantry.

Q: What is Trotsky's theory of "permanent revolution"?

A: I don't know.

Q: What is the difference between the American Communist Party and our Bolshevik Party?

A: The American socialist party was created out of fragments of the Russian party and from Russian emigrants who fled to America during the reactionary period, but I don't know what the ideological difference is.

---

By decision of the committee Comrade Freiman was transferred "from full to associate membership because of political ignorance and failure to master the fundamental principles of Bolshevism." A month later at a new session, however, the committee decided "to revoke the former decision approving the verification of Comrade Freiman and at the same time explain to him that his political ignorance [was] intolerable."

At the Seventeenth Party Congress, Stalin said that once the correct party line had been determined and the correct way to proceed decided, success depended on how work was organized and on organizing the drive to implement the party line. Any problems remaining would be the result of a breach between the party leadership's directives and the way in which directives were carried out. Such a breach developed, he said, because of organizational weakness, poor selection of personnel, lack of self-criticism, bureaucratism, and criminal negligence on the part of local institutions; all of these caused unerring directives to be subverted. An entire system of categorizing worthless cadres had evolved. There were incorrigible bureaucrats, chatterboxes, even honest ones devoted to Soviet power but incapable of leading and incapable of organizing anything, persons with meritorious ties to the Communist past who had transformed themselves into "grandees," whiners, persons of little faith, and persons who considered that party and Soviet laws were written not for them but for fools. According to Stalin, 90 percent of existing problems occurred because there was no organized system to control implementation of high-level decisions.

On this basis, the main slogan of the Second Five-Year Plan— "Cadres Who Have Mastered Technology Decide Everything!"— was in effect replaced by its abbreviated version: "Cadres Decide Everything!"—a slogan that said more about the nature of the relation between people and authority than anything else. The principal criteria for selecting cadres became the evaluation of one's political profile, assiduousness in firmly and unconditionally following the General Line, and ability to fulfill no matter what the assigned task. New leaders, secretaries of party committees, "captains of Soviet industry," construction chiefs, and so on—all were nurtured in this ethic. Initiative, enterprise, personal judgment, and opinion became extremely dangerous qualities. Administrative zeal, scoldings, reprimands, firings, and arrests took the place of an ability to work with people. Rather than solving problems, these made them more deep-rooted. It was a fairly simple management model, one of crude power techniques.

The Seventeenth Party Congress is noted for yet another important decision: the restructuring of party committees at all levels according to the branch principle. The new system, joining all lines of command under the central party apparatus directly controlled by Stalin, inevitably led to a decline in the role and prestige of all other institutions and organizations, now called upon to function as implementers of the party leadership. Part and parcel of the effort to strengthen party control and discipline was the liquidation of the joint TsKK-RKI commission and its replacement by a Party Control Commission (KPK), subordinate to the TsK VKP(b), but with its own central apparatus and permanent representatives in the republics, krais, and oblasts. The role of KPK chief was reserved for one of the TsK VKP(b) secretaries. Appointed to this post in 1935 was one of Stalin's most devoted promotees, N. I. Yezhov.

While the old ideals of equality and sacrifice in the name of a bright future were still being disseminated as essential qualities of the "socialist way of life," the notion of personal well-being and career began to become paramount in Soviet society. This notion affected the ruling party-state nomenklatura first and foremost, and it expressed itself in the creation of that hierarchy of positions and concomitant privileges that would become one of the distinguishing characteristics of the Soviet regime. In the 1930s this process began to gain momentum, sometimes acquiring monstrous forms, and except for control mechanisms and repressive measures, there was nothing to counter them.

Control over cadres turned into a tidal wave. Various types of verifications and the appointment of committees with special powers were followed by "organizational decisions" *(orgvyvody)*: reprimands, firings, indictments, and the like. But it wasn't possible to make people—"human material"—conform immediately to the required image and likeness. Persecuting cadres only served to increase the problems of running the state and governing society. Yet coercive mechanisms seemed desirable because they already had proved effective in the fight against opponents of Soviet authority. The number of those persecuted grew precipitously, many of them destined to be labeled "enemies of the people."

Cadres recently appointed to administrative positions in the economy were poorly prepared for their work and were pressured daily by the leadership to fulfill inordinate tasks. Each time planned targets had to be fulfilled or new directives came in, the specter of accusations about violating the law, treachery, and sabotage arose. It was the same up and down the line. Letters in late 1933 and early 1934 between Kalinin and G. S. Onishchenko, chairman of the rural soviet of the village of Tsvetnoe in the Volodarsk Raion of the Lower Volga Krai (on the northern banks of the Caspian Sea), concern problems facing a local administrative official.

# Document 45

Letter from soviet chairman G. S. Onishchenko to Kalinin, 15 October 1933. RGASPI, f. 78, op. 1, d. 524, ll. 2–4. Certified typed copy.

15 October 1933

Mikhail Ivanovich:

Please forgive me if my letter tears you away from a more important matter. I was inspired to sit down and write you personally by a circumstance I can find no way out of. I believe you can give me a clear reply which will be beneficial not only to me but also to my work, to which I am devoted totally. . . . My own personal interests can be postponed, put off to the distant future. I'll describe now the essence of the matter.

I am young as a Communist; I joined the party on 18 January 1931. I am forty years old and have been working for twenty-eight years. I was mobilized by the town party committee [gorkom] to go to the country as chairman of the rural soviet of Tsvetnoe village and have served in this post since 1 January 1933. This work was completely unfamiliar to me, but after nine and a half months I've become somewhat familiar [with it].

To be a worker and to work as an executive are two quite different things. Since 1913 I've worked as a loader with interruptions caused by the imperialist and civil wars. It was easier for me then than it is now. The work I'm doing now requires that you know how to work yourself and to teach others to work, to give sensible answers to kolkhoz members, to be conversant with all the laws, to know the psychology of the village in all matters, to study the people you work with. You have to know how to skillfully expose everything that causes harm, to conduct a daily battle with the kulak element, to study his tactics, to unmask him, and expel him from the kolkhoz ranks. You have to know how not to violate revolutionary legality and order and acquire a lot of other knowledge and sensitivities. You have to know how to forge a new group of party activists, to learn to teach them how to work—to work in a practical way to fulfill the General Line of the party in the countryside.

How I have worked these nine and a half months I will not describe to you. I will only bring up the fact that out of eight rural soviet chairmen working in 1932, four were given sentences of two to three years for misappropriation, theft, and embezzlement.

So, when I came there, everything, as they say, was in a complete shambles, and I have put it all back together solidly.

On the rural soviet's territory there is a fishing kolkhoz which numbers 774 households; the total population here is 3,740 persons, making it the largest rural soviet in the raion. Before the revolution the residents had a substantial fishing industry and caught primarily sturgeon. During the civil war a quarter of them participated actively in the White Army and were infected to the core with acquisitive greed.

## Document 45 *continued*

This rural soviet is under special observation by the town soviet and the town party committee. The raion is populated by national minorities. There are thirty-two rural soviets in all, four of them Russian, including the one described above. Russians also work in the raion center.

And so, Mikhail Ivanovich, I work honestly, devotedly, regardless of time or health, I'm completely aware who and what I'm devoting my strengths to, and I always ask myself if in the end I'll be tried. If you asked why, I'd answer you straight out: because I am the chairman of the rural soviet.

I have received a reprimand from the party RK [*Raionnyi Komitet,* raion committee] for the way I dealt with those deliberately and continually in arrears in payment of state taxes. All I did was produce property descriptions in accordance with the law you signed. The farms I described belong to solidly established peasants of average means; their minds are not going to change—no matter how much propaganda. Further, I'm hanging by a thread with the party because, as much as I would like to, I won't be able to fulfill the plan assignment for mobilizing resources. To give an example: in the third quarter RAIFO [*Raionnyi Finansovyi Otdel,* raion finance department] levied a 13,800-ruble cultural and recreational tax. So we collected the money and [as early as] the second quarter 13,800 rubles was accounted for. The same was true for the other levies. When you tell them that according to law we shouldn't demand any additional taxes, they declare straight out, "If you don't fulfill this, we'll have you tried." In the fourth quarter they assigned in accordance with their plan a rural tax of 6,000 rubles. All we had left was 3,000 rubles; then they charged us an insurance premium of 29,000. I've checked my own and the kolkhoz's accounts, and all we have now is 14,353 rubles. When you raise this question with the finance officials, they state: "We got the estimates from the city. We have to fulfill these levies. We don't go and think up tax figures on our own."

You're between the devil and the deep blue sea. If you add taxes, you're violating revolutionary legality, and you're put on trial. And if you don't fulfill the raion's assignments, you're tried all the same, and besides that you'll be shamed and so forth.

Mikhail Ivanovich, I consider myself worse than someone with an extra-hard assignment. Someone with an extra-hard assignment gets what he's told done so he won't be tried, while even if I get things done I'll still be tried because I added on taxes which is a violation of revolutionary legality. I've come to the conclusion that they'll kick me out of the party and try me because probably I don't know how to work. After all, I haven't taken any training courses and haven't gotten any help so far. To be sure, there've been fifty-two representatives in the last nine and a half months—five of them really had something to offer, the rest were just a waste of government funds. Written directives come down from the raion like this: "Do this by the fifth"—and they send it on the twenty-fifth. It's thirty kilometers to the raion center, and in

## Document 45 *continued*

these directives they don't spell out how to carry things out—they just write five or six lines and nothing more. The consequence: for nonfulfillment an administrative penalty, a trial, the Control Commission (KK) and prosecutor, etc.

You work like you're on the edge of a straight razor. Because of this constant threat I've contracted third-degree tuberculosis, and I've had an attack of neurasthenia. You can't please anybody in this work.

Mikhail Ivanovich, . . . I'm writing you the absolute truth. Maybe I don't understand enough about how to do this work. Maybe we were dispatched to the country simply to be sacrificed at the present stage, maybe this is what the party requires. I've reached a dead end.

I suffer terribly now because of my illness, but still I won't give up working and await your reply to my letter. No matter what form it's in, your reply will be the supreme reward.

Sending you Communist greetings,
Onishchenko

---

Kalinin's reply:

---

## Document 46

Kalinin's reply to Onishchenko, 10 January 1934. RGASPI, f. 78, op. 1, d. 524, ll. 1–1 (verso). Typed copy, corrected.

---

10 January 1934
Dear Comrade Onishchenko:
Please forgive me for taking so long to respond to your letter of 15 October 1933.

It is really and truly difficult to reply to your letter since there are no specific, practical, or fundamental questions raised in it. To tell the truth, I don't understand how my reply will identify a possible tactic for you to employ in the future.

Judging by your letter, your understanding of the rural soviet chairman's responsibilities is correct. And the Raikom did not err in sending you to the rural soviet. I think you will be able to cope with this work and cope adequately. Evidently, you are already coping with it. I don't agree with your assessment that the chairman of a rural soviet cannot avoid transgressing party and Soviet rules and regulations. Indeed, the facts you cite are not at all persuasive. To put it bluntly, problems surrounding the execution of a financial plan in reality are the ones least likely to lead to a trial. At any rate, this is the

## Document 46 *continued*

first letter I've received of this sort. Look, according to your letter your predecessors were tried for misappropriation—that is, for actions that have to be brought to trial, for actions like that must be fought in the most decisive way possible.

That the post of rural soviet chairman is difficult cannot be denied. And it isn't difficult because you don't know the laws. That you'll overcome before long. The regulations concerning rural soviets are not all that difficult, and the main thing is that you understand party policy and know how to make it work. Now that's not so easy. The most important thing is not to let this predicament lead you astray and to find the proper way to proceed. And in the countryside the proper way to proceed is to strengthen collective agriculture, raise collective farm workers' material level by improving kolkhoz management, using fully, or in a maximally efficient way, resources at hand, both natural resources and manpower. Practical work is inseparable from the state's interests which, in turn, represent the general interests of both workers and peasants.

The lot of rural soviet chairman has improved significantly this year. One shouldn't view the pay increase only in a material sense. This was the way the highest Soviet institutions emphasized the importance of rural soviets in the overall structure of the Soviet system, and it will certainly have the effect of strengthening the authority of the rural soviet.

My sympathetic attitude toward your letter is to a significant degree determined by your poor state of health, which makes the situation you find yourself in seem bleaker than is actually the case. Obviously, you do not consider your appointment as rural soviet chairman right or just. From my vantage point I cannot decide how appropriate the appointment is. To do this I'd have to know the specific details. You are obviously a good chairman, however, which means that the raion had serious grounds for sending you to do this work.

Don't talk about sacrifices. That's not serious and is unfounded. There's no reason for this. If you have reached the point that you don't have the physical endurance to continue the work, then go and have a heart to heart talk with the secretary of the party and the RIK chairman: Say "I'm not good at this, I can't do it any longer, give me a job that's small and peaceful." But then don't claim to be a party activist, for you'll be joining the rank and file.

With Communist greetings,

M. Kalinin

---

Obviously, Kalinin's letter is both consoling and evasive. Why did he need more specific information in order to be convinced that the existing system of local soviet rule was ineffective because of the pressure applied from above by the centralized bureaucracy? The country's "Head of State" was trying to talk his way out of the matter with such phrases as finding "the proper way to proceed." But as Onishchenko's letter makes clear, he already was following the "proper way." Virtually constant party purges also did not help matters any.

In the mid-1930s various initiatives were undertaken within higher education, the result of the increase in the number of higher educational institutions and mass graduation of specialists of the new stamp. Meanwhile, universities and other institutions of higher learning remained as always hotbeds of free thinking and new ideas. A 1935 party review of higher educational institutions in the Azov–Black Sea Krai, the materials of which were sent to the Party Control Commission of TsK VKP(b), evaluated student political opinion in the following manner:[5]

## Document 47

Party review of higher educational institutions in Azov–Black Sea Krai, 1935. RGASPI, f. 17, op. 114, d. 695, ll. 31–40. Typed original.

During December 1934 and January of this year in higher educational institutions and technical colleges there were a number of antiparty and counterrevolutionary sallies and speeches, most of which were not repulsed properly or in a timely fashion by party and Komsomol organizations. The faculties of higher educational institutions are severely infested with Trotskyists and the student body with class-alien and hostile elements who have easily infiltrated these institutions thanks to poorly organized admittance procedures.

Sixty thousand students are concentrated in the higher educational institutions of the Azov–Black Sea Krai. There are cities such as Novocherkassk where approximately 60 percent of the party organization consists of students. Despite this, until the end of December, the krai committee and city and raion committees concerned themselves very little with these institutions and then only with matters related to their everyday needs. The appointment and verification of faculty (especially in the social sciences and humanities), recruitment of personnel, the work of the institutions' party and Komsomol organizations, and mass political work were areas completely neglected.

More than a few alien and hostile elements had wormed their way into a number of these institutions' Komsomol organizations (and the portion of

## Document 47 *continued*

Komsomol members in most of the institutions is significant: 30 to 40 percent). This explains why there have been quite a few instances of counterrevolutionary statements and speeches by Komsomol members. . . .

On 30 December 1934, during the examination period, V. Khriukin, a member of the Komsomol and a third-year student in the History Department at the Rostov Pedagogical Institute, openly defended Zinoviev and Kamenev. He declared that Zinoviev and Kamenev rendered enormous services to the revolution, were friends of Lenin, and that now all this was being obliterated. Khriukin further declared that Zinoviev had no tie with the terrorists who killed Comrade Kirov, that in general members of the opposition cannot be champions of terror, and that the judicial procedure used to establish an ideological tie between the terrorists and the Zinoviev-Kamenev group was improper.

On 3 January a Komsomol meeting took place to which Khriukin was admitted even though he had already been expelled from the Komsomol and the institute. The meeting's presidium afforded Khriukin the opportunity to present his counterrevolutionary views despite protests from the Komsomol members present.

After Khriukin's arrest, in the process of the investigation, it was determined that Khriukin was closely connected with the following group of students at the pedagogical institute: Yelin, Chalov, Ustimenko, Gavrilov, and K. Khriukin. All these individuals (not bona fide party members), the investigation determined, got into the institute by means of forged documents. In 1932, on Elin's and K. Khriukin's initiative, the individuals named stole from the party committee of the "Comintern" Mine (Shakhty Raion) a large quantity of blank associate party member and registration cards, filled them out in their own names and, having prepared false documents about graduating from nine-year schools, gained admission to the institute.

In the Rostov Financial and Economics Institute on 1 January 1935 at a conference of party and Komsomol organizers and individuals assigned by the party, student Kondeev (a Komsomol member) declared: "One must also pay attention to the contributions of Zinoviev and others. Why do you only consider their faults? Zinoviev is a great leader. He was president of the Comintern." Having said this, he left the meeting. That same day Kondeev assembled groups of students and passionately defended Zinoviev, [Leonid] Nikolaev [assassin of Sergei Kirov, Leningrad party secretary, on 1 December 1934], and other counterrevolutionaries.

In the evening at a meeting of a Komsomol group the question of excluding Kondeev from the Komsomol and the institute was raised. In spite of the fact that Kondeev's counterrevolutionary position was quite clear, he was afforded the opportunity of delivering an unabashedly counterrevolutionary sermon. At the end he said straight out that the purpose of his remarks was "to show the students that the party and government and our party committee in particular had wrongly judged the members of the opposition." After his expulsion from the Komsomol and from the institute, Kondeev immediately went underground, disappeared. [Accounts follow of "counterrevolutionary agitation" at several Novocherkassk institutes.]

The Akimov incident illustrates how weak is the political vigilance of party members at the Novocherkassk Industrial Institute. Akimov (not a party member), a recent graduate of the institute's Aviation Department given an appointment in plant no. 22, time and again expressed counterrevolutionary views when he was among party members, especially of late:

"Soviet authority can exist without communists. It's much better for engineers to work for capitalists than in our industries. . . . Kirov's murder wasn't connected with Trotskyists; that's all nonsense. Zinoviev is a good man. He truly acted on behalf of the masses."

Akimov was expelled from the institute in 1934 for rowdiness, but several Communists vouched for him and he was readmitted and allowed to graduate. These Communists (Serdiukov, Gurenko, and Kabanov) have since been severely reprimanded by the party.

In Krasnodar, at the Kuban Pedagogical Technical College, student Diakov, ex-Komsomol member, systematically carried on counterrevolutionary conversations. This was known to a number of Komsomol members and Communists, but they did little to rebuff Diakov. As Diakov left the hall where a memorial service occasioned by Kirov's murder was in progress, he said to a group of students: "One's been done in, soon they'll all be done in. They'll all be killed off."

Who is Diakov? It turns out he was expelled twice from a kolkhoz, once for acting under false pretenses, the second time for fouling up work records that caused a work brigade to fall apart. Yet this didn't prevent him from being admitted as a student.

A student of the workers' and peasants' preparatory department [rabfak] at the Kuban Pedagogical Institute named Kriukova, who had been a member of the Komsomol since 1931, gave a note during class to the student next to her which read, "I salute Nikolaev for the murder of Kirov."

In November 1934 NKVD organs uncovered in Krasnodar a counterrevolutionary fascist youth group made up chiefly of students from the Kuban Pedagogical Institute, with the pretentious name of "labor-democratic party." This group (twenty people in all) had something in the way of a "program," attempted to establish ties abroad, set up a press, obtained weapons, hatched schemes to kill local party and Soviet officials, and so on. The basic goal of the group's program was restoration of private property and the overthrow of Soviet power.

The principal organizer of this fascist group, Zorbidi (not a party member), had been arrested as early as 1932 for counterrevolutionary work among the youth of Kholmsk stanitsa. At the end of 1932 he was freed (because he was a minor) and immediately got himself admitted to the Kuban Pedagogical Institute, where he furthered his counterrevolutionary work on a much broader scale.

By sentence of the military tribunal of SKVO [*Severo-Kavkazkii Voennyi Okrug*, North Caucasus military district] in January 1935, Zorbidi and another organizer of the "labor-democratic party" were condemned and shot; the remaining members of this group were sent to concentration camps for various periods of time.

What elements were these counterrevolutionary youths, age nineteen to twenty, recruited from? They were primarily children of class enemies, filled with hate and spite for Soviet power from childhood. In his testimony defendant Kanshin (b. 1916), for example, talks about this very fact:

"My father had a bakery. My family life affected the formation of my ideology, even while I was still in school. More than once when I was still a child I would hear this or that expression of dissatisfaction with the existing Soviet order. These sentiments were passed on to me as well."

Approximately the same picture emerges from an inquiry A. Stetsky conducted in the Ivanovo Oblast city of Rybinsk in March 1935, as the following memorandum demonstrates:

# Document 48

Memorandum from A. Stetsky on counterrevolutionary attitudes among students in Rybinsk, March 1935. RGASPI, f. 17, op., 114, d. 695, ll. 75–77. Typed original.

Concerning Manifestations of C[ounter]-R[evolutionary] Sentiments among Students of the Aviation Institute and [Aviation] Technical College in Rybinsk

In accordance with instructions from the Bureau of KPK I was dispatched to Rybinsk to verify the report sent by the secretary of the party's Rybinsk GK [*Gorodskoi Komitet*, city committee], Comrade Kostiukov, to Comrade Kaganovich, disclosing that a number of persons in the Rybinsk Aviation Institute and Aviation Technical College had expressed counterrevolutionary and terrorist sentiments. There I acquainted myself with all the materials [involved], questioned Director Dushinov, the leaders of the institute's party organizations, and student party and Komsomol members connected with the facts reported by Comrade Kostiukov. I talked at length with Comrade Kostiukov and his deputy, Ortenberg, GK officials, NKVD Commissioner Comrade Ivashchenko, and also with plant no. 26's party organizer,

Comrade Kozlov, the immediate supervisor of the institute's party organizations.

As a result of acquainting myself with the situation there, the following became clear: At the Aviation Institute among the students (about 750 in all) it was revealed that two, Nekrasov and Voronov, carry on counterrevolutionary conversations with their classmates. Nekrasov is the son of an Orel railroad office worker. He is a member of the Komsomol. He was reared in kulak surroundings: his mother is from a kulak family, one uncle is a dispossessed kulak. A year or two ago Nekrasov also expressed counterrevolutionary views to Komsomol members he was living with. About the building of the White Sea–Baltic Canal, he said, for example, "They built the Canal on human bones."[6] This is the language of the enemy. In connection with the murder of Comrade Kirov he began to make vile comments about how "it wasn't worth risking anybody's life to kill Kirov. The main leaders, not the accessories, need to be killed." As a result of statements like this he was exposed by students who were party and Komsomol members as early as December 1934.

The second, Voronov, is the son of a specialist, his year of birth 1912, a member of the Komsomol, originally from the Azov–Black Sea Krai. In Voronov too counterrevolutionary sentiments manifested themselves a long time ago. He was expelled from an institute in Novocherkassk. He refused to take part in a day of voluntary labor *(subbotnik)* and was a blatant individualist who refused to participate in community work. Voronov too after 1 December made comments about the murder of Comrade Kirov that were out-and-out counterrevolutionary. He said: "In my opinion [it] was poorly organized. They bungled the whole business. But this won't be the end of the matter." Students who were Komsomol members argued with Voronov, but they did not unmask him completely, and only after 1 December when he revealed himself more clearly did they tell the NKVD about him.

A third manifestation of counterrevolutionary sentiments came to light at the Aviation Technical College. This case concerns a student at the college named Gruzdev. Gruzdev is a Komsomol member, born in 1915, the son of a kulak, from Kovrov Raion. Once again, Gruzdev expressed counterrevolutionary sentiments long before to a group of Komsomol members he lived with in a dormitory, and until recently these Komsomol members likewise listened silently to his counterrevolutionary comments and did not refute them. . . .

The first conclusion to be drawn from this is that in the party and Komsomol organization of both the institute and the technical college, the party and mass educational work has been extremely poorly organized; party and Komsomol members were not equipped with a proper understanding of party objectives nor prepared to be vigilant and uncompromising. The work of the party education network was extremely weakly organized. As a result, when party and Komsomol members heard direct attacks and speeches by the en-

## Document 48 *continued*

emy, they did not go on the offensive, did not seize the counterrevolutionary by the hand. I conversed with these Komsomol members, and now they understand their political negligence and curse themselves for their lack of vigilance. Special attention must be paid to the political education of Komsomol members. The importance of this is evident from the following: only 11 out of the 450 students at the Aviation Technical College are party members, 300 are Komsomol members. In the Institute, out of 750 students, 120 are party members and 400 Komsomol members. Meanwhile, work with them is badly organized. I happened to be present when leaders of Komsomol study groups were being quizzed, and few had any conception of the party's fight against the Zinoviev and Trotskyist influences, against the rightists.

However, most of the blame for the fact that counterrevolutionary opinions were voiced at higher educational institutions was placed on the cadres of those institutions. A purge of instructional staff was initiated based on the facts reported here by Stetsky who, as we shall see, was extremely active in this sphere.

## Document 49

Memorandum from A. Stetsky on social and economic sciences faculty, 9 March 1935. RGASPI, f. 17, op. 114, d. 695, ll. 15–21. Typed original.

To the Secretaries of TsK VKP(b):
I. V. Stalin
Comrade L. M. Kaganovich
Comrade A. A. Andreev
Comrade A. A. Zhdanov
Comrade N. I. Yozhov
Recently, numerous facts have demonstrated that social and economic sciences faculties are infested with former members of the opposition, double dealers, people who once belonged to other parties, and so forth. This points to a lack of proper leadership and to the slipshod way in which faculty members are appointed both on the part of the central administrative bodies responsible for educational institutions in various commissariats and Narkomproses and on the part of krai and oblast party committees.

As a rule issues related to the appointment of faculty have not been of great concern to central administrative bodies until recently. These bodies do not have an accurate picture of who is teaching the social and economic sciences. Glaring testimony to this is contained in a report submitted by them regarding ninety-eight departmental heads at higher educational institutions. In more than 60 percent (fifty-seven of ninety-eight) of the cases, "No information was available" about who had belonged to other parties, had been in the opposition, or had received a reprimand from the party. But even the statistics that were compiled signal the fact that a pressing and unresolved problem exists among the institutions' administrators: twenty departmental heads (out of the forty-one about whom the central administrative bodies have information) have been subjected to party penalties, were expelled by the party, or belonged to other parties. Among twenty-one instructors who seemed from available information to be politically irreproachable were such persons as Zagorulko, who was twice expelled from the party, Algasov, an ex-SR, Aleksandrov, an ex-Menshevik who was expelled from VKP(b), and others like them.

In the RSFSR's Narkompros, appointment of departmental heads is given more attention, but the matter is very badly organized. Comrade Orakhelashvili, the Narkompros Administrative Chief, approved departmental heads for twenty-six of the sixty-four teacher training colleges. But the actual result of this "approval" was as follows: (1) departmental heads not approved by Narkompros continued to hold their posts for a year or more, and (2) half of those recently approved by Narkompros have been dismissed for sneaking antiparty views into their teaching.

This is how matters stand with the selection and "approval" of departmental heads by Narkompros.

The following information from Moscow shows how badly departmental heads as a group are tainted: out of 126 heads verified by a commission of the Division of Culture and Propaganda of Leninism of MGK [*Moskovskii Gorodskoi Komitet*, Moscow City Committee] VKP(b), less than a third were deemed fit to remain in their posts.

Things are even worse regarding the appointment and assessment of faculty proper. Information provided by the Narkompros central administrative bodies concerning the 433 faculty members at fifty-four higher educational institutions under their charge shows that up till now the commissariats' central administrative bodies have not studied the party profile of faculty members in the social and economic sciences. Recently information was collected about the social makeup, education, and number of party members (79.4 percent), but there is little information about what these party members represent. . . . We provide several illustrations that characterize the nature of the commissariats' leadership in this matter.

1. On 22 September 1934 Comrade Novikov, the chief of the Division of Higher Institutions of Technical Education in Narkomtiazhprom [*Narodnyi Komissariat Tiazheloi Promyshlennosti*, People's commissariat of Heavy Industry], sent the director of the Energy Institute, Comrade Dudkin, the following memo:

# Document 49 *continued*

"Dear Ivan Ivanovich, I've known Professor Zagorulko, professor at the Kiev Polytechnical Institute, since '21. I recommend that you not lose this valuable teacher and scholar." Thus Zagorulko, once an active Trotskyist, twice expelled from the party, happened to become head of the Department of Leninism.

2. In response to an inquiry by the All-Union Higher Technical Education Committee, an official letter was sent by Narkomzem (signed by Vitievsky, the deputy chief of the Special Higher Educational Institutions Administration, and Mladentsev, a teaching methods specialist and an inspector):

"According to available information received by NKZ RSFSR, both from personal, firsthand inspection and reports by the leaders of higher educational institutions, there have been no instances of misinterpretations in the teaching of the social and economic sciences. However, this does not mean that . . ." etc.

Meanwhile, all one needs to do is glance at one Narkomzem institute (the Institute of Agricultural Mechanization) to discover serious political deviations in teaching. Evidence of the bad state of affairs in the appointment of faculty is provided also in information available about professors at fifty-seven agricultural higher educational institutions. In these institutions fourteen departments in the economic disciplines (political economy, economic policy, and others) are headed by non–party members. Subjects such as agricultural production methods are primarily in the hands of non–party members, which include such "nonparty" people as the saboteur Chaianov [quite possibly Aleksandr Chaianov (1888–1937), who in the 1920s directed the Timiriazev Academy of Agricultural Economics and was the leading exponent of the "organization and production school" of agrarian economists]. Even among the heads of departments of Leninism and dialectical materialism there are five non–party members.

3. In Narkompros there are pro forma personal files for departmental heads, but one can judge how credible these "personal files" by a single example: In one document it is recorded that Professor Singalevich has been a party member since 1926, in another since 1928, and in a third since 1931.

Such is the style and organization of the commissariat's files and faculty hiring practices. [Descriptions follow of similar deficiencies at the Bauman Institute of Mechanical Engineering, at the Institute of Nonferrous Metals, and in Tashkent's higher educational institutions.]

During recent years an enormous number of comrades received positions who had studied at the Institute of Red Professors [IKP], Ranion [*Rossiiskaia assotsiatsiia nauchnogo issledovaniia obshchestvennykh nauk*, Russian association of scientific research in the social sciences], or done graduate work in social and economic science institutions, and so forth. But these comrades are not being utilized as they should be. From information available about 315 who graduated from IKP, it is evident that three-quarters of them are to be

# Document 49 *continued*

found doing party, trade union, governmental, and every other type of work except teaching. More often than not, the worst—not the best people in terms of party consciousness—are left to do the teaching.

Voronezh Oblast serves as a striking illustration. Here out of forty persons who studied at IKP, only two are teaching. The other thirty-eight occupy governmental and party posts and, as a rule, do not teach even when they hold joint appointments. This is how matters stand with regard to engaging a qualified party work force as faculty.

The current state of affairs with regard to how faculty are appointed in the social and economic sciences and the current practice of leaving the teaching to those who cannot be used for other work must come to an end.

It is imperative to:

1. Oblige krai committees, oblast committees, and the Republic TsKs' party committees, on the one hand, and the Narkomproses and central administrations in charge of higher educational institutions of the people's commissariats, on the other, to conduct a review and issue verification on the basis of an investigation of higher educational institution faculty in the social and economic sciences.

2. Establish the following procedure for appointing and approving faculty in the social and economic sciences in higher educational institutions:

    Department heads in the social and economic sciences should be approved according to party recommendations: by a decision of the krai committee bureau, the oblast committee bureau, and the Republic TsKs' party committees, and according to governmental recommendations made personally by the heads of the Commissariats' Central Administrations in charge of higher educational institutions, and in institutions of the Narkompros system made personally by the deputy commissar.

    Faculty in the social and economic sciences should be approved personally by the institution's director in agreement with the director of the department of culture and propaganda of Leninism of the krai committee, oblast committee, and Republic TsKs' party committees.

3. Propose to oblast committees, krai committees, and the Republic TsKs' party committees that they establish a procedure to attract qualified and verified officials from party and government organizations and from industry and business to teach social and economic sciences (Leninism, history, economics, and economic policy) in higher educational institutions.

4. Not permit comrades sent by TsK VKP(b) to teach in educational institutions to transfer to other work without permission from TsK VKP(b).

Director of the Department of Culture and Propaganda of Leninism, TsK VKP(b), A. Stetsky

9 March 1935

As we see, special attention was paid to faculty in the social and economic sciences, faculty who were duty-bound to cultivate an "unshakable" Marxist-Leninist vision. Every departmental head in these disciplines now became part of the special TsK nomenklatura. Future teachers, called upon to cultivate the younger generation, were accorded no less attention, as is evident from the following document:

## Document 50

Memorandum "Concerning the Moral and Political State of Pedagogical Institutes," 23 March 1935. RGASPI, f. 17, op. 114, d. 695, ll. 83–92. Typed original.

To the Bureau of the Party Control Commission, TsK VKP(b),
Comrade N. I. Yezhov
Comrade M. F. Shkiriatov
Memorandum Concerning the Moral and Political State of Pedagogical Institutes

### I. Anti-Soviet elements in the student body of Moscow pedagogical institutes

At the end of January of this year, the KPK's Subcommittee on Education and Public Health received the following letter, which had been sent to Comrade Germogenov, director of the Moscow Oblast Pedagogical Institute, by second-year student Zavalishin:

> I ask that you make it possible for me to leave the Pedagogical Institute painlessly. I promise to pay back the money spent on me. . . .
> I ask this because, as a result of intense study of the natural sciences—especially physics, astronomy, and biology—in particular, from acquainting myself with the works of Einstein, Mises, Eddington, Jeans, Gans, Driesch, Berg, Chelpanov, and also from studying the philosophy of Spinoza, Hegel, Bergson, Husserl, W. James, Vladimir Solovev, S. Frank, and others, I seem finally to have become an objective idealist. To be sure, I am far from thinking that my *Weltanschauung* is completely defined, . . . but nonetheless I have good reason to believe that it will continue to develop in this direction, that of intensified idealistic convictions. . . .
> For all practical purposes I think it will be difficult for me to work as a pedagogue with this philosophy. I want to leave the institute while there is still time to do so.

# Document 50 *continued*

Upon receipt of this letter, we ascertained that Zavalishin is a priest who wormed his way into the institute with counterfeit documents. Zavalishin's noble and humble demeanor had attracted the attention of faculty and students earlier, but no one had questioned his idealistic utterances. Even after the letter was received, Kuprenina, the director of the office of academic affairs, kept repeating to the students that Zavalishin was an original thinker and that Communists could learn a thing or two from him. A month and a half later he was still a student at the institute. He was expelled without any public announcement.

Our inspection revealed that three Moscow higher educational institutions administered by Narkompros (the History and Philosophy Institute, the Moscow Oblast Institute, and the Bubnov Institute) are infested with alien and anti-Soviet elements and that their activity has increased greatly since the murder of Comrade Kirov. Dozens of students in the classes and in the dormitories of these institutes have carried on counterrevolutionary conversations ranging from an open defense of bourgeois theories to direct threats against Comrade STALIN. At the History and Philosophy Institute 50 percent of the students in the literature department did not participate in Comrade Kirov's funeral. In this department an anti-Soviet group consisting of twelve persons was formed at the end of October 1934 by a first-year student and Trotskyist named Tager and a non–party member named Rudiakova. The group gathered several times as if for a party at the apartment of Rudiakova and of someone named Nikulina. In the Bubnov Pedagogical Institute after the murder of Comrade Kirov some twenty students with an anti-Soviet orientation were exposed. The reasons that such a political situation exists at the institutes are (1) infestation of the institutes due to admissions practices, (2) the presence of antiparty and anti-Soviet elements among members of the institutes' faculty, and (3) the absence of Bolshevik vigilance on the part of the institutes' party organizations and weak mass-party work.

## II. Admissions practices

. . . In the Bubnov Institute the admissions committee managed to consider 2,500 applications in ten days. No wonder then that the majority of students turned out to be children of disenfranchised persons and counterrevolutionaries, while those who were workers and the children of workers constituted as little as 27.4 percent. Komsomol member Zaks, the son of a rich merchant who was disenfranchised, managed to stay until his last year of graduate work. Party member Inozemtsev and Komsomol member Abakumov studied in the institute for several years before it was revealed that they were sons of disenfranchised persons. Ex-Komsomol organizer Shemelina was found to be the daughter of a White Guard officer. The nonparty student Vagner was found to be the son of a rich merchant who had been deprived of his voting rights, etc.

## Document 50 *continued*

A timely purge of alien and anti-Soviet elements from the institutes was not conducted, due to weak party committee work and to infestation of the institutes' administration by antiparty Trotskyist elements.

### III. Alien and anti-Soviet elements on the institutes' faculty

The History and Philosophy Institute was headed by former "Bundist" and Trotskyist [A. G.] Prigozhin, who had been an influential participant in an illegal counterrevolutionary Trotskyist organization until 1927. A double-dealer, he repudiated Trotskyism in the books he wrote, yet later, in his lectures, defended his Trotskyist views. When he came to the institute, he concealed from the institute's party organization his former struggle against the party and thereby succeeded in becoming a member of the raion council. As the institute's director he continued to pursue the Trotskyist line, transforming the institute into a mecca for Trotskyist faculty (twenty-five in number) and of bourgeois specialists (eleven). These included Sten, a representative of the right-left bloc; Torbin, a Trotskyist expelled from the party who introduced Trotskyism into his teaching; Burtsev, assistant professor of political economy and formerly a very active Trotskyist; [A. F.] Ryndich, instructor of the history of the peoples of the USSR, and [M. B.] Goldenberg, instructor of Leninism, both ex-Trotskyists; [N. V.] Novikov, professor of dialectical materialism, an ex-Menshevik who sneaked idealist views into his teaching; Grishin, professor of Leninism, an ex-Bundist, who on 7 January of this year at the Higher School of Communist Police [Komvuz militsii] passed counterrevolutionary Trotskyist directives with regard to a Zinovievist counterrevolutionary group; [Ya. S.] Feigelson, expelled from the party in 1927 for belonging to a Zinovievist group; [S. V.] Gingor, ex-Trotskyist, exiled in 1929; [G. F.] Dakhshleger, a prominent ex-Menshevik recently fired for fascist, anti-Soviet attacks; Professor [D. P.] Kanchalovsky [*sic*], who in his classes drew an analogy between slavery in ancient Greece and the economy of the Soviet Union; [S. V.] Bakhrushin and [Yu. V.] Got'e, professors of ancient history from former merchant families at one time exiled from Moscow; [P. G.] Liubomirov, an ex-SR; [N. P.] Gratsiansky, at one time purged from VSNKh's staff; [V. F.] Asmus and Dynnik, ex-Menshevik sympathizers and idealists; Rubin, who was connected with the anti-Soviet group in the Literature Department; [B. I.] Gorev, who from 1907 to 1920 had been an active member of the Menshevik Liquidator faction; [V. V.] Yegorov, recently fired for teaching contraband Trotskyist views; Iskrinsky, the son of a priest who graduated from the Moscow Theological Academy; and so forth.[7] All these faculty members worked unmonitored by the office of academic affairs and their departments and could day after day freely exert their corrupting influence on the backward part of the heterogeneous student body, stirring up anti-Soviet sentiments.

Trying to make a "name" for himself, Prigozhin announced at a general student assembly that "instructors ought to give the students facts, and we'll deal with questions of methodology on our own." He approved programs which, instead of the vulgar sociology of past years, were full of fresh new bourgeois empiricism and positivism. Interpreting TsK VKP(b)'s resolution about the teaching of the historical sciences to be a repudiation of Marxist-Leninist methodology, Prigozhin legalized the counterrevolutionary bourgeois teaching of history, particularly in the literature department, where the teaching of ancient and medieval history and the history of ancient and medieval literature and art is the monopoly of old nonparty professors, who in fact pursue bourgeois political directives, skillfully disguising them with "witticisms" and an "objective" exposition of the subject matter.[8]

Thanks to such completely unmonitored work by the old professoriat and their young "pupils," like nobleman-clerk Mikhalchi, our young literature department students have received an erroneous orientation, one essentially alien to us.

If one takes into account the unacceptably weak social composition of the literature department, the absence there of party and Komsomol mass propaganda, and the presence of faculty alien to us, then it is not surprising that it was namely this faculty where the Trotskyist-Zinovievist group built its counterrevolutionary nest.

Prigozhin's policies thus meant that a department in a Soviet ideological higher educational institution was handed over to a large group of enemies of our party and of Soviet power.

Preparation of new teaching and research cadres is not ensured by the way graduate study is organized. Out of 132 graduate students, only 28 are children of workers, and among the others are offspring of priests and gentry.

In the literature department only 1 of 29 graduate students is a Communist. There are no study plans (except individual ones), no programs, no faculty assigned to answer for the work of graduate students, nor any monitoring on the part of the administration. As a result there are instances in which graduate stipends are received from two institutes, and eternal student types who have already graduated from as many as three institutes (Streletsky). Unmasked Trotskyists (Nazarov, Leibman, Krepsky, Ziubin, and others) have continued graduate study while Communists have left. The associate dean who was fired for Trotskyist views is still a graduate student. In the absence of defined courses, the faculty's work with graduate students is reduced to individual consultations and the grading of papers. Each faculty member conducts this work in any way he wishes. [A discussion follows of Trotskyist and bourgeois theories propagated at the Moscow Oblast Pedagogical Institute and the Bubnov Institute and sections on the "Political Blindness of Party Organizations in the Institutes" and "The Shortcomings of Narkompros' Leadership."]

## Document 50 *continued*

In view of our inspection it is perfectly obvious that a series of measures must be taken without delay.

These measures should be aimed at

1. fundamentally changing the way in which admissions committees in higher educational institutions do their work;
2. carefully verifying faculty invited to teach, especially in the social and economic sciences;
3. organizing party propaganda and ideological education among students;
4. reviewing and strengthening leading cadres in pedagogical institutes;
5. making accountable a number of officials both at the pedagogical institutes and at Narkompros.

Chairman of the Subcommittee on Education and Public Health, Shokhin
Chief Controller
(Volunteer)
23 March 1935

---

As a result of such inspections and memoranda, there began mass expulsions of faculty and specialists from higher educational institutions and scientific research institutes. Dismissed were all those whose "explanation gave evidence" that they had a "non-Bolshevik past" or "denigrating ties." The campaign swept away an ever larger number of people, causing significant damage to the development of various branches of science and higher education. This tougher political control spread to all spheres of public life. Inspections like those described above occurred in publishing in particular, and in connection with them, the attention of party organizations was focused on the cadres of Glavlit, the main organ of censorship.

---

## Document 51

Memorandum to Orgburo "Concerning the Work of Glavlit," 2 January 1936. RGASPI, f. 17, op. 114, d. 731, ll. 72–77. Typed original.

To the Organization Bureau [Orgburo] of TsK VKP(b)
Concerning the Work of Glavlit
Printed works published in this country are reviewed twice by the organs

of censorship. There is the so-called preliminary censorship carried out by authorized representatives of Glavlit who work in actual publishing houses, and the final censorship carried out by the central staff of Glavlit. (Daily newspapers are an exception: here the censorship review of the authorized Glavlit agent attached to each newspaper is final.)

An inspection of the work of Glavlit's central staff shows that the state of censorship in the country is totally unsatisfactory.

Glavlit's central staff carries out the final censorship of books coming to it that have been reviewed by Glavlit's agents working in publishing houses proper and at newspapers and krai (and oblast) censorship bureaus. Therefore, one can judge by the work of Glavlit's central staff the results and quality of the work of its agents in publishing houses and in organizations peripheral to Glavlit who carry out the preliminary censorship.

Glavlit's staff is made up of four basic sections: the political and economic section, the artistic literature section, the agriculture section, and the regional inspection section. Supervision of the work done by preliminary censors is also a function of these sections. How does the central staff of Glavlit fulfill the tasks assigned to it?

The political and economic section carries out final censoring for thirty-two publishing houses, ranging from Sotsekgiz (State Economics Publishing House) to Medgiz (State Medical Publishing House) that publishes the Medical Encyclopedia, publications of the Central Committee of Esperantists, and so forth. Four people work in the section; none is an economist. Neither the number of section staff nor their training guarantees competent review of material for publication. Therefore, the vast majority of material received is simply not examined but goes into the "overflow" pile. (In the political and economic section the "overflow" pile reaches 70 to 75 percent of material received.) Nonetheless, even with so insignificant a percent of books being reviewed by the section, during 1935 thirty books were held up that had been passed by the preliminary censoring, whereas during this same time period only twenty-five books were held up by the preliminary censor.

This indicates the extraordinary weakness of the preliminary censorship and the careless attitude toward work by its staff.

Until very recently someone named Less worked as a political editor in the political and economic section. Less was expelled from the party after his party documents were checked for his tie with Trotskyists. The section head, Comrade Kazansky (fired by order of the Orgburo), did not organize the work of the section itself nor that of supervising the preliminary censorship. Kazansky indulged the self-seeking, antiparty activities of Glavlit's authorized agent at the State Financial Publishing House, Zaretsky, who has been exposed by the Party Control Commission. The section passed Mezier's bibliographical dictionary, which recommends Trotskyist literature.

The agriculture section reviews all literature related to agriculture. Four persons work in the section: three have a smattering of knowledge about agriculture, one is a graduate of the History and Philosophy Institute. Serious reviews are not provided by this inadequately equipped section. Suffice it to say that there is not a single specialist in issues of animal husbandry in the section. "Overflow" in this section reaches 60 to 65 percent. "By and large" the majority of literature concerned with the most pressing agricultural issues is reviewed. Nonetheless, the section holds up a large number of books: 116 for 1935.

The artistic literature section: of the four staff, only the section chief, Comrade Spassky, is a graduate of the Institute of Red Professors. The other staff members lack special training. Authorized agents at the main literary publishing houses also are not trained to analyze fiction.

The regional inspection section. This section reviews all material published in krais and oblasts, everything from social and political literature to veterinarian, medical, etc., literature. Naturally, it would seem that the people working in this section (five persons among whom the responsibilities are divided on a territorial basis: each political editor has a group of krais) possess some kind of universal knowledge enabling them to review all the heterogeneous material for which they are responsible. Inasmuch as this is not and cannot be the case, final censorship is reduced to a cursory review and disclosure of only the crudest blunders, of which there are many in books of the local krai publishing houses. Yet even with this poor work organization the regional inspection in 1935 held up and withdrew seventy-nine titles, eighteen of which were in languages of the national republics.

Until quite recently the deputy chief of the regional inspection section was Orlov, who was expelled from the party after his documents were checked, and who turned out to be not Orlov but Olshevsky, the son of a now-exiled tsarist police officer who had been an officer in the tsarist army. Olshevsky maintained ties with his brother, a White Guardist who had illegally returned to the USSR.

As a result of poor work by Glavlit agents at publishing houses, the state has suffered large material losses, and the book trade has been choked with low-quality literature. In twelve central book publishing firms for eleven months in 1935 as a result of final censorship, sixty-nine titles were withdrawn and sent to be pulped at a cost to the state of 413,510 rubles. Held back for revisions were eighty-five titles costing 148,300 rubles.

As one can see from the survey of Glavlit sections' work cited above, it is by no means evident that the composition of the central staff's employees is optimal, but what is evident is that the authorized agents doing the preliminary censoring are very ineffective and do not work well.

This makes it all the more necessary for Glavlit's central staff to concern itself not merely with catching the preliminary censorship's mistakes—a sluggish business, which costs the state large sums—but with organizing and strengthening the work of the preliminary censorship and with the selection of cadres for the latter, because the present cadres are extremely tainted and almost all hold down more than one job. Now until very recently Glavlit has not concerned itself with this work. Those working for the preliminary censorship, that is, authorized agents and political editors affiliated with publishing houses, newspapers, and in peripheral organizations, not only were never duly verified but were not even registered. Only now is registration of them beginning to be organized, and what immediately came to light was the fact that forty-six out of the eighty-eight Moscow preliminary censorship staff for whom there are personal files have received party and administrative reprimands (sometimes several) for grave political errors.

At the "Academy" publishing house, Glavlit's authorized agent is Rubanovsky, who has received several party reprimands for Trotskyist errors and sympathy with the opposition's views. (He worked in the publishing house while Kamenev was there and continues to work there even now.) Glavlit's authorized agent at the Children's Literature Publishing House [Detgiz], Gorodetskaia, has received a severe reprimand and warning for permitting disclosure of a military secret. During a check of her party documents, her party card was withheld.

Many political editors assigned to the leading newspapers are not sufficiently discerning in a political sense. They have a poor understanding of what they are supposed to do and often have a careless attitude toward their work. Because of this, a lack of uniform standards is quite often observed in the instructions given by political editors of various newspapers (one political editor passes what another prohibits); there is a huge number of anecdotal instances of very innocent things being prohibited, while strictly confidential information continues to find its way into newspapers.

The thriving practice of holding down a second position by virtually every preliminary censorship staff member is totally unacceptable. Out of 126 preliminary censorship employees in Moscow, 76 have a second position. At the same time, in publishing houses of technical literature, 35 out of 42 authorized agents or political editors have a second job, and the same holds true for 25 of the 34 staff members in military censorship.

If the state of censorship at the center of the country is clearly unsatisfactory, then in the provinces, and especially in the raions, it is utterly catastrophic. With the exception of Leningrad, Sverdlovsk, Smolensk, Gorky, and Rostov, Glavlit has no real control over what is published. Almost everywhere in the raions control over the newspapers is entrusted as a tag-on job to the chairman of the raion ONO, the military commissariat, or the raion party committee staff. Out of 3,250 authorized raion agents in the RSFSR, Ukraine, Belorussia, Transcaucasia, Uzbekistan, Turkmenistan, and Tadzhikistan only 297 work full-time.

In most instances oblast committees, krai committees, and the TsKs of the party's nationalities committees underestimate the work of censorship, do

## Document 51 *continued*

not assign it staff, or assign it people who have made reprehensible errors and by and large are not qualified to do any kind of work.

The existing system of remuneration for political editors' service in the preliminary censorship is a sore spot in the work of Glavlit because political editors receive their salary not from Glavlit itself but from the publishing houses in which they work. This system not only leads to a lack of uniform standards of remuneration for work done but also makes the political editors dependent on the publishing houses and, at the same time, gives rise to corrupt practices on the part of censorship staff, to fraud, and to botched work. Zaretsky, the Glavlit agent in the State Financial Publishing House, is a good example: he was getting paid a total of some three thousand rubles a month and was unmasked by KPK. Akselrod, the agent at the Foreign Workers' Publishing House, earned five thousand to six thousand rubles a month.

The existing system of remuneration for this work has to be stopped at once. This was clearly demonstrated by the investigation KPK conducted in connection with the Zaretsky affair.

Thus, in its present state, censorship lags severely in the tasks assigned to the publishing sector by the party.

Director of the TsK's Department of the Press and Publishing Houses
B. Tal
Deputy Chairman of KPK, TsK VKP(b)
2 January 1936

---

A memorandum revealing that Tal himself could not escape responsibility for Trotskyist infiltration was produced by his successor as director of TsK's Department of the Press and Publishing Houses. It "untwists" the story of publishing a political dictionary for workers and collective farm members, a dictionary that was supposed to be an important tool of mass political education.

---

## Document 52

Memorandum from L. Mekhlis to TsK secretaries "Concerning the Political Dictionary for Workers and Collective Farm Members," 28 December 1937. RGASPI, f. 17, op. 11, d. 833, ll. 115–117. Verified typed copy.

---

To the Secretaries of TsK VKP(b), Comrades Stalin, Kaganovich, Andreev, Zhdanov, and Yezhov

Concerning the Political Dictionary for Workers and Collective Farm Members

## Document 52 *continued*

On 10 May 1935, TsK VKP(b) passed a resolution about publishing a political dictionary intended for workers and collective farm members. Tal, Knorin, and Kh. N. Kantor were appointed as its editorial board.

Even before the TsK VKP(b) resolution, Tomsky and his associated Trotskyist spies did "a good deal of work" on this dictionary. Of the sixteen section editors both Tal and Knorin enlisted, chose, and presented to TsK VKP(b) for approval, the overwhelming majority were Trotskyist spies. Many other persons who in the process of work were enlisted as editors or senior staff members also turned out to be enemies.

The editors of the following sections were arrested:

Butkevich, editor of the military section;

Gorin, editor of the history section;

Fainberg, editor of the Komsomol section;

Smoliansky, editor of the Comintern section;

Tivel, editor of the international section;

Ioelson, editor of the world economics section;

Gurevich, editor of the agricultural section;

Berman, editor of the Soviet construction and law section;

Tulepov, editor of the Soviet nationalities section;

Kozlov, editor of the general history section.

The following section editors were expelled from the party:

Dinamov, from literature;

Kostko, from Leninism;

Zenkevich, from the general section.

The writing staff was also infested with enemies of the people: Tankhilevich and Tumanian (both arrested), who wrote entries about topics in party history; Frolov and Vanag (both arrested), who wrote on topics in the history of the USSR; Gurevich and Iosifov (both arrested), who wrote on topics in agriculture.

On the editorial staff of the dictionary two technical staff members were left, both non–party members. The rest, politically discredited, have been dismissed.

This hostile editorial staff recommended counterrevolutionary, anti-Marxist entries and deliberately delayed publication of the dictionary. In the entry "Organized Capitalism," for example, a detailed account is given of this counterrevolutionary theory, and it is also contended that the theory failed only "as a consequence of the crash brought about by the world economic crisis and as the result of fascist rule in 'democratic' Germany and other capitalistic countries." The words *Counterintelligence* and *Gestapo* are used as if they function solely within the borders of their own countries; not a word is said about their subversive anti-Soviet activities. There are counterrevolutionary concoctions in other entries written for the dictionary. An associate of

## Document 52 *continued*

Tal, the bourgeois nationalist and spy Tulepov, who edited the nationalities section, did not include in the subject matter of the dictionary such topics as "Nationalism" and "Bourgeois Nationalism."

During three years of work, 450,000 rubles were expended on preparing the dictionary. The material prepared will have to undergo serious alteration; much will have to be written all over again. The list of terms needs to be gone over and supplemented with new items resulting from the Stalin Constitution, election campaigns for the Supreme Soviet of the USSR, from changes in the international and domestic situation, resolutions of the Seventh Congress of the Comintern, and events in Spain and China.

The Department of the Press and Publishing Houses of TsK VKP(b) considers it necessary to

1. Entrust leadership of all work pertaining to the publication of the political dictionary to the Department of Party Propaganda and Agitation;
2. Approve a new editorial board for the dictionary, consisting of N. L. Rubinshtein, V. P. Potemkin, and Klimov (Kh. N. Kantor);
3. Approve sections editors in accordance with the enclosed list;
4. Oblige the Department of Party Propaganda and Agitation and the new editorial board to finish all the work of publishing the dictionary within a three-month period.

Director of the Department of the Press and Publishing Houses of TsK VKP(b)
L. Mekhlis
28 December 1937

---

Obviously the accusations brought against the compilers of the dictionary are ridiculous. No anti-Marxist ideas, much less counterrevolutionary ones, were to be found there. Nonetheless, work on the dictionary was enough to warrant ideological scolding, if not expulsion from the party and arrest. By this time not even those who had rendered services to the revolutionary movement and subsequently were among the outstanding organizers of the industrial leap forward were immune from arrest. For example, there are two denunciation letters in the personal file of A. D. Bruskin, who in the 1930s quickly worked his way up from mere engineer to people's commissar of machine construction. The first was written by someone named S. A. Drakin from the city of Grozny:

# Document 53

Letter of denunciation from S. A. Drakin to TsK, 18 August 1936. RGASPI, f. 17, op. 100, d. 39599. l. 9. Original letter.

How are you, Ivan Alekseevich? I send you greetings from the North Caucasus and congratulate you on your recovery.

I write as a senior comrade wanting to share the following with you:

Having learned from the press how the Trotskyist-Zinovievist gang continues its counterrevolutionary work proceeding now to terror, making attempts on the lives of our leaders, organizing counterrevolutionary groups. [The sentence is grammatically incomplete in the original—*Trans.*] The press speaks about the unmasking of a counterrevolutionary group at the Khar'kov locomotive works, where participation in and complicity of members of the party has been brought to light. That has compelled me to write you and to cite an example of protection of a Menshevik and a Trotskyist on the part of party member Comrade Aleksandr Davidovich Bruskin, appointed deputy people's commissar of heavy industry from 8 July 36. His protection of these individuals consisted of the following:

Bruskin, after graduating from the Khar'kov Technological Institute, worked at the Khar'kov locomotive works together with his institute comrades Efros, who has been expelled from the party for being a Menshevik, and Dusavitsky, who was expelled from the party for being an ardent Trotskyist. When Comrade Bruskin was transferred to the Khar'kov tractor plant, Efros and Dusavitsky also transferred there to work, and this protection expressed itself even more obviously in the following example: after Comrade Kirov was killed by the Trotskyist Nikolaev, Trotskyist Dusavitsky transferred from the Khar'kov tractor plant to the Cheliabinsk tractor plant, where Comrade Bruskin at the time was director, though Comrade Bruskin was well aware that Dusavitsky was a Trotskyist. Perhaps I am mistaken about something or other, Ivan Alekseevich, but I wanted so badly to share my thoughts with a senior comrade since at the current moment one needs to be more sensitive and vigilant.

Respectfully with comradely and Communist greetings,

S. Drakin

Ivan Alekseevich, you must be surprised when you see who has written you this letter. I think you'll recall me. When you were chairman of the Provincial Department of Miners in Artemovsk and later chairman of the VUK [*Vseukrainskii komitet,* all-Ukrainian committee] of miners, I was the representative of the students of the mining departments in the city of Khar'kov, because at the time I was studying at the Khar'kov Technological Institute. I had often to discuss certain questions with you concerning student matters, and that's why I decided to approach you now. I await your response.

More than a year later another letter came to TsK VKP(b) from A. B. Krikunchik. In both instances it is worth noting the telling surnames of the writers, suggesting that they may have been invented people. Drakin derives from the Russian word *draka,* "fight, scuffle," Krikunchik from *krikun,* "shouter, babbler." An excerpt from the second letter follows:

---

## Document 54

Letter of denunciation from A. B. Krikunchik to TsK, 9 November 1937. RGASPI, f. 17, op. 100, d. 39599, l. 11. Original letter.

---

Doubtless when making appointments to the higher state posts, the Central Committee of the VKP(b) verifies comrades in the most thorough manner possible and the committee is aware of all their past political activity down to the smallest detail. The remarks of Comrade Akaev while proposing the people's commissar of machine construction, Aleksandr Davidovich Bruskin, as a candidate for election as a deputy of the Supreme Soviet published in issue N255 of the newspaper *Izvestia* for 1 November of this year force one to doubt that the TsK VKP(b) is aware of everything about A. D. Bruskin's political past. This circumstance has prompted me to send the TsK the present declaration.

Comrade Akaev's remarks are reported in the following way by the newspaper *Izvestia:*

"I am proposing as a candidate for election as a deputy of the Supreme Soviet People's Commissar of Machine Construction Aleksandr Davidovich Bruskin, who has shown himself to be a staunch Bolshevik. In the revolutionary underground he actively fought for the Leninist-Stalinist cause. He participated in the liberation of Ukraine from Denikin's bands." In fact, in 1920 A. D. Bruskin was still an active Menshevik. He was a member of the Khar'kov City Committee of Mensheviks. In September or October 1920 he was arrested in Khar'kov by the Cheka for being a Menshevik. And only in November or December 1920 did he submit a request to the party organization of the Khar'kov Technological Institute to become a member of VKP(b), and he was made a VKP(b) member without going through the candidate probationary period.

I remember the facts I have cited because I attended that meeting of the technological institute's party organization, very small at that time, at which the matter of accepting A. D. Bruskin as a VKP(b) member was decided.

---

On the basis of these two signals in the TsK VKP(b)'s records section for leading cadres, Bruskin was interviewed and information about him sent to G. M. Malenkov, director of the TsK's Department of Leading Party Organs.

---

## Document 55

From TsK investigation of A. D. Bruskin, 1937. RGASPI, f. 17, op. 100, d. 39599, l. 10. Typed original.

---

Regarding the substance of the declaration received concerning A. D. Bruskin, from a review of materials from the master file of party personnel it has been ascertained that Bruskin did not conceal his membership in the Menshevik Party. This information is consistent in all the documents.

Bruskin joined the Menshevik Party after the February Revolution and was a member until December 1920. In December 1920, as a student at the Khar'kov Technological Institute, he joined the Bolshevik Party. He was made a member without going through the candidate probationary period. His acceptance into the party upon leaving another party was approved by the TsKK(b) of Ukraine. As he indicates in his autobiographical statement, while a Menshevik (in N. N. Popov's group), A. D. Bruskin volunteered to go to the front to fight Denikin. He was in the 3d Lugansk International Regiment as a Red Army soldier from March 1919 until August 1919. After that he remained in White territory and from September 1919 until October 1919 worked as an inspector in a Khar'kov student cooperative society. In October he was arrested by Denikin's counter-intelligence (at that time he was still a Menshevik) and was incarcerated for one month. After prison, from December 1919 until May 1920, he worked as a technician for the Ukrainian Economic Council before entering the Technological Institute—and it was there that he joined the Bolsheviks.

Whether Comrade Bruskin was a member of the Khar'kov City Committee of Mensheviks could not be established because in his personal file there are no pertinent documents, and he does not write about this in his autobiographical statement. There is nothing indicated as well in the registration form for changing party documents.

Regarding his arrest by the Cheka in 1920 for being a Menshevik, there is also no information. He himself states that he was arrested by Denikin's secret police (in October–November 1919, and not in September 1919 as is written in the declaration).

As for the matter in question, on 29 September 1936 Comrade Shkiriatov called in Bruskin and established that he had worked with the individuals named in the declaration, that he had even invited Efros to work with him, and that Efros had Dusavitsky in tow. In conversation with Comrade Shkiriatov, Comrade Bruskin maintained that at the Cheliabinsk tractor plant he did not work with the individuals named.

Somewhat later Bruskin was arrested. It is impossible to conclude that the investigation resulting from the letters' denunciations was the real reason for this, but that they were used as incriminating material cannot be doubted. This is how the slaughter of cadres was prepared during the period of the Yezhovshchina, and it was prepared to a great degree by the cadres themselves.

The losses that the mass repressions inflicted on the cadres were of course substantial, but they were compensated for by the avalanche of new administrators and specialists striving to make a career for themselves. The *Short Course of the History of the All-Union Communist Party (Bolsheviks)* published in 1938 states that during the years of the Second Five-Year Plan the party succeeded in implementing Stalin's slogan "Cadres Decide Everything!"

# CHAPTER THREE

# Stalin's Constitution

THE DISCUSSION AND ADOPTION of a new Soviet Constitution was one of the most important public events of the 1930s. Arguments about the document continue unabated to this day, reflecting not only its own complexity but the complicated and contradictory nature of those times. Graced from the moment of its birth with Stalin's name and called "the most democratic in the world," the constitution was designed to consolidate the principles of the new socialist state and social system and to give socialism an attractive image for the working people of the USSR and the whole world.

Less than thirteen years separated this version from the first federal constitution of the USSR, issued shortly after Lenin's death in January 1924. At the core of the earlier document had been its provisions for a unified governmental structure that nonetheless preserved forms of ethno-territorial representation. Class was an important component as well. While workers, peasants, and the (loyal) intelligentsia were guaranteed the full plenitude of rights accorded by the constitution, former exploiters, kulaks, officials of the tsarist regime, and the clergy were denied the franchise and the right to hold elective office. The constitution of 1936 was less discriminatory. Reflecting the new "correlation of class forces in the

USSR"—that is, the elimination of landlords, kulaks and capitalists in the intervening period—it proclaimed a system of universal secret-ballot suffrage, albeit under the aegis of the Communist Party, "the leading core of all organizations of the working people, both public and state."[1]

The new "basic law" of the land also reflected changes in official thinking about the role of law in a socialist society. Reversing the trend toward "legal nihilism" that was much in evidence during the First Five-Year Plan, the government's edict "On Revolutionary Legality," issued on 25 June 1932, swung Soviet jurisprudence decisively toward statutory stability, formality, and correspondingly the professionalization of jurists. The main spokesman for the new approach was A. Ya. Vyshinsky, whose appointment as procurator general of the USSR in 1935 symbolized the ascendance of that philosophy. Taking his cue from Stalin's assertion that "the withering away of the state will come not through a weakening of state authority but through its maximum intensification," Vyshinsky worked tirelessly to make law the cornerstone of the burgeoning bureaucratic apparatus. He clashed repeatedly with the commissar of justice, N. V. Krylenko, over what Krylenko considered excessive borrowing of forms and norms from bourgeois legal systems. Vyshinsky engaged in bureaucratic turf battles with both Krylenko's commissariat and the NKVD.[2]

The Constitutional Commission, formed at the Seventh All-Union Congress of Soviets in February 1935 and headed by Stalin, comprised thirty-one members, including both Vyshinsky and Krylenko. Twelve subcommissions were also established, focusing on economic, financial, legal, and other issues and consisting mainly of specialists in those fields. After a year's work, a new draft of the constitution was ready, and by decision of a Plenum of the TsK VKP(b) and the Presidium of the TsIK, was submitted for a nationwide debate, which lasted five months. On 5 December 1936, the Eighth Extraordinary Congress of Soviets unanimously adopted the new basic law.

The constitution epitomized the new Soviet legal thinking. As one Western scholar has noted, it provided for "a strong and stable criminal law for the protection of public property, and a predictable and differentiated civil law for the protection of the . . . right of 'personal property.'"[3] Beyond this, the emphasis on stability and predictability was entirely consistent with a whole series of measures adopted by the regime in 1934 and 1935. These included reconciliation with former oppositionists at the Seventeenth Party Congress, the issuing of a kolkhoz statute, the convocation of a Writers' Union congress and its preaching of literary toleration, and the rejection of the Comintern's "class-against-class" strategy in favor of the more ecumenical antifascist popular-frontism. Together, they constituted a strategy of political moderation that distinguishes the mid-1930s from both earlier and later in the decade.

But other factors were involved as well. The desire to add luster to the triumph of statism—or, as Stalin characterized it, the achievement of socialism—seems obvious. No less so was the need to forge a common bond with the "bourgeois democracies" via this classically bourgeois institution, as the Soviet Union pursued a policy of collective security against fascist aggression. Finally, as was the case with so much else in Stalinist political culture, the constitution gave the appearance of stability, order, and respect for human rights that redounded onto all of Soviet law.[4]

The invitation for people to speak out on the most urgent problems of concern to society—to say openly what was on their minds and send in their proposals, letters, and comments—conjured up an illusion of democracy. Even the draft itself gave grounds for optimism, for it promised universal suffrage, equality among all categories of the population, freedom of expression, of the press, and of assembly, and the elimination of all previous restrictions of "the dictatorship of the proletariat." Many believed that the articles of the new constitution embodied the essential features of socialism, which now merely had to be "strengthened." The proclamation that kolkhoz farmers and independent peasants were USSR citizens with equal rights could be viewed as an oblique acknowledgment by the authorities of the injustice of collectivization with a logical corollary that people could leave a kolkhoz and recover the property that had been taken from them. The proclaimed freedom of conscience seemed to signify a condemnation of past persecutions of religious believers and a renunciation of militant atheism. The Bolsheviks' turnaround from war communism to NEP was still fresh in people's memories. Maybe something similar was about to occur again now?

Discussion of the draft constitution gradually developed into one of the regular campaigns that were so characteristic of the Soviet period. Rallies by working people and expressions of unanimous support and approval were trumpeted at full volume by the press, which reported the triumphal progress of "the great historical document" throughout the country. The leadership tried to use the new constitution to incite a new wave of public enthusiasm and give a second wind to the Stakhanovite movement, which seemed to personify the new system's creative potentialities. It had to be shown that the advance of socialism was marked by unparalleled feats of labor, brilliant records and achievements by Soviet people. Here are a few snippets from the reports that moved through all the news media: "Sayenko, master driller first class at the Dzerzhinsky Mine, . . . has fulfilled thirty-two monthly norms and earned about twelve thousand rubles since the beginning of the year." "More than one hundred Stakhanovite brigades, named for the Eighth Congress of the Soviets, are working in Leningrad." "The Stakhanovites' wages have risen accordingly; for example, the wages of the Stakhanovite Koval'chuk at the Lenin plant are 996 rubles a month, Vdovenko 1,024 rubles." Such reports cultivated an illusion of unanimous approval of the draft.

Information about doubters and malcontents—the "bad apples in the barrel"—was meted out only in small doses. At the same time other analytical material was laid on the desks of Stalin and his bureaucracy that bore little similarity to the ideologized pap to which Soviet newspapers and magazines treated readers, and it attested to an extremely wide range of opinions, lines of reasoning, and events related to the adoption of the constitution. This is precisely the import of many of the documents included in this chapter.

The nationwide discussion of the draft constitution, of course, was tightly controlled from above. Detailed information about attitudes in society was provided in the form of summaries by the NKVD and surveys of letters, comments and proposals sent to the country's leaders, primarily Stalin himself, as well as to institutions and organizations. For purposes of publishing material in the press, special attention was paid to "fine-tuning" and furnishing a "correct assessment" of the facts that were being reported. The censors vigilantly tried to prevent anything inappropriate from appearing not only in central newspapers but also in local newspapers and even large factory newspapers. A report on the Moscow press in 1936–37 noted that "large-circulation newspapers committed serious errors and distortions during the preparation and discussion of the 1936 USSR Constitution and the Supreme Soviet elections," and as a result up to thirty issues of newspapers were held up and reprinted.[5]

Of course, the fate of the document that had been prepared inside the bureaucracy was predetermined before its nationwide discussion began. To be precise, the decision of the Plenum of the TsK VKP(b) in the summer of 1936 "to approve in the main the draft of the constitution" meant in the vernacular of the time that no more substantive revisions could be made to its text. Nevertheless, if Stalin said "nationwide debate," then it would be debated nationwide. While opening the gates slightly for a mass expression of people's opinions, the authorities had to ensure mass participation in the campaign and simultaneously channel the popular will in the needed direction—not an easy task. The scope of the campaign was unprecedented. Probably no adopted constitution had ever left in its wake such a vast trail of documents, which lie in the archives to this day.

The figures on the participants in the discussion of the draft are mind-boggling. According to official data, 623,334 meetings were held around the country; they were attended by 42,372,990 people, who produced 169,739 proposals, comments, and prospective amendments.[6] But such precise statistics can only bring a skeptical smile to a specialist analyzing mass events. The numbers are obviously inflated, though not quite to the same extent as can be found in later Soviet literature.[7] The campaign's organizers themselves resisted the temptation to claim that every individual participated in debating the constitution, even though endless summaries came in from localities describing its success and unprecedented public involvement. For example, it was reported from Moldavia that "the discussion involved 70.5 percent of voters"; from Dnepropetrovsk Oblast, "public involvement ranges from 76 to 100 percent"; from Voronezh Oblast, "meetings of working people . . . have been attended by 1,130,000 people, or

71 percent of voters"; from Khar'kov Oblast, "19,166 meetings have taken place, and they have been attended by 2,002,304 people, or 83 percent of working people"; and from Stalingrad, "80 percent of the working people . . . have visited meetings to discuss the draft Constitution." It was noted, in addition, that "in Odessa mass debates of the draft constitution were held outside in parks, . . . the January Uprising Plant conducted eighteen outings for workers to the countryside, where the draft constitution was debated." As we see, there was an effort to create an informal atmosphere, to combine "work with pleasure" and to attract people with fresh air and recreation. Besides general meetings, events were held for the purpose of conducting a more detailed study of specific sections and articles of the draft. In ethnic areas, the draft constitution was debated in the indigenous languages. In Cherkessia, the summaries said, the discussion proceeded "in the Cherkess, Abazin, and Nogai languages, and at village soviets populated by ethnic minorities, in the language of the respective ethnic group. At four Mordvinian village soviets in Pil'na Raion of Gor'ky Krai, the discussion was conducted in the native language. We should take note of the great amount of work that has been done in Blagoevo Raion of Odessa Oblast, for the discussion and study of the draft constitution in Bulgarian. . . . In addition to meetings, discussions, and readings in a number of places . . . there have been radio link-ups, special lectures on the radio, etc." The reports mentioned the huge number of speakers and of people who submitted suggestions and the active participation by deputies of soviets, members of deputies' groups and special-assistance groups.[8] The same references are made in the reports on the conduct of the campaign in localities which can be found in the archive of TsIK's Presidium.[9]

These reports may leave the impression not only that the public was extremely active but that it did in-depth work on the articles of the constitution. In this regard eyewitness testimony describing how these mass events often proceeded is of interest. The picture painted here is far from glowing. This is evident, for example, from a letter written to *Krest'ianskaia Gazeta* in July 1936 by a man named Ivan Vasil'ev, which smacks more of a humorous short story:

# Document 56

Letter from I. Vasil'ev to *Krest'ianskaia Gazeta* on discussion of the constitution, July 1936. RGASPI, f. 17, op. 120, d. 232, ll. 77–78. Typewritten copy.

"The Ghost That Is Not Coming Back"

A film drama by that title was to be shown on 5 July of this year in the Park of Culture and Recreation at Prokhladnaia Station in Primalkinsky Raion, Kabardino-Balkarian Autonomous Oblast.

Well, the raion leaders decided to use this movie to work on the Constitution. They began to assemble people at about 4 P.M. Some organizations arrived in an organized manner, in formation and singing songs. They were taken to the summer theater, and the order from above was not to let anyone leave the hall, yet by about 8 P.M. it had emptied out. What should they do? The decision was, when the people come in for the movie, we'll do some work with them. After two bells the people took their seats based on their tickets. The theater was full, the presidium was assembled and exultant, but the audience was perplexed at seeing a table draped in red and the raion leaders on the stage instead of a screen. The secretary of the VKP(b) RK was Comrade Kashkozhev; the chairman of the RIK was Comrade Biriun, and his deputy, Comrade Opal'ko [was also present].

After the third bell, instead of the movie, Comrade Kashkozhev made introductory remarks, basically saying, we're going to work on Stalin's Constitution. One person in the audience dared to point out that people don't pay money to work. Comrade Kashkozhev shot back that anyone who didn't wish to could leave—and many people left the theater to get their money back at the box office, but the box office had been warned not to give refunds.

Just look at how lacking in consciousness our people are: they don't want to double their pleasure for their eighty kopecks and both work on the constitution and see a movie. Instead they demand their money back.

Comrade Opal'ko, needless to say, delivered a good report. At a raion level she is a brilliant speaker, but people listened involuntarily, because they didn't want to see their eighty kopecks go to waste. The movie, too, was a good one, based on Henri Barbusse. [Barbusse (1873–1935) was a writer and veteran of the First World War who joined the French Communist Party in 1923. Afterward he worked tirelessly to defend the USSR. Many of his realist novels were translated into Russian and were widely known in the USSR.] The report lasted an hour. The presidium appeals, urges, and requests the public to speak out, make statements and express its opinion. That took half an hour. Finally some factory worker, whose name wasn't announced, came up and began to speak; but the way he spoke did a disservice to the presidium. The theater was filled with an incredible din, shouting, laughter, and hissing.

The militia appeared, and so did Comrade Samarinko himself, chief of the

## Document 56 *continued*

Narkomvnudel RO [district branch of the People's Commissariat for Internal Affairs (NKVD)], surrounded by his associates. They spread out among the crowd, kept an eye on the people who were acting restless, and after the movie, at one o'clock in the morning, certain people were detained to provide an explanation.

Comrade Biriun, the RIK chairman, seeing that no one was making any statements, made his own statement and declared: I am the head of the raion and tomorrow I will make you all chew on the constitution at shop-floor meetings. Where do you think you have come to, to some wretched movie? . . .

This is the cinema, which Lenin said is the best of all the arts, yet to Comrade Biriun it is a wretched movie. So we never did work on Comrade Stalin's constitution at Prokhladnaia Station on 5 July, the raion's workers flopped and made a spectacle of themselves and, it must be said, the way things came out was not nice.

---

This instance of "working" on the constitution with the participation of the NKVD was probably far from unique. One can imagine how the experience colored the would-be moviegoers' sense of participatory democracy. The organizers of the assembly unwittingly exposed their true purpose—to make everyone "chew" on the constitution and to report to higher bodies that the largest possible number of people participated in the discussion. If something went wrong for the "supreme leaders" of Primalkinsky Raion in Kabardino-Balkaria, at least they were not alone in resorting to coercion to work on the constitution. A special report by an oblast office of the NKVD in October 1936 said that at the Maksim Gor'ky Textile Factory (Gavrilov Posad Raion, Ivanovo Oblast), "in order to ensure that a sufficient number of workers attended the meeting after work, the doors to the factory courtyard were closed and a guard was placed in front of them. The meeting merely went through the motions. Only three workers made statements." There were also reports of frequent breakdowns of meetings and poor attendance at them. "At the Voroshilov Kolkhoz [Yur'ev Pol'sky Raion, Ivanovo Oblast] . . . they began to assemble people for the meeting at 8 P.M., when most of the kolkhoz farmers were already asleep. The result was that only six out of one hundred kolkhoz farmers came to the meeting."[10] There need be no doubt, however, that in terms of official statistics everything was in perfect order.

The sources make clear that the local nomenklatura, which shouldered the bulk of the work in discussing the draft constitution and conducting the appropriate meetings, found itself between a rock and a hard place. On the one hand, there were demands that it ensure the greatest possible number of participants and an impressive number of speakers and suggestions. On the other hand, the broader and more open the debate, the more likely various critical and negative assessments of Soviet reality became, and that could entail unpredictable consequences. An instinct for self-preservation prompted the leaders to arrange everything in advance and to vet all speakers beforehand. The result was overcautiousness, excessive organization, and formalism. NKVD summaries noted "the stifling of initiative from the masses and the artificial separation of them from direct participation in the discussion on the Basic Law of the Land of the Soviets."[11]

Local leaders also had their own reasons for avoiding a broad debate. They were deathly afraid that such a discussion might develop into criticism of their own rule and its divergence from the provisions of the constitution, and as the documents demonstrate, they had grounds to be afraid. In Sosnovka Raion alone in Gor'ky Krai, 331 people made statements at meetings criticizing shortcomings, "calling attention to the poor work in consideration of complaints, about violations of democracy, failure to fulfill voters' mandates, the low level of inclusion of women in soviets, etc." During the discussion of the draft constitution at a general meeting of the Year of the Great Turning Point Kolkhoz (Karlovka Settlement Soviet, Chutovo Raion, Odessa Oblast), "kolkhoz farmers, while welcoming the new constitution, emphasized in their statements the unsatisfactory work by their deputies Mariukhnich and Miroshnichenkova, and warned them of the possibility that they would be recalled from the soviet unless they improved their work." Many such cases were reported.[12]

Thus the discussion of the constitution may also be viewed, to some extent, as part of the Stalin leadership's overall campaign against local administrators, their incompetence, bureaucratism, and inability to carry out the directives of the ruling bodies. At least that was the practical result. In this case the criticism rained down on the low-level soviet bodies, whose activities were out in the open for everyone to see. It is no surprise that, according to official data, more than fifteen thousand deputies of local soviets in twenty-one krais and oblasts lost their seats during the brief period of the draft debate.[13]

The sources clearly display the political incompetence, lack of training and low cultural level of the "purveyors of Soviet democracy," as well as their inability to answer the most elementary questions or make a decision on their own. The content of the articles of the constitution aroused in them a mixture of vexation and fear regarding the charges that might emerge in the course of debate. Hence the frequent instances of flustered and confused reactions from meeting organizers. Secretary Gostev of the Chernukha Raion Executive Committee in Gor'ky Krai, when asked how the work of the Supreme Soviet and the Sovnarkom would be divided under the new constitution, handled the difficult situation by declaring: "They'll sort out for themselves who does what." A speaker on the constitution at the Engine of the Revolution Plant in Gor'ky first congratulated workers on their successful completion of the Second Five-Year Plan, then unloaded on them the following interpretation of the class makeup of Soviet society: "Classes in our country have been wiped off the face of the earth, . . . but our peasants are not working people." When a better-informed listener asked in puzzlement whether there were any classes in the USSR, the speaker became altogether embarrassed and repeated uncertainly that there were no classes.[14]

The local nomenklatura took a long time to grasp what was really wanted of them: they were supposed to simulate democracy, but in such a way that it turned into a multimillion-strong demonstration of devotion to the cause of socialism and to Comrade Stalin himself. Many evidently chose the path of least resistance, which was to simulate discussions. A representative of the Alma-Ata City Soviet in Kazakhstan named Rudinsky was supposed to organize a joint rally of kolkhoz farmers from suburban village soviets. The kolkhoz farmers began to gather in the morning and waited the whole day for the meeting to begin, which it finally did at 6 P.M. By making the five thousand attendees cool their heels for so long, Rudinsky obviously intended for everyone to get tired, listen to the regular speaker and then, with a sigh of relief, get up and leave. But the kolkhoz farmers wanted to comprehend everything and tried to insist on a debate—which did not suit the representative from above, and he did not allow anyone to make a statement. Similar incidents were reported from a number of cantons in the German ASSR in the Volga Region. "Suggestions for revisions to the articles or amendments to the draft may not be made," said one of the leading functionaries at a meeting of sovkhoz workers. "The draft covers every aspect of life, so no amendments are to be submitted," said a resolution of another meeting, even though the participants made a number of suggestions. Executive committees in many raions of Orenburg Oblast, instead of arranging discussions of the draft constitution, confined themselves to adopting a decision to "work" on the draft. A kolkhoz chairman in Buriatia found such a discussion unnecessary, because the party bodies had already approved it. Quite a few instances were reported of falsified minutes from meetings and the removal of certain suggestions from minutes.[15]

One curious document indicates how a discussion of the draft constitution could come out if no "organizers" were taking part. This is a letter to *Krest'ianskaia Gazeta* from Pavel Ivanovich Voronov, a farmer at the Karetovo Kolkhoz in Soligalich Raion, Yaroslavl' Oblast, written on behalf of all his fellow villagers.

## Document 57

Letter from kolkhoznik P. I. Voronov to *Krest'ianskaia Gazeta* proposing revisions to the constitution, 1936. RGASPI, f. 17, op. 120, d. 232, ll. 74–75. Typewritten copy.

The farmers of our kolkhoz welcome Stalin's constitution with great joy. The kolkhoz farmers listened to me and approved this constitution. Altogether twenty-five people took part in the meeting, but none of them could express themselves, and then I, kolkhoz farmer Voronov, suggested adding a few more clauses, and they started asking me to write these clauses and send them in. So with the consent of all the kolkhoz farmers, I wrote them down, and when I read everyone what I wrote, the entire meeting sang the Internationale and resolved:

1. That we kolkhoz farmers enjoy no lesser rights than city workers, that we kolkhoz workers work for money rather than labordays.

2. That we kolkhoz farmers all be made trade union members and have trade union booklets, so that we can have full rights like city workers.

3. That lumber distribution for the kolkhoz be free of charge for all kolkhoz needs, [or] at least a certain percentage for kolkhoz needs should be issued free of charge.

4. That there be an uninterrupted supply of goods for sale in our villages, especially flour, because we get flour very seldom here, and for bread kolkhoz farmers have to travel thirty kilometers to get baked bread to feed their family, a number of other goods are never available at the cooperatives, and as for leather footwear we never see anything like it anywhere around here.

5. We also ask that the work be set up at our kolkhozes so that we do not work all together but each person works on his own attached plot, which would be attached to us for the whole summer, and that entries be made in our labor books every ten days and they be given to us so that every kolkhoz farmer can know, otherwise we work all summer and don't know who earned how much. We tell the brigade leader to give it to us every month and every ten days. He says, I don't have time, I have too much work, but what does he do? He doesn't do anything on our kolkhoz. We have a chairman and an accounts clerk and a brigade leader, but we don't see anything getting done. The chairman gallivants around, so does the brigade leader, and the accounts clerk we don't see anywhere. They gave him 225 labor-days—he doesn't do anything and we ask for help and getting rid of all the shortcomings on our kolkhozes. We have just twenty workers on our kolkhoz. The kolkhoz chairman and the brigade leader set themselves up nicely when there are just twenty workers on the whole kolkhoz, but as for us nobody gives any help to straighten things out; the village librarian lives on our kolkhoz, but even she doesn't take any part—these problems, of course, exist all over Soligalich Raion.

The document is permeated by a sense of anticipated change as a result of the new constitution, and with each new point the resolution of the kolkhoz meeting drawn up by the writer becomes transformed into a complaint about the hard life on the kolkhoz. This blending of big issues with people's mundane concerns and everyday scenes is highly characteristic of much of the material that spontaneously arrived from below in connection with the discussion of the new constitution.

The Presidium of the TsIK was the main headquarters to which all the suggestions, comments, amendments and revisions were supposed to flow and where they were tabulated and systematized. But it began to operate only after a lengthy delay, when the campaign was already at its height. The Presidium staff included only 43,427 suggestions on the draft constitution in its summary report.[16] This figure represents only a quarter of the materials that flowed in during the campaign. A number of documents that have survived in the archives contain the notation "not relevant to the draft constitution." It is also clear that many materials that were sent to various bodies did not receive proper attention, and some were simply ignored. Hence the inescapable conclusion that in order to evaluate public opinion properly, we must consider the entire spectrum of documents related to the adoption of the constitution and not only those that relate directly to its individual articles and provisions.

In any case, the quantity of materials that was submitted in connection with the discussion of the constitution proved to be enormous—and coercion and window dressing were not the only reasons. What was going on? Was there a sincere desire for change and an illusion that it was possible to overcome past injustices? Undoubtedly, but that is not all. If there was an opportunity for candid talk, then why not talk, even if there was a threat of punishment for having a "big mouth." Another factor was the long-standing tradition of communication between the simple folk and the authorities, especially through correspondence. During the discussion quite a few suggestions were made: practical and trivial ones, very specific and utterly fantastic, absurd ones.

What is perhaps most eye-catching of all is the difference between published and archival materials. While the published comments were dominated by cities, the working class, and large enterprises, as the country's leadership wished, the archival documents clearly attest to more intensive activity by the countryside, which, despite the bitter lesson of the confiscation of property and collectivization, took up the leadership's new venture with alacrity.

The public actively responded to the leadership's call to sum up the progress that the country had made toward socialism. The leadership, however, could hardly have expected to receive the variety of opinions that emerged. There were, of course, quite a few positive comments that reflected the diversity of people's life experiences before and after the Revolution. Some of them bear traces of having been initiated from above, of "editing corrections," easily identifiable by the abundance of stock newspaper phrases and clichés. Political functionaries who made sure the campaign followed the "correct course" so as to avoid accusations of deliberately collecting negative information were compelled to include communications of roughly this kind in their summaries: "Comrade Smolianikov, a medal recipient from Dobrinka Raion in Voronezh Oblast, writes: 'I have studied the draft of Stalin's constitution well. Every article of the draft is imbued with the thoughts of a great mind—of the genius of the proletarian revolution, Comrade Stalin. In every article one can sense the great achievements of [the] October [Revolution] and a genuine achievement by mankind—the construction of a classless socialist society.'"[17]

There is no real point in citing any more such approving comments, because the newspapers overflowed with them under the rubrics: "The Dreams of Working People Throughout the World Are Becoming Reality"; "We Are the Luckiest People in the World"; "Thanks to Comrade Stalin" and so forth. Approving comments about the draft constitution from members of various ethnic groups of the USSR and from foreign workers and specialists were carefully chosen and edited.

The letters that came in from the provinces often made up a very peculiar genre—a bizarre mixture of bureaucratic paperwork and independent creativity, heavily larded with the propaganda clichés of the day. Try to figure out, for example, where the resolution of a kolkhoz farmers' gathering ends and the literary exercises by rural correspondent Pyotr Grigor'evich Shcheglov of Voronezh Oblast begin in his letter sent to *Krest'ianskaia Gazeta*:

---

## Document 58

Letter from rural correspondent P. G. Shcheglov to *Krest'ianskaia Gazeta* proposing revisions to the constitution, 1936. RGASPI, f. 17, op. 120, d. 232, ll. 59–60. Typewritten copy.

---

We, the farmers of the Red Fighter Kolkhoz, have heard a report on the adoption of the new Constitution of the USSR of 1936.

## Document 58 *continued*

Resolved:

To approve for us the joyful draft of the new constitution and to approve the chairman of the Constitutional Commission, Comrade Stalin. We see in the person of Comrade Stalin and in the draft of the new constitution a keen sensitivity to all working people of the USSR. We know that there is no difference in our country in labor discipline either for women or for men. Women also enjoy the same rights as men.

We see with our own eyes that women along with men are building a socialist society at all enterprises and institutions. We know that in a capitalist country women bear an eternal burden, the poor things have nowhere to appeal or complain, because they are looked upon the way women in our country were looked upon before the Revolution.

Comrade Stalin correctly noted in the draft of the new constitution that the people who count in our country are those who march forward together with us and build a socialist society, while whoever doesn't work, doesn't eat. We kolkhoz farmers are waging a struggle in our socialist fields. We kolkhoz farmers want to give the country seven to eight billion poods of grain, and we will give it.

We will not go to borrow grain from capitalist countries and we will not bow to the kulaks, who have had their day. We know that there is nothing frightening for hands hardened by toil. Our Red Fighter Kolkhoz has subscribed 100 percent to the new loan. We have finished stacking the winter grain and have started threshing, above all we are fulfilling the grain [quota] for the state, the payment in kind for the MTS, and we will provide grain through the cooperatives. Last year each kolkhoz farmer produced three kg, eight hundred g, per laborday, and in money terms, one ruble, three kopecks. Today we plan to distribute five kg of grain and in money terms, one ruble, fifty kopecks. In the future we are going to make more use of agricultural machinery so we can turn the Red Fighter Kolkhoz into a Bolshevik kolkhoz and make kolkhoz farmers prosperous.

We know that our country is surrounded all around by capitalist countries, and we see how the enemy is doing everything it can to get closer to the border of the USSR to live off our plot of land. In 1929 I was on the KVZhD [the Chinese and Eastern Railroad] myself. We succeeded in defending the USSR border and will always succeed in strongly repulsing the enemy. We know that the capitalists of all countries can never accept us, they are rabidly preparing to make war on us, but we are ready.

But as soon as Europe threatens us first, we will say excuse us to those who are bringing us war rather than peace, we will say without hesitation that our bayonets are sharp and our powder is dry too and we will point the way back with our bayonets.

For rural correspondent Shcheglov, of course, this muddled torrent of words was not only the fulfillment of a public duty but also a stab at belletristic writing, as well as hope. The hope was that someone would notice his letter, publish it and possibly call attention to his outstanding talent. Probably because it was totally confused and impossible to turn into anything coherent, the letter was not printed, although it became one of the tabulated approving comments on the draft constitution. We have included this document as an example of thousands of approving resolutions—some of them arriving spontaneously, some of them on a voluntary-coercive basis, most of them formal, often barely coherent and far removed from real life. What is distinctive about such documents is that virtually none of them contain any specific suggestions for the draft constitution.

Unlike these comments, a letter to *Krest'ianskaia Gazeta* from Fyodor Mikhailovich Postnikov, a seventy-year-old peasant who describes his difficult life and small pleasures, is hard to suspect of insincerity.

## Document 59

Letter of appreciation from F. M. Postnikov to *Krest'ianskaia Gazeta*, 1936. RGASPI, f. 17, op. 120, d. 232, ll. 58–59. Typewritten copy.

It's a pity that I am seventy years old, the young people are lucky to have such a free life and to have such a leader as Comrade Stalin. But still I did have some good life during Soviet rule. After all, it is awful to remember how I lived in the old days under the tsar. I was born to a poor family, my father led a very hard life, he didn't have much land, he was illiterate and didn't teach me. From the time I was very little I had to work as a farmhand and for no less than fifteen years I worked as a shepherd. There was nothing to live on at home, I had one son, who died for Soviet rule, he was killed at the front in the ranks of the Red Army. He left a wife and child, and his wife died too, so my granddaughter remained in my care, and I brought her up and freely taught her and now she is a student, she even helps the old woman and me. And even as an old man I am still making a living. In 1934 I produced 200 labordays, and in 1935 I had 150 labordays, and I also caulked a school and the village soviet and earned quite a bit. I get two or three bonuses for my honest labor on the kolkhoz, and this year my life has gotten even better; I got a piglet as a bonus, which I've never had before. Then I take part in olympics [competitions of amateur artists, orchestras, choirs, dance ensembles and theatrical troupes, often on a national basis]. I take part in the singers' chorus, I perform alone and when they put me on in our village of Morozovka, the culture people liked it and they took me to the raion together with all of our performers. Our chorus and our performance in the raion won first prize. As for me, they gave the old man a prize of twenty-five rubles for my separate song "Cheryomushka" [little bird cherry tree], and they promise to take me to the krai besides.

So that is where a happy life is, comrades. If I were young, I would definitely study to be a fine performer and singer, but I am already on in years. But if I go to Arkhangel'sk, I will take a good look at those cars, which I have never seen, and all that building. Thanks to Comrade Stalin, although I am an old man, I still managed to get myself a bit of a happy life, and I suggest the constitution not forget about us old people.

To the writer, the new constitution is a favor, a good deed. It was the embodiment of the positive changes in his life under Soviet rule. One should only note that the notions of "freedom" and "happiness" are highly relative. The way different people have conceived of these values at different times and in different countries has varied a great deal. But the overall pattern is obvious: the more people have suffered and the more privations and adversities have befallen them, the lower their standard of "happiness" has been. For F. M. Postnikov, his bonus piglet, the opportunity to take part in amateur shows and public recognition of his singing talent proved to be sufficient. Social emancipation and the opportunity to study and develop one's abilities was of no small importance in one's self-evaluation and the evaluation of the consequences of the Revolution that were presented in the comments about the draft constitution. Here, for instance, is the worldview of an old worker named Berman from Dnepropetrovsk Oblast in connection with its adoption: "People say we were young once, but it's not true. I don't remember any youth in my past, I didn't have any. Youth came at an advanced age. I am young because only in 1934 did I graduate from a technicum, I am young because one of my sons is a professor, another is the director of an enterprise, the third is a mining engineer and the fourth is a student at a transport institute. I am young because it is a joy to live in our country."[18]

Both worker Berman and peasant Postnikov expressed a very important psychosocial phenomenon of Soviet society in the 1930s. Youth is a period of expectations, real and fuzzy, a time of study, growth and first accomplishments. Hopes were pinned on young people, and the country indeed felt young and lived for the future, with the dynamic tempo of a vigorous young person who thought anything was possible. Part of this attitude was transmitted to the middle-aged and older generations. For the sake of the future many people were ready to make sacrifices, overlook any abominations and justify loathsome behavior. From this standpoint, the adoption of the new constitution was well timed. In addition, the notion was hammered into people's heads that they just had to press on a little bit further to reach communism.

Along with such positive comments, however, there proved to be quite a few that could hardly have pleased the campaign organizers. For example, F. M. Plindina, a kolkhoz farmer from Boguchar Raion in Voronezh Oblast, offered a different assessment of the countryside's progress under Soviet rule:

---

## Document 60

Letter of complaint of F. M. Plindina, Voronezh Oblast, 1936. RGASPI, f. 17, op. 120, d. 232, l. 83. Typewritten copy.

---

Maybe some people are shy about writing, but I will write the real truth, the whole opinion of the people: everybody thanks Soviet rule for the fact that the government took all the enterprises away from the landowners, and everybody thanks it for saying that there should be no war. But people on the kolkhoz are not happy that everybody is hungry and are quietly saying, but are obviously afraid to say, that because the whole enterprise belongs to the state, the peasant does all this work and has to give a certain amount from each hectare to the state, so that there will be no war.

Because I see that people don't want to work on kolkhozes, is it really possible that people at the newspaper haven't heard this—peasants want to put in the new constitution, I hear it from the people, but everybody's afraid of saying at the meetings that we don't want to be on the kolkhoz, we work and work, and there's nothing to eat. Really, how can we live? Everybody says we have almost no bread on the kolkhoz now, and where are we going to scrape together a ruble per kilo?

---

The fact that kolkhozes had failed to solve many of the country-side's traditional problems and had even added new ones is illustrated by a letter from K. F. Shestakova in Sverdlovsk Oblast:

## Document 61

Letter from K. F. Shestakova to *Krest'ianskaia Gazeta* proposing revisions to the constitution, 1936. RGASPI, f. 17, op. 120, d. 232, ll. 80–82. Typewritten copy.

I, the undersigned kolkhoz farmer, have decided to write you a letter and tell you about my life. I have a very hard life. Every spring there is not enough bread. I have two sons, the first sixteen years old, the second five. It is very hard for me to raise them. I have no husband—he died. I hear from the news-papers (my son reads them) that kolkhoz farmers write that they are well off and pass their own law. In the old days the poor people kept quiet at meetings, and the folks who were well off managed everything. Now we poor people are electing poor people to the administration, but we don't get much joy out of it. For instance, I am a poor widow, and every winter I starve. My son was in the fifth grade in the raion six kilometers away, and in the fall he was happy to go, as long as it was warm and there was bread, but midway through the winter the bread ran out and the cold weather was brutal, and my son stopped going to school because he wasn't eating enough, he began to slow down as far as understanding his studies, he had no boots, and he had no warm overcoat either. These were the main reasons he didn't finish his studies.

Who is going to help me, a poor widow? The kolkhoz board gave sixteen kg for my two sons for a month, and I ate with them. They write that our law is not only not for the poor, it is for the well-off. We poor people say that we're not able to pay for milk and meat and wool, the poor should be relieved of this. But our words are not taken into consideration, whatever the well-off people say, that is what is resolved. At the general meeting of kolkhoz farmers things are not done our way either. I have lost all my strength from not having enough to eat, and it's hard to work at the same level as the others.

I often remember Lenin, how kind he was for us, for the peasants; he took the land away from the landowners, gave it to the peasants, and ordered them to divide it among everybody. In those days everybody was well fed, nobody went hungry. Lenin died too early. Now things are worse for us, poor widows, than they were before the Revolution. At that time the capitalists were in charge and didn't ask anything of us: no wool, no meat, no milk. Now the Communists are in charge and ask for absolutely everything. There is no bread. They order us to turn in the milk, and even to deliver meat. We have to buy the meat and turn it in. Why do the Communists treat us so badly, in a way that the capitalists didn't—they didn't starve poor peasants?

You write that we should write our suggestions to *Krest'ianskaia Gazeta*. So I deem it necessary to insert in the draft—exempt low-capacity poor farms from milk and meat deliveries, exempt farms ruined by White bandits. Why has it come about in the USSR that there are two classes—one liberated and the other oppressed? The state buys everything at low prices from us and sells to us at high prices. It buys grain for six rubles a centner and sells bread to us for ninety-five rubles a centner.

The new draft refers to freedom of expression and freedom of the press. And we poor people are asking the editors to write our letters in the newspaper. We have a hard life, we want to live better, so that we can also see a well-to-do life in our families.

We need the freedom to sell only our surpluses, and not this way—leaving our children hungry and turning in and selling the milk to the state. We are all working people, like the workers and office clerks and kolkhoz farmers—a kolkhoz farmer is a human being too, he also needs to eat well. Don't leave the poor kolkhoz farmers to go hungry. Only the ones with children and families are poor. Lenin felt sorry for the peasants with many children and ordered that the land be divided among everybody. The peasants without children said it should be divided among those who work. Right now the peasants without children have a very easy and good life, they are the only ones giving praise, but there are hundreds of thousands of poor people, hungry and unclothed.

Please put into the draft: any farm that suffered at the hands of a White gang in 1919 for the cause of socialism is to be exempted from deliveries to the state of milk and meat and wool. Exempt poor farms with three or four small children, they need to eat well, but we don't have enough milk and our children often get sick.

A widowed kolkhoz farmer, half-starved, I write and wash myself in tears.

As a kolkhoz member, the writer expresses thoughts and feelings about herself that date back to the old social categories, and specifically she places herself in the class of the poor, the deprived, and the oppressed, although she has heard secondhand through the newspapers that somewhere people are well off. These well-off people are personified for her by the Communists and are to blame for all the woes and miseries of the poor widow, who has plainly found life completely unbearable since her husband's death and much worse than before the Revolution. In those days there were no compulsory deliveries to the state of grain, milk, meat, and wool. The state, she writes, buys everything at low prices and sells everything to peasants at high prices. It is not even clear from the letter where the kolkhoz farmer places the dividing line between what is public and what is personal. One thing is obvious: the writer wants a better lot for her family and argues that "a kolkhoz farmer is a human being too." Her only hope for the new constitution, about which she has a very fuzzy conception, is that it seems to include freedom of expression and freedom of the press. She needs them to tell the newspaper about her grim situation and, with its help, to propose clauses in the draft that would exempt poor people such as her from deliveries to the state. Alas, the letter ended up in the "hostile comments" category.

NKVD summaries also reported such "anti-Soviet" demands for the elimination of compulsory deliveries to the state of grain, milk and meat.[19] They contained a fair amount of information, however, about the kind of excesses that often occurred during the pre-fabricated discussions of the constitution when one of those assembled (frequently women) suddenly lost composure: "After the draft constitution was read at a plenum of the Kulamzin Village Soviet in Bulaevo Raion (Karaganda Oblast), one of the speakers shared his recollections of the past, describing the conditions in which men used to serve in the tsarist army for up to twenty-five years, at which point an independent female landowner named Khuli-upova angrily shouted out: 'So what if people served twenty-five years, at least everybody was well-fed and had clothing and shoes to wear.'"[20] The call to evaluate the past in comparison with current achievements, as the material on the discussion of the draft constitution makes clear, showed that people had not forgotten at all the requisitions of foodstuffs, the grain-procurement campaigns, the "going to extremes," the starving countryside that was left to the mercy of fate in 1932–33, and the much more recent ration-card system.

The articles of the constitution that affected citizens' immediate interests elicited the greatest attention from the public, and hence the largest number of comments. Substantially fewer letters pertained, for example, to the governmental and administrative system of the USSR. According to data from the Presidium of the TsIK, chapter 10 of the constitution ("Basic Rights and Obligations of Citizens") attracted 53 percent of all the suggestions. Close behind it were articles 7–10 of chapter 1, which dealt with property relations, and article 12, which spelled out the principles of socialism: "Whoever doesn't work, doesn't eat" and "From each according to his ability, to each according to his labor." The proportions are similar to those found in NKVD summaries and citizens' letters to newspapers and magazines. But the comments on these articles often proved to be completely different from what the leadership expected. They contained clear reverberations from the total collectivization that had just recently been completed. This is understandable, since kolkhoz members—former peasants—still made up a majority of the population. The discussion focused on the issues of inequality between workers and kolkhoz farmers and of ensuring that payments actually conformed with the quantity and quality of output.

Recall the suggestions by kolkhoz farmer Voronov cited above. On the one hand, they seem to contain an acceptance of the kolkhoz system—"we can work on a kolkhoz"—but on the other, they include a request to set up work "so that we do not work all together, but each person works on his own attached plot," a system by definition contrary to that of the kolkhoz. And take note of the first two points of the letter. The writer is asking to equalize peasants' rights with those of workers in terms of both wages (work for money rather than for labordays) and social protection (membership in a trade union). This theme was very common in letters. The NKVD summaries eloquently bear this out as well. According to one such summary, a woman named Pogrebnaia from the New Life Kolkhoz in Kozelets Raion, Chernigov Oblast, declared: "Kolkhoz farmers who work in field crop cultivation don't make enough from their labor compared to everybody who works in factories. We work twenty hours a day, and they work eight hours a day. All of us need clothing and shoes, we go around in torn dresses and shirts, while they, the factory workers, are supplied with everything they need. There are no available places for us at the resorts, but there are for factory workers."[21]

She is echoed by I. Savurin in a letter from Voronezh Oblast: "What should be added to the constitution is the wage for a laborday, because we work and we don't know for what. Every spring they always promise us a lot, but when we start getting paid, it isn't enough to cover hominy grits for a year."[22] Toiling for labordays was usually criticized as a breach of the principle of equal compensation for equal labor. Moreover, many people in the countryside sought to prove in their letters that their labor was much harder and more meaningful to the country and asked that this fact be reflected in the constitution. It was precisely this type of comment that was often set aside as irrelevant to the draft.

The rural population was enormously enthusiastic about the articles in the constitution that provided for small-scale private farming, which was based on personal property and precluded the exploitation of other people's labor (article 9). To some, this was tantamount to a partial admission of guilt for the coercion used during the period of "kolkhoz development," while others saw in it hope for acquiring their own farm one day. The few remaining independent peasants also took heart, naively believing that the constant pressure on them would now come to an end. Others simply expressed the hope that they would not be "drowned" now—as was, for example, a group of twenty-five independent peasants in Chuvashia.[23]

NKVD summaries contain the following kind of remarks: N. I. Obukh, an independent peasant in the village of Sil'chenkovo (Chernigov Oblast, Ukrainian SSR), declared: "Well now, under the new constitution, an independent peasant will be able to live, the time when we were abused is over, and now we will show people how to live." M. P. Pilipenko, an independent peasant from the Maksimovka Village Soviet in the same oblast, whose property was sold by the village soviet because of tax evasion, told kolkhoz farmers during the discussion of the draft that under the new constitution the property would have to be returned to him, that independent peasants would now be allocated land, and for those without horses, land would be carved out of the village itself. In the village of Losevo, independent peasant N. A. Nesen, in a conversation with another independent peasant, named Nosach, a former Red partisan, said this: "Now the new constitution says you don't have to join a kolkhoz, the land will be doled out equally, and the main thing is that there will be no assault on independent peasants the way there was before, and whoever was stripped of his right to vote will have it reinstated. Now we will start living the way we used to." In the village of Mysharovtsy, Vinnitsa Oblast, a kolkhoz farmer appeared at the village soviet and asked when land would be parceled out for people who wanted to work on it on an independent basis.[24]

Letters show the same pattern. S. I. Glistin, an independent peasant from Voronezh Oblast, referring to article 9, which spelled out the right of citizens to small-scale private farming, wrote to *Krest'ianskaia Gazeta:* "I would add this to that article: all remaining independent working farms . . . shall be allotted a standard state land allotment, and illegally confiscated draft animals and all other property shall be returned to them." Because the new constitution seemed to place collective and individual peasant farms on an equal footing, A. I. Fedanov of Kursk Oblast wrote: "I submit the following amendment [to article 8]: and a land allotment for permanent use shall be attached to independent farms so that they, too, do not lag behind kolkhozes, either in tilling or in fertilizing the land."[25] And I. N. Sosenkov, an independent peasant from Kuibyshev Krai, went even further, suggesting an interesting future coexistence between the two forms of ownership:

## Document 62

Letter from independent farmer I. N. Sosenkov to *Krest'ianskaia Gazeta* proposing revision to the constitution, 1936. RGASPI, f. 17, op. 120, d. 232, l. 65. Typewritten copy.

. . . In every village soviet there are independent farms that have not yet been absorbed by kolkhozes, that are scattered among kolkhoz farmers and fenced in by kolkhoz land and whose land is not close by, which hampers the tilling of the land and the breeding of some cattle, because an independent peasant's cattle, living among kolkhoz farmers and not having any land of its own close by, may invade the kolkhoz cropland at any time, for which fines are imposed. I request an addition to the article to allow the existence of independent farms, so that by a village soviet's order an independent settlement can be established with all the conveniences for living.

NKVD summaries show that the discussion of the constitution resulted in widespread remarks and rumors to the effect that dispossessed kulaks could now return from exile, their rights would be reinstated, property would be returned and there would be "complete freedom for everybody." From 20 to 22 August the raion executive committee of Putivl' Raion in Chernigov Oblast received from independent peasants in the village of Nizhniaia Sloboda "nineteen requests, including a collective one from thirteen people, to have their property and farmsteads returned." And "a kulak named Zabavsky (from the village of Malaia Poboina in Min'kovtsy Raion, Vinnitsa Oblast), upon returning from exile, demanded that the village soviet return his house and property."[26]

As a result of such expectations, according to the summaries, responsible functionaries traveled to the provinces to provide "clarification."[27] What kind of "clarifications" were given is not reported, but the mere fact that such utterances were classified as "anti-Soviet" speaks for itself. The summaries also cite these remarks by peasants: "Things will not work out in our favor anyway" and "Whatever Stalin said, that's the way it will be."[28]

Most comments gave ardent support to the article in the constitution about the state's protection of citizens' personal property. Many people, recalling the recent "excesses," interpreted it as a guarantee that such things would never happen again. Kolkhoz farmer I. L. Luk'ianov from the Young Pioneer Kolkhoz in Usviaty Raion, Western Oblast, wrote to *Krest'ianskaia Gazeta:* "Our kolkhoz has gone over the new constitution of 14 June 1936, and we have gone over every clause in detail. There was an excited reaction to clause 10 in chapter 1, where all the kolkhoz farmers said that houses and gardens are covered by the law, i.e., they are protected, since kolkhoz farmers were afraid to build houses in the past, saying that all houses would soon be taken over by the *zhakta* [housing cooperative society]." Recognition of the right to a personal garden plot signified in some measure to the kolkhoz farmer the preservation in miniature of the previous independent peasant farm. At the same time it seemed to perpetuate the countryside's long-standing problems. In a letter to *Krest'ianskaia Gazeta,* kolkhoz farmer I. F. Torochin of the Tractor Driver Kolkhoz in Voronezh Oblast contended that "the statutes of the agricultural artel with respect to household gardens are incorrect. A family of ten members and a family of two members each receives 0.40 of a hectare. I feel this is a big mistake. My suggestion is [either] to take away the kolkhoz farmers' household gardens completely and in their entirety for the kolkhoz or allot larger household plots to large families than to small ones. I will give an example from my own family. I have eleven members in my family, while Putintsev has two members; they don't need any kolkhoz work, they provide for themselves from their farmstead, but most of my family concentrates on kolkhoz work." He was echoed by N. M. Danilov in the same oblast: "I submit a suggestion to add to the draft constitution in the second clause of the agricultural artel for big families to at least increase a little the size of garden plots of half a hectare. For a household of two or three members that is fine. But for eight or nine members half a hectare is very insulting because that small family will live in clover, while the big family will be hungry."[29]

It should be noted that the kolkhoz system had already put down roots in the countryside. During the discussion of the constitution quite a few kolkhoz farmers called for the elimination of any opportunity to maintain either a personal garden plot or a small-scale private farm. At one kolkhoz meeting a man named Shugal'sky said: "I don't know why the constitution envisions the existence of an independent peasant. I think he should be either a kolkhoz farmer or a factory worker, because this Five-Year Plan envisions the liquidation of classes." Shugal'sky took a purely "theoretical" approach to this issue, based on ideas that were highly popular at the time. But aside from fears that they would have to answer for previous mistakes or return property that had been unjustly seized, many kolkhoz activists faced a moral defeat in the years-long war for total collectivization. "In my view," one of them wrote to *Krest'ianskaia Gazeta,* "there should be an addition here [to article 9] that says in view of the final inclusion of all working people under socialism, it should be the duty, based on personal conviction, of independent peasants to join kolkhozes and of small-scale artisans to join socialist associations of artisans and craftsmen in the socialist sector. In my opinion, this is due to the fact that here in the USSR there should be no separate categories of working people, for there is a single authority and we need a single spirit. It is apparent from the available facts that we have under our village soviet fourteen independent peasant households, and if you examine their work, they don't seem to be living in the Land of the Soviets." This insistence upon conformity was echoed by I. Yermakov from Kursk Oblast, who wrote: "I am stating my opinion that article 9 should be written in a way that independent farms in the Soviet land should not exist for long, because small-scale private farming by independent peasants could influence the kolkhozes."[30] The writer didn't say how it could influence them, but perhaps that was not necessary.

Another, no less contentious problem stemmed from the proclamation of freedom of conscience and religious practices (article 124), which elicited a wave of responses. They were often linked to article 125 (on freedom of expression, of the press and of assembly) and with article 135 in chapter 11, "The Electoral System," which promised all citizens, regardless of religious affiliation, among other factors, the right to participate in elections. "How are we to understand the clause in the draft of the new constitution about freedom of assembly?" asked V. F. Novozhilov from the village of Khmel'nitsa near Chernigov. "Does this clause permit freedom of religious assemblies to worship outside the walls of a church, i.e., in private homes, where there is no church building? Currently one must get permission from the appropriate bodies of Soviet rule for such assemblies, but they are never permitted."[31]

The NKVD summaries show that a substantial segment of the public concluded that the war against religion was ending and that the policy of shutting down churches and mosques and banning activities by religious communities had been acknowledged to be a mistake. As a result, those who felt that they were being mistreated in Soviet society started to feel resentful: "There is no difference in the new constitution for kolkhoz farmers—the road has been opened for kulaks and priests, but nothing has changed for us."[32]

At the same time the believers themselves began to take heart. Here, for example, is a petition submitted by a group of peasants to the Putivl' Raion Executive Committee in Chernigov Oblast:

---

# Document 63

Petition to Putivl' RIK, Chernigov Oblast, 15 August 1936. RGASPI, f. 17, op. 120, d. 232, l. 49. Typewritten copy.

---

We believers, making use of the directive by our esteemed general ruler, Comrade Stalin, who says in his dear constitution in paragraph 124 that the church is separated from the state and schools and churches may freely prac-

## Document 63 *continued*

tice all cultural services, in view of this hereby request that Father Ioann Krotov, our elected priest, be registered to perform all Christian rites and services for us.

---

At a brigade meeting of kolkhoz farmers in the village of Beryozovka (Odessa Oblast), according to one summary, citizen Novikov interpreted article 124 this way: "Now our day off will only be on Sunday, so the church can be opened up and services held there, and Beryozovka is such a big village that new churches can be built." Said another: "In the village of Troianovtsy in Gritsev Raion, Vinnitsa Oblast, hostile-class elements have started to organize backward kolkhoz farmers to open a house of worship (a church) that was shut down by a resolution of the Ukrainian SSR TsIK and has not operated for several years. The same demands have been made, under the influence of priests and hostile class elements, by certain backward elements—male and female kolkhoz farmers in [other] villages."[33]

Similar incidents occurred in many areas of the country, irrespective of religious affiliations:

---

## Document 64

Excerpt from summary report on religious activity among Germans in Volga Region, 1936. RGASPI, f. 17, op. 120, d. 232, l. 52. Typewritten copy.

---

In the village of Gnadentau in Zel'man Canton, situated in the Republic of Germans of the Volga Region, the chairman of the church council, a man named Shefer who had formerly been stripped of his voting rights, raised a question at a villagers' meeting: can they now reopen a church that had been closed down for refusing renovations that were needed to preserve state property and for refusing to pay appropriate taxes. Can the church council now assemble church meetings without permission from the village soviet and the KIK [canton executive committee]. [punctuation per original]

This same Shefer, a man named Klaub, and Karpukha, bookkeeper for the Staraia Poltava Canton Consumers' Union, have been and are agitating to the effect that churches should now be opened without turning in the appropriate taxes and renovating the church; that the pastor (priest) will now come back [and] regain his voting rights; and that religious meetings, processions, and so forth may be freely organized at any time without permission from the village soviet and the canton executive committee.

The aforementioned Klaub tried to teach kolkhoz farmers to demand for themselves from the kolkhoz board a seven-hour workday and ten to fifteen rubles' pay per day, and at least six kg of bread per laborday.

The above-mentioned Shefer held a gathering of Betbrüder [devotees] in his house without any permission from the village soviet or the canton executive committee.

Betbrüder assembled in the same village of Gnadentau without any permission, and to call the meeting they used a church bell that was in decrepit condition and had not been used for several years.

---

The summaries stated that sectarians had become more active. "Members of the Molokan sect have submitted requests to open houses of prayer, specifically in the town of Rasskazovo in Voronezh Oblast."[34] But the sources make clear that such desires were not the dominant ones. Even the formal proclamation of freedom of religion in the constitution often met with an unsympathetic reaction. Almost two decades of intensive assault on religion, harassment of believers, and destruction of houses of worship were having their effect. People refused to believe their eyes when they read in the draft that it permitted not only freedom of conscience but also participation in elections by clergymen who had previously been stripped of their voting rights. At one meeting in Voronezh Oblast a question was asked to the effect of whether it was really true that "priests are going to vote too." The "knowledgeable" representative of the village soviet explained that by election day they would be stripped of the right to vote. This answer showed that the principle of universal suffrage set down in the constitution was so patently at odds with the spirit of the times that the man thought it best to rely on his "proletarian instinct." One NKVD summary reported that the representative of a raion executive committee in Vinnitsa Oblast began to talk complete rubbish. In answering a question about who the mentally ill were and why they were deprived of the right to vote, he explained that they were "everyone who believes in God."[35]

Vasily Stepanovich Kolesnikov, the party organizer at the Stalinist Kolkhoz, demonstrated the feelings of such people especially strikingly in his letter to *Krest'ianskaia Gazeta:*

# Document 65

Letter from party organizer V. S. Kolesnikov to *Krest'ianskaia Gazeta* on "perverse" understandings of the constitution, 1936. RGASPI, f. 17, op. 120, d. 232, ll. 71–73. Typewritten copy.

I wanted to personally write to the Central Committee about the draft of the new constitution that has been released, with regard to the way it is understood in various backward areas, especially here by the minority Greeks on the Stalinist Kolkhoz, where I work as a party organizer, under the Prokhladnoe Village Soviet in Grechesky [Greek] Raion. First I will take the blame for the fact that I have not yet educated the masses, but in three months it is impossible to do that, because people have lived for centuries and re-education comes very hard, and besides I am myself not completely literate, both politically and especially in general education. You can conclude this from my letter. But now I will go on to the main issues.

When the new constitution came out in the provinces, it was badly perverted, for example, article 136 has been understood and interpreted a hundred times to say that everybody takes part in elections, so priests can be voters too, not understanding that the church is separated from the state. And because priests live on unearned income, they should be deprived of voting rights and of being elected.

Articles 9 and 10 are being perverted to mean that in the spring everyone who wants to be independent peasants, they can quit the kolkhoz, and add article 10, that citizens' personal property is protected by law, which means that we are going to pay the same taxes as kolkhoz farmers. The articles relating to krai, central, and other organizations are distorted less, because these are issues right close to them, and that of course is completely understandable. But in general there is a lot of idle talk on the part of certain leftover sons of plantation owners and former exploiters, who have sort of edged their way onto kolkhozes and are setting down roots in socialism as crooks. The long-haired priests and church elders are playing an especially big role in this. Soon after the constitution [evidently after publication of the draft] they managed to take up renovation of the church and restoration of the fence, and on that basis they conducted agitation to the effect that all churches should be restored and special schools established for priests. The self-proclaimed apostle Yura in particular had to appear at our kolkhoz about these inventions, and a private discussion was held with him three times. . . .

You will especially run into a lot of talk on the part of the ataman's drazhnily [meaning unclear] or the older factory workers, as they call themselves. But these are workers in quotation marks, and they walked around with sticks and beat up workers, but by various excuses they stayed on the kolkhoz. Such individuals are first Aleksei Shkrum and second Potap Nedel'sky. These individuals were not left much land, half a hectare. But what is typical is that Shkrum worked only since the spring until the crops ripened in his truck garden, then he quit the kolkhoz altogether and is working exclusively in his own garden, and the labor-intensive crops that are sown to 0.50 [of a hectare] are quite enough for him and his wife; they have only to cultivate and sell them at the market for profiteers prices, and such people have crops, as well as grapes, fruit trees, strawberries, vegetables, and various other combinations, and if he and his ilk are given a hectare or more of land, then of course he will not find the time or the need to work on the kolkhoz, so that is why they spread the word that the government was wrong to leave 0.50 of a hectare of land apiece for personal use by kolkhoz farmers. Of course, we managed to rebuff such shenanigans on the spot and expose such people and their ilk. But these elements don't want to understand and go, to put it crudely, underground, although they aren't dangerous, but there are already plenty of sneaks like that. [A discussion of abortions follows.]

---

Let us ponder why this man perceived as "perversions" the correct interpretation in the villages of many articles of the draft constitution. It was because he continued to rely on the already assimilated dogmas and traditional behavior of the less-than-literate party activists. Not long before, the Kolesnikovs were the mainstay of collectivization and other such "socialist reforms," breaking their compatriots across their knees. When Stalin condemned "excesses," these people felt cheated and betrayed. Reared on blind hatred toward "long-haired priests," "exploiters," and "their ilk," who are "putting down roots in socialism as crooks," these people were probably never able to come to terms with the principles that were laid down in the constitution. At the same time, they certainly would have been comforted and less racked by doubt if they had known that all manifestations of religious feeling, attempts to restore churches, and efforts to avoid ending up on a kolkhoz and to uphold independent opinions were meticulously noted by the NKVD.

But what that agency recorded with particular care as "anti-Soviet utterances" were people's opinions about changes in the political system and citizens' personal rights and liberties. The comments themselves on this topic sometimes take on a very strange, hybrid form. One example is a letter from S. Kirillovsky, a sixty-four-year-old disabled man from Morshansk Raion. The handwriting of the original document is marked by a somewhat archaic ligature, which, incidentally, provides some idea of the man's personality.

# Document 66

Letter from S. Kirillovsky praising the constitution, 1936. RGASPI, f. 17, op. 120, d. 232, ll. 56–57. Typewritten copy.

I am hastening to share thoughts which I have developed as a summary of all the tenets in Stalin's great creation. Unprecedented in the history of mankind, this greatest of state laws could have been produced only by a brilliant personality. What is potentially set down in it, so to speak, are all of the wishes and thoughts of working people on kolkhozes that have been expressed or could be expressed, so they may become part of the constitution only as a footnote to one article or another. Here is an example: article 123, in principle, provides for unprintable profanities and hooliganlike insults to religious feelings and female modesty and other manifestations of savage barbarism and crude manners in the sense that it displays hatred, contempt, and disrespect for citizens as individuals, and this could be added as a footnote to article 123. Exceptional cases of murder, theft, and other excesses, which so to speak upset normal life, also come only under accountability based on articles 128, 130, and 131, and therefore the working people's desire to detain such individuals without the prosecutor's sanction, in order to prevent them from eluding justice and protect life, honor and property, can be entered as a footnote to article 127. The village soviet can detain them on its account as abnormal individuals and enemies of the people until a trial. The desire of working men and women on kolkhozes to reduce the powers of deputies are [sic] envisaged by article 142, under which a deputy who does not fulfill the hopes of voters may be recalled at any time. Other desires of the working people, as material for the forthcoming congress, may be submitted to the congress upon final approval of the draft. . . . [gap in the text; Apparently the text immediately preceding the sequel is to the effect that "there are proposals which if they were"] to be implemented, would be a fly in the ointment, but time affords an opportunity to everybody to speak their piece and to think over what is good, the unclear and misinterpreted aspects become clear, everything, so to speak, is digested in the popular consciousness, and the constitution appears in even greater brilliance and majesty. With this constitution Comrade Stalin, and I will put it in the words of Pushkin, "has erected himself a monument not of human hands; the people's trail to it shall not become overgrown."

While the 1861 reform gave rise to disturbances by peasants, and in some places to revolts that were brutally suppressed, Stalin's constitution produced a huge upsurge in morale and enthusiasm. This draft, as the esteemed Comrade Kalinin has said, laid bare the ranks of classes alien to the Revolution and won over those who have a conscience and talent and previously were frustrated by a life of deprivation but were eager to join socialist construction. The atmosphere of socialism has lifted up the popular masses and united them into a single entity, as though by a law of physics . . . [apparently a gap in the text: the meaning of the reference to "a law of physics" is unclear] moving, it lifts up all objects, and this law is binding both on the physical world and it is binding on the world of the psyche. While the 1861 reform sent many people to prison and hard labor, Stalin's draft constitution will release many inmates from imprisonment and forced labor with a broad amnesty for this year's anniversary of 7 November [date of the 1917 Revolution]—these are the desires and hopes of the working people. It is time for citizens to realize that no matter who they were in the past, the road is open for everyone to public activity and the construction of socialism. That is what esteemed Comrades Molotov and Kalinin said at workers' rallies. Aside from his other beneficial activities, the name of dear, brilliant Comrade Stalin should be recorded in the history of mankind in conspicuous lettering for the draft constitution alone, and our century should rightfully be called the century of Lenin and Stalin.

---

This letter produces a conflicting impression: either it is self-deception—and in that case, the ease and readiness with which a man who is unquestionably well read and well acquainted with Russian history yields to it is striking—or it is a cautious ploy to criticize the regime by means of extolling Stalin and his associates. Between the lines one can read what concerns the writer: the need for the state to protect citizens' religious beliefs (he may be a believer himself) against "manifestations of savage barbarism and crude manners." After lauding Stalin for the openness of the discussion of the draft, Kirillovsky gives a "cue"—seemingly at random—for the next step that the people expect of the leaders: an amnesty for political prisoners.

A letter to *Krest'ianskaia Gazeta* from "ordinary kolkhoz farmer Vasily Yefimovich Mel'nikov," seemingly residing in the depths of the countryside, is more candid:

---

# Document 67

Letter from kolkhoznik V. Ye. Mel'nikov to *Krest'ianskaia Gazeta* proposing revisions to the constitution, 1936. RGASPI, f. 17, op. 120, d. 232, ll. 83–85. Typewritten copy.

---

The published draft of the USSR Constitution of 12 June 1936 is one of the most precious gifts from Soviet authority to the peoples of the Union since its rule began.

# Document 67 *continued*

If the coming congress of soviets will see fit to approve it in its entirety after a general discussion, a new era in life will indeed begin for the peoples of the USSR, because the thoughts and aspirations of the progressive minds of the old and new world will be realized and implemented.

Then we will be entitled to say to the Westernizers: Citizens! We are not slaves without rights, either, but are free citizens who are building our life in our own way, and with our flesh and blood are forging the rights of citizenship and our homeland, which we will cherish and protect as the apple of our eye. These inalienable rights of citizenship will definitely be mighty and strong in every respect of public life and if anyone thinks [of raising a hand] against the USSR with such a constitution, either from within or from outside, he will get a devastating rebuff.

Under the coming elections to the soviets, based on article 134, the peoples of the USSR will be the supreme holders of power, and consequently the future bodies of power will have the source of the people's will.

Of all the different forms of government one must consider the best to be the one that fulfills the people's happiness and security more completely and that provides the most guarantees against bad administration.

After all, everyone thinks and feels that an encroachment on the basic most important rights of the human individual and citizen not only dulls civic-mindedness but even causes a person to build up a feeling of hatred toward the state and a desire to demolish and destroy the state authority that nullifies the main purpose of human and civic existence.

In order to make the government's laws and directives more sensible and stable, I think this should be added to chapter 3, article 34: people elected to the Supreme Soviet shall be at least fifty years of age and have a higher education.

To the Council of Nationalities, at least thirty years of age, with a broad life experience.

Add to chapter 9, article 102: The death penalty shall be abolished, as a measure of social protection that is degrading for mankind in the twentieth century, and replaced by the penalty of exile from the USSR, with confiscation of property.

Add to article 108: When krai or oblast courts consider cases from People's Courts, the assessors in any session shall consist of four workers and six peasants. Ten percent of people's judges shall have a higher education.

Chapter 10, article 125, should be amended because freedom of the press is one of the greatest underpinnings of political freedom; therefore any restriction on the press should be regarded as an act of tyranny, and all citizens should be granted the right to express their opinion in the press without any censorship and without any obstacle to subscribing to and receiving from abroad newspapers and magazines of various parties and shadings.

Add to article 129: All citizens of the Union shall be granted the right freely to go abroad, to work, travel or for scholarly purposes, to any country in the world.

Add to article 141: In each election district, not only organizations but private individuals shall enter nominations in the lists of candidates, because not all organizations know all of the good people around them.

My sincere request to the esteemed editors of *Krest'ianskaia Gazeta* is the following: provide a broad introduction for our newspaper's readers in the immediate future to the constitutions of the advanced countries throughout the world, because most of the population does not even have the slightest inkling of the principles of these states. In particular, people should be familiarized with the French Constitution of 1789 [presumably either the Declaration of the Rights of Man and Citizen (1789) or the Constitution of the Constitutional Monarchy (1791)] and the American, published in 1772 [*sic*], as one that was fostered in the struggle for independence against English dominion in the colonies.

---

Clearly, the writer should hardly be considered an "ordinary kolkhoz farmer," given his profound reflections about the present and future of a country for which his heart aches. On the one hand, the letter is a cry of despair; on the other, it is an expression of hope for a miracle. The writer endorses the draft constitution in full, calling it "one of the most precious gifts from Soviet authority to the peoples of the Union since its rule began," then focuses primarily on those of its provisions with which the Soviet state was plainly at odds. How much courage it must have taken to write of the need to get acquainted with the constitutions of the "advanced countries throughout the world"—which were supposed to be described, rather, as the countries of "decaying capitalism." In addition, the writer went beyond the draft and suggested laying down in the constitution provisions that were totally unacceptable to the regime: abolition of the death penalty, abolition of censorship, and freedom to travel abroad among them.

An equally seditious letter arrived at the Constitutional Commission from a Leningrad engineer named Glebov, who deemed the publication of the draft of the new constitution to be "the beginning of great reforms." An excerpt from his letter found its way into an NKVD summary: "People's representatives elected by universal suffrage constitute a prodigious force that is capable of influencing the most sturdily organized governments. In considering the future and major state reforms, it is preferable to take account of all possible consequences. That is why it would be useful to ponder the formation under the protection of the legislative chambers of other political parties besides the Communist Party. It is better to provide conditions for their formation by overt means. Otherwise this manifestation of independent activity by the populace will take cover under public organizations of another kind."[36]

Similar comments and suggestions can be found in the materials on the discussion of the constitution. Someone named K. N. Tsenttsel' argued in his suggestions that general-education schools be made independent of the state and that freedom to criticize the activities of the highest and central bodies be guaranteed; he also called for the abolition of the death penalty and for not just public organizations but individual citizens to have the right to make nominations to the soviets, and he advocated an amnesty for political prisoners.[37] A. I. Basharin of Armavir openly wrote that "there is a ten million–strong army of prisoners in the country—the majority [victims of] false denunciations." He contended that this situation had stemmed from a settling of personal accounts and from criminal, irresponsible work by the local investigative agencies, courts, and procurators' offices; he asked that an inquiry be conducted and order restored.[38] There were suggestions for a provision allowing for a rejection of military service based on conscientious objection.[39] Opinions were offered that there should be a clause in the constitution guaranteeing the freedom to choose one's place of work and residence. There were objections to the compulsory assignment of young specialists. Many kolkhoz farmers complained that it was impossible for them to go to work in a factory.[40]

The "hostile comments and suggestions" included a letter from I. A. Tiushin of the Sunrise Kolkhoz in Breitovo Raion, Yaroslavl' Oblast. What is curious about the letter is that it shows how tenacious the idea of creating a Peasants' Union still was among the peasantry, even after the nightmare of collectivization:

# Document 68

Letter from kolkhoznik I. A. Tiushin proposing a Peasants' Union, 1936. RGASPI, f. 17, op. 120, d. 232, l. 79. Typewritten copy.

I propose, according to the draft sent down by the Constitutional Commission, that article 126, which refers to developing organized independent activities, be amended to give all kolkhoz and independent peasants the right to organize a Peasants' Union under every village soviet and which would directly handle all needs and clarifications with the central land administrations in view of the bureaucratic attitude of village soviets and kolkhoz boards, which in most cases lead kolkhoz peasants not to a prosperous, cultured life but to the collapse of the kolkhozes and their deterioration, and the provision of public services for peasants should not be considered in a general way—[on a] nationwide scale—but according to living conditions, especially in the northern oblasts.

Antibureaucratic sentiments, partly encouraged by the press, could be heard fairly often in society during the discussion of the draft constitution. True, people could level accusations only at a specific Soviet bureaucrat who had acted in a high-handed way or committed abuses. They were not allowed to criticize bureaucratism as a phenomenon of Soviet life, under threat of being blacklisted, especially if they went so far as to criticize the power structure.

A certain exception was made for Stakhanovites. The press, for example, conducted an active discussion of the persecution of the famous Stakhanovite A. K. Busygin, whom his management tried to dismiss for overfulfilling norms without the shop floor head's permission. "There are hundreds of thousands of cases," Stakhanovite M. F. Golosov wrote in this regard to the Eighth Congress of Soviets, "in which bosses, acting on a spontaneous whim, dismiss working people." Golosov claimed that he too was subjected to a lot of baiting. One might raise questions about the "spontaneous whim," but it is obvious that the leadership at the time was on the side of the Stakhanovites. Incidentally, ordinary workers sometimes complained that the creation of special conditions for the Stakhanovites and their constant travels to propagandize their experience were breaches of the right to work. "They're skipping work," went the complaint, "while we pay for their labor."[41]

Meanwhile, a new leadership stratum was rapidly taking shape, and it began to assert itself and its interests and tried to incorporate them into the constitution. For example, Chairman Chubukov of the Dedinovo Village Soviet in Lukhovitsy Raion, Moscow Oblast, made the following suggestion for the draft: "Article 10 should be amended to say that comfort and luxury, which used to be a sign of a bourgeois life and now under socialism reflect prosperity and culture, are also protected by law."[42] After many years of preaching of asceticism and universal leveling, this was an unprecedented statement.

In many letters people noted the birth of a "new Soviet bourgeoisie." Kolkhoz farmer N. G. Zhiliaev of the Azov–Black Sea Krai, outraged by this development, naively suggested combating this group by a tried and true method—stripping it of political rights:

---

## Document 69

Letter from kolkhoznik N. G. Zhiliaev proposing revision to the constitution, 1936. RGASPI, f. 17, op. 120, d. 232, l. 70. Typewritten copy.

---

A special paragraph needs to be included in the constitution saying that all able-bodied men and women who do absolutely no work and are not engaged in any activity for the general benefit shall be deprived of political rights. The point is that a new Soviet bourgeoisie—loafer-parasites—is taking shape.

At our kolkhoz, for example, blind sixty-year-old women are sent out to go spear tobacco stalks while these tortoises are growing fat and don't want to lift a finger, in two years at the kolkhoz they have not logged a single laborday, and through their husbands they are always the first to pull out of the kolkhoz pantry whatever goes in there. They are citizen Il'ina, the wife of the kolkhoz bursar; Shevchenko, the wife of the kolkhoz party organizer; and citizen Ivereva, the wife of the kolkhoz chairman. The last one worked on the kolkhoz in 1935 and she had about two hundred labordays, but in 1936 she hasn't had a single laborday. She says to her husband, why aren't their wives working on the kolkhoz, and you after all are more their boss, well then I won't go, either.

---

The letter is also noteworthy for the fact that it touches on the problem of differentiation within the kolkhoz and refers to those

who are living an easy life off "kolkhoz grain." Red Army soldier
F. L. Schastlivyi wrote from Chita that "the wives of many directors,
managers, engineers and technicians don't work and have a servant. . . . This is out-and-out exploitation."[43] Even though the draft
constitution stated that exploiter classes had been completely eliminated in the USSR, kolkhoz farmer M. Ye. Filippov insisted on an addition that would cite the need for protecting the working people
from red tape and bureaucratism, because bureaucrats and red-
tapists, in his opinion, exploited the working people with illegal decisions and resolutions and were "offshoots of the capitalist classes."[44]

The following excerpt from a letter by the aforementioned I.
Savurin of Voronezh oblast colorfully describes the kind of abuse —
verbal and otherwise—to which kolkhoz farmers were subjected:

## Document 70

Letter from kolkhoznik I. Savurin proposing revisions to the constitution, 1936. RGASPI,
f. 17, op. 120, d. 232, l. 87. Typewritten copy.

. . . A kind of constitution should be put out so that everyone can live freely
and so that the brigade leaders don't shout at us—Hey, why don't you go to
work, otherwise I will deal with you. You can't say a word in your own defense, or they will start to threaten: "Don't talk so much, or I will nail you with
article 58. Van'ka got ten years of pulling wheelbarrows and it's time for you to
land up there. Grishka did five years, so now he's not saying Why doesn't
your wife go to work? We're going to let people like that have it soon, all we
need is a scrap of paper and you'll find yourself on the canal" [the White Sea–
Baltic Canal project]. For my part, political prisoners need an amnesty. The
kind of politicos we have, they are fifty-eight times a fool, and he was charged
with article 58 and got ten years. I can't read or write very well, I read the
newspaper and some old men talk about how bad life used to be, you would
owe money to a shopkeeper, a village chief would demand his debt, and if you
didn't pay he would slug you in the teeth. Now, if the litter hasn't been swept
up around the farmstead, they put you in the bughouse for about fifteen days,
I got to thinking and I started feeling ashamed, we live in a free country, but
there are so many prisoners and for what. If your crops get diseased it's ten
years, if your horse wears out its withers it's ten years, if you didn't give somebody a cigarette it's ten years, and so on, if our dear leader Comrade Stalin
knew what is going on in the countryside, he would never forgive it.

One can imagine how easy it was in such an atmosphere, on the one hand, to fan the flames of hatred in society and incite subordinates against their immediate superiors, and on the other, to pin the blame on those superiors for going too far and for supposedly misinterpreting leadership guidelines. Very often the poorest and half-starving segments of society were those who articulated antibureaucratic sentiments. By complaining about the total dominance of the kolkhoz and sovkhoz system and the annual famines, they hoped to rectify the situation with the aid of the new constitution.

How were people supposed to avert the conversion of so-called socialist property into a feeding trough for the elect? How were they to prevent it from being plundered and squandered? The material on the discussion of the draft shows that no levers were found in Soviet society for this purpose other than to toughen punitive policies. Suggestions on this topic poured in, and the sheer quantity of them drowned out the voices that called for legality, mitigated punishments, persuasion, and mercy. When the constitution was adopted, this development was reflected in an addition to article 131: "Persons who encroach on public or socialist property are enemies of the people."

Yakov Oguz, a young technician at the Moscow State Ball-Bearing Factory no. 1, went even further, urging that persons who encroached on citizens' personal property acquired with earned income also be declared enemies of the people. "This addition," he wrote, "will play a big role not only for our everyday life but also will have an enormous resonance in the future. Indeed, there are no rich people and no poor people in the Soviet Union. Everybody toils equally. Therefore a thief is a parasite, an enemy of the people. With the introduction of the constitution a thief—let it be a thief of [personal] property—should be declared an enemy of the people, and just like a thief of socialist property he should be punished to the full extent of revolutionary law. It must be made clear that we have no unemployment, and consequently there is no reason for thievery. And that thievery is a grave crime against the state (there must be no thieves under socialism), against the people."[45] This is the logic of the dogmas of historical materialism, which the writer has mastered, taken to the point of absurdity and colliding with reality and common sense. But his prediction that the struggle against enemies of the people will "have an enormous resonance in the future" was exactly right.

Sometimes one is simply astonished by the literal, straightforward interpretation of the principle "Whoever doesn't work, doesn't eat" and the related excess of brutality and implacability in the society of the 1930s. There was a high degree of readiness in the public consciousness for a new war—this time against "enemies of the people." "Stalin's constitution is a historic document," reported G. I. Proskuriakov, a staffer with the newspaper *Udarnik* [Shock Worker] in Chistoozyornyi Raion, Western Siberian Krai. "Upon completion of work on it, the activists submit an addition to article 12—all individuals who persistently shirk work and do not want to toil honestly (loafers, self-seekers, bunglers, careless workers) shall be considered enemies of the people."[46]

A great many comments came in with respect to articles 120 and 122, which concerned the rights of the elderly and women, family problems and the protection of motherhood and childhood. This was undoubtedly a reflection of the social and demographic problems that worsened during the 1930s. The experimentation in the preceding years in the realm of the family and marriage was attributed by many as the reason for an increase in divorces, a flippant attitude toward family duties, and a drop in the birthrate. So concerned was the leadership about these developments that it decided to take measures, including the adoption of new laws, aimed at strengthening the family's foundations. True, in keeping with the spirit of the times, administrative bans and coercive elements were incorporated into these measures. Among such acts was the newly adopted law "On the Protection of Motherhood and Childhood," best known for outlawing abortions.[47]

All these measures could not help but elicit interested comments during the discussion of the draft constitution. Some letters voiced protest against the abortion ban as a violation of citizens' rights. But most of the comments carried the flavor of household squabbles and complaints on this subject. For example, Maria Stepanovna Khudiakova of Cheliabinsk wrote that she had made a mistake choosing a husband—"He was married to two other women besides me and they had one child apiece, I found out too late—I was already pregnant, and now he has gotten himself a fourth one and taken off."[48]

Meanwhile, the roughly five hundred women who took part in a meeting on the constitution in Berdiansk Raion, Dnepropetrovsk Oblast, apparently discussed everything thoroughly and drafted a letter with suggestions to the TsK of the VKP(b) that included a section "On Alimony and Libertinism":

## Document 71

Collective letter from women of Dnepropetrovsk Oblast to TsK VKP(b) on alimony and libertinism, 1936. GARF, f. 3316, op. 41, d. 82, ll. 13–15. Original manuscript.

. . . About alimony and libertinism, which is at a high level in our country, it is wrong that the constitution says one-quarter [of a couple's earnings] are used for the first child and one-third for two, because this has led to the point where they only judge everywhere about alimony; i.e., they let men change wives, after all divorce is expensive, so men do not get a divorce or do not register—they just get together and then break up, but they bring orphans into the world, and they are given the shameful name of "bastard"; in order to destroy this libertinism and the shameful name of bastard for a child we submit this suggestion:

1. If a girl gives birth from an unmarried man (the marriage is unregistered)—she gets 50 percent of his wages "so that there are no snickers at women." If he does the same thing with another one, the second one gets one-quarter for her child (so she knows that he has a child and so his wife doesn't get any ideas that he left one girl but not me, he won't leave me, and this will make men settle down). But if he does it with a third one, then the child is to be placed in a foundling hospital, and he and she are to pay the hospital three hundred rubles apiece, plus they must both do forced labor for three months.

2. If a widow or a girl begets a child with a family man, it is the same thing—he does three months and four hundred rubles, and she does three months and three hundred rubles for child rearing. When men paid one-third of their wages for alimony, men settled down a little, but when it became one-quarter, the level of libertinism rose by 50 percent—"men were given freedom"—we demand a stop to it. For an abortion a woman should get three months in prison, for abortions have now become very common and the strangulation of the newborn is continuing. We ask especially that the unmarried men be hit, what is going on is unbearable, they have five children apiece. The level of libertinism has reached the point where a man begets five children with five women. . . .

The women concluded by asking that notations on children be recorded on men's internal passports and military cards so that alimony payers could be sought out more easily. The letter is surprisingly consistent with such landmarks of common law as the ancient "Russian Truth," or "Rus' Justice," dating from the eleventh to thirteenth centuries.

Now here is a document of a completely different kind. Lev Vladimirovich Kashkin, a resident of Leningrad, decided to do his bit for the solution of demographic problems. "Population policy has never had a place in history," he wrote. "Every government has handled it the way an ostrich saves itself from a pursuer. I suggest that more effective means be used for population policy than hiding one's head under one's wing." He suggested incorporating into the constitution an entire special chapter (10-a) outlining the responsibility of citizens for their health and longevity and establishing a People's Commissariat of Capacity for Work and Longevity (Narkomtrudolg). The writer sent down from on high a theoretical substantiation in the form of a "note," in which he tried "creatively" to develop the thesis that the organs of the human body are natural tools of production. The "note" consisted of seven chapters, whose content could have competed with Aldous Huxley's Brave New World—published, incidentally, in 1932. The writer realizes, he wrote, that he may be accused of encroaching on citizens' personal liberties and rights, but concern about the interests of socialist society and the state are, to him, paramount.[49]

We cannot reproduce this document in full, but will summarize it and quote a few excerpts. In the process, the following point should be kept in mind. To ensure that he is not misunderstood and to "avoid a narrow interpretation" of his ideas, Kashkin deliberately replaced the words mother, father, parents, children, "and other synonyms" with innovative terms, thereby creating a kind of new language.[50]

The note began with a proposal that the norms of Soviet law incorporate citizens' responsibility for their health in order "to assist the Soviet government in eliminating a social evil that inflicts enormous harm on the construction and defense capacity of the homeland." The evil was illness that resulted from "violations by citizens of the requirements of health discipline," whereas "the tasks of socialist construction and its pace require good health." Because illness stemmed in most cases from violations of health discipline, illness might fairly be deemed a crime, unless there were extenuating circumstances, because "anyone who is ill causes harm to society in many ways": he falls short in production, "he doesn't work but eats," he is "a burden for the country's defense capacity," and so on.[51]

The writer proposed setting up three categories of citizens: *zdravniki* (the "healthy ones"), who preserve and fortify their health; *zdravseredniaki* (the "in-betweens"); and *protivozdravniki* (the "antihealth people"), who do not preserve or fortify their health and include "not very reliable or hopeless, covert or overt health hooligans, . . . a sad legacy of our historical past." The health campaign requires a Stakhanovite-type socialist competition that calls for "producing individual achievements." Every citizen's health level must be determined "with the aid of instruments," and society must be informed "so that everyone knows." The reasons identified for violations of health discipline include ignorance about health, health-threatening behavior (unhealthy habits: gluttony, drunkenness, a dissolute lifestyle, unsanitary habits), antihealth ideology ("justification of violations by accusing zdravniki of overemphasis on biology [*biologizm*], of racism, etc.") and pointless sacrifices of one's health (becoming worn out for the sake of excessive earnings). Measures are also suggested for overcoming these causes: first, a campaign to stamp out ignorance about health and to instruct the people in hygiene, including folk hygiene, physical fitness, proper diet, and vitamins; second, the elimination of wage leveling and the use of a socialist health competition; third, a study of the works of Marx, Engels, Lenin, and Stalin.[52]

"Bodily organs," said Kashkin, "are a kind of equipment that the toiler carries with him in every field of activity, so to speak, the country's corporal industry," which "should be public socialist property." The Narkomtrudolg system required special bodies that "would set up precise accounting of the growth of the population's capital of working capacity." In the writer's view, this called for the establishment of an extensive network of measuring laboratories to determine the health level of all citizens, divide them into categories and move them from one category to another, depending on their health. The creation of a people's commissariat could be based on the model of Soviet defense construction.[53]

How, asked Kashkin, are a specific person's efforts to take care of his health to be evaluated? "To do this, one must compare two health levels: that which prevailed at the time of the citizen's birth with what prevails now. The difference will show whether the efforts were positive or negative. But at the same time the natal level as a starting point is an indicator of the mother's care for the embryo and the fetus and her behavior during pregnancy."[54] The degree of citizens' responsibility was based on age groups, of which he defined four:

---

## Document 72

Proposals on demographic policy submitted by L. V. Kashkin, Leningrad, 1936. GARF, f. 3316, op. 41, d. 79, ll. 56–57, 59, 61, 69–71. Typewritten original.

---

1. Natal citizens—from conception to weaning. Until now neither the embryo nor the intrauterine or extrauterine fetus was recognized as a citizen. This, of course, is wrong. Excluding this age from a citizen's lifetime and depriving it of rights have no legal basis. But the responsibility of natal citizens, because they cannot take care of themselves, equals zero, while the responsibility of the birth mother for them equals 100 percent.
2. Young citizens—from weaning to real maturity. Subgroups are children, adolescents and young people. Their responsibility for their health increases from zero to 100 percent.
3. Mature citizens—their level of responsibility equals 100 percent.
4. Old citizens—our goal is to achieve universal longevity for the population and to eliminate senility while maintaining people's capacity to work. But for the present their responsibility for their health declines from 100 percent to zero.

[The writer went on to the regulation of birthrate processes under socialism:]

The health of a natal citizen relates to the health of the same citizen's other ages roughly in the same way as the country's natural riches relate to their future exploitation. The magnitude and quality of the internal riches that are extracted from the depths of the maternal organism are decisive for the development of the capacity to work in maturity. But a poorly organized extraction of natural riches may lead both to their nonproductive loss during the extraction process and their spoilage. . . .

Absolutely everything in a woman's behavior is reflected one way or another in the composition of her blood and in the uniformity and regularity with which all parts of her body and the fetus are supplied with blood. Hence it is the woman's duty to take care of the health of new generations. . . . As for the man, he has no duty to the new generation, since children are produced not by him but by the woman. The man bears responsibility in health terms only for the quality of his fertilizing impregnation. That is the man's duty.

["Society has the right to provide better for its best citizens at any age," wrote Kashkin, and he concluded his theory with zeal:]

The very first steps of the new population policy along the path of eliminating these social vices, which are detrimental to the population's capacity for work and longevity, will completely change the public face and social status of Soviet women. Their awareness that childbearing production is being converted from a private matter to a state matter, that by conscientiously performing their duties in this production they can increase, in an unlimited way, our homeland's might in every field that requires a capacity for work and longevity from citizens, will give them an awareness of their dignity that they have never had before in the history of the human race.

Women in the highest childbearing categories—Stakhanovites of childbearing production who set the highest standards in it—will enjoy a level of honor and respect in our country that has never been conferred on any queen. Our new population policy will transform the slogan "Clear the way for the woman!" from a pretty phrase into an actual practice, into living, concrete reality. Women from other countries will have to marvel at our country, where women and children are "paramount." During the difficult minutes of their lives they will remember this.

[Kashkin's draft chapter, comprising thirteen articles (compared with the sixteen contained in the official draft of chapter 10, "Basic Rights and Obligations of Citizens"), followed. We may dispense with articles 1–5, which dealt with the rights—or rather obligations—of citizens to be healthy and "produce civic progeny," in order to quote the next three articles in full:]

Article 6. Every natal citizen of the USSR shall be listed in one of the categories established by the government, based on his natal health level. The natal health level shall be entered in the citizen's birth certificate, and subsequently in his [internal] passport as a permanent fact about his identity. The natal health level shall serve simultaneously as an indicator of the citizen's future capacity for work and, on the other hand, as an indicator of his producer's (in everyday language: his mother's) fulfillment of childbearing discipline.

Citizens who were born before the law on women's childbearing responsibility takes effect and whose natal level is unknown shall be listed in the category based on their current health level.

An improvement or decline in a current health level resulting from the personal health efforts or health negligence of young citizens shall entail, on a mandatory basis, a corresponding rise or fall in his childbearing category and the amount of social security for childbirth.

Article 7. A woman's childbearing right to produce citizens and a man's impregnation right to fertilize an embryo, as a socialist right, shall be separated from the personal, individualistic conjugal right to sexual cohabitation between spouses. Childbirth-capable women and impregnation-capable men shall make a commitment, upon entering into matrimony, to take the necessary preventive measures against conceiving an embryo.

In the event that a childbirth-capable woman who is married decides to give the country a new citizen, she shall be required, prior to conception, to apply to the childbirth bureau for a formal divorce and for certification of the impregnation ability of the man she has designated for impregnation and for certification of the normal natal level of her future child.

The marriage shall be permitted to resume only upon termination of the citizen's natal age, i.e., after weaning. Liability for violation of this law shall remain in effect even in the event that the natal level of the infant does not fall into the lower categories.

Article 8. Every male citizen of the USSR shall care for the quality and fullness of his fertilizing agent. Based on the fullness of their agent, men shall be divided into officially established categories, which shall be registered by the childbirth bureau.

Both the category of the childbearing woman and the category of the impregnating man shall be considered in the establishment of a normal natal level for a future natal citizen.

---

Article 9 dealt with state social security for childbirth, based on citizens' childbearing categories; Article 10, the obligation of men to pay a childbirth tax proportional to their earnings and the termination of their payment of individual alimony; Article 11, the obligation of women to produce "progeny" whose level "is not lower than the standard indicated to [them] by the childbirth bureau." Article 12 cited the right of citizens not to exercise their childbearing and impregnating right, but it provided for the introduction of a universal, compulsory childbearing obligation for women "in the event that two-thirds of women capable of childbearing demand this and the government deems this to be expedient"; Article 13 would have outlawed sterilization and declared it to be a state crime.[55]

One might just laugh and put this document aside as an oddity and a manifestation of sick idiosyncrasy, but two considerations make this response untenable. First, the writer was not alone in his ideas. A man named A. Mikhailov from Tula submitted this proposal: "For the purpose of full justice and equality among people, introduce an article making it compulsory or a human duty for every man and woman, to the extent of their ability, to fertilize and be fertilized and have at least two children together before the age of forty."[56] Second, the extreme literalism of Kashkin's materialist outlook is reminiscent of some of the intellectual currents of the late 1920s and early 1930s—Vladimir Vernadsky's projections of the transformation via the application of science of the "biosphere" into a new state, the "noosphere," or sphere of reason, and Andrei Platonov's dark parodies or "despairing farces" of revolutionary romanticism are two examples. One might add that combating entropy, or literally overcoming mortality, was a philosophical and literary theme that continued to exercise its attraction, actually gaining greater currency as the 1930s progressed.[57] The constitution, by proclaiming that a socialist society had been achieved, encouraged such flights of fancy. If the class question had been resolved, why not begin to tackle the (even more fundamental) biological question?

The Eighth All-Union Extraordinary Congress of Soviets opened on 25 November 1936 and approved Stalin's report, which he delivered at the behest of the Constitutional Commission. The 220 members of the editorial commission spent about a week on an article-by-article discussion of the amendments and additions that had been submitted. The overwhelming majority of them were not accepted. The congress approved the new constitution on 5 December. That date was declared a national holiday. The adoption of the constitution was immediately followed by a new campaign for its "elucidation to the masses" and for preparation of elections to the new bodies of power. The party organs seemed to attach no lesser importance to this campaign than to the discussion of the draft; its chief purpose appears to have been to solidify in mass consciousness the idea of the leading role of the VKP(b) in Soviet society and the good deeds that the party had bestowed on the people. Many articles and provisions of the constitution were only partly operative, for the conditions and mechanisms did not exist to enforce them, while others remained completely on paper. Real life often proved to be too far removed from the idyll of constitutional norms. Subsequent events showed that the constitution utterly failed to provide legislative obstacles to the mass repression that swept the country right after its adoption. The irony of history was that most of those who drew up the new basic law were consumed in the fire of the Yezhovshchina.

Nevertheless, the significance of the constitution was immense, because it served for many years as the starting point for resistance to illegalities, abuses of power, deprivation of rights, and arbitrary rule. Attempts to reform the system began, as a rule, with appeals to the constitution.

1. A young worker at the Magnitogorsk Metallurgical Factory.

2. "Don't forget about maternity assistance and consultation in kolkhozes and sovkhozes." The tractor and the day nursery are identified as the "engines of the new village." The new fictive village depicted here in 1930 contains a club, cafeteria, dormitory, day nursery, midwife station, and maternity consultation.

3. "Freed-up labor of the kolkhozes to industry." The hand in the lower left is writing a contract between a kolkhoz and an industrial enterprise. The system of "organized recruitment" *(orgnabor)* was supposed to regulate the supply of labor to industry but was widely circumvented by all parties concerned. Note that although the factory is modern and presumably mechanized, the recruits are wielding the tools of manual labor.

4. These iconic workers are part of an exemplary shock brigade striking blows against the "antedeluvian way of life of laziness."

5. Leading cadres from one of Moscow's factories.

6. A secretary at her desk at Moscow's Machine-Tool Factory. Note the abacus to her right.

7.  A purge of cadres.

8.  "You work like you're on the edge of a straight razor." Last page of a letter from soviet chairman G. S. Onishchenko to Kalinin, 15 October 1933 (doc. 45).

9. A young engineer posing at Moscow's Machine-Tool Factory. The photograph on the right is of Stalin. The white bust in the middle is of Lenin.

10. The draft of the constitution was discussed at countless meetings throughout the Soviet Union. Here a "meeting" is held in the open air.

11. A demonstration in Moscow celebrating the adoption of the constitution on 6 December 1935. The banner reads "Long Live the Constitution of Freedom, Joy, and Happiness."

12. *Notables of the Country of Soviets.* This panel, painted by a collective under the direction of V. P. Yefanov for the Soviet pavilion at the New York World's Fair of 1939, foregrounds outstanding Stakhanovites, aviators, scientists, writers, and musicians.

13. The fish department of the Yeliseev food store on Moscow's Gor'ky Street in the latter half of the 1930s.

14. "Dejeuner sur l'herbe," Soviet-style.

15. Stakhanovites of
Moscow's Machine-Tool
Factory with a motorcycle
awarded as a prize.

16. "Pyramid," one of the most popular forms of amateur talent activities in the 1930s. Groups selected by their respective trade union committees performed on holidays in parades and stadiums.

НА КОЛЛЕКТИВНУЮ РАБОТУ.

17.   "Off to collective work," a Soviet poster.

18.   Picking tomatoes at a kolkhoz on the outskirts of Moscow. The pickers appear to be all women, whereas the two figures standing erect toward the rear are men.

19. The poster quotes (in Ukrainian) a dictum of P. P. Postyshev, Ukrainian party boss: "We must make 1935 a year of bountiful harvest no matter what the climatic conditions."

20. Kolkhoz farmers at work.

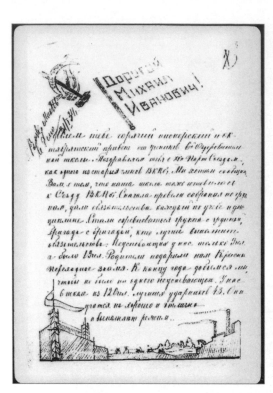

21.    A salutatory letter to Kalinin, written by Young Pioneers at Health-Improvement School no. 6 on the eve of the Seventeenth Party Congress in Janurary 1934 (doc. 136).

22.    "To dear comrade M. I. Kalinin" from ten-year-old Boria Moskalev, a pupil in the fourth grade at a factory training school in Moscow, 1934.

23. A children's demonstration on a kolkhoz on the outskirts of Moscow during the period of collectivization. Banners read "We will increase the harvest on the kolkhoz" and "In celebration of Red Navy Day sing more merrily, sing to the harvest on the collective fields."

24. A parade under the banners "We will liquidate the kulaks as a class" and "All to the struggle against the wreckers of agriculture."

25. Theory: A class studying agriculture.

26. Practice: Kolkhoz children mowing.

27. A kindergarten at
a Moscow factory.

28. A summer camp for Young Pioneers. The sign over the
porch reads "Thank you comrade Stalin for a happy and joyous childhood."

29. Shaming: Winners of the "infamous banner for a tortoise's pace."

# CHAPTER FOUR

# Love and Plenty

IN MARCH 1939 an amateur poet sent a poem to the Eighteenth
Congress of the VKP(b) in which he wrote:

> Heroes grow all over our land.
> And if you suddenly ask each one:
> "Tell me, who inspired your exploits?"
> With a happy smile, he will joyfully reply:
> "He who is the creator of all that is wonderful,
> The masterful architect, our friend and father
> Comrade Stalin. We are Stalin's children."[1]

Many regard the second half of the 1930s as the shining hour
of Stalinist socialism, notwithstanding the mass repressions, the
Yezhovshchina, the atmosphere of latent fear, suspicion, the very
clear sensation of approaching war and the related preparations,
and the sudden friendship with yesterday's worst enemy, Nazi Germany. The adoption of the new constitution raised many hopes. The
winds of change, which were often contradictory and variable, made
the situation in the country extremely complicated and tense, but the
overall mood was definitely optimistic. This was the apogee of the
prolonged tumult that the Revolution had set off, a tumult that was
exultant at the dawn but later became apathetic and gloomy.

There were triumphant welcomes for conquerors of the Arctic, the culmination of enormous campaigns to explore the natural resources of the northern and eastern regions, lay new transportation lines, and open up the Northern Maritime Route. Zealous participants in these endeavors became heroes, "notable people of the Land of the Soviets." Newspapers began to put the spotlight on geologists, scientists, fliers, and navigators who had pioneered the exploration of the Arctic, and children were named for them. Exotic names appeared, such as Oiushminal'd (for Otto Yul'evich Shmidt *na l'dine,* on the ice floe)—a vivid sign of the times. The Arctic heroes became models to emulate and idols for the young generation.[2] The prestige of such occupations as fliers and sailors was extraordinarily high.

Strengthening the USSR in every possible way became the major, if not sole, theme of literature, art, and the movies. A pompous form of painting and architecture, intended to glorify the nation's grandeur and its leaders and create awe among the population, asserted itself. Music and the theater played a big role in ideological education. The main requirement was accessibility. Special attention was given to songs—upbeat, buoyant, majestic, and lyrical. They evoked the heroic spirit of the civil war and the romanticism of the workaday routine of socialist construction, and everyone, especially young people, was supposed to hear them every day. Movies, literature, and the mass media were used to "perfect" the ideas that were being instilled in the masses about Stalin as "the father of the nation," about the party's concern for people, about their happy childhoods and altogether happy life in the USSR.

The flights of fancy stimulated by such ideas are well illustrated by the celebration of the twentieth anniversary of the October Revolution. A five-volume work was prepared for the occasion, at the initiative of Maksim Gor'ky, to show the results of socialist construction and the achievements of the USSR. The fifth volume was to be called *A Look to the Future* and was to contain "scientifically based fantasies." Several meetings of the group of authors are known to have been held, and at these sessions the most famous scholars, cultural and artistic figures, and economic leaders tried to describe what was in store for Europe and the world in the immediate future. The writer Vladimir Kirshon touched off a whole debate on the topic "Will the whole world be socialist in fifteen or twenty years, or just Europe?"[3] Equally intriguing was the discussion that conjured up a future socialist outer space, the Arctic, and agriculture overhauled "according to the principles of [Ivan] Michurin" (1855–1935), a self-taught horticulturalist whose grafting techniques and successful hybrids formed the basis for the ambitious and unsubstantiated claims of phylogenetic transformation advanced by Trofim Lysenko and a corresponding rejection of Mendelian genetics; predictions were also offered about the diet, architecture, theater, and art of the future. As for the USSR's natural resources, the well-known filmmaker Aleksandr Dovzhenko related that "while I traveled around the Far East, I thought a lot about its physical features and came to the conclusion that the Tatar Strait must be eliminated" in order to improve the climate of Primor'e by making it subtropical. It turned out that Dovzhenko had already conveyed this idea to the Vladivostok Oblast Committee of the VKP(b). Just one obstacle troubled him: "If this is written about, the Japanese, after all, will kick up a fuss." The future of Soviet prisoners also came up. Specifically, the GULAG official S. G. Firin, who had presided over the White Sea Canal construction project, attributed to Comrade Stalin its initiation as well as that of the Moscow-Volga Canal: "He also set the task, about a year and a half ago, of building a canal between Moscow and Vladivostok," Firin said confidentially, although he did not clarify how many prisoners this would require or whether, in fact, the labor resources that were still at liberty would be sufficient.

The history of the Soviet state and the ruling party were constructed in the same vein. Prominent academicians "demonstrated" that Marxism-Leninism and state patriotism, as personified by Stalin, were one and the same. Writers set to work producing historical novels that fleshed out this notion. Among the important milestones in this campaign were *Istoriia fabrik i zavodov* (IFZ, the history of factories and plants), *Istoriia grazhdanskoi voiny v SSSR* (IGV, the history of the civil war in the USSR), and *Kratkii kurs istorii VKP(b)* (a short course in the history of the VKP[b]), the last of which played a huge role in imposing a new version of the country's history.

The transformation of society's historical consciousness in the second half of the 1930s is a subject for a separate discussion. Both from above and from below, history was reworked on an enormous scale, simplified, and presented exclusively in black-and-white terms. All "enemies" and "undetermined persons" were lumped together and portrayed as supporters of historical idiocy. Any work that did not conform with the canonized version of the Revolution and socialist construction, the role of the party, and Lenin and Stalin was withdrawn from circulation. Everything that had been created in the USSR was depicted as a natural result of the class struggle over the preceding centuries. It was on this basis that the continuity of pre- and postrevolutionary history was restored. Whether a certain event had actually occurred or not was of little importance. Something similar had taken place, and that was what mattered. This kind of history was more akin to psychological suggestion and merged at times with the mythmaking of folklore.

Here, for example, is a letter to *Krest'ianskaia Gazeta* from I. K. Karniush. (Most spelling errors and some grammar in the original have been corrected for clarity in the translation.—*Trans.*):

---

# Document 73

Letter from I. K. Karniush to *Krest'ianskaia Gazeta* outlining the history of modern Russia, 30 October 1938. RGAE, f. 396, op. 10, d. 97, ll. 34–370b. Original manuscript.

---

Day 30 month 10 year 1938

Comrade Uritsky, I sincerely thank you and our valiant Comrade Stalin for your such hard efforts for us peasants. How our valiant Comrade Stalin shows concern for every person tirelessly day and night so that every peasant can only take care of himself and so that no peasant can give himself up to another saboteur turns over all his resolutions to you Comrade Uritsky as his faithful friend so that you can distribute to the whole population through *Krest'ianskaia Gazeta* and you teach so that we can all be literate. For this I sincerely thank you a hundred times I am already an old man, sixty-eight years old and through your *Krest'ianskaia Gazeta* I have learned to read and write a little it's just too bad that I've lost my eyesight.

So I subscribe to *Krest'ianskaia Gazeta* not just because I want to read it but I ask you Comrade Uritsky whatever little articles I send you that are worthy that you print them in *Krest'ianskaia Gazeta*. [A discussion of the rise of the Romanovs follows.] Now let's talk about the sovereigns. When he took over the sovereign Peter I he was already sovereign not with the boyars but with the ministers and the generals and Peter wanted to develop Russia so when he rode around the German kingdoms he liked the cultured German manners and he took teachers from the German states to educate Russia and from England, Germany, from France and Italy, and gave them the power to run all of Russia.

Then after reigning until he was twenty-nine he remembered what kind of sovereign am I when teachers are ruling all of Russia but I am the tsar and he thought about how to take power into his own hands. He gives the order to divide the troops into four parts and do maneuvers but with empty weapons and we will fight and whoever takes the most prisoners will have the power. So they went out to the maneuvers he thought they would all fight for themselves but they only fought for Peter and when they pressed him up against the Neva so he would surrender he didn't surrender but set strict discipline for his soldiers, didn't allow himself to get caught then jumped into the Neva [with] his detachment and in the Neva there were rafts floating so he floated down the Neva on the rafts for a whole week and came ashore across the border where maneuvers were set. Then he waited for nightfall with his detachment [words unintelligible] he checked all around him and poured a flask of alcohol for his soldiers and orders his soldiers go to the battle line and get the whole line drunk but make sure you don't drink anything yourself. The soldiers did just that and when the whole battle line was drunk and passed out then Peter and his detachments surrounded the whole [word unintelligible] and cried out surrender you are all my prisoners and power is mine.

After these maneuvers he took ill and three years later he died and his wife Catherine was very thin and bony. Two men with outstretched arms could not reach around her. She not only gave up power to the leading bodies but also gave up her peasants to serfdom. The peasants lived in serfdom under the sovereigns first Catherine's son Paul, Paul's son Alexander, and Alexander's son Nicholas. When war broke out with the French in Sevastopol', Nicholas died. Alexander his son took power and got rid of serfdom and wanted to take land away and give it to the peasants but the leading bodies killed him.

Now Alexander III ruled supposedly he was a peacemaker. Then Nicholas [II] took over who gathered the State Duma so many times [three words unintelligible]. The State Duma didn't take place and so he received the command that you don't give power and you don't remove us from it when he left the throne himself he smashed everything now the entire old government has been hanged and shot. And our valiant Comrade Vladimir Il'ich Lenin smashed all of the old gang took power put party people in the posts and as much as he struggled for the people when he ended his life he couldn't beat his enemies.

Now Comrade Lenin left a faithful and true friend to fight for us against saboteurs and said we must have millions and millions of Communists then we can have the idea of the people's life.

## Document 73 *continued*

So our valiant Comrade Stalin already tightened all the faucets so tightly both on the border and inside the country with his faithful Stakhanovites and it seems as though there shouldn't be any breakdowns anywhere. But there are.

Here is an example. Again in Siberian Oblast, Kuibyshev Raion, Yepashin Village Soviet, at the Bliukher Kolkhoz in the village of Konstantinovka, grain was threshed during the 1937 harvest you might say in the months of April and May, and this grain threshing was not given for labordays or for anything, they just left it for too long to rot on the *ladoshki* [open, tamped-down, clayey areas where grain was poured during the harvest] more than two hundred centners of rye about twenty-five or fifty centners of wheat—and the rest were oats that just lay there probably then they will send people to inspect and I, Karniush, am accountable [to the point] of capital punishment. . . .

Signed Ivan Kirillovich Karniush

The writer, evidently an ethnic Belorussian, only recently had begun to learn to write and did not know a number of letters or the rules of grammar. In addition, only in places does his narrative faintly resemble what actually occurred; most of it is more like a Russian folk tale. But significantly, he tacks on to this extremely schematic version of events an account of very recent occurrences at the Bliukher Kolkhoz, thereby aligning himself with the class struggle against enemies of the people.

At the same time, what people had really experienced during all those years did not vanish but shifted to a subconscious level and sometimes was manifested in completely unexpected situations. This was vividly illustrated by a clinical case that was recorded at the Voronezh Medical Institute:

## Document 74

Clinical case recorded at Voronezh Medical Institute, 1935. S. G. Zhislin, *Ob alkogol'nykh rasstroistvakh: klinicheskie issledovaniia*, Voronezh, 1935, pp. 113–14.

Case 14. Patient Z., forty-five years old.

Brought in from the train-station infirmary at 4 A.M.

. . . First contact with alcohol was at age twenty. Seldom drank. Drunkenness intensified at approximately thirty-six, thirty-seven years of age.

. . . Spent past few weeks in Moscow, where he was visiting his brother and was trying to get a job. Prior to leaving Moscow he drank for four consecutive days (up to a liter a day). Did not sleep well, and ate irregularly. Had his suitcase with belongings stolen at the [Moscow] train station. With a few rubles in his pocket, the patient got on a train. He hoped to find a job in Voronezh, counting on help from old friends. He was wrong: when he arrived in Voronezh on 27 September, he could not find his friends and spent four days at the train station. Felt physically ill, and grew very weak. Did not sleep at all for four nights. Ate very little during this time.

On the night of 30 September–1 October the patient was overcome by extraordinary fears: passengers were running and bustling by, and a hurly-burly atmosphere developed. It began to seem to him that certain agents were infiltrating the hall. First they were dressed in sailors' uniforms, then they were dressed in civilian clothes and briskly rushing by. The patient unmistakably recognized all of them, however, by their raised collars, in which they tried to bury their faces. Soon the patient heard (amid the hubbub) a conversation; he listened more closely. It was about shooting a young woman and an old man who was a passenger. The agent was insisting that the shooting take place, and he asked the train station director to set things up so that there would be minimal panic; the latter promised to send engines to the platform (the engine whistles would drown out the shots). A few minutes later the engine whistles let out an alarming roar. Through the din and hubbub the patient managed to hear three shots. The hubbub and chaos intensified; people crowded together and screamed. The patient noticed something in the corner that was covered with a horse blanket, and decided that these were the bodies of the passengers who had been shot. People all around were talking over each other; deafened by the shouting, the patient could not understand anything. Nor could he figure out the meaning of the gestures and signals that passengers were giving him. Shortly afterward he spotted an "agent" in front of him. The latter screeched: "Take him, we'll show him." The agent threatened the patient with a gun that had red smoke curling out of its muzzle. Mustering all of his remaining energy and racked with fear, the patient jumped up on a table, begged for mercy and appealed to people for help. During the effort to subdue him he put up heavy resistance, after which he yielded to force and was brought to the clinic.

The entire illness thus came to an end within three to four hours.

---

In the phantasmagorial picture that arose from the man's drunken delirium, one can easily recognize scenes reminiscent of actual occurrences.

In 1938 *A Short Course in the History of the VKP(b)* was published. Active study of the course began everywhere from the time the first chapters appeared in *Pravda* in September 1938. The party, the Komsomol and all the working people received visual aids on how they were to struggle to build socialism and fight "enemies of the people." Vigorous efforts were made to recruit veterans of the Revolution and the civil war for study of the course. Among them was an old man named P. P. Zagumennov, who joyfully and selflessly responded to this appeal, as his letter to *Krest'ianskaia Gazeta* attests (misspellings and some grammar have been corrected):

---

# Document 75

Letter from P. P. Zagumennov to *Krest'ianskaia Gazeta* on *Short Course in the History of the VKP(b)*, 15 November 1938. RGAE, f. 396, op. 11, d. 26, ll. 545–547ob. Original manuscript.

---

15 November 1938 to the editors V. Poliany at *Polianskaia Pravda* from Pyotr Prokhorovich Zagumennov, Panderka station under Asipersky Village Soviet, Viatskie Poliany Raion, answer to the editors of *Krest'ianskaia Gazeta* to your appeal to me of 3 November 1938 about the importance of the new book on the history of the All-Union Communist Party of Bolsheviks. The importance of that history of our party is very great as we were told by the propagandist Ivan Ivanovich Selivanov in whose circle I am in the history of the VKP(b) for the study of the new textbook. We had three classes and I had to attend one of them where it made a tremendous impression on me the struggle that our Communist Party went through. By studying this book of the history of the VKP(b) we will eliminate even faster the shortcomings in every sector of our national economy especially in agriculture we now have a great many shortcomings in agriculture where I live on a kolkhoz. The name of the kolkhoz is Red Ear of Wheat under the Asipersky Village Soviet in Viatskie Poliany Raion. What kind of shortcomings do we have at our kolkhoz: a lot of drunkenness by our leaders, grain hasn't been harvested from the field which has rotted from the rains. They let all the fodder rot in 1938 both the rye straw and the spring straw and all of the roughage in the storage bins ... they divide the wheat by labordays for good wheat they give 150 grams and for rotten they give 150 grams. As for rye, they gave only five hundred grams and kept promising to pay two rubles forty kopecks for a laborday. But they gave only forty kopecks they badly cheated the kolkhoz farmers. I hereby sign Pyotr Prokhorovich Zagumennov.

[But the letter did not end here. Before sending it, Pyotr Prokhorovich evidently received some more political education and agitation and continued his opus:]

# Document 75 *continued*

I heard another reading of history from the new book at a class in the Asipersky Village Soviet. There was a study of people's judges of the V [probably Viatsky] section by Kuznetsov. I heard it from the book of new history of the VKP(b) that such an important resolution of the TsK came out about studying the history of the VKP(b). You can only welcome it and thank the party and government and Comrade Stalin personally for issuing such a document as the history of the VKP(b). I am an old man already seventy, semiliterate. I feel that without studying such an important document as the history of the VKP(b) it is impossible to manage in any institution. When you read the textbook you can see that everything written in it can be applied to any sector in work so I a seventy-year-old man suggest everybody study this textbook and every party and nonparty member, every worker, office clerk, kolkhoz farmer and nonkolkhoz farmer should know it. Learn this textbook [and] we will not have any distortions in work. I am an old man I pledge to learn it beginning with the first group of what is recommended in the party resolution on the study of history, and then I will go on to the second and third group and call on all the other old people of my age to follow my example. Dear editors I would like to get acquainted with you. Please give my regards to our dear Stalin and Kalinin ardent greetings through the newspaper. I am a pensioner and have no children with me. My old lady and I live alone we receive twenty-five rubles a month but it still is not enough to support old age. Is it possible through you to raise it a little[?] I will describe my idea. I am Pyotr Prokhorovich Zagumennov, seventy years old, my wife is also seventy years old. We have no children with us. I [became one of the] organizers of the kolkhoz when I in 1918 was elected to the first soviets when Red Army deputies brought [Soviet] rule to our volost . . . from the town of Malmyzh. I was elected to the commission to elect the power of the soviets so the kulak couldn't get in. They elected me from complete poverty. I fought the kulaks they were liquidated as a class in 1919. Kolchek [Kolchak] Admiral advanced on our area. The kulaks all went out to fight and they fingered all the soviet functionaries and our people in authority. The kulaks betrayed us to be executed. I was chairman of the poor. Five people sat in a punitive detachment for three days but the forest manager spared us. Instead of a bullet they gave us fifty birch rod lashes on the backside and they took all my things, livestock and all my seeds, and took my son because I was a Communist. My son escaped from the butchers but I vowed to take revenge until I die. We will root out the enemies and bury them under a green spruce. We had them on our kolkhoz we found them and gave them article 58 clause 10 [propaganda or agitation containing a call for the overthrow, subversion, or weakening of Soviet authority or for the commission of specific counterrevolutionary crimes], 58 clause 8 [commission of terrorist acts aimed at representatives of Soviet authority]. The Zagumennov brothers [presumably not related to the letter writer] got eight years and were stripped of their rights for two years.

## Document 75 *continued*

Dear editors forgive me that I wrote badly but I still ask you to answer what will you do but I apologize for taking a long time to answer. We seldom had these classes and I will also tell you when a deputy came to visit us Comrade Solodilov I was entrusted to run the meeting and I would also like to know how you found out about me an old man an Activist. Tell me or did *Polianskaia Gazeta* tell you.

---

The fact that the old man was semiliterate and could not express his thoughts in any coherent way did not matter at all in this case. The correctness of the history campaign had to be demonstrated with "real-life examples" so that not only Communists but also soviet and economic cadres, students and especially those involved in government could firmly master the "axioms of Bolshevism." The lesson to be derived from the case of P. P. Zagumennov, who never forgot his "flogged backside," is obvious from the letter.

Such sentiments played a considerable role in creating an appropriate social atmosphere for the mass repressions. The unbridled and vociferous campaign to unmask and destroy enemies of the people attested to anomalies in the development of society. The campaign's causative factors included the periodic purges of the party and the apparatus; the persecutions for social and political reasons; the encouragement to inform, both openly and secretly; the constant hammering at people over shortcomings and distortions of the party line; the previously organized show trials; and the constant temptation to use methods of coercion and force, in addition to persuasion, education, propaganda, and agitation, on "members of society lacking in consciousness" and to identify them as enemies of the existing system, and hence of the people. Since the civil war, Soviet authorities' dialogue with political opponents had been downright brief—a bullet in the head or a welcome mat for them at prison and camp entrances. So while the Yezhovshchina as a whole was an unprecedented phenomenon, all of its ingredients were already familiar.

Still, why was the mass terror launched specifically in 1937? There were a variety of reasons, linked in no small measure to the declaration that socialism had been built in the country. The notable economic reasons included the constant difficulties in production and in everyday life—the failures in various areas that in theory should not exist in a "socialist society"—and the need to ease the mounting tension and irritation, the contradiction between what had been promised and what really existed. The misfortunes and failures had to be blamed on the schemes of subversive elements, on traitors who had betrayed the cause of socialism. The numerous difficulties and contradictions developed into the idea of enemy encirclement, spy mania, and the need to unmask and destroy enemies of the people, and to pin this label on anybody at the slightest pretext.

It should be kept in mind that the promulgation in the 1936 constitution of universal suffrage, freedom of religion, and equality among all forms of property (even if only on paper) produced no more of a clear-cut reaction in society than did the 1935 amnesty for exiled kulaks. Many militant atheists, activists of collectivization and dekulakization, and workers took this as a slap in the face and thirsted for revenge so they could finish off the "dirty bourgeois who are still hanging on."

Complex processes were taking place among factory workers, as the instances of persecution of Stakhanovites suggested. The formation of the Soviet nomenklatura was proceeding apace in the center and in the provinces, and its members promptly assumed a lordly lifestyle. People were especially resentful about the wives of responsible functionaries, who often did not work, had a servant, and sought to copy the attire and behavior of the ladies of leisure in the half-forgotten, prerevolutionary society. Talk about the appearance of a new, "Soviet bourgeoisie" was not uncommon. Finally, the mass repression proved to be an excellent pretext not only for settling personal scores but also for upgrading one's living standards and moving up the career ladder. All these factors became tightly interwoven and at the same time encompassed broad areas of social existence.

An example of how personal vengeance could be made political is provided by the two statements submitted by railway trackwalker S. Mukhartov to *Krest'ianskaia Gazeta*. They were handwritten in a large, calligraphic style, but with a large number of errors and with old spellings in some places. Nearly every word was followed by a period or a comma, which have been removed in or-

der to improve legibility. The first statement dates from April
1936. (Misspellings have been corrected—*Trans.*):

---

## Document 76

First letter from S. Mukhartov to *Krest'ianskaia Gazeta* on the death of G. Mukhartova, April
1936. RGAE, f. 396, op. 10, d. 41, ll. 141–145ob. Original manuscript.

---

Statement to the *Krest'ianskaia* Editors of *Gazeta* on the political banditry
case of Nikolai Rudochenkov

I request representatives of *Krest'ianskaia Gazeta* to come to the site of the
case, to investigate and impose their just and Proletarian show trial on the
bandit Nikolai Stepanovich Rudochenkov, a former educator at a children's
home, and his concealers, like State Procurator and people's investigator
Comrade Kozopoliansky, people's judge Comrade Vakatov, and the main cul-
prit Comrade Vladimir Barvin, the principal of this school, in the case of an
accusation against the Teacher and Komsomol member Galina Grigor'evna
Mukhartova, who died a martyr's death in the performance of her important
duty at the hands of the scoundrel and bandit Nikolai Stepanovich
Rudochenkov. The teacher and Komsomol member Galina Mukhartova, from
a poor Proletarian kolkhoz family, twenty-two years old, was in her fourth
year of teaching at Elementary [incomplete; that is, only to grade seven] Secondary Uspenskoe school in Kalinin Oblast under the Rzhev RIK and the
Lunacharsky Village Soviet. This is how it happened. Starting at her job in
September 1935, Galina Mukhartova to her great misfortune met this Rudochenkov, who was an Educator at the children's home there, I don't know who
put him in his job. He is twenty-four years old, a native of the City of Taganrog
in the Azov–Black Sea Krai. And so from the very first days after they met, be-
having like a hooligan and a boor, this Rudochenkov began to offer his love
and did everything he could to persuade her to marry him. But Galina Grig-
or'evna Mukhartova, being an intelligent, modest girl, and foreseeing in Rudochenkov a dishonorable and good-for-nothing future husband, replied to
all this by declining and put an end to any acquaintance with him. But Rudochenkov did not let up. As a natural hooligan, he did not let Mukhartova
alone. He often burst into her room and inflicted all kinds of abuse and even
beatings on her, which was confirmed in court by the witness and teacher
Beryoznikova, her girlfriend, who lived in one room with her. Galina Mukhartova tried to complain about all these insolent acts to the school principal
Vladimir Barvin and asked him to transfer her to another school, since Rudochenkov was not letting her have a life, but principal Barvin did not pay
any attention to this, and meanwhile Rudochenkov started threatening to kill
her unless she married him. Seeing that the situation was dangerous, Galina

Mukhartova decided to personally go to the raion public-education department to complain about Rudochenkov. Upon finding out about this,
Rudochenkov decided to take brutal revenge on her. So on 9 March 1936,
while he was washing himself in the presence of principal Barvin's wife
[Barvina], Rudochenkov said, as Barvina herself recounted as a witness in
court, that I have made a specific decision today, but she did not exactly understand what he was talking about, and Rudochenkov also said in the presence of the bookkeeper that we will have two dead bodies today. And so on 9
March at 9 A.M. 1936, when Galina Mukhartova was getting ready to go to class,
Rudochenkov suddenly entered her room and carried out his heinous plan.
He heinously throttled and strangled her on the floor, since nobody saw her in
the noose, and he said she had hanged herself, supposedly she had locked
herself in, and when he found out that she had hanged herself he took a knife
and chisel and, after prying open the door by himself with the chisel, cut
down the towel from which Mukhartova was hanging, removed her from the
noose and rushed to get the nurse Silanova, and after grabbing some medica-
tion, they ran to administer artificial respiration. When Silanova entered the
room first, Mukhartova was lying on the floor, and the scoundrel also told
Silanova that if she said anything I will kill you. Silanova herself confirmed
this in court. And so, Representatives of *Krest'ianskaia Gazeta,* if Mukhartova
locked herself in and hanged herself, did Rudochenkov have the right to enter
the room alone and remove her from the noose, who personally threatened to
kill her, and based on this, the murderer was obvious, and all that needed to be
done was to use a just Proletarian Court against him. But things turned out differently, the Proletarian Court botched this case. On 11 April 1936 this case was
considered in open session by the Rzhev People's Court with Comrade Vakatov presiding and Comrade Kozopoliansky as State Procurator and Investigator, and it did not find us to be the injured parties, the mother Fedos'ia
Gur'ianova and the brothers Aleksandr Mukhartov and Stepan Mukhartov. He
did not allow us to speak in court. Mother was in court as a witness, but her
words were a cry in the desert, and when I, Stepan Mukhartov, asked to speak,
Comrade Vakatov fined me thirty rubles and ejected me from the courtroom.
Comrade Kozopoliansky and Comrade Vakatov did everything they could to
acquit Rudochenkov, in spite of the fact that he got confused in his testimony.
They even coached him in the presence of the court about what to say and
made it clear to him that they could acquit him. But thanks to Rudochenkov
himself, who proved in everybody's presence that Galina Mukhartova really
did hang herself through me, I drove her to it and knew in advance that she
would hang herself, and only for that reason was it impossible to acquit him
and they gave him a four-year term in labor colonies. They didn't want to give
us, the injured parties, a copy [of the court decision], but seeing that we insisted, they gave us a copy, but the murder was covered up with a suicide and
therefore they committed a crime against the entire Proletarian community. In

## Document 76 *continued*

exchange for some wine they let down their class vigilance, and therefore, guided by your just court, as you applied your just court in 1935, I don't know what month, against manager Fast of the rural consumer society and Police chief Kruzhkin, the murderers of rural correspondent Belyi, and therefore we ask representatives of *Krest'ianskaia Gazeta* not to send away our case to any procurator's office, otherwise we will be victims just as our sister and daughter Galina Mukhartova died at her glorious post, in which she carried light and culture to the future young generation, and therefore we ask you from the bottom of our hearts to hear our voice and take control of and look into the political banditry case which we only entrust to you as the most honest and just Organ of Soviet rule and ask you to personally come to the site of the case and apply your Proletarian court and give the guilty parties what they deserve. This is what we sign our names to. Brother Stepan Mukhartov. Daughter Anastasia Mukhartova has signed for our illiterate mother Fedos'ia.

Our address: city of Rzhev, Kalinin Oblast, of the Rzhev RIK, under Lunacharsky Village Soviet, Yesipov Station, village of Vlasovo.

The miserable family's grief is understandable. It is also obvious that a crime was committed. The decision of the Rzhev People's Court seems to have been justified, especially since the defendant admitted that it was his actions that had led to the young teacher's suicide, for which he received a four-year prison term. But this seemed inadequate to the Mukhartov family, and in order to get more they tried to give the case a political flavor. In fact, the main target of their attacks was no longer so much the accused as the "enemies of the people," the school principal, the investigator, and the judge. And so to the second statement:

## Document 77

Second letter from S. Mukhartov, 17 May 1936. RGAE, f. 396, op. 10, d. 41, ll. 152–154ob. Original manuscript.

Statement

17 May 1936

Once again I ask representatives of the workers' *Krest'ianskaia Gazeta* to urgently look into the criminal political case involving the heinous murder of the teacher Galina Mukhartova, about whom I told you in the letter you received on 26 April 1936. I received a reply from you on 29 April in which you reported to me that the case had been turned over for investigation. But three weeks have gone by already and we don't know anything, while the enemies of Soviet power, like People's Investigator Kozopoliansky and People's Judge Vakatov and principal Barvin, are celebrating their heinous victory. They are cocksure that we ignorant kolkhoz farmers cannot get justice, and therefore they fearlessly commit Crimes. When we turned over their copy to the Kalinin Court, it was suitable, then afterward they realized the copy was not in order, and when mother traveled to the Kalinin Court on 28 April 1936, this copy could not be found at the court, and some completely different, fabricated testimony was there instead. The Copy said that Rudochenkov removed Mukhartova from the noose by himself, while the Kalinin papers had him along with Silanova removing Mukhartova. When mother heard all of this nonsense and said that these are all lies, and crying bitterly before the court, said that there is proof that her daughter was murdered in broad daylight on the job, but you can't get justice, then the Kalinin Court refused to consider this case and left it in its previous form without taking any action. And so, workers' and peasants' government, everything is clear here. It is bad enough that the enemies botched the case in Rzhev, and they planted fake papers in Kalinin as well, and therefore I, Mukhartov, hand over to your justice these three fine fellows as traitors and enemies of Soviet power People's Investigator Kozopoliansky, People's Judge Vakatov and principal Barvin, and I ask the workers' and Peasants' government, as soon as you get this letter, to immediately remove these bandits from their jobs and severely punish them with a Proletarian court for the fact that these Bandits did not [sic] deliver their blows against the very heart of the revolution. . . .

Also Representatives of the workers' *Krest'ianskaia Gazeta* here is a short biography of my life. I, citizen Stepan Mukhartov, am from a poor proletarian family, just like my dead sister Galina Mukhartova. I am forty years old. At the present time I am working as a trackwalker for the Yesipov Station one kilometer from my village. In 1919 on the front lines against Kolchak I was willing to give up my life for Soviet power and shed blood when I was wounded. After recovering I was in the revolt in Smolensk Gubernia and we performed our duty with honor there. Now, comrades of workers' and Peasants' power, when such a crime has been committed before my eyes and the Investigator and the People's Court botched and played down the whole case, I am outraged to the depth of my soul by these people's behavior. These people, while enjoying the trust of Soviet rule, have openly embarked on the path of counterrevolution. They were cocksure that no kolkhoz farmer would dare to write about them what I, Mukhartov, wrote, because they have attacked a person with an open heart, who is ready to die for a just cause before the Proletarian court and Soviet rule in order to see the enemies found and punished. I am the undersigned Mukhartov, give me an answer, will you come or not[?]

The statements lay for almost a year without any movement or action. But 1937 arrived, and the case of G. Mukhartova once again attracted attention. On 5 April 1937 the following letter was sent to the procurator of the RSFSR (copy to the TsK of the VLKSM):

---

## Document 78

Letter from *Krest'ianskaia Gazeta* to procurator of RSFSR, 5 April 1937. RGAE, f. 396, op. 10, d. 41, l. 148. Certified, typewritten copy.

---

We are sending you a correspondence regarding the case of the murder of Komsomol member and teacher Galina Grigor'evna Mukhartova. We believe that this case involves not only a common crime but a political one as well. You can judge from the materials in the possession of *Krest'ianskaia Gazeta* this case has by no means been fully investigated and the guilty parties in the tragic death of Komsomol member Mukhartova have remained unexposed and no charges have been filed against them.

We request that you call in this case through the procurator of Kalinin Oblast and review it for purposes of oversight, because the Kalinin Oblast Procurator's Office, in our opinion, was not attentive enough to this case and completely overlooked the political aspects of this case and the indirect culprits in Mukhartova's death.

---

The psychological climate changed drastically in 1937, for the danger that anybody—or anybody's relatives—could be arrested tended to suppress emotions and created an atmosphere of psychosis and suspicion. Like a conflagration, the repression first affected a narrow range of individuals and then began to envelop an increasing number of people. Just like the campaigns to discuss the constitution, to hold elections for the Supreme Soviet, to carry out a successful harvest, to lay in fodder and so forth, a campaign was conducted to unmask and expose enemies of the people. Quotas were even set to determine how many of them should be unmasked in each territory. A kind of competition developed to determine who could display the greatest vigilance by exposing the greatest number of people. Leaders who remained aloof from this campaign ran the risk of being repressed themselves. Nevertheless, it proceeded rather sluggishly in a number of places.

Under these conditions the initiative shifted to the NKVD apparatus. Special representatives, along with NKVD agents, were sent from the center to the outlying regions to "smoke out and destroy the nests of Trotskyist-fascist bugs." The campaign initiated by the leadership quickly got out of control and swept across society. Leaders at every level became vulnerable to criticism both from above and from below. But even ordinary party members could not feel safe, as the campaign heated up and pitted people against one another. In this respect the Yezhovshchina was a radical and hysterical reaction to the increase in bureaucratism and abuses, to incompetence and other defects in the system that had been created. The waves of repression combined many elements: chaos in management, red tape, stupidity, hatred of bosses who committed abuses and behaved high-handedly, and naive hopes that the harsh measures could radically correct the situation. The absence of truthful information was accompanied by secrecy regarding what was happening at the top. Primitive clichés came into play—"there is no smoke without fire" or "too bad they don't put people in jail"—and contributed to a forced and phony enthusiasm in the campaign to unmask and expose enemies of the people.

Many areas of public life were paralyzed. A typical situation occurred at OGIZ, the Association of State Publishing Houses, to which the TsK of the VKP(b) sent P. F. Yudin in November 1937 to take over as its head and "restore order." Yudin's role in history is still awaiting its researcher. During a career that began in the 1920s and ended in the 1960s, he left his stamp wherever he had been. Lacking any traits that distinguished him from his contemporaries, the student at the Institute of Philosophy of the IKP (Institute of Red Professors) built a meteoric career on a merciless struggle against "non-Marxist philosophers." Once he was appointed to the Association of State Publishing Houses, he hastened to justify the trust that had been placed in him.

On 10 November 1937, a few days after his appointment, he held a conference at which he declared that the entire OGIZ system, from the main administration to the publishing houses, was "contaminated to the utmost degree." "There are Trotskyist-Bukharinist, Kadet, Socialist Revolutionary, Menshevik, Bundist, and German-Japanese organizations, every kind you want, but no

Soviet organizations," said Yudin. "For years traitors and spies have sat here, beginning with [Artashes] Khalatov, [Mikhail] Tomsky, Bron, and Bykov, while other enemies sat in the publishing houses: Vikhirev (at Uchpedgiz [State Textbook and Pedagogical Publishing House]), Laz'ian (at Sotsekgiz [Socioeconomic Literature Publishing House]), Bela Kun, Tardyi, Mikhailov (at Sel'khozgiz [Agricultural Literature Publishing House])." Taken aback by such an energetic beginning, the heads of the subdivisions of OGIZ meekly tried to object, but they received a stern rebuff: "The political situation is defined by the fact," said Yudin, "that not a single scum must have an opportunity to hide in an institution. . . . And if you have scum sitting all around you, you cannot say that the political situation is all right." For more than an hour Yudin, the philosopher and future diplomat (he was the USSR's ambassador to China in the 1950s) splattered mud at completely innocent people from head to toe. "Scum are sitting one on top of another," he kept repeating, evidently his favorite expression.

> Yerofeev was here. He came to me to complain that he had been mistreated, that he had been expelled from the party. I said: "You are an honest man, you have been in the printing trade for a long time, so write down and show what is wrong." And he wrote it. The son of a bitch, the grade A vermin, he even tried to justify Tomsky and Bron in an official document and claimed that there was no sabotage. . . . That son of a bitch Yerofeev. I don't understand why he can still write memos. . . .
>
> Now Mel'man, he is Tomsky's lackey, he managed a resort house. . . . When the son of a bitch Tomsky shot himself, he [Mel'man] sent flowers to his grave. . . . He must not be allowed within a hundred versts of the publishing industry. . . . And Bykov himself, who was Bron's deputy here? He is the crook of all crooks. We took away his party card at a meeting in this room and drove him to prison.

Yudin demanded that "all scum and riffraff be kicked out" of the OGIZ system, "burned out with a red-hot iron." The heads of subdivisions were required to submit within three days "lists of people who have been in any parties or opposition groups or were expelled from the party, people who have come from abroad, foreigners, even if they have lived in the [Soviet] Union for fifteen years, people who have been in exile. . . . Let production managers provide information on serious political misprints, . . . this will show counterrevolutionary work." Yudin's hour of triumph arrived soon thereafter. The entire "nest of enemies" in OGIZ was liquidated.[4]

The purge of OGIZ was far from unique. Trying to play it safe, many managers, contrary to the law, dismissed individuals whom they considered to be "suspicious." One example is the story of the mass layoffs of specialists from the research and educational institutions of the system of the Ukrainian SSR Narkomzdrav. This was discussed in a memorandum addressed to Yezhov on 17 November 1937 from N. I. Propper-Grashchenkov, deputy people's commissar of public health of the USSR:

## Document 79

Memorandum to Yezhov on dismissals of medical personnel, 17 November 1937. RGASPI, f. 17, op. 114, d. 833, ll. 132–134. Typewritten original.

Throughout the month of October the U[krainian ]SSR Narkomzdrav received a number of complaints about mass dismissals of staff members of the Kiev Medical Institute and the Odessa Sanitary and Bacteriological Institute. At the Kiev Medical Institute, for example, in a single day director Shashko dismissed thirty-two people "for failing to be in compliance with requirements placed on instructors of Soviet higher schools"; thirty-five people were dismissed from the Odessa Sanitary and Bacteriological Institute in two days with no reasons specified.

An investigation conducted by a special commission of the U[krainian] SSR Narkomzdrav, with the participation of a representative of the All-Union Committee for Higher Education, confirmed the aforementioned facts.

All of the individuals dismissed from the Kiev Medical Institute were immediately dismissed from Kiev's other medical institutions as well, and when they attempted to secure any medical job, they received rejections everywhere.

Of the forty-seven individuals from the Kiev Medical Institute who were considered by the consolidated Commission of the USSR Narkomzdrav and the Ukrainian SSR Narkomzdrav, twenty-six were reinstated in their former jobs, while the commission assigned the other twenty-one to practical work and the previous formulation of their dismissals was canceled.

The individuals who were dismissed and reinstated by the commission in their former jobs include many prominent specialists who are honest workers and are devoted to Soviet rule. The prominent bacteriologist Sheremet, who has a certificate from the USSR TsIK for developing bacterial filters and has been decorated by Comrade Ordzhonikidze for introducing them into industry, declared with certainty to the commission, "My dismissal is the act of a class enemy."

Professor of physics Rudenko was removed from Kiev Medical Institute no. 1 (reason: he supposedly was drunk once at a lecture), and the director of Medical Institute no. 2, covering himself, immediately removed him from his job at Medical Institute no. 2 for . . . holding a second job at Medical Institute no. 1.

When bacteriologist Skibinskaia, a physician with a twelve-year service record and scientific works, was removed from her job at the Kiev Medical Institute and was denied in her request that the city health department assign her to another medical job, she went to work as a seamstress at a factory, flaunting this and angering the workers.

At the Odessa Sanitary and Bacteriological Institute, institute director Anina, on the instructions of the local department of the NKVD, dismissed thirty-five people from their jobs in two days, including four managers of major departments of the institute and eleven physician-researchers.

What all of the dismissed individuals have in common is that they have relatives abroad, although many of them do not maintain contact with their relatives.

The dismissed people include prominent specialists, and some of them (Professor Palavandov, docent Kupershtein, staff scientist Grinfel'd) had worked at the institute for more than fifteen years, had repeatedly received bonuses and were good producers and actively participated in public life.

Employees were removed from the Sanitary and Bacteriological Institute immediately, they were forbidden to hand in their current projects, and some of them were recalled from their vacations ahead of schedule to be dismissed. The dismissed employees were forbidden to enter the institute, wages and other monetary compensation were sent to their homes, and the local party committee opened a reception desk in a little park near the institute to receive trade union dues, issue registration cards, and so forth. The dismissed individuals were not told the reason for their dismissals.

Despite the fact that the institute director told all of the dismissed individuals that they had not discredited themselves in any way as honest specialists and that they could work at another institution in their specialty, the local health agencies are not hiring any of them and at present these individuals are, in point of fact, unemployed.

If the aforementioned individuals had to be dismissed from the Sanitary and Bacteriological Institute for political reasons, it could have been done gradually, by transferring them to other jobs.

But these methods of "purging" higher educational and research institutions, as a result of which about seventy specialists have lost their right to a job, only causes panic and bitterness among the research workers and can benefit nobody but the enemies of Soviet rule.

Deeming these facts to be a counterrevolutionary act, I request that you call [them to] the attention of the TsK KP(b)U [Communist Party (Bolsheviks) of the Ukraine] and ask it to take urgent and necessary measures to prevent such acts in the future.

---

In spite of the protection by the deputy people's commissar of public health, the dismissals continued. The dismissals did not only mean that the families were left without means of subsistence, because no one would hire the dismissed individuals; more dangerous was the fact that a dismissal for "political unreliability" often became the first step on the path to the GULAG.

The sources show that not just the party and state nomenklatura and military cadres suffered from the Yezhovshchina, but also those in scientific and cultural institutions. The report by the Moscow City Committee of the VKP(b) for 1937, for example, said that of the total number (2,524) of Academy of Sciences staff members in Moscow at year's end, almost one-sixth, 420, had been arrested, and the arrests were continuing.[5] An enormous percentage of "enemies of the people" were archivists, librarians, and members of the creative and technical intelligentsia.

The mass repressions affected industrial enterprises to a somewhat lesser extent (in terms of the percentage of repressed individuals). In this sector they were more localized, perhaps because, after all, the Five-Year Plan had to be fulfilled. But the atmosphere in this sector as well was overheated to the limit, especially at large enterprises in the industrial centers. After the trial of the so-called Trotskyist-Zinovievist bloc, for example, the MGK of the VKP(b) sent enterprises a secret letter that referred, in particular, to the organization "by the damned scum of the counterrevolutionary White Guards and fascist agents" of terrorist groups at factories and plants and set objectives for exposing them. On 17 August 1936 a party meeting of the Moscow Three Hills Cotton Factory adopted a resolution: "Work must be organized in such a manner that attitudes and behavior at the factory and in each worker's everyday life can be comprehensively studied."[6] The mass news media openly urged citizens to display vigilance, to expose enemies of the people and to report on suspicious individuals and facts to the NKVD. Meanwhile the media published cases that had led to the unmasking of foreign agents. The grounds for arrest are astonishing in their obvious innocuousness: possession of a typewriter, binoculars, or any weapon; correspondence or any contact with relatives abroad or with foreign embassies. Everything was suspicious. One factory worker wound up in a cell for nothing more than neatness: he regularly ironed his trousers and other clothes—so much so that his neighbors decided he was using the iron to "develop assignments from enemy intelligence written with invisible ink." Another worker, a participant in the 1905 Revolution and a repatriate from America, received a term for "anti-Soviet agitation" because he had told friends that he had had his own car in the United States.[7]

The situation proved to be especially tragic during the mass repression of émigrés from Germany, Italy, Spain, the United States, and other countries who had come to the homeland of all working people to escape from persecution or with a sincere intention to build socialism.[8] Now that NKVD instructions have been made public, it has become obvious that émigrés were destroyed in a premeditated manner, and those who did not acquire Soviet citizenship in time were pitilessly deported back to the countries from which they had fled. The following letter is a cry of despair, a plea, and at the same time an epiphany about what the constitution and legality really meant in 1938. The letter was written in German, then translated to Russian; our translation is from the Russian document.

---

## Document 80

Letter from Yeva Friedländer to Presidium of Supreme Soviet, 16 May 1938. GARF, f. 7523, op. 23, d. 201, l. 49. Certified, typewritten copy.

Magnitogorsk 16 May 1938
To the Presidium of the USSR Supreme Soviet
On 30 April of this year I wrote you a letter with a fervent plea to commute the sentence of deportation that was handed down for my husband Walter

## Document 80 *continued*

Friedländer, a physician and a repatriate from Hitler's Germany. I could not imagine that this was the will of the party and the government: a man who fled from Hitler's Germany, who has legally found refuge in the USSR for two years already, who has lived and worked with all his strength honestly and well, who acquired a child in the USSR, is to be thrown out, into the devil's maw of fascism. Hold up his deportation before it is too late. On 13 May I found out at the Cheliabinsk prison that he had already been sent to Minsk. He is already at the border, and this means death for him and his family. Hold up his deportation, otherwise this could happen any day to our year-old baby and to me. Have you given this treatment to all foreigners who have applied for Soviet passports and received them?

My husband is mentally ill, gravely mentally ill. His illness is not outwardly detectable, and it was not detected by investigator Dolgov in Cheliabinsk, it does not show up in fevers or in rashes, but it suppresses his desire to live. In such a sick condition my husband is in no state to seize the slightest opportunity to write me, his wife, and more importantly, to submit a request to the Supreme Soviet for commutation of his sentence.

In Cheliabinsk I did not receive a single report on him either at the NKVD itself or from the director of the NKVD or from investigator Dolgov. If I called on the telephone in my native Russian for the sole purpose of making an appointment, I was turned down every time, and this has been going on for five months. They would start screaming at me louder and louder, so I would understand less and less, and they would hang up the phone.

How can this be, that the theory of communism that is proclaimed to the whole world, that is contained in Stalin's constitution, in holiday slogans, in speeches by members of the government about granting the right of asylum to emigrants from fascist countries, has been so flagrantly violated, and now in Cheliabinsk this theory is completely distorted by the NKVD, for example, by the deportation of my husband. You must not allow us to become victims of fascism here in the USSR.

Detain my husband at the very border. But your most urgent assistance can still save him and his family. In the greatest despair I plead with you to do this.

Yeva Friedländer, temporary teacher at a music school in Magnitogorsk

---

One highly typical phenomenon in the atmosphere of mass repression was "self-exposure." People were supposed to report on family relationships and friendly ties with "enemies of the people" to the party committee, which would look into the case and make a decision in conformity with "the degree of guilt and repentance." In the circumstances of denunciations and universal suspicion, many people tried to play it safe. So an already elderly female worker wrote a statement admitting her guilt to the party committee of the Three Hills factory: her sister, who worked as a cleaning woman in the Kremlin, while filling in for her coworker who was ill, once cleaned up the office of a high-level supervisor, who was arrested shortly afterward as an enemy of the people.[9] People reported on direct and distant ties of kinship with repressed individuals and on friendships and acquaintances with members of their families. As a result of these investigations, therefore, millions of citizens were directly or indirectly drawn into the orbit of mass repressions. And although not everyone became prisoners of the GULAG, everyone without exception had to make a difficult moral choice: only an unconditional condemnation of "betrayers and traitors to the homeland," no matter how close they were before the court's decision, could save a person from punishment. The families of repressed individuals found themselves in truly desperate straits: the threat of arrest constantly hung over them as members of a family of traitors to the homeland. They had to publicly disown arrested relatives, psychologically betraying them, but even in this case the imprint of the repressed person lay on the family, closing off, as a rule, access for the children to the Komsomol, to education and prestigious, responsible work. Passersby would turn their backs on them as though they had the plague, yesterday's friends would cross to the other side of the street, and coworkers would try to avoid contact. Not everyone was able to endure such a psychological blockade. The hopelessness of the situation pushed some into suicide and others into voluntary cooperation with the NKVD as a possible way of surviving. But as an analysis of the investigative files shows, the punishment for informers who wound up behind bars for any reason, even a trivial one, was especially cruel. The authority of the NKVD soared, and fear was equated with respect.

The desire to play it safe even in an innocuous situation became common. Typical was an admission by a staff member of Narkompros named Arbuzov at a session of the commissariat's party committee on 17 January 1939. In his line of work he had repeatedly spoken at orphanages for Spanish children in 1937–38: "I said a few words at this meeting, and I had asked the NKVD in advance what I should say and do. I was told to drink to the health and prosperity of the Spanish Republic."[10] If people consulted the NKVD even about making toasts, it is easy to imagine how great that agency's influence was in solving other, much more important problems.

Propagandists made the utmost effort to convince people that "the NKVD does not take away people for nothing." This postulate of infallibility seemed to be fully consistent with the notion that the party handpicked the best of the best for this important and responsible work. The arrest of relatives brought many Communists to an especially agonizing collision. Should they put more faith in "the infallibility of the NKVD" or in their husbands or sons, with whom they had lived side by side for dozens of difficult years and whom they felt they knew as well as themselves? Each person made her or his own choice. In the depth of their souls many people did not believe their relatives were guilty, but they were afraid to say so publicly. Others, while regarding their relatives' arrest as a tragic mistake, continued to believe in the fairness of the NKVD. And only a few, such as Kh. Ivanova, wrote to the party's TsK about the outrages perpetrated by the NKVD and demanded that the high-handed practices stop:

---

## Document 81

Letter from Kh. Ivanova to TsK VKP(b) on NKVD, 1937. RGASPI, f. 17, op. 120, d. 298, ll. 93–95. Typewritten copy.

---

To the Central Committee of the party

I am writing you, old party members, and I think you will pay attention to all of the actions by our NKVD. Is it really possible that you haven't heard yet about all the horrors that are going on in our provincial cities, where horrors in the literal sense of the word are taking place, so that it is even hard to believe that we live in a "land of joys." After all, we are living in a happy time, yet our NKVD is perpetrating total outrages. For some reason lately they have begun to arrest only old party members, who have acquitted themselves well among the people, have worked in conformity with the party line honestly and conscientiously, have not had any party penalties, have a party service record of twenty to twenty-five years apiece behind them, and suddenly are made enemies of the people in just fifteen or twenty days. How are we to take this, either he is an enemy of the people, or the enemies of the people got him out of the way because he was interfering with them. But his arrest sets off a whole series of sufferings: the family is immediately evicted from its apartment, and persecution of the children and all kinds of other abuse begin. But in point of fact their father is the most honest worker, he carried out all party tasks conscientiously, the people know him as the most honest worker, but our NKVD doesn't take any of this into account.

Comrades, you would do better to pay attention to what is going on in our NKVD and check whether an enemy of the people hasn't wormed his way in there or whether a kulak hasn't taken cover there and is doing all sorts of vile things there in order to undermine Soviet power.

I am writing on behalf of a hundred women, who have shed rivers of tears, who call a Soviet prison a "wall of tears," where young investigators try to advance themselves and supposedly display their vigilance by abusing people who have been arrested—it's awful even to think about—for what? They also abuse the arrested men's wives if a wife comes to an investigator and asks what his crime is, you will get the answer, he is an enemy of the people, for which he will be punished, but what act he committed, they don't say—it's a secret. Yes, we, women of the Soviet Union, demand of the authorities that our husbands be tried in open court, so that we know that our husbands are really enemies of the people and then we will be able to rip them out of our hearts and break off with them forever. But after all, it is not being done this way, but somehow it is all secret: neither he nor his family nor his acquaintances know what he is being tried for. We women ask, why? If our husbands are guilty, why aren't they being tried in open court? After all, at one time the Industrial Party and the Trotskyist-Bukharinist Party were tried in open court, after all, there was an opportunity to name them plainly: skunks, vermin, lowlifes, that's what you get, don't encroach on our country. But they have begun to try our poor husbands in secret, so that nobody knows. Yes, we women have no faith in this court: all of the charges that are being pinned on them are nothing more than malicious slander, just in order to get ahead at work and display their vigilance. These are lies, we don't have as many enemies as our young investigators are making just in order to protect their own skins. All these little boys have been produced, but now they are abusing the people too much. You should see what is going on and hear all of the horrors that are taking place outside our prisons, when a hundred women all have the same words on their lips: for what? We wouldn't take pity if he were guilty—if he's guilty, then put him on trial, but so that we also know what he is guilty of.

Comrades, old Communists, remember that our husbands are old party members too and worked just like you for the benefit of their state and loved their homeland and what are these young boys trying to pin on them? And when you talk to candidates for party membership, they are happy they

## Document 81 *continued*

didn't get into the party, because party members are now being persecuted—that is why applications to the party have slowed to such a trickle.

The women are writing to our dear Stalin, to Yezhov and Vyshinsky, but apparently none of these letters are getting there. They are obviously being destroyed in the localities, so that is why I have decided to turn to old party members. I hope that you will pay attention, because you are not guaranteed protection from these horrors either. But after all, the best people are leaving the party, people who once defended their country and shed blood alongside Lenin and come from workers themselves and their fathers are workers, in short, they are from the most proletarian family, and became people only thanks to Soviet rule, and suddenly they have become enemies of the people. It's not true! It's a lie! Sometimes I feel like shouting out in public, they are no enemies of the people, but he is being made an enemy of the people by the scoundrels, the lowlifes, who want to get ahead and receive the title of vigilant, or rather pseudovigilant.

Pay close attention to the provincial bodies of the NKVD, for the provinces have always known how to bend the resolutions of the party and the government. That is the way it has turned out in our province.

Pay attention to the cries and moans of the weeping women, who are shedding tears and waiting in vain for your protection from the center. A thousand women are stretching out their arms to you, help us, save us! Don't let us shed tears in vain!

---

The letter bears witness to the intricacies of the typical Bolshevik mentality at the height of the mass repressions. Although the people who were repressed included many members of the Bolshevik old guard, Kh. Ivanova was not quite correct in one respect: the mass repressions did not result from the conflict between generations alone. A large number of young people and minors also found themselves behind bars. The newspaper *Sovetskaia Sibir'* (Soviet Siberia) reported on 21 February 1938, for example, on a trial of a children's counterrevolutionary organization in Leninsk-Kuznetsky, in which 160 schoolchildren were accused of distributing leaflets, fascist insignia, and portraits of enemies of the people. The youngest member of the organization was ten-year-old Vitia Logunov, who had supposedly conducted counterrevolutionary work. While noting that the defendants had "slandered happy Soviet tots," the court did not allow itself to be prodded by the investigators, who insisted from the very start on applying article 58 of the criminal code to the children. They were convicted only of hooliganism. At the same time, in Moscow, a case was trumped up against an alleged Hitler Youth organization, and about fifty children of German émigrés, sixteen to twenty-five years old, were arrested. Most of them were executed. R. M. Traibman, a former agent of the Moscow NKVD, described the details of this fraudulent case in 1957 during an interrogation. In 1937–38 Traibman worked in Department 7, which was "in charge of" secondary and higher educational institutions. "I was especially outraged by the following incident," he said.

> One evening a policeman who had been dispatched to arrest one of the young Germans called Smirnov (Vasily Alekseevich Smirnov, head of Department 7 of the NKVD bureau for Moscow Oblast) on the telephone and reported that the German wasn't home, but was at the plant on the night shift. . . . When Smirnov asked from whom he had learned this, the policeman replied that the brother of the man to be arrested had told him. After inquiring how old the brother was, Smirnov instructed the policeman . . . to arrest the brother and bring him in to the bureau, while leaving the other policeman as a lookout. . . . I remember that not long afterward the policeman brought into the bureau a young (about eighteen), frightened boy, who soon afterward "gave" a statement dictated by Smirnov to the effect that he was a participant in the counterrevolutionary Hitler Youth organization and that he had been recruited into this organization by his brother, that is, the very brother for whom the arrest warrant had been issued and who was not at home. . . . When they brought in the elder brother, they confronted him at the bureau with his younger brother. . . . After that the elder brother . . . was beaten up by Smirnov and then corroborated his younger brother's statement, and supplemented it by giving evidence against a number of other individuals.

This is how the NKVD operated as it fulfilled the plan in conformity with assigned quotas and often showed independent initiative as well. In the Hitler Youth case, according to Traibman, the bureau was following the directive of the NKVD to "uncover a counterrevolutionary, nationalist formation among young Germans in barely two days."[11]

There is another aspect to the letter from Kh. Ivanova quoted above that must not be overlooked. She was writing on behalf of women whose husbands and sons had been arrested. The juggernaut of mass repression did indeed affect the male segment of the country's population to a greater extent. But even the women who did not end up in camps for members of families of traitors to the homeland underwent incredible hardships—psychological, financial, and physical. After all, they had to both raise children and support their husbands. A typical example of this kind of inconspicuous feat was the experience of Anastasia Koch, the wife of a German émigré worker who was arrested by the NKVD in early 1938. "I have worked myself at the Electric Lamp Plant since I was twelve (since 1915)," she wrote to N. A. Bulganin in early 1940.

> I have given the plant twenty-four years of my life, I have felt like it is my own family, and now they have tossed me out and forgotten me— or even worse, they despise me, and for what, I don't know. I was a party member since 1930. I was expelled merely because I dared to say that I found it hard to believe that my husband could be an enemy of the people. When he was arrested, they confronted me at a party meeting with a choice: either you have to disown him and find him guilty or we will expel you from the party. I don't know whether I did the right thing at the time, but I couldn't find him guilty without any evidence, and not just because he was my husband. Honestly, believe me, because this would mean giving up on a man who could have been taken away by mistake. I asked them at the party meeting to tell me, what is he guilty of? They replied that we don't know ourselves, but if the NKVD took him, it means there was a reason. This answer did not satisfy me, but just the opposite, it tortured me even more. I asked another question: for what can he be considered an enemy of the people, after all the machines at the plant were almost all from his design and are still working without a hitch, and in public work he was considered the most honest and conscientious worker. Again they replied: "You see, all of our enemies will always try to be good producers and public-spirited citizens, in order to give themselves a better cover." No doubt about it, that is a jesuitic explanation.[12]

Anastasia never did disown her husband, continuing to believe in his innocence. The knowledge that he had not been betrayed and that someone was waiting for him may have helped Willi Koch, as well as thousands of other inmates of Stalin's camps, to survive.

Yet not everyone could be so steadfast. L. S. Tsel'merovsky, an eighteen-year-old factory worker, described the adversities that befell his family in his letter to the Presidium of the USSR Supreme Soviet, dated 13 September 1938. His letter is also noteworthy for its detailed account of how the state treated exiles, a barely studied category of repressed individuals, in the late 1930s.

---

## Document 82

Letter from L. S. Tsel'merovsky to Presidium of Supreme Soviet, 13 September 1938. GARF, f. 7523, op. 123, d. 202, ll. 16–20. Original manuscript.

---

Autobiography

I was born in 1919 in the city of Petrozavodsk to the family of the city's assistant commandant. At the age of two I moved to Leningrad and when I was eight I went to school and finished seven grades and entered an energy technicum. I left in my second year and went to work at the Russian Diesel Plant as an apprentice model maker. As a Komsomol member promoted at work, I was then sent to a flying club for pilot training. But at that point the whole affair . . . [words obscured] my father (he was arrested and I am exiled as a family member without trial) (I wasn't even interrogated).

A few words about my father.

My mother told me that he was banished to the Northern camps for being a malcontent. I personally would never believe it (he was arrested under [article] 58), because I myself heard him [tell] his sisters how he fought the Whites in the North. He told us about his exploits. When S. M. Kirov was assassinated, he cried. He was an inventor a shockworker and received bonuses several times. Recently he was working at military plant no. 7 as an assembly worker.

It is hard to decide what kind of person he is; maybe all this is a clever cover. He told me a few times that he had been in Warsaw. [An account follows of Lev's separation from his mother and his (unsuccessful) attempts to be reunited with her.]

What I think is that because my father is guilty of something, let him answer for himself, but I am by no means going to suffer the disgrace that he has caused. I want to serve in the Red Army. I want to be a Soviet citizen with equal rights because I feel that I am worthy of that title since I was educated by a Soviet school in a Soviet spirit and therefore my views are obviously completely different so therefore it is heartbreaking for me to have the papers of an alien person.

Then I also have two little sisters, poor girls. They are both thirteen years old and both of them are in school either in the sixth or seventh grade. Both are Young Pioneers and are good students. I am afraid that by the time they are

## Document 82 *continued*

supposed to get a[n internal] passport they will be issued some kind of soiled document (they live with their mother in the city of Kazalinsk).

Now it is just about time to register [for the military draft], and next year is the call-up. So I ask you to consider my status and restore the title of Soviet citizen to me.

Life is hard for me now. I have even become depressed. It hurts the way people look at me as somebody alien and my heart is beginning to ache. After all I am just eighteen and I have already been stripped of the rights of a Soviet citizen. I have completely lost my grip because I make enough just for bread and now my mother too is writing that if you have a spare kopeck then send it to me but I am barely staying alive myself and sometimes my heart aches so badly that I feel like crying and it goes without saying that if you do not help me I will not turn into a human being but will turn into some kind of tramp. It's very hard but I am bearing up; I remember my dream of being a shipbuilding engineer. I ask you Mikhail Ivanovich Kalinin to consider my status, I ask you not to deny my request.

When I was in school I attended a riflery club and was considered the best shot in school with a small-gauge shotgun. When I'm needed I won't miss with a military rifle either. I know the Red Army needs snipers.

Lev Sigizmundovich Tsel'merovsky

Chimkent, Kazakhstan general delivery

---

The letter was written unevenly, with a large number of cross-outs, corrections and incomplete words. Here is another describing the tragedy that was occurring in the country and the NKVD functionaries who had completely let themselves go:

---

## Document 83

Letter from V. Antipov to TsK VKP(b) on banished families, 12 December 1938. RGASPI, f. 17, op. 120, d. 298, ll. 87–88. Certified, typewritten copy.

---

To the TsK of the VKP(b)

While traveling for my job around a number of oblasts and raions during this summer and fall, but especially lately, I had occasion to observe some awful scenes at train stations in large and small towns.

Thousands of families had taken shelter and in some places women, children and sick old people are still taking shelter near railroad stations and inside the stations.

## Document 83 *continued*

These are all people who were exiled from various cities because they had family members who were once on trial or convicted and are serving sentences.

The Novgorod NKVD is apparently displaying particular zeal in banishing people. No matter where I stayed, I encountered dozens of Novgorod families everywhere. According to the exiles themselves, about a thousand families were banished between the middle of October and 1 November, and people are moving who knows where, they have no housing, no jobs, and no means of subsistence, people are wandering around with no shelter, and there are many thousands of them. In Kotel'nich, Viatka, Glazov, Bui, and other small towns—everywhere they are packed, apart from those who are banished to specific places.

It is proper to banish people from border areas when they are politically dangerous and have been tried for counterrevolutionary acts, but to banish absolutely everyone who has been tried, their families, sick elderly, and old people is the handiwork of some wrecker.

I observed about fifty people of various ages in Kotel'nich. They were wandering around the railroad station with children. A group of foreigners was passing through and went up to them, asked them some questions, and shook their heads. People and all the exiles have arrived—they have no apartments and no jobs, and it is fall. If any of them are fortunate enough to find shelter in cold sheds or village bathhouses, they are very lucky.

When I passed through these towns in November, I was curious and found out that people had traveled on and were probably wasting away in other places, if half of them haven't died.

I daresay that the TsK of the party doesn't know about this, and therefore I decided to write you because this is something unhealthy and apparently the functionaries of some NKVD bureaus have completely let themselves go, even engaging in high-handed behavior, especially in Leningrad Oblast.

They give you twenty-four hours to leave, and people in a panic sell their property for a song and start traveling anywhere, just to get out.

They don't even spare sick people.

The TsK should give some definite instructions to the NKVD so that there is no high-handed behavior in the provinces, otherwise things turn out badly. V. Antipov . . .

---

As early as January 1938 a plenum of the TsK of the VKP(b) did take some steps, adopting a resolution that condemned the mistakes of party organizations in expelling Communists from the party and the formally bureaucratic treatment of appeals by expelled members. It also condemned scandalmongers and careerists, who were contributing to an atmosphere of distrust and suspicion in the party. It mentioned functionaries of the NKVD, the procurator's office, and judicial bodies that were under the thumb of the NKVD and committed "mistakes" in convicting honest Communists. But only when the situation threatened to get out of control and the NKVD had become a liability to Stalin, did he acknowledge the excesses, as he had once done in March 1930, and accuse Yezhov of causing them. In August 1938 Yezhov was effectively removed from the NKVD leadership, and in the fall he was ousted as people's commissar for "mistakes made." Society reacted turbulently to this decision with a new outpouring of exposures and complaints. Here is one of them, over an illegible signature, sent to the party's TsK in late 1938:

## Document 84

Letter to TsK VKP(b) on arrests in Tula, 1938. RGASPI, f. 17, op. 120, d. 298, l. 92. Certified, typewritten copy.

Neither the policies nor the laws of the Soviet state, nothing justifies what happened in Tula in this year of 1938. Thousands of arrests in a month or two, of which a very small percentage were based on law and substance. Information, rumors, and facts are seeping into the masses and only create unhealthy attitudes and distrust. Even in the party ranks there is a lot of cautious talk about excesses and a lack of faith in the claim that people are being fairly tried and exiled. After rumors spread among the masses about the removal and arrest of the chief of the NKVD bureau and the removal of the former people's commissar of the NKVD and the arrest of representatives of the authorities in other cities, people began speaking openly that thousands of people are languishing in prisons and in exile. Completely Soviet people, devoted people to the Soviet state, sense that something is wrong here, something is the matter. One gets the impression that everything here has been deliberately muddled, that large enterprises have been deliberately stripped.

Comrades, none of this helps Soviet rule, but only alienates people. I am a party man, but I am beginning to vacillate, I am starting to feel some kind of apathy. I know what kind of talk and sentiments there have been in our party organization since totally honest people have been arrested and exiled. If somebody says there are no shoes to be had, that is not anti-Soviet agitation.

After all, we knew the people who worked with us, we trusted them, the whole party organization trusted them, just one person doesn't trust them and

## Document 84 *continued*

they are held for a year, often coerced to admit to something, but they never even knew what.

Everything is done in secret, but a great deal is still known.

Something has to be corrected, the common cause of the Soviet system has to be helped, people must be compelled to respect legality and to release people who were wrongly taken away.

If a person is not trusted, something should be done so that he is a friend of the Soviet system rather than making him an enemy.

Dear Comrades! Discuss this letter, show it to Iosif Vissarionovich Stalin. Send a commission, believe me that I want to live in a way that I can be happy and continue to build up our life.

A copy of this letter has also been sent in Moscow, because people say letters are not reaching the center, which may be incorrect.

Another letter, from Odessa, on the same subject:

## Document 85

Letter from V. Chernousov to TsK VKP(b) on removal of Yezhov, 10 December 1938. RGASPI, f. 17, op. 120, d. 298, ll. 90–91. Certified, typewritten copy.

To the Central Committee of the VKP(b)

Esteemed Comrades!

As an ordinary citizen of the USSR I cannot help but comment on the removal of Yezhov from the NKVD leadership—an event of no small importance.

Appointed to the job to uncover betrayers and traitors and to purge the country of enemy elements, he himself caused as much harm as maybe all of the betrayers and traitors combined.

Along with elements hostile to Soviet rule, hundreds of thousands of absolutely innocent, honest people, some of them even devoted to Soviet rule, have been arrested and exiled. After all, there is now virtually not a single home in the country from which somebody is not in prison. The final result is a picture in which the whole country is against Soviet rule. Unheard-of brutalities have been committed in the process. People have been forced under severe torture to "confess" to crimes they never did. A wife is arrested only because her husband is in prison. Children have been left to the mercies of fate. None of the exiles' relatives knows anything about them.

The result is a sharp contrast between what has been declared in our constitution and the brutal, high-handed behavior that prevails in the country.

## Document 85 *continued*

Not only do we have extremely low wages, not only are basic necessities unavailable, but to top it off nobody can be sure of not being in prison tomorrow. It is hard after this to figure out what kind of attitudes exist among the masses. And this attitude was created by Yezhov. Two or three years ago the attitude was different.

According to tens and hundreds of thousands of people, Yezhov overlooked real spies and saboteurs. The fires and explosions at enterprises have not stopped, and they are undoubtedly plotted by saboteurs. It is naive to think that the country has been completely purged of them. But Yezhov had his agents specialize in taking innocent citizens from their beds, while they forgot how to catch real saboteurs. On the contrary, they are even openly allowed into the country. The case of the pilot Lindbergh is a very striking one. When [special British representative Lord] Runciman sent a report from Prague to London, Hitler knew what was in it, that is how the Gestapo works, but when an out-and-out spy and our enemy plans to slip into our country we just twiddle our thumbs, and we don't know what he is bringing.

We will hope and want to hope that with Yezhov's removal the nature of the NKVD's work will change as well. We want to hope that Yezhov's mistakes will be eliminated and corrected, that the NKVD will begin to really fight elements hostile to Soviet rule and that honest workers will be assured normal and tranquil working conditions.

V. Chernousov . . .

---

The vicious circle had been completed—the fight against wreckers proved to be the handiwork of the wreckers themselves. An analysis of many letters shows that people did not raise doubts about the practice of repression itself, ascribing "excesses" in this area only to certain individuals.

More than 1.7 million people were arrested in 1937–38 altogether, mostly under article 58—that is, for counterrevolutionary crimes. In the same period the courts sentenced 1,345,000 people to various penalties. The country's prisons, with an official capacity of 155,000 inmates, held 549,000 at the end of February 1938. The number of those sentenced to death—execution or "ten years without the right of correspondence," which in practice also meant a death sentence—amounted to 682,000 in 1937–38. The population of the GULAG increased by about 600,000 inmates.[13] But even after the Yezhovshchina the NKVD, under the leadership of the new people's commissar, Lavrenty Beria, conducted the same work in the same tenacious and systematic manner. True, its methods became more secretive and hence more sinister. As the documents cited above show, all of the previous repressive factors—wrecking, spy mania, and so forth—remained in the public consciousness. Thus the repressions continued, contrary to a widespread opinion that they subsided after the Yezhovshchina. The prisons were "unloaded" as some people were actually released and some were pardoned, but there were not many of them. In 1939 the GULAG lost only 120,000 people.[14] Most of the "enemies of the people" remained in the camps and colonies.

In spite of the broad sweep of the repressions, they did not affect the so-called fifth column, the active opponents of the Soviet system, who secretly dreamed of staging a mass slaughter of the Communists. By putting on a show of loyalty and even pandering to the repressive policy, they had no trouble eluding the alert eye of the NKVD and extra-vigilant citizens. This is illustrated by a rather amusing incident described by a man named P. A. Misov in a letter addressed to Kalinin. The location of the letter writer has not been determined, but its content suggests the city of Gor'ky. The letter was written in July 1938 and is reminiscent of the disclosure—albeit an unsuccessful one—of the gladiators' plot in Raffaelo Giovagnoli's novel *Spartacus,* which was popular in those years. (All of the peculiarities that highlight the writer's personality—including the lowercasing of Stalin's name—have been left intact, except for passages that could not be deciphered because of sloppy handwriting.)

---

## Document 86

Letter from P. A. Misov to Kalinin on overheard conversation, July 1938. GARF, f. 7523, op. 23, d. 212a, ll. 96–97. Original manuscript.

---

To the People's and All-Union Elder Mikhail Ivanovich Kalinin

Mikhail Ivanovich I am sorry that you don't know me maybe you have more serious things to do but my heart cannot keep it in I want to write somebody about an incident but I don't know who I decided to write you knowing your simplicity. It happened at the end of June I was on statutory leave the day was hot I like to go fishing I took my fishing rods and headed for the river but after

I walked about two or three kilometers I decided to take a rest there was a little gully and some thick bushes I went down into these thick bushes it was really hot and I thought I would sit awhile and have a smoke I sat for about twenty minutes and I hear somebody talking above me at first I didn't pay attention but then I hear they are talking about war I started listening to what the people are saying about war I took out a notebook and a pencil I always carry these things with me. One of them says you want war to start soon but in my opinion it is better if it drags out for a year or two during that time we will be able to create spontaneous cadres so that our victory will be guaranteed. There are more than two million prisoners . . . no more than 40 percent of ours ended up there the rest are stalin's toadies . . . This material is no good for us whoever they do release will not go anywhere they will be afraid of being put in prison the rest of the cadres will come from relatives, friends, and lovers, they're going to avenge their fathers there's a double benefit here they love their relatives and they will choose stalin's honest functionaries from work. Everything will fall apart. Think about it yourself Lenin spent his whole life taking revenge on tsarism for his brother's death imagine how many such Lenins we will have. . . .

Even now in prison they are dropping like flies from malnutrition the weak ones so they are done now we have to work and work in a way so that one of ours is joined by twenty stalinists there will be a lot of bitterness and this will play a big role they will take even the emptiest denunciation and an enemy of the people will not be able to get away and his goose is cooked one of every two hundred people get out. The investigation drags on for nine months and then even though he is not guilty they send him to prison on an administrative basis as unreliable a lot of them have already been exiled that way. Let them punish and beat them so that they pull out the whole cabbage with the weeds they won't realize what they're doing for a while they've gotten carried away which is better for our people. And the situation is like this at work now if the NKVD took somebody away then it means he's an enemy of the people and if he's an enemy of the people then you can't say anything good about him even if he is one of the most honest workers otherwise they will take you away as well for consorting with an enemy of the people at this point they started to talk quietly I decided to follow these skunks and I also heard them talking about something here the workers' center and all the plants will work for defense and the people in Gor'ky need spontaneous cadres but what is spontaneous I don't understand this word they began to talk really quietly I dropped down into the gully so that I could come out from the other side as if it was by chance but when I went around the gully these scoundrels were already gone the gully was alongside the road two passenger cars and one truck passed by on the road maybe they were in a car I don't know where they went I even started crying what an old fool I am I wasn't able to follow them I got so upset that I took my fishing rods and went home. But after all it's true something is wrong in our country look they took away the son of one acquaintance of mine a young fellow he did a year they released him with galloping consumption and soon after he died his relatives are still crying it hurts after all if a man dies for no reason it's hard for the relatives he caught a cold in prison they took him away in the summer and they would not allow parcels through he slept on a cement floor after catching a cold another office worker was in for nine months they would not allow any food through they released him and he is already in stage three.

I could write a lot of examples like that to you my dear Mikhail Ivanovich but I can see that I've let myself go on for nothing I didn't want to talk about it but I couldn't keep it in so I wrote you don't be angry. Now I also wanted to write you about something else they are not thinking through what they broadcast on the radio for example they were broadcasting about Kuibyshev to honor his memory they said when Kuibyshev was sitting in a tsarist prison his sister brought him food, cigarettes, and even a bouquet of flowers I listened to this and didn't take notice I came to work and one Komsomol member says to me under tsarism as we see it was nice even in prison all the food was allowed through cigarettes and a bouquet in the bargain not like what we have if you're guilty or not once you go you are gone and relatives are not told where a person went but there is no reason for all this now we old people didn't notice but the young people have stored it away my heart aches for all these mistakes I am not a party member but my heart aches badly for Soviet rule I live well and I could not have even dreamed of this under tsarism I feel that everything is not right here is an example about that conversation and as we can see [somebody] is working and working hard to make the people angry who is happy to make them into an enemy forgive me an old man if I knew that you are not angry I would write another time about everything that seems bad to me and that the people are saying.

The fact that little had changed in the social atmosphere since Yezhov's removal was borne out by the continued outpouring of letters, despite a toughening of prison and camp regimens, from people who said they were innocent victims. For example, in a letter written to the TsK of the VKP(b) in 1940, a prisoner named Arkhangel'sky described abuse during his arrest and the customs that prevailed among camp guards.[15] Complaints kept coming in about illegal actions by the NKVD. Party organizations continued to impose reprimands and other penalties for contact with repressed individuals.[16]

Among the letters depicting the situation in the provinces, our attention was drawn to a memorandum by G. L. Skriabin addressed to Stalin in 1940. Skriabin, along with a number of other individuals, was assigned by the TsK to the Kuibyshev party organization to strengthen the party line, and he became a member of the plenum and the bureau of the Kuibyshev obkom. Skriabin found himself in a "nest of spiders" and he was forced out in short order. But during his stint he managed to make interesting observations about the customs of the local nomenklatura. Skriabin may have laid it on a little thick, but the general nature of the provincial apparatus's work nonetheless comes through clearly enough. Several examples from the document follow:[17]

## Document 87

Memorandum from G. L. Skriabin to Stalin on Kuibyshev Obkom, 1940. RGASPI, f. 17, op. 121, d. 19, ll. 95, 98, 100–101, 102–103. Typewritten original.

Because I have been compelled to transfer to the Leningrad organization and am thereby deprived of an opportunity to continue a direct struggle against the nonparty line of Comrades [N. G.] Ignatov [first secretary of the Kuibyshev Obkom and gorkom of the VKP(b); in January 1941, transferred to the post of first secretary of the Orel Obkom of the VKP(b)] and Mel'nikov, secretaries of the Kuibyshev Oblast Committee of the VKP(b), I consider it my party duty to disclose to you certain facts so that they may be investigated by the Central Committee of the VKP(b).

For a long time Ignatov and Mel'nikov have been waging an unscrupulous struggle with each other for the job of obkom first secretary. The struggle between them has reached the point where one calls the other a double-dealer at official meetings. This struggle could not help but lead to intrigues, to abuses against certain functionaries of the apparatus, and to the forcing out of unwanted people from the apparatus of the obkom of the VKP(b). . . .

The struggle between Ignatov and Mel'nikov has compelled them to curry favor with cadres, securing their support on an improper basis. In January 1939 Comrades Ignatov and Mel'nikov organized a drinking spree at which ORPO [*otdel rukovodiashchikh partiinykh organov,* department of leading party organs] head Surin beat up two policemen on guard duty. This was repeated during the May holidays, with the sole difference that policemen were not beaten up, but they avoided a fistfight between themselves only by chance. This also occurred in the past. After one drinking party at the home of Comrade Ignatov, Comrade Ignatov along with Bocharov and Detkin [an arrested NKVD representative and his deputy] drove down to the Volga and began taking motorboats from people riding down the river. . . .

## Document 87 *continued*

One would have thought that the extremely flagrant mistakes that Ignatov made when he was an enemy of Postyshev [first secretary of the Kuibyshev obkom of the VKP(b) from 1937 to early 1938; removed in January 1938, expelled from the party in February and executed a year later] taught him something. Unfortunately, that was not the case. Personal and professional ties and joint drinking binges with Zhuravlyov [former representative of the NKVD for Kuibyshev Oblast], and then with the enemies Bocharov and Detkin, prevented Comrade Ignatov from becoming head of the obkom of the VKP(b). . . .

Ignatov and Mel'nikov proved to be too "modest" about the criminal activities of Bocharov, Detkin, and other NKVD functionaries. Bocharov's arrest was kept secret for a long time from certain members of the obkom bureau. The NKVD bureau for our oblast, under the leadership of Zhuravlyov and his deputies—and enemies of the people—Bocharov et al., perpetrated extraordinary outrages: drunken revelries lasting several days at a time; an assembly-line system of interrogation; physical beatings of arrestees; frequent cases in which cold water was poured on individuals who had been beaten up; intimidation; the staging of confrontations between arrestees with conflicting statements; the falsification of interrogation summaries; the theft of belongings from arrested individuals, and others. These perversions and improper arrests, it seems to me, are directly related and linked to the consideration of the appeals by former arrested Communists and to holding the slanderers accountable. I must assure the TsK that the slanderers "have not been found" in Kuibyshev Oblast and almost none of the NKVD functionaries have been held accountable for their extremely flagrant perversions. The reason for this is to be sought in the fear of the Kuibyshev leaders over their mistakes. . . .

I would like to call the attention of the TsK to how Ignatov and Mel'nikov managed certain areas of work.

People are our most valuable assets. Take a look at how they are treated in our oblast. In 1938, one hundred kolkhoz farmers who are members of ethnic minorities in Baranovka and Kuznetsk raions, incited by class elements, got into a brawl among themselves. The incident did not end without fatalities. In 1939 in Krasnoiarsk Raion, kolkhoz farmers beat up Kazakhs for taking their straw. The court and procurator's office did not attach significance to these cases and dragged their feet in looking into them.

Two raions in the oblast—Chelnovershiny and Novyi Buian—are especially plagued by murders and suicides. There have been thirty-five homicide and suicide cases in Chelnovershiny in the past two and a half years. And typically, the investigative agencies drop all the cases because the murder and suicide victims are represented as mentally disturbed. I remember one suicide case in that raion. Comrade Gerasimov, a Communist who managed a school, and his wife committed suicide under the following circumstances: after being persecuted and wrongly expelled from the party and finding no support from the raion committee of the VKP(b), Gerasimov by

## Document 87 *continued*

agreement with his wife first shot her in bed and immediately killed himself. A note left after their death gave some details of their persecution. The homicide and suicide cases are all different. You will find murders of children by their mothers, seductions of minors, murder with armed robbery, terrorist acts and others. How attentive the investigative agencies are in these cases is apparent from the fact that one arrested individual in the same raion committed suicide in a pretrial-detention cell. Absolutely savage methods were used during the investigation. In one homicide case the deputy oblast procurator and the raion procurator enacted a murder in front of a deaf-mute in a pretrial-detention cell. The deputy oblast procurator donned bast sandals and rags, sat down on a chair, then the raion procurator walked in, rushed at him, removed the bast sandals, pulled a noose around his neck and choked him. . . .

The situation is almost the same in Novyi Buian Raion, where thirty homicides took place in 1938–39. Such incidents also occur in other raions of the oblast. For example, the party organizer of the TsK for Maina Raion committed suicide, and a policeman committed suicide in Inza Raion.

---

A letter to Stalin from K. Pol' describes the ordeal of a woman and her family who were unconditionally devoted to the regime but found themselves "tainted" by contacts with people who had been repressed:

---

## Document 88

Letter of appeal from K. Pol' to Stalin, 21 January 1939. RGASPI, f. 17, op. 121, d. 19, ll. 41–43. Typewritten original.

---

Dear Comrade Stalin!

Permit me, on the basis of your directive about the importance of the experiences of ordinary people, to describe to you what some rank-and-file party members and Komsomol members must go through with regard to certain complex issues of our time. [A lengthy discussion follows of the notion that relatives of enemies of the people and of people living abroad should not be persecuted, based on a variation of Stalin's words "The son is not responsible for the father."]

As an illustration, I will describe what my son, a Komsomol member nineteen years old, and I have had to [go through] and are [going through]. I have been a member of the VKP since 1919. I was in party work until 1926, and in 1930, upon graduating from the party-history department of the Institute of

## Document 88 *continued*

Red Professors, I went into research and journalistic work. In 1936, when I learned from a letter from the Moscow Committee about the arrest of [G. I.] Sokol'nikov, I reported to the party committee of the RSFSR People's Commissariat of Education, where I was working at the time, that Sokol'nikov was a first cousin of mine but that I had had nothing to do with him and had not seen him since 1924. Because of this I was expelled from the party and fired from my job. I had no party card for a year, and I was without work for eight months. Only after the January plenum did the Party Control Commission under the TsK reinstate me in the party, and it did not impose any penalty on me. But despite my request for a removal of the stern reprimand that had been imposed on me in 1936 by the enemies of the people who were sitting in the party committee of the Vuamlin [*Vysshee upravlenie assotsiatsii marksistsko-leninskikh institutov,* Higher Administration of Associations of Marxist-Leninist Institutes] (Dzenis, Gittel' et al.) "for letting down Bolshevik vigilance," the Party Control Commission did not remove this stigma, even though the entire gang that imposed it has long since been exposed. Before this I was unable to obtain a removal of this penalty for a year in the party committee of the People's Commissariat of Education, because the party committee was in the hands of enemies of the people (Romanov, M. Orakhelashvili, et al.). Now I have been teaching the history of the USSR and the constitution in school no. 332 in Krasnogvardeisky Raion for a year. I have been an excellent teacher the whole time and I have done active party work. I have been in the party organization of the raion department of public education for eight months. My request to have the penalty stricken has been raised four times in the party committee, and each time it has been denied on the grounds that they don't know me well enough. I have visited Comrade Stepanenko, the secretary of the raion committee, three times on this issue. He promised to help me and use me in party work, but nothing has been done. Before the Institute of Red Professors I graduated from the history and philology department of Petrograd University, and I have a good command of German and French and can read English. I have experience in research work, teaching the history of the VKP and Leninism in higher educational institutions, journalism and propaganda work, and mass-agitation work at enterprises. Nearly a year has passed already since my reinstatement in the party, but all of my attempts to get a production job or party work in my profession have been in vain. It's the same story everywhere: they need people very badly, they are downright joyful to greet you, but when you tell them about your relative and penalty, they turn you down, either openly or on some other pretext. Here are examples. I submitted a proposal to the international-law section of the Institute of Law of the Academy of Sciences to write a doctoral dissertation under their direction on the foreign policy of the USSR and to compile an anthology called "Lenin and Stalin on the Struggle of the USSR for Peace." I have been working on these issues for a number of years and I fer-

## Document 88 *continued*

vently want to write a book suitable for the broad masses on the history of our struggle for peace. First I was told there was a vital need for such a book, but then they turned down the idea. True, I am working as a member of the section and I actively participate in the discussion of other comrades' works, but I don't get any research assignments.

During the summer I brought articles on international issues to [the newspaper] *Rabochaia Moskva*. I asked, where is the head of the foreign department? They said, he isn't here. "What about his deputy?" "He's not here either." "Then some staff member of the department?" "No one's there."

Then I went to the editor of the newspaper. After questioning me about my qualifications, he immediately started talking about [my] managing the international department, but once he heard about my relative he wrote down my telephone number and . . . never called. I went to the journal *Propagandist*. I was commissioned to write an article about the Rostov strike [a general political strike from 4 to 26 November 1902 in Rostov-on-Don, organized by the local committee of the RSDRP]. When they read it, they ordered a second from me about the Obukhov defense [a clash lasting several hours between workers of the Obukhov plant in St. Petersburg and police on 7 May 1901, considered to be one of the first politically motivated mass actions in Russia]. They accepted both articles and offered me a job on the staff. But when I told them about my relative and especially the reprimand, they did not print either article, even though they had found them to be good. In the eight months that I have been in the Krasnogvardeisky Raion party organization, the raikom has not given me a single assignment and has not had me conduct a single discussion or report. I have not been at the plants for three years, whereas I used to hold two or three discussions a week at enterprises. Is all this proper, Comrade Stalin?

Now a few words about my son. He has been a member of the VLKSM since 1936. He is a third-year student at the Moscow Institute of Geological Exploration. Although he has never seen Sokol'nikov in his life and reported this connection of his own accord, he was expelled twice from the VLKSM because of this and because of my expulsion, and was reinstated without any penalty after the January plenum. . . .

---

Material from the discussion of new draft statutes of the VKP(b), drawn up by a commission headed by A. A. Zhdanov, paints a very complex and contradictory picture within the party itself.[18] A. Karaulov of Tambov wrote: "Comrade Stalin said in 1935 that the son is not responsible for the father. Yet thanks to the play-it-safers, in practice the party organizations have made brother responsible for brother, even if their lives are completely separate from each other. A Communist per se is irreproachable, and such a Communist begins to be viewed as a second-rate Communist only because some of his relatives have been repressed, he is not elected to anything, he is not trusted and is constantly rebuked for the crime of his brother or other relatives." In this connection he proposed adding to the statutes: "A party member shall not be responsible for the actions and crimes of his relatives unless his personal guilt in this regard is proven." A. Smaga of Baku insisted on "protecting the rights and lofty title of party member—eradicating the 'theory' of dividing Communists into two or three grades, stopping the practice of compiling secret cases against Communists and prohibiting the release of party information about Communists to nonparty organizations." V. Sedov of Sverdlovsk wrote of the need "to change the actual treatment of individuals reinstated in the party: surround them with a comradely atmosphere, do not leave them isolated from the party rank-and-file, do not trample on their human dignity by demanding eternal repentance. Is it not time," he asked, "to 'reduce' party-related questions in the application forms of Soviet institutions—Have you incurred party penalties? When and for what? Who rescinded it?" Severov of Leningrad noted that the TsK was continually tardy in correcting the mistakes of local organizations. This was the case, for example, with regard to party expulsions. Mistakes were corrected only when their magnitude became too great. A railroad worker named S. Lipenkov called for a stipulation in the statutes that raikoms could not bypass a primary organization to expel someone from the party and that the question of expulsion in a primary organization would be settled only by secret ballot. Another railroad worker, A. Khripin, and Kamalov of Ufa made the same point and also urged that an appellant be granted the right to recuse from the organization considering his case individuals he suspects to be prejudiced. As a response to the beating of cadres during the Yezhovshchina, M. Roshchin of Leningrad deemed it imperative to include a clause in the statutes to "ensure considerate treatment of experienced, old party members, representatives of the Leninist-Stalinist Bolshevik guard, former members of the underground, and participants in the civil war of 1917–21."

All these proposals reflected a certain impulse to democratize the party. But there were also proposals of a completely different kind. P. Lutskevich of Kirovograd proposed renaming the party the All-Union Leninist-Stalinist Communist Party (Bolsheviks). I. Gurevich of Voronezh wrote: "A procedure exists for a party member or candidate member who has proved to be an enemy of the people and has been exposed by NKVD organs to be expelled from the party at a general meeting of the primary party organization. What is the point of this formality?" He proposed inserting this amendment to the statutes: "If a party member proves to be a person who has betrayed the party and has fought against the party and Soviet rule for subversive purposes, he shall be automatically excluded from the party, and the party organization shall be informed thereof." Naturally, such a procedure would substantially "simplify" the fight against "enemies of the people." G. Kiselyov, a serviceman from Chita, insisted that any expulsion from the party be accompanied by a stipulation—"with the right to join" or "without the right to join the VKP(b). Individuals who have been expelled for political reasons shall be admitted on the same terms as individuals who have come from other parties." Because individuals who had belonged to other parties were being arrested for just that reason, this was tantamount to an arrest warrant. N. Kuznetsov proposed inserting a stipulation in the statutes that "party members who have engaged in factionalism or attempts to organize factional work in the party shall be immediately expelled from the party as enemies of the socialist homeland."

Some proposals on the statutes mirrored the changes that had occurred in society. Although the working class had been clearly favored in the past with respect to party membership, the new draft statutes called for broader access, which made the path to the top easier for members of the nomenklatura and their children. As a reaction to the low educational level of Communists in previous years, S. Zhizhkin of the village of Shevchenko proposed inserting a requirement in the statutes that every Communist have at least a secondary-school education by the end of the Third Five-Year Plan. There were also negative reactions to this proposal. Romanov of the Main Administration of the Northern Maritime Route was concerned that the party might become contaminated with the kind of free access to it that is prescribed by the theses in Comrade

Zhdanov's report, and that its fighting capacity might suffer. F. Shapovalov of Lipetsk proposed setting up a second category for people from alien classes with regard to applications: they would need five sponsors with ten years of service (including two workers) and would be admitted under a two-year period of candidate membership. I. Furman of Novograd-Volynsk supported the retention of three categories for party admission: (1) for workers who had worked in production for three years, admitted to a six-month period of candidate membership under two sponsors with three years of party service; (2) for peasants and members of the intelligentsia, admitted to a one-year period of candidate membership under three sponsors with five years of service; and (3) for people from other parties, the same provision as in the old statutes.

This clause in the statutes was adopted at the congress in a simplified version. Moreover, the leadership began to express annoyance with the small chinks in the armor of the "dominant force" (workers), citing a decline in discipline at factories, laxness, turnover, and an increase in a number of negative factors—drunkenness, crime, and so forth. Under a resolution adopted by the SNK in January 1939, any tardy arrival at work of twenty minutes was equated with an unjustified absence, and a second late arrival led to the employee's dismissal. A decree of the Presidium of the Supreme Soviet on 26 June 1940 provided for even stricter measures. Any unjustified absence at work was to be taken up in a People's Court. Those found guilty were to be sentenced to correctional work at their workplace for up to six months, with 25 percent of their earnings withheld. At the same time, because of the difficulties that had cropped up in production, the seven-hour workday—a "gift" from the party that coincided with the tenth anniversary of the October Revolution—was replaced by an eight-hour day. The decree also prohibited the unilateral termination of labor contracts for hired workers, which meant, in effect, that workers were tied to the enterprise. In August 1940 a decree was adopted that increased criminal liability for minor crimes, such as drunkenness and hooliganism. These measures resulted in another rise in the population of the GULAG. While 108,000 people were convicted under the hooliganism article in 1939, almost 200,000 people were convicted under it in 1940. A sizable percentage of those convicted were individuals accused of crimes related to violating social and administrative order.[19]

That the mass repressions produced a supply crisis and a kind of "economic fever" in production is quite apparent from the documents. The arrests of production organizers, technical and engineering personnel, and skilled workers could not fail to have an impact on the operations of labor collectives and on the quantity and quality of output, both in industry and agriculture. The top and middle echelons of the planning and managerial sector of the recently created "socialist economy" were hit especially hard. As the sources make clear, advanced enterprises of national importance in the capital that were packed with sophisticated, imported equipment, such as the *Elektrokombinat* (Integrated Electrical Equipment Plant), the Avtozavod (Auto Plant) and the GPZ-1 (State Ball-Bearing Factory no. 1), found themselves so disorganized by the repressions that they made a total mess of the plan and were unable to recover completely until the very beginning of the war.

On the eve of the war there was a clear increase in the lopsided nature of Soviet industry and in the lag of sectors producing consumer goods. In addition, the "economic fever" coincided with war preparations, which required a sharp rise in the share of military output at the expense of civilian production. As numerous letters from the provinces show, by 1939 the country was on the brink of returning to a rationing system for distributing consumer goods and food. But this would be tantamount to an acknowledgment of failure by the leadership and a retraction of its loud declarations about taking better and better care of the Soviet people, whose lives were supposedly improving and becoming more cheerful with each passing year. This was a step that Stalin could not take. As letters from the provinces made clear, many people believed that the situation was critical only in their locality rather than throughout the country, and that the shortage of goods was the handiwork of wreckers and profiteers or the result of ineptitude by local authorities. The shortage of foodstuffs produced huge lines. Desperate citizens themselves asked to have a rationing system introduced so that they would not starve to death. The letters repeatedly emphasized that the authorities' refusal to deal with the situation was making the public bitter and was stirring up anti-Soviet sentiment.

As a result, in spite of obvious opposition from the center, local leaders were forced to introduce, without prior authorization, rationing of foodstuffs and goods for categories of the population that were not covered by closed commerce and special distribution centers. When scarce goods were thrown into the open market, people often lost not only all signs of socialist morality but any resemblance to human beings as well. M. I. Apen'ko, a resident of the Cossack village of Belaia Kalitva in Rostov Oblast, painted this typical picture of everyday life in a letter to M. I. Kalinin at the end of 1938:

---

# Document 89

Letter from M. I. Apen'ko to Kalinin on kolkhoz market in Rostov Oblast, 1938. GARF, f. 7523, op. 23, d. 209, l. 70. Typewritten original.

---

A kolkhoz fair was held in the village of Belaia Kalitva in Rostov Oblast on 26 and 27 November this year, and several thousand kolkhoz farmers and factory workers gathered there to buy consumer goods, since the local newspaper *Stalinsky Klich* [Stalin's call] announced that a sufficient quantity of consumer goods had been delivered to the kolkhoz market.

A red cloth over the shopping stalls bore the slogans, in enormous lettering, "For a High Standard of Soviet Trade in the City and Countryside!" But in reality I witnessed unprecedented abuse against citizens, to wit: lines to the dry-goods stalls began to form during the night. They began to bring in dry goods at 10 A.M. The horse-drawn cart broke up the line, and whoever was first wound up last, and the ones at the end wound up first. So profiteering elements and people using their connections were able to buy the fabrics, for many individuals passed themselves off as members of police-support teams. There was no price list for the goods, so shoppers were inevitably overcharged.

When people began to buy the fabrics and the merchandise was tossed over their heads, the lines broke up completely and the result was total chaos and a solid mass of human bodies, which gave people a chance to crawl over other people's heads in dirty boots and dirty clothing. Specifically, on 26 November Roman Leonov and Nikolai Chernikov crawled over people's heads.

Marfa Belousova was pulled out unconscious, with her clothes tattered, and citizen Aksyonov (from the Krutinsky settlement) had his nose smashed, causing a lot of bleeding, because the lid of the bin was not fastened.

On the morning of 27 November citizen Mazolevsky, dressed in a railroad worker's uniform, [also crawled] over people's heads and especially cynical abuse was inflicted on a fifteen-year-old citizen named Natal'ia Kakicheva from the Forshtad settlement. She was tossed onto people's heads and rolled over them (her legs were exposed).

The raion organizations knew about all this, but nobody reacted.

I consider that this is the work of the class enemy, specific counterrevolutionary agitation was done in practice, which I wrote about to Comrade Molotov, the chairman of the Council of People's Commissars. Comrade Molotov's secretariat sent it to the oblast procurator for investigation, and it is still stuck there. I also reported to the Oblispolkom, and the latter required the Oblast Internal Trade Administration and the Oblast Consumer Union to develop proper Soviet trade in Belaia Kalitva Raion. But none of this was carried out. I request that you let me know of your next directive.

---

As we see, it is again the "class enemy" who is to blame. Meanwhile, the problem of shortages of various foodstuffs and consumer goods continued to worsen. Limits were introduced everywhere on the amount of goods allowed any individual, forcing people to run around to dozens of stores in order to stock up on groceries and not wait on countless enormous and angry lines. A kind of vicious circle took shape: the more reserves of goods that were thrown into the marketplace, the longer the lines became. The planned growth of trade turnover could not meet the public's needs even to a small degree. The snatching up of goods was intensified by constant rumors of war, which in reality was edging ever closer to the borders of the Soviet Union.

The leadership battled the shortages chiefly by administrative and punitive means. The Decree of 26 June 1940 was also targeted at those who stood in line instead of working at enterprises and institutions. On the eve of the war the leadership even decided to pro hibit queues and combat them with the police's help. This campaign had intermittent success. People invented thousands of ways to get what they needed. A kind of science evolved in how to accomplish this by applying a fair amount of time and resourcefulness. There was an increase in the number of people who tried to stick their hands in the state's pocket.

The sources show that the economic situation in the late 1930s generated several serious social problems that should receive particular emphasis. First, it intensified social and vocational conflicts within Soviet society. The trouble can be traced to the decision by the Politburo to create a system of closed shops and food-service establishments for military servicemen, functionaries of the NKVD, workers at military-industrial facilities, railroad transport, and several other strategically important sectors. In other words, privileged social and vocational groups were singled out for special care from the state. This, at a time of a real threat of famine, inevitably produced an outraged reaction from the public. As Boris Morozov, a schoolboy from Gomel' Oblast, wrote to A. I. Mikoyan, railroad workers, "while telling outsiders and educators to go to hell, are getting bread from their own canteen. And who gave them the right to disgrace the country! No, with this way of doing things and these shortcomings we will never triumph, we will never build communism!" concluded the ninth-grader. Of course, the top nomenklatura had no intention of sharing the hardships and adversities of life with the rest of the people, but they were not alone. A resident of Kazan' named Zaichenko wrote to SNK Chairman Molotov in the spring of 1940 that profiteering had become widespread. Store employees, uninhibited by shoppers, let relatives and acquaintances get merchandise without waiting on line and stashed away items for resale with the connivance of the police and local authorities. People were forced to buy goods from profiteers at triple the normal price. While ordinary citizens waited on line all night for bread on the eve of the 1940 May Day holiday, local authorities obtained fine caviar, sausages and pastries at their own special distribution center. S. D. Bogdanov of Fergana reported to the people's commissar of the food industry in November 1940 on the spectacular growth of string-pulling and the use of official positions in a half-starved city: "On 22 October factory workers and office employees were waiting on line for consumer goods at the raion store. . . . The chief of the police, the head of criminal investigation, the procurator and the judge came in, picked out the most valuable goods and left. After that the crowd became agitated, people started saying that there is no justice and you can't get it anywhere. The rest of the merchandise was taken to some unknown place, and the workers were unable to get it."[20]

The terrible shortages did in fact revive a profiteering environment, stirring up widespread discontent and notions of enemy schemes—thoughts that were natural in an atmosphere rife with rumors of mass repressions. "Again somebody's criminal paw has upset the supply lines for Moscow," S. Abuladze, a Muscovite, wrote to Molotov on 19 December 1939. This was the simplest and most accessible explanation for the problems that were occurring. We should note that this explanation was also most convenient for the authorities, because it distracted people from pondering the real reasons for the shortcomings. Abuladze continued:

> Once again there are overnight queues for fats, potatoes have disappeared, and there is no fish at all. The market has everything, but not much of it either, and at four times the price. As for consumer goods, more and more you see in the endless lines people who aren't working, some kind of tough-looking men and janitors, early-morning cleaning women and unoccupied people. . . . What is an office worker supposed to do? We don't have the time to stand on line for hours or pay outrageous prices at the market. Viacheslav Mikhailovich! Is it really impossible to regulate the supply of food and consumer goods? We ask you as our [legislative] deputy to help eliminate all the machinations and misconduct in the supply system, after all, queues develop the worst qualities in people: envy, anger, rudeness, and they completely wear out people's nerves.[21]

The capital was in considerably better condition than the rest of the country. People from other regions who came to the capital to visit relatives or on assignment were openly envious of Muscovites and incensed at the same time: what made them and their children worse than their Moscow counterparts, why didn't they ever see sugar or milk?

The supply crisis, accompanied by a noticeable increase in prices, led to a certain deterioration in relations between city dwellers and the kolkhoz countryside. Many factory workers, as in the past, began to pin the blame on the rural dwellers. Kolkhoz farmers came to the city to sell produce from their garden plots and bought up scarce goods, which obviously annoyed the city residents. "The countryside is buying up all of the goods that appear at the market. . . . A city dweller can't buy clothing or shoes even in Moscow"—such were the complaints heard during the discussion of the new draft statutes of the VKP(b). Apparently on the basis of official statistics, A. Sazonov, an instructor from Moscow, pointed to what he regarded as an unjustified increase in the income of kolkhoz farmers and proposed securing an income reduction of 10–12 percent a year in the countryside for the next four years.[22] We will see in the next chapter what the real situation of kolkhoz farmers was and why they traveled to the city for food.

The system of social services at the end of the 1930s appeared by no means to be smoothly functioning. The sources cite a shortage of kindergartens and nursery schools, tremendous waiting lists to place children in them, and complaints about the privileges that certain groups enjoyed in this process. As has been mentioned, the state during this period set a policy of strengthening the family. The measures along these lines included a resolution of the TsIK and the SNK dated 27 June 1936 "On the Prohibition of Abortions, an Increase in Financial Assistance to Women Giving Birth, the Establishment of State Assistance to Large Families, the Expansion of the System of Maternity Hospitals, Nursery Schools, and Kindergartens, an Increase in Criminal Penalties for Nonpayment of Alimony, and Some Revisions in the Divorce Law." It is obvious from the title alone that the measures that were laid out were largely of a prohibitive and repressive nature. It is not surprising that they had little effect in the long term. A memorandum sent to the party's TsK in 1940 by Miterev, the USSR people's commissar of public health, noted that infant mortality had risen since the mid-1930s. In 1935 the mortality rate was 146 infants per one thousand newborns, whereas in 1938 it was 162. Materials reporting on implementation of the above-mentioned resolution showed that in 1935, before it was adopted, 1,932,305 abortions were performed in the country. After the resolution there was first a sharp drop, and then another upswing: 570,000 in 1937, 685,000 in 1938, and 755,000 in 1939.[23] And these figures reflect only officially recorded abortions. A set of instructions that was drawn up for combating so-called "criminal abortions" established criminal liability for performing them. A telegram from a serviceman named Anisimov to the USSR Supreme Soviet perhaps provided

the best illustration of what kind of everyday conflicts could flare
up in this situation:

---

## Document 90

Telegram from Anisimov to Kalinin requesting wife's abortion [n.d.]. GARF, f. 7523, op. 23,
d. 209, l. 60. Original telegram form.

---

To Kalinin, Supreme Soviet Kremlin Moscow
During [a] vacation [in] Kislovodsk [my] wife Anisimova had affair[.] Result [was] pregnancy[.] Have family two adult children after twenty years. Because [of] pregnancy Anisimova left family[.] Request decision terminate
pregnancy[,] restoring family [of] four people [to] normal life[.] After termination Anisimova returns [to] family[.] Send your decision[:] Anisimov[,]
army medical office[,] Khabarovsk

---

The resettlement movement in the country continued in the
1930s, and by the end of the decade it had become organized on a
more coercive basis. One of the most significant surprises to come
from the documents was the outbreak of interethnic conflicts. The
problem became so serious that in many cases ethnic strife caused
the mass return of resettlers and a de facto breakdown of the resettlement policy.

The local population's hostility toward new arrivals stemmed in
large part from general economic difficulties: housing and food
shortages and the supply crisis discussed above. The local population feared that newcomers with many children would eat them
out of house and home, that housing would have to be vacated for
them and that the already skimpy ration of food and consumer
goods would have to be shared with them. A half-starving country
still had the psychological phenomenon of the queue in which
everyone waited but not everyone obtained goods. In this way economic and ethnic problems became tightly interwoven, producing
periodic flare-ups of hatred. Lazarev, the head of the Resettlement
Department under the SNK of the Chuvash ASSR, reported that
966 households moved in 1940 from the Chuvash ASSR to the Altai Krai, and 318 of them, or 32.9 percent, moved back.[24] This re-

port came with three copies of letters attached to it, and it commented that such letters came in almost daily. One of them said the following:

---

## Document 91

Copy of letter in report on resettlement from Chuvash ASSR to Altai Krai, 1940. RGASPI, f. 17, op. 123, d. 42, ll. 59–590b., 61. Certified, handwritten copy.

---

It will soon be a year since we moved from Chuvashia but if you take how we live at the present time [sentence incomplete in original]. We have no livestock at all, because the board doesn't help us. [A section follows on the use of benefits for new settlers to write off the kolkhoz's debts and arrears.] Basically are we to blame for their arrears last year or something? We live in shabby apartments, the frigid winter has hit us hard, the shacks are in disrepair and haven't been fixed, the windows too, but the kolkhoz has received glass for us but hasn't fixed it for us, instead they used the glass meant for us for livestock breeding and after that we had to board up the windows and seal them with clay. . . .

We have no bathhouse and we don't have a horse to go for firewood and they don't even give us one, we wash ourselves in the bathhouse once every four or five weeks, and there are even unpleasant things that occur. Our clothing is all worn out, but we can't get any at the store, they always throw us off the line because they say you haven't paid your share dues, even the raion functionaries don't think about us, but lately we are ashamed to go outside, everything we wear is tattered, but there is nowhere to buy anything, yet when they recruited us to come here they said clothing would be sold to us above all, but when we arrived there was nothing to be had.

Basically we are not considered needed people here, we are considered the same as swine, for example: when new settler Pyotr Sergeev was standing by the warehouse to receive five kg of flour, the attendant refused to give him any, instead he kicked him in the chest and knocked him down and said Chuvash they are just like swine so live on potatoes, but flour is needed for Russians, well then where is Stalin's constitution on equal rights[?] . . .

While [we] were sitting at a table with new settler V. A. Alekseev and S. Kh. Aleksandrov we were approached by A. L. Zhirov and he yelled at us get up from the table, we will eat first, and the leftovers will be for the new settlers, he said, all you new settlers are eating other people's bread. . . .

[Accounts followed of new settlers who went back home:]

1. Yekaterina Kupriianovna Kozlova moved from the Dmitrov Kolkhoz in Ibresi Raion to the Anatoly Kolkhoz under the Talitsa Village Soviet, Zalesovo Raion, in Altai Krai. I fenced in a garden together with Il'in Zakharovich Shir-

tanovsky, and with Yegor Nikitin from the village of Nizhniaia Vysla. But some peasants and younger fellows who have lived there for a long time got together, a drunken mob, and tore up the fence around the garden with these wooden poles, smashed windows and used the poles to wreck the ovens of Pavel Trofimov and Fedot Denisov.

These men from the area said you should be kicked out, what the hell did you come here for, you think money grows on trees here or something[?] We complained to the raion and they didn't take any measures there and we were forced to come back here. . . .

2. Yemel'ian Gavrilovich Gavrilov (old man).

I came to resettle, moved into a house there were windows, there was a little oven, as soon as I moved in they smashed all the windows in one day, they wrecked the oven and turned the house into a toilet. . . .

We had cases like this we temporarily had no bread for seventeen days (the old man wept as he spoke). There were cases when new settlers ate carrion. For example Fedot Denisov ate a dead heifer, and so did Nikolai Nikitin.

---

A meeting of the Altai Kraikom bureau of the VKP(b) on 18 December 1940 confirmed in full the instances of abusive treatment of new settlers in Altai Krai's Zalesovo Raion. As the minutes noted, the result was that 361 of 769 families went back home in 1940. It was pointed out that the local authorities had violated the resolution of the party's TsK and the SNK, dated 4 June 1940, on personal management of the task of receiving new settlers and providing for them economically. A comment was made that no one welcomed the settlers' families. They lived at the train station for ten days. They had baggage stolen. It was noted that the local administration had insulted the ethnic feelings of the Chuvash. They were not issued loans or food, and fifteen children of settlers died as a result.[25]

The Chuvash ASSR people's commissar of internal affairs, Senior Lieutenant of State Security Barsukov, reported to NKVD People's Commissar Beria on 6 March 1941 that "it is apparent from materials that have come in to the NKVD of the Chuvash ASSR that the resolution of the TsK of the VKP(b) and the SNK on resettlers is being violated in a number of oblasts and krais of the Soviet Union, to wit: in Krasnoiarsk and Altai Krais and in Sverdlovsk and Kustanai Oblasts." He went on to say that "the local population is giving a poor reception to the new settlers. There has been rude treatment and abuse, even to the point of beatings," and many had left: "Of the 2,839 households from the Chuvash ASSR that resettled in the aforementioned krais and oblasts in 1940, 859 households went back." "Afanasy Yakovlevich Vorob'-yov, a new settler at the Chkalov Kolkhoz in Zalesovo Raion, Altai Krai, recounted that at first he got a normal reception, but then the treatment changed drastically. Children and old people were left without foodstuffs. They were not allowed into the public cafeteria, merchandise was not sold to them at the store, they were not provided with fuel, and they had to carry firewood from the forest themselves. Nothing was issued them for labordays." N. P. Yanbashev of Mendygarinsky Raion, Kustanai Oblast, "among other new settlers, lay in dust and in the rain for eight days, and for four days his family had absolutely no bread and he didn't even have money to buy any. Beginning on 8 July of last year (the day of the new settlers' arrival) they were not allowed to buy a single meter of dry goods." At the New Path Kolkhoz in Verkhoturovo Raion, Sverdlovsk Oblast, new settler Aleksandr Osipov, describing instances of abuse, reported that the kolkhoz vice chairman, A. G. Shubikov, had declared at a kolkhoz farmers' meeting: "New settlers are coming with very big families, they want to live off our backs, let them eat potatoes and drink water."[26]

All these circumstances demonstrate that the social processes in Soviet society in the late 1930s, contrary to the proclaimed commonality and supposedly growing unity of the society, remained internally tense, and existing conflicts not only were not being ironed out but were on the increase. The mass repressions, the supply crisis, and other factors, without question, catalyzed these processes.

With the public "on guard" against profiteers, spies and other enemies of the people, it is not surprising that anti-Semitism was rife, as one report to party bodies claimed.[27] Moreover, NKVD directives from the late 1930s that have been declassified show the almost total repression of such nationalities as Germans, Italians, Austrians, Poles, and Finns. Indeed, all "foreigners" were under suspicion, regardless of nationality, or of their services to the USSR and the Comintern. Hatred toward them as potential terrorists and agents of foreign intelligence was deliberately whipped up. This was in marked contrast to earlier in the decade. As recently as 1934 members of the leftist paramilitary group *Schutzbund* of Austria, for example, were welcomed as national heroes, yet three years later they were turned into the worst enemies of the USSR. The repressive machine lumped all foreigners together. In 1938–39 families of Russified Germans and Italians, many of whose ancestors had come to Russia in the time of Peter the Great, were banished from the USSR, even though these people knew neither the language nor the culture of their ancestors and had not had any contact with those countries. The sole basis for expulsion was a foreign surname.

It is worth focusing in particular on the social and ethnic problems that resulted from the USSR's annexation in 1940 of territories from eastern Poland, and then of the Baltic states and Moldavia. Occupation was followed by "Sovietization," collectivization, the slapping together of kolkhozes, dekulakization, and so forth—the same processes that the rest of the country had undergone ten years before. It would seem that certain lessons could have and should have been learned in order to avoid the numerous problems and absurdities that had accompanied the socialist offensive and produced justified outrage among the public—especially given that the 1936 constitution appeared to have indirectly acknowledged as much.

The documents indicate, though, that nothing changed. Moreover, the Sovietization of these regions was further complicated by military conflicts and ethnic prejudice.[28] Most of the people repressed in western Ukraine and Belorussia proved to be ethnic Poles. Special trains carrying exiled Poles, Estonians, Lithuanians, and others headed eastward, to Kazakhstan and Siberia. We learn from a secret letter Beria wrote to the party's TsK in September 1940 that, under a resolution of the SNK dated 10 April of that year, members of twenty-five thousand Polish families—old people, women and children—were exiled from the new western oblasts of Ukraine and Belorussia. All they were guilty of was that their men had served in the Polish army or the state apparatus, or had been classified as "bourgeois-landowning, counterrevolutionary-insurgent elements" and were in concentration camps or had been executed. In March and April 1940 alone, sixty-two thousand old people, women, and children arrived in Kazakhstan with the standard term of exile: ten years.[29] The repressed people themselves unquestionably perceived what was happening as an unjust "punishment" based on their ethnic background among other reasons. And they were right, judging from secret NKVD instructions. Excerpts from a secret report by an instructor named Kheilo in the agricultural department of the party's TsK dated 21 August 1940 describes the everyday life of exiled Poles:

---

## Document 92

Report on exiled Poles in Kustanai Oblast, Kazakh SSR, 21 August 1940. RGASPI, f. 17, op. 123, d. 42, ll. 7–8. Certified, typewritten copy.

---

On the Demoralizing Influence on Kolkhoz Labor Discipline of Kulaks and Bourgeoisie Exiled from the Former Poland to Kustanai Oblast in the Kazakh SSR. . . . Exiled kulaks are put up in the homes of kolkhoz farmers, often without the latter's consent. There have been cases in which one kolkhoz arranged such a cordial welcome for exiles that it gave them a day's milk yield from the dairy section, so that the kolkhoz farmers' children at the open-air kindergarten were left without milk. There have been cases in which certain kolkhoz chairmen have taken exiles into their apartments. Combine and tractor operators and other kolkhoz activists have married exiles.

Exiles are credited with labordays and paid on an equal footing with kolkhoz farmers for their work on the kolkhoz.

In the vast majority of cases these bourgeois and kulaks don't do anything on the kolkhoz. Many of them arrived with enough money, clothing, and other belongings, and some of them receive money transfers of two thousand to three thousand rubles each, evidently from relatives.

They buy foodstuffs from kolkhoz farmers, but they don't want to work and nobody makes them.

Twenty families of exiles [at the Dzhanaul in Karabalyk Raion] did not do anything, explaining that they were not used "in their vocation" . . .

At the Magnai MTS in the same raion, a former officer arrived with his orderly, and the latter continued even here to make coffee for him and to polish and remove his boots, and when the NKVD transferred his former orderly to another kolkhoz, the officer did not take off his boots for a week, and when his feet became swollen, he took the boots off and has not put them on for two weeks. . . .

There are many exiles in Fyodorovka Raion, in the raion center itself, who have also been placed in kolkhoz farmers' homes, who don't do anything,

## Document 92 *continued*

spend entire days sitting in a restaurant and strolling around the market and around offices. . . .

There are cases in the oblast center itself, the city of Kustanai, when exiles are hired as office typists and clerks and are even hired to work in such organizations as Zagotzerno [the All-Union Bureau for Grain Procurement and Sales], where possible acts of sabotage by them are not out of the question. . . .

---

We should take note of the good treatment, on the whole, that the Poles who arrived got from local residents. Having themselves gone through dekulakization and exile, the majority of Russians helped the newcomers adjust to their new environment. Mixed marriages between exiled Poles and local residents were convincing evidence of the lack of ethnic animosity. As the document makes clear, none of this pleased the authorities, as suggested by the title of the memorandum.

The numerous, previously secret materials that we examined concerning the situation in the ethnic regions and republics of the USSR at the end of the 1930s offer a stark contrast to what the newspapers of the time wrote about friendship between peoples. One can infer from the sources that ethnic problems worsened during this period. An especially difficult situation persisted in the Northern Caucasus. A secret letter provides specific facts about the situation in Kabardino-Balkaria:

---

## Document 93

Report "On Manifestations of Bourgeois Nationalism and Great-Power Chauvinism" in Kabardino-Balkaria, 16 September 1940." RGASPI, f. 17, op. 122, d. 2, ll. 24–30. Certified, typewritten copy.

---

Manifestations of bourgeois nationalism and great-power chauvinism have been noted lately in a number of raions of the republic. . . .

Here are some of the numerous incidents that have been uncovered in recent months:

On 11 July 1940, at the Tyrnyauz Integrated Works, M. P. Kardanov beat up Comrade Sofronov, head of the food-supply department, supposedly for refusing to give him [Kardanov] a job because he is a Kabardin (Kardanov did not have his papers with him: no passport, labor book, etc.). He tried to stab Comrade Sofronov. Kardanov was sent to the El'brus Raion police, but the chief of the police, Comrade Dzhaboev, released him, and he went into hiding. It was learned that Kardanov is the son of an exiled kulak.

There have also been instances of great-power chauvinism. On Navy Day a mass rally was held in which more than five hundred people took part. A plasterer named Gladkov, while inebriated, tried to gather Russians for a fistfight among Kabardin, Balkar, and Russians. Gladkov was sent to the El'brus Raion police, but was also released. . . .

On 16 August 1940, S. M. Divnich, Pfeifer, and Sidorenko were returning home to Chegem Pervyi while intoxicated. As they walked along the street, some young boys began to badger them, and one of them struck Divnich in the back with a rock. The latter went to chase the boy, who ran into the yard of Buzha Bogotov and hid in the corn while screaming "Urus, Urus." A Kabardin responded to the boy's screaming by running out with a stake in his hands and he stabbed Divnich in the shoulder. Pfeifer heard the screams, ran to the scene of the fight and saw Divnich surrounded already by a whole mob of Kabardin, who also attacked Pfeifer and beat him up, cracking his head open. Divnich and Pfeifer decided to complain to the village soviet, where, however, not only were the appropriate measures not taken, but they were beaten up again by the village soviet chairman Tamash Mazanovich Pekov, village soviet secretary Ibragim Makoev, Komsomol secretary Bogotov, a driver, the kolkhoz assistant manager Khabaz Kishev, and others.

During March and April of this year many Russian workers at the Eastern Akbash bast fiber factory were beaten up by Kabardin, and the methods used in the beatings were identical. The individuals would accost a Russian leaving the factory at night, ask him for a light and, upon making sure he was Russian, beat him up, saying over and over: "Now take Finland, now take the Ukraine, now take Poland and Turkey."

At 10 P.M. on 2 May a group of Kabardin attacked workers returning from the bast fiber factory and threw rocks at them, injuring Vasily Yefimovich Kvint, a driver for the factory, in the head. . . .

A group of nationalists in the village of Kenzhe, Nal'chik Raion, headed by Tkhamokov, the chairman of the village soviet, destroyed the gardens of Russian workers from the Peplo-Pemzovoi mine. There have been a number of incidents in which Kabardin have beaten up Russians waiting on line at shops while they shouted out patently nationalist phrases (Leskensky, Baksan, Urvansky, Nal'chik, and other raions).

In the Balkar raions and several others, schoolteachers who have resettled are persecuted even by the heads of Soviet organizations. The teachers are denied an opportunity to buy food, insulted and so forth. . . .

Among the measures suggested to combat manifestations of nationalism, the need for intensifying systematic educational work was cited. "It should be kept in mind," said the letter, "that *the repressive measures that judicial bodies will take against the nationalists will naturally cause an increase in their subversive work among the masses and make them want to use this for their own, nationalist purposes.* (Underlined in the document, and the question is raised in the margins, apparently in Zhdanov's handwriting: "What if they crack heads open?")

The authorities became particularly concerned in the late 1930s about mass evasions of service in the Red Army by draftees from the ethnic regions, something that was regarded both as a criminally punishable offense against the state and as a manifestation of nationalism. Consider this letter from deputy chief Kuznetsov of the Red Army's Main Administration of Political Propaganda to the party's TsK:

---

## Document 94

Letter to TsK VKP(b) "On the Results of an Investigation of Mass Evasions of Service in the Red Army by Draftees in the Chechen-Ingush ASSR," 1940. RGASPI, f. 17, op. 122, d. 2, ll. 31–39. Certified, typewritten copy.

---

A group of functionaries of the USSR People's Commissariat of Defense has conducted an on-scene inquiry into mass evasions of service in the Red Army by draftees in the Chechen-Ingush ASSR.

The inquiry determined that 6,246 men were enlisted in the Red Army in Chechen-Ingush ASSR from the 1939 draft; of that number, 3,325 men were dispatched to Red Army units in 1939, and 2,921 men were left in the reserves. On special duty for the Northern Caucasus Military District command, the reserves were dispatched in small units to the Red Army in February and June of 1940. The dispatching was extremely disorganized; there was no verification that draftees showed up at assembly points. As a result, 529 men failed to appear at the assembly point during the dispatching process or fled from the train-departure sites.

In addition, eighty-four of the draftees from the Chechen-Ingush ASSR who had previously been dispatched to the Red Army deserted their units.

As of 18 September, 180 of those who fled or failed to appear had been arrested, and thirty-seven of them had been convicted by Military Tribunals. The rest are being sought by the police and the NKVD. . . .

# Document 94 *continued*

In Itum-Kalinsky Raion (Comrade Magomadov, secretary of the raion committee of the VKP[b]), sixty-two men failed to appear to be dispatched. Fifty percent of the total number in hiding are Communists and Komsomol members, seven are village schoolteachers, one is a technical functionary for the VKP(b) raion committee, one is a bookkeeper, and one is a statistician.

Comrade Sel'murzaev, secretary of the Shali Raion Committee of the VKP(b), insisted that deserters Dokuev, Yunusov and Makhmatkhazhiev be released from custody, justifying this by the fact that one of Dokuev's brothers is the chairman of the village executive committee and a VKP(b) member and another brother is a school principal and a VKP(b) candidate member, while Yunusov's mother is a member of the plenum of the VKP(b) raikom.

The same thing occurred in Shatoevsky Raion.

Many Communists in that raion are harboring deserters. Gerikhanov, an instructor for the VKP(b) raion committee, knew that VKP(b) member Demel'khanov was protecting deserter Dubaev, and began to speak with Demel'khanov about his behavior unbecoming a party member. Demel'-khanov responded: "What do you need from me, you're a Chechen and I'm a Chechen, so why on earth should we talk about Dubaev's desertion and his affairs. We should keep quiet about that."

The most shameful incident involved raion procurator Davlitgireev, who adamantly refused to go to the draft commission. Only when the raion military committee demanded it did Davlitgireev appear at the commission for an examination, and he was found fit to serve in the army. He disagreed, however, with the draft commission's decision and went to see medical specialists in Groznyi, where he was also found fit to serve in the Red Army. After that Davlitgireev went to the republic procurator's office and asked to be hired as a responsible functionary. The republic's deputy procurator, Comrade Shcherban', agreed to this and, in a strictly secret letter to the chairman of the raion executive committee, Comrade Sapaev, wrote: "I request that Davlitgireev be attached to the procurator's office of Shatoevsky Raion." . . .

The chairman of the Guchum-Kalinsky village executive committee, El'saev, concealed seven first cousins from the draft. Under this village soviet one hundred draftees failed to appear at assembly points.

## Harboring of Relatives

. . . On 22 February 1940 the chairman of the Red Hammer Kolkhoz in Urus-Martan Raion, Kagirmanov, and accountant Guchigov issued a certificate to Guchigov stating that "he is authorized to travel to any city in the USSR to acquire goods." After receiving the certificate, Guchigov went into hiding. In May 1940 the same individuals issued Guchigov a second certificate stating that "Guchigov is not hiding from the authorities." In June 1940 they issued Guchigov a third certificate to the effect that Guchigov had gotten married on

## Document 94 *continued*

22 February and, in keeping with Chechen custom, had to hide from his parents for two weeks. A military tribunal sentenced Guchigov to five years. [Information follows about shortfalls in conscriptions according to year of birth, and defiance of restrictions on the size of household plots among ʼolkhoz farmers.]

Of course, evasions of service in the Red Army by people in the Caucasus had occurred before. What apparently turned this into a mass phenomenon was the USSR's participation in the war against Finland and other conflicts involving fatalities. Meanwhile, all the documents depicting everyday life convey a sense of the approaching storm of war: the defensive measures that were continually being taken, the reports on the sentiments that the measures produced, and the information sometimes mentioned in passing. The government decided in the mid-1930s to lift various restrictions on military service for Cossacks, who had once constituted the most effective fighting units of the Imperial Army. Special Cossack units could be set up, comprising the Cossacks of the Don, the Kuban', and the Terek. The Cossacks, of course, had had mixed feelings about Soviet rule. Many Cossacks had supported the Whites. Cossack areas had suffered heavily during collectivization and the famine of 1932–33. A secret summary by the Migulin Raion branch of the NKVD reported on the discussions that this had precipitated (all the syntactic idiosyncrasies of the original have been preserved):

## Document 95

NKVD summary report on reactions of Cossacks in Migulin Raion to lifting restrictions for service in Red Army, 26 April 1936. GARF, f. 1235, op. 141, d. 1789, ll. 74–79. Typewritten original.

Special Summary
On the Sentiments of Various Segments of the Population of Migulin Raion Based on the Government's Decision to Lift Restrictions on Cossacks for Service in the RKKA [*Raboche-Krest'ianskaia Krasnaia Armia*, Workers' and Peasants' Red Army] and the Order of Comrade Marshal Voroshilov, the

USSR People's Commissar of Defense, on the Establishment of Cossack Divisions

The Government's decision to lift restrictions on the Cossacks for service in the RKKA and the order of Comrade Voroshilov, the people's commissar of defense, on the establishment of Cossack divisions were greeted by the population of Migulin Raion with great enthusiasm.

Even though explanatory work and study sessions on the government's decision and the order have not been set up well enough yet, a large portion of the kolkhoz farmers know about them. They are having spirited discussions about them, mostly expressing positive sentiments. They are responding to the government's decisions and the order of Comrade Voroshilov, the people's commissar of defense, with production indexes.

Before the discussion of the government's decision to lift restrictions on service in the RKKA, kolkhoz farmer Roman Brekhov of brigade no. 2 at the Kirov Kolkhoz under the Mrykhovsky Village Soviet did no more than five hectares of row planting, but the day after a study session on the government's decision and the order by the people's commissar he began to do 7.8 hectares of planting in a shift without changing oxen.

A kolkhoz farmer in brigade no. 1 at the same kolkhoz, Roman Ivanov, was doing up to 4.5 hectares of row planting before the study session on the government's resolution and the order by the people's commissar, and began to do no less than 5.5 to six hectares after the session.

Kolkhoz farmer Tat'iana Udovkina, twenty-five years old, was doing 3.5 hectares of harrowing before the study session and began to do five and 5.5 hectares on one harrow after the session.

"Why didn't they take me into the service a year ago, I would have been in the army for almost a year now and would be learning, I was terribly hurt that the commission didn't allow me into the ranks of the RKKA during the call-up. Well, that's all right, I will go serve in the army in the fall anyway."

(Ivan Ivanovich Zelenkov, a Cossack from the settlement of Alekseevsky, born 1913, poorly literate.)

"I want to go into the Red Army very much, but I have these really fine uncles, damn them. Two of them were removed by the NKVD, the third one vanished somewhere, and my father is no better he was also a Cossack sergeant with the Whites, don't worry, they will take me into the Army too."

(Vasily Semyonovich Nasonov a kolkhoz farmer at the New Life Kolkhoz born 1914 called up into the RKKA on 24 April 1936 and enlisted in the cavalry.)

"Well that is very good, now more of our Cossacks will come out of the Red Army developed and literate. They'll get taught there not like we used to get taught, so that we came out of the army and forgot even what we knew when we went into the service."

## Document 95 *continued*

(Grigory Osipovich Babkin, a Cossack fifty years old, a kolkhoz farmer at the New Life Kolkhoz under the Alekseevsky Village Soviet.)

"Cossacks are people just like the rest of us. They have also realized that Soviet rule builds a comfortable life, that's why the Government met them halfway."

(Pelogeia Ivanovna Plakhova thirty-five years old, a milkmaid at m.[eat] and d.[airy] state farm no. 22, non-Cossack.)

Most of the kolkhoz Cossacks, especially young people, in expressing positive sentiments often show a desire to go serve in the Red Army as volunteers. In certain cases this desire is so great that young Cossack kolkhoz farmers are demanding very persistently that the village soviets petition the Red Army to allow them to enlist.

"Why don't they want to take us into the Red Army now, we want to serve too, fellows our age are being dispatched today, but for some reason they don't want to take us. Let the soviet petition them to take us too. Now all Cossacks except people stripped of their rights may serve, and we want to go into the army on our own without waiting for the call-up."

(Gavril Zemliakov, a kolkhoz farmer at the Podtelkov and Krevoshlykov Kolkhoz under the Verkhnekovsky Village Soviet and Yevgeny Pshenov born 1914. They were not called up on 24 April 1936 due to a limited call-up. A total of twenty-five men were taken into the RKKA from Migulin Raion.)

The urge to volunteer for the army is coming not only from young people but also from adult Cossacks. This segment of the Cossacks is especially interested in serving Soviet authority and definitely in the newly established Cossack units. Among old Cossacks people are showing a desire to volunteer for the army—they are promising to achieve, honestly and through dedicated service, the highest medal the Order of the Red Banner.

"Ivan Kabkin kolkhoz farmer at the October Revolution Kolkhoz thirty-seven years old Cossack submitted a request to the village soviet addressed to Comrade Voroshilov asking him to admit him into the ranks of the Red Army and without fail through his dedicated service to achieve his decoration with the Order of the Red Banner."

Only an insignificant segment of the Cossacks and non-Cossacks, mostly people on file and from the mining works, consider the government's decision and the order of Comrade Voroshilov, the people's commissar of defense, to be a sign of "the weakness of Soviet authority" in the event of war regarding the government's measures distrustfully, and in most cases with hostility, as plain pandering to the Cossacks for fear of complications on the impending homefront.

"Soviet authority always strangled the Cossacks put them on trial and exiled them, and now that things look bad in the west and in the east, let's praise the Cossacks. They don't know that a Cossack must get a little praise then they can say he will follow us and things will be taken care of on the home-front too. And the Cossacks if they get a little praise will be happy to try, they will go all out."

(Semyon Fyodorovich Merkulov, fifty-six years old, independent peasant working temporarily at a grain-procurement facility. On file as a [former] member of a punitive detachment, a counterrevolutionary-minded element.)

"With this resolution and order Soviet authority is taking notice and trying to gain favor with the Cossacks, laying the groundwork for the coming war. They are creating divisions made up of the whole population, but they know themselves that there are now more non-Cossacks than Cossacks in the Cossack villages and settlements. Now, they are saying that they're creating divisions made up of the whole population in order to mix Cossacks with non-Cossacks, then they say it will be more reliable. But nothing will come of this effort. As soon as they start mixing a Cossack with a Russian peasant, they will end up with some kind of riffraff. If we have no Cossack blood, they can't serve together with the Cossacks."

(Kulak Stefan Filipovich Chikunov, born 1875, Cossack on file as a kulak.)

A segment of the Cossacks, mostly older ages, active White Guards and kulaks speaking out negatively about the government's measures in most cases are circulating provocative reports about war coming soon and the demise of Soviet rule.

"They can write a hundred resolutions and orders, nothing will come of this. We know the young people are for Soviet authority as it is, but these orders have no effect on the old people. As soon as war starts we know who will go into the woods with us, and from there we will show them on the home-front no matter where they run to."

(Aleksei Khizhnikov, fifty-six years old, Cossack Meshcheriakovsky settlement, main facility at the Nikolaev Cossack mining works.)

"Soviet authority is now praising the Cossacks because war is about to break out. Well that's all right as soon as the war starts, and it is around the corner, they haven't started pandering to the Cossacks for nothing, they've sensed that there is a smell of gunpowder in the air. We will show them in the rear without waiting for the war to end on the front."

"Cossack units are being organized from three oblasts because the rest of the Cossacks are closer to Japan and Germany and Poland, but these are farther away and more reliable but the others in the event of war might take off for those countries. Japan and Germany should crush them, but they are afraid of this Bolshevik plague."

There are only a few isolated negative sentiments among young people and the village intelegentsia, those among the first group are caused by a lack of work with the masses and the influence of their parents, and among the second group the a-s [anti-Soviet] minded segment of the intelegentsia by distrust of the measures that are being carried out.

## Document 95 *continued*

"In case the Cossacks have to fight, the old Cossacks will not go to fight for Soviet rule with enthusiasm but the young ones will fight with great enthusiasm, and even now you might say there are no Cossacks left all of them have either been convicted or exiled."

(Vasily Vodurin Cossack, kolkhoz farmer, eighteen years old, resident of Podgorsky, son of an active White Guardist.)

"As soon as Soviet authority started having a hard time they remembered about the Cossacks, but they forgot how they set fire to our brother and exiled him, so let them manage without our brother now there won't be a lot of people willing to go into the army if they force us to go serve, we will have to serve like it or not."

(Vasily Mrykhin, son of a kulak Podgorsky settlement in Migulin Raion placed by us on file.) [A section follows on attitudes toward the old Cossack uniforms and whether they should be retained.]

Head of the Migulin Raion Branch of the NKVD
Sergeant of State Security
(Signed) Osipov

---

The ranks of the RKKA grew rapidly during the 1930s. From 1932 to 1938 its armed forces increased fourfold, numbering 2.1 million at the beginning of 1939.[30] An even greater increase (larger than in the preceding ten years) occurred in 1939, when a universal military obligation for adult males took effect, and 1940. The army took in sizable contingents of young draftees from the countryside and the cities. On the eve of the war the total number of people under arms was close to five million. The army's role in the life of society grew more conspicuous. It became prestigious to be a serviceman. This image derived from the education of the army in a heroic and patriotic spirit and the exaltation of past military victories. The restoration of ranks for generals and officers and the abolition of the institution of military commissars were part of the same trend. The army was also undergoing reorganization in the direction of imperial traditions, which included combined military and political command and strict hierarchy.

The army's condition, however, left much to be desired. More than 70 percent of the officer corps was made up of hastily trained specialists. In addition, there was a substantial shortage of middle-level and junior commanders. Real combat training was often replaced by regimentation and jingoistic political campaigns, with such slogans as "From the taiga to the British seas, the Red Army has no peer!" The repressions of 1937–38 inflicted significant losses on military cadres. During the Yezhovshchina twenty-four thousand men were arrested and "discharged for associating with plotters." In addition, more than four thousand commanders of Polish, Latvian and other "undesirable nationalities" were purged. As a result, the army lost 8 percent of its commanders. The condemnation of the Yezhovshchina seems to have pertained primarily to army cadres. By 1 May 1940 twelve thousand repressed individuals had been reinstated.[31] Yet the repressions in the army continued, albeit on a smaller scale. They produced an extremely nerve-racking atmosphere, shackling initiative and provoking distrust, suspicion, and unhealthy rivalries and denunciations.

In spite of the increasing rearmament and "motorization" of the Red Army, military production in the country often seemed to emphasize a quantitative buildup. There were long delays in the introduction of new types of airplanes and tanks. The quantitative and qualitative expansion of the armed forces required training of appropriate command and technical personnel, and special courses, general and military schools, and academies were failing to keep up.[32] The Soviet-Finnish war of 1939–40 exposed the army's problems with particular starkness. The documents of the time continually mention various defense-oriented measures: setting up television in the USSR for military purposes, bringing the radio-engineering industry up to standard, or producing torpedoes for the navy. Lists of enterprises and specialized factory shops were drawn up with a view to attaching engineers, technicians, and workers in the leading vocations to them; there were lists of specially recruited people at the oblast, krai, and union republic levels to be sent to infantry, flying, armored-tank, and naval schools; horses were requisitioned from kolkhozes to establish a reserve for the Red Army.

As was the case everywhere else, there was a great deal of disarray, "excesses," and high-handedness in the implementation of defense measures. Here, for example, is a letter to Stalin from Red Navy sailor I. Kotov, who describes the measures that were used to ensure "constant combat readiness":

# Document 96

Letter from Red Navy sailor I. Kotov to Stalin on confiscations of books and postcards, 1940. RGASPI, f. 17, op. 121, d. 26, l. 43. Typewritten copy.

Dear Iosif Vissarionovich!

On 31 August an inspection of the premises aboard the battleship Marat of the Red Banner Baltic Fleet was conducted, and in the process lockers, belongings and training manuals were inspected and I don't understand why textbooks that the Red Navy sailors need were taken away and they were forced to tear them up and burn them.

Iosif Vissarionovich! I decided to describe to you how this business was organized in the artillery subunit, where the political leader was Comrade Sheptunov. [A demand that works by Stalin and Marx that the sailors purchased be turned in to the ship's library follows.]

Iosif Vissarionovich! Most of the sailors in our subunit had a third- or fourth-grade education, more than 50 percent of the personnel, many sailors had acquired textbooks, some had taken them out of the library, Red Army sailors, they said during the inspection, "turn in all textbooks to the library, and whoever doesn't want to is to dump them out of his locker, tear them up, throw them in the sack (in the middle of the crew's quarters), carry the sack aboard the tugboat Yakobinets, which is standing alongside the battleship, and burn them."

Iosif Vissarionovich! Petty officer Kovtun of the [inspection] group found a postcard in sailor Yusov's locker which pictured you with Comrade Voroshilov in front of the Kremlin building. The petty officer asks what is this for? The sailor replies what do you mean this is allowed it's Comrades Stalin and Voroshilov. The petty officer flings the postcard onto the deck at people's feet. Comrade Stalin, why did this happen?

The sailors had postcards, they bought them in the city of Kronstadt, you and Comrade Voroshilov are in a submarine, then a postcard of Comrade Voroshilov and Comrade Kirov in military construction, and they were ordered to tear them up and throw them out, for heaven's sake why?

Iosif Vissarionovich! I had a postcard of Sergei Mironovich [Kirov] among Young Pioneers, I've had it for a long time since I was a Pioneer and I saw Sergei Mironovich a few times, but they are not allowing me to keep it, they go so far as to order me, well of course sailors are not happy to throw them in the garbage bag. I ask Comrade Sheptunov, the senior political leader, why can't we have them? What's the reason? I say these are our supreme leaders, loved by all the people and by the working people of the whole world. It's an order, says comrade political leader, an order from the people's commissar, not to have anything extraneous. Have two or three notebooks, a textbook on the history of the peoples of the USSR, since I'm in my second year of service, and then I can also have The Short Course in the History of the VKP(b).

Iosif Vissarionovich! The crew's quarters had framed portraits of Comrades

## Document 96 continued

Voroshilov, Molotov, and Kalinin, under glass, so they broke the frames, ripped up the portraits and burned them in the tugboat's furnace, the politburo of the VKP(b) was also framed, they gave orders to break it, rip it up and burn it. [An account follows of the destruction and burning of posters and slogans that the Red Navy sailors had prepared for the celebration of International Youth Day, extra blank notebooks, and so forth.]

There are a great many such examples. You ask the commanders, they reply it's an order from the people's commissar, but Iosif Vissarionovich I don't know, I don't think the people's commissar of the USSR Navy gave orders to break, rip up, and burn the portraits of beloved great people who we sailors treasure, so why does this happen?

Comrade Stalin maybe I didn't write smoothly, but I wrote the truth about everything that I would like to say.

Red Navy sailor I. Kotov

---

The civilian population was also preparing for the coming war, primarily young people, through a far-flung network of the most diverse volunteer organizations and "support" activities, including those that combined military and athletic elements: OSOAVI-AKhIM (Society to Support Defense, the Air Force, and Chemistry), PVKhO (chemical warfare defense), GTO (labor and defense preparedness), GSO (medical defense preparedness) and others. But the cadres and the physical assets that were required for proper, universal training did not exist, especially in the countryside. Here is another document describing the situation that the defense measures produced. It is a letter to *Krest'ianskaia Gazeta* from Komsomol member N. Timokhin of the village of Smirnovka in Dedinovsky Raion, Tula Oblast:

---

## Document 97

Letter from N. Timokhin to *Krest'ianskaia Gazeta* on defense measures on kolkhoz in Tula Oblast, 8 October 1938. RGAE, f. 396, op. 11, d. 56, ll. 1–2. Original manuscript.

---

Esteemed comrades, I send you my prosperous kolkhoz greetings and wish you the best in your happy city life.

Dear comrades,

I got your letter in which you ask me about military activities in the people's consciousness including our Yezhov Kolkhoz under the Smirnovka Village Soviet. You ask me to write you at the newspaper do you have on your kolkhoz an Oso[a]viakhim organization, a GTO, PVKhO, GSO, and others. Let me explain: we don't have these organizations at our kolkhoz and if they appear, it will be unbelievable, because things at our kolkhoz have gotten to the point where the whole kolkhoz discipline has fallen apart. Our kolkhoz doesn't even have a red corner [a recreation and lecture room] where the kolkhoz's young people and the kolkhoz farmers themselves could have some fun. Our kolkhoz is the poorest one in the whole raion, it doesn't have many horses or harnesses, and the harnesses it does have are all worn out. A labor-day at our kolkhoz today fetches 150 grams, as for money they don't give any at all, because the kolkhoz itself borrows from other kolkhozes. Our village soviet has kolkhozes that are all right and they do have Komsomols, but they don't have a Oso[a]viakhim organization either. Propaganda sessions on military affairs have not been set up at all, because there are no people to conduct them, and besides all the kolkhoz farmers get upset when they come to a meeting because they don't feel like human beings, the same person has to be begged to come two or three times, but never mind all that. Explain to me in detail in your next letter where and how to get this Oso[a]viakhim organization, what to teach and how. Our segment of the kolkhoz farmers will take part because there are interesting issues involved. And I would take part myself in an Oso[a]viakhim organization, since I'm with the Komsomol, and I'm dying of boredom, there's no place to have fun, no place for any culture, and in the countryside this will only lead to street hooliganism with the young lads on the street, nothing else.

It's clear that if you get wet it's going to take a long time to dry off in rainy weather, and that's the case here. When there is no guiding instrument, it is a wall newspaper, it corrects all the failings on the kolkhoz, and they can't even do that properly. The kolkhoz board does not subscribe to the most interesting newspapers and magazines and there is nothing to entertain us and the Yezhov Kolkhoz under the Smirnovka Village Soviet doesn't have enough funds for a red corner and they don't allocate money for any *kruzhki* [small cultural or recreational groups] either. They still have failed to finish sowing the winter crops and haven't threshed the grain and turned it in for procurement, and haven't started to dig up potatoes, and as for vegetables there are none at all in the gardens. And if you ask why don't you agitate yourself about all these problems? I will answer you because I can barely cope with my own job, I'm a letter carrier, I cover five villages, and all on foot, I subscribe to newspapers, and where do I read them in the brigades, and if there is time in the evening, but I am the only Komsomol member in the village I don't do anything, I do after all need an assistant, and on top of it there is no office where I can be based. In my next letter I will describe to you where our Komsomol organization is situated and where the raikom at which I joined the

## Document 97 *continued*

Komsomol is, but our young people don't even want to think about going there, because it's too far to walk. Meantime ask some more questions don't be shy. We wish you the best in your work.

With friendly regards Timokhin

---

This letter is depressing to read, not so much because of the lack of defense measures as because of its description of the "prosperous" life on the Yezhov Kolkhoz.

In light of what was occurring in the country, the situation in the border areas is of particular interest, especially in the territories that had recently been incorporated into the USSR (Western Ukraine, Western Belorussia, the Baltic republics, Bessarabia and Northern Bukovina, and part of Finland), where an all-out effort was under way to impose a new Soviet order. This is described in a letter to *Pravda:*

---

## Document 98

Letter to *Pravda* on "Mistakes in . . . Viipuri Party Gorkom," 15 January 1941. RGASPI, f. 17, op. 122, d. 8, ll. 16–19. Certified, typewritten copy.

---

Mistakes in the Activities of the Viipuri (Vyborg) Party Gorkom

It is especially important that every resident of Viipuri is always on alert and display Bolshevik vigilance. Fires or major disasters occur almost daily here at the power plant, the gas plant, or on the water pipeline. This is not by chance, of course. There are still a lot of suspicious people, a lot of chiselers and crooks in the city.

Things are not calm at the border. Almost every day border guards detain spies and saboteurs who have been sent in by the White Finns [the standard Soviet term for the Finnish government against which the Soviet Union had been at war during the winter of 1939–40]. There was a case in which three Finnish airplanes crossed the border and reconnoitered in the area between Sortavala and Viipuri.

Under these conditions the gorkom should orient Communists toward intensifying their vigilance. Unfortunately, this is not happening. An intolerable complacency and lack of concern are being displayed. Recently Comrade Yushchenko, a staff member of the local newspaper, a nonparty member, was talking with Comrade Ivanov, an engineer who is a Communist, a responsible functionary of the power plant. Without even finding out who he was talking

## Document 98 *continued*

to, Ivanov blabbed out over the telephone the contents of a secret resolution by the gorkom bureau on the work of the power plant. This kind of excessive, unhealthy trustfulness exists in the gorkom, at enterprises (the Johannes integrated works and the shipyard) and on the river steamship line. They talk about everything: the capacities of plants and factories, defense measures, and the fortification of the border.

Or take this fact: there are still dozens and hundreds of Russian-language books published in Helsinki, Riga, and Berlin that are left in people's homes. The content of these books is anti-Soviet. But no one is really getting down to removing them. The pupils in school no. 1 are taking up the works of Charskaia. The principal's office at a vocational school has in it what are obviously fascist books (in Finnish), which should have been removed long ago. What is more, for a long time a board with an "incomprehensible inscription" hung on the wall of the school's gymnasium (there used to be a lycée here). Actually the inscription read: such-and-such pupils from the lycée died in the struggle against the Bolsheviks. . . .

Nonchalance is displayed even when people are appointed to responsible posts. Comrade Parshina, a nineteen-year-old girl who had just arrived from Piatigorsk, came to see the director of the river steamship line Sukharev. She wanted to have a job. Without checking her [internal] passport or getting a clear idea of where she had come from to Viipuri and why, the director of the steamship line decides:

"You will go to the Saimaa Canal."

And a nineteen-year-old girl who graduated from the tenth grade [the final grade of secondary school] this year goes . . . to the border to be the director of a canal lock.

During the summer a lot of adventurers and chiselers arrived in the city. Some of them set themselves up in trading organizations and began to sell trophy property. To this day there are embezzlers and thieves working at the trust for cafés and cafeterias. . . .

---

The letter went on to describe poor ideological and educational training and complained that the "Short Course" was not being studied and that local leaders, in effect, were ignoring the instructions of the TsK. The denunciation was most likely written at the instigation of the Viipuri Raion Committee of the VKP(b), which for some reason was unhappy with the gorkom's activities. We find a somewhat similar situation in Peremysl' (Western Ukraine), judging from a report to the republic people's commissar of state security from Jr. Lieut. of State Security M. A. Vitkov, head of the Special Border Department (SPO) of the NKVD City Department (GO):

# Document 99

Denunciation of NKVD officer in Peremysl', Western Ukraine, 30 April 1941. RGASPI, f. 17, op. 122, d. 8, ll. 91–96. Typewritten original.

From the moment Khimenko arrived as head of the city department he made a system out of rudeness, foul language, and insensitive treatment of his subordinates. While he has referred repeatedly to the need for maintaining strict secrecy, especially in the conditions of Peremysl'—a border city—Khimenko himself does not follow even the elementary rules of secrecy. For instance, he might run into any staffer in the guard room and in the presence of watchmen and other service personnel demand a report on operational work. Comrade Sokolovsky, a detective officer of the SPO, as well as other employees can confirm this.

There was even a time when Khimenko got into a car, taking Comrade Kolosov, the head of the KRO [Department of Counterintelligence] branch, with him, and rode to a village to hear information from an important domestic agent on the OUN [Organization of Ukrainian Nationalists]. Arriving in a forest, he left the car and in the presence of driver Stan'ko—a local Ukrainian whose brother is abroad, and he himself has had suspicious ties with German intelligence agent Plishke (under arrest)—received material from the agent, and Comrade Likhouzov, a KRO detective officer, can confirm this.

Plishke was in the KRO files as a German intelligence agent, nonetheless this man had free access to the building and the courtyard of the city department for auto repairs. He was brought to the city department by the aforementioned driver Stan'ko.

Once on a day off Plishke entered the city department building, but instead of going to the garage, he went into the internal prison and began to look through the peepholes of the cells. City department watchman Goropadsky noticed this, locked him in a cell, and reported what had happened to me. I reported all this to Captain Sizov, the deputy head of the city department, and he called Khimenko at home on the telephone and told him that Plishke, who was known to us as a German intelligence agent, had slipped through to the internal prison cells and peered in there, and as a result was detained and locked up in a cell. Upon hearing this, Khimenko ordered that Plishke be released from the cell and that an apology be issued to him for the fact that he was detained, supposedly by mistake. I will not begin to draw conclusions about what this response indicates.

In April 1941 we called in for questioning a man who is known in Peremysl' as a Trotskyist. In the process of working with him, he described his Trotskyist ideology and stated that he had never been a Bolshevik, just as Trotsky never was a Bolshevik. Khimenko, who entered the room during this time, began to carry on a conversation with him, explaining that Trotsky, Bukharin, and the others had supported Soviet rule both before the revolution and after the revolution until the reconstruction period, but then deviated from the general line and started playing a double game. This kind of "explanation" can only come from a politically illiterate person, or one ideologically close to the Trotskyists. Comrade Chekushin, an SPO detective officer, was present during Khimenko's polemics.

It should be pointed out that Khimenko is unscrupulous when it comes to acquiring things. I will now cite an interesting example:

A well-known merchant and administrator of buildings named Unger used to reside in Peremysl'. Khimenko cultivated close ties with Unger and the latter could always be found either at Khimenko's apartment or in his office. Unger would supply Khimenko with various goods.

Later complaints poured in about Unger, and Khimenko issued a directive to investigate the matter. It is evident from the city department file so far that Unger, a man who is hostile to Soviet rule, had contact with the Polish police and based on the conclusion of Comrade Kolosov, the head of the KRO, he should be dismissed from his position at the combined trading office where he worked and should be placed on file. In reality, though, Unger stayed at his job, nobody placed him on file and nobody took an interest in him, but on the other hand Khimenko did issue him a permanent entry pass to the city department building so that he could visit Khimenko regularly and supply him with "stuff."

As a result the procurator's office arrested Unger and others and by decision of the oblast court Unger was sentenced to be executed.

Everybody in the city department knew about Khimenko's connection with Unger and there was even an article in the wall newspaper, but the party organization hushed up the matter, because the secretary is Kolosov, a bootlicker of the most extreme kind. . . .

---

One gets the impression that all of the negative phenomena that accompanied the development of Soviet society were especially conspicuous in the territories annexed by the USSR. In fact, all the documents cited here testify to the fact that the war caught Soviet society at a time of high tension, of colliding trends and currents. A great deal of disorder and chaos stemmed from what happened when Germany's well-equipped war machine invaded the country. Logic demands a closer examination of the Soviet countryside, where, even though the USSR had been declared "a mighty industrial power," the majority of the population still lived—a majority that would have to carry the brunt of new tribulations.

CHAPTER FIVE

# Bolshevik Order on the Kolkhoz

THE SOVIET COUNTRYSIDE was mostly collectivized by the mid-1930s. The process of "de-peasantization"—the liquidation of the last individual peasant farms—continually increased the proportion of rural households belonging to collectivized farms. In order to strangle the independent demon once and for all, the state intensified pressure on independent peasants. Year after year they were compelled to reduce their output and forbidden to sow all of their arable land. Forced to use up previous earnings to buy food, many went elsewhere in search of seasonal work, or left altogether for the cities and other regions of the country. Only 10–15 percent of the number of peasant households that existed before collectivization were still afloat by the middle of the decade. Even though the 1936 constitution allowed for the existence of small peasant enterprises owned by independent peasants and artisans based on personal labor (article 9), the fate of independent owners was already predetermined. Taxation "on an individual basis" gradually encompassed everything: income from agriculture, haymaking, the fur trade, self-made products, and so on. One could not take a step without running into the taxing bodies. The bulk of letters and petitions from independent owners to raion tax commissions and higher offices concerned the calculation of "extra-hard assignments" and complaints about persecution by the kolkhoz and raion administrations.

For example, in October 1933 NK RKI received a complaint from thirty-six citizens of the village of Lomaty in Dubensky Raion, Mordovian Autonomous Oblast, about flagrant violations of the law on grain deliveries and the confiscation of grain after obligations for deliveries to the state already had been fulfilled. The complaint interpreted these acts as a "distortion of the class line." A commission of the Mordovian Obkom that was formed to conduct an on-site investigation of the complaint determined that "the report that counterplans were given to independent farms in the village of Lomaty was confirmed in its entirety." Based on the commission's material, NK RKI drew up a memorandum addressed to Stalin , which said in part:

---

## Document 100

Memorandum from NK RKI to Stalin on complaints of independent farmers in Mordovian Autonomous Oblast, 1933. RGASPI, f. 17, op. 114, d. 661, ll. 3–5. Typewritten original.

---

. . . The commission found unlawful activities of the same kind in other village soviets as well: Kochkurovsky, Tazinsky, Parakinsky, Yengalychevsky, and others. Furthermore, the violations of the resolution of the TsK of the VKP(b) and the SNK occurred on a mass scale. The commission concluded that "at certain village soviets these irregularities reached monstrous dimensions, and the fulfillment of grain deliveries was transformed into outright *prodrazvyorstka*" [requisitioning of farm produce according to quotas]. The commission determined that grain was confiscated solely from compliant grain deliverers, "from poor and middle-level peasants' farms."

Especially outrageous are the abominations perpetrated at the Parakinsky Village Soviet, where houses, horses, potatoes, and so forth were confiscated on a mass scale. Here, as at other village soviets, the fulfillment of grain deliveries by a segment of the independent peasants lagged far behind schedule. But searches of their premises turned up no grain. Then Comrade Kriukov, the raion representative, summoned the chairmen of eleven kolkhozes and required them, "by way of kolkhoz trade," to deliver 171 centners of grain for the independent peasants at a price of sixty to ninety rubles a centner. This money was recovered from the independent peasants by selling their property, and specifically potatoes, although the delivery plan for potatoes had not yet been fulfilled. Thus by Kriukov's directive thirty-five centners were collected from the Kaganovich Kolkhoz, thirty-five centners from the Veitse Kolkhoz, forty centners from the Red Pine Kolkhoz, and so forth—long before kolkhoz trade was permitted. The director of the Parakinsky MTS knew about this, but failed to react to it in any way.

At the Tazinsky Village Soviet, grain was taken from every compliant grain deliverer. In fact, no receipts were issued for the grain collected, no records were kept, and there were possible abuses.

At the Kochkurovsky Village Soviet, where the secretary of the Komsomol Raikom was the representative of the Raikom, searches were conducted on the premises of all compliant deliverers and even kolkhoz farmers. The team would come to the house, calculate the amount of grain received and used, determine a dietary norm of three to five poods per person, and if a surplus remained, they would seize it. In this manner twenty-six kg were confiscated, for example, from M. Z. Naumkin, sixty-seven kg from A. A. Ageev, eleven centners from A. F. Samatkin, who has nine members in the household and, like the others, had honestly fulfilled his obligations to the state, and so forth.

Grain was confiscated in this way from eighty-one farms. The teams made the rounds of the homes while drunk with bottles of vodka in their pockets. They flung raw eggs at the residents.

At the Yengalychevsky Village Soviet (the party-cell secretary Khripunov is a kulak's son who has already received a severe reprimand with a warning for distorting the class line), a concealed area of 114 hectares was uncovered. This area was parceled out among the farms in proportion to their respective numbers of tenants. The cell, under the leadership of Comrade Chekashkin, the Raikom representative, launched a mass seizure of all grain without the approval of the RIK or the issuance of supplementary obligations by the village soviet.

All told, the commission of the obkom and the Oblast Control Commission has received 629 complaints, covering six village soviets, about the unlawful confiscation of grain and property (546 of them, or 86.8 percent, have been satisfied). "Similar grain seizures have occurred in other settlements as well: Kabaeva, Turdaki, and Nekliudovo," writes the commission, "but we determined there was no point in going there because the methods of grain seizure were the same." According to a statement by the second secretary of the obkom, similar distortions of the party line have occurred at twelve village soviets. [A discussion follows of the measures taken and the fact that party penalties were imposed and legal proceedings initiated against the guilty individuals.]

Although the "unlawful activities" in this case seem to have been corrected, they continued elsewhere. The following letter to *Krest'ianskaia Gazeta* describes what happened to a specific independent farm in the intervening years:

# Document 101

Letter from independent farmer Grebenev to *Krest'ianskaia Gazeta* on harassment by local officials, 22 September 1938. RGAE, f. 396, op. 10, d. 57. ll. 231–233ob. Original manuscript.

Moscow

To the editors of *Krest'ianskaia Gazeta*

From citizen independent owner Afanasy Fyodorovich Grebenev, village of Loboshan under the Shalegovsky Village Soviet in Orichi Raion, Kirov Oblast

Statement

I request that you print a reply to my written statement in your highly esteemed newspaper. I am a natural laborer a peasant born in 1879, I have worked in farming since childhood, all I knew is how to fertilize and work the land with my own hands, a middle-level peasant and I didn't have an extra-hard assignment imposed on me. I have a family of six, my wife was born in 1881, I have a son sixteen years old and two daughters both nineteen, all three attend a school for adults, and I have a sister seventy-one years old. In 1932 my farm had back-breaking taxes levied on it that we could barely handle. In 1935 the local authority increased the taxes [on me] as an independent peasant, and I could not handle them so they distrained all of my property: the horse, the cow, the young animals, the ewe with its lambs, all the farming implements, the harness, the furniture, and the stockpile of timber for repairing structures and other items, and they sold them for the taxes. For 1936 they sold all of the buildings: the storehouse, the granary, the stable, the farmstead, and the fencing with the small outbuildings. Our kolkhoz bought them for a stable, which still exists for fourteen horses. For 1937 there were two adjoining *izbas* [huts] under one roof, it [evidently the roof] was sold and taken to another village soviet for five hundred rubles. The entranceway was not distrained or sold but was taken away. Our Loboshan Kolkhoz took all this without authorization. My family still has to make its way into the izba with a stepladder. There is no place to fix yourself up. On 1 July 1936 I was forced to abandon my land and get a regular job, leaving my house to the mercies of fate, for I had to give the state my grain procurement and there was nothing left for seeds, no farming implements and no horse. Since then I have been working at the raion hospital as a watchman for ninety rubles a month. My farm has fallen into decay, I have no money or workers to raise it again. It would be nice to teach the children, but now two years have passed with no money for studies, I have to make money for bread. I have a farmstead. This year I am tax exempt as a service worker.

In March 1937, for [nonpayment of] tax they took my second izba, which was attached under one roof to the izba we live in, demolished it and hauled it away. Now there is a danger that everything could collapse. The buildings are decrepit, dating to 1874. That one was not a izba for habitation, it had a small stove, was built with plaster, covered with planks, the interior was painted and it was solid, but what is left to me is decrepit and rotting. I appealed to the Kirov Oblast Financial Department to stop the transfer of the izba, and it issued an order to stop the demolition and transfer and to investigate the matter. The raion executive committee jointly resolved with the village soviet that the demolition and transfer were to be stopped, because not all of the izba was removed. On 12 June 1937 the Presidium of the Raion Executive Committee resolved that I was to be issued 1,096 rubles based on an insurance appraisal and the remnants were to be hauled away. I did not agree to this, although I did receive the money. I petitioned the raion and the oblast about the izba, to the effect that the removal of the izba was wrong, which is supported by the eighth all-Russian party congress on 25 November 1936 [the Eighth All-Union Congress of Soviets]. Comrade Stalin is for middle-level peasant farms and the inviolability of dwellings in his constitution, yet here the authorities completely violated this article.

In June 1937, after collecting all of the documents, Comrade Valev, a defense attorney with the People's Court, wrote a complaint for me and collected seventy rubles [from me] at the People's Commissariat of Finance. My second complaint got an answer: "Your case has been sent to Kirov and there will be a response by 20 September." A response did in fact come at the end of September: "All calculations were correct, you are not exempted from the tax, but for the improper seizure of the izba you will receive an insurance indemnity of 1,096 rubles." I asked for five thousand rubles in my complaint. Refusing to accept this response, I wrote my second appeal of the year in June [1937] and pointed out the resolution of the Eighth All-Union Congress and the violation of Stalin's constitution, and sent a confirmation and certificate from my neighbors that the izba's value was five thousand rubles. The People's Commissariat of Finance replies: "As the enclosed copy of Paragraph 40, which was in effect in 1936, indicates,["] but my izba was hauled away in June 1937: "Your demand for the replacement cost concerning seizure of the izba cannot be met."

So I request that the editors answer me, was everything done fairly and who broke the law against bringing middle-level peasant farms to ruin: the local authorities or the supreme authorities? And where, if it is a higher level, should I appeal to recover my property? That is the first point.

Second. In February of this year the raion financial department granted the right to purchase structures that our kolkhoz has used since October 1935, which it bought at auction for 870 rubles. In February I paid the kolkhoz five hundred rubles, and the rest with a markdown of forty-one rubles the markdowns were for destroyed ceilings and interior walls and other objects. I think 30 percent of all the buildings are destroyed. But I decided to make the purchase with the money received for the seized izba, only I have not been able to pay the remaining 329 rubles for seven months already, and the kolkhoz farmers are not leaving my farmstead, for they have not finished

## Document 101 *continued*

building their stable. Am I entitled to ask them to leave my farmstead while withholding the remaining payment for seven months from the date of purchase, because I have no opportunity to manage my household?

22 September 1938

I have another question, how do I get the central cammishin to investigate my farm, bringing it to ruin and replacing it, why was it done and who did it?

---

The reply to Grebenev's letter was terse: "We find no grounds for a further appeal of your case. If you are unhappy with the response from the RSFSR People's Commissariat of Finance, you can appeal to the USSR People's Commissariat of Finance."[1]

The most amazing aspect of the above letter is how tenaciously the man continued to fight for his property. Grebenev was still able to muster the strength to battle, but a complaint by O. P. Semyonova, a peasant woman from Smolensk Oblast, exudes utter hopelessness and testifies to the flagrantly high-handed behavior and ruthlessness of the government machine. *Krest'ianskaia Gazeta* received the complaint in July 1938:

---

## Document 102

Letter of complaint from independent farmer O. P. Semyonova to *Krest'ianskaia Gazeta*, 15 July 1938. RGAE, f. 396, op. 10, d. 133, ll. 102–102ob. Original manuscript.

---

To the printing plant of *Krest'ianskaia gazeta* comrade Uritsky from citizen Ol'ga Petrovna Semyonova, village of Shishkino, Kostkinsky Village Soviet, Viaz'ma Raion.

Complaint.

No. 2. [The first complaint was not found among the letters.]

I, citizen Ol'ga Petrovna Semyonova, request the publishing house of *Krest'ianskaia gazeta* to pleeze look into my complaint. I, citizen Semyonova, have three children, i.e., three daughters, the oldest daughter is nineteen years old, she is blind, the middle daughter is sixteen, this daughter was born lame, and another daughter is twelve, I am fifty-seven, I have no man in the house: it has already been five years since he died, he was also a crippel from the civil war. So we live independently. I, citizen Semyonova, am complaining that all my property was taken away on 1 September 1936, they took from me 336 kg of rye, forty kg of oats, a sewing machine, two sheepskins from sheep, a suit with trousers, a seelskin sport coat, a cloth-lined fur coat, six

## Document 102 *continued*

sackfulls of rye, and they distrained the hay in the shed as well. These individuals were present during the seizure: Comrade Yegorov, chairman of the village soviet, Comrade Navazhilov [evidently Novozhilov], inspector of the Viaz'ma Tax Commission, and three witnesses: Ivan Mikhailov, Mikhei Stepanov, and Aleksandr Sokolov. When they arrived and started picking out things, I asked why, and they reply for arrears on 1935 tax and for payment of 1936 tax. I, citizen Semyonova, am illiterate and asked them to wait before taking things: the two smaller girls will come home from school and they will show you receipts for the payment of tax in 1935, but they said that we cannot wait a single minute, and in 1936 I did not receive any notices about the payment of tax, they came to take away property without notice, when I started asking Comrade Navazhilov, the Viaz'ma inspector of the tax commission, are they doing the right thing, he replies that they are doing the wrong thing, grandma. They are all my people, and I can't do anything about it. On 1 January 1937 they took away 150 poods of hay, which was distrained on 1 October 1936 together with the seized property. Comrade G. Ya. Il'in, secretary of the village soviet, and Ivan Mikhailov, a witness, were present when the hay was seized, and they didn't even tell me, they arrived without a word, broke the lock on the shed and turned over this hay to the chairman of an outside kolkhoz Golosov, without any bargaining and without weighing it they called it a hundred poods. Why my property, hay, and grain was taken I don't know and to this day I have no idea, they didn't give me receipts for the rye or the property and didnt even retern the six sacs or the money for the rye to me. I have appealed more than once to the oblast, to Moscow, and to the raion executive committee and said, why don't they settle with me at all, they keep promising, we will, but in reality nothing happens. They only reterned eighty-six kg of rye and that was growing its own sprouts, but they refuse to make any other settlement with me, they are mocking an illiterate and sick woman. I wonder, when will these outrages end? [Repeated appeals for investigation and help follow.]

Written for her by Maiorova . . .

---

In 1938 there were officially 1,347,000 independent peasant farms still left in the country; the number had fallen to 960,000 by 1939 and to 641,000 by 1940.[2] One of the last advantages of an independent farm was the opportunity to keep a horse as a work animal and conveyance and to use it as a source of supplementary earnings. But in August 1938 the Second Session of the Supreme Soviet adopted the law "On a State Tax on the Horses of Independent Farms." Exorbitant taxes were already in force for keeping just one horse, and the levy was almost twice as large for each additional one. This forced the remaining horse owners to ask to join kolkhozes. It is no surprise that the decisions of the Eighteenth Party Congress (March 1939) defined independent peasants as people who were at the crossroads between the kolkhoz and the factory. The final act of violence against them was the liquidation of farmsteads in the late 1930s and early 1940s. Those who had held out until then were shadowed by the "kulak" stigma.

Meanwhile, the majority of labor settlements in the northern and eastern regions of the country had long since been converted to kolkhozes and sovkhozes. But letters from people who were, as they said, "improperly de-kulakized" poured into various agencies with requests that they be allowed to return to their former places of residence, especially after the adoption of the 1936 constitution. These letters drew the standard response that exiles regained their civil rights beginning in 1935, but without the right of return. It was no longer possible, however, to stop those who wanted to go back. As a rule, family ties and friendships were used for this purpose. "Former kulaks" dissolved into kolkhozes, sovkhozes, plants, and factories while carefully concealing their past exile. The sources reveal no mass acts of wrecking by these people, but the myth to this effect remained alive and was used to justify repression.

A Politburo resolution dated 2 July 1937 stated that "a large segment of the former kulaks and common criminals who were once exiled to the northern and Siberian regions and then returned to their oblasts upon expiration of the term of their exile are the main instigators of all kinds of anti-Soviet and sabotage actions both on kolkhozes and sovkhozes and on transport vehicles and in several industries." The resolution recommended that these people be placed on file, and that the most active ones be placed under arrest and either exiled again or executed. Six days later, as a result of work by the three-judge courts [*troiki*], a circular was distributed indicating that, for example, in Omsk Oblast 479 people were scheduled for execution and 1,959 were slated for exile. According to the list drawn up at the NKVD, by 30 July a total of 72,000 people had been scheduled for execution and 270,000 for a second exile.[3]

That was how the final pages of the history of the independent countryside were written. It gave way to a new form of rural life—kolkhozes and sovkhozes. Their names were introduced to replace the names of former settlements and villages. Garish terms from the era of the Revolution and the civil war, names of famous political leaders and military commanders, and memorable dates all produced bombastic echoes of the onetime struggle for world revolution and for people's happiness throughout the world. The entrenchment of the kolkhoz system also dates to the mid-1930s. In February 1935 the Second All-Union Congress of Kolkhoz Shock Workers adopted model statutes for the agricultural artel, more often called "Stalin's statutes for kolkhoz life," which were to serve as the basis for building a "Bolshevik order on the kolkhoz"—probably the most common stock phrase applied to the Soviet countryside in the 1930s. In July 1935 the Council of People's Commissars adopted a resolution calling for state certificates to be issued to kolkhozes authorizing the use of the land in perpetuity. The campaign for granting kolkhozes these certificates was given great publicity in the newspapers during the second half of the 1930s.

An ongoing stream of reports and letters trumpeted the successes of the kolkhozes under such rubrics as "Growing Stronger Every Day," "Ready for Spring Planting," "Hauling Manure onto the Fields is the Best Present for the Eighteenth Party Congress," "Stalin's Harvest," "Let's Greet the Harvest Fully Armed," "Let's Retain Snow," "Let's Prepare the Horses Well," "Life Is Better, Life Is Brighter," "The Planting Was Done Superbly," "Ready for Spring," "The Fruits of Stakhanovite Labor," and so on and so forth. Much was made of the shock work of Stakhanovite teams and of the scientific benefits to kolkhozes and sovkhozes resulting from the work of experimenters and breeders. Reports were often submitted by kolkhoz chairmen themselves, as well as agronomists, livestock experts, top laborers in the kolkhoz fields, shock workers and Stakhanovites, village librarians, and ordinary rural correspondents. A large stack of documents was assembled in connection with the All-Union Agricultural Exhibition, which opened in Moscow in August 1939 to display the achievements of kolkhozes and sovkhozes. The documents were used to compose articles that appeared under the standard heading "Let's Earn the Right to Participate in the Exhibition," for material that publicized and reviewed agricultural literature, and for the albums "Donkey Breeding and Mule Production," "Camel Breeding," and other popular, scientific, and pseudoscientific books.

Many scholars believe that these reports and letters, which were often published in the press, sketched what were for the most part Potemkin villages similar to the one that was depicted in the popular film "The Swineherd and the Shepherd" (1941). But apparently this is not quite true. To be sure, the achievements of the Soviet countryside were highly relative. Many of them derived from general progress in agriculture, the use of machinery, and the growth of people's cultural and educational levels, but some of them actually came about thanks to the consolidation of individual farms into kolkhozes and sovkhozes.

Probably more letters came in from the countryside on comparing past conditions with the present than on any other topic. We must pay close attention to them. In an item titled "The Soviet Village," I. Popov of the village of Khvoshchevatka in Berezovka Raion wrote that his village today "has schools, both primary and secondary, a pharmacy, a kindergarten, a farmers' cooperative store, a reading room, and a veterinary clinic." People "don't go anymore to the old wise woman. There is an infirmary on the kolkhoz, and a maternity clinic on the neighboring kolkhoz." The village also has its own intelligentsia: "teachers, physicians, a veterinarian, an agronomist, bookkeepers, secretaries, combine operators, truck drivers, tractor drivers—everybody came from the common folk."

"Many people from Khvoshchevatka who graduated from secondary school," the writer remarked, "can be found at educational institutions around the Soviet Union. U. Koltakova attends Voronezh State University, S. Vasil'ev is completing his studies at Leningrad Military School, A. Vasil'ev is a student at the Institute of National Economic Accounting, K. Vasil'eva is a student at a medical institute, and N. Koltakov is completing a construction engineering institute. There's no way to list them all!" he exclaimed.[4] Rural correspondent Ya. P. Kashirskikh of the Bolshevik Kolkhoz in Voronezh Oblast wrote about how everyday life in the countryside had changed, specifically on the theme "Winter Evenings on the Kolkhoz." He described a kolkhoz club, where people would enjoy themselves in the evening, sing songs and ditties, and listen to visiting lecturers discussing the Red Army and hostilities in China and Spain. Among the kolkhoz farmers, reported the writer, "there were conversations about increasing the sugar-beet harvest, about hauling manure and snow retention." The writer concluded: "It will get even better, we will purchase a radio, a portable gramophone."[5] These were the kinds of letters, edited by experienced hands, that were published in the press most often. But not every episode from the "happy kolkhoz life," especially of the bizarre variety, had a chance to land in the press. Here, for instance, is an item from rural correspondent Glukhov in the village of Shevyrialovo in Sarapul Raion, Udmurt ASSR:

## Document 103

Letter from rural correspondent Glukhov to *Krest'ianskaia Gazeta* on "A Happy Life," 24 December 1938. RGAE, f. 396, op. 10, d. 12, l. 12. Original manuscript.

A Happy Life

Matvei Fyodorovich Rusinov has already passed seventy years of age, he has been a kolkhoz farmer since 1929.

Before the Revolution Matvei Fyodorovich because of his advanced years grew a beard all the way down to his chest and had his hair cut evenly all around which made him show [look] like an old man. He is a hard working man before 1 December 1938 by himself he made it past four hundred labordays. He has on his farm a milking cow, poultry, and a piglet. His house is covered with an iron roof, but Matvei Fyodorovich was still missing one thing he was a widower.

Matvei Fyodorovich asked advice from people close to him and he made up his mind to take what is already his third wife. In the first few days of December 1938 he performed a modest Soviet-style wedding he trimmed his beard, trimmed his hair, and that made him seem just about right for his third wife who is forty-two years old.

In the old days the priests would never permit a wedding in December. It was considered Advent, and besides a man like that who is seventy-four years old would have been denied for getting married. We truly have a happy Soviet life.

Young people, too, joined the wave of reminiscences of their former joyless life and its comparison with today. One example was the memoir "The Story of My Life" by Prokofy Gur'ianovich Shatrov, who was drafted into the Red Army from an unidentified remote village and served with a unit in the Belorussian Military District. "I was born in 1916," writes the author. "I have really had some interesting things happen to me during the years of Soviet rule." But a large part of his reminiscences consist of copied newspaper phrases on the country's achievements under the leadership of the party of Lenin and Stalin, interspersed with trivial everyday vignettes. It is extremely difficult to read the reminiscences, because the writer, having completed the fourth grade in elementary school, obviously did not learn how to read and write very well and could not set forth his thoughts on paper clearly:

---

## Document 104

Letter from P. G. Shatrov to *Krest'ianskaia Gazeta* on benefits of Soviet rule, 1938. RGAE, f. 396, op. 10, d. 13, ll. 334–335ob. Original manuscript.

---

I will discribe. When I was six-seven years old I was babysitting with my younger brother and sisters. When I got bigger eight-nine years old I began to help out my housework. Then my father [crossed out] hired me out to a rich peasant I. M. Vlasov for summer work so I worked him for two years, I harrowed and so on. In one summer I earned two poods of oats from him plus meals. In those days there were no metal plows, everybody worked the land with the old plows and wooden harrows. We would mow the whole day with nothing but sickles at a slant. We harvested everything in our arms. The rich peasants made to help, they gathered people to harvest with their arms. They harvest all day and for a long time a month at night. When they get drunk the drunkerds harvest fast and they start cutting their arms, almost just about everybody mutalates their arms.

Our locality was very much under the influence of religion. We had this kind of religion—old men would come around. The old men are yung and old, they are called by the teknical name sectarians. They preached. They told of a whole lot of different sins: smoking tobacco, dancing, and singing songs. Whoever had a samovar, they would not visit them, that was a sin too. They talked about you couldnt count how many sins. Ther will be a special punishment from god in the next world for thees sins: some people will burn in hellfire, some will sit among the wurms, some will boil in tar. One side will burn, the other will gro. They talked most of all about how the anticrist will walk upon the earth and put a stamp on people. This means they will be given Soviet vacsine.

At that time the contagious disease smallpox was very common. This disease did away with people, especially the little ones. Whoever would remain alive, if they did, would be covered with skratches, their whole faces covered with pockmarks. Whoever remained alive was called lucky.

Soviet authority began to take care of people, they started coming to the villages to vacsinate them, to protect them from death and mutalation.

One day a doctor came to our village from the hospital to vacsinate people. So our parents hid almost just about everybody wherever they could, but I was a little bigger, so I got on my skis and took off to the woods, and I came very close to freezing.

There was one mor insident. I was already in school. Suddenly a vaksinater arrived and everybody scattered. I took off to the village and hid in a pile of straw, and my comrade, even though the school was 3 km away from us, took off in winter in nothing but his underwear. . . .

---

The writer goes on to describe how he was appointed the kolkhoz letter carrier and messenger after completing the fourth grade: "Our kolkhoz was three km from the village soviet and it was all woods. One night I was carrying a report at midnight. The night was very dark, and the birds were wailing with different voices. I didn't notice a fir tree in front of me, and I ran right into it." Apparently the collision with the fir tree was so violent that it was what he remembered most about his job as a messenger. Two years later he was sent to take bookkeeping courses, after which he worked as a bookkeeper right up until his call-up into the army. The writer mentioned in passing that he joined the Komsomol. By that time, he wrote, machinery and tractors had already appeared on the kolkhoz fields. The sectarians said that "the devil has arrived." One old woman, rather than walk straight through a field, "walked an extra kilometer to go around." The writer constantly blends such trivial details with "big-time politics." "The kolkhoz farmers," he wrote, "have learned to run the machinery. Only under the party's leadership did this rout and distroy forever those theories of the sectarians and the priests." And now, the writer concludes, "I am in the most honorable workers peasants Red

Army, I arrived in October 1937. What a good life they dress you, feed you, educate you. I pledge to serve honestly, as the statutes call for."[6]

A large quantity of documents attest to the fact that the advent of the kolkhoz system did not bring about much change for the better in the countryside, and in many places the situation even grew worse. Here are the observations of engineer Matiukhin:

## Document 105

Letter from M. Matiukhin to Kalinin on conditions in his home district, 16 December 1932. RGASPI, f. 78, op. 1, d. 430, ll. 45–46. Original manuscript.

In July I visited my home region, whose fields I have not roamed for many, many years. I covered about sixty to eighty square kilometers on foot. I went to the settlement where I was born, I went to the village where I grew up until the age of fifteen, I visited the village where I was a farmhand for two summers. I roamed around the settlements and villages where I used to collect food for myself and my family forty years ago in the name of Christ. I will not try to convince you how skimpy the kolkhoz and sovkhoz fields are and how sickeningly barren the so-called suburban fields are, or how hard to get through the main roads are. But now the figures show that they are the most convincing arguments. Thirty-seven years ago, leaving the village for the Briansk plant, the thirty-five farmsteads in the village of Popov-Klinok had sixty to sixty-five work horses, thirty-five to forty cows, there were more than a hundred one-, two-, and three-year-old foals and calves and about 250–300 sheep and pigs. The landowner Leonov had twenty-five to thirty horses and the same number of cows on his farmstead. In July when I asked the villagers how many horses they had, the reply was twenty-seven, and about thirty cows. They had no young of either animal. . . .

My home region is a producer of hemp. Hemp is a plant half again as high as you or me. That is the way the hemp was thirty-seven years ago. Now I saw unprocessed hemp three-quarters of a meter [thirty inches] high. Maybe a meter, but no more. Thirty-seven years ago you would never see unprocessed hemp in July. By the feast of Nicholas and no later the entire hemp crop would be at the merchants' shops in the city of Briansk. Two poods of hemp were equal to a pair of sixteen-vershok [twenty-eight-inch-high] boots.

When I asked whose blackened hemp that was in the mud, the reply was it belonged to the Goritsky kolkhoz farmers, and we independent peasants turned in ours on a contracting basis at eight rubles a pood.

There is also a great deal of evidence that residents of the countryside resigned themselves to the kolkhoz system. As a group of peasants from Pukhovichsky Raion in the Belorussian SSR wrote to M. I. Kalinin in 1935 on the eve of the Seventh Congress of Soviets, "It has become clear that peasants cannot avoid the kolkhozes, so human living conditions have to be created on the kolkhoz. While this may have been impossible to achieve before, this year, in our opinion, it can be done." The peasants attributed the deterioration in their situation to the fact that after a segment of the peasantry was "dekulakized and banished," a second segment that did not wish to move to a kolkhoz headed for the city to join the ranks of factory workers, leaving the land that was allocated to them to the remainder of peasants who had to cultivate it, which meant they had to work day and night.[7]

Then again, the information about labor intensiveness on the kolkhozes is contradictory. One gets a different impression from a letter by someone named Malov to *Krest'ianskaia Gazeta*, from November 1938:

---

## Document 106

Letter from Malov to *Krest'ianskaia Gazeta* on kolkhoz labor in Komi ASSR, 21 November 1938. RGAE, f. 396, op. 10, d. 4, ll. 196–196ob. Original manuscript.

---

May Day Kolkhoz
The May Day Kolkhoz, whose territory comprises the villages of Vampy, Kuispel', and Mishko Ivan, is situated on the Pechora River one hundred km below the city of Troitsk in Komi ASSR. What can the aforesaid kolkhoz boast? As for achievements—there aren't any here. The kolkhoz farmers here have no concept of socialist competition, about fulfilling assignments, or about production norms in general. The kolkhoz farmers' cultural level is low, there is no reading room, and besides, nobody is interested in this, although the raion leaders are well aware of this, and of everything else. Apparently they don't pay attention either.

Hence the consequences. Drunkenness and carousing are flourishing in the villages, and you can say that the entire village drinks from old to young, which especially is striking to somebody passing through. There is no discipline, brigade leaders do not listen to the kolkhoz chairman, and there is constant wrangling and swearing. Not a single assignment gets fulfilled. During the busiest time for a kolkhoz, the haymaking and harvest campaign, no more than three or four kolkhoz farmers went out to work. The hay was left under the snow, 35 percent of it unmowed. The kolkhoz did not allocate haymaking fields to independent peasants and livestock was not provided with hay. Some of the potatoes were left in the field without being dug up. In spite of the good summer, the grain harvest is smaller than last year's, for the reason that the kolkhoz did not take fertilizers into the fields. There are no buildings for grain threshing and the grain is threshed the old-fashioned way, in the winter out in the open. The kolkhoz has just one New Ideal haymaking machine, and more than once during the summer it broke down and had to be repaired. They finished mowing, it snowed, and the mower has been lying and rusting under the snow for two months already, there is nobody to take it away. It is strange that the leaders riding by have seen all this more than once, but they don't take any measures—the machine is still there.

The kolkhoz facilities have fallen apart: there are not enough sleighs or horse collars, and the ones we have look pathetic, there is nobody to fix and repair them because no kolkhoz farmer is in charge of it.

On 15 November the following outrageous incident occurred: the woman who tends the livestock took ill, and sixteen milking cows and other animals were left unfed for three days and the cows unmilked and only on the fourth day the sick woman came out on crutches to feed the livestock and milk the cows, and this was right before the eyes of the kolkhoz board in the village of Vampy. Neither brigade leader V. Mezentsev nor bookkeeper V. Yudin was able to give instructions to replace the sick woman, and kolkhoz farmer Pyotr Yudin bluntly said, the Tatar didn't feed the livestock for three days and they still survived, and it's the same with us. No doubt about P. Yudin's personality, he is an old Psalm reader, a former White bandit, his personality is a clear indicator of his deeds, but what is surprising is that Kalinovsky, the chairman of the Savinoborsky Village Soviet, still nominated him as a candidate for chairman of the kolkhoz. If you look at the output by the kolkhoz farmers, it is also a pathetic picture. [Space was left for output figures in labordays, but there are no figures.] The rest of the days were frittered away on drunkenness and absenteeism. All this attests to an unhealthy atmosphere on the May Day Kolkhoz and the proper person must set about revitalizing the kolkhoz.

I confirm the above facts in full with my signature:
Malov

What were the reasons for the unsatisfactory state of affairs? What was hampering the establishment of a "Bolshevik order" on kolkhozes and sovkhozes and the attainment of impressive successes in building socialism in the countryside? Noteworthy in this regard is the view of P. M. Grebennikov, a kolkhoz activist and rural correspondent who sent *Krest'ianskaia Gazeta* an essay on changes in the life of the Voronezh Oblast village of Kazinka under Soviet rule. The writer focuses on the problem of the application of machines, which was considered one of the main advantages of the kolkhoz system. The essay is clearly weighed down by the "iron syndrome" that was typical of the times. The piece included futile attempts at a metaphorical description of reality in imitation of writers' essays and novels about kolkhoz life that were common in those years—a practice, incidentally, which many correspondents followed. We shall omit the writer's "lyrical digressions" describing the countryside and various vignettes on abstract topics, but certain excerpts of the document deserve attention.

The essay begins by stating several facts:

"In 1934 the combine mowed twelve hectares and stood abandoned until October. Every year the fields that were to be harvested with the combine have been finished off by hand with scythes, and the fall plowing has never been done completely. The most has been 60 percent. In 1937 combines harvested 225 hectares."

The writer goes on to describe the village, which he says is shaped like "a triangle in the plain on the left bank of the Don, intersected by the small stream called Kazinka":

---

# Document 107

Essay on life in Voronezh Oblast village sent by rural correspondent Grebennikov to *Krest'ianskaia Gazeta*, 1939. RGAE, f. 396, op. 11, d. 7, ll. 35–370b. Original manuscript.

---

. . . The Kazinka people's labor was well known not only in their own village but far beyond the boundaries of the former Voronezh Gubernia, in the Manich [Manych] and Kalmyk steppes, to which leased boats would carry them down the Don as soon as the gardens blossomed.

Driven by hope, they would travel there to the Martynovka fairs like human merchandise, where they would bunch together like sheep and wait for somebody to buy their labor, wholesale or retail.

And were even considered lucky if they returned home, after covering hundreds of kilometers, with a wretched pittance in the bosom of their tattered shirts that had been worn away by perspiration, so that they could pay tax and rent to the landlord Sukhanov.

And in the spring they would again leave the half-orphaned village of

Kazinka and their native fields, which were sliced up by gullies, and go off to harvest hay and grain for the rich men the Korol'ki [the Korol'kovs] and the Bezuglye [the Bezuglovs].

At that time Kazinka numbered [among] its villagers 320 seasonal mowers, eighteen shepherds, five horse herdsmen, seven ox drivers, and three draymen.

Witnesses to all this who are still alive and who tasted the Bezuglov kandery [meaning unclear] and their grain, which was black as the earth, are grandpa Koz'ma Matveevich and grandpa Timokha Shkurin.

And only Soviet rule loosened the grip of the landowners, which for many years squeezed the village of Kazinka, and only Soviet rule allowed the people of Kazinka to breathe freely in their own expansive domain. The people of Kazinka understood this and were always in the forefront in establishing the Kalinin Kolkhoz. They took more than one kolkhoz in tow and allocated more than one shock brigade to help sovkhozes. The kolkhoz itself had a Red Banner fluttering at its board office for several years with the inscription: "Labor is a matter of honor, a matter of valor and heroism!"

But some people began to find the kolkhoz farmers' labor offensive and harmful. People who wormed their way into the leading raion organizations, now exposed as enemies of the people, the Polish spy Sandlir, the enemy of the people Shapkin, Riabinina, and Zhuzhalov, who did their foul deeds and stooped to the worst act of nastiness they could think of. Making sure it was in the middle of the coldest frost, they summoned two hundred carts to the raion under court order, supposedly for essential matters of national importance. Without preparing any shelter, they left people and horses out in the open air around the clock, and for two years these tricks deprived the Kalinin Kolkhoz of draft animals.

The people of Kazinka have seen quite a few such abominations, often at the height of harvest time. They have seen a combine come in because some simple part is broken and stand idle while the procedures began—daily expeditions to the raion and the MTS for parts, and carts would be sent. Brigades were assigned every day to service the combine. People would come with pitchforks and rakes and would wait for a part. By evening a cart would come back, but without the part.

On more than one occasion, grandpa Timokha Shkurin, swinging his shoulders with an eagle sketched in sweat glistening on his back, and boldly wielding a scythe, mowed down more than the idle combine. You can often hear people say things like, they all mow that way, they just write to us that we mow, but everybody can see their work.

But in May 1938 the glorious Soviet intelligence agents exposed the people who were perpetrating these outrages and they must bear their proper punishment. And only in 1938 did the people of Kazinka, after heaving a sigh of relief, freely set about their work, proving that labor is valor in heroism. Plow-

## Document 107 *continued*

ing was completed by 15 May. By 1 July all of the spring crops had been weeded three times, and on 6 July the kolkhoz began the harvest and finished it in seventeen days, and only in 1938 did the Kalinin people see the combine and tractor operate.

Combine operator N. F. Aleksandrov harvested 631 hectares on the Stalinets combine in seventeen days, and combine operator V. P. Drugalyov harvested 428 hectares on the Komunar combine in seven days.

After the harvest was over, when Comrade Aleksandrov was departing, he was seen off not only by the brigades that serviced the combine but also by the nearby production brigades. Everybody crowded around to shake his hand, and then they did not disperse for a long time, gazing after him until he was out of sight and listening to the comments of grandpa Timokha, who commented with amazement: "See, they told you that everybody can see the work of the combines. No, brother, if people work, and they love their work, then there will always be work." Upon learning that Aleksandrov was a student in the workers' department of the agricultural engineering institute, he added: "Now he will really be an engineer! He knows what's what."

---

As Kazinka welcomed in the new year of 1939, the writer reported, it

> counted its achievements. The former shepherds and mowers have sons and grandsons who break down as follows: two engineers, three air force lieutenants, five construction technicians, ten secondary school instructors, twenty-nine schoolteachers, two physicians, two students at a military aviation-engineering school, two land surveyors, seventeen students at higher educational institutions, forty-eight tractor drivers and combine operators, twelve truck drivers, and 450 people are attending a full-length secondary school, which is the pride of the settlement, replacing the "den" of deceit and depravity, and in a year thirty-six people from Kazinka will emerge from it with a secondary education, . . . followed by as many as a hundred people every year thereafter.

Kazinka, the writer also said, "has a club that holds up to a thousand people, a library for four thousand books, a splendid new rural department store, a pharmacy and a hospital with a maternity ward for as many as twenty women giving birth. The settlement has the following members of the intelligentsia: eleven secondary school teachers, thirteen primary school teachers, two midwives, and an agronomist."[8]

The changes in the life of Kazinka, of course, were not at all related to the exposure of the wreckers in May 1938; they resulted from many years of development in the settlement during the years of Soviet rule. What did the "wrecking" in this case consist of? The death of the kolkhoz draft animals seems to have been primarily a consequence of intemperate administrative zeal in fulfilling state obligations, callous bureaucratism, and ineptitude, and neither the lack of parts nor the low quality of machinery in the fields can be attributed to wrecking, either.

Yet a great deal of the correspondence from below dealt precisely with wrecking and abuses at kolkhozes, sovkhozes, and machine-tractor stations. As Grebennikov wrote, people were preoccupied "not so much with their joyful future as with killing all the enemies of creative and working people." It seems as though the immense tribe of wreckers thought about nothing other than where and how they could inflict damage on socialism.

Land-management expert P. Anisimov of Arkhangel'sk Oblast wrote to the People's Commissariat of Agriculture in late 1938 that "the elimination of the consequences of wrecking in land management is proceeding at a sluggish pace." Oddly, the writer refers to himself in the third person, thereby seeming to express the views of a certain segment of specialists in the field of agriculture:

---

## Document 108

Report of land management expert P. P. Anisimov to Narkomzem on wrecking in Arkhangel'sk Oblast, 1938. RGAE, f. 396, op. 10, d. 13, ll. 44–45ob. Original manuscript.

---

Soviet land-management techniques have made big strides in recent years. Our government annually appropriates enormous funds to the establishment of a Bolshevik order on kolkhoz soil. Thousands of members of the intelligentsia and toilers in the land of socialism have emerged from the milieu of the people. Our party and government surround land-management personnel with concern and create all the conditions for fruitful work. But the thrice-cursed enemies of the people, the Trotskyist-Bukharinist scum and other vermin who have been operating in our Arkhangel'sk Oblast have been wrecking agriculture and land management. The enemies of the people did everything they could to make the people angry at Soviet rule. But the enemies miscalculated. Under Stalin's leadership the glorious organs of the NKVD under the

# Document 108 *continued*

leadership of Stalin's people's commissar N. I. Yezhov smashed and destroyed the main nests of wasps. Tarasovsky, an exposed enemy of the people, former raion agriculture chief and head of a land-management detachment in Pinega Raion, did a lot of filthy things. Tarasovsky never regarded producers who issued state certificates as people. He gave them the nicknames "Fascist," "Hitler," "Big Nose," and so forth. This guy would not pay wages for three or four months at a time, he didn't create any working conditions, and he would take half a year to approve advance-payment reports. State certificates would be turned in unsigned by the raion executive committee, with muddled data, for example to these kolkhozes: the Leunovo, the New Life, the Zavrazhsky, the Red October, the Sovpol'e, Kar'epol'e, and others. The Zavrazhsky, Vonsky, Trufanogorsky, and Val'tegorsky village soviets have gotten entangled with alternating strip holdings. The Kar'epol'e Kolkhoz was issued a state certificate for an area six thousand hectares less than it actually had allocated to it. The Red October received fifty hectares more than it did in actuality. It must also be mentioned that the state certificate on that kolkhoz burned up and to this day none of the leaders of the raion organizations in Pinega knows about it. The senior technician on that kolkhoz, Mariukhin, established the boundaries of the kolkhoz, eliminated the alternation, and then Tarasovsky arrived and restored the alternation again. He gave the kolkhoz eighteen hectares of hayfields eighteen km out, and snipped off another eighteen hectares from the kolkhoz boundaries. The presidium of the raion executive committee treated this matter in a short-sighted manner, approving Tarasovsky's plan while violating the plan of land-management expert Mariukhin, which had been drawn up properly. The presidium also violated the statutes of the agricultural artel. Two hundred kilometers of tracts, rivers, and streams within the boundaries of kolkhozes in this raion have not been surveyed with instruments, and were recorded in state certificates based on rough estimates. Three thousand hectares of hayfields along remote streams were attached for long-term use, and the areas were derived by polling people.

P. P. Anisimov twice sounded the alarm about Tarasovsky's machinations to the krai newspaper *Pravda Severa,* but the letters got lost somewhere, and he never received a reply. Tarasovsky is now under arrest. But the situation in the system of the land-management department has not changed. Technician Anisimov has been working for more than four years, and during this time he has not attended a single meeting or conference where producers have shared their experience. He wanted to go for schooling, but his hopes were in vain. Nothing happened. Now he has submitted two letters of resignation, and he hasn't gotten a reply to them, either. Personnel turnover at the land-management department is very high. A young man promoted from the rank and file, Aleksandr Ivanovich Karel'sky, is now the raion land-management chief in Pinega. He knows little about the work. No suitable conditions were set up [for him]. He submitted a letter of resignation—no reaction. Nobody is helping him. Instead of help he received a reprimand. Senior technician Nemirov is now the raion land-management chief in Karpogory Raion, and nobody helps there either. None of the land managers are studying anywhere. The oblast land-management department (the chief is Kyz'iurov, his deputy Maklakov) plans and writes up stacks of directives, but they do nothing to help specialists. There was a parceling out of personal garden plots. They did not start this task until 21 March. They were supposed to finish it by 1 April, but the oblast land-management department didn't deign to send out instructions on this work until 10 April. They weren't able to do the job, of course—they messed it up. There were tons of irregularities in this matter. [Here follow a description of the allotment of hayfields to kolkhozes and a report that, because of bureaucratic ineptitude, land managers themselves had to do this without pay instead of foremen.]

The people in Pinega are not guiding the subdivision of kolkhozes, either. The subdivision process has been dragging on for two years and to this day nothing has been done in this matter. The leaders (the head of the raion land-management department is Kalinin) are violating the kolkhoz farmers' democracy. The New Countryside Kolkhoz under the Leunovo Village Soviet was subdivided by Tarasovsky in May 1937. There are documents on the subdivision. Another kolkhoz that was separated out received more land than the New Countryside (especially hayfields). The Second Five-Year Plan Kolkhoz under the Chapol'e Village Soviet was subdivided by Tarasovsky. Alternating strip holdings resulted. Now the kolkhoz farmers are writing to the raion executive committee and the raion land-management department on this matter, but there is still no one coming to them to subdivide.

---

The letter illustrates a number of curious facts. First is the existence of substantial friction between different generations of specialists who were fighting for their place in the sun by various means, including "alarms" about each other to higher-ups and to the press. In this case Anisimov's "alarms" apparently did their bit to eliminate the "wrecker" Tarasovsky, whose crudeness, petty tyranny and incompetence played into the hands of his opponents. Second, the letter attests to the survival in kolkhoz and sovkhoz management of such phenomena as alternating strip holdings and remote land use. Part of the reason was that the farm heads themselves had an interest in concealing additional areas of plowed lands and hayfields because of onerous deliveries to the state. Denunciatory letters came in from various regions of the country, reporting that kolkhozes were making "hiding places" on remote plots of land in ricks, stacks, and piles of hay. Third, Anisimov's letter bears witness to the fact that the work to subdivide kolkhozes and bring their boundaries into line with customary settlements and villages was a long way from completion. Finally, the letter points to the tremendous scale of work involved in separating out and allocating personal plots—a vital issue for the survival of the rural population.

It should be noted that the peasants themselves were ardent champions of subdividing kolkhozes. Kolkhoz farmers in Pukhovichi Raion, Belorussian SSR, offered these arguments: "The more land there is, the worse the land is cultivated and the more grain has to be paid in the form of tax to the state and the more payment in kind has to go as well to the MTS for cultivation and the less a kolkhoz farmer gets per laborday. And on this kind of kolkhoz there is more mismanagement and more rude and outrageous treatment of kolkhoz farmers by the administration. On this kind of kolkhoz a kolkhoz farmer not only does not have time to cultivate his own little plot, which is still his main livelihood, but does not have the right to talk about it."9

The small payments to kolkhoz farmers for labordays were usually regarded as a consequence of wrecking. Yet the statutes of the agricultural artel stated that kolkhozes above all must provide deliveries to the state, remit taxes to the state, make insurance payments, and repay loans; next they were to cover current production needs and administrative and operating costs, outlays for cultural needs, and allocations to the indivisible fund; only then were they to allocate output for labordays. It is no surprise that little was left to pay for labor, especially in years with poor harvests. But sometimes even bumper crops were no salvation. The following letter illustrates this:

---

## Document 109

Letter of rural correspondent A. P. Alekseev to *Krest'ianskaia Gazeta* on violations of law on Northern Oblast kolkhozes, 19 September 1937. RGAE, f. 396, op. 10, d. 4, ll. 345–347. Corrected, certified copy.

---

To the editors of *Krest'ianskaia Gazeta* from Aleksandr Petrovich Alekseev, member of the Baklanka Kolkhoz under the Ramenovo Village Soviet in Lesha [Lezha] Raion, Northern Oblast

19 September 1937

The kolkhozes of Lesha Raion in Northern Oblast this year are getting a very abundant harvest, that even our grandfathers do not remember such an abundance of produce, but the enemies of the people, seeing that the kolkhozes are growing stronger, the kolkhoz farmers are becoming well off and are becoming even more devoted to the party and its leader Comrade Stalin, at the same time are trying to muck things up, prevent the harvest from being gathered and stir up the masses on the kolkhoz. Take [for example] at our machine-tractor stations the enemies of the people Trotskyists Bukharinists have put machines out of commission, machines as decisive in the harvest as the seventeen VNIL-5 flax pullers. Flax has been harvested from only thirty-five hectares for the season. Combines are not being used, they are standing in the fields and the manager is doing nothing. MTS contracts with kolkhozes are not being honored and MTS leaders have yet to give a single accounting to kolkhoz farmers, fearful that their wrecking work will be exposed to the masses. The statutes of the agricultural artel are being violated on the kolkhozes and nobody wants to do anything about it, take for example on our Baklanka Kolkhoz the kolkhoz farmers did not elect the kolkhoz chairman Mikhailov, but who has already been working since 15 January of this year and has systematically violated Stalin's statutes and in revenge against Stalinist shock worker and Komsomol member Il'ia Ukhanov. [The nature of the alleged revenge is unspecified, as is the ostensible motive for it.] And the raion organizations, instead of protecting Ukhanov, are conniving over Ukhanov, conducting an investigation and playing up his mistakes. They harass rural correspondents like rural correspondent Krasulin was ousted from his job as a bookkeeper for the village cooperative store because he often criticized the leadership and others.

I Alekseev have been a rural correspondent since 1926. On 10 July 1936 I cut up my foot in a mower, but I could not get any help in treating it anywhere, instead of help I got gibes like from the same Baklanka village cooperative store it was a member of the auditing commission. I was taken off supposedly due to illness, but this is wrong, because to replace me they brought in An. Iv. Serov who just arrived from a concentration camp and who is now doing all he can to ruin the village cooperative store, and director Koshel'nikov of the Sidorovskaia MTS branded me a Trotskyist at the MTS council for a letter [I wrote] to the USSR People's Commissariat of Agriculture, and the raion land-management department's horse expert says that Alekseev should be dragged by his feet into the river for that letter. But in spite of all this the masses of kolkhoz farmers themselves are struggling with all their might to preserve the abundant crop and the harvest is going through to completion. Then the enemies of the people took another method of struggle to irritate the masses. They are setting fire to villages, the biggest and the most packed [densely settled], so that they burn more, like the village of Otemetenikovo recently

## Document 109 *continued*

burned down, a fire was set in a nonresidential structure, today 19 September 1937 the village of Ramenovo burned down, the fire was set in a nonresidential structure, it burned down in the village of Antipino, the same thing on the same night a threshing barn with grain on a kolkhoz was set afire. And what is no secret is that there used to be SR [Socialist Revolutionary] groups in these villages, and apparently their offspring are the ones that are operating. [The fires most likely became more frequent because of the dry weather that prevailed in 1937.] But our raion leadership hasn't come down much to the localities yet, so far it has only handled the problem in the raion itself, but after all Comrade Uritsky correctly noted in his article, to eliminate the consequences of wrecking in agriculture and what must be done, or there is no other way.

I ask that the editors handle my letter themselves personally, because if you sent my letters on for investigation, I never received anything after that, it's like they're mocking me and not to disclose my name right up until the facts are checked. Because I already reported what happened to me over this and do not contact me directly while the facts are checked.

And a great many other violations of revolutionary law can be cited.

---

The letter provides evidence of rather serious conflicts and a constant quest for people to locate blame for the failures, setbacks, and reasons for the difficulties that arose.[10] In an appeal to *Krest'ianskaia Gazeta* from May 1938, the board of the Il'ich Kolkhoz in Il'insky Raion, Ivanovo Oblast, blamed everything, as was often the case, on wreckers who had settled in at the MTS and their protectors in the raion. (On the letter is a resolution: "Urgently send off to oblast organizations for investigation.")

---

## Document 110

Appeal from kolkhoz board in Ivanovo Oblast sent to *Krest'ianskaia Gazeta,* 2 May 1938. RGAE, f. 396, op. 10, d. 36, ll. 15–16. Corrected, certified copy.

---

*Krest'ianskaia Gazeta*
Help the kolkhozes of the Khlebnitsky Village Soviet and the Rozhnovsky Village Soviet to unmask our mortal enemies and wreckers who have settled in at the Gorskaia MTS of the Il'insky RIK in Ivanovo Oblast, and at the same time their protectors all of the raion organizations of the Il'insky RIK in Ivanovo Oblast.

## Document 110 *continued*

What happened was that the spring plowing and planting in our area began on 15 April, and there are no tractors on the fields to this day 2 May. And no word about when we will get them. In 1937 the worst sort of wrecking flourished at our Gorskaia MTS and the Il'insky Raion Executive Committee. Based on an alarm sent to the newspaper *Pravda* the wreckers were unmasked and incurred the punishment they deserved from ten to five years in prison and were ousted from their jobs. The population was able to breathe freely, the wreckers were gone, but the spring of '38 brought them back. They have felled trees, heaps of suckers have come out of the roots, there are more wreckers and they are worse than in '37. The stock of tractors was left in the fields in the local villages, and they just stood there all winter, and some of the machines got all rusted. The same wreckers filched and pilfered them and only in the second half of February and in March did the MTS start thinking about repairs and taking the motors apart. They removed them from the tractor to send them off for repairs.

And when the kolkhoz boards started saying at meetings see the kolkhozes have repaired their equipment but the MTS ruined the spring planting, the raion organizations, the MTS of the raion executive committee, and the village soviets made a vow that everything will be ready on time, and it ended up the other way around, and when the kolkhozes asked the Gorskaia MTS why there were no tractors, the latter replied that the tractors were under repair, and when they come out we will bring them to you, but you should plow with horses, and plant by hand and take the old mama scythe out of the museum and work with that.

On the basis of the foregoing we request that you urgently untangle this mess with the wreckers at the Gorskaia MTS and Il'insky Raion, which are covering up and hushing up all the acts of wrecking and laying waste to the kolkhoz stock of horses. They are wearing out the horses which are already weak as it is with overwork, dragging out the sowing indefinitely. They have ruined all the plans for spring work. Is this abomination going to continue much longer, the kolkhoz boards and kolkhoz farmers are outraged and demand an investigation.

Chairman of the Il'ich Kolkhoz Khalistov
Bookkeeper [signature]

---

As the letters show, there was constant friction between the kolkhozes and the machine-tractor stations. Compared with the kolkhoz farmers, MTS employees enjoyed a relatively privileged status, as defined by a resolution of the TsK and the SNK dated 13 January 1933. MTS tractor drivers and combine operators had guaranteed minimum wages, both in kind and in cash. Although labordays were recorded for them just as they were for kolkhoz farmers, the calculations were done by MTS accountants, the reports were sent over to the kolkhoz, and based on them kolkhozes were billed for the transfer of funds to the machine-tractor stations. During the work period equipment operators had to eat at the kolkhozes and receive one kg of bread a day, two hundred g of meat, fifty g of animal fats, one liter of milk, 400–450 g of millet and a quantity of potatoes depending on how much was required for soup. Then, for all this, one ruble fifty kopecks in cash per day was deducted from earnings. The kolkhozes delivered payments in kind to equipment operators at home, regardless of where they lived. A considerable portion of the correspondence between machine-tractor stations and kolkhozes involved mutual grievances and resentments. The kolkhozes continually complained about the poor quality of work done by the machine-tractor stations and that the latter imposed various fees on them (for overconsumption of fuel, for damage to equipment, and so on). There were constant complaints that kolkhoz farmers who were sent to MTS courses were, in effect, lost to the kolkhoz, and the MTS was not making proper use of them. MTS employees complained that the kolkhozes were not fulfilling their obligations, were late with payments, "laid waste" to equipment and did a poor job of feeding tractor drivers and combine operators.

Many letters touch on the problem of the operations of the machine-tractor stations themselves—the lack of facilities, the dearth of repair resources, the enormous turnover of personnel and the shortage of gasoline, which because of its scarcity was distributed mostly according to personal connections. The female Stakhanovite A. Kon'shina from the Thälmann MTS in Bolkhov Raion, Orel Oblast, reported on the poor condition of dormitories for MTS equipment operators, where, moreover, "men and women live together." *Krest'ianskaia Gazeta*'s advice to complain to the management resulted in the fact, according to the writer, that "now everybody despises" her.[11]

Agronomist G. I. Taranov (from the Talo-Pisarevskaia MTS in Pisarevsky Raion, Voronezh Oblast) complained that the raion organizations were not creating proper conditions for specialists. The MTS, he wrote, had six agronomists, but only two of them had a means of transportation to the kolkhozes, and the rest of them had to hitchhike to work. Taranov found at his disposal a horse, he writes, "that is undernourished, a saddle with no bellyband, and a cart with no wheels." The workday as described by this sort of specialist is of interest:

## Document 111

Letter of complaint from agronomist G. I. Taranov sent to *Krest'ianskaia Gazeta*, 1938. RGAE, f. 396, op. 11, d. 7, ll. 101–102. Certified, typewritten copy.

I arrive an hour or two before the start of the workday, my first duty is to collect and repair my gear. The setting up and repairing take at least three to six hours, and after that I set off around the kolkhozes over a distance of ten to fifteen km. It takes about two hours, sometimes three, to cover this distance, instead of getting right down to work at the first kolkhoz I start to repair my cart again, i.e. you have to look for wheels on the kolkhoz or a harness maker to fix the horse's collar, and with that the workday is over.

You continue riding on to another kolkhoz, now things are already worse, the horse starts to pull up or the wheels have broken down, and these kinds of things keep happening every day.

On top of all that they don't provide fodder for the horse, you have to get it yourself, nobody gives it to you.

You cannot buy anything at the store, everything they bring in goes out the back door. Therefore an agronomist has to go around in an Adam shirt [without a shirt] and in his father's shoes. There are no apartments. You have to do your own repairs on the lodgings they allocate. It is no surprise that agronomists quit their jobs and go into schoolteaching. Five agronomists have fled recently.

This state of affairs grew even worse on the eve of the war as a result of industry's conversion to military needs and the mass call-up of skilled tractor and truck drivers into the army. Under these conditions, naturally, the machine-tractor stations could not provide proper support for kolkhoz production even without wreckers.

Sometimes the letters cry out about the countryside's problems. Letters selected for storage often served as material for an investigation and for initiating criminal proceedings. The category of acts of wrecking was applied to losses of grain, epidemics and deaths of livestock, the poor condition of fodder and seed supplies, grain rotting in the field, frequent fires in the villages, and so forth ad infinitum. There were plenty of problems in the countryside to fuel accusations.

A man named P. S. Rogudilin, who fled from a kolkhoz to Moscow, continued to shower the newspapers with letters. In spite of the writer's lack of literacy, the nature of his complaints is unmistakable:

---

## Document 112

Letter from ex-kolkhoznik P. S. Rogudilin to *Krest'ianskaia Gazeta* on abuses on K. Marx Kolkhoz, Orel Oblast, 3 November 1938. RGAE, f. 396, op. 11, d. 41, l. 29. Original manuscript.

---

I have been writing to you for four years already but you have taken no measures at all on the especially important remarks, for which people wanted and are wanting to take revenge on me. In 1936 I was forced to leave, or otherwise the enemies wanted to lock me up for the fact I was unmasking enemies. But evinso [even so] I feel sorry for my beloved kolkhoz where the enemies are ruining it and want to ruin it like in the spring of 1937. Didn't I write you that the people at K. Marx Kolkhoz of the Kalabinsky Village Soviet in Zadonsk Raion, Orel Oblast, with crimanil intent sowd ordanary wheat instead of high quality. Also I received more than one letter from home where they write me that the kolkhoz chairman on our kolkhoz swapped all of the chaff for drink. Whoever gives half a liter gets chaff from him, and although there were no labordays, wheat chaff was pilfered from forty hectares nobody knows where he pilfered all of it to, but he did not give it out for labordays.

---

What is striking about the letters is the ordinariness of the shortcomings and the assessment of them as acts of wrecking, banditry, and the like. Almost invariably tacked on to them was a past connection to Whites or kulaks, sometimes dating virtually to infancy. As a rule, this was done in a way that was extremely difficult to verify either because it was in the form of innuendo or because, as in a letter from Novosibirsk Oblast, the events in question occurred all the way at the other end of the country.[12] If, however, the raion administration failed to take any measures on the "facts" reported in the letters, this signified to the writers that wreckers had entrenched themselves there as well, and also had to be dealt with. Often the remnants of "wasps' nests of wreckers" that had been smashed in the capitals and large cities tried to hide from mass repressions in the provinces. But the wave of exposures reached there as well. This is illustrated by an "alarm" dated 9 January 1939: "There resides on the Vil'na Ukraina Kolkhoz under the Plautinsky Village Soviet, in Mokhovsky Raion, citizen Pyotr Grigor'evich Korchak previously repressed with his wife, has a divorce but lives together, resided in Moscow until 1936 and worked in kolkhoz work in 1937–38, but has not yet been approved by the general meeting." And the vigilant editor of *Krest'ianskaia Gazeta* sounds an alarm of his own: "Leonid! This case may turn out not to be an isolated one."[13]

The constant threat of repression gave rise to a particular way of thinking that was closely linked to the everyday life of the countryside. S. G. Reshetnikov of the Reshetnikovsky Kolkhoz in Svecha Raion, Kirov Oblast, reported that "their potatoes burned up this year [1938], but deliveries of them to the state are being taken in the form of rye instead." This is unfair, he concluded, for there would be nothing to eat, and he cited an example: "If an elder brother has been sentenced to ten years in prison but he went and dropped dead, should the younger brother then serve the time for him? In my view, absolutely not."[14] This kind of analogy is highly revealing.

In order to somehow ease the burden on the kolkhozes, boards often tried to establish auxiliary trades. The skills gained from these sideline activities, however, were largely wasted because their pursuit could be construed as violating the very purpose of kolkhozes. This is borne out by an article that was prepared for publication in *Krest'ianskaia Gazeta* under the rubric "Trial," but for some reason was marked with the decision "won't run."

---

## Document 113

Unpublished article "Violators of Stalin's Statutes of Kolkhoz Life," 20 December 1938. RGAE, f. 396, op. 11, d. 34, ll. 102–105. Certified, typewritten copy.

---

The Voroshilov Kolkhoz in Mytishchi Raion, Moscow Oblast, was established in 1930. In terms of the number of consolidated farmsteads, the kolkhoz was a small one, numbering thirteen farmsteads. The kolkhoz had all the prerequisites for it to gain financial strength and thereby to provide a prosperous life for the kolkhoz members. The kolkhoz had 107.6 hectares of land, it had work animals, agricultural equipment and, finally, most important, the kolkhoz farmers had a fervent desire to forge, through harmonious, collective labor, a new happiness for themselves.

People on the make who worked their way into the leadership decided, with the direct connivance of certain leaders, to take a completely different path, a path of crime, deceit, and crooked activity.

Former chairman of the kolkhoz board Markov, aware that the direct purpose of the kolkhoz is agricultural production and that the establishment of any auxiliary enterprises whatsoever that are not related to agriculture is not envisaged by the kolkhoz statutes and is directly prohibited by a government resolution, decided that none of this applies to him in the least. After seeking out a clever swindler named Gaivoronsky (who is now under arrest as an enemy of the people), Markov developed boundless energy in setting up auxiliary enterprises of the most varied kind, knowing that something from this venture may come his way as well.

On 12 April 1937 Markov secured the kolkhoz farmers' consent, misled them, collected from them cash and working capital for a future enterprise and sent out representatives to all the republics of the Soviet Union to sell the yet-to-be-produced merchandise—contour maps and classroom blackboards.

Without a single map produced, Markov sent out twenty-two representatives, who accepted orders for the manufacture of thirty-six thousand maps worth 1,480,000 rubles. Taking advantage of a flawed accounting and reporting system, these agents appropriated 122,603 rubles from the advance payments made and some of them gradually slipped out of the kolkhoz's sight, or to put it more simply, they went into hiding with kolkhoz money.

After still receiving 580,000 rubles in advances instead of 700,000, Markov set about making the geographical maps. Production proved to be rudimentary and as a result 85.8 percent of the output in 1937 was defective.

Markov, dissatisfied with this and clearly aware that the auxiliary enterprises were not working out, opened a new production line, now already without the knowledge of all of the kolkhoz farmers, for the manufacture of small rugs on the theme of the Three Little Pigs. The fate of this new production line was roughly the same—the kolkhoz lost more than three thousand rubles.

Nevertheless, Markov, following the enemy's bidding, laid down grandiose "projects" that called for the kolkhoz to build a huge, integrated plant for geographical maps, a vegetable storehouse, a livestock yard, etc. He sought workers to hire, and took on completely unknown individuals as agents for timber procurement, and they went into hiding after failing to account for 24,635 rubles.

Instead of properly organizing agricultural production, kolkhoz chairman

## Document 113 *continued*

Markov, auditing commission chairman and brigade leader Zhiganov, and bookkeeper Serebriakov go on drinking binges in close matrimony [*sic*] with Gaivoronsky. Agriculture, i.e. the basis of kolkhoz production, is regarded as a secondary matter. As a result, in 1937 ten out of fifteen hectares of potatoes remained under snow and the per-hectare yields of oats and other crops dropped sharply. While he was drunk, brigade leader Zhiganov plowed half a hectare that had already been sowed to onions. The drunkards and criminals made the situation so bad already that the value of a laborday has dropped sharply and losses totaling 439,788 rubles have been inflicted on the kolkhoz.

The outraged kolkhoz farmers ejected the bankrupt leaders Markov, Zhiganov, and Zhiganova from the kolkhoz leadership. But the newly elected chairman Gavrilenko was not much better than his predecessors. Instead of establishing Bolshevik order on the kolkhoz, Gavrilenko continued a course of setting up auxiliary enterprises. New orders were accepted for map production, a contract was signed for the manufacture of colored chalk, membership cards in the MOPR [International Organization for Assistance to Revolutionary Fighters], etc. The previous practice also produced the previous results. In 1938, during Gavrilenko's tenure, losses totaling 14,634 rubles were inflicted on the kolkhoz.

Bookkeeper Serebriakov and accountant Zhiganova brought accounting and reporting on the kolkhoz to a state of chaos. Requirements for financial discipline were violated, and accountable individuals wound up with arrears of 135,000 rubles.

Thus the criminals, ignoring the interests of kolkhoz farmers and deliberately violating Stalin's statutes of kolkhoz life, drove the kolkhoz into a grave condition and devalued the kolkhoz farmer's laborday.

They will all appear before the Moscow Oblast Court in the very near future.

The case is being heard with the participation of the prosecution and the defense in assizes in Mytishchi Raion.

V. N. Markov, S. S. Serebriakov, and I. I. Gavrilenko have been charged with abuse of their positions under article 109 of the RSFSR Criminal Code. Accountant A. A. Zhiganova and auditing commission chairman V. A. Zhiganov have been charged with neglect of their official duties under article 111 of the Criminal Code.

The impending trial is yet another confirmation of the correctness and timeliness of the Union Government resolution of 23 October 1938 "On the Illegal Establishment Under Kolkhozes of Industrial Enterprises Not Related to Agricultural Production."

This trial graphically demonstrates what breaches of Stalin's statutes of kolkhoz life lead to.

Nik. Sudarikov, member of the Moscow Oblast Court

In this way the state condemned the practice of setting up auxiliary enterprises as an impediment to the principal purpose of kolkhozes—producing as much agricultural output as possible. Notwithstanding the fact that matters came to a sad end for the leaders of the Voroshilov Kolkhoz, even in the ensuing years chairmen persisted, often clandestinely, to resort to this practice. On the eve of the war, cases of underground *biznes,* misappropriations, embezzlement, and illegal profiteering, according to NKVD summaries, became more frequent.

Yet another conflict gradually developed in the kolkhoz economy: between work in the collective sector and labor on personal garden plots. The meager—for the most part—compensation for labordays compelled people to clutch at the scraps of land that these farmsteads represented (0.5 hectare for kolkhoz farmers, 0.4 hectare for factory workers and office employees) and focus their utmost labor efforts there. These farmsteads became the main livelihood and turned into a kind of peasant microfarm—an object of special care in detriment to work in the kolkhoz fields and livestock sections. A huge number of letters dealt with how to provide firewood for personal plots and fodder for cows or small domestic livestock. "Invasions" of the kolkhoz for grain were even observed; otherwise there would have been nothing to feed livestock. Many inquiries came in regarding the inheritance of personal plots. Kolkhoz farmers did not miss an opportunity to secretly "tack on" some scrap of land to their plot or to illicitly collect hay. The authorities did not let these occurrences go by unnoticed. In 1939–40 measurements of personal plots were conducted, and as a result roughly one-quarter of their total area was snipped off. The gathering of the "timber harvest" and the sale of berries and mushrooms at so-called "kolkhoz markets" became a great help in supporting village dwellers.

Although they occupied a minute portion of crop areas and had much less livestock and poultry, kolkhoz farmers' personal plots accounted for almost half of the country's agricultural output. They also provided peasants with the bulk of their monetary income and enabled them to subsist.[15]

At the same time personal farm plots became a target of intensified tax exploitation by the state. Just as independent peasants had complained about their heavy taxes in the past, kolkhoz farmers now protested against their increasing tax burden. But the letters show that people defended every centimeter of land allotted to them and argued with their neighbors to the point of fisticuffs. A kolkhoz farmer was permitted to keep only one cow on the personal plot. Any attempts to increase this number were vigorously rejected. One tearful letter from Tambov Oblast contained a complaint that a kolkhoz had taken away a calf that had been raised with great effort.[16] On the eve of the war the number of livestock in personal use declined rather sharply.

In May 1939 a resolution was adopted that mandated a minimum number of labordays to be worked on kolkhozes—something that already resembled a *corvée*. A great many letters came in on the theme: people had to work from one morning until the next, there were no days off and no time to elevate one's cultural level to that of urban workers. The majority of village dwellers, especially young people, found this situation extremely painful. Watching their parents tormented by arduous labor and unwilling to accept psychological degradation, constantly digging around in manure and seeing nothing but cows' backsides, young people in the countryside aspired, whatever the obstacles, to go to the city, which enticed them with its relative freedom, clean offices, higher educational institutions and theaters. Despite all of the hurdles, therefore, the exodus from the countryside mounted. Various methods were used to produce this trend, and as a result specific migratory "channels" took shape within Soviet society. One channel was organized recruitment, *orgnabor*, the employment of workers on kolkhozes for construction projects, for seasonal jobs, for timber procurements, and so forth by special representatives, with whom the kolkhoz administration did not have the right to interfere. Three kolkhoz chairmen—those of the Red Sword, the Second Five-Year Plan, and the Engels—in Zamtechinsky Raion, Tambov Oblast, reported that "many kolkhoz farmers have gone elsewhere to work without the board's consent, especially men. There is nobody to do the work."[17] Reports by NKVD organs regularly described mass "departures," or rather mass escapes, from the countryside in quest of work.

Another channel for outmigration was the continuation of studies at secondary schools, factory-training schools, higher institutions, and technicums. This made the goal of continuing education a steady means of avoiding life on the kolkhoz, a method that is quite apparent from the documents cited here. Yet a third channel, which came into especially wide use in the ensuing years, was service in the Red Army, after which few people returned to the kolkhoz. There were also intermediate forms, specifically work at machine-tractor stations, from which equipment operators could transfer to a factory. Thus the most active, competent, and youthful segment of the adult population poured out of the countryside.

The rest of the kolkhoz farmers ruminated fairly often about how they might leave their kolkhoz. Ivan Pirogov of the settlement of Lebedinka in Tektovsky Raion, Novosibirsk Oblast, formulated his questions in a letter this way:

## Document 114

Letter from kolkhoznik I. Pirogov to *Krest'ianskaia Gazeta* asking for explanation of kolkhoz policy, 1938. RGAE, f. 396, op. 10, d. 97, ll. 151–152. Original manuscript.

1. Can a kolkhoz member go to work in a factory?
2. If he can leeve to work in a factory then why doesn't the board give out certificates permitting people to obtain their [internal] passports and why don't the raion bodies order them to give out certificates?

Example a kolkhoz farmer dusn't take to som things about this kolkhoz like living under climatic lokel conditions he wants to leave and asks for a certificate then the kolkhoz Board says we wont give you a certificate go work and the kolkhoz farmer says I wont work give me a certificate I'm leaving. The kolkhoz farmer doesn't go to work then they start to enfriten [scare] him and keep him until the kolkhoz farmer has nuthing left and at last they expel him from the kolkhoz and the village soviet taxes him right away like an independent and he even is left without nothing he spends everything on food. Please explane did they do the rite thing or the wrong thing.

While young people, who were ready to move at the drop of a hat, considered it a stroke of luck to leave the kolkhoz, for the older generation, which had established roots in the countryside, expulsion from a kolkhoz created major problems. Realizing this, kolkhoz boards used the practice or the threat of expulsion on an increasing scale to punish those who did not suit them. A great many letters came in on this topic. One letter reported the expulsion of a full 160 kolkhoz farmers, a measure that went through without investigation. Those expelled included the family of the complainant, Kuz'menkov, a former Red partisan, whereas the family of Makarov, a former officer of the Imperial Army, remained.[18] The kolkhoz administration also looked askance at people whose children did not work on the kolkhoz. A letter to *Krest'ianskaia Gazeta* from Orel Oblast from January 1939 dealt with this subject:

## Document 115

Letter from S. N. Gretsky to *Krest'ianskaia Gazeta* seeking restoration of kolkhoz membership, 11 January 1939. RGAE, f. 396, op. 11, d. 41, ll. 91–910b. Original manuscript.

I Stepan Nikitich Gretsky Have sevin sons whoo eech wirk at there own jobs. The oldest son Grigory wirks at the Mitkovsky emtiess [MTS] as the brigade leeder of a traktor Brigade. The second son Nikolai wirks as a forge hand at the same emtiess. The third son Vasily got discharged ahead of schedule from the Red Army in '38 as a tankman. He works at the same Mitkovsky emtiess. The forth son Dmitry was called up into the Red Army he serves in one of the units of the far east Army. The fiffth son Ivan is in the sevin grade at seckondary school. The six son Stepan is in the six grade at the same school, the sevin Nikikhvor is in elimentary school in the third groop. I the father Stepan Gretsky am an invalid of the World war in the second group, and in December 1938 I was expelled from the kolkhoz. But my plot is worth 220 laberdays. I ask the editors of Krest'ianskaia Gazeta to explane and get me back on the kolkhoz. Red Riverbank Kolkhoz Klimovo Raion Orel Oblast.

In this case the board's decision was deemed improper and Stepan Nikitich was reinstated on the kolkhoz. The letter is of interest with regard to sociodemographic dynamics and the niche occupied by each of the seven sons. At the same time one senses the emergence of a serious demographic problem in the kolkhoz village—the large accumulation of old men and women. The older sons were already outside the kolkhoz, and the younger ones who are still in school were clearly following a different path, away from the kolkhoz.

Within the village structure the village administration occupied a preeminent position. For the most part, collective farmers viewed it as the offender or guilty party for the numerous calamities and misfortunes and served as the target for various kinds of exposures. The primary targets were the chairmen of kolkhozes and village soviets and the directors of sovkhozes and machine-tractor stations. If, so it was commonly believed, the newspapers were reporting on the successes of the kolkhoz system and the happy kolkhoz life, who was to blame for the fact that at a certain farm things were not working out? The victims in 1937 included Polikarp Parmenovich Sergeev, chairman of the Lenin Kolkhoz, Zalegoshch' Raion, Orel Oblast, who wrote the following letter:

---

## Document 116

Letter from kolkhoz chairman P. P. Sergeev to *Krest'ianskaia Gazeta* on his persecution, 23 January 1938. RGAE, f. 396, op. 10, d. 110, ll. 96–1010b. Original manuscript.

---

To *Krest'ianskaia Gazeta*
Statement
I hereby request that the following be taken up for consideration. My year of birth was 1887 I am the son of a (middle) peasant. My father was enslaved his whole life by neighboring kulaks unable to escape bondage under the Davydkin brothers, who forced him to work for entire months for a pood of flour and it went on this way his whole life until he died. I became a farmhand at the age of eleven. In 1900 I found myself in Moscow under a rich boss named Artamonov in Gruziny on Kondrat'ev Lane and worked there all the way until 1904. In 1904 due to illness I went to the countryside and my illness lasted until 1906, and in 1906 I went back to Moscow for work. In 1909 I was called up for military service and served in the city of Blagoveshchensk on the Amur in the 4th East Siberian infantry regiment, where I met Sergei Yermolaevich Suvorov, who had refused to serve military service and had been in prison, which I paid serious attention to. I had thoughts before this: why am I serving, what for, and who am I serving? After that I had occasion to read some brochures by Tolstoy that denounced the church, priests, and landowners. I decided to write a letter to L. N. Tolstoy. Tolstoy quickly answered me, where he confirmed my thoughts even more. Upon returning from military service, I again found myself in Moscow, where I went to work at a vegetarian cafete-

ria as a doorman. After working at the cafeteria for a year, we established a farming artel outside Tula at the village of Khmelyok. The artel soon broke up because of harassment from the tsarist authorities and we were persecuted and subjected to frequent searches by the police. I went back to the cafeteria, and in 1914 war was declared, and mobilization was announced I went into hiding in Siberia. I felt that an imperialist war would not be of any benefit to us and I thought it was unnecessary, even harmful, to defend the tsars, landowners, and kulaks. [A section follows describing his jobs and contacts in Siberia during the war.] After the revolution I returned to Moscow again and worked in a children's colony at the Chuchkovo station (the children's colony was attached to a factory). Some time later I left for the countryside with my whole family, where I have been farming to this day. When I arrived in the countryside I set up a village reading room, and for two years I was a librarian and got involved with the land question. The settlement of Glubki, where I used to live, had a very poor life and was located far from the fields. I broke up all the land into four sections with new settlements, and in 1931 I was elected chairman of the Lenin Kolkhoz and a member of the Grachevsky Village Soviet as chairman of the field-crop section, where I worked until 7 December 1937. On 7 December I was ousted as [kolkhoz] chairman (75 percent of the kolkhoz chairmen in our raion were removed in 1937, and nobody was given any reasons for it), and on 13 January 1938 I was expelled from the kolkhoz (but I am still a member of the village soviet) by stirring up the public [against me] as a sectarian, wrecker, and enemy of the people by a resolution of the general meeting of kolkhoz farmers. The kolkhoz had a total of forty-five members, and only nineteen attended the meeting. I consider this action both by chairman Yeliseev of the Grachevsky Village Soviet and the meeting of kolkhoz farmers to be a mockery and persecution of a living human being. This only plays into the hands of the enemies of the people, I consider it wrong. Under the agricultural statutes of the artel any expulsion from the kolkhoz requires two-thirds to be present, and only nineteen out of forty-five were present. Second it is not according to Stalin's constitution.

I don't belong to the sectarians anyway, and I have been and am the most mortal enemy of any fonaticism. I began to fight against this trend myself back in 1909. I see the word god itself as an invention by the priests and the dirty bourgeois and so on. This served their purpose so they could fleece the working people better and keep the masses in the dark. I declare once again that I do not believe in any gods or any lackeys of the bourgeoisie. In the old days, i.e. before the war, I even had to take gibes from fellow villagers and neighbors, they called me an antichrist and godless.

My struggle during my time as kolkhoz chairman. In 1932 a gang of thieves was organized in our area, and they hid in the woods, about twelve of them. They stole the property of kolkhozes, sovkhozes, and kolkhoz farmers. In our

# Document 116 *continued*

former Novosil' Raion they stole a lot of cows and all kinds of property. I was the first to decide to fight, I reported to Novosil'—an investigation corner still existed there at the time [The letter writer interprets *ugrozysk (ugolovnyi rozysk)*, in this case a criminal investigation department, in a most peculiar way as "*ugol rozyska*," investigation corner or desk.]—I fought for a full two years and in the end defeated this gang: some of them were locked up again, and some escaped. At the time they wanted to shoot me. I reported this more than once, but they didn't pay much attention to my calls for help. Later I also exposed two kolkhoz farmers for stealing state property. In court they messed up the case. The two brothers each got six months at forced labor to be served at the kolkhoz, and I also exposed two kolkhoz farmers for stealing potatoes on the Rusty Marsh sovkhoz farm. They each got one year at forced labor and one had to be present during dekulakization. All these people are now living on our kolkhoz. And on 18 June 1937 I wrote a report on Stefan Ivanovich Davydkin about a counterrevolutionary act: he referred to Comrade Stalin by all kinds of derogatory names in the presence of the following individuals first V. M. Glotov, Yegor S. Kochergin, St. Yegor. Gorokhov, V. Pav. Savina, and Ivan Serg. Glotov, and previously this citizen was making statements during road construction, corrupting other kolkhoz farmers. This matter is still being worked on, and that is where the whole struggle started against me and so did all kinds of persecution of me. More than once I was subjected to all sorts of repressions and threats, they threatened to cause me trouble in kolkhoz work. More than one time there was a work stoppage. I have sent alarm signals to the raion about all of the outrages that are taking place, but to this day nobody has wanted to help me and nobody has paid any attention. Our kolkhoz, village soviet, and the raion have received very few visits, and nobody has wanted to know what life on our kolkhoz is like, and I have been left helpless to my own devices for a full six years, so I request that you pay serious attention to the foregoing and I feel that I alone may be wiped off the face of the earth, so I request your intervention and get to the heart of the matter and give me assistance and sort things out on a fair basis.

23 January 1938

---

Enclosed with the letter is a denunciation of improper work by the kolkhoz auditing commission, which treats financial violations (or what the writer depicts as violations) as schemes by enemies of the people on the kolkhoz.[19]

Chairman Sergeev is not particularly appealing as a personality, although his background is unusual and of interest. He does not realize that his methods of managing the kolkhoz are deficient, and as we see, he was not ousted because of that at all but because of a lack of purity in his background. Usually people with more prosaic lives became chairmen. Many of them were recruited from among village activists who had distinguished themselves on the "collectivization front" or were "specialists" dispatched from the city with a hazy knowledge of agriculture and limited education. Often the people who ended up as chairmen had no qualifications; they could barely read or write, had little culture and were dissolute. At times they treated kolkhoz farmers the way the old, tyrannical landowners did. Thus one of the demands that letters put forth was "to introduce on a mandatory basis courteous treatment of kolkhoz farmers on the part of the kolkhoz chairmen and the brigade leader so that a kolkhoz farmer is not called a kulak or a kulak-saboteur."[20]

Nominally all chairmen were supposed to be elected by a general meeting of kolkhoz farmers, but "kolkhoz democracy" did not work very well, and it was also rather difficult to assemble people. For the most part kolkhoz farmers acquiesced without a murmur in the candidacy that was imposed on them from above. There is an abundance of various kinds of testimony about how such chairmen "managed" kolkhozes.

One archive file contains the special summaries of the Migulin Raion branch of the NKVD (Azov–Black Sea Krai) for 1935–36 that were cited earlier. Compiled by the NKVD raion branch chief, Sergeant of State Security Osipov, they contain various bits of information, including reports of abuses, violations, and distortions of the law that were perpetrated by local leadership bodies. Below are excerpts from these documents, which describe the practices of the kolkhoz administration:

---

## Document 117

From NKVD summary report on kolkhozes in Migulin Raion, 1936. GARF, f. 1235, op. 141, d. 1789, ll. 66–73. Typewritten original.

---

Profiteering with Kolkhoz Produce and Crooked Machinations by the Leadership of the Kolkhoz Farmer's Banner Kolkhoz under the Nazarovsky Village Soviet

... The leadership of the Kolkhoz Farmer's Banner as represented by Klimoshenko, the kolkhoz chairman, and Nazarov, a candidate member of the

VKP(b), the business manager and a kulak and White Guard, who accidentally wormed his way through as a party candidate. As soon as the kolkhoz received a truck, the latter organized systematic profiteering with produce that was intended for the kolkhoz. In the process they obtained the produce on the kolkhoz at reduced prices and took them to the bazaars in the cities of Millerovo, Rostov, and Lugansk, where they sold [it] at profiteering prices. Kolkhoz chairman Klimoshenko did not stop there, and in October he set up the sale of kolkhoz products—butter, ham, apples, and fleece—in the city of Rostov, to which he personally transported the above products in a kolkhoz vehicle. In addition, he sold the products at the market price that prevailed during that time at the market in Rostov, whereas he accounted for these products at slightly above their cost on the kolkhoz. For instance, he sold butter at fifteen rubles a kilogram, but the report he submitted for the seventy kg of butter he sold was based on three rubles a kilogram. This enabled Klimoshenko to appropriate 3,200 rubles of kolkhoz money from the trip to Rostov. Klimoshenko's machinations were exposed by us with the aid of a thorough inspection of the kolkhoz and an interrogation of witnesses who traveled with Klimoshenko and who confirmed that Klimoshenko sold products at several times higher [prices] than he indicated in his report. [An account follows of similar profiteering with kolkhoz grain and apples.] (Klimoshenko and Nazarov were sentenced to eight years each.)

On Stavropol' Regiment Kolkhoz under the Meshkovsky Village Soviet

... Testimony by [female] witness Konovalova: "At the end of August or the beginning of September, I don't remember exactly, I along with kolkhoz farmers Gorina and Batal'shchikova were separating seed rye. The granary where we were working is in the courtyard of the kolkhoz board. That evening just before the end of the workday kolkhoz chairman Zemliakov came into the granary and started joking with me. Seeing this, kolkhoz farmers Gorina and Batal'shchikova decided not to wait for me and headed home. A while later, Zemliakov's carriage driver Pavel Kuznetsov came over and closed the door to the granary where I and Zemliakov were. Seeing this, the latter started to strenuously badger me and [tried to persuade] me to have sexual intercourse with him. Since I knew from the kolkhoz farmers that Zemliakov had venereal disease, I told him that, to which the latter replied that that was incorrect and that just yesterday he had sexual intercourse with Yefrosin'ia Pozdniakova. I did not agree for a long time, but then I did the sex act with him after all. A few days later, doubting the plausibility of Zemliakov['s assertion] that he was not sick, I went to a doctor in the hospital, who examined me and told me that I had the venereal disease gonorrhea and that I had to be treated."

In addition to Zemliakov's infection of kolkhoz farmer Konovalova, there is evidence that he infected Ul'iana Chibizova, Yefrosin'ia Pozdniakova and other female kolkhoz farmers of the Stavropol' Regiment Kolkhoz. (Zemliakov was sentenced to five years in prison.)

# Document 117 *continued*

Georgy Andreianovich Veshchunov, chairman of the Kaganovich Kolkhoz under the Verkhniakovsky [Verkhnekovsky] Village Soviet in Migulin Raion, has engaged, throughout the months of April and May [1935], i.e. from the time he took the position of kolkhoz chairman, in criminal, hooliganlike activity, which was manifested in coercing women into sexual relations.

Veshchunov, by his filthy, brazen, criminal, hooliganlike actions, terrorized female kolkhoz farmers, suggesting [to them] during their first encounter that they must be sure to spend the night with him. Veshchunov's most brazen abuses include the following:

As soon as Veshchunov took over as kolkhoz chairman, he marked his very first days by going on a drinking binge with former kolkhoz chairman Klimantov, now the business manager.

In April citizen Mrykhin married the daughter of a kolkhoz farmer at the Kaganovich Kolkhoz. Aware that Veshchunov might not admit him to the kolkhoz because Mrykhin had been convicted, the latter decided to buy some vodka and invite Veshchunov to his house. Despite the fact that the kolkhoz was behind in its planting, Veshchunov engaged in a drinking spree at Mrykhin's house. During the drinking, Veshchunov suggested to Mrykhin's wife that she go sleep with him in the shed, otherwise he would not only refuse to admit her husband to the kolkhoz but would make him return to the Urals. The flustered woman was left in a quandary and made this statement to her husband Mrykhin: "What on earth should I do, go to bed with Veshchunov and buy you off or you will be sent back to the Urals?" Mrykhin replied: "If you have something going with him, then go screw, I won't have anything against it."

That same day, with evening setting in, the nearly drunk Veshchunov entered the apartment of shoemaker Yegor Nazarov and, as he walked through the entranceway, he struck a tub of water with a lash, splashing himself all over and he started swearing at God, Christ, and so forth, saying: "There are so many tubs scattered around here that you can't get by." As he entered the hut, Veshchunov sat down next to kolkhoz farmer Babkina, a young girl who was Nazarov's sister-in-law, and started right in, harassing Babkina in front of Nazarov. He put one arm around Babkina's shoulders, and with the other he began to lift her skirt, saying: "Let me try you out, you're still pure, untouched, tight, let me f— you for a while and you'll get well." (Babkina was ill.) To avoid that defilement, Babkina went out into the courtyard, and Veshchunov followed right on her heels. In the courtyard Veshchunov again started to harass Babkina and invite her to the shed, but Babkina refused. Then Veshchunov declared: "Now you can stop considering yourself a kolkhoz farmer for the Kaganovich Kolkhoz."

The female kolkhoz farmers on the field-crop brigades were frightened when Veshchunov came to see them. As soon as Veshchunov would ride up, the women would declare: "Get going, girls, every which way, Veshchunov is coming, he's going to take somebody down right away."

Female kolkhoz farmer Uvarova says: "The kolkhoz women of our settlement say Veshchunov is 'all hard,' he has inseminated part of the settlement, and soon he will get to the top part of it as well." (In court, Veshchunov was acquitted.)[21] . . .

On Violations and Distortions of Revolutionary Law

. . . In September 1935 milkmaid Beschotnova of the Stalin's Path Kolkhoz, daughter of the commander of a punitive *sotnia* [Cossack squadron] under the Whites, fed a dead ram to kolkhoz farmers on the above kolkhoz, as a result of which some of the kolkhoz farmers became ill after consuming it as food.

Characteristically, Beschotnova's father Andrei Beschotnov not long before this incident was manager of the MTF [commercial dairy section], who was ousted from his job for fraud. When the best kolkhoz farmer and shock worker Brovkin was nominated to take his place, the daughter of the member of the White Guard punitive squadron, Beschotnova, began to take revenge on Brovkin for her father. And when a ram died at the MTF, she brought it to the kolkhoz storehouse and turned it in as a healthy ram. Our case against Beschotnova and Brovkin has been completed. The chief [defendant] in the case was Beschotnova. Brovkin was charged with negligence.

When it took up the case at trial, the court acquitted Beschotnova, and it gave the minor participant Brovkin, who was victimized by Beschotnova, a three-year prison term.

During the grain harvest in 1935 a kulak woman, the wife of a White bandit named Merkulov, who was executed by our organs, threw a cushion at a combine. The combine was out of commission for two or three days. When charges were brought against Merkulova, the court acquitted her, but the best combine operator, Tret'iakov, was sentenced to six months at forced labor— for what, no one knows.

---

Sergeant Osipov reported on another case of abuse by kolkhoz officials, but went further by seizing the opportunity to insert information about the desperate food situation in the raion:

---

# Document 118

Report of NKVD Migulin Raion branch chief, Sergeant Osipov, on suicide attempt and food shortages on kolkhozes, 13 June 1936. GARF, f. 1235, op. 141, d. 1789, ll. 56–59. Typewritten original.

---

To Captain of State Security Comrade Volkov, head of the special political section of the Azov–Black Sea Krai Bureau of the NKVD, City of Rostov-on-Don

To Senior Lieutenant of State Security Comrade Avtonomov, head of the North Don Okrug Bureau of the NKVD, City of Millerovo

13 June 1936

On a suicide attempt by kolkhoz farmer Aleksandra Polikarpovna Kharitonova of the Comrade Kaganovich Kolkhoz under the Verkhniakhovsky [Verkhnekovsky] Village Soviet as a result of abuse by the brigade leader of brigade no. 2 Iliushchikhin and hardships regarding food.

On 10 June of this year our source "Ivashchenkov" reported to me that the brigade leader of brigade no. 2 on the Comrade Kaganovich Kolkhoz, Iliushchikhin, systematically abused kolkhoz farmer Aleksandra Polikarpovna Kharitonova to the point where Kharitonova, upon finishing work on 2 June, came home and attempted to hang herself and only thanks to her husband who entered the apartment in time did he succeed in preventing his wife's suicide.

Upon receiving this information I immediately traveled to the Comrade Kaganovich Kolkhoz. During an interview with kolkhoz farmer Kharitonova, her husband Kharitonov and kolkhoz chairman Yazykov I determined the following:

While kolkhoz farmer Kharitonova was working on brigade no. 2 of the aforementioned kolkhoz she was subjected to completely unjustified abuse on the part of brigade leader Iliushchikhin, who in the presence of the brigade's kolkhoz farmers repeatedly rebuked her and her husband Kharitonov for "loafing and malingering," even though Kharitonov was working on the kolkhoz all the time and there was never a case when Kharitonov would refuse to perform an assignment.

Iliushchikhin did not stop there. He was well aware that the food situation on the kolkhoz was strained, and when, on 1 June, Kharitonova did not finish eating her ration of noodles while with the brigade, but took it home in a coffeepot so that she could eat it with her husband, Iliushchikhin spoke on 2 June at a joint kolkhoz meeting of brigades nos. 1 and 2 after a discussion of the draft law on the prohibition of abortions, on assistance to women giving birth and the expansion of the network of maternity clinics and nursery schools, and declared: "And we're supposed to help thieving women like Kharitonova, who steals noodles from the brigade and feeds it to her malingering loafer."

The Komsomol organizer of the kolkhoz, Yazykova, who was present at the kolkhoz meeting, failed to give an appropriate rebuff to the kulak-type assault and abuse by Iliushchikhin against Kharitonova.

Kharitonova, who was insulted without any basis, was compelled to leave the meeting with tears in her eyes. When she came home, Kharitonova decided to do away with herself, so she tied a rope to the ceiling in her hallway, placed a chair under it and was already intent on hanging herself. It was only thanks to her husband Kharitonov who returned from work that he succeeded in preventing his wife's suicide.

In a talk with me about the reasons that prompted Kharitonova to decide on such a thoughtless act, the latter stated to me:

"My husband and I have been dependable workers on the kolkhoz. Even though my husband was ill, he still earned 250 labordays. This year he has already earned a hundred, and I have fifty labordays. No housewife on our kolkhoz has more than fifty labordays, because we barely worked during the winter and spring, and they only began to call us to work this past April. My husband doesn't have many labordays because he himself isn't very well developed: he works wherever they send him to, and in addition we are all worn out from an extremely hard situation with our finances and food. We have not had a single gram of flour, potatoes, or butter at home for a month already. Life is very difficult, and now the undeserved abuse from brigade leader Iliushchikhin on top of it. The extremely hard situation with food and the fact that we aren't getting any help are what forced me to do away with myself."

It was also determined that Kharitonova and her husband were abused not only by brigade leader Iliushchikhin, but also by the leadership of the kolkhoz board in the person of kolkhoz chairman Yazykov. The raion's functionaries, particularly the head of the raion farming department Prusakov, not only knew about this, but he himself, in effect, supported this abuse, and the following facts may serve as proof of that:

"To keep the kolkhoz farmers going, the kolkhoz board issued them *makukha* [refined sunflower seeds] for food in April or the beginning of May. After I found out about this, I (A. P. Kharitonova) told my husband to apply to the kolkhoz board for makukha. In Prusakov's presence, kolkhoz chairman Yazykov and business manager Mrykhin began to take an interest at the bookkeeping department in how many labordays my husband and I had. Bookkeeper Kalmykov reported incorrect information, that supposedly we had no labordays, whereas my husband at the time had about 100 labordays, and I had about 50. In discussing this question of whether to give us makukha or not, the aforesaid individuals started calling my husband a loafer and the like at a kolkhoz farmers' meeting.

"I told brigade leader Iliushchikhin, who was present at the meeting, to get up and say that they were wrong to call us loafers. To this Iliushchikhin replied: 'I didn't hear them call you loafers.' And they never did give us makukha." (From the testimony of A. P. Kharitonova.)

The actual food situation on the kolkhoz is so grim that a number of kolkhoz farmers on the kolkhoz are starving. In 1935 this kolkhoz issued one kg fifty g [of grain] per laborday. The kolkhoz board, instead of taking measures through the appropriate organizations and improving the situation by obtaining a food loan, deemed it necessary to "sustain" the needy segment by handing out to needy kolkhoz farmers makukha that had previously been delivered for hogs. All told, thirty-one tons of makukha was distributed to kolkhoz farmers.

## Document 118 *continued*

This abusive treatment of kolkhoz farmers has led to the point where certain shock workers have been without grain for more than a month and are literally starving. Another group is selling its calves, hogs, and the like and buying bread at the village cooperative store.

It should be noted that this kind of food situation applies not only to the Comrade Kaganovich Kolkhoz but also to a number of other kolkhozes in our raion.

According to our data, the raion has fourteen kolkhozes that need food assistance. Of those, the following kolkhozes are especially in need:

|     |                                      | Grain received per laborday |
| --- | ------------------------------------ | --------------------------- |
| 1.  | Budyonnyi Kolkhoz                    | 780 g                       |
| 2.  | Kolkhoz Farmer's Banner Kolkhoz      | 1,200 g                     |
| 3.  | Stavropol' Regiment Kolkhoz          | 700 g                       |
| 4.  | Lenin's Precepts Kolkhoz             | 900 g                       |
| 5.  | Molotov Kolkhoz                      | 1,050 g                     |
| 6.  | Podtelkov and Krivoshlykov Kolkhoz   | 1,000 g                     |
| 7.  | October Revolution Kolkhoz           | 2,000 g                     |
| 8.  | Seventeenth Party Congress Kolkhoz   | 1,400 g                     |

In addition, it was determined that, two days before it received information on the abuse of the Kharitonovs, the newspaper *Stalinsky Put'* [Stalin's path] had an official statement from Kharitonova's husband Kharitonov, who reported on the abuse of his wife and her suicide attempt resulting from Iliushchikhin's abuse and asked that measures be taken. The deputy editor, Comrade Zemliachenko, conveyed this to the secretary of the VKP(b) raion committee, Comrade Yerofeev, but no measures were taken until we uncovered this matter, investigated it and raised it with the VKP(b) raion committee and the RIK.

Our Actions

Thanks to measures taken, Kharitonova has been provided with financial and medical assistance through raion organizations and normal working conditions have been set up for her on the kolkhoz.

Legal proceedings are being initiated against brigade leader Iliushchikhin through the raion procurator.

The matter of the chairman of Kaganovich Kolkhoz, Yazykov, and the head of the raion farming department, Prusakov, has been raised with the VKP(b) raion committee.

Chief of the raion branch of the NKVD
Sergeant of State Security Osipov

---

To judge by the letters, the largest contingent of "wreckers" in the countryside seem to have been chairmen, and they were primary targets of the onslaught of punishments during the Yezhovshchina. Still, as suggested by the following letter, high-handed and outrageous behavior, crooked machinations and embezzlement persisted:

## Document 119

Letter of appeal from five female kolkhoz farmers in Ivanovo Oblast to *Krest'ianskaia Gazeta*, 21 November 1938. RGAE, f. 396, op. 11, d. 19, ll. 323–324. Original manuscript.

A Hooligan is Being Concealed

Former kolkhoz chairman N. Kh. Panteleev of the Stalin Kolkhoz under the Gorkinsky Village Soviet in Yur'ev-Pol'sky Raion, Ivanovo Oblast, abused kolkhoz farmers in every way, scolded them with foul language and called them thieves. He hit the kolkhoz accountant a woman and a herdsboy. He called some women thieves. Like he scolded Anna Matveevna Osipova right at the general meeting: "Bitch, thief, pilferer," and she is not guilty of anything. This kolkhoz chairman N. Kh. Panteleev engaged in padding of labordays in his favor and appropriated fifty-six rubles of kolkhoz money. Because of him a horse died, a seven-year-old mare. One girl on our kolkhoz stated that this kolkhoz chairman N. Kh. Panteleev tried to rape her, and the militia station made them confront each other. And now a year will soon have passed, but all the cases have been covered up. An investigation was under way for six months, the investigation ended, the file was turned over to the procurator of [the town of] Yur'ev-Pol'sky, but it has been lying in the procurator's office for two months and the whole case has faded away. And this hooligan brags and taunts us women: "Whatever rottin things you do to me, nothin will ever happen to me and I will never be locked up."

We women ask for help through *Krest'ianskaia Gazeta* to start legal proceedings against this hooligan for his abuse of women, for beating the accountant and for all his wicked actions, we ask you to look for all of the lowdown things he has done.

Signed: [five signatures by female kolkhoz farmers]

An enormous number of letters touch on the problem of bribe-taking and self-supply by chairmen from kolkhoz granaries. By bribing the chairman, somebody could get firewood or coal, mow some hay for himself, obtain a horse, and so on. On the basis of deceit, corruption, and drunkenness, the village and raion administrations covered up for each other, something that could not escape the notice of kolkhoz farmers. In one letter, which was headed "They Drink Vodka Day and Night Like There's No Tomorrow" and was sent to a deputy of the Supreme Soviet, two kolkhoz farmers who said they were "exhausted from writing" described how investigators responded to their complaint that "a *zafatchik* [*zakhvatchik,* invader], a kulak's son, mowed more for a bribe than he was supposed to": "an instructor arrived, they filled him up with vodka, and he forgot about his job and lost his mind." He showed the complaint to the board members, and "they laughed awhile, and lambasted us." And with that he took the complaint back home. Then "the deputy head of the raion farming department came, he also drank some vodka too and he left without doing anything too." After that "the first alcoholic was sent again, and he got even more drunk the second time."[22]

One archive file contains a set of letters from Dmitry Afanas'evich Khalatov, a rather interesting storyteller. The letters help to determine a few facts about his background. He was a member of the Labor Kolkhoz in Zhizdra Raion, Orel Oblast, which he joined in 1929. At first, he writes, "we led a wealthy and fun-filled life, but since then we have had eleven chairmen, who have spelled disaster for the kolkhoz and kolkhoz farmers." Sometimes measures were taken in response to his calls for help. But that made the raion and local administrations angry at him. With a blacksmith's vocation and a wife and six children, he "reached the limit with this bad life, left the kolkhoz," and in late 1936 went to work on the railroad in Briansk. From that time on he visited the kolkhoz on his days off and observed the life of his and neighboring kolkhozes, reporting to various bodies on how they were being victimized by thieves and embezzlers. That was apparently why Khalatov's family and his two brothers were expelled from the kolkhoz in September 1937 as kulaks and wreckers. But, Khalatov writes, "If I am a wrecker, then I could do more wrecking in transportation than on a kolkhoz. In point of fact I am a dedicated nonparty Bolshevik, as Soviet law and Stalin's constitution allow. In my family my wife worked, my daughter worked as director of a nursery school, and I had four working schoolchildren, and on my days off I worked, too, at a smithy. Altogether we earned 450 labordays."[23]

Khalatov regularly wrote about troubles not only at his own kolkhoz but also at surrounding ones, which, he said, were "on an equal footing with ours like brothers."[24] For instance, in a letter of 26 January 1938, he wrote that after frequent changes of chairmen the May Day Kolkhoz was taken over by M. N. Kondrashev, a former accountant, "a friend and pal of I. N. Larin, a leftist Socialist Revolutionary who was put away by the Soviet authorities." Khalatov accused this Kondrashev of every mortal sin. The accusations included some that were not unsubstantiated. Here is what he reported:

---

## Document 120

Letter from D. A. Khalatov to *Krest'ianskaia Gazeta* on abuses on kolkhoz in Orel Oblast, 26 January 1938. RGAE, f. 396, op. 5, d. 110, l. 161. Corrected, certified copy.

---

Tractor driver Kirill Vasil'evich Lun'kin works at the Zhizdra MTS. He had to bring his earnings from the kolkhoz: grain and potatoes to his family. The problem was horses. Vasily Lun'kin, the tractor driver's father, couldn't get horses at his May Day Kolkhoz. Then he invited the whole board to his home, served them wine with snacks, as much as they could take in. The drunken board led by Kondrashev decided to give Lun'kin four wagons, but the next day, when he came to get a note authorizing the horses, he was allowed only two horses, and whatever he could not transport, he was told, he could sell on the spot. Lun'kin agreed to that. The offended drayman went to the corral with the note and showed it to the stable boy Zaitsev. Another dead end here. Zaitsev demanded a quarter-bucket of vodka for each horse. That was paid and Lun'kin got two horses. Pyotr Dmitrievich Talalaev, who is serving in the Red Army, visited his wife, then went back. A long time after her husband [had left] the Red Army man's wife Yefrosin'ia Ivanovna gave birth, and after she recovered some she was hit by winter. Yefrosin'ia got a document to take a horse and fuel. She went to the stable boy Zaitsev. Like the law, Zaitsev was not shy about asking two quarter-buckets from the Red Army man's wife. . . .

---

Khalatov's numerous reports and a request by *Krest'ianskaia Gazeta* for an investigation met with this response from the Orel Obkom: "An inquiry established that Khalatov comes from a family of merchants. He has a dishonest attitude toward work, was exposed for stealing kolkhoz property and engaged in corrupting

activities on the kolkhoz, for which he was expelled from it. Khalatov's brother Yefim is under arrest by the NKVD." Nevertheless,
the complaint was taken up, and the secretary of the raion party
committee was ousted from his job "for keeping silent."[25]

A letter from Komsomol member V. I. Guliaev to *Krest'ianskaia
Gazeta* described the way kolkhoz administrations treated new
settlers. He was representing not just himself but a group of
kolkhoz farmers who had arrived on the New Ear of Wheat
Kolkhoz in Sivashsky Raion, Dnepropetrovsk Oblast. To lend
weight to his "statement," the writer made abundant and inappropriate use of bureaucratic phrases and expressions, and in addition
he failed to insert a single comma. To make the letter at all comprehensible, we have supplied this deficiency:

---

## Document 121

Letter from V. I. Guliaev to *Krest'ianskaia Gazeta* on reception of new settlers in Dnepropetrovsk Oblast, 20 June 1937. RGAE, f. 396, op. 10, d. 33, ll. 136–137ob. Original manuscript.

---

Statement
I, Vasily Ivanovich Guliaev, came to the New Ear of Wheat Kolkhoz from
Gor'ky Oblast, and a number of families have also come from other oblasts.
When we arrived at the kolkhoz, the kolkhoz board promised the new settlers
it would provide them with all food and grain, and with apartments as well.
As a result it turned out that the kolkhoz board began to treat the new kolkhoz
farmers in a bureaucratic manner, to wit: instead of apartments, the families
were housed in stables, as a result of which small children are taking sick and
are dying. In addition, the kolkhoz has nursery schools where the children of
new settlers are treated in a predatory way, to wit: my wife and I were at work
in the steppe about four kilometers from the hut, and the children were in
nursery school. At twelve noon the nannies released a two-year-old boy by
himself, who had to walk home from the nursery school for about a kilometer,
which it is unknown how he arrived home and found the way by himself, but
when he arrived he could not get into the hut, in view of the fact that it was
locked. He sat down in front of the hut and started screaming, i.e. crying.
Thanks to the fact that a neighbor heard him crying and took him into her
apartment, otherwise the boy could have sat crying in front of the hut until
evening. After which the boy is still sick to the present time. And besides that,
an eight-month-old boy was allowed to catch a chill at the nursery school and

the boy died. And when the children were sick and I went to the head of the kolkhoz and asked him to give me a liter of milk for the sick children, he did not even attent the words. And if any new settlers were given an apartment not in a stable, the head of the kolkhoz, having foisted it on kolkhoz farmer Karpukhin for eight hundred rubles after the kolkhoz bought it from the village soviet for two hundred rubles, after which he also put a tenint there, and the head of the kolkhoz told Karpukhin, kick out tenint Cheprov, but he told Cheprov don't leave, i.e. he cauzed trouble between kolkhoz farmers, who go at each other with knives, and a board member is brazen, he is also the business manager, he goes around to the newly arrived kolkhoz farmers, telling them that, if you have money, buy huts from them on the kolkhoz, and if you don't have money, you can be out of the kolkhoz, we don't need you, and the head of the kolkhoz says the same thing. And if [a new settler] comes to the board for food, it does not treat them quite nicely, declaring to the newly arrived kolkhoz farmer that we accepted you not to supply you but for work, so you must buy the grain, as a result of which kolkhoz farmers are hungry are not going out to work, and ten families of newly arrived kolkhoz farmers had to move from the kolkhoz to other kolkhozes. In regards to all this the kolkhoz farmers went to the raion and the village soviet, but there are no improvements on the part of the kolkhoz leadership. There is no accounting on the kolkhoz, labordays are not written down for kolkhoz farmers, and when a kolkhoz farmer wants to ask, he spends weeks going to the board and gets no result.

In addition, the brigade leaders on the kolkhoz abuse the newly arrived kolkhoz farmers. [A description follows of beatings of kolkhoz farmers administered by brigade leader Kalinkin.] Kalinkin forces the wives of new settlers into sexual relations, saying to them that you don't go to work, I will write down labordays for you, and if you don't have sexual intercourse with me, then I won't write down labordays for you at all. And it is brigade leader Kalinkin who is not giving a dwelling on the kolkhoz to new settler Aleksandra Guliaeva [evidently the wife of the letter writer], he comes to her apartment, forces her into sexual intercourse, who stopped staying in the apartment by herself, stating to her husband that I will not live here. And besides that there are other abominations as well.

---

In close proximity with the village administration was the so-called rural intelligentsia: schoolteachers, doctors, livestock experts, managers of cultural clubs, village librarians, and the like. This was the most literate, educated, and youthful segment of the rural population. A sizable number of rural correspondents were recruited from this milieu. One example was Andrei Ivanovich

Poluektov, a staff rural correspondent for the Voronezh Oblast newspaper *Kommuna* [Commune] and the raion newspaper in the town of Pavlovsk, *Krepi Kolkhoz* [Strengthen the kolkhoz]. After he became dissatisfied with his success in this job, he decided to write to the central *Krest'ianskaia Gazeta.*[26] But let us give him the floor:

---

## Document 122

Letter from A. I. Poluektov to *Krest'ianskaia Gazeta* on his life and Dzerzhinsky Kolkhoz, Voronezh Oblast, 10 November 1938. RGAE, f. 396, op. 10, d. 19, ll. 189–1950b. Original manuscript.

---

More than a year ago has passed [*sic*] since I wrote a letter to *Krest'ianskaia Gazeta* about our achievements in agriculture in 1937. The editors answered me, thanked me for the letter, and asked me to write more about the good, as well as the bad, which must be rooted out, but I just did not dare to answer you until now for the following reason: I, Andrei Ivanovich Poluektov, am a member of the Dzerzhinsky Kolkhoz in Losevo Raion, Voronezh Oblast working at present as head of the laboratory-hut [an agronomy station, typically run by nonprofessionals, for preparing seeds for sowing and disseminating information and propaganda among kolkhoz farmers] and biolaboratory. First I will describe the capacity of our kolkhoz to you, and then the reason for my silence. In the middle of 1929 our kolkhoz was established by Red Army men who had come from Briansk Gubernia and who served in the city of Voronezh in the Dzerzhinsky Commune, which included the little village of Tumanovka, as it was called under the landowner Tushnev, with fifty-five to sixty farmsteads, and the neighboring village of Livenka three km away, where the village soviet is located, with 1,500 farmsteads. But when the floodwaters receded in the spring of 1930 all of the neighboring villages dropped out and all that remained in the Dzerzhinsky Commune was the little village of Tumanovka, along with the Red Army men's five families. In addition, each Red Army man brought in his relatives from Briansk and [so] there were twelve families. The aforesaid commune in the village of Tumanovka occupied the land area of former landowner I. D. Tushnev, of which there was 650 hectares and thirty-three hectares of fruit gardens, plus twenty-nine hectares of barren land. In addition, there were the farmsteads of the landowners Mazurin and Sviridov, whose land was in other locations, as well as a forest, which after the revolution was added to the Shipovsky Forestry Management Enterprise. The area of the commune itself is situated next to the Shipovsky Forest, famous for its shipbuilding wood, borders the commune on three sides, except for the western side from the village of Livenka, in 1931 four families [came in] from the raion center, the settlement of Losevo, and in 1932 five families came from other raions, so in 1933 there were already more than 120 families. Most of the arable land is flat, consists of black soil and is fertile, and there is also twenty hectares of dry-valley meadowland and two hectares of wooded shrubbery.

With regard to socialized livestock, commune members and the commune have established these animal-husbandry sections: a commercial dairy farm with seventy-five cows, a hog-breeding farm with a hundred hogs, a sheep-breeding farm with 150 sheep, a commercial beekeeping farm with two hundred bee colonies, and sixty-five horses. In 1931, structures socialized by the commune members on a completely new site were used to build a fine stable for one hundred horses, a cowshed for 120 cows, a pigpen for 150 hogs, a winter apiary for 150 colonies, twelve storehouses, a grain-milling facility, a hulling mill and a mechanical creamery that was driven by a motor from which a dynamo electrically illuminated an office, a school, a club, a dormitory for twenty families, and all of the livestock-breeding farms. The club had a standard film projector, there was also a brickyard that produced up to two hundred thousand burned bricks, a fruit dryer, a greenhouse for growing early vegetables, and there was also a breeding farm that yielded twenty-five thousand to thirty thousand roots a year of fruit seed stock, which contained the best varieties of apples and peaches. Recently they have also developed Michurin varieties, of which there are more than two hundred apple-tree roots.

In 1934 the commune converted to the statutes of the agricultural artel, after which all of the kolkhoz farmers who had arrived were each allotted half a hectare of vegetable gardens, and for those who were still socializing their structures, the kolkhoz used its own funds to build houses as well on the newly formed street. In this manner the kolkhoz doubled its size during the collectivization period. In addition to the foregoing, there were also three Fordson tractors [designed by engineers from the Ford Motor Company, Fordson-Putilovets (FP) tractors were produced at Leningrad's Red Putilovets factory between 1931 and 1934], three engines of ten, twelve, and eighteen horsepower, and a complex thresher. When the MTS was established, the commune turned in one engine, three tractors, and a thresher.

Thus, for the eight years of collectivization the kolkhoz has consisted of the following: 140 families, seventy-five horses, forty-five cows, twenty head of young cattle, eighteen pairs of working bulls, two hundred sheep, 120 hogs, 250 bee colonies, and two hundred chickens, plus, at the personal disposal of kolkhoz farmers, a hundred cows, 150 sheep, five hundred chickens, 120 hogs, and twelve bee colonies—in short, the kolkhoz became Bolshevik, and its farmers became prosperous. This was in fact because the kolkhoz actually placed first in all of the raion's campaigns throughout the years of collectivization, but in 1938 our kolkhoz ran last in the raion in all of its operations.

It would seem from the economic position of our kolkhoz as described above that there is nowhere we kolkhoz farmers would rather live, but in point of fact the exact opposite is true.

What on earth were the factors that slowed down the favorable economic growth of our kolkhoz? The reasons were as follows:

1. From the very early days of the commune's establishment and to this day the hostility has continued unabated between the old residents of the village of Tumanovka, who saw three families dekulakized and exiled during collectivization and whose closest relatives remained, and the new families that arrived and established the commune. They often hurl abuse at each other, and the old-timers say: "The devil must have brought you here, if it hadn't been for you, there wouldn't even be a kolkhoz here," so the new residents tell the old-timers: "This isn't your landowner Tushnev who you worshiped like God and stole whatever you wanted from him."

The Dzerzhinsky Kolkhoz was ethnically Russian and the founders of the commune were ethnic Russians. We Ukrainians had four families that arrived from the settlement of Losevo and to this day we are called "khokhly" [a derogatory term for Ukrainians, derived from the word for "topknot," a reference to the Cossack hair style—*Trans.*], despite the fact that while the Voronezh NKVD was still acting as patron of the commune in its early days, an NKVD representative said at a general meeting of all kolkhoz farmers that ethnic dissension on a kolkhoz is harmful, but it still continues to this day. "You khokhly, the devil made you come here," some kolkhoz farmers say. In addition, the new street which has been settled by about sixty farmsteads, has been named May Day Street, but the old-timers of the village of Tumanovka never call it by that name but have dubbed it "Devil's Horn" and in every conversation that is all we hear: "Devil's Horn," "Let's go to Devil's Horn," and so forth.

2. Since 1933 there has been no suitable person for the job of chairman, which has seen four people come and go, and all of them were self-suppliers, kept toadies and embezzlers around them, etc. Take the following conduct as an example. In 1933 chairman V. Ye. Kuznetsov was ousted by the raion organizations for the fact that he rode to the apiary on a trotter horse and the bees there stung it to death. In 1934 another [chairman] M. D. Rusanov this one started to do some hard drinking and go around to different women. The MTS politotdel [*politicheskii otdel*, political department] ousted him too, and after Rusanov the raion organizations also appointed G. I. Boiko, who seemed to be all right as a manager, but his personality did not please the kolkhoz farmers, and nearly every party member asked the raikom to remove him, which they did. He was removed, and they say that he later turned out to be a Trotskyist. Next after him the MTS recommended the deputy director of the MTS, but he also turned out to be a self-supplier and embezzler, and when he resigned, the court fined him 750 rubles. After him the general meeting again elected

the former chairman Kuznetsov, who also turned out to be dishonest and the party organization lambasted him, as a result of which the People's Court sentenced him at the end of 1937 to two years, and he served out his punishment in the first half of 1938 and is already living at home. After Kuznetsov Comrade K. V. Nikul'shin, a candidate member, and since April 1938 a full member of the party, has been on the job for all of 1938. He is a man who is devoted to Soviet rule and is trying to do well for the kolkhoz, but for some reasons his work is going very badly, and as I indicated above, [the kolkhoz] is running shamefully behind all of the kolkhozes in every campaign in the raion. Comrade Nikul'shin himself is from the neighboring village of Livenka, from which our kolkhoz has up to thirty families and even has relatives of his, for whom he makes allowances, of course, which causes bitterness among the other kolkhoz farmers. Discipline has grown lax. In spite of the fact that there has been good weather for the whole summer, the harvest has been protracted, the fall plowing for spring planting is still not finished, the fodder for the threshing barns has not been collected from the fields, the threshing barns are empty, and the chaff in the field is getting soaked by the rain half a kilometer away. There is enough winter fodder for the livestock to last only half the winter, and the leaves in the forest have not been collected and the forest is a kilometer away. The winter livestock buildings have still not been prepared and some have not even been puttied. All of the agricultural equipment is scattered about and the kids are ruining it, and all the mowers and winnowing machines with sifters are sitting out in the rain. There is a nice bathhouse, but it has not been heated for more than half a year, and the kolkhoz farmers have forgotten when they last bathed there, and instead they go to Uncle Afonia and ask him to let them into his bathhouse. [Nikul'shin] does not take advice from kolkhoz farmers and does everything on his own authority, without asking either the board members or a general meeting of kolkhoz farmers. For example, he began in the spring, of his own accord, to move the brickyard to another ravine, which has clay and sand, but everybody knows that clay is not good for bricks. Now there were two sheds under way: the carpenters worked for a whole month, and they did not make it before the winter so they began to pull them down. One shed is almost down on the old site, and they are starting to pull down the second one. The furnace is half-collapsed. In 1938 the factory did not operate and bricks were brought in from other villages. According to the estimate of revenue and expenses, they overspent by seventeen thousand, for which the procurator announced in the local raion newspaper as far back as June that he would put the chairman and accountant on trial, but there has still been no word about it, and at the insistence of raion functionaries S. P. Bobrovsky and S. I. Bobrovsky a reprimand for all the crimes was delivered during the third-quarter report. [An account follows of the depletion of livestock and other violations by Nikul'shin of kolkhoz regulations.]

# Document 122 *continued*

As the kolkhoz chairman and a board member of the Livenka village cooperative store, [Nikul'shin] set up another man from Livenka in a stall to sell his wares—S. A. Krynin, who was a livestock breeder in 1932 and squandered fifty-one pigs, for which he was convicted [*sic*] for five years, but he served out his punishment in two years, was expelled from the kolkhoz and has still not been readmitted, but is living on the kolkhoz and is selling his wares at the stall not on the board's say-so but on the kolkhoz chairman's say-so, as a result of which all of S. A. Krynin's children have clothing and shoes, while a widow from Briansk, whose husband Comrade F. A. Zaitsev was a party member and died back when the commune was being established, simply cannot manage to get even one outfit for her three schoolchildren, and they, incidentally, were available.

There have been plenty of other abominations, but even they would not be enough to prompt an investigation and put a stop to them. Incidentally, the kolkhoz farmers are writing about all these abominations to the raion newspaper *Krepi Kolkhoz* and to the Voronezh Oblast newspaper *Kommuna,* but so far there have been absolutely no results, so I decided to write to the central *Krest'ianskaia Gazeta.* I hope it will put an stop to these abominations, which are bringing down our kolkhoz.

[It is immediately apparent that Andrei Poluektov is an uncommonly observant man, but unquestionably a typical son of his times. The writer regards ethnic frictions as one of the reasons for the unsatisfactory state of affairs on the kolkhoz. But the problem lay not so much in ethnic background as in the persistence of the old communal mentality, the division of people into "our own" villagers and the newcomers, who were "outsiders." Part of the blame for what had occurred in the countryside in recent years, naturally, was pinned on the latter group. The newcomers, in turn, were struck much more by the nepotism, favoritism, and mutual cover-ups that had found their way from the old countryside into kolkhoz life. By and large, the newcomers were far more sensitive to the outrages that were perpetrated in the countryside and wrote about them to newspapers, deepening the mutual hostility, and if matters reached the point where they criticized the administration, there was no end to the ensuing persecution. Yet Poluektov sees the main reason for the collapse of kolkhoz operations in the personnel problem, the endless shuffling of chairmen and the inept conduct by the various farm managers. Also of interest is the autobiographical portion of the letter:]

Now I will talk about myself as a person and why I moved from Losevo to the Dzerzhinsky Kolkhoz.

I am a peasant from the settlement of Losevo, I lived in the center of the settlement. My father was a poor man, he had a seasonal job driving logging rafts from Kalach down the Don River to Rostov. I was born in 1886. Before 1897 I graduated from the rural school and in 1898, egged on by my father, I went to work as an apprentice to the merchant Mikhail Yegorovich Mikushin in the town of Pavlovsk on the Don, served for more than two years with him for nothing, as was the arrangement at the time or was the system for compensating apprentices, that in exchange for learning how to sell wares, boys came and worked for nothing. After I worked for the merchant for more than two years, my father took me home from the merchant in the winter of 1900, you are all I have, he says, and you are having a hard time here, all covered with tar, kerosene, and coal: the shop was filthy. When I moved to Losevo, and we got into agriculture, in the summer a fire broke out by accident at the mill in the beginning of August already, and the fire burned down 450 farmsteads— almost the whole center of the settlement, and our whole property also burned down to the foundation, since we lived pretty close to where the fire started. Besides our real property, all of the personal property we had in livestock burned up, as well as all our belongings in the hut. My father and I were eight km away at the time. Left with one mare that had one eye, which we immediately sold for seventeen rubles, as I recall it today, we moved to live with my grandfather on my mother's side. He was a solid middle peasant, and I made an arrangement with a local merchant again and started working for him right up until the Russo-German war, from whom I was taken for the war in 1916. After the fire and until the war my father and I earned enough to buy a horse and a cow, and we also built a hut: the front room was made of wood, and the second was all made of pickets. During my service [with the merchant] I had no ambition to work in agriculture anymore, and I began to study commerce. I subscribed to magazines on merchandising and, in addition, subscribed to bookkeeping courses, which I completed already before the war, but I wasn't able to get an accounting job, since I was taken for the war. My father, though, kept pushing me into agriculture, and when the Stolypin law on securing individual land allotments came out, my father secured three allotments: his, my mother's, and mine. [The land reform of 9 November 1906 was designed by Prime Minister P. A. Stolypin to facilitate the establishment of individual peasant holdings in place of communal tenure.] I started arguing with my father that I didn't need it, but the law gave fathers the right to not even get their children's consent to secure. So even now some kolkhoz farmers, whom I insult in the newspaper or at a general meeting over infractions, call me a Stolypinite because of my father's action, and they threaten me, we'll teach you. Some even claim out of spite that I went into hiding from the Losevo settlement so that they would not touch me there, but the situation is completely different and does not pertain to what my enemies accuse me of.

During the war I went through a training detachment and was promoted to junior noncommissioned officer and tried to gain favor with the old-time commanders, but when the February Revolution came I was in a reinforcement company with the 189th infantry regiment, which was posted in the city of Mtsensk in Orel Gubernia and I met a factory worker from Moscow by the name of Sergeev, who explained the importance of the February Revolution

## Document 122 *continued*

to me. [Note the parallel with the encounter of P. P. Sergeev (unrelated) with a draft dodger (p. 318)]. I attached myself to him, and the company elected us the first deputies to the soldiers' assembly, and when our company was sent to the front, I was elected as well by the front company committee to the cultural and educational commission of the 2d Finland rifle regiment and as librarian of a machine gun detachment, where I began to read contemporary revolutionary literature. I delivered a speech at a revolutionary rally during the Kerenshchina [a derogatory term for the period of the Provisional Government headed by Aleksandr Kerensky—*Trans.*], for which they wanted to arrest me, but I went into hiding, for the rally of the two regiments took place in the forest. A witness to this—my comrade in Losevo—is still alive. I spoke against the offensive, against the continuation of the war. Before the October Revolution our regiment headed for Petrograd to defend the Provisional bourgeois government, but on the way it broke up over Bolshevism and stopped at Shklov station, where it stayed until the demobilization after the October Revolution. Upon being demobilized I came to Losevo settlement, where I actively began to participate in revolutionary affairs, after which I was elected to the first Losevo Village Soviet. In the village soviet I was elected to the commission for confiscation of bourgeois property, where the first thing I did was to confiscate the property of my [former] master. While the front was shifting I hid from the Cossacks, and when they took off and the Red Army men came to our area, I went back into soviet [work]. My little brother first joined the Red Guard, then the Red Army, where he served for seven years and he was accused because of [our] father too, they didn't believe he was a partisan. In 1919 I was at the Pavlovsk Uezd Congress of Soviets, after which I stayed to serve in the town of Pavlovsk and held various positions all the way up to head of the Ukusprom under the Uezd National Economy [Bureau of Cottage Industry under the uezd council of the national economy]. I served in Pavlovsk for three years. Before serving in Pavlovsk I put together a family of sixteen people and life was very hard for me in Pavlovsk, where I had only four children, the rest were in Losevo. I was starving terribly and had to leave my job in Pavlovsk and moved to Losevo. At the time I had neither a horse nor a cow. During my service in Pavlovsk we, four comrades from Losevo, established a kolkhoz of fifteen households and during a raid by the Kolesnikov band on Losevo one of our kolkhoz farmers was murdered by the band in the center of Losevo in the square, while we, the founders, were still working in Pavlovsk. When we all arrived in Losevo after the band left, we were unable to save our kolkhoz, the whole thing fell apart—all the kolkhoz farmers handed in their notices of withdrawal from it. That was in 1922. But the uezd organizations would not let us leave Pavlovsk at the time. The uezd party organization was inviting all office employees to join the party, but my comrade with whom I shared an apartment so destroyed my desire that I tore up the application, and it later turned out that this comrade was dekulakized and deported to Karaganda. Of course, I subsequently realized the party's role in the socialist revolution and reapplied, but the application was not examined with me there and one comrade, as I was told afterward, criticized me for my Stolypinite father. With that, the matter just dried up. When I moved to Losevo, I was immediately elected a board member of the Losevo Credit Association, where it was reorganized along Soviet lines. I organized commerce on behalf of the credit association as a specialist in this area, where I engaged in commerce for a year, and then I was a member of the auditing commission of the credit association for two years, and then I was elected a member of the auditing commission of the Losevo Raion Consumers' Union, where I worked for two years. During collectivization I joined the Red Village Kolkhoz in 1929, worked for the three fall months as an accountant, and then in January 1930 during full-scale collectivization the kolkhoz was renamed Red Losevo and I was elected a board member of the kolkhoz and deputy chairman. During the exodus [from kolkhozes in the spring of 1930] the board was reelected, and I was again elected deputy chairman and manager of plot no. 1 of the kolkhoz in the center of Losevo settlement—more than five hundred farmsteads. After a year's work on the kolkhoz, where I was one of the first to socialize agricultural equipment and draft animals, I was reelected again as a member of the kolkhoz auditing commission. The party organization gave me the principal accounting work for the Losevo farmers' cooperative store.

I had two sons—both tractor drivers. One of them worked almost a year on a tractor, and the other, a Red Army man, took tractor courses, and then the chairman of the Dzerzhinsky commune started trying to lure them to the commune, after which they agreed to go with the consent of the raikom, since Losevo had extra tractor drivers and the commune did not have enough. After they worked there in 1931, they were invited to become members of the commune and in August 1931 they were enrolled. Then the chairman began to invite me as well into the commune. When I agreed, the commune board demanded that I be removed from my job at the Losevo cooperative store and that I come work for them, which I did on 10 January 1932. First I worked as a field-crop specialist [*polevod*] for two years, then as manager of the commercial dairy farm, then as secretary of the board for two years, and after that the MTS appointed me manager of the laboratory hut, which I also established, and in 1938 the oblast land department added a biology lab to the laboratory hut. Throughout my time on the Dzerzhinsky Kolkhoz I was very active in studies for kolkhoz farmers, for two years I led an agricultural study group, a member of a drama group, a member of a choir, and then I was a member of all the voluntary societies: the MOPR, Radio Amateurs, Down with Illiteracy, and Osoaviakhim. I have made all voluntary and compulsory payments to the state ahead of the others since 1920. Recently the newspaper *Krepi Kolkhoz* has announced more than once that I have made my payments ahead of schedule. At present I am in a deputies' group of the Livenka Village Soviet in the commerce and procurement section. I am also a rural correspondent for my kolkhoz wall newspaper, for the raion newspaper *Krepi Kolkhoz* and the oblast's *Kommuna* in Voronezh. I have endured a great deal of financial losses in my family due to my work as a rural correspondent. In early 1938 I was elected a member of the editorial board of the kolkhoz wall newspaper. I organized work on the wall newspaper so well that the newspaper *Krepi Kolkhoz* cited it a week ago as one of the best wall newspapers in the raion. I complained to *Krepi Kolkhoz* about harassment against me in my work as rural correspondent. Nothing comes of it, because the party organizer or the chairman is summoned to the raion, and they deny everything, so I am to blame again. Next I turned to the oblast procurator, but so far I see no results. With regard to the kolkhoz farmers for whom the kolkhoz was supposed to build houses, as I indicated above, they were built illegally, which I wrote about to the newspapers, but the situation has not been corrected and has created quite a lot of bitterness. My stories, which I wrote for *Krepi Kolkhoz,* I write them openly and I properly sign my name. I feel that the truth must be written everywhere and all over and I am carrying out the words of Comrade Stalin that the press is the most powerful weapon, which uproots all malingerers, self-suppliers, blabbermouths, usurpers, and wreckers. That is why I do everything this way. But those people who stand against the truth, they have become so surrounded by untruth that even a twelve-inch cannon will not get through to them, because they have such an army of toadies that when you start to speak the truth they interpret it as the opposite and even brand you a counterrevolutionary.

A week ago I was elected a member of the auditing commission, they wanted to elect me chairman, but I said I was working as manager of the biolab hut and it was very difficult for me, then they replaced me with someone else, a tractor driver, and the general meeting issued an order to audit all sections of the kolkhoz, because there has not been a proper audit on the kolkhoz from the beginning of the commune to this day, and that is why, I feel, the kolkhoz is falling apart. I will carry out this task, of course, but I need help from above. If I don't get any, it will come out the way it came out in 1932, when the auditing commission began to do a thorough audit and to affect certain people, it came under the purview of the NKVD and was locked up for two months, while the enemies celebrated.

10 November 1938

Poluektov's biography depicts to some extent the life of a non-party economic leader who is loyal to the authorities. And yet, if one judges by the fact that the writer regrets not joining the party and afterward is hampered in this objective by his Stolypinite father (in the usual lexicon, a "kulak," and of a prewar vintage at that), his ambitions extend further, which apparently explains, to a large degree, his itch to be a correspondent.

The letters contain a great many examples of the rural intelligentsia nobly and honestly serving the cause, but there is a fair amount of evidence pointing to the opposite. Letter writer Yefim Koniukh, a village schoolteacher, wrote in this regard to *Krest'ianskaia Gazeta:*

---

## Document 123

Letter of denunciation from village schoolteacher Ye. Koniukh to *Krest'ianskaia Gazeta*, 18 February 1938. RGAE, f. 396, op. 11, d. 49, ll. 208–209. Corrected, certified copy.

---

Esteemed Comrade Editor!

I am writing to you with the following question. Will you argue with these facts?

A Soviet schoolteacher is the figure whom the party, Soviet authority and the entire people have entrusted with an honorable task—the task of educating the rising generation in the spirit of communism, raising a patriot and at the same time instilling fine human qualities in students. If not, then you cannot deny the fact that the teacher himself must be an example for children.

We have (albeit rare) "specimens" that serve as an example, but this example has nothing in common with a person who not only carries the title of teacher, but with a Soviet person, either.

It is impossible to keep quiet about this matter. V. I. Tolstov, the principal of the Dubrova village NSSh [incomplete secondary school] in Lamsky Raion, Riazan' Oblast, is a very "prudent" man. At a teachers' conference on 6 February 1938 he laid down an ultimatum for teachers: "I categorically forbid teachers to stroll on the street after 10 P.M., otherwise I will hit the ceiling."

But he does such outrageous things himself. In 1937 he worked in the settlement of Paslovka, got "married," lived that way for three months and for some reason became a bachelor again. He came to Dubrova village as a bachelor to take the principal's position, got "married" again, except not for the entire day but only "for nights." The woman became pregnant by him, and when she saw that he would not marry her, she had an abortion and is ill. In the past Tolstov said to her: "I am studying you," but now he has refused her once and for all: "I am married, my wife is coming to join me soon." These facts do not outrage the manager of the Lamsky Raion Public Education Department, which Tolstov petitioned to transfer a female teacher from the Lelenovskaia NSSh to the Dubrova NSSh, on the grounds that he wants to marry her. But

Tolstov has said, I will marry her (I just won't register), I'll live [with her] until the spring, and then I'll kick her out.

Let Tolstov get married with the awareness that his actions also have an effect on the students.

This outrageous action elicits no response from the raion organizations.

---

The document attests more to a general breakdown of family principles and an incipient, sanctimonious, and hypocritical struggle to reinforce them. Other letters are full of complaints from abandoned women and of requests to track down men who are not paying alimony. The campaign to reinforce marriage was often manifested merely in an obligation to "register"—to endorse the marriage certificate with signatures. Young female teachers, who appeared in the countryside in abundance, often became the targets of sexual demands.

Correspondence between various official bodies contains a huge number of documents from village activists, from people who "by their mere existence have proven the correctness of the party line." A great many letters on various topics came in from front-rank production workers, "the Stakhanovites of the kolkhoz and sovkhoz fields." On the eve of the Stakhanovite era, the Department of Meat and Dairy Sovkhozes of the People's Commissariat of State Farms (Narkomsovkhoz) and the three corresponding trade unions of sovkhoz workers launched a contest for best production achievements in animal husbandry. A specially formed Central Contest Commission (TsKK) toted up the results of the contest in the spring of 1935 and handed out prizes to a number of front-rank production workers. They included Vladimir Afanas'evich Sychov, a senior herdsman at Armavir dairy and meat sovkhoz no. 32. The TsKK awarded him four hundred rubles in cash and a hunting shotgun. At the same time the leadership of the meat and dairy sovkhoz workers' union of the Center and South (essentially covering the European part of the Soviet Union) decided to get better acquainted with the winners of the contest and initiated a correspondence with them, asking them to write about themselves, their families and—most unusually—their needs.[27] As a result the following letter arrived from V. A. Sychov:

# Document 124

Letter from livestock and dairy sovkhoz worker V. A. Sychov to Odintsov, 13 September 1935. GARF, f. 7689, op. 11, d. 50, ll. 34–36. Original manuscript.

Livestock Breeder Sovkhoz no. 32. Section 1. Herd 1.
Sychov.
13 September 1935.
Deer Comrade Odinchov [Odintsov].

I give great thanks to the Ts.K.K. for the prizes awarded to me and in the future I pledge to wirk even better as I did to strugle for [reproduction] of the herd and fulfillment of all state plans and to bring all the lagging herds up to the forefront;

I have worked on the sovkhoz since 5 May 1930. [Here, as elsewhere, punctuation has been added to facilitate comprehension.] My family I have with me four members a Mother a brother and my wife. My wife worked as a milkmaid until 1 September and on 1 September she went to dismissal. My brother gos to school in the seventh grade in the town of Armavir. Our wages were an averige of 220 rubles [per month].

My herd left the section I went with it to the full steppe where I built with a brigade a House of four rooms of which I occupy one. The setup in the room is a table and two chairs. A wooden bed etc. Because we seldom go to town, the setup in the room is unenviable. In regard to footwear our situation is bad. The brigade is all barefoot because we have noware to buy, we buy at artisans who have socks three to five days, and we pay alot of money at the Cooperative. We have nothing not even matches.

Us people with the herds don't get any food in the summer period excep tomatos and cabbige but we have that ourselves in our gardens, I had a garden but we had a drout so we harvested very little from it.

I have the following livestock: two pigs one sleepy hog and a wild boar. There is 1 wild boar with the herd which we will slauter in a months. I have chickens and nothing else. As for fodder for the hogs they dont give us anything we buy at the bazar to feed them.

I myself was born Voronezh guberni. Born 1907 cant read or write much finished third class in the village [school]. Right now we dont have tech. training and probaly wont But in future I want to learn and raise my seniority since I dont know anything besides practical work because nobody trains us.

I dont feel sick at all excep I have some weakness that I dont have anything to fix it either from not enough fats or from my herd being restless. Now I report on my production work. I have in my herd a hundred head of cattle of which eighty-four head calved, all the calves at the presint time are alive and none is sick. There will be late calving. I will have november december calving twelve head. The calves now are not allowed to suckle, they are fed milk by hand and the ones that were suckling we already weaned them from the

## Document 124 *continued*

mothers and the cows are giving milk without the calves. So far I havint had a seasonal job during the winter and summer period. The plan for milk deliveries is not getting fulfilled. In the first six months I fulfilled and overfulfilled the plan but in the second six months it was fulfilled to 55–60 percent only because we had a severe drout and theres no water for my herd which [means] we have to drive them seven kilometers to the Kuban' thru big mountins where only mountain animals can go and I said so much about water but no measures were takin in my brigade. There are three milkmaids and one junior herdsman who got promoted who are now distinguished people of our sovkhoz. The other brigades dont want to share experince with me and are jelous at me because in their herds some livestock run away and young ones to. My livestock even tho it oftin dosnt drink enuff has averige fatness. Our livestock is a mix of the Ukrainian breed and mongril. There is a mix of the German breed but not a lot of young ones now. The mixed breed gained from seven hundred g to one kg a day.

Regards
Senior herdsman
Armovir dairy meat sovkhozes no. 32
Vladimir Afanas'evich Sychov

---

Naturally, the fact that a front-rank worker was in the kind of situation described in the letter angered the union's leadership. The following official letter was sent to the local administration:

---

## Document 125

Official letter to Armavir Dairy and Meat Sovkhoz no. 32 administration, 26 October 1935. GARF, f. 7689, op. 11, d. 50, ll. 33–330b. Certified typewritten copy.

To the Director, the Head of the Political Department, and the Chairman of the Workers' Trade Union Committee of Armavir Dairy and Meat Sovkhoz no. 32

Copies to: The director and deputy director of the Northern Caucasus Dairy and Meat Trust's political section and to the Northern Caucasus Kraikom of the Union

According to our information, the best shock worker on the sovkhoz, who has been awarded prizes by the Central Contest Commission, Comrade Sychov, has yet to be provided with the necessary cultural and living conditions, training has not been set up for him, etc.

# Document 125 *continued*

We direct that:

1. The room occupied by Comrade Sychov be given a proper look and be completely and appropriately furnished at the expense of the sovkhoz.
2. Assistance be provided in purchasing footwear through the sovkhoz workers' cooperative or in the town stores.
3. Comrade Sychov be provided with an improved diet, while an improved diet is simultaneously arranged for the shock workers of the sovkhoz.
4. Comrade Sychov be assisted in securing the necessary fodder for his hogs.
5. A cow or calf be sold to him with an extended payment term of 1.5–2 years.
6. Instructors be assigned to Comrade Sychov to advance his general education so that he can be prepared for technical animal-husbandry courses.
7. An appropriate environment be established for Comrade Sychov in his work by organizing an exchange of work experience among brigades.

At the same time we call your attention to the absence of veterinary training for workers on your sovkhoz. It is directed that this area of work be activated immediately.

You are to report on measures you have taken and the results no later than 1 November 1935.

Deputy Chief of the Main Administration of Dairy and Meat Sovkhozes, Mesunov

Chief of the Sector for Dairy and Meat Sovkhozes of the Puns [Political Administration of Narkomsovkhoz].

Shakhgil'dian

Chairman of the TsK of the Union of Dairy and Meat Sovkhoz Workers Trubacheev

---

The measures taken were also reported to Sychov himself. At the same time the message contained a request that he report what new features the proliferation of the Stakhanovite movement had contributed to his work, what kind of cultural services had been set up for front-rank production workers, and so forth.[28]

The alarmed sovkhoz leadership tried to respond as well as it could to the stern directives. The deputy director of the sovkhoz, Rassvetaev, reported in a message to the union's chairman, Trubacheev, that on 14 November 1935 individual apartments, renovated and furnished at the expense of the sovkhoz, had been assigned to a number of distinguished people on the sovkhoz, including V. A. Sychov. The message said Sychov had received a clothes closet, a table, four chairs, and a children's bed, and the sovkhoz workers' committee reported in addition that, at its expense, "a library was aquired for Comrade Vladimir Sychov," as well as a "portible gramaphone" and "portrits of all the leaders," and, in addition, he was "awarded a nickel-plated samovar during the October Revolution holidays." It was also reported that "evry section has a culture room and four sections have a radio," and "every section has an acordeon and a string Orkestra."[29]

These measures resulted in a letter from Sychov, which we quote below. Lessons with a teacher seem to have actually made his writing skills worse (we again have added punctuation marks), although the enhanced sense of pride and importance stemming from the attention shown him comes across clearly:

---

## Document 126

Letter from V. A. Sychov to Trubacheev, trade union chairman, 16 November 1935. GARF, f. 7689, op. 11, d. 50, ll. 39–40. Original manuscript.

---

Mosko [Moscow] Palace of Labor
of dairy/meat sovkhozes
of central and southern olosts [oblasts]
To chair. of Ts. K of the union
Comrade Trubachev

fram distinguished herdsman
of sovkhoz No. 32 in Armavir Roion [Raion]
ACh. K. [Azov–Black Sea Krai]
Livestock specialist
Section 1 herd 1
Vladimir Afanas'evich Sychov

I am reporting to you that I recieved the leters and presints you sent for wich V. A. Sychov my Wife mother and brother send you their deep gratatude.

To the letter recieved fram you what the triangle of our sovkhoz must do they done the following mesures:

They bought for my apartment one table four chairs one clothe closit and a portabil gramophone. They assined me to a teecher who started working with me. I walk six kilo[meters] to studie. As for geting footwear we are in bad shape because there is nowhere to buy it because we live a long way fram town. As for food I am not in need. As for selling a cow or calve the Manigemint of our sovkhoz cant do it without the Trusts permishin. Fodder for our hogs costs sixty-five rubles a centner of barly. A club was setup in our section. It oftin has producshins and films. The politikil department and the workers committee supplied us with a library and they oftin give us talks on the stakhanovite movement.

At the presint time I want to join the ranks of stakhanovites to. For the summer period ninety-one out of one hundred head calved. As of 15 november 1935 all the calves are alive. I turned over seventy-two calves on 24 october 1935 to the generil herd in fine shape. The other nineteen are with me. The whole summer I didnt have one head run away or aborshin. Seven head are calving this munth.

We are rasing the calves byhand. I am fullfilling the november milk plan to 103% in liters. I got temparary shelters all reddy for the winter. They are putteed inside and outside and witewashed. They just didnt get glass put in because the maniger says theres no glass. The calf shed is reddy to but dosnt have glass either.

Fodder for the winter was delivered to storehouses 1 km away and 80% closer.

The sovkhoz divied up the livestock but they didnt form the herds yet and I dont know what livestock Im going to spend the winter with. They want to give me a crossbreed calf born 1933 but we dont have them in our section. My livestock is 86% covered for 1936 because there are cows that calved recintly in november and there are pregnint ones that Im not counting for 1936. I have four recordbraking cows that are mongrils. For two and three burths they produced eighteen liters and the calf suckled and just now I discovered another recordbraker a firstimer calved on 25 March 1935. I put her under speshil observation and brought up her level fram seven lit to sixteen lit with a norm of four kl [kg] of bran and one k of oilcake and in futur we will work like Comrade Aleksei Stakhanov.

These are the shortcumings here on the part of the administrashin and the buro for rasing calves: there are no drinking bowls for cows, no towls, no cheescloth. There is no soap during milking [and] no kerosine. The milkmaids dont have overalls either. There never even were any handbasins. There are no troffs for the cows to drink fram at the storehouses. The above mentioned shortcumings may cause losses to our sovkhozes and the whole country too. Maybe I was wrong to write and made mistakes then dont pay attenshin because I cant read or write much.

Regards Signature

---

Enclosed with the correspondence is an article in the raion newspaper, which in a smooth and streamlined manner re-created the persona of front-rank production worker V. A. Sychov, who "has joined the ranks of the Stakhanovites": "All his facilities are already prepared, the calf shed has been well equipped. All of the livestock shelters have been puttied, whitewashed nice and clean, and are well heated from the outside."[30] In reality, as we can see, in spite of the assistance that had been rendered, the living and working conditions of the front-rank production worker had not improved very much. Similar sets of documents were collected in connection with prizes awarded to a stable hand on the Kirov Sovkhoz (in the town of Cherven', Minsk Okrug, Belorussian SSR), Ignat Karlovich Adamovich, whom the sovkhoz proved altogether powerless to help in any way.[31] "Stalinist shock worker" Klavdia Fyodorovna Maksimovskaia, meanwhile, wrote the following to an instructor from the TsK of the trade union:

## Document 127

Autobiographical letter from livestock and dairy sovkhoz worker K. F. Maksimovskaia to Odintsov, 1 November 1935. GARF, f. 7689, op. 11, d. 129, ll. 133–137ob. Original manuscript.

Dear Comrade Odintsov!

I received the letter you sent on 25 October and I thank you very much for this letter. In connection with the spreading Stakhanovite movement in our country your letter fortified me even more for the future struggle to strengthen socialist animal husbandry and turn our sovkhoz into a profitable enterprise. Comrade Odintsov you ask if I have children. I am not married, I am still twenty-one years old and I live alone. I don't have anybody else, no kin. I lost my parents when I was one year and three months. I was brought up for five years at the Totemsky orphanage in the Northern Krai and then lived as a nanny at strangers' houses. It hurts even to remember now what I had to go through in my childhood living with strangers.

After going through a harsh school of life in my childhood I was very glad that I survived to the time when I joined the Victory Sovkhoz to work as a milkmaid. I was only seventeen years old.

I started trying to work and got to be the best milkmaid on the sovkhoz, but I couldn't read or write. The Komsomol organization on the sovkhoz required me to learn to read and write and I had a passionate desire to learn reading and writing and I quickly did. Then they made me a brigade leader for a milk herd, and again I started trying to make my brigade the leading brigade on the sovkhoz. And I did it. My brigade was the leading brigade on the sovkhoz throughout the period of my work. The Victory Sovkhoz has four young girls shirkers whom I took into my brigade and now they are all shock workers.

One of them got a certificate of honor from the political department and one is now a candidate for Stalinist shock worker. I have received awards fifteen times for good work, I have a certificate of honor as one of the best shock workers and a certificate of honor for builders of socialism issued by the political department of the Victory Sovkhoz.

I have always won the competition although after sharing my experience with a competing brigade leader at one time they beat us in milk output but after that we started using other new methods to beat them again. At first the agreement on socialist competition was checked once a month but then we started checking it every ten days in spite of the fact that we were working in different sections and were getting good results in both brigades. Then I was sent off to take six months of brigade leaders courses, where I got excellent grades in all the exams.

After mastering the techniques of my field I started performing even better.

But the class enemy has not been finished off yet and in February there turned out to be large crumbs in a can of milk that was sent to the collection facility. The sovkhoz administration did not attach much importance to this but in May some water was poured into one of my cans of milk and people started saying right off that Maksimovskaia is fulfilling the plan with water. We have had a lot of dekulakized people working at the Victory Sovkhoz who were admo-exiled [administratively exiled], who do not like shock workers and who tried to spread these rumors as widely as possible.

Comrade Odintsov! You can imagine how hard it was to endure this when I sat at home by myself for the whole day and nobody from the administration came to see me. They at least could have asked how this happened. The section's party organizer came and . . . asked to borrow some money and didn't say anything else. When I asked him if they had started sorting out this matter he replied: there will be time to give attention to you right now it's sowing time.

Only some Young Pioneers came with tears in their eyes and said that the old women at the shop are saying that the Komsomol brigade is fulfilling the plan with water and at that time a letter carrier brought me a newspaper where they wrote about an Order of Lenin being awarded to the Komsomol of the [Moscow] subway. And my Komsomol brigade was just defamed.

Comrade Odintsov! I couldn't endure this anymore. I recalled my unhappy childhood. The sovkhoz took me in, raised me, educated me. The sovkhoz was dearer than life itself to me, I lived and breathed the sovkhoz.

I looked at the weeping Young Pioneers and it became painful for me that everybody else forgot, those who saw that I devoted all my energies to the sovkhoz, and I made up my mind to commit suicide but thanks to timely assistance I was saved.

Of course I now realize that I did not conduct myself like a Komsomol member should. After I recovered, the Northern dairy/meat trust transferred me to a permanent job in Dikoe where I have worked since 7 June 1935. I am working on the Dikoe Sovkhoz as the brigade leader of a calf shed and the delivery section. When I arrived there were a lot of sick calves, I started a competition among calf attendants and entered into a brigade agreement on socialist competition with the brigade leader of a calf shed at the Bushuikho Sovkhoz, Comrade Viktorova. As of today I defeated Viktorova, the losses from sickness stopped, the diseases have been eliminated. I had an average weight gain in my calf shed of 715 gram that has never happened in Dikoe, but that is not the limit. I will attain an even better fatness level. But Comrade Odintsov my goal is not only to make the calf shed where I work a model production area but to make it a school for training personnel so that they are not afraid of difficulties. Raising Stakhanovites I am trying to see to it that every member of my brigade becomes a Stalinist shock worker. I already have results on this sovkhoz. A few days after I arrived in Dikoe there was a Komsomol meeting and the issue up for discussion was the expulsion from the Komsomol of a girl Galina Sedunova. She wasn't able to work anywhere. Either she was being kicked out for a negligent attitude or she ran away herself and got to the point where even her mother started to kick her out of the house. I spoke with the secretary of the Komsomol committee that I will take her into my brigade and spoke with her and the Komsomol organization assigned Sedunova to me. Now Sedunova is producing models of fine work and is a candidate for shock worker.

Comrade Odintsov the trade union organization on our sovkhoz is not doing a good job. In my five months of work here the chairman of the Workers' Committee has not visited my brigade a single time, there has yet to be a review of shock workers in my five months of work, and new shock workers of animal husbandry have yet to be named, and there are a lot of workers who deserve the title of shock worker.

There has been no meeting of the section's workers either that would sum up the results of work for the month and where workers could talk about achievements and shortcomings. The chairman of our R.K. [raion committee] exists only on paper, he is also the assistant bookkeeper and doesn't do anything in trade union work with the masses. He doesn't stay in touch at all with the trade union group organizers, doesn't give them assignments, doesn't get them together, doesn't hear them report on their work, and the group organizers don't even know their duties.

My living and everyday conditions: a small room, a table, a bed, a bookcase, and stools. I am satisfied with my room but it is only a room and there is no place where I can keep vegetables or anything else.

I eat at the cafeteria. There is no difference in eating there from any others, they won't even give you priority in serving lunch in the cafeteria or at the bread store. You come to the store or to the cafeteria, and standing in line there are housewives and even people who don't work on our sovkhoz and if you ask to be served without waiting, the salesperson replies "only when your turn in line comes."

I don't have any animals or poultry, and there's nowhere to keep them anyway.

I didn't study much. I studied by myself under the dept. for elimination of illiteracy and compleeted six month courses for brigade leaders in animal husbandry. I passed all the exams with excellent grades, now I am preparing to take the technical veterinary minimum exam under the Krai land bureau, to earn the title of master of socialist animal husbandry.

I attend the political circle in the history of the VKP(b) I read the newspapers: *Komsomol'skaia Pravda* and *Sovkhoznaia Gazeta* and the krai's *Severnyi Komsomolets* I read newspapers in my brigade where I work and in the milkmaids dormitory.

I would like to go further in my studies but right now they are taking people with no less than seven years of education. That is first of all and second of all I really don't want to leave animal husbandry because lately my health has gotten very poor and I am trying rite now in my brigade to raise a deputy for myself. I need treatment very badly right now. My heart is giving me trouble. I have "heart disease." At the Victory Sovkhoz Gorokhovskaia the chairman of the R.K. promised me a voucher to the senatorium but I never got to go so if you could give me a voucher please Comrade Odintsov life rite now is so intiresting and I want to live so much and life is already so hard for me because I'm sick but in spite of that I can do any job even as well as a man. And one last thing I am informing you that I didn't get the prize yet that was sent out by the central contest comision and I don't even know if I will get it. I asked the director of the trust so he promised to reply and he still hasn't given me any reply.

Well so long all the best!

With Komsomol greetings [signature]

I am sorry that I wrote so much I wanted to let you know about my autobiography and my work.

---

The letter was written in an unsure hand with frequent corrections and insertions, which may be an indication of the writer's poor physical and mental health. In addition, its content shows what kind of conditions shock workers and Stakhanovites had to work in—on the verge of nervous exhaustion and collapse. In this case intervention by the trade union's Central Committee resulted in Maksimovskaia's receiving a resort voucher for health purposes, which led to the following letter:

# Document 128

Letter from K. F. Maksimovskaia to Odintsov, 25 December 1935. GARF, f. 7689, op. 11, d. 129, ll. 132–132ob. Original manuscript.

To instructor of the Union Ts.K. Comrade Odintsov
From Klavdia Fyodorovna Maksimovskaia.
Esteemed Comrade Odintsov!
First of all I send you warm greetings and my shock worker's thanks for the attention you rendered me and the practical assistance.

I am not writing you anymore from Dikoe but from Abkhazia.

I am at a resort in Novyi Afon. I am so happy that, besides the Northern Krai, I have a chance to see other parts where there is never any winter. And apart from that I saw a lot of intiresting things, on the way, when I was traveling, as for example: Donbass-Konstantinovka and other industrial cities.

Comrade Odintsov! I am so grateful to you that I cannot even express it in words.

Well, really, can you possibly write about your feelings in words? I will be able to express my gratitude when I return back to the sovkhoz, in my shock work. I will again spare no effort to struggle for strengthening our sovkhoz so that our sovkhoz can be profitable and the most advanced sovkhoz in the Northern Krai.

My health is improving noticeably I feel well.

It is very warm here, almost like it is in the summer at home, and that's all for now.

---

The file includes a copy of a letter from the chairman of the union's TsK, Trubacheev, to the Northern Kraikom dated 29 December 1935. It asks the kraikom to determine why the trust's deputy political director, Comrade Liustrov, was advising Dikoe's director and the chairman of the workers' committee not to promote Comrade Maksimovskaia to a more important job and not to give her special privileges.[32]

This letter is one of many that were sent to the provinces with the twin aims of providing real assistance to shock workers and Stakhanovites and of instigating investigations of those suspected of opposing the Stakhanovite movement. Letters similar to those quoted above also came in from kolkhozes. One file contains correspondence from a Stakhanovite milkmaid named A. G. Yufereva, whose "aunt Ye. O. Yufereva is also a Stakhanovite, a decorated worker, currently a student at the Socialist Academy of Agriculture in Moscow." A. G. Yufereva herself, she wrote, had overexerted herself in kolkhoz work, contracted tuberculosis and was no longer working. She wrote that she had no means of supporting her children and asked for a voucher to a sanatorium. As a result of measures taken, she was hospitalized in the city of Kirov.[33]

The documents often produce a highly contradictory portrait of the people who were in the vanguard of kolkhoz and sovkhoz labor. Maksimovskaia tried in her letter to blame the crumbs in her can of milk and the addition of water to it on the schemes of the class enemy who had not been finished off. And in a letter titled "They Are Disrupting the Stakhanovite Movement," sent to *Krest'ianskaia Gazeta* in May 1938, its author, O. S. Mokrousova, whose life story closely paralleled the biographies of other front-rank workers, was fighting "enemies of the people" out in the open:

---

## Document 129

Letter from O. S. Mokrousova to *Krest'ianskaia Gazeta,* 16 May 1938. RGAE, f. 396, op. 10, d. 32, ll. 248–249. Typewritten copy.

---

From 1936 until 6 May [1938] I was in charge of the hog-breeding section on the Victory Kolkhoz in Kamenskoe-on-Dnieper Raion, Dnepropetrovsk Oblast. My section was first in the whole raion, I made pledges every year and overfulfilled them every year, and I received three prizes: one time a pig, one time a watch, and the third time a voucher to a resort from the oblast executive committee worth 1,500 rubles. The disruption of my work started in the person of a former secretary of the RPK [raion party committee], now an enemy of the people. He tried to remove me from the hog-breeding section and sent me to work at the village soviet as chairman, where I worked for two months. Based on my personal request, for health reasons, I asked that I be relieved of this job. During this span of time the section went into decline, and the board of the Victory Kolkhoz repeatedly asked me to accept the hog-breeding section. I love that job, and, seeing the condition the hogs were in, I agreed. The kolkhoz has the acceptance report and what kind of condition the hogs were in (terrible). I took up the job again, went at it selflessly myself, sparing no effort and, of course, demanded work from support personnel and demanded everything from the board that the hog section needed. This annoyed board chairman I. Kuz'min and business manager N. Sidel'nikov and they started persecuting me: "Everybody can fatten their livestock with our grain." They are conducting agitation among the kolkhoz farmers to the effect that the section is very costly for them. "She is"—i.e. I am—"an outsider" (I am a refugee from Grodno Gubernia, I have lived in Dneprovka since 1916), but I am still an "outsider." And as a result of its work, this campaign has had its effect. At a kolkhoz farmers' meeting on 6 May 1938, a resolution was passed to remove me from my job. What on earth did they base their resolution on? All kinds of rubbish. Nobody can say anything about my work and nobody did. "She demands work of the hog tenders," "she doesn't work much herself," in short, the resolution wasn't based on anything. When I went to get a copied passage from the minutes, accountant Likhatsky wrote something that never happened at all and nobody said anything of the kind. I complied with the decision of the general meeting and gave up the section, of course, in accordance with the document, but decided not to let this matter go and to expose in your newspaper all of the injustice, all of the filth that is being poured on me, a Stakhanovite. The hostility started already with the fact that my brother, a captain who has served in the Red Army for twenty years, came to visit while on leave, exposed many wreckers, former kulaks in leadership work—and they were ousted from their jobs. After an article was printed in your newspaper, "Enemies of the People and Their Protectors," on 2 October 1937, life just became impossible for me. I had to endure so many insults, and for the sake of the work I tolerated and endured all of it. And, finally, the board members found another solution—to remove me from the hog section, [because] I interfered with them getting drunk, with their perverted behavior, etc.

I used to be a farmhand, I had to break my back for the landowners, could it really be that I won't get my well-earned right and protection in the USSR[?] Who gave them the right to abuse a Stakhanovite woman?

I ask the editors to report in your newspaper on the basics of my case. An article in your newspaper will give a jolt to an investigation of this case.

O. S. Mokrousova

Dneprovka, Kamenskoe-on-Dnieper Raion, Dnepropetrovsk Oblast

---

It is unknown to what extent the accusations against shock workers and Stakhanovites of poor-quality work were justified. For the most part, their selflessness and readiness to give themselves wholeheartedly to their work were not open to question, but occasionally people "skipped" their shock work, and the livestock were left without feed or drink. But one thing was obvious: such accusations provoked an especially outraged response and a desire to punish the accusers.

# CHAPTER SIX

# Happy Childhoods

PEOPLE WHO WERE BORN after the Revolution were destined to live under communism. The Great Lenin promised them this. But first they had to *build* this unprecedented society of social brotherhood, equality, and justice. They had been designated for this mission by the Revolution, through which the older generation had suffered. They were not supposed to be like their parents; they were to become completely "Red"—that is, utterly devoted to revolutionary ideals and free from the influence of the "accursed past." That period had been left far behind—its image had been zealously pounded into the new generation since infancy and was, at best, associated with the Big Bad Wolf in the fairy tale about Little Red (!) Riding Hood. Everything this generation had, starting with the beautiful and vivid names that were given them at birth, was to be unlike what previous children had. Later, too, everything was supposed to be different—nursery school and kindergarten, the schools, which were to educate a new person, the higher institutions, which trained the best specialists in the world.

Students were expected to memorize the "ABCs of communism" instead of the biblical commandments, to go to Young Pioneer Palaces instead of churches, and to stand with nervous anticipation in Young Pioneer lineups instead of attending services. In addition, they would wear kerchiefs, sing impassioned new songs, and not only "study, study, and study" but, starting from the time they were in diapers, "fight, fight, and fight" for a new society and against everything that was considered a "birthmark of capitalism," including fathers, mothers, grandfathers, and grandmothers who were lacking in the proper social consciousness. Moreover, they had someone to emulate: instead of the icons that formerly hung in the "sacred corners" of people's homes, there were portraits of the steadfast and unshakable fighters for the liberation of working people throughout the world—Lenin and Stalin.

The children of the Revolution breathed its air, soaked up its slogans, and swore to uphold its ideals. But even in those days children were children and, like all children in the world, they craved parental affection, demanded a pretty fairy tale with a happy ending, and fell asleep more easily to a lullaby than to the strains of a revolutionary march. As they grew up, they got into mischief and acted like hooligans in moderation and without moderation, fought over boyfriends and girlfriends, secretly read the poet Sergei Yesenin, and learned forbidden "bourgeois" dances. They "went astray," smoked, and took a fancy to the bottle. Their peers in both the street and the courtyard influenced them no less than before and played an active role in their upbringing. All this existed, and yet it did not seem to exist, because little was written about it in the books aimed at these youths. The Second World War was also to blame for the fact that we know so little about the generation of the Revolution. It was they, the boys and girls born between 1915 and 1924, who absorbed the horrifying brunt of the Nazi onslaught. They died and they triumphed.

When one closely examines the documents below, two principal factors stand out. First, adults often tried to make children hostages to their ideas and political games; after all, the Pavlik Morozov phenomenon is more complex and contradictory than is usually believed.[1] And the children, who were more vulnerable and fragile than grown-ups, were the ones who had to pay the price, whether they liked it or not, for the outcomes of the often brutal games. Second, contrary to the voluminous Komsomol literature, the sources show how varied and heterogeneous this generation was, how diverse their notions of life were, and what different twists their biographies took.

Most children in the 1930s remained in the countryside, which was going through a process of devastating upheaval, and the way their lives took shape determined, in large part, the paths of social development for Soviet society. Village children, along with the grown-ups, had to endure the hardships and privations of full-scale collectivization. One can see from the letters to a newspaper that was fittingly called *Kolkhoznye Rebiata* (Kolkhoz kids) how children lived on the kolkhozes—not from the bombastic reports that were published in every issue but rather from the messages that were shelved as soon as they came in. Mitia Ivanov, a Young Pioneer in Yalano-Kataisky Raion, Cheliabinsk Oblast, was one of those who were taught from early childhood to tell the truth and fight against shortcomings. "What is life like for us children of kolkhoz farmers in Yalano-Kataisky Raion?" he wrote to the editors in 1936. "Many of us do not go to school. We don't have bread, and some of us don't have shoes or clothing. There aren't even any hot breakfasts at school, and when you come home, there is nothing to eat either, because we had a bad grain harvest this year. The kolkhoz gave out five hundred grams per laborday. We have long since eaten it up. . . . Who will help us so that we don't starve to death? There are already people around the raion who are getting swollen from hunger. Some widows abandon their children and go into hiding in some unknown location so that they can at least save themselves from starving to death."[2]

The government was aware of the critical situation with regard to meals for school-age children, and it decided to supply schools with hot breakfasts. This undertaking was carried out with great fanfare and was accompanied by a propaganda campaign demonstrating concern for children. Indeed, the gradual introduction of hot breakfasts, above all in city schools, was an extremely urgent and, to a certain degree, forced measure, for many children were dropping out of school due to hunger. But even this program had major problems, and testimony about the quality of the breakfasts by the children themselves has been preserved. Vasily Shibanov, a third-grader at the Zagor'e Secondary Boarding School in Nagor'e Raion, Yaroslavl' Oblast, wrote to *Kolkhoznye Rebiata* in 1936: "I am reporting that there is something wrong at our school. We always eat meat lunches, but for some reason there is no meat in our soup, what happens to the meat, we don't know. And they make this soup every day, we are so tired of it that we can't look at it. Right now there is a shortage of baked bread at the shops in our raion. Our parents did not get any grain from the kolkhoz due to the fact that there was a severe drought. At school they give us only 0.2 gram [apparently 0.2 kilograms, two hundred grams] of bread apiece. That isn't enough for us, which is why some students have stopped going to school."[3]

Every child's letter reveals a great thirst for knowledge. Life's hardships and the immense psychological burden of the country's political upheavals all weighed heavily on children. Yet the difficulties did not kill their enormous desire to study. By and large, the prestige of having an education and mastering a good vocation was extremely high in the 1930s. This was related both to the objective needs of a developing industrial society and to the long-standing dream of poor people, whose talents had never dried up, to obtain an education. The Soviet state's programs during the 1920s and 1930s in the area of schooling and education seemed to be aimed at meeting these needs. In reality, however, the situation was much more complicated. The system that was taking shape interfered with getting an education, especially a higher and specialized secondary education, for children of *byvshie* (formerly privileged groups) as well as dekulakized individuals, the disenfranchised, exiles, and other categories of repressed people, a subject that will be discussed below. But kolkhoz life, with its constant rush jobs requiring all hands and its heavy demand for labor, also hampered kolkhoz farmers' children in obtaining a quality education. Continuing to attend the village school beyond the fourth grade was especially problematic. N. K. Krupskaia, Lenin's widow, was aware of this problem, which was a serious one everywhere, and sounded the alarm in 1932, appealing not only to various bodies but to the country's leadership as well. In a letter to Ukrainian party boss P. P. Postyshev in the fall of 1932 she wrote:

> The children of kolkhoz farmers are flooding us with letters, saying that they are not allowed to leave the kolkhozes to go to school because they are needed for work. Youngsters twelve and older (who have completed the fourth grade) are being required to produce labor-

days and the youngsters are forced to drop out of school. In the spring all the ShKM youngsters [students at peasant youth schools] were mobilized (school vacations are not timed to coincide with the harvest period) and they had to drop their studies at a number of kolkhozes because they were required to produce labordays. We have sought to bring the countryside closer to the city, but it is precisely in the countryside and on kolkhozes that we are imposing cruel barriers which make it impossible for youngsters who have completed the fourth grade to continue their studies. The children of independent peasants are free to go to school, while the children of kolkhoz farmers are not. We end up with an intolerable contradiction. I am enclosing a letter from a girl, a Young Pioneer, who doesn't know what she should do, she wants to go to school but she is not being allowed to do so. I cannot write to the kolkhoz, of course. But some kind of general resolution is needed. The Kolkhoz Center does not have a policy in this regard. Last year child labor was under the control of schools, but this summer the schools were removed from this issue. There are no officials whose job is to protect child labor, and it is exploited inordinately. The beet harvest is done by child labor. How can they even think of doing any schoolwork?[4]

As we see, beginning at age twelve children on the kolkhozes had to work full-time, while getting paid much less than adults and only dreaming of continuing their studies. Krupskaia realized that the exploitation of child labor was inevitable, so she proposed at least establishing official posts for protecting labor that would bar "inordinate exploitation."

Thus the actual plight of kolkhoz farmers' children stood in stark contrast to the laws on child protection, as well as to the pretty rhetoric about the party's concern for the young generation. Krupskaia aptly compared them to people who had been stripped of their rights. "The children of kolkhoz farmers are to all intents and purposes disenfranchised," she wrote to Postyshev, "not to mention the fact that the plight of kolkhoz youngsters in general is a difficult one. Recently the chairman and secretary of a kolkhoz named for me showed up here from the Central Black Soil Oblast to petition for dry goods for shock workers. They make a report boasting how well they are doing. The kolkhoz breeds livestock. They turn over all the milk somewhere, to the Butter Center, maybe. I recalled Il'ich's [Lenin's] phrase 'Provide every child with a bottle of milk,' and I ask, 'But are you leaving some milk for the children?' 'No, we turn in all of it down to the last drop!' And half of the kolkhoz's population has fled."[5]

Of course, the kolkhoz enterprises varied around the country, but most of them eked out a semidestitute existence, while turning in the entire harvest to the state. Could anybody afford to worry about children if people could lose their heads for failing to fulfill the plan? But once the harvest was over, it would seem that in the winter, kolkhoz farmers' children would be able to devote themselves entirely to schoolwork. In practice, though, the arrival of cold weather presented new problems: children often had nothing to wear when they walked to school, which, as a rule, was located several kilometers from home. Thirteen-year-old Ivan Nemchinov from the Cossack settlement of Spirova decided to write about this to M. I. Kalinin:

---

## Document 130

Letter from thirteen-year-old I. Nemchinov to Kalinin, 13 January 1933. RGASPI, f. 78, op. 1, d. 456, ll. 10–11. Original manuscript.

---

Dear grandfather Kalinin. I will now describe my whole life to you. Grandfather Kalinin we have a big family, four children. I have no father—he died fighting for the workers' cause, and my mother too almost died, she is sick. Grandfather Kalinin, I really want to go to school, but I have nothing to put on to walk there. I had old boots, but even those got completely tattered, and there is nobody to fix them. My mother is sick, we have no money, no bread, but I really want to go to school. Dear grandfather, we are told to study, study, and study. So said Vladimir Il'ich Lenin. But I will have to stop going to school. We have no relatives and nobody to help us, I will have to go to work in a factory so that the whole family doesn't starve to death. Dear grandfather, I am thirteen years old, I am a good student, with no failing grades. I am in the fifth grade. Well so long, I have nothing else to write. Our address: Spirova village, 4 Kooperativnaia Square, Ivan Vasil'evich Nemchinov.

[After thinking awhile, this precocious young fellow, who was the oldest in the family and therefore felt responsible for the rest of the children and his ailing mother, added a postscript:]

Dear grandfather, they give us very little bread—300 grams a day. We have to eat only twice a day, and it is hard to study without bread.

In January 1933 people in the countryside could already sense the approach of mass famine, but Ivan Nemchinov was thinking more about schooling, which was hampered by the bread shortage.

By the end of the 1930s the situation had improved somewhat, but not a great deal. The most realistic way for rural (male) children to learn a reliable vocation and acquire some prospects in life was to go to take courses for tractor drivers, combine operators, and truck drivers. This was the subject of a letter written by a student at a school for combine operators in the town of Mtsensk, Orel Oblast. As the postscript indicates, it was sent by the student's uncle to *Krest'ianskaia Gazeta*:

---

## Document 131

Letter from student at combine-operator school to his uncle and aunt, forwarded to *Krest'ianskaia Gazeta*, 17 January 1939. RGAE, f. 396, op. 11, d. 41, ll. 284–284ob. Original manuscript.

---

Hello uncle Fedia and aunt Sonia. Uncle Fedia I recieved the letter in which you write [that I should] describe how many of us there are in the courses and how I am dressed. There are only 150 of us in the courses, and there are supposed to be three hundred. There were three hundred but they all leaved to get away from the bad conditions since they just got bread to eat, the dormitory are cold and the lighting is bad. But we sent it to the oblos [oblast] newspaper the case was turned over to the Oblos Land Administration for investation [investigation].

I am dressed well and have shoes but it is not so good in the courses we always have to go hungry for three days right before payday because there is no cafeteria and in town there is only one restaurant where 1 b[owl] of soup is 125 kopecks. There is no lawndry so I have to go around dirty and with lice but I am trying to finish school because next time [I want to] take a course for truck drivers or a mechanic.

The money I earned all together with my food that I ate for the summer was one thousand rubles, four hundred rubles Millets [apparently four hundred rubles' worth of millet] and I got 250 rubles in the summer after my Grandfather died. I will get the rest in the end of January. I earned seventy-two poods of bread I earned thirty poods of forage twelve poods of hay five poods of straw. All to gether they were earned for four hundred days. Uncle Fedia thank you very much for the paper and thank you again. Without paper it's like being without hands. Well so long goodby stay alive helthy. Give regards to Polina and aunt Varia and Zhenia and All the rest.

---

In reading the letters rural dwellers wrote to *Krest'ianskaia Gazeta,* one constantly encounters complaints about the kolkhozes' lack of funds for maintaining children's institutions—maternity clinics, nursery schools, and kindergartens, which often existed thanks only to the enthusiasm of the operating personnel. The situation at factories and plants in the cities was, on the whole, a little better. Paradoxical as it may seem, the supply of food was better than in rural localities. But here too, especially in new neighborhoods, workers' children were continually undernourished, especially during the famine years. A month before Ivan Nemchinov sent his letter, schoolchildren from Volkhovstroi (the Volkhov Hydroelectric Station construction project, now the town of Volkhov) wrote to Kalinin:

## Document 132

Collective letter from schoolchildren at Volkhovstroi to Kalinin, December 1932. RGASPI, f. 78, op. 1, d. 432, ll. 4–40b. Original manuscript.

To the All-Union elder M. I. Kalinin from the school-age children at Volkhovstroi.

To our dear proletarian leader M. I. Kalinin.

We school-age children as the progressive vangart ask you to impruve our food situation, for we children at Volkhovstroi don't have any food for anybody. We go to lunch in the general cafeteria, we get soup there with sour cabbage, and theyve flavered in salid [apparently, flavored it with salad ingredients]. Its gotten unbearable for us to study with such food. They feed us like pigs. Consider our food situation, give some animal fats for us. . . . Mikhail Ivanovich Kalinin, we look forward to your answer. We ask from our heart for your help with food, to improve the food.

As the letter indicates, the children at Volkhovstroi were being fed, albeit inadequately, and they were not in danger of starving to death. Because they ate in a general cafeteria, it is clear from the letter what the Volkhovstroi workers ate and what their "working mood" was like after lunch.

The appendixes to the conference on Young Pioneer work organized by the party's TsK on 7 May 1933 reported that at one school in Saratov in 1932 "Youngsters led by a Young Pioneer ravaged the cafeteria one night. When asked 'Why did you do this?' they replied, 'The food is bad.' 'And why didn't you say anything about it?' 'We did complain, but nobody pays attention. But now they paid attention right away,'" the children explained.[6]

It is well known that children often repeat what their parents say at home, taking in not only the general tenor and subject matter of conversations but also the typical expressions, which they have picked up from the earliest age. In this regard the material drawn from the minutes of the conference of the Extrascholastic Sector under Narkompros in February 1935 is of enormous importance not only in terms of the situation in kindergartens, where children under seven years of age were sent, but also as a valuable source on the history of social consciousness in the 1930s as a whole.

One kindergarten in Moscow had an "extraordinary" incident —"a child flung a boot at a portrait of Comrade Stalin. The child is a difficult one, and he did it in a fit of agitation," the document says. But at the Lenin Raion kindergarten, a child did not just rip a portrait of Stalin off the wall in the presence of a teacher, he also explained his actions in an apparent reflection of what he had repeatedly heard from his parents: "He doesn't give us any bread." At the Reutov Raion kindergarten in Moscow Oblast, inspectors uncovered more trouble—ethnic hostility among the children.[7] One wonders how small children came to exhibit this behavior when they had little life experience and lacked a clear notion of ethnic differences.

Another example of children, almost from infancy, being drawn into a discussion of "grown-up" problems, was the assassination of S. M. Kirov. On this issue, at the model kindergarten in the town of Shchelkovo, one could hear the following children's version, which was not devoid of meaning: "One guy told another one: 'Kill Kirov, I'll give you money. He killed Kirov, but didn't get the money.'"[8]

The teachers at Kindergarten no. 1 in Moscow's Stalin Raion ran into a problem that put them in a state of shock and fear at the same time: a child refused to participate in the Red Army holiday together with the other children, declaring that "he wants to be a White Guard. This started after a viewing of the motion picture

*Chapaev,*" a kindergarten employee recounted at the conference, alluding to the 1934 film starring Boris Babochkin in the role of the eponymous civil war hero, based on the book by Dmitry Furmanov. "They ascertained in the family that the mother was in despair." Also in despair was the teacher, who was in danger of receiving a serious punishment. In an effort to play it safe, teachers held any initiative to a minimum, strictly following, to the point of absurdity, the plan for working with children that had been approved "at the top." Thus, any unforeseen events in the country became a genuine natural disaster, for they could not be anticipated by the plan. "I sense that educators are afraid of social events," a representative of Krasnaia Presnia Raion acknowledged at the conference. "There are reports that educators at the kindergarten of the Bolshevik plant covered the windows so that the children could not see the demonstration during Kirov's funeral, because it was not in the program."9

Children got into mischief without realizing that grown-ups would look for a political motivation in their actions and words. They fell in love and wrote what they considered romantic verses to one another for scrapbooks, carried on friendships and got together in groups, discussed grown-ups, and secretly smoked and drank—in short, they led their own lives, which were often hidden from adults and beyond their control. Having read books about Tom Sawyer and Huck Finn, they wanted to live in a children's world of their own invention, governed by their own laws. The problem was, to what extent did all this square with the situation in the USSR in the 1930s, when everyone and everything were supposed to be controlled? Materials discovered in the archives help to sketch an outline of school life in the 1930s.

The above-mentioned appendixes to the conference of 7 May 1933 cited "isolated instances of hooliganism and unhealthy tendencies among children," which in the spirit of the times were blamed on "class-alien elements": "Hooliganism is very widespread throughout the Urals," the documents reported. "The main breeding grounds of hooliganism are Sverdlovsk, Magnitogorsk, Cheliabinsk, Perm', Tagil, Nadezhdinsk, and others." The documents went on to say that children at a number of schools in Sverdlovsk were ruining school property, beating up Young Pioneer activists, disrupting classroom work and pilfering belongings from one another. There was a report that the school in Magnitogorsk had a "gang of bandits and thieves" that "damaged the school and terrorized teachers and students. The gang was led by kulaks, bandits and thieves." In Karabash, near Cheliabinsk, "a group was established that wanted to have fun and lead a carefree life. The group was led by a schoolgirl—a top student. The group called her Lel'ka Atamansha [from *ataman,* Cossack leader]. Her distinguishing feature was that she wore a man's shirt with an unbuttoned collar. Lel'ka was assisted in all of her activities by a thief, a bandit, who was known only by the name Oleg." In Shadrinsk, "two schoolgirls, Galia Skopina—thirteen years old, the daughter of a kulak supporter—and Titov—the daughter of a former officer—set up a society 'of struggle for equality and truth.' They had one slogan in their work: 'Don't believe in the victories of socialism, struggle for faith and truth.' The group recruited members and wrote counterrevolutionary leaflets." In the same town,

> A church-going woman by the name of Vizberg, the former wife of a general, set up a schoolchildren's group in October 1932, supposedly to study music. In reality she planned through her visitors to initiate counterrevolutionary activities in school. At first only five girls were coming to visit her. She taught them to play church canons on the piano, organized games with them, helped them with their homework and gradually began to develop counterrevolutionary agitation. Vizberg praised the old school system and derided Soviet schools. She arranged excursions to the cathedral and told stories about saints, their relics and about religion in general. She regularly served tea to her visitors, later planned to set up a skating rink, and the local priest assisted her in her work. The group grew from five people to eighteen, and they included Young Pioneers.[10]

The notion that the children's behavior was related to "counterrevolutionary activities" is highly questionable; more likely these were typical examples of daily life for schoolchildren at major construction projects, and in cities and towns.

The same situation was to be found in the capital. A report received by the Moscow City Soviet in 1932 cited classroom shenanigans by students and even beatings of Young Pioneers and teachers. It also pointed to the existence of anti-Soviet organizations called the Society of Strikes and Proclamations, the Liberal-Democratic Alliance, and the Black Crescent Society.[11]

Materials supporting the report of the Moscow City Committee of the VKP(b) for 1937 cited the establishment at several Moscow schools of "unlawful" (that is, not established on the instructions of adults) organizations—the Gold Tooth at school no. 313 and the White Button Society at school no. 610—as well as the dissemination of amateur manuscript journals and wall newspapers (school no. 59). School no. 232 in Moscow's Dzerzhinsky Raion had a literary circle comprising students from the ninth and tenth grades during 1936 and 1937, which the report labeled as "underground."[12]

It was common at many schools to compile scrapbooks of sentimental verse, candid confessions, and the like, which naturally were of great interest to educators. The writers of a memorandum to the Central Committee of the Komsomol on shortcomings in school operations took notice, for example, of the following candid confession in the scrapbook of Raia Novokuptseva, a sixth-grade student at the Atiashevo Secondary School in the Mordovian ASSR:

> I love you like a Yid loves herring,
> I love you like a German loves sausage,
> I love you like a Russian loves vodka . . .
> I couldn't love you more than I do.

Instead of giving the student the top grade of 5 for taking a curious look at the object of such an unusual love, the inspectors, shocked by the mundane national stereotypes, immediately made a big political case out of the poem. Yet it is obvious that the student's earthiness was rooted in the adult environment, primarily that of her parents. It is equally difficult to blame the writing of anti-Soviet ditties on a fourth-grade schoolgirl at the remote Kuliasovskaia Elementary School (Mordovia), who, to the horror of the audience at a raion competition of children's performing arts, innocently sang a ditty that was popular in her home village:

> Five-Year Plan, Five-Year Plan,
> The Five-Year Plan in ten years.
> I won't go to your kolkhozes:
> Your kolkhozes have no bread![13]

As the sources make clear, the favorite prank of little brats during the 1930s was to use slingshots to strafe the portraits hanging in the school hallways and classrooms. It was fortunate if they chose lesser figures, such as writers or scientists, but if they hit leaders of the party and the state, the consequences were grim. A memorandum stamped "Top Secret," from an inspector named Alekseev who worked for the Narkompros administration of elementary and secondary schools, is worded like a war communiqué. Dated 2 November 1935, it was sent to People's Commissar Bubnov and Moscow City Board of Public Education director Dubrovina: "It has been determined that on 26 October of this year, at secondary school no. 4 in Stalin Raion, Moscow, a group consisting of six pupils in grade 4-C—Bylinkin, Klochkov, Artamonov, Somov, Sineev, and Mikhail Markelov—conducted a fusillade with slingshots upon the portrait of Comrade Kaganovich. This anti-Soviet assault was organized by pupil Markelov, the son of a VKP(b) member who is a board member of the Consumers' Society."[14] It is doubtful whether any of the youngsters had personal grievances against Comrade Kaganovich; they simply felt like doing a little shooting with their slingshots. The result was that the naughty behavior was classified as anti-Soviet activity, and teachers and parents alike suffered the consequences.

Similar incidents were reported by other schools as well. We learn, for example, from a secret letter by the Gor'ky City Committee of the Komsomol that "sixth-grade pupils made fun in various ways of our leaders' portraits on school premises in Sverdlovsk Raion on 28 September 1934." A memorandum on incidents at certain schools in Mordovia reported on 21 February 1937: "In November [1936] there was an incident in which a portrait of Comrade Yezhov was pelted with pieces of bread. A few days ago a pupil in grade 8-A named Savchenko drew a mustache with chalk on a portrait of N. K. Krupskaia (which hangs in the classroom). It was also discovered that a portrait of Comrade Voroshilov was torn to pieces." In all likelihood, none of these pranks was politically motivated, but they do attest to an obvious lack of piety among the young generation with regard to the leaders. At the same time there is something to ponder in the fact that nothing similar was done to the portraits of the dead founders of Marxism-

Leninism, whom the children spared—or else such incidents did not come under investigation.

Another troubling symptom of school life in the 1930s that was not supposed to be discussed was the prevalence and popularity among schoolchildren of the swastika. An inspector who visited one school in Mordovia in 1937 was shocked by this fact and decided to conduct a genuine investigation. "For example," he wrote in a memorandum,

> I personally detained a pupil in grade 4-A named Pyotr Grishin in the hallway of this school during recess on 13 February 1937. He was pressing his hand (the fascist symbol had been written in chalk on his palm) on the back of a fourth-grade pupil in the school named Chertopolokhov. In a conversation with pupil Grishin, the latter said that this has been common in school for a long time and indicated that insignia are also imprinted by Cherniaevsky, Cheprygin, Kolzakov, Lytkin, Sitnikov, Glazov. . . . Such incidents have also taken place in the upper classes. For instance, on 28 January 1937 pupil Sobolev in grade 7-B drew a fascist swastika with chalk on a desk, and pupils Savchenko and Moiseev in grade 8-A drew fascist symbols with chalk on a desk. It was also established that a fascist symbol was drawn on the heater in the 5-C classroom at the beginning of January 1937. In addition, during my inspection of the school's rooms I personally noticed a fascist swastika on the walls in the hallways.[15]

There are similar reports about pranks by schoolchildren involving the swastika in other schools and regions as well, indicating how widespread the phenomenon was. It was turned into a political issue, of course, and the guilty individuals were punished.[16]

The reasons for the swastika's prevalence among schoolchildren in the 1930s derived largely from the forbidden, unhealthy interest that adults showed toward this symbolism as they went to incredible lengths to play it safe. We are alluding here to the "adult games" over Young Pioneer symbols that flared up in earnest and did not go unnoticed by children. On 14 November 1937 *Komsomol'skaia Pravda* deputy editor Porel'shtein received a letter from the newspaper's Leningrad correspondent, Finogenov, the gist of which had long been an open secret for school and Young Pioneer functionaries. "We have learned that Young Pioneer leaders and Komsomol organizers at many schools in Leningrad and the oblast have demanded that Young Pioneers immediately turn over to them their Pioneer kerchiefs and badges, for a directive to that effect had been received from higher organizations. In making this demand, they explained that the badge was a fascist symbol because it depicted a hammer and sickle burning in a bonfire. The kerchief, if held up to the light, is supposed to show a silhouette of Trotsky."[17] The correspondent, astonished by the obvious nonsense and mysticism, went to school no. 21 in October Raion and determined that the Young Pioneer leaders had indeed taken the kerchiefs and badges away from the Pioneers the day before, in accordance with instructions from the Komsomol's raikom, which in turn had received a directive from the Komsomol's obkom, and the obkom had been ordered to carry out all this by telephone from the TsK of the Komsomol. The correspondent continued:

---

## Document 133

Letter from *Komsomol'skaia Pravda* correspondent Finogenov to deputy editor Porel'-shtein, 14 November 1937. TsKhDMO, f. 1, op. 23, d. 1267, ll. 44–45. Typewritten original.

---

... The story of this infuriating case was the same in the rest of the schools as well. After ascertaining these facts, the obkom of the VKP(b) censured Comrade Liubin, secretary of the Leningrad Obkom and City Committee of the Komsomol, for unacceptable conduct. But the Komsomol obkom and city committee are not checking even now to see how the correction of outrages that have occurred is proceeding on site. At some schools, such as school no. 21 in October Raion, instead of immediately returning the kerchiefs and badges to the Pioneers, Komsomol organizers and Pioneer leaders are conferring on how best to do this in an educational sense, and they have yet to communicate anything to the youngsters.

Today [Leningrad's] Mosraiono [Moscow Raion Board of Public Education] distributed the following directive to schools and kindergartens: remove pictures of Comrade Stalin with Young Pioneer Markizova from the walls, because her father is an enemy of the people. Rather than expose this vile provocation, the raion's kindergarten and school functionaries immediately began to carry out the directive. People at the Mosraiono say that they were told to do this by the Moscow Raikom of the Komsomol and the department of schools of the VKP(b) raikom. Only late in the evening did someone telephone from the party's city committee to the raiono and demand immediate cancellation of this absurd and patently counterrevolutionary order.

## Document 133 *continued*

The new directive from the party's city committee canceling this provocative order has not yet reached some schools, so what took place at many other schools is now happening there. Certain people seized on the counterrevolutionary directive to advise youngsters to burn their kerchiefs, which several youngsters did.

The materials supporting the report of the Moscow City Committee of the VKP(b) for 1937 suggest that a similar situation prevailed in Moscow, where "a provocation about supposed fascist symbols pictured on Young Pioneer kerchiefs assumed a massive scale."[18]

The schools of the 1930s were, of course, a cross-section of society at large, but an unusually vivid and revealing cross-section. Working as a schoolteacher in the 1930s was not only a difficult but also a perilous job. Supervisory bodies reported in detail to the top on extraordinary incidents in class and on conversations among students. A memorandum to Comrade Frenkel', the representative of the Party Control Commission under the TsK, reported:

## Document 134

Memorandum to representative of TsK KPK on anti-Soviet statements by students in Mordovia, 21 February 1937. TsKhDMO, f. 1, op. 23, d. 1265, l. 38. Typewritten copy.

On 22 November 1936, several students made outright anti-Soviet statements during the classes of teacher Babin (Mordovia). To the question, "Why will a war against the Soviet Union be the most dangerous war for the bourgeoisie?" student Yurenev gave this response: "The bourgeoisie will attack the Soviet Union, the kulaks will rise up, recruit the kolkhoz farmers to their side, and everyone together will take action against Soviet rule." He was supported by students Medvedev and Zaikin, both members of the Komsomol. Teacher Babin, instead of exposing the counterrevolutionary substance of this answer, got into a debate with the students by asking them a new question: "What do you base that on?" And this response followed: "The situation in the countryside is bad, and you should take off your riding breeches, go visit the countryside and listen to what the peasants are saying. Just don't dress too nicely, and you will find out everything."

Such classroom discussions and revelations by students were not a rarity. In their naive candor—and sometimes as a show of bravado—schoolchildren would blurt out things to their classes that would make teachers clutch at their heads and rush to carry out their professional duty as purveyors of the party line. When teacher Beliaev, a former Red Guard and a participant in the October Revolution, was appointed principal of school no. 119 in Moscow, he concluded that the student environment harbored anti-Soviet attitudes. In a letter addressed to Stalin and Komsomol secretary A. V. Kosarev, dated 26 August 1937, he hastened to report: "With regard to those who graduated from the tenth grade (103 students) in 1937, I have become convinced that 90 percent of them are not our young people, and this will be proven by reality and by their activities at higher educational institutions and in the workplace." In denouncing his own students, the vigilant school principal took the trouble of enclosing with the letter lists of the graduates' home addresses.[19]

Some administrators displayed admirable creativity in their effort to establish tight discipline in schools. At one school in Omsk Oblast in 1935, a decision was made, "in order to strengthen discipline," to arrange mandatory haircuts for all schoolchildren, both boys and girls. It is not at all surprising that, as a memorandum reported to Kosarev, "the haircuts caused great unhappiness among parents and the students themselves, especially girls. School attendance on the haircutting days dropped to 60 percent."[20]

The memorandum noted that jokes and inventions aimed at discrediting Soviet authority and its leaders were continuing to circulate in the schools of Omsk Oblast. "Lenin liked to wear shoes, but Stalin prefers boots. Why?" Such brainteasers were highly popular among schoolchildren. The document provided the answer for the slow-witted adults: "Because Lenin led us along a dry, clean path, but Stalin more and more is taking us through a swamp."[21]

The archival documents that were reviewed include a considerable number of references to suicides by schoolchildren and teachers. What was obviously distinctive about the 1930s was the incredible physical and psychological overload, and the exaggeration of the significance of many ideological problems. Each suicide, however, had its own background, its own causes, which we may never learn. The official documents usually cited official—that is, more convenient—causes. "On 20 November 1937, sixth-grade student

Vasil'tsev, a Young Pioneer, hanged himself at School No. 313," said one memorandum on the situation in Moscow schools, sent to the TsK of the VKP(b) on 28 November 1937. "The reason was that he was kicked out of the classroom by the mechanical-drawing teacher, and because his situation at home was a hard one (he was growing up without a father, his family was in financial need) and he was afraid of trouble at home, he committed suicide. On 25 November Kirsanov, a Young Pioneer in the fourth grade at school no. 525, hanged himself in his apartment."[22] The wording in this document is extremely laconic, like communiqués reporting war casualties.

The fact that Stalin's terror was just then at its height may or may not be relevant here. But in other instances it would appear that the reasons for taking one's own life were far more "material" or mundane. A memorandum addressed to Stalin, Andreev, and Kosarev reported one such case in Omsk Oblast:

---

## Document 135

Memorandum to Stalin, Andreev, and Kosarev on suicide of teacher in Omsk Oblast, 31 July 1935. TsKhDMO, f. 1, op. 23, d. 1129, l. 63. Typewritten copy.

---

On 8 May of this year Komsomol member Vorob'yov, a teacher at the local first-stage school, committed suicide under the Sedinsky Village Soviet in Novo-Zaimka Raion. In a suicide note that Vorob'yov left, he wrote that he was unhappy with the local Soviet authority, because he was in financial need. Agents of the [state-security] organs who investigated the suicide performed an autopsy for the purpose of confirming that Vorob'yov was in financial need. The result of this farce was recorded as follows: "During the autopsy on Vorob'yov no food was found in his stomach. The investigation also determined that Vorob'yov lived in very bad conditions, and local teachers sometimes were not issued their wages for several months at a time."

---

If the authorities wanted to figure out whether someone was starving or not, did they really have to wait for him to commit suicide and then rummage through his stomach? What if he had happened to eat something and therefore hanged himself not out of starvation but, for example, as they attributed to Vorob'yov, because he had read "decadent literature (Yesenin)"?

One of the most powerful and indisputably effective organizations engaged in educating the young generation in the new, Communist principles was the Young Pioneers. Its cells existed in the 1920s and 1930s on kolkhozes and in schools, children's homes, and other educational and child-care institutions. Though nominally autonomous, the Young Pioneer organization was one of the key links in the chain from Pioneers to Komsomol to the party. In giving top priority to the indoctrination of children in a spirit of devotion to the socialist homeland, the grown-ups in the party's Central Committee understood perfectly well the importance of the basic worldview that was instilled at a young age. That was precisely why relevant symbolism and attributes, along with discussions and other forms of work, were so prominent in Young Pioneer detachments. Typically in the 1930s, political education was based on devotion not so much to ideas as to specific leaders who were identified with them. Thus the traditional slogan went: "Pioneer, in the struggle for the cause of Lenin and Stalin, be prepared!" which was invariably followed by: "Always prepared!"

The archives still contain a large number of salutatory letter-reports from Young Pioneers to party and government leaders suggesting that an idyllic atmosphere prevailed inside the Young Pioneers organization. Although they were written by children—in the calligraphic handwriting of the best pupil and devoid of the usual juvenile errors—these letters were often dictated by adults. One striking sample of this correspondence was a salutatory letter to Kalinin, written by the Young Pioneers at Health-Improvement School no. 6 on the eve of the Seventeenth Party Congress in January 1934:

---

# Document 136

Salutatory letter from Young Pioneers to Kalinin, January 1934. RGASPI, f. 78. op. 1, d. 526, ll. 3–30b. Original manuscript.

---

Dear Mikhail Ivanovich!
We send you warm Young Pioneer and Little Octobrist greetings from the pupils of Health-Improvement School no. 6. We congratulate you on the opening of the Seventeenth Party Congress as one of the old members of the VKP(b). We want to report to you about how our school has also prepared for the VKP(b) Congress. First we held meetings in groups, and each of us made pledges for our studies and discipline. We began to compete, group against group, team against team, to see who fulfills their pledges better. We have

only nine students with failing grades, and before we had nineteen. Our parents gave us the Red Challenge Banner. By the end of the year we will make sure that there will not be a single student with failing grades. Out of the 120 students in our school, forty-three are the best shock workers. Their grades are good or excellent and they follow regulations. We do community work. Everybody has joined the MOPR. We are helping the Chuvash Kolkhoz Banner of the Revolution, have opened up nursery schools, have sent money and toys, and are helping the school: we have sent an erector set, textbooks, and money for seeds to be planted in the school vegetable garden. The kolkhoz school sends us its projects. We correspond with them all the time. Right now we are preparing for the spring sowing campaign, we are doing a collection for the kolkhoz and we are working in our pet corner. Grandfather, we are the happiest children in the Soviet Union. Our school was established after [the] October [Revolution]. We study here and get treatment. Our school is the school of the future. The open schools pay attention to children's health, and so they have sent us weak children to the Health Improvement School.

Mikhail Ivanovich! Please make mention at the Congress of the VKP(b) how the children of working people study, get health care, and receive instruction so that they will be ready to replace their fathers.

Always prepared in the struggle for the workers' cause!

[Signatures of twenty-one children]

---

The most interesting of the numerous letters from children were those that were written without instigation or participation by adults—parents, teachers, or Young Pioneer leaders. These letters were by no means models of proper spelling or political consistency, but they were disarmingly direct and sincere, and they painted a realistic picture of Young Pioneer life in the 1930s as the children themselves saw it. For example, Liza Zarubina and Zhenia Smirnova, from the village of Tropa in Ivanovo Industrial Oblast, got together one day in March 1933 and decided to write a letter to Kalinin. Why him? They explained this themselves:

---

## Document 137

Letter from L. Zarubina and Zh. Smirnova to Kalinin, March 1933. RGASPI, f. 78, op. 1, d. 456, l. 4. Original manuscript.

---

Hello Uncle Misha!

We send you warm greetings and all the best in your big projects. Uncle Misha, we recently heard about you that you are a good guy, everybody praises you, and we felt like writing you a letter. You probably won't get angry at us that we wrote to you, but we badly want to see you and have a look at Moscow. We have never been anywhere but our village and never saw anything nice. We want to see the grave of sweet uncle Volodia [a diminutive form of Lenin's first name] too, and there are a lot of you good uncles there besides.

We saw in pictures and whenever somebody said they were in Moscow and saw everything, we listened with envy. Uncle Misha, write an answer to us right away. At least we will take a look at your letter, if we never get a chance to see you in person. Goodbye, we are looking forward to your answer. Give our regards to Uncle Stalin and all the others.

Liza Zarubina and Zhenia Smirnova. Our address: Village of Tropa, N. Tropa Village Soviet, Mimoshino Post Office, Volodarsk Raion, Ivanovo Industrial Oblast

Goodbye dear Uncle Misha

"We are the happiest children in the Soviet Union," wrote the Young Pioneers at Health-Improvement School no. 6. "We have never been anywhere but our village and never saw anything nice," came the counterpoint from the girls in the Ivanovo area. For them, as well as the overwhelming majority of children in the 1930s, going to a large city, especially Moscow, was tantamount to finding themselves in a fairyland. Paradoxical as it may seem, children's letters sometimes captured the pulse of everyday life in the Soviet hinterland more clearly than piles of reports did. A letter to Kalinin from Herrmann Roland not only describes the difficulties of organizing Pioneer detachments in the provinces but also provides a three-dimensional portrait of attitudes on an ethnic German kolkhoz.

# Document 138

Letter from Young Pioneer H. Roland to Kalinin, 23 November 1934. RGASPI, f. 78, op. 1, d. 526, ll. 6–8. Original manuscript.

Dear Grandfather M. I. Kalinin!

In the newspaper *Pravda* no. 310 of 11 November 1934 I read in your report at the ceremonial meeting about the achievements of our Soviet Union. About the output of metal, agricultural machine building, the chemical industry, etc. Allow me to report on our achievements at our little Rosa Luxemburg Kolkhoz, under the Koltunovka Village Soviet in Georgievsk Raion, Obilenskaia MTS, in the Northern Caucasus Krai. Our kolkhoz is small, there are only 150 members on the kolkhoz and sixty of them are able to work. And you know, almost none of the Germans like Soviet rule. I want to write you first about how our Young Pioneer detachment came about. My papa has been a teacher in Koltunovka for ten years already. He himself is not a party member, but he takes part in all the Soviet political activities. I have been a Pioneer for two years already. This year I succeeded on the eve of May Day in recruiting two of my comrades, who declared themselves Pioneers at a general meeting. The next day my papa and I recruited eleven more pupils at school, but you know how the Germans [are] without their parents' permission, some pupils could not join the Pioneers, papa had to visit the parents at home and change their minds and get their consent. In this way we ended up with a detachment of fourteen Pioneers. Of course our boards of the kolkhozes Rosa Luxemburg and Karl Liebknecht[,] Slizhevsky, Huber, and Otto Heck did a lot to help us. Right away they bought Pioneer outfits, a bugle and a drum for all the Pioneers. I became the leader of these Pioneers. At the ceremonial meeting on May Day all the Pioneers declared themselves patrons of the colts and piglets, and the girls became patrons of the poultry farm. In addition we Pioneers worked and helped the kolkhozes. We guarded the harvest and helped with the mowing, weeding, and horseback riding. Now after all the work of the political campaigns we spend our free time in the kolkhoz yard, where we clean the animals under our care and teach them to jump over obstacles, so that if they grow up they will be ready for the Red Army. Since we Pioneers started helping our kolkhozes, they have taken first place in Georgievsk Raion. But we are not lagging in our studies either. Through socialist competition and shock work, our schools have taken first place in the raion. Most of our pupils are shock workers, and all our kolkhozes have also taken first place in the raion in all of the economic and political campaigns, and we Pioneers will not allow this top position to be given up. We wanted to have a writing exchange with our foreign comrade Pioneers, but we don't know how to write there, to what address. Grandfather Kalinin I am sorry to bother you, I don't know what interests you the most in our little detachment, I could write everything to you. If I finish my studies, then I will also come to Moscow, right now I am in the fifth grade of the N.S.Sh. [incomplete secondary school] in the settlement of Mikhailovsky, which opened just in the fall, so it is still poorly equipped and has absolutely no visual aids. The breakfasts are still not set up well. I have to walk three km each way every day. All my grades are good or excellent. Just as our advanced kolkhozes have received prizes several times for taking first place, so our Young Pioneer detachments under the Koltunovka Village Soviet and several individual Pioneers have received prizes for good work.

I was awarded a balalaika as a prize at the Georgievsk Raion rally of Young Pioneers, ten rubles from the Koltunovka Village Soviet, and a certificate and five rubles from the Rosa Luxemburg Kolkhoz. That is all for now, next time, if I get an answer from you, I will write more often.

With Young Pioneer greetings. Be prepared! Young Pioneer leader Herrmann Roland.

From the time they were in diapers, the young generation of the 1930s was taught to be truthful, uncompromising about shortcomings, and prepared to expose and fight the enemies of socialism. For many children this turned into an amusing game, and if they succeeded in doing something serious, it also bolstered their self-esteem. Often these "games" became second nature to the children, generating a stereotyped pattern of behavior and view of reality. "And you know, almost none of the Germans like Soviet rule," the German boy Herrmann Roland wrote, thinking of this not as a denunciation but as the unvarnished truth, and not even suspecting that he might thereby doom the entire village. Enlightenment came, as a rule, when trouble knocked on the door at home and affected one's relatives and loved ones. But in the meantime the tradition of Pavlik Morozov was continued by the Young Pioneers and Komsomol members of school no. 35 in the city of Kuibyshev, who in September 1936 composed a letter exposing the counterrevolutionary work of a kulak:

# Document 139

Letter of denunciation from Young Pioneers and Komsomol members to director of forestry department, September 1936. TsKhDMO, f. 1, op. 23, d. 1188, l. 102. Typewritten copy.

To the director of the forestry department.

We have information from the Zubchaninovsky Village Soviet that citizen Aleksandr Aleksandrovich D'iakonov is a kulak, a very harmful parasite for our construction. Your duty is to do a purge of your institution, we the young generation are growing, but these kulaks are still hampering our studies and training with their proclamations. I, Misha Gorbunov, Zina Strelkova, and many other Young Pioneers and Komsomol members of ours saw him pasting

## Document 139 *continued*

up proclamations that "war is coming soon, we'll strangle the Bolsheviks, we'll hang Stalin, and we'll shoot down Krupskaia and her lovers," "Celebrate Easter—it is bestowed by God," and other absurdities. I wanted to rip them down, he noticed that we were watching him, and he quickly tore them up. He clipped one of us on the back of the head and yanked another one's ears, claiming that we had supposedly done it. This is a clever kulak, but we found out where he works and decided to write you that he should be taken out of there and fired. We keep track of everybody, that is our duty to Soviet authority.

The Young Pioneers and Komsomol members of Soviet School no. 35 of the city of Kuibyshev

As soon as we ripped away this proclamation, he quickly tore it up, that is how hard it is to fight a kulak, he is more clever and resourceful than us, and he turned around and accused us. Well that's all right, we won't leave our post, but party members, come to our aid.

---

As the documents make clear, local Pioneers did indeed provide a great deal of help to farms, especially in bringing in the harvest and breeding young animals. But the general politicization of life in the 1930s unfortunately also affected the activities of Young Pioneer organizations, which lost whatever autonomy they had had. Bureaucratism and overorganization drove out the remnants of Young Pioneer romanticism left over from the 1920s. The political indoctrination work in many organizations became dominant, while many activities were conducted as formalities, for the record. As a result of petty supervision by adults, children stopped feeling that they were in charge of the Young Pioneers organization, which was increasingly turning into an obedient appendage of the Komsomol and the party. Special attention was paid to forming cadres of Pioneer leaders, who were actually supposed to disseminate party policy in Pioneer detachments.

These leaders, however—obedient implementers of instructions from the top—were often deficient not simply in talent but even in an elementary education for working with children, with whom they lacked authority. Many of these young people, who had viewed a Young Pioneer leader's job as the initial step in a political career, were more than anything frightened of making a mistake. So they sought to follow the plan and instructions approved at the top.

They were afraid of creativity and initiative from below, which could lead to unpredictable consequences. Many children, especially sensitive to fakery and window dressing, despaired of the possibility that anything could be changed and withdrew into a shell. As a result, despite the outwardly quite prosperous picture and continuing growth of the Young Pioneers, the early 1930s were marked by a crisis within the movement. Just as in adult life, double standards of behavior and a dual morality were becoming increasingly widespread among children. Yet educators were surprised that the schoolboy who was best in conduct could come home and, upon removing his Pioneer kerchief, turn out to be an out-and-out hooligan. Party and Komsomol leaders became concerned about the decline in the authority of the Young Pioneers organization and hence in their ability to influence and control the young generation, and they discussed the issue "On Young Pioneer work" at a session of the Orgburo of the TsK of the VKP(b) on 7 May 1933.

The exchange that follows between L. M. Kaganovich and a Young Pioneer leader named Dorfman from Moscow's October Raion is of interest on many levels. It is a kind of cat-and-mouse game in which Kaganovich insists that Dorfman describe the situation in the Young Pioneer milieu "not the way you're supposed to" but as it really was. The Pioneer leader, who apparently was attending such an important meeting for the first time in his life, was clearly nervous as he adjusted to the conversation, and kept trying to ingratiate himself with the sly Kaganovich without slipping up, but it didn't work very well. So there was general laughter already when he asserted that the youngsters did not care whether they danced with boys or girls, or that nobody danced the "bourgeois" foxtrot:

---

# Document 140

From stenographic report of Orgburo session "On Young Pioneer Work," 7 May 1933. RGASPI, f. 17, op. 114, d. 236, ll. 193–201. Typewritten copy.

---

KAGANOVICH: What interests us the most is to hear from you what the Pioneers themselves are unhappy about; what kinds of opinions they express and what are they unhappy about?

## Document 140 *continued*

DORFMAN: The major shortcoming is this. What does the Pioneer demand? That he be the master of his organization.

KAGANOVICH: Look at the kind of language you are using. We are not asking about this formula. Tell us in plain language, the way you talk with the youngsters and they talk with you.

DORFMAN: They are unhappy that there are no special technical groups.

KAGANOVICH: That's all they're lacking? That's all they miss?

DORFMAN: There's no color in their work.

KAGANOVICH: What does color mean?

DORFMAN: There's no club.

KAGANOVICH: Now you tell us, do they want to dance, and with whom? Do the boys want to dance with the girls, or don't they care?

DORFMAN: That of course makes no difference (laughter).

KAGANOVICH: Please, Comrade Pioneer leaders, don't be shy, describe things in plain terms, don't try to use language that plays up to us. Tell us what Pioneers want. Do they want to have dancing, do they want to go to a museum, study art, or go to the theater or to the pictures? What do they want? Do they want to go to the pictures by themselves or to be taken, how many times do they want to go on their own, on their own without supervision, or under supervision? Do they want to be under supervision or not, and if so, how much?

DORFMAN: What do Pioneers want? They want to see a good picture. They don't like to go on an organized basis.

KAGANOVICH: Do they go on an organized basis?

DORFMAN: Yes.

KAGANOVICH: Are movies shown in school?

DORFMAN: Yes. Our school, for example, has a movie projector.

KAGANOVICH: What movies are shown?

DORFMAN: Most of all we run scientific pictures, as an aid, related to the study of some subject.

KAGANOVICH: But what pictures do the Pioneers like the most?

DORFMAN: Fights. Wherever there are fisticuffs, wherever people are leaping around.

KAGANOVICH: What else?

DORFMAN: Usually you can hear this kind of talk among the Pioneers: William Hart appears there, American actresses are in that. Now they'll spread the word, get about ten kids together and go to the pictures on their own.

KAGANOVICH: On what basis do they get together?

DORFMAN: The Pioneer unit has a work plan to go to the pictures three times a month. They fulfill that. But apart from that three or four youngsters get together and when classes are over they run to the movie theater to see a picture that interests them.

# Document 140 continued

KAGANOVICH: What pictures do the girls like the most? Or won't they say? What else do the kids want? Are they interested, for instance, in dancing?

DORFMAN: They're not very interested in dancing on a mass scale.

KAGANOVICH: Do they get to dance often?

DORFMAN: At every school dance.

KAGANOVICH: How many times a month are these dances held?

DORFMAN: Twice a month, but there are other evening functions as well.

KAGANOVICH: What functions are those?

DORFMAN: A shock worker's evening, a Pioneer detachment evening, and a school evening.

KAGANOVICH: Where are these functions held? Describe some specific function.

DORFMAN: Well we had an evening at school that was devoted to the issue of implementing the TsK's decision on the work of the Young Pioneer organization. This evening was arranged and conducted together with parents and the community. There was a short report at this function by the secretary of the party cell on implementation of the TsK's decision, then a representative of the TsK of the Komsomol spoke and afterward there was a brief report on the work of our Pioneer base. We awarded radios to the best shock working Pioneers as prizes. Five radios were handed out, and altogether twenty-eight people received prizes. After that there were amateur performances by the youngsters themselves.

KAGANOVICH: What kind of performances were these, and how did they manifest themselves?

DORFMAN: The units performed, they did physical-fitness exercises, they performed dances, there were individual dances, say from the ballet The Red Poppy and The Little Apple [a dance performed to a sailor's song of the same name—*Trans.*], and there was dancing for everybody. Then there was a stage production by the youngsters themselves and there was a living newspaper. And later, of course, there were refreshments for the youngsters.

KAGANOVICH: But does your school allow dancing in general? Where can the youngsters display some bravado and show off some tricks—is such dancing allowed? For example, the Kazachok ["The Cossack," a folk dance with an accelerating tempo—*Trans.*]? You don't have dances like that?

DORFMAN: The youngsters don't know the Kazachok, but they like to dance the russkaia ["The Russian," any of several Russian folk dances of varying tempos—*Trans.*]. They like "The Little Apple" and there are people who like to dance the Shamil' [named after the North Caucasian Muslim leader who defied Russian conquest in the mid-nineteenth century].

KAGANOVICH: And what about the foxtrot in your school? Do they dance it legally or illegally?

## Document 140 *continued*

DORFMAN: They don't dance the foxtrot, and they don't dance it illegally, either.

KAGANOVICH: They probably dance it, you just don't know about it. Well, what else are the youngsters interested in? You referred to technical groups, what kind of groups are those?

DORFMAN: A radio group, a sawing group, and the cinema.

KAGANOVICH: What else?

DORFMAN: A percussion orchestra has been organized. They are very interested in this.

KAGANOVICH: Which children are most interested in these groups? Do these groups encompass a small group of children?

DORFMAN: The fifth and sixth groups.[23] I would say that these groups do not encompass the majority, of course, and here is why—for one thing there are no leaders, for another there are no funds.

KAGANOVICH: What else are they interested in?

DORFMAN: They are interested in a lot of things.

KAGANOVICH: And the children, the Pioneers, how do they get along with each other? Are they indifferent, or are there serious arguments, animosity, egotism, this kind of selfishness? What predominates the most? Maybe you could give a few examples from your work.

DORFMAN: I can describe an incident of a political nature and an incident of an academic nature. The first incident. This was the situation. One girl stopped coming to school. She was a girl from the second group—twelve years old. She didn't come in for three days, some old woman dragged her to church and she went around there with the priests, collecting money, cleaning windows, washing floors and so forth. I dealt with this matter myself. I went with two other Pioneers, we ascertained the reason, and we discovered that the well-known priest Vedensky and another priest twenty-two years old were exploiting this girl. We managed to find out where she lived. They were giving her packages to distribute, and what they were putting in the packages were prayers and crosses to distribute to adults.

KAGANOVICH: And you persecuted this girl in school, of course?

DORFMAN: On the contrary.

KAGANOVICH: Did she admit her errors? Did she write a declaration or not?

DORFMAN: We did not distribute wide notification of the detachment's meeting on this matter. We just had a preholiday rally. We just had a preholiday rally where we described this incident in passing. True, it was very easy for us to uncover this. The second incident has to do with how youngsters relate to other youngsters. We have situations like this one. A girl at our school is the chairman of the student committee [*uchkom*], and based on the fact that she is the best student they began to persecute her: they started saying that she goes with somebody and that is how she gets good grades.

## Document 140 *continued*

KAGANOVICH: How old is she?

DORFMAN: Fifteen, she is in the sixth group.

KAGANOVICH: Are there fights between the boys, and if so, what causes them?

DORFMAN: Fights break out for no special reason. [Somebody says:] "Come out, let's fight." They just go for a fistfight to see who is stronger, who will beat whom.

KAGANOVICH: But in general, on what basis do fights occur, is there any hatred toward each other?

DORFMAN: Yes, there is.

KAGANOVICH: Based on what?

DORFMAN: We had an incident at school. A group got together—two boys and two girls. They got together at one boy's home on the pretext that they gathered to study subjects in which they were behind, and they shut themselves up in a separate room and took vodka in there. Their mother discovered these goings-on, she discovered that one boy came with half a bottle of vodka.

KAGANOVICH: How old is he?

DORFMAN: Thirteen. But they were not able to drink it, because the mother knocked, they opened the door and she found the vodka, took it away and gave them a real tongue-lashing. Somebody at school let the cat out of the bag, told a girl, the girl told the teacher, and they began to take up the issue in class. And after that they wanted to arrange a fistfight. There are also fights that are related to thefts.

[BORIS] ROIZENMAN [a member of the party's Central Control Commission]: But are there any fights based on envy, say, somebody is doing better in his studies or eats better or dresses better? Do fights occur because of that?

DORFMAN: As an example, let's look at one class. We have boys who are well provided with money and pens and notebooks, they are fully provided for, yet they still steal, and not only in school, but from their own parents as well.

KAGANOVICH: You don't seem to be able to describe relationships in general between the children, meaning their very essence.

DORFMAN: I did describe them.

KAGANOVICH: I am asking how much our children have already progressed in truly human terms with respect to how they relate to one another, with respect to getting rid of the mentality of the past, egotism, vanity, selfishness, with respect to getting rid of all the bad elements that have lingered from the past. After all, we have to say that in regard to the human psyche 80 percent still survives from the past in our country. So I would like to find out how things are going with respect to ridding our children of these vestiges of the past.

## Document 140 *continued*

DORFMAN: I have already cited this case. Because a girl is a good student, people try to take the wind out of her sails and begin to taunt her to the effect that she supposedly used to go with somebody or that she has a good relationship with the chairman of the uchkom and he is giving her good grades. Another situation has to do with thievery, when even well-to-do youngsters still steal. We have these cases too. Children sometimes assemble not only from a single building but from a neighboring one and organize attacks on children from other buildings.

KAGANOVICH: Are there ever any arguments at your meetings?

DORFMAN: Almost never. Somebody will give a report, people will ask questions, some people will have their say and at that point the meeting ends.

I would also like to say something on another issue. We have special-education schools. Nobody is working with these schools. Yet this issue is very important and it requires a lot of attention. It is mostly workers' children who attend these schools; retarded children, underdeveloped and handicapped children. There are many cases of thievery among them, they act like hooligans. I would like to figure out what needs to be done for them, some definite framework should be set up, and the issue of special-education schools in general must receive serious attention. We also have to raise the issue of books, the issue of literature for these children. We have five such schools in our raion. It is very hard to work in these schools. The children act very much like hooligans and do nothing but steal. These are sick children—they have handicaps. There must be very intensive work done with them.

---

So Kaganovich, who was trying to find out "how much our children have already progressed . . . with respect to getting rid of the mentality of the past, . . . the vestiges of the past," could easily conclude that they had not progressed very much. It turned out that the Young Pioneers could not bear overorganization and petty supervision; they clearly preferred American action movies to the scientific films that were crammed into them at school; they were less interested in classical music than in a "percussion orchestra"; they danced the forbidden foxtrot on the sly and drank vodka; they not only got into fights "for no special reason"—as a test of strength— but also often acted like hooligans and stole things.

The speakers at the meeting proposed ways to intensify Young Pioneer work. Komsomol secretary Kosarev, for example, sharply criticized formalism and overorganization, proposing that an emphasis be placed on initiative from the Young Pioneers themselves and that they be granted more autonomy and freedom of creativity:

---

## Document 141

Speech by Kosarev at Orgburo session "On Young Pioneer Work," 7 May 1933. RGASPI, f. 17, op. 114, d. 236, ll. 185–186. Typewritten copy.

---

. . . Finally, I want to say a few words concerning children's recreation. This area is in extremely poor shape. Nobody is interested in how youngsters want to spend their recreation time. The Pioneer leader decides this issue. Instead of assembling the Pioneers and asking them how they would like to spend their recreation time, the leader presents them with a plan, which he has drawn up himself or has received from the organization.

The children have all been lumped together. It is impossible to figure out where the good Pioneers are and where the bad ones are. Nothing sets the good Pioneers apart. We are debating this issue in the TsK—maybe we should follow the Boy Scouts' example and introduce some kind of medals for Pioneers. Right now all Pioneers look alike. The top people in a detachment are usually not children. Who are these top people? There is a leader, an assistant leader and older Pioneers—who are already Komsomol members. The heads of Pioneer detachments also include nice youngsters, but for the most part they are appointed in a bureaucratic manner from the top, they do not have adequate pedagogical experience, and often these are already overage youngsters and it is very hard for them to manage children, and uninteresting besides. Such heads, understandably, lack authority with the Pioneers.

A few words about voluntariness in the Pioneer detachments. There is no voluntariness. The detachments have existed for twelve years already. And what do they do? Still the same assemblies, the same discussions, and in the summer, group gatherings around a campfire. There are Pioneer groups that are interested in mathematics, in all kinds of inventing, and there are groups that are interested in studying nature. So the children establish their own associations and all kinds of groups for these purposes. This is the most precious thing that should enliven the Pioneer organization, that should make it breathe at full strength. This is lacking in the Pioneer detachments.

So the problem is not that there isn't enough assistance. A better job could be done, of course, in helping the Pioneer organization. But the problem is that we are applying a number of mistaken premises to the work of the Pioneer organization. These mistaken premises must be eliminated. The problem is that we are not selecting the best Komsomol members as Pioneer leaders. We don't have many leaders, and those we have quickly leave and a large number of detachments don't have any leaders at all.

## Document 141 *continued*

I want to come back to children's recreation. The situation in this area is very bad. Just take Moscow. It has only one or two children's theaters, and morning movie showings for children are almost never organized. Nobody is involved in producing special children's movies, movies that interest children and educate them. Children's theaters don't have appropriate plays, either. You will recall, five years ago "The Bluebird" was produced at the Art Theater and how delighted the children's reaction to it was. We—and that includes the Narkompros—are not concerning ourselves enough about children's recreation.

Krupskaia also viewed formalism, window dressing, and excessive organization as an evil that hurt the Pioneers. She correctly pointed out that Pioneers at their meetings tried to imitate adults, and the result was becoming a farce. It was also typical that the Pioneers were afraid to tell her the truth about which books they liked to read, because "adventure literature was forbidden." But the main conclusion that Krupskaia drew from numerous children's letters was that the Pioneer organization failed to satisfy youngsters:

## Document 142

Speech by Krupskaia at Orgburo session "On Young Pioneer Work," 7 May 1933. RGASPI, f. 17, op. 114, d. 236, ll. 206–208. Typewritten copy.

KRUPSKAIA: What shortcomings do I see in the Pioneer organization? First, we have a mechanical quality: whoever wants to can join the Pioneer organization. As soon as he reaches ten years of age, he joins it. Whether he knows anything politically or not, either way he is accepted. There is no probationary period. There is no period when he aspires to be a Pioneer. There is no practice of having somebody briefly sum up at the time of acceptance: now such-and-such a child has completed this and this, let's elect him to this, he has done such and such well. This doesn't exist. And so the most diverse kinds of people turn up at Pioneer meetings: people from the older groups, people from the younger groups, they don't listen to one another, everybody talks at once. I have attended several meetings. All these general detachments discuss within each detachment so-called political issues and they are discussed in the same formulations as adults discuss them. No connection is made between a political issue and real life. Our Pioneer organization used to be different. The Pioneers in the countryside, if one of them saw something that was wrong, he would take the floor and speak. But now at a ceremonial meeting they single out a group that begins to recite the latest resolution of the TsK. It will finish reciting, walk by to a drumbeat and that ends it. There is no real political work being done.

Now they are saying here that a Pioneer leader is unable to give an answer if a Pioneer asks him a question. But after all, there is nothing terrible about that, it is very easy to deal with that situation: say that the leader doesn't know this, he will read up or ask someone and then will give an answer. No, [people say,] that must not happen. He cannot do that. There is an awful lot of formalism. For example, with respect to reading books. There were these courses for juvenile correspondents. I asked them what kind of books they like a lot. Everybody kept quiet. I kept asking and asking, and they were silent. Finally one of them said: *Katorga i ssylka.* ["Hard labor and exile" was a journal of the Society of Former Political Prisoners and Exiles that was published between 1921 and 1935. It carried articles about the revolutionary movement in tsarist Russia.] Well, all right, I said, and the books that interest you, the kind you can't put down? No discussion ever got going. Yet there is a lot that interests the youngsters.

KAGANOVICH: He didn't answer because he was afraid, because adventure literature is forbidden.

KRUPSKAIA: But who knows, if you say any book, you could get into trouble, but if you say *Katorga i ssylka,* that's all right.

The youngsters are formalistic about expressing their opinions. A certain number of kids speak, always the same ones. And they ask hackneyed questions. I was recently corresponding with some Pioneers and I've written for *Pionerskaia Pravda.* I have written some letters, particularly about relations between boys and girls. The people at *Iskra* [The spark] and *Pionerskaia Pravda.* sent me a pile of letters, and some of the letters are formalistic while some are very interesting. You get the impression that the Pioneer organization is not satisfying the youngsters. They are not finding their kind of work there. They are afraid of organizing groups, they don't think it is related to the Pioneers. . . .

There is somehow no initiative, good beginnings and good ideas are not picked up and there is no community work at all. There are work assignments, but no real work. For example, they will assign Pioneers to collect refuse for use as raw materials. A little girl climbs onto a table and reads off how much refuse she has collected. But stirring up an idea, having a child outraged about something—that doesn't happen. It is this situation that must be changed, we must rethink the work itself so that there is no situation like the one now, so that there is every possible kind of group, and not just on paper, but groups that actually function in real life. We have to carefully rethink the programs of these groups and organize them well, so that initiative develops on a wide scale there and organizational abilities and skills develop there. After all, the Pioneer organization is of tremendous importance because it can begin to mold organizers in the early years. And in some places where the work has been set up well, we see children developing organizational abilities. It is an abnormal situation when all youngsters are doing is deciding how to sew on a kerchief or where to hang a banner and they are not doing any really useful, really essential work.

The Pioneers have laws and an oath that in large part have been copied from the Boy Scouts. But now that the Boy Scouts have degenerated into totally bourgeois organizations, it seems to me that we should repudiate these laws for the Pioneers.

We must do a tremendous amount of work to reorganize the Pioneer organization and do away with the formalism that now constitutes the principal evil in our Pioneer organizations.

---

Although they properly diagnosed the disease of the Young Pioneers and proposed what were in principle proper methods of treatment, Krupskaia and Kosarev—unquestionably competent people who were aware of all the subtleties of the issue—said nothing about the causes or predictability of this critical situation in the Pioneer organization. The people who were really to blame for the disease were the adults who "directed" the work of children's organizations in accordance with the party's instructions and in the spirit of the times. This meant that the proposed methods for treating the "Pioneer disease" were patently unfeasible. What was needed first was treatment for the underlying problems, among them homeless children.

Homelessness among children became a genuine plague for Soviet society in the 1920s and 1930s, creating a breeding ground for an increase in juvenile delinquency—and later, of adult crime. And whereas the homelessness among children of the 1920s related to wars, revolutionary upheavals, and deaths from epidemics and famine, the homelessness of the 1930s—already an offshoot of the new system—deserves a separate discussion for the additional reason that this phenomenon was assiduously kept under wraps for a long time. Yet the archival materials not only discuss how serious it was but also provide food for thought about the many latent sources of government policymaking at the time.

A report on the work of the Children's Commission of the VTsIK for 1932–34 acknowledges that "a relapse of child homelessness" occurred during that period.[24] The materials from the commission and Narkompros show that the network of institutions for homeless and neglected children expanded significantly. In the Northern Caucasus alone, a major upsurge in homelessness led in late 1932 and early 1933 to the establishment of twenty-six new children's homes and eight infant-care homes and the expansion of the network of raion children's homes.[25] From 1932 to 1934 appropriations for these purposes on a nationwide scale increased by 150 percent.[26] But why did such a surge of homelessness occur specifically in the first half of the 1930s? The sources attest that the principal causes were, first, collectivization, which was accompanied by the dekulakization of peasants and mass deaths at special resettlement centers, and, second, the famine of 1932–33, which was also mainly attributable to the state. In reading the documents, one cannot help but be astonished at how skillfully the country's leadership created hardships and problems for its citizens, only to solve them with considerably less success.

Distressed by the explosion of homeless children, the state established a network of children's address registries in large cities in 1934 to help search for children and parents. Here is an example of a notice that sparked a search by staffers of the registries, the police, and a children's home:

---

## Document 143

Letter of L. M. Pisanka to Children's Commission of VTsIK on disappearance of daughter, 28 June 1935. GARF, f. 5207, op. 1, d. 727, l. 54. Original manuscript.

---

In the spring of 1933 my daughter twelve years old Maria Lukitichna Pisanka from the village of Deregivka in Novo-Vodolazhsky Raion, Khar'kov Oblast in Ukraine, came to the city of Khar'kov because of the famine, and disappeared; it might be surmised that either she starved to death or she ended up in some Soviet shelter, but to this point I have not heard anything about her, although I am not changing my residence. I don't know whether she knows my address. I earnestly request the Commission to make an inquiry about her and report to me at my address: Luker'ia Moiseevna Pisanka.

---

Such was the tragedy of a mother who had lost her daughter. There were countless such mothers throughout the country, who sent their children to the cities, realizing that there lay the only hope for salvation. According to a report by an NKVD inspector of labor colonies, sent to the Children's Commission of the VTsIK, 312,472 homeless children were caught and delivered to child-rearing institutions in 1935–36, and more than half of them repeatedly ran away from children's homes during these years and were caught again. Typically, of the nearly 196,000 homeless children who arrived in 1936 at children's homes, 68,000 had run away from parents who were still alive.[27] Under these circumstances the TsK of the VKP(b) and the SNK considered a number of measures for the elimination of child homelessness and child neglect, and adopted a special resolution on the issue on 31 May 1935. But as a secret memorandum to the SNK dated 12 April 1941 makes clear, implementation of the resolution during the ensuing six years was unsatisfactory.[28]

The situation in children's homes and other special child-rearing institutions, in which hundreds of thousands of young people found themselves during the 1930s, deserves a separate discussion. Depending on the contingent, these institutions were part of the systems of Narkompros, the People's Commissariat of Social Security, the NKVD and Narkomzdrav. After inspecting medical care and sanitary services at Moscow children's homes in 1935, a special team reported its findings in a memorandum to the Presidium of the Children's Commission of the VTsIK:

---

## Document 144

Report of medical team to Children's Commission of VTsIK on conditions in Moscow children's homes, October 1935. GARF, f. 5207, op. 1, d. 1056, l. 2. Typewritten copy.

---

With outrage the team points out the outrageous [repetition in original— *Trans.*] condition of the only medical children's home—the Dzerzhinsky isolation ward with a capacity of 350, accepted just four months ago by the Moscow City Health Department from the city board of public education (the isolation ward's director is Comrade Brunshtein).

As of the day of the survey, the isolation ward housed 446 children, of whom 377 were ill (287 with trachoma, 71 with herpes, 51 with syphilis) [presumably some patients had more than one disease]; the rest of the children were completely healthy, including 54 preschoolers who were compelled to be around the patients and 33 children who had recovered but had not been removed from this children's home [again, there appears to be some overlap]. As a result, there were 29 recurrences of illness among the 33 children who had already recovered. The healthy children include some who are mentally retarded and deaf-mute. In addition, children who have recovered and are difficult to handle live in the comprehensive school for up to three years and have not been moved to the appropriate institutions.

The school premises are in an exceptionally neglected condition, filthy and unsanitary. Many windows have no glass in them, and there are no tanks for drinking water. The baths are in a cellarlike, filthy area, which has only thirty small tubs.

The Dzerzhinsky school sent two pupils who had ostensibly recovered to children's home no. 3 at the Pravda station, even though they had not been completely cured. As a result, nine pupils at children's home no. 3 contracted herpes.

The school's internal staircase has no railings. On 29 September of this year Vitia Kiselyov, a seven-year-old boy, started walking down from the third floor, but he fell off the staircase to his death. Yet even on 13 October, when our team visited the isolation ward, railings had still not been built for the staircase. The isolation ward also has a shortage of clothing and shoes for the children. There are no dishes, and the children drink tea from deep plates with tablespoons. No child-rearing work is done. Children who disobey are undressed and sent to sit naked in a separate room. Such "practices" result in the fact that even sick children are forced to run away from this isolation ward. For example, between 1 January and 30 September of this year, 105 children ran away. The greatest number of these escapes—fifty-eight (since July)—occurred after this institution had been turned over to the city health department.

---

The situation was no better in the children's homes of Narkompros, especially those located in small towns, raion centers, and settlements—and these accounted for the majority around the country. Year after year these institutions lacked the money for children's basic needs; the selection of caregivers was often haphazard, and there were few dedicated individuals who were ready to sacrifice themselves in order to reeducate difficult children. In a memorandum from the Central Committee of the Komsomol to R. S. Zemliachka at the SNK, we learn the following:

## Document 145

Memorandum from TsK of Komsomol on Narkompros children's homes, 12 April 1941. TsKhDMO, f. 1, op. 23, d. 1472, ll. 49–50. Typewritten copy.

The unsatisfactory performance of the children's homes of Narkompros is borne out by the following fact: the Procurator's Office of Krasnodar Krai has cited the krai's children's homes for serious violations of the law: an inadequate supply of clothing, shoes, and food for children, unsanitary accommodations for them, and in several homes, the embezzlement of state funds that were allocated for maintenance of the homes. Children's home no. 39 in Plastunka Raion had no fuel; the room in which the children slept was cold and dirty, and the air temperature was so low that the water in the washbasins froze and the children could not wash themselves. The business manager of the children's home, Serliuk, corrupted young girls, raping a girl named Alaeva (he has been sentenced for this to five years' imprisonment). It was also discovered that children's home director Korsakova misappropriated 9,500 rubles in state funds; the manager of the sewing workshop misappropriated 7,800 rubles; and the director of studies embezzled 1,500 rubles (all these individuals have been taken into custody). [A description follows of a children's home in Novo-Kuban Raion.]

The following was detected at the children's home in the Cossack settlement of Ubozhenskaia in Uspensky Raion: the rooms in which the children were living were not heated, the rooms in general were dirty, the glass in the windows was broken, the stoves were out of order, the temperature in the rooms was ten degrees below zero [Celsius, or fourteen above, Fahrenheit]; the water in the washstands froze, and the children did not wash themselves and were filthy; during the severely cold period, children burned overcoats, blankets, books, bedsheets, and other belongings in the stoves; in all, ten thousand rubles' worth of various items were burned in this manner. Fifty children had no shoes, did not attend school, and some of them were forced to walk barefoot in the snow; a commission found forty-six children with frostbitten feet. Children were often left without bread; some of them were beaten by children's home director Strel'tsov. Criminal proceedings have been initiated against the individuals who are to blame for these abominations, including children's home director Strel'tsov.

Similar facts have been found at other children's homes as well.

The memoranda on inspections of the children's homes probably paint the most objective and comprehensive picture of everyday life in the homes during the 1930s. The home at Barybino station outside Moscow was an ordinary children's home, not notable for anything, located not somewhere in the Russian hinterland but in direct proximity to the central leadership of Narkompros, the City Children's Commission, the Moscow City Board of Public Education, and other institutions that were responsible for the situation in children's homes. These circumstances make the following memorandum, covering 1936, especially interesting:

# Document 146

Memorandum to deputy chairman of Moscow City Children's Commission on Children's Commune, Barybino, 1936. GARF, f. 5207, op. 1, d. 1293, ll. 7–8. Corrected and certified typewritten copy.

To Comrade Sorokin, deputy chairman of the city children's commission, from instructors Dubinina and Minaeva

Pursuant to your directive, our inspection on 19 and 20 June of the children's home at Barybino station.

The children's home, which bears the name The Children's Commune, is located twenty km from Barybino station and is situated in very good natural conditions: the buildings of the children's commune stand on an elevated site in timberland on the bank of the Severianka River.

The children's commune is designed for six hundred youngsters. Last winter there were 570, and at the time of inspection, 364, for the rest had been sent off to relatives for vacation and sixty had been sent to the Pravda Children's Home. All the youngsters are of school age, from eight to sixteen. The children's commune has 256 Young Pioneers.

The children have an extremely unkempt, tattered appearance. First of all we should note that the youngsters are not dressed according to the season: the boys walk around in long trousers, some even in corduroy shirts. Children are dressed in various ways: some in undershirts worn loose over their trousers, some in jackets, some in shoes without laces worn on bare feet, some just barefoot, and one boy even wore high boots. All the clothing was old and torn. A boy named Minaev broke the record in this regard, for he was walking around in one trouser leg, while the other one, ripped along its entire length, hung off him like a wing. A girl named Temnova walked around in a torn dress in such a way that it barely stayed on her shoulders. The girls' panties have no elastic whatsoever, but the children still found a way to put them on: the girls secure pieces of elastic to their bodies for an indefinite time and then tuck the panties under them so they don't fall down. We should mention that the children tie on the elastics tightly, and they sleep in them and walk around in them the whole day without removing them.

Moreover, this "wonderful outfitting" is not based on any measurements and one can often see a boy who has used a string to draw in trousers that are too big for him, or a girl in a dress that is too long or short.

The youngsters' hands and feet are dirty and weather-beaten. The haircuts also vary greatly: there are "boxer cuts," short haircuts, and shaggy hair down to the neck.

The rooms also look unattractive. The beds are old, the boards on them constantly slide over, and one night a girl even fell on the floor altogether. The mattresses are old and in poor condition; 20 percent of them need to be replaced with new ones immediately. There is only a change and a half of bed linen, which is simply unacceptable. The towels in use are dirty. The night tables and chairs are old, and many of them are completely broken.

Much of the time children are left to their own devices without adult supervision. This has resulted in a number of negative situations that we observed during our visit to the children's commune. The children go swimming in a disorganized manner, without adults. They swim as much as they want, and wherever they want. Some of them choose shallow spots in the river for bathing while others head for deep areas after stocking up on logs and boards. They drop them in the water, then swim around while hanging on to them and knock each other about, so that there is a risk of an accident. Some little kids swim until they are blue and come out of the water totally exhausted. The youngsters immediately start playing on the riverbank, some of them try to catch fish with towels, some wash their clothes, some start campfires; one girl, Tosia Yefimova, brought a pen and ink to the riverbank and many youngsters wrote things on their hands. One such inscription, for example, read: "I swear to love Zhenia Belova," and so forth.

The children also walk in the woods without elders. On 19 June six boys got lost: Karataev, Fedorenko, Shpakov, Spirin, Volkov, and Fadkov. They were all two hours late for supper.

We noticed two black-and-blue marks on the neck of Vera Sokolova. First Vera did not want to explain the reason for these marks, but then, with embarrassment, she said that Liza Ivanova had kissed her in the woods, which resulted in the blue marks on her neck.

There was a case in early spring when two girls from bedrooms 5 and 9 were drowning and Young Pioneer Misha, who by chance was passing by from the village, rescued them.

The children invented a game for themselves that involves hurling a stocking, which has been tightly packed with dust, through the air like a rocket, and as it falls it creates an entire cloud of dust. The youngsters play this game a lot, even though it has been forbidden by the management.

All the facts we have cited indicate that child-rearing work is poorly organized. Yet the children's commune has a work plan for the summer, and a daily schedule for the children has actually been drawn up, but the schedule is often disregarded and the work plan is not always fulfilled.

With the onset of the vacation period, the children's commune opened a Young Pioneer camp. Every morning the Pioneers do exercises, line up and raise the flag. Both in the morning and the evening, the lineup is conducted with great ceremony, accompanied by an orchestra.

With regard to the exercises, we should note that while they are done under a physician's supervision, the youngsters do them in long trousers, and some even in corduroy shirts. Many children knot their shirts at the waist. [A description follows of other outdoor activities.]

On June 19 an evening of performances by the girls' detachment no. 2 was held. The evening took place in the club of the children's commune. The program consisted of a recitation, dancing, a production of song and dance called "The Merry Flower Garden" and, as the program said, a performance of physical exercises by little Octobrists. The evening went well. The youngsters were well prepared. A particular standout was Mania Vlasova, who did a lovely job of reciting the poem "Song of Spain." We find it necessary to remark, however, that the physical-exercise performances by the little Octobrists, in our view, were the most genuine acrobatic number. The youngsters who did it displayed excellent technique and skill. Nevertheless, this number, based on stunts in which the youngsters contorted their bodies into various shapes, was exhausting for them.

In spite of the "failings" and deviations from instructions cited by the two priggish inspectors, the youngsters at the children's commune do not convey an impression of being unhappy, especially by comparison with those who were discussed above. The memorandum is more interesting for its detailed description of the everyday routine of a children's home and the life of a Young Pioneer camp. One point is beyond question: the indigent living standard of these institutions. The documents make clear that this was precisely the case at most children's homes. Government appropriations both for the children's accommodations and for their food, schooling, and so forth fell far short of their needs, and in addition there were not enough caregivers, and their wages were low. All this could be attributed to the overall, grim situation in the half-

starving country and might be understandable if not for the radically different level of support allocated to homes for children of
Schutzbund members and especially for young refugees of the
Spanish Civil War. A political game was played, unfortunately,
even over children's homes, and when the need arose, money was
found, in sizable sums. In 1938 there were 2,200 children who had
been brought out of Spain and were living in eleven children's
homes in the USSR. According to the sources, an army of 1,500
people was helping to rear them—two adults for every three children, a ratio of which an administrator of an ordinary Soviet children's home could not even dream. More than twenty-one million
rubles was allocated from the special fund of the Central Council
of Trade Unions in 1938 to support the Spanish children's homes.
(In comparison, the entire budget for children's homes in the USSR
in 1934 was 169.5 million rubles, and while the prescribed cost for
feeding one Soviet child in a children's home in 1934 was a mere
four hundred rubles for the year, the figure for one Spanish child
was more than 2,600 rubles in 1938.)[29] So much for the myth that
the Soviet state placed equal value on all children. When the world
community lost interest in the events in Spain and Austria, the relevant agencies gradually also lost interest in the children of
Schutzbund members and of fighters for Republican Spain.

The educators themselves knew that the weakest part of child
rearing in children's homes during the 1930s was coldness, formalism, and the lack of individual attention. "Our children's homes
were more stagnant than any other children's institutions, because
even the appearance of our youngsters, the appearance of our institutions, and the appearance of the educators were all stereotyped,
they all bore the imprint of a stereotype that affected a child's psyche, an educator's psyche, and the psyche of anyone who worked in
a children's home. After all, it was no secret to anyone that after
taking a child into a children's home who was normal, the child we
put out was often a difficult one, even though you would think that
the process should be the opposite."[30] Could anyone have been
more eloquent in describing the crux of the problems in children's
homes than the educator who said this at a conference in the
Moscow City Board of Public Education on 4 January 1935?

It was common knowledge that children's homes during the

1930s had a severe problem with hooliganism and were a kind of breeding ground for juvenile delinquency. Educators knew and did not hide the fact that a large percentage of child prostitutes came out of children's homes.[31] Trouble occurred so frequently at children's homes that it came to be taken for granted. On 12 January 1937 a group of five children at the Krasnaia Sloboda Raion Children's Home in Mordovia tried, according to a memorandum, "to get into the storeroom of the children's home in order to get dressed and take off from the home. Upon discovering this attempt the director placed one of the pupils in a cold room. Other children, in protest, began to set fire to children's home property (they set fire to three blankets, thirty-eight mattresses, and several pillows and broke chairs and tables) and beat up the director. When the police arrived at the home, the group of children beat up the police chief. The incident finally ended when a fire brigade that had been summoned hosed down the children with cold water."[32] After this kind of fighting, the kind of behavior by children's home occupants that was reported at a party meeting of Narkompros on 1 December 1935 seems like nothing more than innocent pranks: in one place youngsters constantly referred to Stakhanovites as "Stakanovites" (*stakan* in Russian means "drinking glass"), while in another they "tore up a portrait of Comrade Stalin and wrote pornographic inscriptions on the leaders' portraits."[33]

The children's homes were clearly failing in their effort to reeducate yesterday's homeless children. Then a new idea was promoted—to place children in foster care, not only by specific individuals and families, but also by workers' collectives and especially by kolkhozes. The state did everything possible to encourage this practice, including the awarding of tax breaks and direct bonuses to kolkhozes that took children into their care. It is known that forty thousand children were turned over to kolkhozes for foster care in 1934 alone.[34] The result of this measure is apparent from a letter Krupskaia wrote to Kalinin on 22 November 1934: "Children are being distributed to those who wish to take them. It is still rather difficult to have youngsters on kolkhozes; collective foster care runs the risk of turning into a veiled form of exploitation of child labor."

Whatever one thinks of Krupskaia, there is no denying that she was well informed and competent with respect to the real situation of children in the 1930s. Even a cursory examination of her personal files is enough to see that she received an endless stream of letters, about twenty to twenty-five a day, and most of them from children, caregivers, and teachers. And one more important point: as she was obviously in disfavor during the 1930s, Lenin's widow tried not to waste her talents on minutiae and always raised only the most painful and urgent problems in her messages to the leadership. This meant that exploitation of the labor of children under foster care on kolkhozes was a problem that actually existed and which Kalinin, in his response, tried to brush off with general phrases.[35]

The documents also reveal other instances—uncovered in connection with other subjects—in which the labor of children's home occupants was exploited. Ironically, the gigantomania so fashionable at the time proved to be one of the ways for the directors of children's homes to distinguish themselves, and that is what ultimately destroyed them. Establishing homes of one thousand children each seemed to be the thing to do. Children's homes in Sverdlovsk were especially successful with regard to the number of occupants. Meanwhile, intelligent educators worried that children's homes were turning into flophouses, that it was physically impossible to do any work with formerly homeless children, and that in order to maintain at least a semblance of discipline, authorities were constantly forced to resort to emergency coercive measures rather than educational ones. For example, director Ionin of the Red Dawns Integrated Agricultural Enterprise in Leningrad set up his own modern and profitable operation based almost exclusively on unpaid labor by children's home occupants. He was, however, convicted not of this offense but on the charge that in the heat of the struggle to overfulfill the plan, "Stakhanovite" Ionin often got carried away and punished disobedient youngsters too severely: placing frogs in their mouths or locking them up in the cellar or a lavatory, for example. This kind of practice, as one might expect, was condemned by the party organization of Narkompros in 1938.[36]

Hooliganism and juvenile delinquency became serious problems in the 1930s. Even the games related to politics that children played bordered on mass hooliganism and rioting. A typical example was the situation involving "Chapaev assaults." The release of the film *Chapaev* in 1934 led to a nationwide craze for "Reds-vs.-Whites" battles among children. On 24 January 1935, two hundred youngsters took part in a Chapaev assault in Gor'ky. According to a secret letter from the Gor'ky City Committee of the Komsomol, the youngsters used sticks and fists, "constructed a cannon and stuffed it with ball bearings, but fortunately it did not fire."[37] In Stalingrad, students from ten of the city's schools continually took part in Chapaev assaults in 1935.[38] Many adults winked at the hooliganlike games until a surprising subtext of these "battles" was discovered—in a number of places the "Whites" defeated the "Reds." This was no laughing matter anymore.

Another serious problem that the authorities faced in the early 1930s was so-called "juvenile profiteering," against which an especially fierce campaign was waged. Many children who had been born after the revolution and had not seen capitalism were unexpectedly developing a commercial bent, which the authorities feared more than anything else. "The overwhelming majority of youngsters who sell cigarettes on the streets, who shine boots, and so forth, are schoolchildren. Some of them are Young Pioneers. All of them are children of working parents. The evidence that has been gathered indicates that, as a rule, children go to profiteer on the street not out of indigence or a calamitous financial situation but as a result of extremely poor work by the schools and the Young Pioneer organization in the area of meeting children's needs," said a report prepared for the session of the Orgburo of the TsK cited above. "A poor job is being done of combating juvenile profiteering around Moscow, and in a number of cities, such as Rostov, Novorossiisk, and others, nothing is being done, for the boards of public education and the schools think the police should handle it, the police think the schools and the board of public education should handle it, and the Young Pioneer organization is standing on the sidelines."[39]

Here are examples of "young profiteers" detained around Moscow: "Furshin, a student in class 5-C at school No. 3 in Bauman Raion, regularly sells matches. He buys a pack at twenty kopecks and sells it at fifty. Furshin's parents are quite well-to-do. Kostia Vasil'ev, a student at school no. 29 in Dzerzhinsky Raion, does not go home from school. He heads for the Tret'iakov passage. He lays out matches on the steps, opens a pack of cigarettes and sells them." The youngsters spent the money they made on movies, sweets, cigarettes, and liquor. Yet what troubled the adults was that "if it is not stopped in time, juvenile profiteering . . . could become an end in itself, a habit for making commercial profits," which was manifestly at odds with the principles of socialism. That was why the police in Moscow went out to catch the young profiteers by the hundreds, even though only 1 to 2 percent of them were homeless. According to the report, the number of underage lawbreakers brought in to Moscow police stations for profiteering in 1932 increased by 1,133 over 1931, and most of them were factory workers' children.[40] This figure underscores not only how widespread the phenomenon was but also the increased attention that the police were paying to it.

Distressed by the rise in juvenile crime, the state took a host of measures in the 1930s, the best-known of which was the law of 7 April 1935 "On Measures to Combat Crime Among Minors." But this did not produce results. Data on underage criminals were always classified in the USSR. A memorandum to the SNK dated 12 April 1941, stamped "Secret" details not a decline but a rise in juvenile crime following the adoption of the 1935 law. "Judicial bodies have convicted minors aged twelve to sixteen as follows: in 1936, 15,031; in 1937, 17,234; in 1938, 20,203; in 1939, 24,975; and in 1940, 24,203. The principal reasons among minors at present are the homelessness of many children, the lack of a child-rearing influence by the family, and poor coverage of children with outside activities. A study of juvenile cases has shown that 40 to 50 percent of those who committed crimes were pupils in school, about half were not pupils, and many of them were not doing anything at all prior to the commission of the crime."[41] It was a revelation that, notwithstanding the Law on Universal Compulsory Elementary Education, many school-age children were not in school, and thousands were dropping out every year for various reasons. Another new problem was crime by children under twelve years of age. The memorandum expressed regret that criminal proceedings could not be initiated against them under the law, even though a large number of crimes, especially larcenies, were committed by such small children.

In the second half of the 1930s parental responsibility for child rearing was increased. On 10 January 1937 the newspaper *Rabochaia Moskva* carried an article headed "A Party Rebuke for the Communist Nekrasov." The reporter told the story of a party member who worked at the Pavshinsky Machine Shop and had been given a written rebuke for doing a poor job of child rearing. The case was fairly typical. His elder son had been expelled from school at fifteen for hooliganism, while the younger one, an eleven-year-old child, "swiped some money and on 6 November got drunk." The newspaper focused on the latter incident in particular, because the anniversary of the October Revolution was being celebrated. The night before the holiday, a group of eleven-year-old schoolchildren imitated grown-ups by organizing a "7 November party," buying candy for the girls and wine for the boys. They had a feast to remember. Because eleven-year-olds could not be held accountable, their parents took the full brunt of the punishment.

Stalin's assertions that children were not responsible for their parents may have misled not only people who were far removed from politics but even the likes of Krupskaia. But the documents contain irrefutable evidence of the persecution—approved and sanctioned at the highest level—of children of "formerly" disenfranchised persons, people resettled to meet manpower needs, and numerous categories of repressed individuals. It was common practice to tear children of resettled laborers (read: kulaks) away from their parents by force and place them in special boarding schools for "reeducation." Life in such children's homes is best described by letters from children addressed to Krupskaia and Kalinin. Venia Bushmanov, an occupant of the Krasno-Vishersk Children's Home in Cherdyn' Raion, Sverdlovsk Oblast, wrote one such letter to Krupskaia:

# Document 147

Letter from special migrant V. Bushmanov to Krupskaia, 23 October 1934. RGASPI, f. 78, op. 1, d. 524, l. 98. Typewritten original.

I live in a children's home in the town of Krasno-Vishersk, I want to describe our life how we live at the present time in the northern territory. For now our life here is alright, they feed us well, they give us clothing and shoes

## Document 147 *continued*

and most important they teach us. I, Venia Bushmanov, an occupant of the children's home, am so interested in this life and respect it so much and I really want to learn. I started going to school at seven years of age and finished the fourth group at ten years of age and started going to a FZS [*fabrichnozavodskaia spetsshkola*, special factory school, for the children of special migrants] in the fifth group and finished it at eleven years of age. Now, as somebody who is well disciplined, I have been promoted to courses at an editorial office and now I am working although not completely, but all of us are already working with orders and minutes of meetings and so forth. We were all brought to Krasno-Vishersk from the North and none of us has a father or mother, we are all orphans. Our fathers and mothers and we too were banished into exile and dekulakized. Our fathers and mothers died, and we were all brought to the children's home and now we are living here. But there is cheating on the part of the management both by the head of the children's home and by the caregivers. For example I work in the editorial office and every month the head of the general department writes out thirty rubles to me for the month but I never see it, it is credited to the children's home and I need to buy a pencil or some paper and paints and I have nothing to buy it with. If you ask they will not give it to you but we all thank them, except now the one we got, the new director of the children's home, she takes care of the children and respects them, but the ones we had, the old directors, they cheated us and sold our food for vodka. Now that is cheating and they insulted us too, but this new director is very nice. Also we are in our second year of living in the children's home it will soon be two years that we have lived in the home without fathers and mothers and have already been reeducated in the new way i.e. Soviet functionaries still call us these special migrants wherever we go it is always special migrant but we are very hurt that we all attend school together, and we are called special migrants. What kind of special migrants are we when we have been reeducated in the new way we go to defend the Soviet Union I repeat to you once again that I want to learn very much and I respect Soviet Rule because they give us enough to drink and eat and most important they teach us. I, Bushmanov, an occupant of a children's home, am typing on an Underwood typewriter and ask you to write a letter back to me and send regards to all the caregivers in the children's home and thank our children's home director Baiandina for the fact that they respect the youngsters very well and come to teach us and in short reeducate us in the Soviet way.

For now goodbye Nadezhda Konstantinovna Krupskaia I look forward to a letter from you for which I will thank you very much.

I Venia Bushmanov will study and study.

While he had learned to type on an Underwood—albeit with many mistakes (we have removed some purely technical ones to make the letter easier to read)—Venia Bushmanov did not know that he would never be able to expunge the stain of being a special migrant and that his fervent wish to go on studying was unlikely to come true. But he at least felt well fed and well provided with clothing and footwear. He would probably have been the envy of the special migrants' children living in the children's home at Kokornaia station in Pinega Raion, Arkhangel'sk Okrug, who wrote a letter in 1932 to Kalinin about their everyday life:

---

## Document 148

Letter from special migrants' children to Kalinin, 1932. RGASPI, f. 78, op. 1, d. 432, ll. 8–90b. Original manuscript.

---

To Uncle Kalinin

From children

This is us writing uncle we are special migrants. You live there in the city and we are stuck here with our fathers. We live a long way from Arkhangel'sk. Our fathers all lounge around and moan and groan and we don't have much bread. It's very hard for us uncle really hard. We are twelve years old and some are even younger there is a whole hungry mob of us in the children's home and everybody is asking for bread. We don't even know what to do. And all our hopes are on you. That's why we're writing to you. So uncle Kalinin if they let you go or you can get away yourself please try to find the time in the spring and come visit us in the settlement. Don't come in the winter our settlement is a long way from the city and if you go by sleigh you will definitely catch cold or your hands and ears will get frostbitten. As soon as you arrive come straight to see us. From here we will take you to the city ourselves in somebody's cart and maybe the commandant will give us the next available one. Oh it's so hard and it seems to be too late already. Well come here and you will easily find us we are poor looking little kids. If you can't find the time then send a letter. We will write letters to each other write a lot we will figure out everything. Well uncle we have a secret to tell you we have one thing in mind we will grow big and enlist in the party and we will fight against neediness. Neediness is dirty bourgeois stuff.

Our address is Arkhangel'sk Okrug, Pinega Raion, Kokornaia Station, Children's Home C.

This was written and composed for you by children.

Uncle don't be insulted that we are sending this letter without a stamp we don't have any money.

---

When the children's home occupants composed this letter in the naive belief that "Uncle Kalinin" would help them and that the battle against neediness signified, above all, a battle against the bourgeoisie, they did not realize that they were writing to the wrong person. As Kalinin's correspondence with Krupskaia shows, the All-Union elder did not suffer any pangs of the heart over the migrants' children. His references to the need for strict compliance with laws covering the children of disenfranchised people, at a time when public and secret party directives and high-handed local authorities held sway, seemed like a mockery. It is clear from the letter quoted below that, regardless of the law, the authorities could do anything they wanted with the children of kulaks and "socially dangerous elements." When indisputable reports of high-handed rule landed on the desk of A. Sol'ts, a member of the Presidium of the Central Control Commission of the VKP(b), even this experienced party functionary wrote in outrage to Procurator-General Vyshinsky:[42]

---

## Document 149

Letter from A. Sol'ts of Party Control Commission to Vyshinsky, 5 January 1932. RGASPI, f. 613, op. 3, d. 86, l. 5. Certified, typewritten copy.

---

Esteemed comrade!

In November I received an appeal from citizen Nikulina, a nanny at a children's home in Moscow, concerning the exile of her children—eighteen-year-old Gavriil, who graduated from school last year and afterward worked independently of his parents in the town of Maloarkhangel'sk on a state vegetable farm, and thirteen-year-old Vasily, a pupil in a seven-year school. According to her, these youngsters were suddenly arrested last summer and exiled to Kazakhstan as kulaks.

I asked the local procurator to investigate this case and, if the report is confirmed, to determine who issued this muddleheaded resolution and who carried it out.

To this I received a reply, a copy of which is enclosed, in which Comrade Razoryonov, the raion procurator, justifies the exile of these youngsters by pointing out that their parents (with whom they do not live) used to have—prior to 1925—a kulak farm. Incidentally, the dekulakization of the Nikulins was rescinded in 1930. It is clear from the 1929 inventory that all of their property was appraised at 790 rubles—and this raises doubts, of course, about whether the classification of the farms belonging to the old Nikulins as kulak enterprises was correct.

But irrespective of this, I believe that exiling youngsters for their parents' old sins, youngsters who have been reared or are being reared already in our Soviet school, and, on top of that, exiling them without any connection with the exile of their parents, is the height of muddleheadedness and absurdity, which demonstrates a total lack of understanding of our policy toward young people. It turns out that the procurator, who should have prevented this outrage at the proper time, rubber-stamped it, and is now defending it, thinking that everything, as he says, was correct.

Because I believe that this interpretation by Comrade Razoryonov of his tasks with regard to overseeing revolutionary legality carries the risk of further excesses in the raion, I deemed it my duty to report this to you.

---

The question of whether to allow into schools the children of disenfranchised persons, kulaks and other "socially alien" categories was quite complicated. Many administrators, education officials, and teachers were clearly confused because of the often contradictory instructions from above. The majority, however, perceived the overall trend correctly: "It is better to be overvigilant than undervigilant." Thus the class struggle that had unfolded in the countryside turned into a war on children. Administrators "toss them out of school, as a rule—and imagine that this constitutes a hundred percent class struggle, whereas it is a violation of the party program—or they provoke these elements to drop out by depriving them of paper and textbooks and demanding that youngsters boycott the eight- and nine-year-old youngsters of disenfranchised persons (appalling cruelty) and deprive them of hot breakfasts," wrote a genuinely angry Krupskaia. "A teacher recently asked me whether it was permissible to take the children of kulaks into school and whether it was admissible to instill in them a hatred for exploitation."[43]

During Krupskaia's trips and meetings with teachers and education officials, who were aware of her distinctive position on this issue, they inundated her with notes. She decided to answer one of them in particular detail. A village teacher was complaining that authorities were artificially encouraging an unhealthy attitude toward the children of kulaks and disenfranchised persons in the provinces. "There are instances in which a village soviet holds a teacher accountable for writing in her evaluation of such a pupil: 'has fine abilities and grades.'"[44] Thus the local authorities were forcing teachers to commit fraud by evaluating knowledge on the basis of the pupil's background. In a letter to Kalinin on 24 November 1934, Krupskaia wrote that the issue of the children of disenfranchised persons should be settled:

> According to the instructions, the children of disenfranchised persons are not to be deprived of voting rights, they specify only that great vigilance should be shown toward them. Yet with regard to education, all roads are often blocked for them. About five years ago I raised this issue, there was even a commission set up under the Sovnarkom, and everybody agreed with me, but in practice, more often than not, the youngsters are placed in a very difficult situation. A certain directive should be issued here, and this question should be discussed in the press. I am enclosing three typical little letters. You have also received a fair number of such letters, of course.[45]

Kalinin's reply is astonishing in its formalism:

---

## Document 150

Letter from Kalinin to Krupskaia on rights of children of disenfranchised persons, 13 December 1934. RGASPI, f. 78, op. 1, d. 524, l. 92. Typewritten original.

---

. . . As for the children of persons who have been stripped of their voting rights, the main question with regard to them was the question of granting them political rights, i.e. the right to vote in elections to soviets. At present our law on the voting rights of children of disenfranchised persons has been resolved in the affirmative for them. In this connection the issue of hiring them for jobs is also resolved. We must only try to see to it that Soviet laws are not distorted in the provinces, and in instances when excesses are committed, these excesses must immediately be eliminated. The most important point is not to allow anybody to be dismissed from their job for the sole reason that one's parents are disenfranchised persons.

With regard to education, children of disenfranchised persons cannot be expelled from the system of compulsory education. As for their admission to higher and specialized educational institutions, in consideration of the generally strong craving for studies, when we are obliged to deny places in higher

# Document 150 *continued*

educational institutions, higher technical institutions, and other educational institutions to many children of workers, office clerks, and kolkhoz farmers who have not been stripped of their voting rights, it would be wrong to issue a directive that children of disenfranchised persons are to be admitted. This does not preclude the possibility, of course, that in certain instances the most capable children of disenfranchised persons, who have excelled in their jobs, may be placed in a higher educational institution, technicum, or the like. I don't think there is any reason to raise this issue in the press.

As Kalinin's reply makes clear, discrimination based on social background was legitimized by government policy with respect to admitting children to higher and specialized secondary institutions—a fact that officials preferred, nevertheless, not to publicize. As the letters show, young people took this type of discrimination especially hard, for they did not consider themselves guilty of anything. Here is a typical letter of the kind that Krupskaia mentioned:

# Document 151

Letter from M. S. Gorokhova petitioning Krupskaia to continue her studies, 13 November 1934. RGASPI, f. 78, op. 1, d. 524, ll. 99–99ob. Original manuscript.

13 November 1934
To the Central Committee of the Trade Union of Education Functionaries
Nadezhda Konstantinovna Krupskaia
Moscow, Solianka 12, Palace of Labor, 5th floor
From Manefa Semyonovna Gorokhova
Citizen of the Northern Krai, Sokol Raion
Kadnikov Village Soviet
Village of Podel'noe
Petition
In connection with the dekulakization of our farm and the liquidation of the latter by the village soviet over debts on individual taxes imposed because my parents had a small shop prior to 1913 but in their own village, located under their house, I, as a kulak's daughter who has graduated from a seven-year school, have been deprived of the opportunity to continue my education. Feeling no guilt toward the Soviet government, because I was born in 1916 whereas my father had ended his commerce (1913), because I was absolutely uninvolved in my parents' actions, because my brother served in the Workers

## Document 151 *continued*

and Peasants' Red Army in 1919, because our farm was considered a middle peasant's farm until 1933, I serenely graduated from the seven-year school upon reaching adolescence, firmly confident that I would receive further education, obtain a vocation, and work together with toilers for the benefit of construction and Soviet power.

All of this has been ruled out now. I am now seventeen years old I don't work anywhere, I am burning with shame in front of my girlfriends, because they are continuing their education, while I am deprived of this because of the circumstances set forth above, although my young life demands an education.

In view of the foregoing I ask you to put yourself in my position and give me assistance in continuing my studies and thereby fulfill V. I. Lenin's precepts (study study and study).

M. Gorokhova

The children of kulaks and disenfranchised persons usually ended up as society's pariahs. Not only did they find the road blocked to higher education, to a good job, and to the Komsomol, but their onetime comrades and friends began to steer clear of them. A letter to Krupskaia from Vera Shkuropieva describes the kind of tragedy that this situation produced:

## Document 152

Letter of appeal from V. L. Shkuropieva to Krupskaia, 3 November 1934. RGASPI, f. 78, op. 1, d. 524, ll. 100–1020b. Original manuscript.

Dear Nadezhda Konstantinovna

At a hard time in my young life failing to find any assistance I have decided to appeal to you, hoping that you will be of great assistance to me, I am well aware that you have always cared about children and Young Pioneers, I have read many of your letters, Dear N. K. please show a little concern for me, I will be grateful to you for it until I die.

My autobiography

I, Vera Lavrentivna, was born in 1918 in the village of Shkuropinovka, Reshetilovka Raion, Khar'kov Oblast. My father has a piece of land, a hut, a cow, and worked in agriculture. Our family consisted of six people (my sister died in 1927). We lived in poverty, and our father was an alcoholic. And we suffered a lot of grief from our father. We had a great ability to learn, we were the top pupils. Although we lived in an out-of-the-way village we realized early on that knowledge is light, ignorance is darkness, so we have studied, studied, and studied, as the dear teacher V. I. Lenin said. From 1921 to 1923 my father engaged in commerce for which he was stripped of his voting rights (he had his own shop). I was five years old at the time, and my elder sister Dusia was eight years old. In 1930 my sister completed the seven-year school and went to Zaporozh'e to get a job (at the plant and then bring me and our mother there), but they refused to hire her because she was only fifteen, and she got a job as a maid for a technician named Paladei. She worked there for one year. At the beginning of 1931 my father was told to turn over grain and meat, he couldn't manage it, and for that his property was sold (which consisted of a hut and a cow), and he himself left for the Donets Basin. We lived with our aunt for three months (during this time I completed the fourth group, I was twelve years old). We didn't even have enough money to live with our aunt, and when we found out from an acquaintance where our father was we went to him, he was living here at Fenol'naia station and was working as a watch-man for the Residential Design and Construction Administration. Our father did not take us in and we wrote to Dusia (the one that worked in Zaporozh'e) to come and get a job here. Dusia arrived and got a job here as a cleaning woman at a beer warehouse and took me and my mother in to live with her. Dusia worked (for 1$^1$/$_2$ years) I went to school (in the fifth group) I was the top shock worker student, but it was very hard for me to study because we had no money (Dusia made forty-five rubles a month), but I struggled with these dif-ficulties the best I could and I was glad to be in school. One and a half years later Dusia went to work at a *paistol* [meaning unclear], then in the personnel department at the phenol plant. She joined the Komsomol there and a year later she was transferred to work as a clerk for the party cell. My sister did a good job and was the top shock worker in the Komsomol; she was a model worker many times, she took part in [sociopolitical] campaigns. She had great authority among the workers at our plant. In 1934 I graduated from the seven-year school, when I was in school I was awarded prizes nine times in three years (not counting the fourth) for good grades and [sociopolitical] work. For two years I was the sector head in school and gave a lot of help to lagging stu-dents, and in the Komsomol I was a Young Pioneer leader in the second group and was able to organize all the Pioneers to fight failing grades, in short I was the top student in the whole school. When I graduated from school Dusia (my elder sister) said to me: "Vera I taught you [let you go to school] for three years now it is time for me to go to school." It was painful for me to listen to these words, it was painful for me to leave school, but I knew and understood well that my sister wanted to go to school too and I had to give her help with this, and then she would teach me. With these thoughts, with this goal, I got a job at the phenol plant in the laboratory (as a trainee). During this time my sister (Dusia) worked as a secretary of the Komsomol (temporarily filling in) and then something happened that ruined all of our plans. They fired Dusia from her job and expelled her from the Komsomol (that was on 9 September 1934) after finding out that our father was stripped of his voting rights. The poor thing she cried so hard (mostly over the Komsomol where she worked for three years and where she spent all her free time). After that Dusia got sick for two months. Exactly two weeks later I was fired from my job for no reason and I felt so much grief, I thought so much about everything, Dear N. K. you know that I wanted to end my life (that was my first thought to escape my hard life the terrible torment that I went through during the sixteen years of my life and I can't describe everything in detail. But maybe other people will describe it for me). And so Dear N. K. when I picked up this poison I remembered just one word of Il'ich's [Lenin's]: "Life is struggle" and I decided to struggle to the final victory. And so they fired me from my job (Dusia is also without a job [and] Mama is disabled), winter is coming, then they kicked us out of the apartment in disgrace (Comrade Kisichova) saying: "I will not allow kulaks to live on the premises," and going over all this, in short, thinking over my situation I was going out of my mind, and then I gathered up my courage and decided to struggle to the final victory. On the second day (26 September 1934) I was called back to work (and they ordered me not to tell anybody that they fired me from my job, but of course everybody found out about it). So I have stayed at my job to this day, but I cannot work normally because I am afraid every day that they might fire me (for some little reason) and what am I supposed to do, where will I and my disabled (sixty-five years old) mother go[?] In addition I cannot work normally when I see that everybody is looking at me like an enemy, that they don't consider me a human being, that they make remarks about me like: "That's Dusia's sister their father was stripped of his voting rights, so why is she (meaning me) working here" of course Dear N. K. after I hear such remarks I cannot work normally, but I want to work, I want to study and prove that I am not an alien class element, like I proved it during the seventh year of my studies. So I appeal, to you Dear N. K. and I have my hopes on you that you will give me help in my young life. My hopes are on you because I know well that you have always cared about us Young Pioneers and pupils, I know well how you pointed us in the right direction with your letters. You always asked us to study well and I fulfilled your instructions. Oh dear Nadezhda K. if you only knew how much I want to study. Dear N. K. if you only knew how much I want to be a human being and bring benefit to the state in order to prove that I am not an enemy. Oh dear N. K. please show some concern for me, give me help after all I am still a girl I am just sixteen years old I have not known life yet I can study up and bring benefit to the state, and I want to study (I would give half my life if somebody helped me to study). Oh dear N. K. please show concern for me I will be grateful to you till I die give me maternal help.

Dear N. K. after all I want to live to study to be a shock worker to be a shock worker in the Komsomol (but unfortunately the Komsomol won't admit me) but I consider this wrong because nobody in our family was stripped of voting rights except my father, and we haven't lived with him since 1931 (I was twelve years old) why can't I be a Komsomol member? Why can't I work normally? Why don't they let me have a normal life? Dear N. Kons. I am pinning all my hopes on you. Dear N. K. if possible give me an answer soon. Don't put my request aside. Right now I am sitting in school (I have a day off today) and it is very painful for me why is everybody studying and I can't. Dear N. K. please show some concern for me, so that I can study and be a human being.

Fenol'naia station

New York post office [*sic*]

Coke Plant No. 7, Laboratory

V. L. Shkuropieva

Dear N. K. If possible do all this soon. I will thank everybody.

Dear N. K. I will look forward to your letter every day (with impatience) and your parental help. N. K. I sent a letter to Mikhail Iv. [Kalinin] it's been more than a month already and I haven't gotten an answer this worries me very much is it really possible that I am such a creature that I can't give benefit to the state should I really not be able to live.

With that goodbye dear N. K.

I have my hopes on you that you will give me parental help. My life depends on you.

D. N. K. I am sorry that it is badly written but I am so upset that I can't write.

---

In the conditions of the 1930s, a young person could not obtain a good education and vocation without being a member of the party or Komsomol, not to mention that people who were excluded from the turbulent public life of those years felt defective in many ways. That is why the discrimination in Komsomol admissions had such a painful impact on the children of special migrants and other "socially alien" groups.[46] The problem was exacerbated in those regions where migrants' children predominated among those admitted to the Komsomol. Even after the adoption of the 1936 constitution, which gave everyone equal rights, there was no unanimity among Komsomol officials about whether to admit such individuals to the Komsomol. Sometimes their admission became grounds for repressing "liberals." "There was a pernicious theory in Krasnoiarsk Krai that children of labor migrants can be admitted to the Komsomol because the children's fathers had had their rights of citizenship restored," the secretary of the local kraikom of the Komsomol, Kulikov, reported to the TsK of the Komsomol on 15 November 1937. While acknowledging that "the issue of labor migrants here is a real problem," he informed the leadership that he had not found a decision by the TsK on the issue, so he issued his own directive—don't admit them.[47] Others also played it safe by taking the same stance.

The repressions of the 1930s did not exempt young people. The files of the NKVD show that its officials closely monitored the rising generation's attitudes. They focused especially on collecting information on "unlawful youth organizations" in schools, higher educational institutions, and *rabfaki* (educational facilities to prepare workers for higher education), and at enterprises. There were also cases in which fifteen- to eighteen-year-olds were arrested and repressed on charges of espionage, anti-Soviet agitation, and counterrevolutionary activities. Investigators conjured up full-scale, illegal youth organizations, and the prison conditions in which children were kept and the interrogation methods were no different from those applied to adult inmates and suspects. There was, however, a much larger, and little-studied, category of young people in the 1930s—the "members of families of traitors to the homeland," relatives of repressed persons, who not only were exiled on an administrative basis, without a trial or investigation, but were also kept in special camps. And in their hour of trouble, as the documents quoted below make clear, people's behavior varied: some bravely endured their tribulations and fought for themselves and the good name of their relatives, while some were so eager to return from exile that they would betray people who had been close to them just yesterday. But one point is obvious: every letter was a cry of the heart.

The lot of Ksenia Chekina, a young student at a Leningrad medical institute, proved to be typical of many. With the arrest of her husband under article 58, her happy, cloudless life suddenly went topsy-turvy. The authorities banished her from Leningrad, first confiscating her internal passport and issuing her an exile's "wolf card"—an identity document, originally used in tsarist Russia, indicating that the bearer is politically unreliable. Then they kicked her out of the institute and took her away from her small child. At a loss about what to do next, an innocent victim without a job, shelter, or even a piece of bread, she decided to write Kalinin. Calling what happened to her an "outrage," she still refused to believe that these actions were legal, citing the just adopted constitution:

---

# Document 153

Letter of K. Ya. Chekina to Kalinin requesting return of passport, 1937. GARF, f. 7523, op. 23, d. 202, ll. 96–96ob. Original manuscript.

---

M. I. Kalinin! Please take notice of the outrage that is being perpetrated against us. There is a limit to such outrages. I have already appealed five times to government bodies to look into my case, but to this day for some reason they have kept silent or have brushed me off with some little notes. *I ask you to return my passport,* which the Leningrad Passport Department took away from me on 6 July 1937, and give me an opportunity to graduate from the institute, or to go back to my child, who is now in the Western Oblast at Seshcha station.

I have been without a job, without shelter, without a piece of bread for seven months already. Am I supposed to drop dead just because I have a child from somebody who was sentenced to five years under article 58? Children are not responsible for their fathers. I am a medical student, I was torn away from my studies, why? *I consider my exile absolutely wrong, so I ask you to return my passport* and allow me *to graduate from the institute* and have an opportunity to bring up my child. Innocent people should not be so cruelly punished. Leningrad procurator Rozanov tricked me when he told me that I have a right to study. Where is that right? I know the constitution, and somehow this is not working out that way. I ask you to take an interest in the case of Ivan Yakovlevich Chekin, he was convicted on 23 February 1937, and put an end to my suffering.

My address is the village of Riga, Cheliabinsk Oblast, Galkinsky Raion. Ksenia Yakovlevna Chekina

---

During this cruel time, when they found themselves face to face with calamity, children matured with astonishing speed and learned what was by no means juvenile wisdom and responsibility, which in normal circumstances comes only with the passing years. A noteworthy letter in this regard was written by Boria Trapezontsev, a Leningrad schoolboy who lost his parents overnight, to the Presidium of the USSR Supreme Soviet:

# Document 154

Letter of Boris Trapezontsev to Presidium of Supreme Soviet requesting release of his mother from exile, 8 December 1938. GARF, f. 7523, op. 23, d. 200, ll. 1–2. Original manuscript.

To the Presidium of the USSR Supreme Soviet

cc: Procurator of the Union of the USSR [*sic*]

From Boris Trapezontsev, a resident of Leningrad on Mytnikovskaia Embankment, 3, apt. 5. . . .

I am a pupil in the seventh grade at school no. 14 in Petrograd Raion, Leningrad, I request that you consider my petition.

On 17 January 1938 my mama Anna Pavlovna Trapezontseva was exiled from Leningrad to Liski in Voronezh Oblast in the case of my father Gavriil Borisovich Trapezontsev, who was arrested in Leningrad on 27 October 1937, and in January 1938 he was exiled to the Far East. My mother's sister, who works at the State Hermitage, became my guardian. I spent last summer with my mother in her place of exile. I found her in very grave condition, destroyed by grief and her separation from me. True, she is now working in her vocation—as a teacher at a first-stage school on a kolkhoz at Pykhovo station (Voronezh Oblast). Mama writes me in her letters that the youngsters have come to love her and the school administration values her as an experienced educator, yet she gets no peace thinking of the school that she was forced to leave in Leningrad. She is suffering a lot. I am only fourteen years old. I lived my whole life with my parents. I don't know what my father was guilty of— nobody has given us any answers, even though mama stubbornly tried to get some. I only know that my mama is not guilty of anything. I ask you to review the case and return mama, since it is very painful for me to live and study by myself.

Please, I beg you, answer my letter. I can hardly wait. I am enclosing a character reference from her former job.

Boria Trapezontsev

8 December 1938

While Boria Trapezontsev asked Kalinin as the top official in the government to return his mother to him, the young sailor Aleksei Tsyganov begged G. I. Petrovsky, deputy chairman of the USSR Supreme Soviet, for leniency toward his pregnant wife, who had been imprisoned for the mere fact that she had "showed pity" for her arrested mother:

# Document 155

Letter from A. Tsyganov to G. I. Petrovsky requesting pardon of his wife, 22 October 1938. GARF, f. 7523, op. 23, d. 202, l. 49. Typewritten original.

From Aleksei Yegorovich Tsyganov, junior naval commander, group petty officer, acting chief of the club of troop unit no. 7579 of the Red Banner Baltic Fleet

Grigory Ivanovich I am appealing to you to provide assistance in pardoning my wife, Liudmila Mikhailovna Tsyganovna, who was sentenced to three years in prison and to two years of disenfranchisement. She was convicted for blabbing under article 58, clause 10, section 1.

Her mother a churchgoer was arrested, and on this basis, failing to consider the political essence of being a churchgoer [my wife] showed pity for her and for her girlfriend's mother.

I lived with her for only ten months, and in living with me she didn't have any resentments about Soviet Rule since she is almost the same age as the October Revolution, born in 1916. She is in her fifth month of imprisonment in Leningrad, at Arsenal'naia 9.

She is in her fifth month of pregnancy but there are no exceptions for pregnant women. During this time I visited her twice and each time talked for twenty minutes. During these four-plus months in confinement the woman has been educated and her eyes opened to life so that she has started to appreciate life in a completely different way.

Grigory Ivanovich I appeal to you once again for your assistance, in considering her youth and pregnancy and inexperience in life, and the political ignorance she displayed in her blabbing without being aware of anything. No formal appeal was filed, for the reading of the sentence in court caused her to faint, and she was taken unconscious to her cell and she was in such a condition that she had no idea what was going on or what she should do, and I didn't know when the trial took place, so the time limit for filing an appeal ran out.

These four-plus months have been very educational and have taught us big moral and political lessons.

For my part, I will make every effort to fortify the education that she has received in these four-plus months and lead her along the right path so that we can live together with our happy young people and toil in the Socialist family.

I have served in the navy for four years and have stayed to serve some more, because I am considering the international situation and the threat from the fascist states. But this shameful stigma could make them release me on long-term leave, and I want to honestly serve the Soviet Union and give my life, knowledge, and skills to the cause of defense to protect our homeland.

Grigory Ivanovich allow me to wait for your answer.

## Document 155 *continued*

My address is Leningrad Oblast, town of Oranienbaum, Red Fleet Street, 3, apartment 5, A. Ye. Tsyganov.
Junior Naval Commander Tsyganov
22 October 1938

The monstrous logic of the repressions suggested that if you wanted to keep your life intact, you must forget about your feelings toward your family and master "Stalin's school of survival" instead. A notion of how this actually transpired emerges from a letter by Georgy Tsaplin to Kalinin in 1938. Born in 1917, he was supposed to be drafted into the army in 1938, but his father was suddenly arrested, sentenced to ten years and dispatched to a camp. Consequently, instead of serving in the army, Georgy found himself exiled from Leningrad to a godforsaken corner of Cheliabinsk Oblast, where more than anything else there was time for reflection about the eternal questions of Russian life—"What is to be done?" and "Who is to blame?" Here are a few results of Georgy's reflections, as set forth in his letter to Kalinin. About his repressed father: "If I had known that he was an enemy of the people, I would have shot him dead myself. Soviet authority turned out to be more lenient, yet it treated me, his son, more harshly." About himself: "I am losing my mind from loneliness, it is better to die than to live the way I am living right now. I am twenty-one years old, I attended a Soviet school, I worked in Soviet plants, I believed in what the great I. V. Stalin said, 'A son is not responsible for his father,' and a little more of this and I will be over the edge and I will either end up in a madhouse, where my mother has been since 1932, or I will end my life."[48]

"Why?" With this question he concludes the letter, imploring Kalinin to do something for him and return him to his hometown, where his friends and sweetheart live. Georgy Tsaplin, who is ready to execute his own father, inspires sympathy and loathing at the same time.

The atmosphere in which the repressions took place was accompanied by rumors and fabrications, spawned hatred and aggressiveness and was transmitted through adults to the entire young generation. Here, for example, is an excerpt from a letter to G. M. Dimitrov, general secretary of the Comintern, from M. I. Simenova:

## Document 156

Letter from M. I. Simenova to G. M. Dimitrov, 10 May 1938. RGASPI, f. 495, op. 73, d. 61, l. 18. Typewritten copy.

Comrade Dimitrov!

It will seem odd to you why I am writing to you rather than to Comrade Stalin. I wrote to him too and more than one letter, but apparently they don't pass along letters to him from such little and illiterate [people], and that is wrong: we learned to read and write under Soviet rule and we write the best we can. He himself called on us to give reports on disturbances, of which we still have quite a few in our country, and the truth about the situation is being kept from him.

I work in a plant, a Stakhanovite, and I sympathize with the party. A week ago, during the five-day workweek [rather than the normal six, evidently because of the May Day holiday], my little boy comes home from school and says that all the boys are preparing a pogrom and will beat the other nationalities, the Poles, Latvians, and Germans, because all their parents are spies. When I questioned him about who says this, he said one boy's brother is a Komsomol member and works in the NKVD and said that all the foreign spies who live in Moscow will be put on trial, and their families and children in school will be beaten up like the yids were under the tsar. I went to see the principal at school, and he says the parents are to blame for this, I [he] can't keep track of all the talk that goes on. . . .

And now here is something new that was presented to the young generation during the years of the Yezhovshchina. This is a letter from Vania Vylegzhanin, a fifth-grade pupil at the Khomiakovskaia incomplete secondary school in Mozhga Raion, Udmurt ASSR:

## Document 157

Letter from Vania Vylegzhanin to *Krest'ianskaia Gazeta* on dismissal of Kosarev, 22 December 1938. RGAE, f. 396, op. 11, d. 26, ll. 176–176ob. Original manuscript.

To the editors of *Krest'ianskaia Gazeta*

Dear editors anser this question for me: did they fire Comrade Kosorev [Kosarev] for his mistakes at the Komsomol congres, what mistake it could be

I don't know, I found this out [from] Maria A. Liubanova. And write who they put in Kosorev's place wich leader. Not a single Komsomol member knows here, and the leader of the Komsomol organization of the Khomiakovskaia incomplete secondary school Comrade Maria Andreevna Liubanova probably dosnt know either. She dosnt keep discipline in school. Yegor Libanov a pupil in the seventh grade talks, fools around, and distracts others in class and during recess he dosnt let anybody play billiards he argues kicks gets into fights and insults his comrades.

"Eyewitness"

---

This illiterate letter, written in an unduly familiar and vulgar style by a mere twelve-year-old boy, is a routine denunciation, just like many written in those years by adults. By linking his real point to the rumors about Kosarev's removal from his post as secretary of the TsK of the Komsomol, the writer seems to imply that it would not be a bad idea to take a look at schoolmates whose behavior he doesn't like.

The writer was honored with an official reply: "Kosarev was removed by a resolution of the Seventh Plenum of the TsK of the VLKSM for violating Komsomol democracy, for inertia, for callously bureaucratic and hostile treatment of honest functionaries who are trying to uncover shortcomings, for carrying out a reprisal against one of the best Komsomol functionaries, Comrade Mishanova, and for protecting morally corrupt elements that are alien to the party and double-dealing elements that are in hiding. N. A. Mikhailov was elected secretary of the TsK. Read *Komsomol'skaia Pravda* for 23 November 1938."[49]

The young generation took shape in an atmosphere based on the notion that "enemies are all around us" and on faith in Comrade Stalin. Vania Korolyov of Orel Oblast, who wanted to become a correspondent for *Krest'ianskaia Gazeta,* sent the editors the following little sample of his work in January 1939: "Enemies of the people want to smash our Soviet land and the supreme leader Comrade Stalin but they will never sucseed in doing that because as the saying goes Stalin is made of steel [*stal'*] and nobody will defeat him. Thank you to Comrade Stalin for our happy schooling I would write more but I have no paper. I send warm regards to the chiefs of the editorial office."[50]

The documents, we believe, vividly convey what the "happy childhoods" under Stalin were like, how full of contrasts the generation of the revolution was, how it differed from that of its parents, how difficult and arduous its experiences were, and the emotional and psychological traumas that it suffered.

# Conclusion

NEITHER IN THE 1930s nor in subsequent decades did Stalinism produce a single, uniform way of life. No matter how powerful its transformational thrust, it did not obliterate the variety of attitudes and modes of social existence that antedated its ascendance—hence the complaint by L. M. Kaganovich in 1933 that 80 percent of the "mentality of the past, egotism, vanity, selfishness" had survived (doc. 140). Differences between rural and urban dwellers, Russians and non-Russians, manual and mental workers, the young and the old persisted or even took on new dimensions, sometimes in conformity with official policies and sometimes in reaction against them. The new Soviet man, a construct much employed in the 1930s, correspondingly evolved and was itself multidimensional.

Yet as the documents in this book illustrate, the pursuit of building socialism confronted citizens—no matter where they lived or what their occupations were—with challenges that profoundly altered their daily lives and often were life-threatening. Among these challenges, three were ubiquitous: shortages of basic necessities, above all food; the ascriptiveness of class categories and origins; and the necessity of dealing with the state by inscribing oneself into its grand narratives.

Shortages were hardly unique to the 1930s, but the closing down of private retail outlets, combined with the upheavals of collectivization and inadequate ration levels, universalized what historically had been a regionally or seasonally based problem. There were different degrees of shortage, mainly depending on one's place of residence (Moscow and Leningrad as opposed to provincial cities; provincial cities as opposed to rural locations) and institutional affiliation. The aim of the state, in any case, was to maximize its distributive power in order to create universal material dependency—a relationship between the state and citizen that some scholars have termed socialist paternalism.[1]

The documents refer to some of the more traditional strategies for coping with shortage, such as migration, reliance on kin, connections, exchange of favors, and theft.[2] But far more prominently represented are letters of appeal to authorities. These came mainly from kolkhoz farmers, dekulakized peasants, and orphaned children. The shortages that they mention—"bread," footwear, clothing, paper, and so on—are a poignant reminder of the grave deficiencies of the centralized distribution system during its Stalinist phase, and a devastating commentary on Stalin's claim, amplified in the Soviet media, that life was joyous in the land of socialism. Still, propaganda was not without its effects. Many who wrote letters about shortages and other "black marks" in their villages could not know that they were no worse off than collective farmers in other regions. They were apt to blame local officials (who, after all, were not necessarily blameless) for their suffering. Local officials in their turn faced the unenviable task of realizing instructions from above without being denounced from below. For some the pressure was enormous, or, as one rural soviet chairman put it to Kalinin, "like you're on the edge of a straight razor" (doc. 45). This, too, was a product and a constituent element of Stalinism.

"Who are the term prisoners?" wrote an investigator from VTsIK in 1932 about the inmates at the Nizhni-Novgorod House of Correction. He then listed them: so many workers, hired hands, poor peasants, kulaks, "idlers," and so forth (doc. 31). But kulaks already were becoming ex-kulaks, and collective farms were eroding distinctions between poor and middle peasants. By 1936, when the Soviet Constitution was adopted, Stalin could proclaim that "there are no longer any antagonistic classes in society; . . . society consists of two friendly classes, of workers and peasants . . . that are in power."[3] The old class distinctions nevertheless remained part of Soviet lexical currency for some time thereafter, figuring prominently in the letters to authorities.

Autobiographical narratives frequently cite prerevolutionary class origins to authenticate the Soviet self or reinforce complaints against others. Polikarp Sergeev, chairman of a kolkhoz in Orel Oblast, managed to accomplish both feats by stating that he was the son of a peasant who "was enslaved his whole life by neighboring kulaks . . . the Davydkin brothers," and then denouncing a Davydkin for referring "to Comrade Stalin by all kinds of derogatory names" and "making statements during road construction corrupting other kolkhoz farmers" (doc. 116). Andrei Poluektov went to considerable lengths to explain why his father's decision to take advantage of the Stolypin land reform of 1906 did not make him a "Stolypinite peasant," but the stigma of having been, in effect, a prerevolutionary kulak seemed to bar permanently the door to party membership. The civil war, and particularly service in the Red or White armies, was a second template on which letter writers could inscribe their Soviet identities or "unmask" the pretensions of others. But especially in letters from the countryside, the label of kulak remained a powerful signifier, haunting those against whom it was used long after the (partial) restoration in 1934–35 of their civil rights, or even their parents'.

Stepping back from the substance of the letters, that they were written at all is worthy of comment. Many of the voices we hear would have been lost to us were it not for the acquisition of literacy, which in quite a few cases appears to have been recent. Some writers were apologetic about the limitations of their locution. But others evidently took pride in their ability to read and write themselves into the stories that the nation was telling about itself, stories about good versus evil, about the promises of socialism and who was preventing their realization, about the personal realm mirroring the collective as well as the historical sweep of the period in which they lived.

This proliferation of voices and stories was encouraged from above as part of the twin processes of individuation and working to make oneself a better Soviet citizen that until recently have gone all but unnoticed by scholars.[4] At the same time, the expansion of the reading and writing public made it incumbent on the authorities to get right and codify the master narrative. The fitful and largely disastrous attempts to purge libraries and produce politically reliable calendars in the early 1930s, the evolution of a socialist-realist aesthetic, the 1936 constitution, and that apotheosis of Stalinist catechismic writing, the *Short Course in the History of the VKP(b)*, were all indicative of such efforts. So were the purges in the mid-1930s of faculty and students who had "wormed their way" into educational institutions, and whose removal was a prelude to the more sweeping and lethal actions of 1936–38.

"Worming one's way" was the direct antithesis of coming clean about one's real intentions and past. Yet in a situation of shortage where the paternalistic state adjudicated among supplicants, (re)fashioning oneself to suit the criteria of political authorities (or, as in the case of so many desperate children, worming one's way into the heart of a dear "uncle" or "elder") was often a necessity. Navigating through these two contradictory imperatives shaped many of the self-presentations contained in the documents and became, in effect, a way of life.

In assembling the documents, we frequently found ourselves empathizing with some of their authors and moved to irritation and even anger by others. These emotional reactions, clearly an indication of the transhistorical power of the written word, are probably inevitable and undoubtedly color our contextualizing and linking commentary. Yet one would do well to remember that the constraints under which these people acted, the choices they made, and the sense of themselves and others thereby derived are not entirely reproduceable. Passing judgment on these individuals or even on the political system in which, and moral codes by which, they lived is therefore quite tricky if not presumptuous. Our aim as historians was to understand the mentalities and behaviors that were produced by, and in turn helped to perpetuate, Stalinism, and that is very much the point.

# Notes

1. Hubert Hassner and Evgenia Petrova, eds., *Agitatsiia za schast'e: Sovetskoe iskusstvo stalinskoi epokhi* [Agitation for happiness: Soviet art of the Stalin era], 2d rev. ed. (Dusseldorf: Edition Temmen, 1994), p. 10. See also Gabriele Gorzka, ed., *Kultur im Stalinismus: Sowjetische Kultur und Kunst der 1930er bis 50er Jahre* (Bremen: Edition Temmen, 1994). This is the product of a conference held at the University of Kassel in November 1993 in conjunction with the opening of the exhibition.

2. For a recent history of this concept, see Abbott Gleason, *Totalitarianism: The Inner History of the Cold War* (Oxford: Oxford University Press, 1995). See also Giuseppe Boffa, *The Stalin Phenomenon,* trans. Nicholas Fersen (Ithaca: Cornell University Press, 1992), pp. 60–75.

3. Among the best of these was Barrington Moore, Jr., *Terror and Progress USSR: Some Sources of Change and Stability in the Soviet Dictatorship* (New York: Harper and Row, 1954).

4. See Nicholas Timasheff, *The Great Retreat: The Growth and Decline of Communism in Russia* (New York: Dutton, 1946); Robert McNeal, "Trotskyist Interpretations of Stalinism," in Robert Tucker, ed., *Stalinism: Essays in Historical Interpretation* (New York: Norton, 1977), pp. 30–52. As Boffa (*Stalin Phenomenon,* p. 91) notes, "The idea of Stalinism as a historical phenomenon in its own right first developed within Marxist thought; its origin can hardly be disputed, since practically no one else paid any attention to it for a number of years."

5. The foundational texts are Tucker, *Stalinism;* Kendall E. Bailes, *Technology and Society Under Lenin and Stalin* (Princeton: Princeton University Press, 1978); Sheila Fitzpatrick, ed., *Cultural Revolution in Russia, 1928–1931* (Bloomington: Indiana University Press, 1978); and Sheila Fitzpatrick, *Education and Social Mo-*

*bility in the Soviet Union, 1921–1934* (Cambridge: Cambridge University Press, 1979).

6. J. Arch Getty, *Origins of the Great Purges: The Soviet Communist Party Reconsidered, 1933–1938* (Cambridge: Cambridge University Press, 1985); Gabor Tamas Rittersporn, *Stalinist Simplifications and Soviet Complications: Social Tensions and Political Conflicts in the USSR, 1933–1953* (Chur, Switzerland: Harwood Academic Publishers, 1991). The Smolensk Archive, for decades the sole body of Soviet Communist Party archival documents available to Western researchers, served as the basis for Merle Fainsod's *Smolensk Under Soviet Rule* (Cambridge: Harvard University Press, 1958).

7. Moshe Lewin, *The Making of the Soviet System: Essays in the Social History of Interwar Russia* (New York: Pantheon, 1985), pp. 18, 32, 43, 218–28, 274–76.

8. Other, perhaps less obvious, influences are also worth noting. Russian historians, now freed from the constraints of Marxist-Leninist dogma, have made signal contributions in recent years to our understanding of the Stalin era. Opportunities (including those provided by Yale University Press's Annals of Communism series) to engage in dialogue and to collaborate with them have resulted in mutually beneficial cross-fertilization. The collapse of the Soviet Union itself has precipitated a panoply of new questions about what sustained its existence, the trajectory of the *nomenklatura*, the formation of national identities, and other issues demanding historical perspective. Finally, historians of the Stalin era have not been immune from the shift in the historical optic away from grand narrative and toward the local and marginal, the constructedness and instability of categories, and the pervasiveness and polyvalency of power.

9. Andrei Sokolov, ed., *Golos naroda: Pis'ma i otkliki riadovykh sovetskikh grazhdan o sobytiiakh 1918–1932 gg.* [Voice of the people: Letters and commentary of ordinary Soviet citizens about events in the years 1918–1932] (Moscow: Rosspen, 1998).

10. Andrei Sokolov, *Obshchestvo i vlast' 1930-e gody: Povestvovanie v dokumentakh* (Moscow: Rosspen, 1998).

11. On "speaking Bolshevik" see Stephen Kotkin, *Magnetic Mountain: Stalinism as a Civilization* (Berkeley: University of California Press, 1995), chapter 5.

12. Sheila Fitzpatrick, "Readers' Letters to *Krest'ianskaia Gazeta,* 1938," *Russian History/Histoire Russe* 24, nos. 1–2 (1997): 150; Sheila Fitzpatrick, *Everyday Stalinism, Ordinary Life in Extraordinary Times: Soviet Russia in the 1930s* (New York: Oxford University Press, 1999), pp. 175–76.

13. Fitzpatrick, *Everyday Stalinism,* pp. 164–72, 175–78; Sarah Davies, *Popular Opinion in Stalin's Russia: Terror, Propaganda, and Dissent, 1934–1941* (Cambridge: Cambridge University Press, 1997), pp. 9–17.

14. Natalie Zemon Davis, *Fiction in the Archives: Pardon Tales and Their Tellers in Sixteenth Century France* (Stanford: Stanford University Press, 1987), p. 4.

15. Rossiisky Gosudarstvennyi Arkhiv Ekonomiki (RGAE), fond 7486s, opis' 1, delo 236.

16. James C. Scott, *Domination and the Arts of Resistance: Hidden Transcripts* (New Haven: Yale University Press, 1990).

17. James C. Scott, *Weapons of the Weak: Everyday Forms of Peasant Resistance* (New Haven: Yale University Press, 1985).

18. See, for example, Paul Cohen, *History in Three Keys: The Boxers in History, Experience, and Myth* (New York: Columbia University Press, 1997).

19. The most sympathetic and detailed analysis of peasant resistance is Lynne Viola, *Peasant Rebels Under Stalin: Collectivization and the Culture of Peasant Resistance* (New York: Oxford University Press, 1996). Document collections devoted to, or containing substantial information on, peasant resistance include Valery Vasil'ev and Lynne Viola, eds., *Kollektivizatsiia i krest'ianskoe soprotivlenie na Ukraine, noiabr' 1929–mart 1930 gg.* (Vinnitsa: Logos, 1997); Lynne Viola et al., eds., *Riazanskaia derevnia v 1929–1930 gg. Khronika golovokruzheniia: Dokumenty i materialy* (Moscow: Rosspen, 1998). See also Sokolov, *Golos naroda*, pp. 295–307.

20. These forms are analyzed in Sheila Fitzpatrick, *Stalin's Peasants: Resistance and Survival in the Russian Village After Collectivization* (New York: Oxford University Press, 1994). For immediate post–Second World War rumors of the liquidation of collective farms, see Elena Zubkova, *Russia After the War: Hopes, Illusions, and Disappointments, 1945–1957*, trans. Hugh Ragsdale (Armonk, N.Y.: M. E. Sharpe, 1998), pp. 60–62, 78–79. Zubkova considers rumors to be "fantasies" rather than resistance.

21. Viola, *Peasant Rebels*, p. 235.

22. Sorting this out is no easy matter, as there was considerable overlap psychologically, if not conceptually. Viola (*Peasant Rebels*, p. 235) claims that peasants regarded their antagonists as an "unholy triad of Communism–Antichrist–sexual depravity."

23. Jeffrey Rossman, "The Teikovo Cotton Workers' Strike of April 1932," *Russian Review* 56, no. 1 (1997): 44–69.

24. This issue was explored, albeit without access to Soviet archives, during the 1980s, a high point for the historiography of Soviet labor. See especially Donald Filtzer, *Soviet Workers and Stalinist Industrialization: The Formation of Modern Soviet Production Relations, 1928–1941* (Armonk, N.Y.: M. E. Sharpe, 1986); Vladimir Andrle, *Workers in Stalin's Russia: Industrialization and Social Change in a Planned Economy* (New York: St. Martin's, 1988); Lewis H. Siegelbaum, "Productive Collectives and Communes and the 'Imperatives' of Soviet Industrialization, 1929–1931," *Slavic Review* 45, no. 1 (1986): 65–84.

25. See Sheila Fitzpatrick, "The Great Departure: Rural-Urban Migration in the Soviet Union, 1929–33," in William G. Rosenberg and Lewis H. Siegelbaum, eds., *Social Dimensions of Soviet Industrialization* (Bloomington: Indiana University Press, 1993), pp. 15–40.

26. My thinking about how to understand resistance and alternative strategies has been influenced by Alen Isaacman, *Cotton is the Mother of Poverty: Peasants, Work, and Rural Struggle in Mozambique, 1938–1961* (Portsmouth, N.H.: Heineman, 1996); Ann Stoler, "Plantation Politics and Protest on Sumatra's Coast," *Journal of Peasant Studies* 13, no. 2 (1986): 124–43; and Frank Trommler, "Between Normality and Resistance: Catastrophic Gradualism in Nazi Germany," in Michael Geyer and John W. Boyer, eds., *Resistance Against the Third Reich, 1933–1990* (Chicago: University of Chicago Press, 1994), pp. 119–40.

27. Sheila Fitzpatrick, "Writing to Power: Denunciation, Complaint, Confession, and Other Public Epistolary Genres in Stalin's Russia," unpub., pp. 7–8; Roberta Manning, "The Great Purges in a Rural District: Belyi Raion Revisited,"

in J. Arch Getty and Roberta Manning, eds., *Stalinist Terror: New Perspectives* (Cambridge: Cambridge University Press, 1993), pp. 168–97.

28. Ellen Wimberg, "Socialism, Democratism, and Criticism: The Soviet Press and the National Discussion of the 1936 Draft Constitution," *Soviet Studies* 44 (1992): 313–32. The decision to subject the draft of the constitution to public discussion may have been inspired by the monthlong discussion of the draft decree criminalizing abortion published on the front page of *Pravda* on 26 May 1936. See Janet Evans, "The Communist Party of the Soviet Union and the Women's Question: The Case of the 1936 Decree 'In Defense of Mother and Child,'" *Journal of Contemporary History* 16 (1981): 754–76; Wendy Goldman, *Women, the State, and Revolution: Soviet Family Policy and Social Life, 1917–1936* (New York: Cambridge University Press, 1993), pp. 331–36.

29. J. Arch Getty, "State and Society Under Stalin: Constitutions and Elections in the 1930s," *Slavic Review* 50 (1991): 23–24.

30. Ibid., p. 24. See also Davies, *Popular Opinion,* p. 102: "The show of 'Soviet democracy' did in fact provide a genuine forum for the expression of popular opinion and stimulate consciousness of civil and political rights."

31. Daniel Field, *Rebels in the Name of the Tsar* (Boston: Houghton Mifflin, 1976), pp. 31–33, 208–14.

32. This and the following paragraph are derived from Fitzpatrick, *Stalin's Peasants,* pp. 140–42, 227–30.

33. See Peter Holquist, "A Russian Vendée: The Practice of Revolutionary Politics in the Don Countryside, 1917–1921," Ph.D. diss., Columbia University, 1995; and D'Ann Penner, "Pride, Power, and Pitchforks: Farmer-Party Interaction on the Don, 1920–1928," Ph.D. diss., University of California, Berkeley, 1995. Penner quotes an OGPU agent's report in 1925 that "all Cossacks were viewed as counter-revolutionaries" (p. 206).

34. Fitzpatrick, *Stalin's Peasants,* pp. 183–84, refers to "the Civil War 'command' model" and the "frontier world" as constituent elements of local officials' leadership style. One should add that older models of authority could also shape officials' behavior.

35. See Matt F. Oja, "From *Krestianka* to *Udarnitsa:* Rural Women and the *Vydvizhenie* Campaign, 1933–1941," *The Carl Beck Papers in Russian and East European Studies* 1203 (1996); Roberta Manning, "Women in the Soviet Countryside on the Eve of World War II," in Beatrice Farnsworth and Lynne Viola, eds., *Russian Peasant Women* (New York: Oxford University Press, 1992), pp. 206–35; and Mary Buckley, "Why Be a Shock Worker or a Stakhanovite?" in Rosalind Marsh, ed., *Women in Russia and Ukraine* (Cambridge: Cambridge University Press, 1996), pp. 199–213.

36. See Lewis H. Siegelbaum, "'Dear Comrade, You Ask What We Need': Soviet Paternalism and Rural 'Notables' in the Mid-1930s," *Slavic Review* 57, no. 1 (1998): 107–32; and Mary Buckley, "Was Rural Stakhanovism a Movement?" *Europe-Asia Studies* 51, no. 2 (1999): 299–314.

37. Kotkin, *Magnetic Mountain,* p. 23.

38. Ibid., p. 22.

39. Igal Halfin and Jochen Hellbeck, "Rethinking the Stalinist Subject: Stephen Kotkin's *Magnetic Mountain* and the State of Soviet Historical Studies," *Jahrbücher für Geschichte Osteuropas* 44, no. 3 (1996): 458.

40. For the inappropriateness of simply transferring Michel Foucault's analysis and critique of the bourgeois liberal subject to the Soviet case, see Laura Engelstein, "Combined Underdevelopment: Discipline and the Law in Imperial and Soviet Russia," *American Historical Review* 98, no. 2 (1993): 338–53. I do not subscribe to Engelstein's dismissal of the possibility of an alternative Soviet subjectivity.

41. Jochen Hellbeck, "Fashioning the Stalinist Soul: The Diary of Stepan Podlubnyi, 1931–1939," *Jahrbücher für Geschichte Osteuropas* 44, no. 3 (1996): 344–73. These are Hellbeck's, not Podlubnyi's, words. An abridged version of the diary was published in German as Jochen Hellbeck, ed., *Tagbuch aus Moskau, 1931–1939* (Munich: Deutscher Taschenbuch Verlag, 1996). For a volume containing substantial excerpts from nine diaries (including Podlubnyi's), see Veronique Garros, Natalia Korenevskaya, and Thomas Lahusen, eds., *Intimacy and Terror: Soviet Diaries of the 1930s* (New York: New Press, 1995).

42. Thomas Lahusen, *How Life Writes the Book: Real Socialism and Socialist Realism in Stalin's Russia* (Ithaca: Cornell University Press, 1997), p. 55.

43. On the changing status of the family during the 1930s, see Goldman, *Women, the State, and Revolution*, pp. 296–336. On representations, see Katerina Clark, *The Soviet Novel: History as Ritual* (Chicago: University of Chicago Press, 1981), pp. 114–35. Clark notes (p. 114) the projection of "primordial attachments of kinship" as "the dominant symbol for social allegiance."

44. Robert Conquest, *The Great Terror* (Cambridge: Harvard University Press, 1969).

45. See, respectively, Getty, *Origins of the Great Purges*; Rittersporn, *Stalinist Simplifications*; Oleg Khlevnyuk, "The Objectives of the Great Terror, 1937–38," in Julian Cooper, Maureen Perrie, and E. A. Rees, eds., *Soviet History 1917–53: Essays in Honour of R. W. Davies* (New York: St. Martin's, 1995), pp. 158–75; Kotkin, *Magnetic Mountain*, pp. 280–354; Robert Thurston, *Life and Terror in Stalin's Russia, 1934–1941* (New Haven: Yale University Press, 1996); J. Arch Getty and Oleg V. Naumov, *The Road to Terror: Stalin and the Self-Destruction of the Bolsheviks, 1932–39* (New Haven: Yale University Press, 1999).

46. For suggestions along these lines, see Halfin and Hellbeck, "Rethinking the Stalinist Subject," pp. 460–62.

47. See inter alia Hiroaki Kuromiya, *Freedom and Terror in the Donbas: A Ukrainian-Russian Borderland, 1870s–1990s* (Cambridge: Cambridge University Press, 1998), pp. 201–50; Robert Weinberg, "Purge and Politics in the Periphery: Birobidzhan in 1937," *Slavic Review* 52, no. 1 (1993): 13–27; Robert McCutcheon, "The 1936–1937 Purge of Soviet Astronomers," *Slavic Review* 50, no. 1 (1990): 100–117; Francesco Benvenuti, *Fuoco sui sabotatori! Stachanovismo e organizzazione industriale in URSS, 1934–1938* (Rome: Valerio Levi, 1988), pp. 369–452; Sheila Fitzpatrick, "Workers Against Bosses: The Impact of the Great Purges on Labor-Management Relations," in Lewis H. Siegelbaum and Ronald G. Suny, eds., *Making Workers Soviet: Power, Class, and Identity* (Ithaca: Cornell University Press, 1994), pp. 311–40; Sheila Fitzpatrick, "How the Mice Buried the Cat: Scenes from the Great Purges of 1937 in the Russian Provinces," *Russian Review* 52, no. 3 (1993): 299–332; Getty and Manning, *Stalinist Terror*. Getty, *Road to Terror*, appendix 1, neatly summarizes estimates of the number of victims and provides new evidence.

48. Paul M. Hagenloh, "'Socially Harmful Elements' and the Great Terror," paper presented at annual meeting of AAASS, Seattle, November 1997; David R. Shearer, "Policing the Soviet Frontier: Social Disorder and Repression in Western Siberia During the 1930s," paper presented at annual meeting of AAASS, Seattle, November 1997; Michael Gelb, "An Early Soviet Ethnic Deportation: The Far-Eastern Koreans," *Russian Review* 54, no. 3 (1995): 389–412; Terry Martin, "The Origins of Soviet Ethnic Cleansing," *Journal of Modern History* 70 (1998): 813–61; N. F. Bugai, ed., *Iosif Stalin—Lavrentiiu Berii: 'Ikh nado deportirovat': Dokumenty, fakty, kommentarii* (Moscow, 1992).

49. See Gerhard Simon, *Nationalism and Policy Toward the Nationalities in the Soviet Union: From Totalitarian Dictatorship to Post-Stalinist Society* (Boulder: Westview, 1991); Ronald Grigor Suny, *The Revenge of the Past: Nationalism, Revolution, and the Collapse of the Soviet Union* (Stanford: Stanford University Press, 1993); Yuri Slezkine, "The USSR as a Communal Apartment, or How a Socialist State Promoted Ethnic Particularism," *Slavic Review* 53, no. 2 (1994): 414–52; Francine Hirsch, "The Soviet Union as a Work-in-Progress: Ethnographers and the Category of Nationality in the 1926, 1937, and 1939 Censuses," *Slavic Review* 56, no. 2 (1997): 251–78.

50. Slezkine, "USSR as a Communal Apartment," pp. 441, 448.

51. This term was coined by Aleksandr Zinoviev (see his *Homo Sovieticus,* trans. Charles Janson [London: Gollancz, 1985]) and used in a pejorative sense. It has been adopted by Sheila Fitzpatrick, who employs it "to call attention to the existence of a characteristic set of 'Soviet' practices and behaviors related to the peculiarities of Soviet institutions and social structure" (*Everyday Stalinism,* p. 229).

52. This is also amply demonstrated in Sokolov, *Golos naroda.*

CHAPTER I. THE SOCIALIST OFFENSIVE

1. The most detailed account of the economic dimensions of the offensive is R. W. Davies, *The Industrialisation of Soviet Russia,* vol. 1, *The Socialist Offensive: The Collectivisation of Soviet Agriculture, 1929–1930* (London: Macmillan, 1980), and vol. 3, *The Soviet Economy in Turmoil, 1929–1930* (London: Macmillan, 1989).

2. In-house newspaper *Udarnik Metrostroia,* 29 December 1933.

3. *Pervyi Vsesoiuznyi s"ezd udarnykh brigad (k tridts. s"ezda),* Moscow, 1959, pp. 52–53.

4. Ibid., p. 179. On socialist competition and shock work in the late 1920s and early 1930s see Hiroaki Kuromiya, *Stalin's Industrial Revolution: Politics and Workers, 1928–1932* (Cambridge: Cambridge University Press, 1988), pp. 115–28. See pp. 319–23 for a statistical analysis of shock workers.

5. Magnitka, a popular name for Magnitogorsk, was the "socialist city" built east of the Urals. It is the subject of John Scott's *Behind the Urals: An American Worker in Russia's City of Steel* (Bloomington: Indiana University Press, 1973) and Stephen Kotkin's *Magnetic Mountain: Stalinism as a Civilization* (Berkeley: University of California Press, 1995).

6. RGASPI, f. 17, op. 120, d. 62, ll. 36–54.

7. TsMAM, f. 2090, op. 1, d. 832, ll. 1–2.

8. GARF, f. 1235, op. 141, d. 583, ll. 203, 204.

9. RGAE, f. 7486, op. 1, d. 102, ll. 210, 211.

10. TsKhDMO, f. 1, op. 3, d. 65, ll. 82, 83. On anti-Semitism among Donbass miners before the October Revolution see Charters Wynn, *Workers, Strikes, and Pogroms: The Donbass-Dnepr Bend in Late Imperial Russia, 1870–1905* (Princeton: Princeton University Press, 1992). For its persistence in the Soviet period see Hiroaki Kuromiya, *Freedom and Terror in the Donbas: A Ukrainian-Russian Borderland, 1870s–1990s* (Cambridge: Cambridge University Press, 1998), pp. 147–48, 160, 198, 246.

11. I. V. Stalin, *Sochineniia* [Collected works], 13 vols. (Moscow, 1946–51), 12: 68. For the November plenum, see Davies, *Collectivisation of Soviet Agriculture,* pp. 155–74.

12. N. A. Ivnitskii, "Kollektivizatsiia i raskulachivanie v nachale 30-kh godov," in *Kooperativnyi plan: Illiuzii i deistvitel'nosti* (Moscow: RGGU, 1995), p. 45.

13. Ibid., p. 51. Syrtsov was chairman of the RSFSR's Council of People's Commissars in 1929–30. Ordzhonikidze was Commissar of RKI (1926–30) and thereafter chairman of VSNKh and commissar of heavy industry.

14. RGAE, f. 7486, op. 1, d. 100, l. 55.

15. GARF, f. 3316, op. 1, d. 448, l. 68.

16. Ibid., l. 66.

17. RGAE, f. 7486, op. 1, d. 100, ll. 101, 139.

18. For a sympathetic account of the Twenty-Five Thousanders see Lynne Viola, *The Best Sons of the Fatherland: Workers in the Vanguard of Soviet Collectivization* (New York: Oxford University Press, 1987).

19. RGAE, f. 7486, op. 1, d. 237, l. 373.

20. Ibid., l. 376.

21. RGAE, f. 7486, op. 1, d. 236, l. 58.

22. Ibid., l. 76.

23. Ibid., l. 65.

24. The *Krest'ianskaia Gazeta* summary concerned with organization of work on collective farms can be found in RGAE, f. 7486, op. 1, d. 102, ll. 246–272.

25. Ibid., ll. 269–270.

26. For a more detailed description of rationing and of standards for supplying the population, see Ye. A. Osokina, *Ierarkhiia potrebleniia: O zhizni liudei v usloviiakh stalinskogo snabzheniia, 1928–1935 gg.* (Moscow: Rosspen, 1993).

27. RGAE, f. 7486, op. 1, d. 102, l. 202.

28. Ibid.

29. Scholars have long questioned the veracity of these figures. For an estimate of less than fifty million tons in 1932 see Mark Tauger, "The 1932 Harvest and the Famine of 1933," *Slavic Review* 50, no. 1 (1991): 70–89.

30. RGAE, f. 7486, op. 1, d. 236, l. 11.

31. Ibid., l. 35.

32. Ibid., l. 9.

33. RGAE, f. 7486, op. 1, d. 237, ll. 294–324.

34. N. A. Ivnitskii, "Golod 1932–1933 godov: Kto vinovat?" in Iu N. Afanas'ev, ed., *Golod 1932–1933 godov* (Moscow: RGGU, 1995), p. 61.

35. Quotation from *Don,* no. 6 (1988), p. 61.

36. RGAE, f. 7486, op. 1, d. 100, l. 109.

37. GARF, f. 7952, op. 7, d. 297, l. 47.

38. *Rasskazy stroitelei metro* (Moscow, 1935), pp. 28, 80.

39. This was to be the site of an enormous Palace of Soviets, for which a highly publicized architectural competition was held. Owing to technical difficulties, the palace was never built and the foundation pit became a giant outdoor swimming pool. The church was rebuilt in the 1990s and opened in 1996, in time for the one thousandth anniversary of the Russian adoption of Orthodox Christianity.

40. RGASPI, f. 558, op. 1, d. 2939.

41. *KPSS v rezoliutsiiakh i resheniiakh s"ezdov, konferentsii i plenumov TsK* (9th ed., Moscow, 1984), vol. 5, pp. 407–8.

42. RGASPI, f. 12, op. 1, d. 748, l. 34.

43. Ibid., d. 114, l. 1.

44. Most likely the objection is that mention of "undernourished livestock" on collective farms discredits the kolkhoz system. In one party document we learn that, following publication of an article "How to Put a Stop to the Decrease in Livestock" by a Professor Vasiliev in the Voronezh Oblast newspaper *Kommuna* (Commune) in April 1934, the editor in chief was removed and the mere fact of publication termed "the grossest political error, intended to disrupt meat procurements" (RGASPI, f. 17, op. 114, d. 168, l. 126).

45. RGASPI, f. 17, op. 114, d. 333, l. 54.

46. RGASPI, f. 386, op. 1, d. 57, l. 15.

47. Calculated on the basis of the most recent summaries compiled by NKVD bodies. Cf. GARF, f. 9401, op. 1, d. 4157, ll. 201–205.

48. Ibid.

49. In this and the following two instances the information has been obliterated in the original.

50. TsMAM, f. 528, op. 7, d. 14, l. 1.

51. Calculated using GARF, f. 9401, op. 1, d. 4157, ll. 201–205 in V. N. Zemskov, "GULAG: Istoriko-sotsiologicheskii aspekt," *Sotsiologicheskie issledovaniia,* no. 6 (1991), p. 11. (Cf. also J. Arch Getty, Gabor T. Rittersporn, and Victor N. Zemskov, "Victims of the Soviet Penal System in the Pre-War Years: A First Approach on the Basis of Archival Evidence," *American Historical Review* 98, no. 4 [1993]: 1048.)

52. Calculated using V. N. Zemskov, "Kulatskaia ssylka v 30-e gody," *Sotsiologicheskie issledovaniia,* no. 10 (1991), p. 5.

53. Calculated using V. N. Zemskov, "Spetspereselentsy," *Sotsiologicheskie issledovaniia,* no. 11 (1990), p. 6.

54. Zemskov, "GULAG," p. 11; Getty, Rittersporn, and Zemskov, "Victims," p. 1048.

55. On the Stakhanovite movement see Lewis H. Siegelbaum, *Stakhanovism and the Politics of Productivity in the USSR, 1935–1941* (New York: Cambridge University Press, 1988).

56. TsMAM, f. 150, op. 1, d. 366, l. 266.

57. See Svetlana Boym, *Common Places: Mythologies of Everyday Life in Russia* (Cambridge: Harvard University Press, 1994), pp. 121–59; Timothy Colton, *Moscow: Governing the Socialist Metropolis* (Cambridge: Harvard University Press, 1995), pp. 272–79.

58. RGASPI, f. 386, op. 1, d. 61, ll. 2–3.

59. TsKhDMO, f. 1, op. 23, d. 1070, ll. 29–30.

## CHAPTER 2. "CADRES DECIDE EVERYTHING"

1. RGASPI, f. 355, op. 1, d. 115, ll. 100–101.

2. Kendall E. Bailes, *Technology and Society Under Lenin and Stalin: Origins of the Soviet Technical Intelligentsia, 1917–1941* (Princeton: Princeton University Press, 1978), p. 150.

3. Andrei Platonov, "Iuvenil'noe more" [Juvenal Sea], *Gosudarstvennyi zhitel'* (Moscow: Sovetsky pisatel', 1988), pp. 343–44.

4. GARF, f. 7952, op. 3, d. 240, ll. 65–66. For more on Stepanov and the reconstruction of Hammer and Sickle during the First Five-Year Plan, see Kenneth M. Straus, *Factory and Community in Stalin's Russia* (Pittsburgh: University of Pittsburgh Press, 1997), pp. 44–54, 245–54.

5. The review was conducted in February 1935 by A. Stetsky, director of TsK VKP(b)'s Department of Culture and Propaganda, in connection with the publication of a brief article in *Pravda* with the title "A Trotskyist on the Faculty." Stetsky concluded that the actual situation in institutions of higher education was even worse than reported in *Pravda*. The materials from the review, entitled "Concerning the Political State of Institutions of Higher Education in the Azov–Black Sea Krai," consist of three parts. The first part, quoted here, is devoted to student political attitudes. The second part is entitled "A Teaching Staff Infested with Trotskyists and the Case of Vladimirov." Vladimirov was expelled from the party in 1928 for belonging to the Left Opposition. There is a detailed discussion of who was to blame for the fact that an ex-Trotskyist had been on the faculty of the Higher Communist School of Agriculture in Rostov and of how the city's party organizations had not exercised sufficient vigilance. Also discussed is the expulsion of seven faculty members "for making Trotskyist inroads and smuggling in Trotskyist ideology." The third part of the materials discusses the inadequacy of party and mass political work in Krai institutions of higher education.

6. The White Sea–Baltic *(Belomorsko-Baltiiskii)* Canal was built between 1931 and 1933, primarily with prisoner labor and prisoner engineers. Although it has been estimated that as many as 100,000 of the 280,000 employed on the project perished, the canal's construction was hailed in a lavishly produced, collectively written volume as an example of redemption through labor. See M. Gorky, L. L. Averbakh, and S. G. Firin, eds., *Belomorsko-Baltiiskii Kanal imeni Stalina* (Moscow, 1934).

7. For details on these historians' scholarship, see M. N. Tikhomirov and M. V. Nechkina, ed., *Ocherki istorii istoriograficheskoi nauki v SSSR*, 5 vols. (Moscow: Akademiia nauk, 1955–85), vols. 3–5. The "right-left bloc" consisted of previously loyal Stalinists who criticized the excessive pace and wastefulness of industrialization and the rampant growth of bureaucratism. Bloc leaders were S. I. Syrtsov, a candidate member of the Politburo and premier of the RSFSR, and V. V. Lominadze, first secretary of the Transcaucasian Federation. The bloc was "exposed" in late 1930, and its leaders were removed from their posts.

8. The TsK's resolution "On the Teaching of Civic History" was published in *Pravda* on 16 May 1934. It condemned the schematism associated with the school

of M. N. Pokrovsky and called for the restoration of narrative history. See George Enteen, *The Soviet Scholar-Bureaucrat: M. N. Pokrovskii and the Society of Marxist Historians* (University Park: Pennsylvania State University Press, 1978), pp. 189–96.

CHAPTER 3. STALIN'S CONSTITUTION

1. The first quotation is from V. Molotov's speech to the Seventh All-Union Congress of Soviets on 1 February 1935; the second is from article 126 of the constitution, as cited in Merle Fainsod, *How Russia Is Ruled* (Cambridge: Harvard University Press, 1965), pp. 373, 379.

2. On Vyshinsky's long career as a jurist and legal "theoretician," see Robert Sharlet and Piers Bierne, "In Search of Vyshinsky: The Paradox of Law and Terror," in Piers Bierne, ed., *Revolution in Law: Contributions to the Development of Soviet Legal Theory, 1917–1938* (Armonk, N.Y.: M. E. Sharpe, 1990), pp. 136–56; and Robert Sharlet, "Stalinism and Soviet Legal Culture," in Tucker, *Stalinism*, pp. 163–68. Vyshinsky's trenchant advocacy of a "socialist legal culture" did not preclude his participation in jurisprudential terror, as prosecutor in the infamous political show trials of 1936–38. Nor did it curb the sweeping powers of the police.

3. Robert Sharlet, "Pashukanis and the Withering Away of the Law in the USSR," in Fitzpatrick, *Cultural Revolution*, p. 187.

4. The latter point is stressed by Peter H. Solomon, *Soviet Criminal Justice under Stalin* (Cambridge: Cambridge University Press, 1996), p. 193.

5. TsGAODM, f. 4, op. 49, d. 173, l. 91.

6. GARF, f. 3316, op. 8, d. 222, l. 159.

7. For example, the multivolume history of the KPSS referred to two million proposals on the draft constitution. Cf. *Istoriia KPSS,* 6 vol. (vol. 4, book 2, Moscow, 1971), p. 513.

8. Cf. the information summary of the NKVD on the discussion, submitted to the TsK of the VKP(b): RGASPI, f. 17, op. 120, d. 232, ll. 40–44.

9. Cf. GARF, f. 3316, op. 41, d. 105, 142, and others.

10. *Neizvestnaia Rossia. XX vek.*, vol. 2 (Moscow, 1992), pp. 274, 273.

11. RGASPI, f. 17, op. 120, d. 232, l. 46.

12. Cf. RGASPI, f. 17, op. 120, d. 232, ll. 46–48.

13. GARF, f. 3316, op. 41, d. 105, l. 1.

14. RGASPI, f. 17, op. 120, d. 232, l. 45. In the original draft of the constitution, the rough outline of Article 102 stated that class divisions in the USSR had been eliminated, and this proposition "slipped" into the press, adding confusion for the propagandists, but within a week this theoretical premise was deemed incorrect. Two classes were cited: workers and peasants.

15. Ibid.

16. GARF, f. 3316, op. 8, d. 222, l. 159.

17. RGASPI, f. 17, op. 120, d. 232, l. 37.

18. Ibid., l. 36.

19. *Neizvestnaia Rossia. XX vek.*, vol. 2, p. 278.

20. RGASPI, f. 17, op. 120, d. 232, l. 52.

21. Ibid., l. 50. Sarah Davies, working mainly with Leningrad NKVD materials

from the Central State Archive of Political Historical Documents in St. Petersburg (TsGAIPD SPb), notes that "the discussion seems . . . to have activated peasant 'class' consciousness." Sarah Davies, *Popular Opinion in Stalin's Russia: Terror, Propaganda, and Dissent, 1934–1941* (Cambridge: Cambridge University Press, 1997), p. 105.

22. RGASPI, f. 17, op. 120, d. 232, l. 86.

23. GARF, f. 3316, op. 41, d. 79, l. 510b.

24. RGASPI, f. 17, op. 120, d. 232, ll. 50, 49, 51, respectively.

25. Ibid., ll. 68–69, 65.

26. Ibid., ll. 49, 51.

27. Ibid., l. 49.

28. *Neizvestnaia Rossia. XX vek.,* vol. 2, p. 273.

29. RGASPI, f. 17, op. 120, d. 232, ll. 63, 64.

30. Ibid., ll. 50, 65, 67.

31. Ibid., l. 80.

32. Ibid., l. 86.

33. Ibid., ll. 50, 51.

34. *Neizvestnaia Rossia. XX vek.,* vol. 2, p. 278.

35. RGASPI, f. 17, op. 120, d. 232, ll. 75, 46.

36. Ibid., l. 52.

37. GARF, f. 3316, op. 41, d. 84, ll. 33–34.

38. Ibid., op. 40, d. 14, ll. 100–101.

39. Ibid., op. 41, d. 85, l. 80.

40. Ibid., d. 81, ll. 22, 23, 24, 27, 30, 32, 33, 51.

41. GARF, f. 3316, op. 41, d. 81, ll. 9–90b, 8. On these issues, see Lewis H. Siegelbaum, *Stakhanovism and the Politics of Productivity in the USSR, 1935–1941* (New York: Cambridge University Press, 1988), pp. 76–88, 127–44, 190–204.

42. RGASPI, f. 17, op. 120, d. 232, l. 69.

43. GARF, f. 3316, op. 41, d. 77, l. 96.

44. RGASPI, f. 17, op. 120, d. 232, l. 88.

45. GARF, f. 3316, op. 41, d. 193, l. 55.

46. RGASPI, f. 17, op. 120, d. 232, l. 70.

47. Cf. Wendy Goldman, *Women, the State, and Revolution: Soviet Family Policy and Social Life, 1917–36* (Cambridge: Cambridge University Press, 1993), p. 336: "The state drew upon [a] deep fount of bitterness to justify the resurrection of the family."

48. GARF, f. 3316, op. 41, d. 82, ll. 1–2; d. 79, l. 16.

49. GARF, f. 3316, op. 41, d. 79, ll. 58, 51.

50. Ibid., l. 58.

51. Ibid., ll. 34, 35–36.

52. Ibid., ll. 38, 39, 40–41, 42–43.

53. Ibid., ll. 44, 46–50.

54. Ibid., ll. 55–56.

55. Ibid., ll. 72, 73.

56. Ibid., d. 82, l. 3.

57. See Kendall E. Bailes, *Science and Russian Culture in an Age of Revolutions: V. I. Vernadsky and His Scientific School, 1863–1945* (Bloomington: Indi-

ana University Press, 1990); Thomas Seifrid, *Andrei Platonov, Uncertainties of Spirit* (Cambridge: Cambridge University Press, 1992); and Irene Masing-Delic, *Abolishing Death: A Salvation Myth of Russian Twentieth-Century Literature* (Stanford: Stanford University Press, 1992).

## CHAPTER 4. LOVE AND PLENTY

1. RGASPI, f. 477, op. 1, d. 43, l. 1.

2. See John McCannon, *Red Arctic: Polar Exploration and the Myth of the North in Soviet Russia, 1932–1939* (New York: Oxford University Press, 1997).

3. RGASPI, f. 386, op. 1, d. 65, ll. 29–31.

4. GARF, f. 4581, op. 1, d. 18, ll. 2–9, 13–17, 41–43.

5. TsGAODM, f. 4, op. 9, d. 173, l. 221.

6. TsGAODM, f. 369, op. 1, d. 162, ll. 22–26.

7. Materials were used from the case files of individuals repressed in 1937–38, which are stored in the Archives of the Bureau of the FSB RF (Federal Security Service of the Russian Federation) for Moscow and Moscow Oblast.

8. For more on the fate of political refugees in the USSR, see William J. Chase and F. I. Firsov, *The Comintern and Stalinist Repression, 1934–1939* (New Haven: Yale University Press, forthcoming).

9. TsGAODM, f. 369, op. 1, d. 161.

10. TsGAODM, f. 1934, op. 1, d. 184, l. 57.

11. Archives of the FSB RF (Federal Security Service of the Russian Federation) for Moscow and Moscow Oblast, case file P-33352.

12. Anastasia Koch's letter requesting a review of her husband's case is in his case file in the Archives of the FSB RF for Moscow and Moscow Oblast.

13. Estimate is based on: GARF, f. 9401, op. 1, d. 4157, ll. 201–205; V. N. Zemskov, "GULAG (Istoriko-sotsiologicheskii aspekt)," *Sotsiologicheskie issledovaniia,* no. 6 (1991), p. 11; J. Arch Getty, Gabor T. Rittersporn, and Victor N. Zemskov, "Victims of the Soviet Penal System in the Prewar Years: A First Approach on the Basis of Archival Evidence," *American Historical Review* 98, no. 4 (1993): 1048.

14. Getty, Rittersporn, and Zemskov, "Victims of the Soviet Penal System," p. 1048.

15. RGASPI, f. 17, op. 161, d. 36, ll. 5–12.

16. Ibid., d. 37, l. 121–123.

17. For the full document, see RGASPI, f. 17, op. 121, d. 19, ll. 95–103.

18. RGASPI, f. 477, op. 1, d. 61. References to page numbers from the file are not provided because the excerpts from the discussion materials are extremely fragmentary and vary in nature.

19. Getty, Rittersporn, and Zemskov, "Victims of the Soviet Penal System," p. 1033. For more on these decrees and noncompliance with them, see Donald Filtzer, *Soviet Workers and Stalinist Industrialization: The Formation of Modern Soviet Production Relations, 1928–1941* (Armonk, N.Y.: M. E. Sharpe, 1986), pp. 139–51.

20. Ye. A. Osokina, "Krizis snabzheniia 1939–1941 gg. v pis'makh sovetskikh liudei," *Voprosy istorii,* no. 1 (1996), pp. 6, 18–19.

21. Ibid., p. 5.

22. RGASPI, f. 17, op. 161, d. 41.

23. Ibid., d. 48, ll. 13, 62.

24. Ibid., op. 123, d. 42, l. 58.

25. Ibid., ll. 67–68.

26. Ibid., ll. 100, 101, 102, 103.

27. Ibid., op. 161, d. 32, ll. 5–12.

28. Cf. Jan. T. Gross, *Revolution from Abroad: The Soviet Conquest of Poland's Western Ukraine and Western Belorussia* (Princeton: Princeton University Press, 1988).

29. RGASPI, f. 17, op. 123, d. 42, ll. 1–2.

30. Calculated on the basis of an information sheet and report by Ye. A. Shchadenko, head of the RKKA bureau for command personnel, on work in 1939. Cf.: *Izvestia TsK KPSS*, no. 1 (1990), p. 177.

31. *Izvestia TsK KPSS*, no. 1 (1990), pp. 182, 187, 188–89. The figures on which the estimates are based are incomplete, because they do not include the air force and navy.

32. Cf. Roger Reese, *Stalin's Reluctant Soldiers: A Social History of the Red Army, 1925–1941* (Lawrence: University Press of Kansas, 1996).

CHAPTER 5. BOLSHEVIK ORDER ON THE KOLKHOZ

1. RGAE, f. 396, op. 10, d. 57, l. 230.

2. M. A. Vyltsan, "Poslednie edinolichniki," in Iu. A. Afanas'ev, ed., *Kooperativnyi plan: illiuzii i deistvitel'nost'* (Moscow: RGGU, 1995), p. 85

3. *Izvestia TsK KPSS*, no. 10 (1989), pp. 81–82; *Trud*, 4 June 1992. Several forthcoming articles by Paul M. Hagenloh and David R. Shearer analyze the background to the Politburo's now-famous resolution and the extent of its execution. We thank them for sharing with us typescripts of these articles.

4. For the letter in full, see RGAE, f. 396, op. 11, d. 7, ll. 31–39.

5. Ibid., ll. 18–21.

6. For the letter in full, see RGAE, f. 396, op. 10, d. 13, ll. 334–341ob.

7. RGASPI, f. 78, op. 1, d. 526, l. 116.

8. For the essay in full, see RGAE, f. 396, op. 11, d. 7, ll. 35–41ob.

9. RGASPI, f. 78, op. 1, d. 526, ll. 116–117.

10. For another such letter, see RGAE, f. 396, op. 10, d. 8, ll. 144–145ob. For the interpretation of trials of local officials as peasant carnivals, see Sheila Fitzpatrick, *Stalin's Peasants: Resistance and Survival in the Russian Village After Collectivization* (Oxford: Oxford University Press, 1994), chapter 11.

11. RGAE, f. 396, op. 11, d. 41, ll. 260–262ob.

12. Ibid., op. 10, d. 97, l. 146.

13. Ibid., op. 11, d. 41, ll. 61, 60.

14. Ibid., d. 26, l. 191.

15. For more on the personal/private plot, see Fitzpatrick, *Stalin's Peasants*, pp. 120–22, 130–36.

16. RGAE, f. 396, op. 11, d. 55, l. 7.

17. Ibid., l. 35.

18. Ibid., d. 41, ll. 61, 89.

19. Ibid., op. 10, d. 110, ll. 102–103.

20. RGASPI, f. 78, op. 1, d. 526, l. 120.

21. It is reported in the section "On Violations and Distortions of Revolutionary Law" that "in June 1935 legal proceedings were initiated against Veshchunov, and the case [against him] was turned over to the People's Court. For unknown reasons the court acquitted Veshchunov, but in October 1935, during a check of the leadership makeup of the raion's kolkhozes, the Krai Commission of the VKP(b) kraikom verified all of the allegations of abuse by Veshchunov against the female kolkhoz farmers. By decision of the commission and the VKP(b) kraikom, Veshchunov was ousted from his job and expelled from the kolkhoz. With regard to his ouster from his job, the decision was carried out. But Veshchunov has yet to be expelled from the kolkhoz and has not been held accountable." GARF, f. 1235, op. 141, d. 1789, l. 69.

22. RGAE, f. 396, op. 11, d. 41, l. 81.

23. Ibid., op. 5, d. 110, ll. 165, 164.

24. Ibid., l. 160.

25. Ibid., l. 169.

26. Poluektov's letter was published (in Russian) along with an analysis of its contents by Sheila Fitzpatrick, "From *Krest'ianskaia Gazeta's* Files: Life Story of a Peasant Striver," *Russian History/Histoire Russe* 24, nos. 1–2 (1997): 215–36. Fitzpatrick characterizes the letter as "a real gift to historians of the Russian countryside."

27. This correspondence is analyzed in Lewis H. Siegelbaum, "'Dear Comrade, You Ask What We Need': Socialist Paternalism and Soviet Rural 'Notables' in the Mid-1930s," *Slavic Review* 57, no. 1 (1998): 107–32.

28. GARF, f. 7689, op. 11, d. 50, ll. 32–320b.

29. Ibid., ll. 39, 38.

30. Ibid., l. 37.

31. Ibid., d. 127, ll. 67–75.

32. Ibid., d. 129, l. 140.

33. RGAE, f. 396, op. 11, d. 26, ll. 69–74.

CHAPTER 6. HAPPY CHILDHOODS

1. Pavel (Pavlik) Morozov (1918–32), the son of a peasant in Sverdlovsk Oblast, reported his father to Soviet authorities allegedly for trying to help other peasants evade the state's requisition of grain during collectivization. The father was consigned to the GULAG. According to the official version, Pavlik was murdered by vengeful kulaks, thereby becoming a Soviet martyr. Various aspects of the official version have been called into question by recent research. See Yu. Druzhnikov, *Voznesenie Pavlika Morozova* (London: Overseas Publications Interchange, 1988).

2. TsKhDMO, f. 1, op. 23, d. 1264, l. 24.

3. Ibid., l. 25.

4. RGASPI, f. 12, op. 1, d. 114, l. 2.

5. Ibid.

6. RGASPI, f. 17, op. 114, d. 346, l. 242.

7. TsGAODM, f. 1934, op. 1, d. 100, l. 590b.

8. Ibid.

9. Ibid.

10. All quotations from RGASPI, f. 17, op. 114, d. 346, l. 242.

11. TsMAM, f. 528, op. 7, d. 37. l. 111.

12. TsGAODM, f. 4, op. 9, d. 173, l. 192.

13. TsKhDMO, f. 1, op. 23, d. 1265, ll. 42, 43.

14. Ibid., d. 1129, l. 59.

15. Ibid., d. 1265, l. 50.

16. Ibid., l. 25.

17. Ibid., d. 1267, l. 44.

18. TsGAODM, f. 4, op. 9, d. 173, l. 192.

19. TsKhDMO, f. 1, op. 23, d. 1265, ll. 31–32.

20. Ibid., d. 1129, l. 60.

21. Ibid., l. 62.

22. Ibid., d. 1265, ll. 33–34.

23. From 1918 until 1934, elementary and secondary education was organized on the basis of groups *(gruppy)* that corresponded to the degree of a pupil's preparation rather than age. A resolution of the TsK of the VKP(b) and SNK of 15 May 1934 "On the Structure of the Elementary and Secondary School in the USSR," restored grades *(klassy)*. See *Narodnoe obrazovanie v SSSR: Obshcheobrazovatel'- naia shkola. Sbornik dokumentov, 1917–1973 gg.* (Moscow, 1974), p. 167. Thanks to Larry Holmes for this clarification.

24. GARF. f. 5207, op. 1, d. 693, l. 85.

25. Ibid., d. 721, l. 47.

26. Ibid., d. 693, l. 86.

27. Ibid., d. 1390, l. 1.

28. TsKhDMO, f. 1, op. 23, d. 1472, l. 48.

29. GARF, f. 5207, op. 1, d. 693, l. 86; TsKhDMO, f. 1, op. 23, d. 184, l. 24.

30. TsMAM, f. 528, op. 1, d. 304, l. 5.

31. Ibid., l. 230b.

32. TsKhDMO, f. 1, op. 23, d. 1265, l. 44.

33. TsGAODM, f. 1934, op. 1, d. 100, l. 108.

34. GARF, f. 5207, op. 1, d. 727, l. 108.

35. RGASPI, f. 78, op. 1, d. 524, ll. 91, 970b.

36. TsGAODM, f. 1934, op. 1, d. 147, l. 46.

37. TsKhDMO, f. 1, op. 23, d. 1472, l. 620b.

38. TsGAODM, f. 1934, op. 1, d. 94, l. 12.

39. RGASPI, f. 17, op. 114, d. 346, l. 245.

40. Ibid.

41. TsKhDMO, f. 1, op. 23, d. 1472, l. 48.

42. Sol'ts is described as an "Old Bolshevik and self-appointed conscience of the party in the legal realm," in Peter Solomon, Jr., *Soviet Criminal Justice under Stalin* (Cambridge: Cambridge University Press, 1996), pp. 121–22.

43. RGASPI, f. 12, op. 1, d. 111, ll. 7–8.

44. Ibid., d. 154, l. 8.

45. RGASPI, f. 78, op. 1, d. 524, l. 97.

46. For the moving account by Stepan Podlubnyi, another child of special migrants, see Jochen Hellbeck, ed., *Tagbuch aus Moskau, 1931–1939* (Munich: Deutscher Taschenbuch Verlag, 1996).

47. TsKhDMO, f. 1, op. 23, d. 1264, l. 13.
48. GARF, f. 7523, op. 23, d. 202, ll. 3–30b.
49. RGAE, f. 396, op. 11, d. 26, l. 175.
50. Ibid., d. 41, l. 152.

CONCLUSION

1. On socialist paternalism see Janos Kornai, *The Socialist System: The Political Economy of Communism* (Princeton: Princeton University Press, 1992), pp. 56, 144; Katherine Verdery, *What Was Socialism, and What Comes Next?* (Princeton: Princeton University Press, 1996), pp. 19, 24, 63; and Lewis H. Siegelbaum, "'Dear Comrade, You Ask What We Need': Socialist Paternalism and Soviet Rural 'Notables' in the Mid-1930s," *Slavic Review* 57, no. 1 (1998): 107–38.

2. For more on these strategies, see Sheila Fitzpatrick, *Everyday Stalinism: Ordinary Life in Extraordinary Times: Soviet Russia in the 1930s* (Oxford: Oxford University Press, 1999); Alena V. Ledeneva, *Russia's Economy of Favors: Blat, Networking, and Informal Exchange* (Cambridge: Cambridge University Press, 1998).

3. Stalin's speech to the Extraordinary Eighth All-Union Congress of Soviets, 25 November 1936, quoted in Merle Fainsod, *How Russia Is Ruled*, rev. ed. (Cambridge: Harvard University Press, 1965), pp. 371–72.

4. Oleg Kharkhordin, *The Collective and the Individual in Russia: A Study of Practices* (Berkeley: University of California Press, 1999), especially pp. 212–38.

# Index of Documents

# Index

Numbers in **bold** type refer to document numbers.